PERSONNEL:
THE MANAGEMENT
OF HUMAN RESOURCES

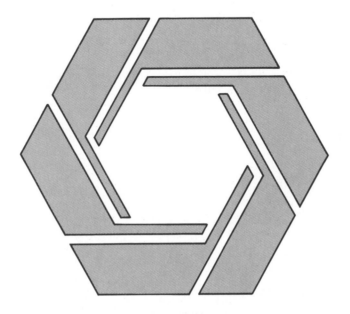

ALLYN AND BACON, INC.

Boston ■ London ■ Sydney ■ Toronto

THIRD EDITION

PERSONNEL: THE MANAGEMENT OF HUMAN RESOURCES

R. WAYNE MONDY, SPHR ▪ **ROBERT M. NOE,** SPHR
McNeese State University · East Texas State University

in collaboration with

HARRY N. MILLS, JR., SPHR   East Texas State University
ARTHUR SHARPLIN   Bentley College

TO MY DAUGHTERS:
ALYSON LYNN AND MARIANNE ELIZABETH
RWM

TO
JUDY LYNNE NOE
RMN

Series editor   Jack Peters
Manufacturing buyer   Andy Rosenau
Editorial-production service   York Production Services
Cover coordinator   Linda Dickinson

Library of Congress Cataloging-in-Publication Data

Mondy, R. Wayne
   Personnel, the management of human resources.

   Includes bibliographies and index.
   1. Personnel management—United States.   2. Personnel management.   I. Noe, Robert M.   II. Title.
HF5549.2.U5M66   1987   658.3   86-17459
ISBN 0-205-08946-1

Printed in the United States of America

10 9 8 7 6 5 4 3 2   91 90 89 88 87

Contents

v

PART TWO: HUMAN RESOURCE PLANNING, RECRUITMENT, AND SELECTION 127

PART THREE:
HUMAN RESOURCE
DEVELOPMENT 249

PART FOUR: COMPENSATION AND BENEFITS 411

PART FIVE: SAFETY AND HEALTH   497

Preface

The third edition of *Personnel: The Management of Human Resources* offers a practical and realistic approach to the study of human resource management. While the book is essentially pragmatic, it is balanced throughout by current human resource management concepts. A common theme—the interrelationships among the various human resource functions—runs throughout the book. Each of the functions is described from the standpoint of its relation to the total needs of human resource management. The book is written primarily for students who are being exposed to personnel management for the first time. It puts the student in touch with the real world through the use of numerous illustrations and company material showing how personnel management is practiced in today's organizations. Some of the highlights of the book are described below.

Chapter 1: Human Resource Management: An Overview An overview of the functions of human resource management (HRM) is provided in this chapter. The importance of HRM in today's business environment is also highlighted.

Chapter 2: The Environment of Human Resource Management This chapter develops a comprehensive model which is used throughout the book to show the many interrelationships that exist in human resource management. Both external and internal environmental factors are examined. A new section deals with the many dynamic environmental factors affecting multinationals.

Chapter 3: Legal Aspects of Human Resource Management This is a new chapter highlighting significant laws, Executive Orders, and Supreme Court decisions. Affirmative Action Programs (AAPs) receive considerable attention. The manner in which human resource management is affected will be described in the appropriate chapter.

Chapter 4: Job Analysis This chapter emphasizes the importance of job analysis to all aspects of human resource management. Newer methods for conducting job analysis are described in this edition.

Chapters 5, 6, and 7: Human Resource Planning, Recruitment, and Selection Current topics relating to planning, recruiting, and selection are included. Particular emphasis is placed on the legal aspects associated with these topics.

Chapter 8: Organization Change and Training and Development In this chapter, the change sequence is discussed along with reasons change is resisted and means of reducing such resistance. The training and development process is presented emphasizing methods of training, orientation, and training and development programs for special groups.

Chapter 9: Corporate Culture and Organization Development The various factors that determine corporate culture are described in this chapter. Types of cultures are discussed with emphasis on the participative culture and quality of work life. Various approaches to organization development are also presented.

Chapter 10: Career Planning and Development This chapter stresses the importance of career planning and development in today's organizations. Meaningful information about careers in personnel management is also provided.

Chapter 11: Performance Appraisal This chapter describes various aspects of performance appraisal with emphasis on the process itself and various methods utilized. Characteristics of an effective system are also presented.

Chapters 12 and 13: Compensation and Benefits A unique model is developed in this chapter to describe the factors which determine an employee's compensation. Both financial and nonfinancial compensation factors are described. This chapter is essentially pragmatic and should provide stimulating reading.

Chapter 14: Safety and Health The importance of safety and health in today's work environment is emphasized in this chapter. Stress management and physical fitness programs are among the topics highlighted.

Chapters 15 and 16: Labor Unions and Collective Bargaining The labor movement is described in a manner that should appeal to students. We are especially pleased with the sections depicting the development of the collective bargaining relationship and the bargaining process.

Chapter 17: Union Free Organizations This chapter is not typically found in personnel management books. However, we believe that students of human resource management need exposure to this topic. The chapter takes a middle-of-the-road approach to the discussion and describes the conditions that typically exist in union free firms.

Chapter 18: Internal Employee Relations This is a new chapter which includes topics related to discipline and the grievance process, termination, transfer, demotion, and promotion.

Chapter 19: Human Resource Research The importance of human resource research in today's business environment is highlighted in this chapter.

FEATURES OF THE BOOK

We have included the following features to promote the readability and understanding of important human resource management concepts:

- A model (see Figure 2–1) is developed which provides a vehicle for relating all human resource management topics. We believe that the overview provided will serve as an excellent teaching device.
- Objectives are listed at the beginning of each chapter to provide the general purpose and key concepts of the chapter.
- Each chapter begins with brief incidents which introduce pertinent human resource concepts and problems.
- Career profiles of human resource professionals are included in each chapter to demonstrate the work that personnel people do and to convey their philosophical comments to students of human resource management.
- Actual company material is used throughout the book to illustrate how a concept is actually used in organizations.
- Illustrations help to make specific points about selected topics.

- Review questions appear at the end of each chapter to test the student's understanding of the material.
- Key terms are listed at the end of each chapter. In addition, a key term is presented in bold print the first time it is defined or described in the chapter.
- Two incidents are provided at the end of each chapter. These cases highlight material covered in the chapter.
- A comprehensive long case is developed which ties all of the sections together.
- An experiential exercise at the end of each section provides an opportunity to put into practice important concepts covered in that section.
- A list of references is provided at the end of each chapter to permit additional in-depth study of selected topics.
- Finally, a glossary of all key terms appears at the end of the book.

IMPROVEMENTS TO THE THIRD EDITION

The first and second edition of *Personnel: The Management of Human Resources* enjoyed considerable success. Many of our users provided us with suggestions for improving the third edition. Topics which have been added or have been given additional coverage are provided below.

- Two new chapters have been added. First, a chapter entitled "Legal Aspects of Human Resource Management" has been included because of its significance to all human resource management functions. Second, the chapter "Internal Employee Relations" has been added because of its importance in today's human resource management.
- External environment of multinationals (Chapter 2).
- Job design, job enrichment, and job enlargement (Chapter 4).
- Human resource forecasting techniques (Chapter 5).
- Matching sources and methods of recruitment (Chapter 6).
- Affirmative Action Programs (AAPs) and recruitment (Chapter 6).
- Hiring criteria to avoid (Chapter 7).
- Expanded discussion of the use of tests in the selection process (Chapter 7).
- Corporate culture (Chapter 9).
- Characteristics of an effective performance appraisal system (Chapter 11).
- Comparable worth, two-tier wage system, and plateauing (Chapter 12).
- Wellness programs (Chapter 14).

All these features were designed to promote and stimulate student interest. The numerous company examples were used to demonstrate how "textbook" concepts are actually being used in the real world. We sincerely hope that students of human resource management derive as much pleasure from reading the book as we did in writing it.

ACKNOWLEDGMENTS

The assistance and encouragement of many people is normally required in the writing of any book. It is especially true in the writing of *Personnel: The Management of Human Resources*, third edition. Although it would be virtually impossible to list each person who assisted in this project, we feel that certain people must be credited because of the magnitude of their contribution.

Our sincere thanks go to many members of the faculty and staff at Northeast Louisiana University and East Texas State University. A special thanks goes to Art Bethke of Northeast Louisiana University who provided valued suggestions, advice, and encouragement through the project. Dean Trezzie A. Pressley, Suzanne H. McCall,

Donald L. Caruth, Robert M. Seay, Raymond L. Ackerman, Bonnie M. Cathey, all representing East Texas State University, encouraged us to see the project through to completion. For their positive influence on our early careers, we thank Frank N. Edens of Louisiana Tech University, C. L. Littlefield of North Texas State University, James R. Young, Dean Graham M. Johnson, and Elton D. Johnson of East Texas State University. Barbara Duncan Pace provided invaluable and professional assistance in typing and editing the manuscript. We deeply appreciate the efforts provided by Mary Jo Gregory of York Production Services in coordinating the production of this edition. The encouragement and advice of Drew M. Young, SPHR, Vice President, Employee Relations, ARCO Oil and Gas Company (retired); Robert E. Edwards, SPHR, Senior Vice President, Drake Beam Morin, Inc.; and Kathryn D. McKee, SPHR, Senior Vice President, First Interstate Bancorp, throughout three editions of the book were especially helpful.

Our wives also deserve a special note of appreciation for their constant patience, understanding, and encouragement. They kept us of sane mind during the arduous process of reviews and rewrites.

Special thanks are due to the following individuals for their in-depth review and critique of the manuscript: Professor Lane Kelly, University of Hawaii at Manoa, Professor Ray Montagno, Ball State University, Professor Art L. Bethke, Northeast Louisiana University, Professor Winston Oberg, Michigan State University, Professor Richard Richardson, Southwest Missouri State University, Professor Wanda V. Smith, Ferris State College, Professor Matt Amano, Oregon State University, Professor Thomas Chacko, Iowa State University, Professor Patricia Corcoran, Embry Riddle Aeronautical University, Professor Naomi Berger Davidson, California State University at Northridge, Professor Carol M. Ondeck, George Mason University, and Professor Eileen Aranda, University of Phoenix.

Part One

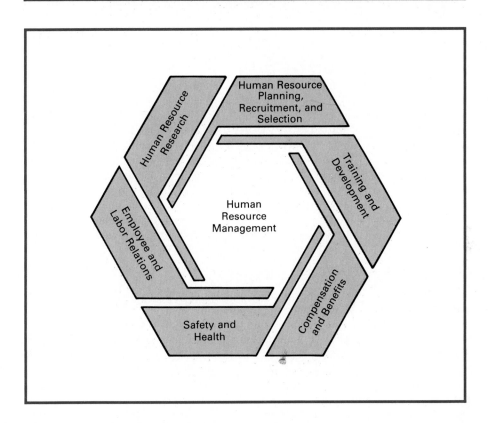

Human Resource Planning, Recruitment, and Selection

Human Resource Research

Training and Development

Human Resource Management

Employee and Labor Relations

Compensation and Benefits

Safety and Health

INTRODUCTION

CHAPTER OBJECTIVES

1. Define *management* and state its basic tasks.
2. Explain the relationship of management, human resource management, and the personnel manager.
3. Define the functions of human resource management.
4. Describe changes that have taken place in the personnel field in recent years.
5. Define *personnel executive, specialist,* and *generalist.*
6. Describe the changes that occur in the personnel function as a firm grows in size and complexity.
7. Express the nature and direction professionalization of Personnel has taken.

Chapter 1

HUMAN RESOURCE MANAGEMENT: AN OVERVIEW

David Curtis, personnel director for Nelson Enterprises in New York City, has just learned that his firm intends to open a new plant in Mobile, Alabama. When the plant is completed, 1000 new employees will be hired in addition to the 200 personnel who will be transferred from New York to Mobile. David's job is to ensure that the best qualified people are hired and trained by the time the plant opens.

Carl Edwards is the supervisor of fifteen convenience stores for a grocery chain in Houston, Texas. He is in charge of all employment activities for these stores. If one of his store managers fails to show up for the assigned shift and Carl cannot find a replacement, he must work the shift. It is Friday afternoon and Carl is hurriedly attempting to locate a replacement as one store manager has just resigned after giving five minutes notice.

Judy Lynley is vice president for industrial relations of Axton Manufacturing Company, a unionized firm that employs 15,000 workers nationwide. She has been negotiating with union leaders for five weeks under the threat of a strike. The union members have threatened to walk off the job, if the contract is not resolved by midnight. However, if Judy's firm agrees to all the union's demands, it will no longer be in a competitive position in the industry because of a higher wage level.

David, Carl, and Judy all have one thing in common: they are deeply involved with some of the challenges and problems related to personnel and human resource management. Managers must constantly deal with the often volatile and unpredictable human element. Managing people in organizations is more complex than ever in our rapidly growing, changing, and complex work environment.

WHAT IS MANAGEMENT?

The title of this book, *Personnel: The Management of Human Resources*, implies that an understanding of management is required in the study of Personnel. This being the case, what do we mean by management? We define **management** as *the process of getting things done through the efforts of other people.* The management process consists of four functions: planning, organizing, influencing, and controlling. A function is a type of work activity that can be identified and distinguished from other work. Management functions are:

Planning: *Determining in advance what should be accomplished and how it should be done.*

Organizing: *Acquiring human, material, and financial resources and specifying the relationships among them in order to get things done.* A most important aspect of organizing is ensuring that people with the appropriate qualifications are available at the specific places and times to accomplish the organization's objectives. This aspect of organizing is called staffing.

Influencing: *Determining or affecting the behavior of others.* This involves the areas of motivation, leadership, and communication.

Controlling: *Comparing what is happening with what should be happening and taking necessary corrective action.*

All successful managers perform these four functions, regardless of whether the person is a manager of marketing, production, finance, or human resources.

THE PRACTICE OF HUMAN RESOURCE MANAGEMENT AND THE PERSONNEL MANAGER

Before we progress further, we should make a distinction between two terms: human resource management and the personnel manager. **Human resource management (HRM)** is *the utilization of the firm's human assets to achieve organizational objectives.* All managers in the organization are vitally concerned with human resource management (HRM is also referred to as personnel management). They must get things done through other people's efforts. The production manager ensures that products are manufactured in sufficient numbers and quality; the marketing manager works through sales representatives to sell the firm's products; and the finance manager obtains capital to ensure that the business has sufficient operating funds. In all of these instances, managers have certain specialized functions as their primary responsibility. They are "line managers" because they are responsible for achieving their firm's primary objectives. These individuals must also be concerned with human resource management. Carl Edwards, the convenience store supervisor from Houston, Texas, fully understands the problems a line manager has with personnel management. As a line manager, if he cannot find a replacement, Carl will have to work the Friday night shift. William B. Pardue, senior vice president for American General Life Insurance Company, says, "The real personnel manager's game is played by the line manager. The personnel manager's role is to develop policies and programs — the rules of the game — and to function as a catalyst and energizer to the relationship between line management and employees."

Personnel managers are *individuals who normally act in an advisory (staff) capacity when working with other managers regarding human resource matters.* They have the primary responsibility of coordinating the firm's human resource management activities. Jane Kay, formerly vice president of employee relations for Detroit Edison Company, states, "The personnel manager acts more in an advisory capacity, but should be a catalyst in proposing human relations policies to be implemented by line managers." The distinction between human resource management and the personnel manager becomes clearer when the following situation is considered:

> Bill Brown, the production supervisor for Ajax Manufacturing, has just learned that one of his machine operators quit. He immediately calls Sandra Williams, the personnel manager, and says, "Sandra, I just had a Class A machine operator quit down here. Can you find some qualified people for me to interview?" "Sure, Bill," Sandra replies, "I'll send two or three down to you within the week and you can select the one that best fits your needs."

In this instance, both Bill and Sandra are concerned with accomplishing organizational goals but from different perspectives. Sandra, as a personnel manager, identifies applicants who meet the criteria specified by Bill. Yet Bill will make the final decision as to who is hired because he is responsible for the machine operator's performance. His primary responsibility is production, whereas Sandra's is personnel. As personnel manager, Sandra must constantly deal with the many human resource related problems faced by Bill and other managers. She must view the human resource needs of the entire organization. In this book, we will refer to her function as personnel, human resource management, employee relations, or industrial relations.

HUMAN RESOURCE MANAGEMENT FUNCTIONS

As previously mentioned, all managers are concerned with human resource management. The personnel, or human resource, manager is at the heart of a human resource management system. Today's personnel problems are enormous. The personnel manager is suddenly "grappling with discontented and restless employees and unions, myriad government regulations dealing with everything from safety standards to minority hiring, new trends in executive recruitment and compensation, and much more."[1] These areas are now receiving top priority by management. The personnel executive who is able to cope effectively with these problems is often recognized as one of the firm's top managers. As Frederick W. Bahl, director of personnel administration for Alumax, Inc., states, "Actions taken by personnel executives nearly always affect every stratum of the organization."

Personnel managers work with the firm's human resources to help achieve the organization's goals. The firm must attract, select, train, motivate, and retain qualified people. At the same time, employees must be permitted to satisfy personal needs.

There are six functional areas associated with human resource management (see Figure 1–1). The sound management practices required for successful performance in each of these functional specialties will be discussed next.

HUMAN RESOURCE PLANNING, RECRUITMENT, AND SELECTION

An organization must ensure that individuals possessing appropriate qualifications are available at specific places and times to accomplish the objectives of the organization. Some of the primary tasks involved in accomplishing this are human resource planning, recruitment, and selection. Human resource planning (HRP) is the process of systematically reviewing personnel requirements to make sure that an appropriate number of employees possessing the required skills are available when they are needed. Recruitment is the process of attracting individuals, in sufficient numbers and with appropriate qualifications, and encouraging them to apply for jobs with the organization. Selection is the process through which the organization chooses from a group of applicants those individuals best suited both for the open positions and for the company. David Curtis, personnel director for Nelson Enterprises, will be required to become deeply involved in planning, recruitment, and selection. These three tasks must be carefully coordinated if his firm is to satisfy its work-force requirements.

TRAINING AND DEVELOPMENT

Training and development (T&D) programs are designed to assist individuals, groups, and the entire organization to become more effective. Training

---

[1] "It's Hell in Personnel," *Dun's Review* 97 (March 1971): 40–43.

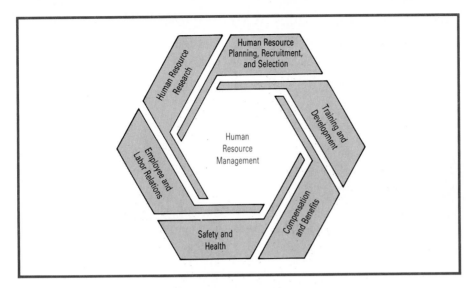

Figure 1–1. The human resource management system.

is needed because people, jobs, and organizations are always changing.[2] T&D should begin when individuals join the firm and continue throughout their careers. Large scale T&D programs are referred to as organization development (OD). The purpose of OD is to alter the environment within the firm to assist people in performing more productively.[3]

Other aspects of T&D include career planning and development and performance appraisal. Career planning is a process whereby personal goals are set and the means to achieve them are established. Individual and organizational careers are not separate and distinct. Organizations should assist employees in career planning so that the needs of both can be satisfied.

Through performance appraisal, employees are evaluated to determine how well they are performing their assigned tasks. Identified deficiencies can often be overcome through effective training and development programs.

COMPENSATION AND BENEFITS

The question of what constitutes a fair day's pay has plagued managers for decades. Employees must be provided with adequate and equitable rewards for their contributions to organizational goals. As used in this book, compensation includes all rewards individuals receive as a result of their em-

[2]Thomas A. DeCotiis and Richard A. Morano, "Applying Job Analysis to Training," *Training and Development Journal* 31 (July 1977): 20.

[3]Lester A. Digman, "Let's Keep the OD People Honest," *Personnel* 56 (January–February 1979): 23.

ployment. As such, it is more than monetary income. The reward may be one or a combination of the following:

- *Pay:* The money that a person receives for performing jobs. It is the cash that you can jingle in your pockets.
- *Benefits:* Additional financial rewards other than base pay, such as paid holidays and medical insurance.
- *Nonfinancial:* Nonmonetary rewards that an employee may receive, such as enjoyment of the work performed and a pleasant working environment.

SAFETY AND HEALTH

Safety involves protecting employees from injuries due to work-related accidents. Health refers to the employees' freedom from illness and their

Executive Insights

Robert L. Berra
Senior Vice President,
Administration
Monsanto Company

There was never any doubt in Bob Berra's mind about what profession he would pursue as a career. "Personnel played to my strengths as I perceived them," he says. "I felt I had strong communications skills and an ability to sense the meaning behind complex relationships — in other words, being able to cut through to what people really say and mean."

Berra received a B.S. degree in commerce and finance from St. Louis University in 1947 and an M.B.A. degree from the Harvard Graduate School of Business Administration that same year. "I took all the courses in personnel administration that Harvard offered at the time — both of them," he notes. He has also done graduate work

in psychology at Washington University in St. Louis. He joined Monsanto in 1951 as assistant training manager for the company's Springfield, Massachusetts, plant and subsequently served there as employee relations manager, director of sales training, and director of sales administration. In 1959 he was appointed director of personnel for the Plastic Products and Resins Division. He was appointed director of administration for the division in 1966 and was named assistant director of the Corporate Personnel Department in 1967.

From 1970 to 1974, Berra was employed by McKesson, Inc., as corporate vice president of personnel and public relations. He rejoined Monsanto in 1974 as vice president of personnel and was named senior vice president, administration, in 1980. As the "chief morale officer," as he describes it, for an organization of 60,000 employees worldwide, Berra is ultimately responsible for all personnel policies and programs, Executive

general physical and mental well-being. These topics are important because
employees who enjoy good health and work in a safe environment are more
likely to be efficient. For this reason, forward thinking managers have long
advocated advanced safety and health programs. Today, because of federal
legislation, all organizations have become concerned with their employees'
safety and health.[4]

EMPLOYEE AND LABOR RELATIONS

In 1985, approximately 19 percent of the workforce was unionized — and
a downward trend is expected to continue. Some estimates are that by the

[4]The key law in the area of health and safety is the Occupational Safety and Health Act of
1970. The effect of this act will be discussed later in this book.

Services, and the Corporate Public Affairs
Department. He is a prolific author of arti-
cles in the area of management and motivation and has served as guest lecturer at
numerous universities.

He is a past president of the Industrial
Relations Association of Greater St. Louis
and a past president and member of the Executive Committee of the American Society
for Personnel Administration. "Monsanto
gets first call on my time, but you have to
feel strongly enough about your profession
to take the time to contribute to it," he says.
He also serves on the Board of Directors of
Fisher Controls International, Inc., on the
Advisory Council of St. John's Mercy Medical Center in St. Louis, is an adjunct faculty
member of Washington University, and
works with other civic organizations.

Berra has witnessed and participated in
the evolution of the personnel function from
specialty area to profession and senior management responsibility. "Today," he says,

"the personnel executive wears many hats:
manager, member of top management, advisor, employee representative, corporate
officer, and professional. The successful human resources executive must be intelligent, sensitive, and healthy enough to handle the pressures. He has to be willing to
stand up and be counted when the chips
are on the line. Above all, he has to exercise
good judgment and then make things happen." An essential element of good judgment, he says, is to seek "in-depth exposure
to all parts of the organization to assure
properly balanced decisions."

He stresses the importance of getting the
right experience at the right time, forcing
the issue if necessary. "In most careers, it's
necessary to do this only once or twice; but
when the need is obvious, don't delay."

year 2000, unions will represent only 13 percent of all nonfarm workers.[5] Even with the projected decline in union membership, a business firm is required by law to recognize a union and bargain with it in good faith if the firm's employees want the union to represent them. This relationship has become an accepted way of life for many employers. And, as Judy Lynley, vice president for Axton Manufacturing Company, has discovered, there are often difficult problems to solve when dealing with the union. If the workers walk off the job, the firm's products cannot be manufactured. On the other hand, agreeing to all the union's demands may mean that the firm's products cannot be competitively priced. Judy must be a skilled negotiator to solve these problems. When a labor union is present, the personnel activity is often referred to as industrial relations. As in Judy's case, the personnel department typically serves as a coordinator between union and management.

Nonunion organizations are often knowledgeable about union goals and activities. These firms typically strive to satisfy their employees' needs in every reasonable manner to make it clear that a union is not necessary for individuals to achieve their personal goals.

HUMAN RESOURCE RESEARCH

The personnel manager's research laboratory is the work environment. The need for effective research permeates every personnel function. For instance, research may be conducted to determine the type of workers who will prove to be most successful in the firm.[6] Or it may be directed toward determining the causes of certain work-related accidents.[7] Because of the growing need for human resource research, personnel professionals are beginning to develop greater quantitative skills and are becoming much more adept in using the computer. As will be seen in chapter 19, there are numerous quantitative methods that are appropriate for use in human resource research. This function is expected to be increasingly important to all forms of organizations in the future.

THE INTERRELATIONSHIPS OF HRM FUNCTIONS

The previously mentioned functional areas of HRM should not be considered separate and distinct because they are highly interrelated. Decisions in one area must be made in light of the impact they will have on the others. For instance, it will do little good to emphasize the recruiting and training

---

[5]"Beyond Unions: A Revolution in Employee Relations Is in the Making," *Business Week* 2902 (July 8, 1985): 72.

[6]R. Wayne Mondy and Frank N. Edens, "An Empirical Test of the Decision to Participate Model," *Journal of Management* 2 (Fall 1976): 11–16.

[7]Dan Cordtz, "Safety on the Job Becomes a Major Job for Management," *Fortune* 86 (November 1972): 114.

of the firm's sales force while neglecting to provide adequate compensation. In addition, if a firm's goal is to remain nonunion, management must certainly ensure that a safe and healthy work environment exists. Throughout the book we will emphasize the high degree of interrelationships that exist among the six HRM functional areas.

THE REVOLUTION IN HUMAN RESOURCE MANAGEMENT

One of the major changes on the business scene in recent years has been the increase in the amount of time and effort that managers must spend in dealing with human resource problems and challenges. Every manager has been affected by this trend. Line management increasingly needs and expects greater support from Personnel. The personnel department has had to respond in a positive manner.

Not many decades ago, individuals engaged in human resource work had titles such as "welfare secretary" and "employment clerk." Their duties were rather restrictive and often dealt only with such items as workers' wages, minor medical affairs, recreation, and housing.[8] Personnel was generally held in low esteem and its organizational position was typically near the bottom of the hierarchy. "In the past," says John L. Quigley, vice president of human resources, Dr Pepper Company, "the personnel executive was the 'glad hander' or 'back slapper' who kept morale up in a company by running the company picnic, handling the United Fund drive, and making sure the recreation program went off well." These days are over in many organizations. The personnel director's position is no longer a "retirement" position given managers who cannot perform adequately anywhere else in the organization.[9] The overall increase in the personnel function's value is emphasized in the following article.

Business

Personnel Jobs Gain Ground

Once upon a time, the personnel department was the graveyard of the business world. Workers were expected to process application forms and cherish few hopes for advancement. No longer. The rapid increase in job discrimination suits, pension laws, federal regulations, and labor disputes has made the personnel worker's job more demanding and more important to the company than ever before.

Big corporations often have a sizable staff of personnel specialists who handle recruiting, employee counseling, psychological testing, wage and

[8]Henry Eibirt, "The Development of Personnel Management in the United States," *Business History Review* 33 (Autumn 1969): 348–349.

[9]Lawrence A. Wangler, "The Intensification of the Personnel Role," *Personnel Journal* 58 (February 1979): 111–119.

salary administration, training, affirmative action, fringe benefits, and compliance with government regulations. Training in business or personnel administration can be good preparation for entry-level jobs — but the personnel field is still open to ambitious graduates with liberal arts degrees.

Advancement often requires more education, however. Highly paid negotiators who handle collective bargaining contracts often hold either a law degree or a master's in industrial relations.

One thing seems clear, though: the personnel department is no longer a corporate backwater. In fact, some companies have decorated their top personnel staffer with the lofty title of Vice President for Human Resources.[10]

Perhaps going one step further, Lester B. Korn, president of the consulting firm Korn/Ferry International, has stated:

> Personnel is now one of the most exciting functions in the entire business world. It has become the focus of the highest level thinking and policy making, and the best thing about it for the personnel chief is that more and more he or she is the one doing the best thinking and making the most important policies.[11]

Salaries for practitioners depend on company size and the responsibility level associated with the job. According to Heidrick and Struggles, a New York-based international executive search firm, the average annual salary and bonus for top personnel executives is $140,000. However, the average for industrial personnel executives is higher at $170,000, while the average for nonindustrial firms is $111,000.[12] As impressive as these figures may appear, the salaries of individuals engaged in personnel work typically continue to lag behind those in other major functional areas. However, their relative compensation position is improving.

Numerous individuals have progressed from Personnel to other top executive positions. For instance, Ernest F. Boyce, a former vice president for personnel, is now chairman of the board and chief executive officer for Colonial Stores, Inc., the billion dollar southwestern supermarket chain. William L. Mobraaten, formerly personnel vice president at Pacific Telephone and Telegraph Company, became president and director of Bell Telephone Company of Pennsylvania.[13] W. T. Beebe, former chairman of the board of Delta Airlines, was vice president of personnel for Delta from 1954 to 1966.

The increased status of the personnel field is not limited to the United States. In his research on Japanese industry, William Ouchi found that "ordinarily, the most senior and the most respected managing director is

---

[10]Gina Pera, "Business: Personnel Jobs Gain Ground," *Ford's Insider: A Continuing Series of College Newspaper Supplements* (February 1979). Published by 13-30 Corporation.

[11]"Personnel — Fast Track to the Top," *Dun's Review* 105 (April 1975): 74–77.

[12]"Anatomy of a Human Resource Executive," *Training* 22 (May 1985): 146.

[13]"Personnel — Fast Track to the Top," p. 74.

in charge of Personnel."[14] Another study showed that in Germany, Scandinavia, Switzerland, and the United Kingdom, over half of the top personnel executives were also directors in their companies.[15] This trend is expected to continue as human resource management grows in importance.

THE CHANGING WORLD OF THE CHIEF PERSONNEL OFFICER (CPO)

The importance of human resource management appears to be receiving ever-increasing attention. A recent survey involving 50 of the top chief personnel executives found that 70 percent of chief executive officers (CEOs) and 66 percent of company presidents are spending more time on human resource matters. And, none are spending less time.[16]

The CPOs were also asked, "What are the principal human resource areas attracting top management attention?" The results are shown in Figure 1–2. Note that the top concern related to compensation, while succession planning (planning for the replacement of key employees) was a close second. All of the major topics covered in this text were mentioned.

In the survey, the CPOs were also asked to identify the major changes they see occurring in their management responsibilities and organizational relationships.[17] Their responses are summarized under the following five major headings:

1. *Greater emphasis and more time spent on human resource strategic planning and management succession planning.* Integrating human resource strategic planning into the corporate strategic planning process is apparently taking on greater importance.
2. *More involvement in all aspects of the business.* Just as production and finance are important to the success of the business, so is personnel, and it is achieving similar respect.
3. *A significant member of the management team.* Top level managers have begun to realize the contribution of effective human resource management.
4. *Key role as consultant to the CEO on organization and succession planning.* Chief personnel officers have become key advisors and counselors to the CEO.
5. *More emphasis on cost-related issues and control of costs.* The emphasis here is on workforce management.

[14]William G. Ouchi, *Theory Z.* Reading, Mass.: Addison-Wesley, 1981, p. 30.

[15]Sandra Salman, "Personnel: A New Route to the Top," *International Management* 32 (May 1977): 25.

[16]John S. Hellman, ed. "The Changing World of the CPO," Spencer Stewart & Associates special report, 1984, pp. 3–4.

[17]Ibid., p. 13.

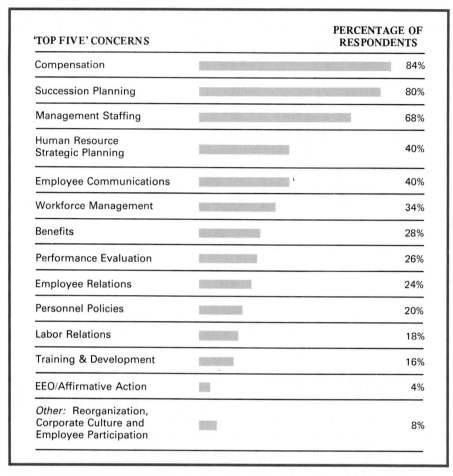

'TOP FIVE' CONCERNS		PERCENTAGE OF RESPONDENTS
Compensation		84%
Succession Planning		80%
Management Staffing		68%
Human Resource Strategic Planning		40%
Employee Communications		40%
Workforce Management		34%
Benefits		28%
Performance Evaluation		26%
Employee Relations		24%
Personnel Policies		20%
Labor Relations		18%
Training & Development		16%
EEO/Affirmative Action		4%
Other: Reorganization, Corporate Culture and Employee Participation		8%

Figure 1–2. Principal human resource areas attracting top management attention. Source: John S. Hellman, ed. "The Changing World of the CPO," a Spencer Stewart & Associates special report, 1984, p. 6. Used with permission.

Chief personnel officers are taking on greater responsibility, facing tougher challenges, and working harder and smarter. But, as one CPO stated, the job today is "a lot more fun."[18]

PERSONNEL EXECUTIVES, GENERALISTS, AND SPECIALISTS

Within Personnel, there are various classifications that should be understood. Throughout this book, we will refer to personnel executives, generalists, and specialists. **Executives** are *top level managers.* They report

[18]Ibid.

directly to the corporation's chief executive officer or the head of a major division. A **generalist** (who often is an executive) is *a person who performs tasks in a wide variety of personnel-related activities.* This individual is often involved with several or all of the six personnel functions previously described. On the other hand, a **specialist** is *an individual who may be either an executive, a middle manager, or a nonmanager who is typically concerned with only one of the six functional areas of human resource management.*

Figure 1–3 helps clarify the nature of executives, generalists, and specialists. The vice president of industrial relations, in this example, specializes primarily in union-related matters. He or she is both an executive and a specialist. The personnel vice president is both a generalist and an executive because he or she is responsible for a wide variety of functions. The manager of compensation and benefits is a specialist, as is the benefits analyst. An executive may be identified by his or her position level in the organization. Generalists and specialists are distinguished by their positions' breadth of responsibility.

The distinction made between generalists and specialists may become even clearer by referring to the Monsanto example in Figure 1–4, which lists the type of general work assignments at various levels in the organi-

Figure 1–3. Personnel executives, generalists, and specialists.

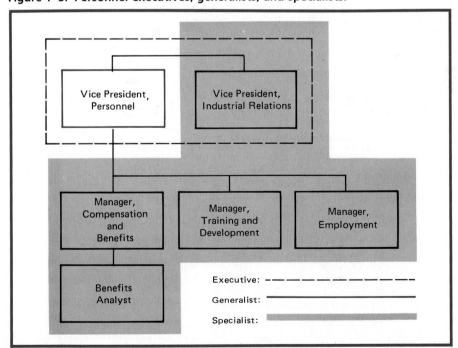

Starting Assignment

Specialist	Generalist
Work for a supervisor in an area like labor relations, employment, training and benefits. This would be at a larger location, where the function is broken down into areas of specialty.	Work for a supervisor or superintendent in several areas. You might be responsible for training, communications, employment, benefits, safety. This would be at a smaller location with two or three personnel professionals on the staff.

Later Assignments

Specialist	Generalist
Manage one or two areas of responsibility, such as labor relations, training and development, a combination of employment and benefits. Again, this would be at a larger location.	Manage the total personnel function ■ For a sub-unit within the location (such as for the maintenance department, or for a geographic area within the location), ■ For a smaller Monsanto location, ■ For a larger location.

Operating Company/Staff Department

Specialist	Generalist
Manage one or two functions such as personnel planning, compensation, recruiting, or an entire company or staff department.	Manage the total personnel function for a sub-unit within a company (e.g., a division) or for the entire company or staff department.

Corporate

Specialist	Generalist
Work in or manage an entire area of expertise for the corporation, such as labor relations, equal employment opportunity, development, benefits.	Manage the total corporate personnel function.

Two bits of advice:
   ■ Don't get hung up on whether you begin your career as a specialist or generalist. The lines between generalist and specialist are not as neat as the chart would indicate. For example, as an employment "specialist," you would daily become involved with questions of labor relations, compensation, personnel planning and equal employment policy—and much more! Or as a small-plant "generalist," you would have to learn the basics of several specialties. Also, the overwhelming odds are that you will get both types of exposure—specialist and generalist—in your career.
   ■ Career development will not always be "up." It's to the professional's advantage to get as much experience and exposure as possible—and many times, this will mean lateral moves into different areas of specialty.

Figure 1–4. Career development at Monsanto. Source: Used with the permission of Monsanto Company.

zation for both generalists and specialists. Note the "two bits of advice" that Monsanto gives to personnel professionals with regard to career development.

THE PERSONNEL FUNCTION IN DIFFERENT SIZE ORGANIZATIONS

All firms from the small corner grocery store to General Motors Corporation are concerned with human resource management. However, the personnel function's structure tends to change as firms grow in size and complexity and as the function gains importance. The basic purpose of Personnel remains the same, but the approach followed in accomplishing its mission is often altered.

In small businesses, there is usually no formal personnel unit. Rather, executives in the company bear the entire burden of handling their own personnel activities. These activities include ensuring that capable people are hired and retained (see Figure 1–5). Some aspects of the personnel function may actually be more significant in the smaller firm than in larger organizations. For instance, if a small business hires its first and only full-time salesperson, and this individual alienates the firm's customers, the company might actually go out of business. In a larger firm, such an error would be less devastating.

A separate personnel staff function may be required to coordinate human resource activities as the firm grows in size. The individual chosen will be expected to handle most of the personnel activities (see Figure 1–6). For this size firm there is little specialization. A secretary may be available to handle correspondence, but the personnel manager is essentially the entire department.

When the personnel function in an organization cannot be adequately performed by one person, separate sections are created and often placed

Figure 1–5. The personnel function of a small business.

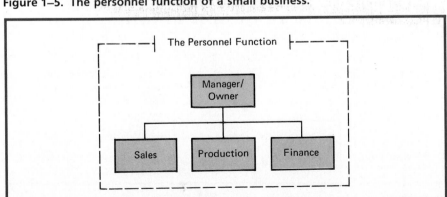

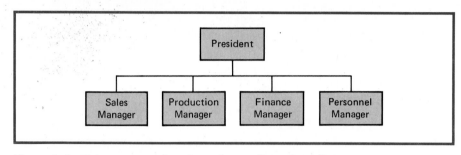

Figure 1–6. The personnel function of a medium-sized firm.

under the direction of a personnel manager. These sections will typically handle tasks involving such areas as training and development, compensation and benefits, employment, safety and health, and labor relations (see Figure 1–7).

In large firms, the personnel function becomes a unit using even greater specialization (see Figure 1–8 for the organization chart for Champion International Corporation). For instance, the unit responsible for compensation will most likely include specialists who concentrate on hourly wages and others who devote their time to salary administration. The employee relations vice president works closely with top management in formulating corporate policies. The scope of the duties of the employee relations executive is provided in Table 1–1. As you can see, the scope of the position is quite broad, ranging from the coordination, recommendation, and implementation of plans to auditing performance.

Figure 1–7. The personnel functions of a medium-large-sized firm.

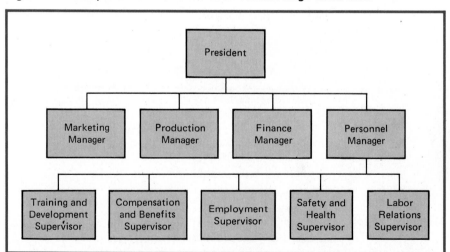

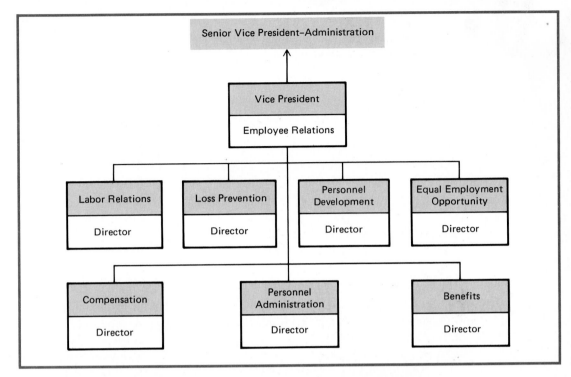

Figure 1–8. The employee relations organization—Champion International Corporation. Source: Used with permission of Champion International Corporation.

Table 1–1. Champion International Corporation corporate employee relations

Charter:

To provide operating and staff management with professional centralized services that will assure the competence and continuity of the company's human resources

Scope:

- To provide expertise and centralized services
- To coordinate plans, recommendations, implementation, and review of corporate projects
- To recommend general policies
- To establish functional procedures for designated activities
- To audit performance and compliance with general policies and procedures for designated activities

Table 1–1. Champion International Corporation corporate employee relations (continued)

Objectives:

- To provide direction and support to each functional director and his department
- To require quality and excellence in total performance of function
- To assure that professional positions are occupied by competent people who can and do respond to the company's needs and requirements

Source: Used with permission of Champion International Corporation.

PROFESSIONALIZATION OF HUMAN RESOURCE MANAGEMENT

A **profession** is *characterized by the existence of a common body of knowledge and a procedure for certifying members of the profession.* Performance standards are established by members of the profession (self-regulation) as opposed to outsiders. A profession must also have an effective representative organization that permits its members to exchange ideas of mutual concern. In Personnel, there are several well-known organizations. Among the more prominent are the American Society for Training and Development, the American Compensation Association, the American Society for Personnel Administration, the International Association for Personnel Women, the Personnel Accreditation Institute, and the International Personnel Management Association.

AMERICAN SOCIETY FOR TRAINING AND DEVELOPMENT

Founded in 1944, the American Society for Training and Development (ASTD) has grown to become the largest specialized personnel organization. The membership exceeds 22,000 and has over 132 local groups.[19] The membership is comprised of individuals who are concerned specifically with the training and development of personnel. The Society publishes the *Training and Development Journal* monthly.

AMERICAN COMPENSATION ASSOCIATION

The American Compensation Association (ACA) was founded in 1954. The membership exceeds 8,500.[20] The ACA is comprised of managerial and personnel professionals who are responsible for the establishment, exe-

[19]Katherine Gruber, (ed.), *Encyclopedia of Associations 20th Edition — 1986, Volume 1: National Organizations of the United States*, part 1. Detroit: Gale Research Company, 1985, p. 259.
[20]Ibid., p. 129.

cution, administration, or application of compensation practices and policies in their organizations. The ACA's journal is *Compensation Review*.

AMERICAN SOCIETY FOR PERSONNEL ADMINISTRATION

The largest national professional organization for individuals interested in personnel and human resource management is the American Society for Personnel Administration (ASPA) founded in 1948. The basic goals of ASPA include defining, maintaining, and improving standards of excellence in the practice of personnel. ASPA membership consists of 33,500 individuals.[21] There are currently more than 390 local chapters. Titles of ASPA members range from corporate vice president to division personnel manager to compensation analyst. There are also numerous student chapters of ASPA on university campuses across the country. The *Personnel Administrator* is published monthly by ASPA.

INTERNATIONAL ASSOCIATION FOR PERSONNEL WOMEN

Founded in 1950, the International Association for Personnel Women (IAPW) was established to expand and improve the professionalism of women in personnel management. Its membership consists of personnel executives in business, industry, education, and government. As of 1984, there were approximately 2500 members.[22] IAPW's journal, *Human Resources: Journal of the International Association for Personnel Women*, is published quarterly.

PERSONNEL ACCREDITATION INSTITUTE

One of the more significant undertakings in the field of Personnel has been accomplished by the Personnel Accreditation Institute (PAI). Founded in 1976, PAI's goal is to recognize personnel professionals through an accreditation program.[23] This program encourages personnel professionals to continuously update their knowledge in the field. Accreditation indicates that they have mastered a validated common body of knowledge. The advantages of personnel accreditation were outlined a number of years ago by a former national president of ASPA, Wiley Beavers, who wrote:

> First, we would benefit at the college and university level. The development of the body of knowledge required for successful practice in the various areas of personnel would provide invaluable assistance in curricula design. The breakdown of the field into its specialties would also allow students to focus on career directions earlier in their educations.
>
> Second, young practitioners would have sound guidelines and information covering areas in which they should be boning up and could avoid the mistakes many of us older types make.

[21]Ibid., p. 259.
[22]Ibid.
[23]Details of the PAI are shown in the appendix to this chapter.

Third, senior practitioners would be encouraged to update their knowledge. (Don't know how many of them will be interested in accreditation. There will be an appreciable reaction along the lines of: "I don't need to take tests to prove I know what I'm doing. I have already proven it by the job I'm doing." And they will be right in about 50 percent of the cases.)[24]

INTERNATIONAL PERSONNEL MANAGEMENT ASSOCIATION

The International Personnel Management Association (IPMA) was founded in 1973 and currently has a membership exceeding 5500. This organization seeks to improve personnel practices by providing testing services, an advisory service, conferences, professional development programs, research, and publications. IPMA sponsors seminars and workshops on various phases of public personnel administration. The organization's journal, *Public Personnel Management,* is published quarterly.[25]

SCOPE OF THIS BOOK

Effective human resource management is critical for every firm's success. In order to be successful, managers must understand and practice effective personnel management. This human resource management book is designed to provide you with:

- Greater knowledge and insight into the role of human resource management in today's organization.
- Increased knowledge of human resource planning, recruitment, and selection.
- An awareness of the importance of training and development in modern organizations.
- An appreciation of how compensation and benefits programs are determined and administered.
- An understanding of safety and health factors as they impact a firm's profitability.
- An opportunity to view employee and labor relations from both union and nonunion standpoints.
- Greater understanding of the role of personnel research in today's organizations.

Students often question whether the content of a book corresponds with the realities of the business world. In our research efforts, we have drawn heavily upon the comments, observations, and experiences of personnel practitioners. Human resource practices followed by leading busi-

---

[24]Wiley Beavers, "Accreditation: What Do We Need That For?" *The Personnel Administrator* 18 (November 1975): 39–41.

[25]Ibid., p. 260.

ness organizations are cited to illustrate how theory can be applied. Our intent is to enable students to visualize actual, everyday business experience.

This book is organized into seven sections (parts) as shown in Figure 1–9. We believe that this approach will provide you with an appreciation of the importance of personnel and human resource management. As you

Figure 1–9. Organization of this book.

I. Introduction

Chapter 1: Human Resource Management: An Overview
Chapter 2: The Environment of Human Resource Management
Chapter 3: Legal Aspects of Human Resource Management
Chapter 4: Job Analysis

II. Human Resource Planning, Recruitment, and Selection.

Chapter 5: Human Resource Planning
Chapter 6: Recruitment
Chapter 7: Selection

III. Human Resource Development

Chapter 8: Organization Change and Training and Development
Chapter 9: Corporate Culture and Organization Development
Chapter 10: Career Planning and Development
Chapter 11: Performance Appraisal

IV. Compensation and Benefits

Chapter 12: Financial Compensation
Chapter 13: Benefits and Other Compensation Issues

V. Safety and Health

Chapter 14: A Safe and Healthy Work Environment

VI. Employee and Labor Relations

Chapter 15: The Labor Union
Chapter 16: Collective Bargaining
Chapter 17: Union-Free Organizations
Chapter 18: Internal Employee Relations

VII. Human Resource Research

Chapter 19: Productivity and Human Resource Research

read this book, we hope you will be stimulated to continue your search for knowledge in this rapidly changing and expanding field.

SUMMARY

All managers in the organization are vitally concerned with human resource management. They must achieve organizational goals through other people's efforts. Personnel managers normally act in an advisory (staff) capacity when working with other managers. They have the primary responsibility of coordinating the firm's human resource management activities. The personnel, or human resource, manager is at the heart of a human resource management system.

In order to fulfill the firm's personnel and human resource needs, the personnel manager must perform tasks in a wide variety of functions. These include: (1) human resource planning, recruitment, and selection; (2) training and development; (3) compensation and benefits; (4) safety and health; (5) employee and labor relations; and (6) human resource research. The personnel department has had to respond in a positive manner to the many major changes on the business scene in recent years. Line management increasingly needs and expects greater support from Personnel.

Within Personnel there are various classifications that should be understood. An executive is a top level manager. Generalists are people who perform tasks in a wide variety of personnel-related activities. Specialists are concerned with but one of six functional areas. Many of these personnel people have progressed to their firm's top level managerial position.

A profession exists when there is a common body of knowledge and there is a procedure for certifying members of the profession. In Personnel, there are several well-known organizations. Among the more prominent are the American Society for Training and Development, the American Compensation Association, the American Society for Personnel Administration, the International Association for Personnel Women, the Personnel Accreditation Institute, and the International Personnel Management Association.

QUESTIONS FOR REVIEW

1. Justify the statement, "All managers are involved in human resource management."
2. Distinguish between human resource management and the personnel manager.
3. What personnel functions must be performed regardless of the size of the organization?
4. Distinguish by definition and example between personnel executives, personnel generalists, and personnel specialists.
5. How does the personnel function change as a firm grows in size? Briefly describe each stage of development.
6. Do you believe the field of personnel management should be professionalized? Explain your answer.

TERMS FOR REVIEW

Management	Personnel managers
Planning	Executives
Organizing	Generalist
Influencing	Specialist
Controlling	Profession
Human resource management	

Incident 1

The day was one of the happiest in Ed Beaver's life. He was told that morning that he was being promoted to corporate vice president for personnel from his present position as personnel manager for his firm's large New York plant. As he leaned back in his office chair, he felt a deep sense of accomplishment. He thought back to the day fifteen years earlier when, fresh out of college, he joined Duncan Foods as an assistant compensation specialist. He had always wanted to be in personnel, but he got his degree in business management because the university did not have a personnel curriculum. Ed remembered how tense he was when he arrived at work that first day. College graduates were rarely given the opportunity to start work directly in personnel and he was the youngest employee in the department.

Ed learned his job well and the older workers quickly accepted him. Three years later he was promoted to compensation manager. Immediately after the promotion he was given the task of designing a new pay system for operative employees. As he remembers, "Designing the system wasn't difficult. Convincing the employees that the new system was better than the old one was the real chore." But he overcame that obstacle.

A few years later Ed moved up again. He was chosen to become the new personnel manager for a small Duncan plant outside Chicago. The move required a major readjustment for his family. Ed's wife remarked, "I sure hate to move in the middle of the school year. And we've just begun to enjoy our new house." Ed was able to find another home the family liked just as well, and the children adjusted quickly. The job was certainly no bed of roses. Six months after Ed arrived he led negotiations for a new union contract. He worked night and day for months to develop a contract that would be acceptable to both the company and the union. Successful signing of the new agreement was one of his most satisfying experiences.

Four years later, Ed was asked if he would accept the position of personnel manager for the large New York plant. This plant employed five times as many workers as the Chicago plant and had many different types of problems. After a family discussion the Beavers were off to new adventures in the Big Apple.

At that moment, Ed's nostalgia came to a halt. The challenge of the new job suddenly came home to him. As vice president of personnel for Duncan Foods he would be responsible for personnel management for fifty plants and warehouses employing 13,000 people. What an overwhelming responsibility he was facing! Personnel management had changed greatly during the previous fifteen years and the rate of change seemed to be increasing. Ed wondered about the problems he would face and what role he would play in solving them as the new vice president for personnel.

QUESTIONS

1. Trace Ed's progression to vice president of personnel. Do you feel that this progression qualifies him well for the job?
2. What problems do you imagine Ed will face in his new role compared to his problems as plant personnel manager?
3. What new challenges do you feel Ed will confront in the changing field of personnel in the future?

Incident 2

Marsha Smith was exceptionally happy the day she received word of her appointment as assistant personnel director at Nelson Electronics in Boise, Idaho. Marsha had joined the company as a recruiter three years earlier. Her degree from the University of Missouri was in personnel administration and she had four years of experience as a personnel specialist.

As she walked to her office, she thought about how much she had learned while working as a recruiter. The first year she was with Nelson she went on a recruiting trip to Southern Idaho State College, only to find the placement director there extremely angry with her company. She was visibly upset when the placement director said, "If you expect to recruit any of our students, you at Nelson had better get your act together." Questioning of the placement director revealed that a previous recruiter had failed to show up for a full afternoon of scheduled interviews with Southern's students. Marsha's trip ended amicably, though, and she eventually recruited a number of excellent employees from the college.

Another important lesson began when the production manager asked for some help. "I need you to find an experienced quality control inspector," he said. "I want to make sure that the person has a degree in statis-

tics. Beyond that, you decide on the qualifications." Marsha advertised the position and checked through dozens of resumes in search of the right person. She sent each promising applicant to the production manager. This went on for six months with the production manager giving various obscure reasons for not hiring any of the applicants. Finally, the production manager called Marsha and said, "I just hired a QC person. He has a degree in history but he seems eager. Besides, he was willing to work for only a thousand a month."

Marsha has learned more with each passing day. She feels that one of her greatest accomplishments is having improved the firm's minority recruiting program. Her ability to do this was based on something of a coincidence. One of her close friends in school had become a leader in the Black Chamber of Commerce. With his advice she was able to develop a recruiting program that attracted blacks to Nelson Electronics.

As Marsha began to clean out her desk, she suddenly realized that the learning process was just beginning. As assistant personnel director, she would be responsible not only for matters related to recruiting but for all aspects of personnel management. It was a little scary, but she felt ready.

QUESTIONS

1. What are the lessons that can be learned from each of the three situations described?

2. How will the problems Marsha faces as an assistant personnel director differ from those she has handled as a recruiter?

REFERENCES

Abraham, Yohannan. "Personnel Policies and Practices in Saudi Arabia." *Personnel Administrator* 30 (April 1985): 101–110.

"Accreditation Counts Among Personnel Pros." *Industry Week* 210 (August 24, 1981): 34.

Alper, S. William and Mandel, Russell E. "What Policies and Practices Characterize the Most Effective HR Departments?" *Personnel Administrator* 29 (November 1984): 120–124.

Akey, Denise S., ed. *Encyclopedia of Associations.* 17th Edition, Volume 1. Detroit: Gale Research Company, 1984, p. 234.

"Anatomy of a Human Resource Executive." *Training* 22 (May 1985): 146.

Bamforth, Mike. "What Future for the Personnel Function?" *Personnel Management* 9 (December 1977): 75–78.

Bell, Chip. "The HRD Manager's 'Rules for Living'." *Training and Development Journal* 30 (December 1976): 38–39.

"Beyond Unions: A Revolution in Employee Relations Is in the Making." *Business Week* 2902 (July 8, 1985): 72.

Cooper, Lloyd. "HRD — Stepping Forward Toward Professionalism." *Training and Development Journal* 33 (February 1978): 30–31.

Evans, P. A. L. "On the Importance of a Generalist Conception of HRM: A Cross-National Look." *Human Resource Management* 23 (Winter 1984): 347–363.

Facha, Austin Ross. "The Mentor's Role in Developing New Leaders." *Hospital & Health Services Administration* 29 (September/October 1984): 22–29.

Franke, Arnold G., Harrick, Edward J., and Klein, Andrew J. "The Role of Personnel in Improving Productivity." *Personnel Administrator* 27 (March 1982): 83–88.

Hellman, John S. "The Changing World of the CPO." Spencer Stewart & Associates special report, 1984, pp. 3–4.

Jain, Harish and Murray, Victor. "Why the Human Resources Management Function Fails." *California Management Review* 26 (Summer 1984): 95–110.

Knicely, H. V. "Employee Relations: It's a Whole New Ball Game." *Dun's Business Month* 119 (April 1982): 121–122.

LaBau, Marilyn L. "Human Resource Accounting: Is Quality of Worklife Profitable? *Management World* 11 (January 1982): 45–46.

McKendrick, Joseph. "The Office of 1990: Human Resources." *Management World* 11 (January 1982): 14–17.

Miles, R. E. and Rosenberg, H. R. "Human Resources Approach to Management: Second-Generation Issues." *Organizational Dynamics* 10 (Winter 1982): 26–41.

Naisbitt, John. *Megatrends.* New York. N.Y.: Warner Books, 1982.

Nardoni, R. "Personnel Office of the Future Is Available Today." *Personnel Journal* 61 (February 1982): 132–134.

Odiorne, G. S. "Human Resources Strategies for the Nineties." *Personnel* 61 (November–December 1984): 13–19.

Ortman, John K. "Human Resources 1984: The State of the Profession." *Personnel Journal* 29 (June 1984): 35–48.

Patten, R. H., Jr. "Human Resource Management and the Energy Crisis — An Ostrich Posture?" *Human Resource Management* 20 (Fall 1981): 2–8.

Pursell, D. E. "Planning for Tomorrow's Personnel Problems." *Personnel Journal* 60 (July 1981): 559–561.

Russ, Charles F., Jr. "Should the Personnel Department Be Abolished?" *Personnel Journal* 64 (June 1985): 78–81.

Salman, Sandra. "Personnel: A New Route to the Top." *International Management* 32 (May 1977): 24–26.

Skinner, W. "Big Hat, No Cattle: Managing Human Resources." *Harvard Business Review* 59 (September/October 1981): 106–114.

Tichy, Noel M., Fombrun, Charles J., and Devanna, Mary A. "Strategic Human Resource Management." *Sloan Management Review* 23 (Winter 1982): 47–61.

Wangler, Lawrence A. "The Intensification of the Personnel Role." *Personnel Journal* 58 (February 1979): 111–119.

White, Harold C. and Wolfe, Michael N. "The Role Desired for Personnel Administration." *Personnel Administrator* 25 (June 1980): 87–97.

Wright, N. B. "The Revolution Around Us: Human Resource Development in the 80's." *Business Quarterly* 49 (Fall 1984): 6+.

Appendix

The Personnel Accreditation Institute (PAI) is a subsidiary of the American Society for Personnel Administration. Since its inception in 1976, the PAI has granted accreditation to more that 6000 individuals. The number of accredited individuals will likely increase substantially as the benefits of accreditation become more apparent.

The Personnel Accreditation Institute's program provides for two levels of accreditation: operational and policy level. These two levels recognize degrees of expertise and responsibility.

Operational: Requires an examination and some experience. The examination covers the general body of knowledge.

Policy: Requires an examination and senior experience. Practitioners must also have policy-developing responsibilities.

> *Specialist:* A practitioner, consultant, educator or researcher who characteristically provides indepth expertise or management in a segment of the field.

> *Generalist:* A senior practitioner or consultant whose responsibilities span the field and whose knowledge is broad-based rather than specialized.

OPERATIONAL LEVEL ACCREDITATION PROFESSIONAL IN HUMAN RESOURCES (PHR)

SPECIFIC REQUIREMENTS

Practitioners.   Four years of professional experience in the field in the last six years. A B.B.A, B.S. or B.A. in personnel management or social sciences may be substituted for experience, allowing two years for a bachelor's degree and three years for a master's degree. The minimum experience requirement is one year of recent full-time professional practice in the field.

Educators.   Three academic years of full-time teaching at the undergraduate level or two years at the graduate level at an accredited college or university. Two current years of teaching in the personnel or human resources field.

Consultants or researchers (academe, business, government, etc.).   Four years of consulting or significant and recorded research related to the field of personnel or human resources. Minimum of one current full-time year of consulting or research in the field.

Combination. Practical experience, teaching, research and/or consulting may be combined. A minimum of one year of recent experience or two recent academic years of teaching in the field of personnel and human resources.

EXAMINATION

Successful completion of the operational level examination of the body of knowledge in the field of personnel and human resources.

POLICY LEVEL ACCREDITATION
SENIOR PROFESSIONAL IN HUMAN
RESOURCES (SPHR) — SPECIALIST

FUNCTIONAL AREAS

1. Employment, Placement and Personnel Planning
2. Training and Development
3. Compensation and Benefits
4. Health, Safety and Security
5. Employee and Labor Relations
6. Personnel Research

SPECIFIC REQUIREMENTS

Practitioners. Eight years of experience in the field. College degrees may be substituted for experience. Minimum experience is five years. Recent three years must include policy-developing responsibility. Recent position must encompass the full scope of the functional area in which accreditation is sought.

Educators, researchers, or consultants. Eight years of experience equivalent to that specified for practitioners.

Combination. Eight years of combined practical experience, teaching, research and/or consulting. Minimum of five years of experience in the functional area in which accreditation is sought. Recent position must encompass the full scope of senior responsibilities in the functional area in which accreditation is sought.

EXAMINATION

Successful completion of an examination at the policy level in one, or possibly two, functional areas. The examination also includes some items from the basic body of knowledge across the personnel and human resources field.

POLICY LEVEL
SENIOR PROFESSIONAL IN HUMAN RESOURCES (SPHR) — GENERALIST

Policy level senior experience in four of the six functional areas plus an examination covering all functional areas and management practices.

Generalists are typically practitioners, although some consultants and educators may qualify.

SPECIFIC REQUIREMENTS

Eight years of experience in the field. College degrees may be substituted for experience (cf., PHR). Minimum of five years of experience in the field. Three years of recent experience with policy-developing responsibility spanning at least four functional areas. Candidates with specialist and generalist policy-influencing experience may qualify with at least two years in each of four functional areas in the last six years.

EXAMINATION

Successful completion of an examination at the senior level demonstrating broad based knowledge across the personnel and human resources field.

Accreditation and reaccreditation, together, sum up personnel professionalism. Accreditation is earned by individuals who demonstrate their mastery of the defined body of knowledge. The personnel field, however, is not static. Rapid change requires new and more sophisticated knowledge and behaviors by personnel professionals who wish to grow and develop. Reaccreditation is a method for accredited individuals to demonstrate their accomplishments in keeping abreast of change and updating their knowledge in the field.

Reaccreditation is required within three years of accreditation. The actual expiration date is June 30 or December 31, whichever date occurs first, following the three-year anniversary of the accreditation. Each reaccreditation period is also for three years. Senior Professionals in Human Resources who are reaccredited twice are not required to be reaccredited again. There are two ways to become reaccredited. One method is by testing. The other method is through a variety of specified activities.

Accreditation examinations are given on the first Saturday of each May and December at designated test sites. Applications must be made with the Institute at least six weeks in advance of the examination date.

For additional accreditation information, contact:

Personnel Accreditation Institute
606 North Washington Street
Alexandria, VA 22314

CHAPTER OBJECTIVES
1. Develop a generalized model for understanding the environment of human resource management.
2. Identify the external environmental factors that affect human resource management.
3. State the changes expected in the labor force that will impact on human resource management.
4. Explain factors in the internal environment and state how they exert pressure on the human resource management function.
5. Describe some external environmental factors that affect human resource management for multinational corporations.

Chapter 2

THE ENVIRONMENT OF HUMAN RESOURCE MANAGEMENT

Bryan Osborn is president of Tempo Manufacturing, a producer of high quality telecommunications equipment. He was disturbed as he arrived at his office one day recently. He had just learned that the firm's major competitor had developed a new manufacturing process. The competitor claimed that the new process would cut costs substantially. The industry had been expanding rapidly, but Bryan knew that the demand for his product was far from automatic. He felt that he could rely on a certain amount of loyalty from his established customers. He also knew that if the new technology was really superior Tempo was in trouble.

As Bryan sat at his desk he noticed a memo from the personnel director. The memo recommended a new training program be implemented immediately because a sufficient number of qualified workers could not be recruited from the immediate labor market. Problems. Problems. Problems.

Bryan Osborne is keenly aware of how the external environment impacts Tempo Manufacturing. A technological breakthrough by a competitor could have a devastating effect on the company. Present customers might switch to the lower cost product. And, because there are not enough qualified workers in the labor market, a new training program may have to be implemented.

In this chapter we first identify the environmental factors affecting human resource management. Then we describe how specific external environmental factors can influence the job of human resource management. In the following section we focus briefly on the major internal environmental factors that can affect the personnel manager's job. Because of the continuing growth of multinational organizations, we devote the final section to describing some major external environmental factors that multinationals confront.

ENVIRONMENTAL FACTORS AFFECTING HUMAN RESOURCE MANAGEMENT

Many interrelated factors affect human resource management. They can be grouped as factors of external and internal environments (see Figure 2–1). The external environment affects a firm's human resources from outside the organizational boundaries. The internal environment affects the firm's human resources from inside its boundaries. In addition, personnel professionals constantly work with people from other functional areas such as marketing, production, and finance. They must understand the different perspectives of people from various disciplines in order to perform their tasks.

Understanding the many interrelationships implied in the model is important as the personnel professional works with other managers to assist them in resolving their daily problems. For instance, a production manager may want to give a substantial pay raise to a particular employee. The personnel manager may know that this individual does an exceptional job, but should also know that if this raise is granted, it will not only affect the department where the individual works but may also set a precedent for the entire firm. The personnel manager may have to explain to this manager that such action is not an isolated decision and that alternatives may need to be considered as a means of rewarding superior performance. Perhaps the personnel manager knows of a higher paying position that this employee would be qualified to fill. The manager may also be able to move the deserving worker into a supervisory position. Whatever the case, the effect of a particular act must be considered in light of its impact on the entire organization. The model provides personnel managers with a framework

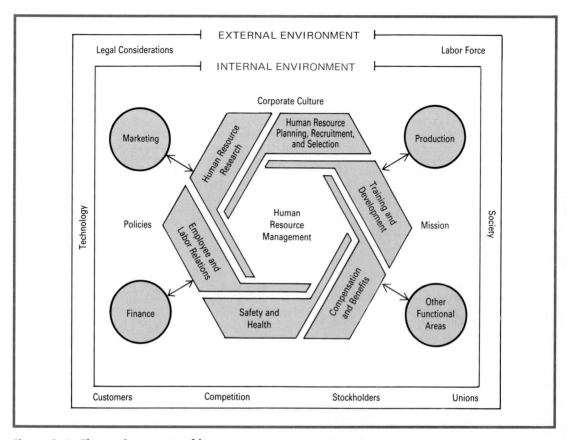

Figure 2–1. The environments of human resource management.

that emphasizes viewing the big picture rather than concentrating on a narrow phase of the company's operation.

The basic tasks assigned the personnel manager remain essentially the same regardless of the impact from either the external or the internal environment. However, the manner in which the tasks are accomplished may be altered substantially.

THE EXTERNAL ENVIRONMENT

The **external environment** is comprised of those factors (see Figure 2–1) that affect a firm's human resources from outside the organization's boundaries. As Figure 2–1 illustrates, they include legal considerations, the labor force, society, unions, stockholders, competition, customers, and technology. Each of these factors, separately or in combination, can result in constraints on the personnel manager's job.

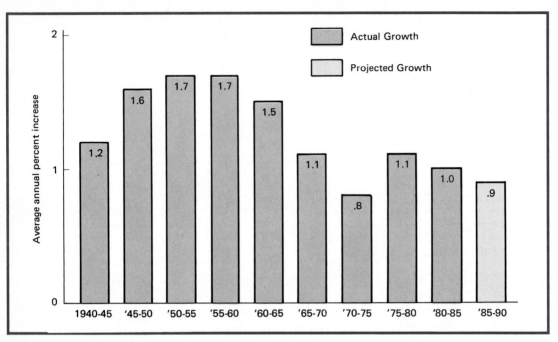

Figure 2–2. Civilian labor force growth and projected growth. Source: Bureau of the Census.

LEGAL CONSIDERATIONS

One of the most significant external forces a manager must face relates to federal, state, and local legislation and the many court decisions interpreting this legislation. In addition, many presidential executive orders have had a major impact on human resource management. These legal considerations affect virtually the entire spectrum of personnel policies. The most significant of these considerations are highlighted in chapter 3, and the manner in which these laws, court decisions, and executive orders affect human resource management will be described in the appropriate chapter.

THE LABOR FORCE

The number and characteristics of individuals in the labor force is another major external factor. The nature of this group may be quite different in the future.[1] By 1990, there will be approximately 119 million people in the civilian labor force. This estimate represents an 18.5 percent increase over the 1978 figure of 100 million. As may be seen in Figure 2–2, although the

[1]For a more detailed discussion of future labor force characteristics, see *Occupational Outlook Handbook*, 1980–81 ed., U.S. Government Bulletin, Number 2075.

population has grown more slowly in recent years, the figures do not tell the entire story. The labor force composition is also changing. While the participation rate for men continues to decline, the participation rate for women is rising (see Figure 2–3).

A recent Labor Department report shows that American women are moving into nontraditional fields, including management, at an increasing rate. In 1984, women comprised 39.6 percent of economists, 35.4 percent of computer programmers, 16.1 percent of lawyers, 16.0 percent of doctors, 10.8 percent of police/detectives, and 6.2 percent of engineers.[2]

Reflecting increased opportunities in business, the number of women receiving bachelor's degrees in business increased from fewer than 4000 in 1960–1961 to more than 73,000 in 1980–1981. In 1960–1961, fewer than 200 women received master's degrees in business, while more than 14,000 received them in 1980–1981.[3]

37

**Chapter 2
The
Environment of
Human
Resource
Management**

[2]*Monthly News on Human Resource Management,* American Society for Personnel Administration (August 1985): 12.

[3]*Newsletter,* Beta Gamma Sigma, the National Honor Society in Business and Management (September 1985): 2.

Figure 2–3. Percentage of total employed persons 16 years old and over, by sex, 1970 and 1981. Source: Bureau of Labor Statistics.

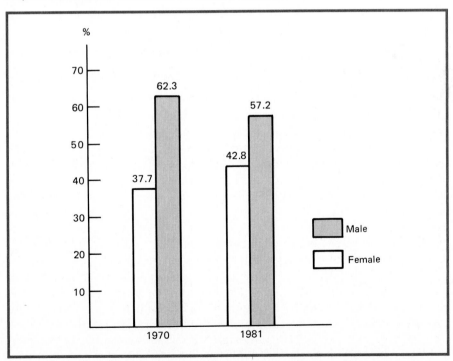

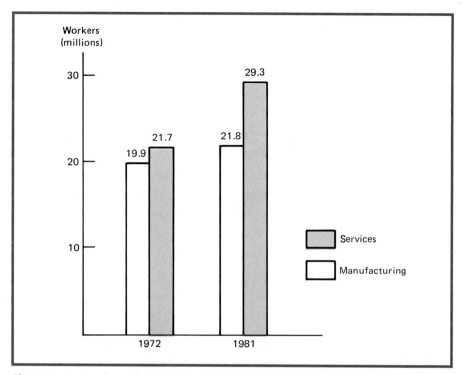

Figure 2–4. Number of workers in the manufacturing and service industries, 1972 and 1981. Source: Bureau of Labor Statistics.

In spite of impressive gains made in business organizations by women, a rather sobering statistic emerged from a recent survey of HRM executives serving the nation's 1000 largest companies: 98 percent of the responding chief human resource officers were male.[4] This indication of almost total male domination is surprising because the personnel field has long been considered one that is perhaps most open to females.

The industries that will be capable of absorbing additional employees will also likely be different from those of today. This change has already begun as job opportunities increase in service-producing industries such as transportation, public utilities, finance, insurance, real estate, and government (see Figure 2–4). By 1990, employment in service industries is expected to have expanded by 30 percent over 1978 figures. In goods-producing industries, employment is projected to increase by 13 percent. A projection of employment growth by industry is presented in Figure 2–5.

Once a small proportion of the total labor force, white-collar workers now represent about half of the total. The number of service workers has also risen rapidly, while the blue-collar work force has grown only slowly and the number of farm workers has declined (see Figure 2–6).

[4]"Facts and Figures: Anatomy of a Human Resource Executive," *Training* (May 1985): 146.

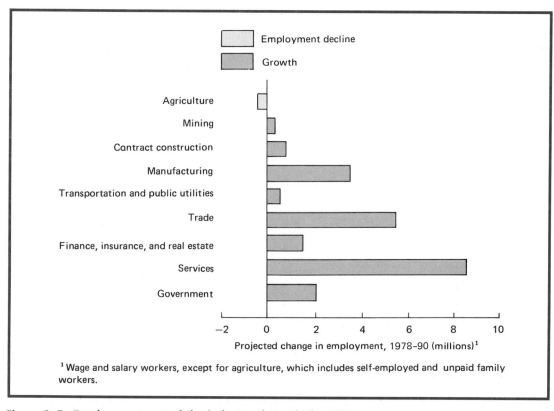

Figure 2–5. **Employment growth by industry through the 1980s.** Source: Bureau of Labor Statistics.

Figure 2–6. **Projected growth of white-collar, blue-collar, service, and farm workers through the 1980s.** Source: Bureau of Labor Statistics.

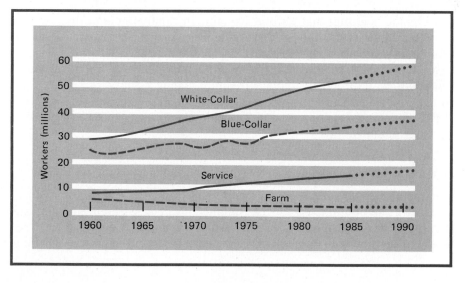

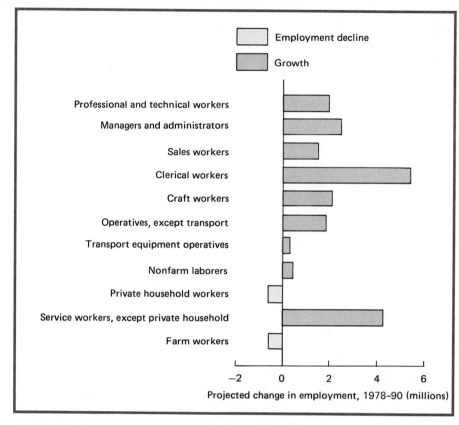

Figure 2–7. Replacement plus growth determine job openings. Source: Bureau of Labor Statistics.

The job openings that will be available by 1990 are determined by the growth of a particular industry and the number of replacement personnel needed. As you can see in Figure 2–7, a large number of industries are projecting growth in employment by 1990. The challenge in filling these job openings will be enormous. Personnel managers must not only adapt to the changing characteristics of the labor force, but the employees comprising this new labor force must be able to adjust to the ever-changing needs of organizations.

SOCIETY

Members of society also exert considerable pressure on personnel management. The public is no longer content to accept, without question, the actions of business. They have found that changes can be made through their voices and votes and that their influence is obvious by the large

Kathryn D. McKee,
SPHR
Senior Vice President
First Interstate Bancorp.

Kathryn D. McKee, former president of the International Association for Personnel Women says, "The field of Personnel is on the cutting edge of major social change." In today's highly complex environment, McKee believes that the programs developed and the decisions made by Personnel can profoundly impact a business firm's profits.

Her extensive background in Personnel includes experience with several organizations. After she graduated from college, her first assignment was as an employment clerk for a major aerospace firm in southern California. After this job, she obtained a position as employment security officer with the State of California, and, as she puts it, she was "out from behind the typewriter at last!" At this job she received a solid foundation for her career in human resources management. She obtained invaluable experience in job classification, employment interviewing, unemployment claims determination, and vocational counseling.

McKee next joined Mattel, Inc., as an employment interviewer. She progressed rapidly to salary analyst and later to corporate compensation manager. While at Mattel, she demonstrated that raising a family and being a business executive are not mutually exclusive — her employment with Mattel was interrupted briefly for two maternity leaves.

The next phase of McKee's career began when the president of a small firm sought her out to serve as director of industrial relations. Three weeks into her job, she was faced with a Teamsters' effort to organize the office employees. "Ironically they picked the day we were to implement the new salary administration plan for *all* nonunion employees to pass out the signature cards, almost as if they knew we were starting to create programs. After a few harried hours of panic and some counsel from our labor attorney, we proceeded to implement our programs and face down the union. Anyone who has been through that experience will attest to the exhilaration and the anxiety it creates. There are so many things employers can't do in such situations. The episode came to a head when, on advice of counsel, we held an open meeting for all nonunion employees and the new president in effect said, 'We're new and we're here to make this company run better. Give us six months to make improvements. If, after that time, you feel you need a union to make it better, then do what you want, but at least give us a chance.' The upshot of that was, acting upon a request from an employee, top management held a series of small-group, open meetings to air problems and respond with what we could do to solve them. The problems ranged from 'The carpet is dirty' to 'We have lousy benefits,' both of which were true at that time. After three months, we had all the issues resolved, the Teamsters had no show of interest, and the organizing attempt was moot."

When Twentieth Century Fox needed to fill the position of corporate compensation manager, they selected Kathryn McKee. After a year of developing, organizing, and implementing a compensation program, she embarked on still another major project, which encompassed designing the company's corporate equal opportunity program.

Later she moved from compensation to establish a management development function as well.

McKee's newest career opportunity came when First Interstate Bancorp recruited her as vice president of compensation and benefits, responsible for designing and implementing benefit programs that affect over 35,000 employees, and for developing corporate compensation policies and administrative tools such as a state of the art quantitative job evaluation plan used to analyze and evaluate work in the financial services industry positions. "It is in this position I am able to draw on all the human resources experience I have. Compensation and benefits planning affects and is affected by all aspects of our profession."

number of regulatory laws that have been passed since the early 1960s. If a firm is to remain acceptable to the general public, it must be capable of satisfactorily explaining its purpose.

A major point that management must consider is that society includes the firm's employees. For instance, if an organization has 10,000 employees, these individuals will have influence over a larger number of people who are not connected with the firm, including friends or members of an employee's family. Therefore it behooves a firm to maintain clear communication with its employees so that the firm's side of a story is told.

The general public's attitude and beliefs can affect the firm's behavior. **Social responsibility** refers to *an organization's basic obligation to ensure that its decisions and operations meet the needs and interests of society.* Considerable pressure can be exerted on a firm to alter its practices if the public believes that it is not operating in the best interest of society. If a firm is to be socially responsible, the interests and welfare of both the corporation and the public must be considered.

You may ask at this point, "Why should a business firm be concerned with the welfare of society? Its goal is to make a profit and grow." It is difficult to question that a business must make a profit in the long run if it is to survive. But, a basic point should also be remembered: If the needs of society are not satisfied, a firm will ultimately cease to exist. A firm operates by public consent to satisfy society's needs. To compound the issue, society's goals, values, and attitudes are constantly changing.

Although these issues are directed at the overall organization, it can easily be seen how Personnel might be expected to become involved in each. The organization is a member of the community in which it operates. Just as citizens may work to improve the quality of life in their community, the organization should also respect and work with the other members of its community. For instance, a high unemployment rate of a certain minority group may exist within the firm's service area. A philosophy of hiring workers who are capable of being trained as opposed to hiring only qualified applicants may work toward reducing unemployment. In the long run this philosophy may actually improve profitability. It is extremely difficult for an individual to purchase the firm's products or services when he or she is unemployed. Human resource managers are becoming more involved in social responsibility issues.

43

Chapter 2
The
Environment of
Human
Resource
Management

UNIONS

Wage levels, benefits, and working conditions for millions of employees now reflect decisions made jointly by unions and management. A **union** is *a group of employees who have joined together for the purpose of dealing with their employer.* Unions are treated as an environmental factor because, essentially, they become a third party when dealing with the company. It is the union rather than the individual employee that negotiates an agreement with the firm. The presence of unions tends to increase labor costs but often improves the welfare of the employees.

There are approximately 20 million union members in the United States.[5] Although unions remain a powerful force, union membership as a percentage of the nonagricultural work force slipped from 33 percent in 1955 to about 19 percent in 1985.[6] This trend is likely to continue for a number of reasons. Young women who become blue-collar workers are often reluctant to join unions because they think unions are dominated by men.[7] In addition, an increasing percentage of the work force is involved in service occupations rather than in manufacturing. Service employees, such as clerical workers and computer programmers, have traditionally resisted unionization.

STOCKHOLDERS

The owners of a corporation are called **stockholders.** Because stockholders have a monetary investment in the firm, they may at times challenge programs considered by management to be beneficial to the organization. Managers may be forced to justify the merits of a particular program in terms of how it will affect future costs, projects, and revenues. For instance, if it is recommended that $50,000 be spent for implementing a management development program, the program may need more justification than merely stating that "managers should become more open and adaptive to the needs of employees." Stockholders/owners are concerned with how expenditure

---

[5]"The Rise and Fall of Big Labor," *Newsweek* (September 5, 1983): 51.
[6]"Beyond Unions: A Revolution Is in the Making," *Business Week* 2902 (July 8, 1985): 72.
[7]Marvin Cetron and Thomas O'Toole, *Encounters with the Future*, p. 265.

decisions will increase revenues or decrease costs. Thus management must be prepared to explain the merits of a particular program in terms of its economic costs and benefits.

Another means by which stockholders can influence a company is through stockholder activism. Such activism was virtually unheard of in the 1960s, but now management has become extremely sensitive to its public image. The last thing most corporations want is criticism of the firm's performance on the front page of a major newspaper.[8]

COMPETITION

Unless an organization is in the unusual position of monopolizing the market it serves, other firms will be producing similar products or services. For a firm to succeed, grow, and prosper, it must be able to maintain a supply of competent employees. But other organizations are also striving toward the same general objective. A firm's major task is to ensure that it obtains and retains a sufficient number of employees in various career fields. A bidding war often results when competitors attempt to fill certain critical positions in their firms. Because of the strategic nature of their needs, firms are sometimes forced to resort to unusual means to recruit and retain critical employees. The poster you see in Figure 2–8 illustrates the extreme approaches that some organizations have used to recruit qualified workers.

On the other hand, because of the competitive nature of many businesses, organizations may feel that they are under considerable pressure to improve their compensation system. In order to meet this challenge, firms not only are improving their salaries but also are emphasizing other forms of rewards. Thus the overall working environment may need to be considered as a portion of the firm's total financial compensation program.

CUSTOMERS

The people who actually use a firm's products and services also must be considered a part of the external environment. Because sales are critical to the firm's survival, management has the task of ensuring that its employment practices do not antagonize the members of the market it serves. There have been instances of consumer boycotts when organizations have limited the number of minorities they employ. Thus legal requirements are not the only consideration when determining the firm's workforce composition. If a certain minority or ethnic group purchases a large share of the firm's products, it may be in the best interests of the organization to make sure that a representative proportion of this group is included within its work force.

[8]David Vogel, "Ralph Nader's All Over the Place: Citizens vs. the Corporation," *Across the Board* 1 (April 1979): 26–31.

45

Chapter 2
The
Environment of
Human
Resource
Management

Figure 2–8. A recruitment poster. Source: Ampex Corporation.

Customers are constantly demanding high quality products and improved service. Therefore the firm must always strive to have a work force that is capable of providing these products and services. Sales are often lost or gained because of product quality, which is directly related to the skills and qualifications of the organization's employees.

TECHNOLOGY

Rapid change has been a significant factor in placing personnel managers in the forefront of organizational decision making. Few firms operate today as they did twenty years ago. Today, change is being experienced at an ever-increasing pace. Of major concern is the effect that technological or state of the art changes have had on businesses. Frederick W. Bahl, director of personnel administration for Alumax, Inc., believes that "During the next decade, the most challenging area in personnel and human resource management will be training employees to stay up with rapidly advancing technology." Products that were not envisioned only a few years ago are now being mass produced. This has caused the task of all managers to be substantially enlarged. New skills are needed to meet new technology demands. These skills are typically not in large supply, and it often becomes difficult to recruit qualified individuals.

As technological changes occur, certain skills are no longer required. This necessitates some retraining of the current work force. For instance, many colleges and universities have experienced enrollment decreases in certain fields of study. To offset these changes, some have begun to cross-train some of their instructors into fields that are experiencing a high level of demand. Math teachers, for instance, are taking additional courses to prepare themselves to teach data processing. Also because of the rapid change, some firms have been forced to emphasize job specialization. This process permits jobs to be broken down into smaller components in order that they may be performed by less skilled employees. However, this approach appears to be a two-edged sword. As jobs become more specialized, employee motivation may become a problem.

THE INTERNAL ENVIRONMENT

The internal environment also exerts considerable pressure on human resource management. The **internal environment** is comprised of *those factors that affect a firm's human resources from inside the organization's boundaries.* As indicated in Figure 2–1, the primary internal factors include the firm's mission, company policies, and corporate culture. These factors have a major impact in determining the interaction between human resource management and other departments within the organization.

MISSION

Mission is *the organization's continuing purpose or reason for being.* Each management level in the organization should conduct its operation with a clear understanding of the overall mission of the firm. In fact, each unit in the organization (division, plant, department) should have clearly understood objectives that coincide with the organizational mission.

The specific company mission must be regarded as a major internal factor that affects the tasks of human resource management. Consider two companies, each having a broad-based objective, and envision how related tasks might differ from one firm to the other. Company A has the goal of being a leader in the industry with respect to technological advances. Its growth occurs through the pioneering of new products and processes. On the other hand, Company B's goal is one of conservative growth with little risk taking. Only after another company's product or process has proven itself in the marketplace will Company B commit itself.

47

Chapter 2
The
Environment of
Human
Resource
Management

Company A needs a creative environment which would encourage new ideas. Highly skilled workers must be recruited and selected to bring about technological advancement. Constant attention to the training and development of the work force is essential. A compensation program designed to retain and motivate the most productive workers is especially important.

The basic tasks of human resource management remain the same for Company B, but the mission dictates that they be altered somewhat. A different kind of work force will likely be needed. Highly creative individuals may not want to work for Company B. Perhaps because the mission encourages little risk taking, most of the major decisions will be made at higher levels in the organization. Thus there may be less emphasis on management development at lower levels in the organization. The compensation program may be different to reflect the requirements of this particular work force. As this comparison indicates, a human resource manager must have a clear understanding of the company's mission before attempting to direct his or her department's activities.

POLICIES

A **policy** is *a predetermined guide established to provide direction in decision making*. It provides guidance for thinking. Policies establish parameters that assist people in the organization as they go about accomplishing their jobs. Policies are also flexible in that some interpretation and judgment is generally required in their use. They can exert significant influence on how managers accomplish their jobs. For instance, many firms have an "open door" policy, which permits employees to bypass their immediate supervisor and take a problem to the next higher level in the organization. Knowing that their subordinates can speak to a higher level manager may encourage supervisors to try harder to resolve problems with subordinates.

Many larger firms have policies related to every major area of their operations. Although policies are established for marketing, production, and finance, often the largest number of policies relate to human resource management. Some potential policy statements that could affect the work of the personnel manager are:

- To provide employees with a place of work that is as safe as possible.
- To encourage all employees to achieve as much of their human potential as possible.
- To provide compensation that will encourage a high level of performance in the form of increased quality and quantity of production.

■ To ensure that present organizational members are considered first for any vacant position.

This last policy is often referred to as a "promotion from within" policy. This type of guideline aids managers when they are faced with promotion decisions. Since policies have a degree of flexibility, however, the manager is not necessarily required to promote an employee currently with the firm. The supervisor may determine, for example, that no one in the firm is qualified and choose to look outside the firm for a replacement.

The tone of a policy can assist managers as they perform their daily activities. Consider, for instance, the policy to ensure "that all members of the labor force have equal opportunity for employment." This policy implies more than merely adhering to certain laws and government regulations. Confronted with this policy, the manager will likely do more than merely conform to the law. Perhaps a training program will be initiated to permit hiring of minorities or women who are not totally qualified to perform available jobs. Rather than just seek qualified applicants, a firm that actively implements this policy has gone beyond what is required by law.

CORPORATE CULTURE

As an internal environmental factor affecting human resource management, corporate culture refers to the firm's social and psychological climate. **Corporate culture** is defined as *the system of shared values, beliefs, and habits within an organization that interacts with the formal structure to produce behavioral norms.*[9] An infinite number of possible cultures could exist, and they might be viewed as a continuum. A closed and threatening culture is at one extreme. In this type of culture, decisions tend to be made higher in the organization; there tends to be a lack of trust and confidence in subordinates; secrecy abounds throughout the firm; and workers are not encouraged to be creative and engage in problem-solving activities. At the other extreme of the continuum is an open culture in which decisions tend to be made at lower levels in the organization; a high degree of trust and confidence in subordinates exists; open communication is encouraged and workers are encouraged toward creativity and solution of problems with other team members. Identification of the type of culture that exists within a firm is important because it affects job performance throughout the organization. Corporate culture will be discussed in considerable detail in chapter 9.

EXTERNAL ENVIRONMENT OF MULTINATIONALS[10]

Multinational organizations often confront environmental factors that are quite different from the environment of firms headquartered and operated

[9]Arthur Sharplin, *Strategic Management.* New York: McGraw-Hill, 1985, p. 102.

[10]This discussion is based on R. Wayne Mondy, Arthur Sharplin, Robert E. Holmes, and Edwin B. Flippo, *Management: Concepts and Practices*, 3rd ed. Newton, Mass.: Allyn & Bacon, 1986, pp. 588–610.

exclusively in the United States. A **multinational company (MNC)** is *a company that conducts a large part of its business outside the country in which it is headquartered and has a significant percentage of physical facilities and employees in other countries.* Multinationals usually operate through subsidiary companies in countries other than their home nation. Some of the names of the largest multinationals have become household words: General Motors, Ford, IBM, General Electric, and Exxon. The world-wide impact of these companies is significant. Their operations create interrelationships between countries, as well as between economic and political systems.

49

Chapter 2
The
Environment of
Human
Resource
Management

MNCs provide a large portion of the total economic output of the world. Some economists have estimated that, by the year 2000, some 200–300 multinationals will account for one-half of the world's total output of goods and services. In recent years, direct investment by multinational firms has grown rapidly, averaging about 10 percent per year. MNCs based in the United States account for more than half of this worldwide investment. In fact, of the top twenty multinational companies, 12 are based in the United States.[11]

HUMAN RESOURCE MANAGEMENT AND MULTINATIONALS

Successful management of an MNC requires that its managers understand the needs, values, and problems of workers in the countries where the company operates. A study of 300 managers in 14 countries found that parent country managers had a low opinion of their subordinates' abilities to take an active role in the management process.[12] Management must recognize that no one style of leadership will be equally effective in all countries. People in various countries have widely divergent backgrounds, education, cultures, and religions and live within a variety of social conditions and economic and political systems. All these factors have a dramatic effect on the work environment.

TYPES OF MNC EMPLOYEES

When filling key managerial, technical, or professional positions abroad, multinationals can choose among three basic types of employees: (1) parent country nationals (PCNs); (2) host country nationals (HCNs); and (3) third country nationals (TCNs). Until the 1950s, it was common for MNCs to fill foreign key posts with trusted and experienced personnel from home (PCNs). Recently, stronger nationalistic feelings have led countries to alter their policies and companies to employ more people from host countries. Ad-

[11]"The Largest Industrial Companies in the World," *Fortune* (August 10, 1981): 205.

[12]Abdulrahman Al-Jafary and A. T. Hollingsworth, "Practices in the Arabian Gulf Region," *Journal of International Business Studies* 14 (Fall 1983): 144.

ditionally, some firms have used workers from countries other than the parent country or host country. Such employees are known as third country nationals; for example, one U.S.-based firm received a contract to build highways in Saudi Arabia using personnel from Turkey and Italy. Still, many companies attempt to keep parent country employees in at least half of the identified key positions, particularly in the financial function. As an example, Renault has chosen to use HCNs in its operations, although a number of PCNs have been assigned as senior managers.

Using workers from the parent nation of the multinational ensures a greater degree of consistency and control in the firm's operations around the world. This is not without its costs because these personnel may experience considerable difficulty in understanding cultural differences. In an attitude survey of personnel in forty-nine multinationals, employees from the host country contended that parent country workers tended not to question orders from headquarters even when appropriate to do so.[13] This enabled them to advance their own long-term interests in the firm by getting better headquarter evaluations and making repatriation easier at the end of their tours of duty. In addition, the common practice of frequent rotation of key personnel intensified the problem of understanding and adapting to local cultures. However, employing PCNs does help in communications with headquarters because both parties share the same culture.

Utilizing individuals from the host country in key positions can improve the MNC's relations with the host country's government. It can also enable a quicker and more effective adaptation to requirements of the local culture. Disadvantages include a lessened degree of central control and increased communication problems with headquarters. In addition, if the HCNs perceive that the opportunity for higher positions is blocked for ethnic reasons, they will use the MNC to gain experience so they can move into higher positions with host country firms.

HUMAN RESOURCE PROBLEMS RELATED TO PARENT COMPANY NATIONALS

One of the most difficult human resource problems for the multinational is that of selecting the appropriate people to send on foreign assignments. Careful plans should be made to ensure that selectees possess certain basic characteristics, such as:

- A real desire to work in a foreign country.
- Spouses and families who have actively encouraged the person to work overseas.
- Cultural sensitivity and flexibility.

---

[13]Yoram Zeira, "Overlooked Personnel Problems of Multinational Corporations," *Columbia Journal of World Business* 10 (Summer 1975): 96–103.

- High degree of technical competence.
- A sense of politics.

51

**Chapter 2
The
Environment of
Human
Resource
Management**

Several surveys of overseas managers have revealed that the spouse's opinion and attitude should be considered the most important screening factor. Cultural sensitivity is also essential to avoid antagonizing host country nationals unnecessarily.

A second major problem that confronts MNCs is the establishment of equitable compensation systems for workers given international assignments. Typically, employees from the parent country receive a salary, an overseas premium of up to 50 percent, and moving expense and living allowances. Individuals from the parent country of the MNC receive higher pay than personnel from the host country. This difference tends to create resentment and reduce cooperation. Many Americans have found their standard of living and social class to be considerably improved in foreign countries over what it had been in the United States. The drop in living standard when they return may make for some difficulties. An important incentive for U.S. citizens to accept assignments in foreign countries is the opportunity to exclude a portion of their income earned in the foreign country from U.S. income taxes. Internal Revenue Service regulations allow a U.S. citizen to exclude certain income earned while working in a foreign country provided that the individual is a resident of the foreign country for 12 months or longer. In addition to financial rewards, foreign assignments often provide career advancement opportunities.

Despite a company's intention to provide career advancement opportunities, there is still some danger that skilled managers assigned to foreign operations will come to feel that their career progress has suffered. Some managers have returned from foreign assignments to find no job available, or they are given jobs that do not utilize skills obtained during the overseas service. To solve this problem, a godfather system has been set up in companies such as Control Data Corporation.[14] Before the person leaves on assignment, a specific executive is appointed as the "godfather" to look after the person's interest while in a foreign country and to assist the executive in achieving a smooth transition upon returning home. A repatriation plan is developed, including the duration of the assignment and the job to which the appointee will return. Ordinarily, the godfather is the person's future boss upon return to the parent country. During the assignment, the individual is kept informed of major events occurring in the unit of future assignment. In this way, a logical career plan is worked out, and there is no feeling on the part of the executive of being lost in the vast international shuffle of the company.

[14]David M. Noer, "Integrating Foreign Service Employees to Home Organization: The Godfather Approach," *Personnel Journal* 53 (January 1974): 45–50.

MANAGEMENT APPROACH AND MULTINATIONALS

Surveys have shown that academic research has not kept pace with the internationalization of industry.[15] Much that is said and written about appropriate management approaches for international businesses is based on common sense and informed conjecture. However, it seems reasonable that a successful international manager should possess the following qualities, among others:

- A knowledge of basic history, particularly that of countries of old and homogeneous cultures.
- A social background in basic economics and sociological concepts as they differ from country to country.
- An interest in the host country and a willingness to learn and practice the language.
- A genuine respect for differing philosophical and ethical approaches.

The multinational company, by definition, is faced with a wide variety of situations: differing cultures, economic and political systems, and religions. Management must capitalize on its unique strength of being able to make worldwide decisions in the selection of markets and allocation of resources. Yet each market has different environmental constraints. Thus multinational managers must adapt to and work with the varying cultures of a multiplicity of nations throughout the world.

A Harvard University study shows that global-centered MNCs generally perform better than country-centered ones. Global-centered companies see the world marketing effort as an integrated set of activities. Country-centered MNCs follow the portfolio approach to their overseas subsidiaries, treating operations in each country as a separate investment. Global companies tend to think more in the long term. They are organized to achieve economy of scale.[16]

The chief executive officer of each foreign subsidiary is confronted by opposing flows of corporate uniformity and cultural fragmentation. If the officer is from the parent country, uniformity is likely to be emphasized. If the manager is from the host country, cultural adaptation may take precedence. Because of growing nationalistic tendencies in many countries, there is an increased chance that the top manager will be from the host country. In Germany, for instance, the chief executive officer must have an engineering degree to be accepted and respected. In France, graduates of the *grades ecoles* are favored. If third country nationals are to be used as chief executive officers, varying mobilities must be considered. A married Frenchman living in Paris is almost unmovable. Most German managers are quite enthusiastic about working in other countries. The English and

---

[15]Nancy J. Adler, "The Ostrich and the Trend," *The Academy of Management Review* 8 (April 1983): 231.

[16]Michael Porter, "Why Global Businesses Perform Better," *International Management* 38 (January 1983): 40.

53

**Chapter 2
The
Environment of
Human
Resource
Management**

Scandinavians are typically willing to relocate, but they require assurance of return to their native lands.

Adaptation is not all one way. Local nationals will have to try to understand and adapt to the culture of the MNC, which inevitably requires some understanding of the culture of the parent country of the MNC. In dealing with headquarters executives of a U.S. MNC, the local national will have to learn to get to the point quickly. Americans are notoriously impatient with lengthy and expanded explanations. Nationals must be positive in approach and must avoid constant criticism. They must also learn to argue with American executives but know just how far they can go.

Effective managers of multinational operations must develop a style of leadership consistent with the needs of the situation existing in the host country. The appropriate managerial style of leadership can be determined only after a careful assessment of the external environment of the host country, the types of personnel to be managed, the level of existing technology, and the specific goals and operational requirements of the company.

SUMMARY

Human resource managers interact with other managers as they strive to achieve the goals of the organization. In a real sense, all managers are managers of human resources. Personnel's job is not accomplished in a vacuum. Many interacting factors affect the performance of specific tasks and can be grouped under two primary headings: (1) the external environment; and (2) the internal environment.

The external environment consists of those factors that affect a firm's human resources from outside organizational boundaries. Major external factors include: legal considerations, customers, unions, society, technology, the labor force, competition, and stockholders. The primary internal factors include company mission, company policies, and corporate culture. In addition, personnel professionals constantly work with people from other functional areas such as marketing, production, and finance. They must understand the different perspectives of people from various disciplines in order to perform their tasks.

Understanding the many interrelationships involved in human resource management is quite important as the personnel professional works with other managers to assist them in resolving their daily problems. The effect of a particular act must be considered in light of its impact on the entire organization. This framework emphasizes the big picture rather than concentration on a narrow phase of the company's operations.

The basic tasks assigned the personnel activity remain essentially the same regardless of the impact exerted from either the external or internal environments. However, the manner in which they are accomplished may be altered substantially. None of the personnel functions should be studied without considering the results of a decision on each of the other functions.

A multinational company (MNC) is a company that conducts a large part of its business outside the country in which it is headquartered and has a significant percentage of physical facilities and employees in other countries. The external environment that confronts multinational firms is diverse and complex. The success or failure of an MNC is determined largely by how it responds to this environment. The majority of the environmental problems that arise can be categorized as economic, political–legal, and social.

QUESTIONS FOR REVIEW

1. What is meant by the statement, "The personnel manager's job is not accomplished in a vacuum?"
2. What factors comprise the external environment of human resource management? Briefly describe each.
3. How is the labor force of the United States expected to change?
4. What internal environment considerations exert pressure on the accomplishment of Personnel's job?
5. How could changes in an organizational policy affect the personnel professional's work? Give an example.
6. Define corporate culture. What affect could culture have on human resource management?
7. What is a multinational company?
8. What basic characteristics should managers who are being sent abroad possess?

TERMS FOR REVIEW

External environment
Social responsibility
Union
Stockholders
Internal environment

Mission
Policy
Corporate culture
Multinational company (MNC)

Incident 1

As the largest employer in Ouachita County, Arkansas, International Forest Products Company (IFP) is an important part of the local economy. Ouachita County includes a mostly rural area of south central Arkansas. IFP employs almost 10 percent of the local work force and there are few alternative job opportunities available.

Scott Wheeler, the personnel director at IFP, tells of a difficult decision he once had to make.

Everything was going along pretty well despite the economic recession, but I knew that sooner or later we would be affected. I got the word at a private meeting with the president, Mr. Deason, that we would have to cut the work force by 30 percent on a crash basis. I was to get back to him within a week with a suggested plan. I knew that my plan would not be the final one, since the move was so major. But I knew that

Mr. Deason was depending on me to provide at least a workable approach.

First of all, I thought about how the union would react. Certainly, workers would have to be let go in order of seniority. The union would try to protect as many jobs as possible. I also knew that all management's actions during this period would be intensely scrutinized. We had to make sure that we had our act together.

Then there was the matter of the impact on the surrounding community. The economy of Ouachita County had not been in good shape recently. Aside from the impact on individual workers who were laid off, I knew that our cutbacks would further depress the area's economy. I knew that there would be a number of government officials and civic leaders who would want to know how we were trying to minimize the harm done to the public in the area.

We really had no choice but to make the cuts, I believed. First of all, I had no choice because Mr. Deason said that we were going to do it. Also, I had recently read a news account that one of our competitors, Johns Manville Corporation in West Monroe, Louisiana, had laid off several hundred workers in a cost cutting move. To keep our sales from being further depressed, we had to ensure that our costs were just as low as those of our competitors. The wood products market is very competitive and a cost advantage of even 2 or 3 percent would allow competitors to take many of our customers.

Finally, a major reason for the cutbacks was to protect the interests of our shareholders. A few years ago we had a shareholder group which disrupted the annual meeting to insist that IFP make certain anti-pollution changes. In general, though, the shareholders seem to be more concerned with the return on their investment than with social responsibility. At our meeting the president reminded me that, just like every other manager in the company, I should place the shareholders' interest foremost. I really was quite overwhelmed as I began to work up a personnel plan which would balance all of the conflicting interests that I knew about.

QUESTIONS

1. List the elements in the company's environment that will affect Scott's suggested plan. How legitimate is the interest of each of these?
2. Is it true that Scott should be concerned first and foremost with protecting the interests of the shareholders? Discuss.

Incident 2

As the personnel director for KBH Stores in St. Louis, Missouri, Virginia Knickerbocker knew that she had her work cut out for her. Company management had just announced a goal of opening ten new stores during the next twelve months. KBH employed 480 people in the 35 stores they then had in operation. Virginia knew that staffing the new stores would require hiring and training about 150 people. She felt that her own small office was inadequately funded and staffed to handle this task.

Virginia found out about the expansion plans from a friend who knew the president's secretary. While she did not like being kept in the dark, she was not surprised that she had not been told. Glenn Sullivan, the president of KBH, was noted for his autocratic leadership style. He tended to tell subordinates only what he wanted them to know. He expected everyone who worked for him to follow orders without question. He was not an unkind person, though, and Virginia had always gotten along with him pretty well. She had never confronted Mr. Sullivan about anything, so it was with some concern that she approached his office that day.

"Mr. Sullivan," she began, "I hear that we are going to be opening 10 new stores next year." "That's right, Virginia," said Mr. Sullivan. "We've already arranged the credit lines and have picked out several of the sites." "What about staffing?" asked Virginia. "Well, I presume that you will take care of that, Virginia, when we get to that point."

"What about my own staff?" asked Virginia, "I think I am going to need at least three or four more people. We are already crowded for space, so I hope you plan to expand the personnel office." "Not really," said Mr. Sullivan, "You will have to get by with what you have for at least a year or so. It's going to be hard enough to afford the new stores and the people we need to staff them without spending money for more office space."

QUESTIONS

1. Evaluate the environment Virginia faces within the company.
2. How does the internal environment affect Virginia's ability to do her job?

REFERENCES

Adler, Philip, Jr., Parsons, Charles K., and Zolke, Scott B. "Employee Privacy: Legal and Research Developments and Implications for Personnel Administration." *Sloan Management Review* 26 (Winter 1985): 13–21.

Atherton, Roger M., Jr. and Scanion, Burt K. "Participation and the Effective Use of Authority." *Personnel Journal* 60 (September 1981): 697–703.

Bairol, Lloyd. "Managing Dissatisfaction." *Personnel* 58 (May–June 1981): 12–21.

Banik, Joseph A. "The Marketing Approach to Communicating with Employees." *Personnel Journal* 64 (October 1985): 62–68.

Beerbower, Albert. "Junk the Jargon." *Supervision* XLIII (May 1981): 7–8.

Bernstein, A. and Schiller, Z. "The Double Standard That's Setting Worker Against Worker." *Business Week* (April 8, 1985): 70–71.

"Beyond Unions: A Revolution Is in the Making." *Business Week* 2902 (July 8, 1985): 72.

Brewer, Richard. "Personnel's Role In Participation." *Personnel Management* 4 (September 1978): 27–29 + .

Brunner, Nancy R. "Blue-Collar Women." *Personnel Journal* 60 (April 1981): 273–282.

Copperman, Lois Farrer and Keast, Fred D. "Older Workers: A Challenge for Today and Tomorrow." *Human Resource Management* 20 (Summer 1981): 13–18.

Copperman, Lois F., Keast, Fred D., and Montgomery, Douglas G. "Older Workers and Part-Time Work Schedules." *Personnel Administrator* 26 (October 1981): 35–65.

Cosijn, Eugene. "European Patterns in Working Time." *Personnel Management* (September 1985): 33–36.

Denova, Charles C. "Develop a Self-Motivating Attitude." *Supervision* 43 (June 1981): 7.

"Dilemma of Management Leadership." *Training and Development Journal* 35 (August 1981): 6–7.

Driver, Russell W. "Opening the Channels of Upward Communication." *Supervisory Management* 25 (March 1980): 24–29.

———. "Employers Urged to Overcome Fears of Favoritism and Identify High Fliers." Management Review 73 (October 1984): 32.

"Facts and Figures: Anatomy of a Human Resource Executive." *Training* (May 1985): 146.

Ferris, G. R. and Curtin, D. "Shaping Strategy: Tie Personnel Functions to Company Goals." *Management World* 14 (January 1985): 32–33+.

Fitz-enz, Jac. "Measuring Human Resources Effectiveness." *Personnel Administrator* (July 1980): 33–36.

Foltz, Roy G. "Labor Relations Communication." *Personnel Administrator* 26 (March 1981): 12.

———. "Productivity and Communications." *Personnel Administrator* 26 (August 1981): 12.

———. "Gainsharing: Is It a Human Resource Strategy or a Group Incentive System?" *Business Quarterly* 49 (Winter 1984–85): 92–95.

Goerth, C. R. "Who Has Access to What Information." *National Safety News* 130 (December 1984): 44–47.

Greene, Jeanne Polston. "People Management: New Directions for the 80s." *Administrative Management* 42 (January 1981): 22.

Hay, Christine D. "Women in Management: The Obstacles and Opportunities They Face." *Personnel Administrator* 25 (April 1980): 31–39.

———. "How Robotization Affects People." *Business Horizons* 28 (May, June 1985): 75–80.

Kandel, W. L. "Preventive Law and Personnel Policies." *Employee Relations Law Journal* 10 (Summer, 1984): 120–128.

Lee, Nancy. "The Dual Career Couple: Benefits and Pitfalls." *Management Review* 70 (January 1981): 46–52.

Lesly, Philip. "Functioning in the New Human Climate." *Management Review* 70 (December 1981): 24–28+.

Lewin, David. "Collective Bargaining and the Quality of Work Life." *Organizational Dynamics* (August 1981): 37+.

Likert, Rensis. *The Human Organization: Its Management and Value*. New York: McGraw-Hill, 1976.

Magnus, Margaret. "Employee Recognition: A Key to Motivation." *Personnel Journal* 60 (February 1981): 103–104.

March, James G. and Simon, Herbert A. *Organizations*. New York: John Wiley & Sons, 1963.

McGregor, Douglas. *The Human Side of Enterprise*. New York: McGraw-Hill, 1960.

Miller, William B. "Motivation Techniques: Does One Work Best?" *Management Review* 70 (February 1981): 47–52.

Monthly News on Human Resource Management. American Society for Personnel Administration (August 1985): 12.

Neudeck, Mariellen MacDonald, "Trends Affecting Hospitals' Human Resources." *Hospital & Health Service Administration* 30 (May, June 1985): 82–93.

Newsletter, Beta Gamma Signa, the National Honor Society in Business and Management (September 1985): 2.

Owens, James. "A Reappraisal of Leadership Theory and Training." *Personnel Administrator* 26 (November 1981): 75–84.

———. "Personnel Trends and the Law." *Office Administration and Automation* 45 (December 1984): 29.

Rhodes, Susan R., Schuster, Michael, and Doering, Mildred. "The Implication of an Aging Workforce." *Personnel Administrator* 26 (October 1981): 19–22.

Rogers, Carl R. and Roethlisberger, J. J. "Barriers and Gateways to Communication." *Harvard Business Review* 30 (July/August 1952): 46–52.

Ruck, Frank J., Jr. "A Participative Management Concept Shares Successes, Responsibility, at ETC." *Personnel Administrator* 27 (June 1982): 65–71.

Sharkpin, A. D. and Wall, J. L. "Serving HRM Purposes through Chapter 11?" *Personnel Administrator* 30 (February 1985): 103–111.

Sharplin, Arthur. *Strategic Management*. New York: McGraw-Hill, 1985: 102.

Sheppard, I. Thomas. "Rite of Passage . . . Women for the Inner Circle." *Management Review* 70 (July 1981): 8–14.

Sinetar, Marsha. "Developing Leadership Potential." *Personnel Journal* 60 (March 1981): 193–196.

Somers, Patricia, Poulton-Callahan, Charles, and Bartlett, Robin. "Women in the Workforce: A Structural Approach to Equality." *Personnel Administrator* 26 (October 1981): 61–64.

Tavernier, Gerard. "Improving Managerial Productivity: The Key Ingredient Is Better Communication." *Management Review* 70 (February 1981): 12–16.

Teresko, John. "Artificial Intelligence: More Fact Than Fantasy." *Industry Week* 224 (January 21, 1985): 53–60.

Walton, R. E. "From Control to Commitment in the Workplace." *Harvard Business Review* 63 (March–April, 1985): 77–84.

Weidenbaum, Murray L. "The True Obligation of the Business Firm to Society." *Management Review* 70 (September 1981): 21–22.

CHAPTER OBJECTIVES

1. Explain the major legislation that affected human resource management before 1960.
2. Describe the major laws passed since 1960 that have affected human resource management.
3. Explain Presidential Executive Orders 11246 and 11375.
4. Describe the purpose of Office of Federal Contract Compliance Programs.
5. Identify some of the major Supreme Court decisions that have had an impact on human resource management.
6. Describe the importance of the Uniform Guidelines on Employee Selection Procedures.
7. Explain what is meant by sexual harassment.

Chapter 3

LEGAL ASPECTS OF HUMAN RESOURCE MANAGEMENT

"I know that on paper Mary Martin is the best qualified," said Art Bethke, supervisor of the maintenance division of Allied Chemical. "But, you can't put a woman with that crew. Those guys wouldn't work with her." Phyllis Jordon, personnel director of Allied, was shocked to hear these comments. She knew that discrimination based on sex was illegal. Not only that, Allied had a policy of nondiscrimination with regard to sex, religion, race, color, and national origin. She also knew that Mary Martin would likely be given a hard time by the men in the maintenance crew. But, something had to be done.

The difficulty that Phyllis now confronts might not have arisen prior to the Civil Rights Act of 1964. Since then, many laws, court decisions, and Executive Orders have been handed down, and virtually all managers—human resource managers, in particular—must be aware of and work within these constraints. The purpose of this chapter is to provide an overview of the major legal developments that impact human resource management. We first describe the significant legislation affecting human resource management prior to 1960. Next, a major section is devoted to presenting HRM legislation passed after 1960. Then the importance of Presidential Executive Orders 11246 and 11375 is described. An overview of the function of the Office of Federal Contract Compliance Programs follows. The remainder of the chapter is devoted to significant Supreme Court decisions and the *Uniform Guidelines on Employee Selection Procedures*.

LAWS PRIOR TO 1960

The public often assumes that the major impact of laws and regulations began with the highly visible legislation of the 1960s. These laws continue to exert a significant impact on human resource management. While the legislation passed after 1960 is important, previous enactments laid the groundwork for government's increased intervention into business practices. A few of the most significant interventions are briefly described in the following sections. Some of them will be discussed in greater detail, as appropriate, in later chapters.

CIVIL RIGHTS ACTS OF 1866 AND 1871

The 1866 Civil Rights Act is based on the Thirteenth Amendment to the Constitution and prohibits race discrimination in hiring, placement, and continuation of employment. Private employers, unions, and employment agencies are covered. The 1871 act is based on the Fourteenth Amendment and prohibits deprivation of equal employment rights under coverage of state law. State and local governments are included. Thus, in the case of *Brown v. Gaston County Dyeing Machine Company* (1972), the court ruled that a black was entitled to back pay for the period during which discrimination occurred. The time period involved was between 1960 and 1961, three years prior to the 1964 Civil Rights Act. There is virtually no effective statute of limitation in filing charges under these acts.[1]

[1]Howard C. Lockwood, "Equal Employment Opportunities," in Dale Yoder and Herbert G. Heneman (eds.), *Staffing Policies and Strategies*. Washington, D.C.: Bureau of National Affairs, Inc., 1979, pp. 4–252.

RAILWAY LABOR ACT OF 1926

This law provided procedures for collective bargaining and for settling disputes between labor and management within the railroad industry. Although the Act pertained to only one industry, it is important because of its pioneering provisions in the area of collective bargaining and settling disputes between labor and management.

DAVIS-BACON ACT OF 1931

The Davis-Bacon Act requires that businesses holding federal construction contracts in the amount of $2000 or more pay their employees the rates offered for similar jobs in the community in which the work is being performed. This act resulted in the establishment of a high minimum wage for workers because "union scale" is normally taken to be the prevailing wage rate.

ANTI-INJUNCTION ACT OF 1932

This act, also known as the Norris–LaGuardia Act, severely restricts the use of injunctions in labor disputes. It defines permissible union activities in very broad terms. As a result of this act, the private injunction ceased to be used effectively as a means to defeat strikes. It also made the **"yellow dog" contract** legally unenforceable. These contracts between the employee and employer prohibited a worker from joining a union or engaging in union activities.

NATIONAL LABOR RELATIONS ACT OF 1935

The National Labor Relations Act (NLRA) of 1935 was passed at a time when the United States was in a severe depression. This act, referred to as the Wagner Act, has become the cornerstone of employer–employee relations in the United States. For the first time, a federal law supported union organization on a broad scale and required employers to recognize unions and to bargain collectively with them over wages, hours, and other terms and conditions of employment. The act also created the National Labor Relations Board (NLRB). This board was given responsibility for conducting representation elections and investigating and dealing with unfair labor practice changes. It also forbids any activity by management that tends to encourage or discourage membership in any particular labor union.

SOCIAL SECURITY ACT OF 1935—AS AMENDED

This act established a federal tax to be placed on payrolls and provided for unemployment and retirement benefits. The act also set up the Social

Security Administration. Employers were to share equally with employees the cost of old-age, survivors, and disability insurance. Employers were required to pay the full cost of unemployment insurance.

WALSH–HEALEY ACT OF 1936

The Walsh–Healey Act covers employers with federal contracts of $10,000 or more for the manufacture or furnishing of materials, supplies, articles, and equipment. As with the Davis–Bacon Act, employers must pay wages at the same rate paid for similar jobs in the community in which the work is being done.

FAIR LABOR STANDARDS ACT OF 1938

This act, known also as the Wage and Hour Law, requires payment of a minimum wage to virtually all workers. It also requires overtime pay at one-and-one-half times the regular rate for work beyond 40 hours in a work week. The act also sets a minimum employment age. Amendments have extended the coverage of the act to an increasing number of employees.

LABOR–MANAGEMENT RELATIONS ACT OF 1947

Twelve years after the labor-oriented Wagner Act, Congress attempted to provide a more balanced approach to labor relations by passing this piece of legislation, even overriding a presidential veto. Also known as the Taft–Hartley Act, this law amended the Wagner Act. The act gives employees the right to refrain from union activities and denies supervisors legal protection in obtaining union recognition.

LABOR–MANAGEMENT REPORTING AND DISCLOSURE ACT OF 1959

During the late 1950s, a series of Congressional investigations uncovered evidence of racketeering, crime, violence, and corruption by labor organizations and employers. As a result, the Labor–Management Reporting and Disclosure Act of 1959 (Landrum–Griffin Act) was passed. This far-reaching law was based upon congressional findings of a "need to eliminate or prevent improper practices on the part of labor organizations, employers, labor relations consultants, and their officers and representatives which distort and defeat the policies of the Labor Management Relations Act, 1947, as amended, and the Railway Labor Act, as amended." The act established very detailed federal regulation of the internal affairs of unions.

LEGISLATION AFTER 1960

The laws passed prior to 1960 were important because they initiated a new era of labor–management relations. These laws paved the way for a proliferation of legislation, which has had a significant effect on human resource management. Major legislation passed after 1960 will be described next.

EQUAL PAY ACT OF 1963—AMENDED 1972

The Equal Pay Act (an amendment to the Fair Labor Standards Act of 1938) made it illegal to discriminate in pay on the basis of sex where jobs require equal skills, effort, and responsibility and are performed under the same or similar working conditions. Exceptions are permitted if the payment is made based on a seniority system, or a system that measures earnings by quality or quantity of production. Pay differentials are also permitted if they are based on any factor other than sex.

The 1972 amendments expanded the act to cover employees in executive, administrative, professional, and outside sales force categories as well as employees in most state and local governments, hospitals, and schools. The act was originally administered by the U.S. Department of Labor but became the responsibility of the Equal Employment Opportunity Commission (EEOC) in 1979. In recent years, the act has been less significant because a violation of the Equal Pay Act is also a violation of Title VII of the Civil Rights Act.

TITLE VII OF THE CIVIL RIGHTS ACT OF 1964—AMENDED 1972

One law that has had an extensive influence on human resource management is Title VII of the 1964 Civil Rights Act, as amended by the Equal Employment Opportunity Act of 1972. This legislation prohibits discrimination based on race, color, sex, religion, or national origin. Women and minorities comprise the majority of people in what are called **protected groups.**

Title VII covers employers engaged in an industry affecting interstate commerce with fifteen or more employees for at least twenty calendar weeks in the year in which a charge is filed, or the year preceding the filing of a charge. Included in the definition of employers are state and local governments, schools, colleges, unions, and employment agencies.

The act created the Equal Employment Opportunity Commission (EEOC), which is responsible for its enforcement. Under Title VII, filing a discrimination charge initiates EEOC action. Charges may be filed by one of the presidentially appointed EEOC commissioners, by any aggrieved person, or by anyone acting on behalf of an aggrieved person. Charges must be filed within 180 days of the alleged act. However, the time is extended to 300 days if a state or local agency is involved in the case.

Once a charge is filed, the EEOC typically proceeds in the following manner. First, an attempt is made for a nofault settlement. Essentially, the

Drew M. Young,
SPHR
Vice President,
Employee Relations
(Retired)
ARCO Oil and Gas
Company (Division of
Atlantic Richfield
Company)

When the term *personnel professional* is used to suggest excellence in the field of personnel, the name of Drew M. Young must certainly come to mind. Throughout his career Young has participated in professional and civic activities. He believes that a person should give something back to the profession and community of which he is a part. As a result of practicing this philosophy, he has held numerous leadership positions in professional associations, including the national presidency of the American Society for Personnel Administration, the presidency of the Personnel Accreditation Institute, and a vice presidency and membership on the Board of Directors and the Executive Committee of the American Society for Training and Development.

Young's long and varied career began in the late 1930s after he received a B.A. degree in English and philosophy from Swarthmore College. He added to his education through the years by doing graduate studies in psychology and music at Temple University, graduating from the Executive Program at Columbia University's Graduate School of Business, and participating in numerous seminars, training programs, and workshops in the human resource field. His first position was that of director of music at Henry C. Conrad High School in Richardson Park, Delaware. The pay was higher for band directors than English teachers, and he thoroughly enjoyed what he did.

During his five years in the U.S. Army, he taught training management at the Signal Corps Officer Candidate School (Ft. Monmouth, N.J.) and was a training supervisor at the Army Signal Corps School AFWESPAC (Oro Bay, New Guinea and Manila, P.I.). These positions marked the beginning of his work in the field of training.

Young's transition to the world of business took place during the two years that he was an area training supervisor with the Veterans Administration. He and the training officers reporting to him were responsible for administering training for 12,000 veterans in Philadelphia, Chester, and Delaware Counties, Pennsylvania.

In 1947 he voluntarily took a cut in pay to enter the private sector as a training assistant with The Atlantic Refining Company (Philadelphia), one of the predecessor companies of Atlantic Richfield Company. As a member of the corporate training staff he found it somewhat frustrating to develop training programs for other company units and then not to see the results when not involved in implementing the programs. Thus, when several years later he was asked to be the training supervisor on the personnel staff of the company's North American Producing Division (Dallas, Texas), he jumped at the opportunity. He found it challenging to initiate the Division's first supervisory training program and even more challenging to convince the management of the Atlantic Pipe Line Company that they needed such a program for their supervisors. One tool used to accomplish this objective was a morale survey of all of their employees. The survey results showed definite needs for improving supervisory skills and changing work procedures. Shortly thereafter they implemented a specially designed supervisory training program.

After six years as supervisor of an ever-growing training function, Young was promoted to the position of personnel supervisor. His responsibilities included all of the personnel functions except safety and employment. After several years in this position, he accepted the assignment of manager of industrial relations for the Venezuelan Atlantic Refining Company (VARCO) in Caracas, Venezuela. During his almost four years in this position, he was responsible for all personnel functions plus the medical department, which operated two hospitals, the schools for employees' children in field locations, and the travel and documentation section. Operating in a different culture with employees whose value systems varied somewhat from those of American employees was a broadening and interesting experience. One thing he had to learn was to be able to say "no" in such a way that the other person could save face. He also found that negotiating collective labor agreements under circumstances where the Ministry of Labor might make the final decisions was a whole new ball game. Young said, "Working overseas provides valuable experience and is enriching in many ways. I would recommend it for anyone who is adaptable and has the opportunity. Many of the lessons that I have learned there stood me in good stead in subsequent years."

Several years after returning to Dallas as general personnel supervisor, he was promoted to the position that he held until he retired in May of 1981. In addition to being responsible for all personnel functions, he was involved in many interesting special projects. Several projects that stood out in his mind were: working on a task force to plan the logistics and personnel requirements for ARCO operations on the North Slope of Alaska; chairing a task force to develop organizational and policy recommendations for the corporate medical department; and overseeing the development and implementation of an integrated personnel planning system.

Young believes that personnel professionals should be well prepared to help their organizations meet three important needs:

- The need for greater, more creative contributions to productivity in the face of rising labor costs, stiffer competition, and economic changes.
- The need for more broadly skilled managers at the top of the company and stable executive succession.
- The need to plan and assimilate changes in status, work, and evolving relationships and expectations of employees.

Since his retirement, Young has remained active in human resource consulting and in the Personnel Accreditation Institute, serving as immediate past president. Over a four-year period, he and his wife Mary have conducted preretirement planning workshops involving more than 600 people.

organization charged with the violation is invited to settle the case with no admission of guilt. Most charges are settled at this stage.

Failing settlement at the first stage, the second phase is investigation by the EEOC. Once the employer is notified that an investigation will take place, no records relating to the charge may be destroyed. During the investigative process, the employer is permitted to present a position statement. After the investigation has been completed, the district director of the EEOC will issue a **probable cause** or "no probable cause" statement.

The next step involves attempted conciliation. In the event this effort fails, the case will be reviewed for litigation potential. Some of the factors that determine whether the EEOC will pursue litigation are: (1) the number of people affected by the alleged practice; (2) the amount of money involved in the charge; (3) other charges against the employer; and (4) the type of charge. Recommendations for litigation are then passed on to the general counsel of the EEOC. If the recommendation is against litigation, a right to sue notice will be issued to the charging party.

It is important to note that the Civil Rights Act prohibits retaliation against employees who have opposed an illegal employment practice. The act also protects those who have testified, assisted, or participated in an investigation of discrimination.

There are certain exceptions to the coverage of Title VII. These exceptions include: (1) religious institutions, with respect to the employment of persons of a specific religion in any of the institution's activities; (2) aliens; and (3) members of the Communist party. Noncitizens are not protected from discrimination because of their lack of citizenship. However, the act does protect them from discrimination because of their national origin. Even with these exceptions, the impact of the law has been felt by virtually every organization.

AGE DISCRIMINATION IN EMPLOYMENT ACT OF 1967—AMENDED IN 1978

The Age Discrimination in Employment Act (ADEA) prohibits employers from discriminating against individuals who are at least forty but less than seventy years old. The act pertains to employers with twenty or more employees for twenty or more calendar weeks (either in the current or preceding calendar year), unions of twenty-five or more members, employment agencies, and federal, state, and local government subunits. Administration of the Act was transferred from the U.S. Department of Labor to the EEOC in 1979.

Enforcement may begin once a charge is filed, or the EEOC can review compliance even if no charge is filed. The Age Discrimination Act differs from Title VII of the Civil Rights Act in that it provides for trial by jury and there is a possible criminal aspect to a charge. The trial by jury is important in that the jury may have greater sympathy for older people who have possibly been discriminated against. The criminal aspect means that an employee may receive more than lost wages if discrimination is proven.

In addition, under the 1978 amendment, class action suits are possible.

There are several exceptions to the ADEA. Compulsory retirement at age sixty-five is permitted for employees who have been high level executives. Individuals falling in this category must have their nonforfeitable annual retirement benefit equal to or exceeding $27,000.

THE OCCUPATIONAL SAFETY AND HEALTH ACT OF 1970

In recent years, no law has been as controversial as the Occupational Safety and Health Act (OSHA). The intent of the law was to make work and the work environment free of hazards. However, the manner of implementation has been questioned on many occasions, especially during the early years following its passage. The act established the Occupational Safety and Health Administration, an agency of the Department of Labor, to set up regulations and standards covering safety and health. OSHA has taken a broad view of interpreting health and safety factors, and virtually all companies are affected. Effects of the act will be described in detail in chapter 14.

REHABILITATION ACT OF 1973

The Rehabilitation Act covers certain government contractors and subcontractors and organizations that receive federal grants in excess of $2500. Individuals are considered handicapped if they have a physical or mental impairment that substantially limits one or more major life activities, or have a record of such impairment. The Office of Federal Contract Compliance Programs (OFCCP) administers the act. If a contract or subcontract exceeds $50,000, or if the contractor has fifty or more employees, an affirmative action program must be prepared. In it the contractor must specify the reasonable accommodations that are being made in hiring and promoting handicapped persons.

This act is expected to have even more impact in the future because the definition of "handicapped" has not been thoroughly tested by the courts. In some court decisions, epilepsy and alcoholism have been held to be covered under the act.

PRIVACY ACT OF 1974

The Privacy Act of 1974 was passed to "provide certain safeguards for an individual against an invasion of personal privacy." The act is limited to the federal government and its contractors. It applies to all executive departments, the military, independent regulatory agencies, government corporations, and government-controlled corporations. Any private business that has a contract with any of these agencies is also covered for the duration of the contract.

The purpose of the act is to limit the amount and type of information that federal agencies maintain in records about individuals and to control dissemination of that information to other agencies. Individuals must be permitted access to any personal records concerning them. Failure to comply with the act can result in litigation. Civil suits can be brought for actual damages or $1000, whichever is greater, plus reasonable costs and attorney fees. The courts can also order that a record be corrected. In addition, certain activities are misdemeanors and punishable by fines of up to $5000.

EMPLOYEE RETIREMENT SECURITY ACT OF 1974

Passed in 1974, the Employee Retirement Income Security Act (ERISA) is one of the most complex pieces of federal legislation to be passed. The purpose of the act is described in this manner:

> It is hereby declared to be the policy of this Act to protect . . . the interests of participants in employee benefit plans and their beneficiaries . . . by establishing standards of conduct, responsibility and obligations for fiduciaries of employee benefit plans, and by providing for appropriate remedies, sanctions, and ready access to the federal courts.[2]

Note that the word *protect* is used here because the act does not force employers to create employee benefit plans. It does set standards in the areas of participation, vesting of benefits, and funding for existing and new plans. Numerous existing retirement plans have been altered in order to conform to this legislation.

PREGNANCY DISCRIMINATION ACT OF 1978

Passed as an amendment to Title VII of the Civil Rights Act, the Pregnancy Discrimination Act prohibits discrimination in employment based on pregnancy, childbirth, or related medical conditions. The basic principle of the act is that women affected by pregnancy and related conditions must be treated the same as other applicants and employees on the basis of their ability or inability to work. A woman is therefore protected against such practices as being fired, or refused a job or promotion, merely because she is pregnant or has had an abortion. She usually cannot be forced to take a leave of absence so long as she can work. If other employees on disability leave are entitled to return to their jobs when they are able to work again, so too are women who have been unable to work because of pregnancy.

The same principle applies in the benefits area, including disability benefits, sick leave, and health insurance. A woman unable to work for pregnancy-related reasons is entitled to disability benefits or sick leave on the same basis as employees unable to work for other medical reasons. Also, any health insurance provided must cover expenses for pregnancy-

[2]*U.S. Statutes at Large 88*, Part I, 93rd Congress, 2nd Session, 1974, p. 833.

related conditions on the same basis as expenses for other medical conditions. However, health insurance for expenses arising from an abortion is not required except where the life of the mother would be endangered if the fetus were carried to term, or where medical complications have arisen from an abortion.

CIVIL SERVICE REFORM ACT OF 1978

The Civil Service Reform Act of 1978 had a great impact on the structure and practice of federal personnel management. The act, and two related agency reorganization plans, resulted in the abolishment of the U.S. Civil Service Commission, the creation of the Office of Personnel Management and the Merit Systems Protection Board, and an expanded affirmative action mission for the EEOC. It also included the first federal employee collective bargaining law enacted by Congress since 1955.

STATE AND LOCAL LAWS

There are numerous state and local laws that affect human resource management. Many individual states (particularly those that are highly industrialized) enact legislation many years before Congress passes a comparable law. In other situations, federal laws predate state enactments and set the pattern for state laws.

Twenty-one states have right-to-work laws that prohibit management and unions from entering into agreements requiring union membership as a condition of employment. In twenty-five states, right-to-know laws require companies to provide information on hazardous substances. Nineteen states have laws prohibiting any mandatory retirement age. Corporate and government whistleblowers are protected in twenty-one states. Nine states give employees access to their personnel files, and twenty states limit use of polygraph tests for job applicants.[3]

FAIR EMPLOYMENT PRACTICE LAWS

A number of states and some cities have passed fair employment practice laws prohibiting discrimination on the basis of race, color, religion, sex, or national origin. Several states also have antidiscrimination legislation relating to age and sex. In New York the protected age group is from 18 to 65, and a company cannot discriminate against anyone based on age. There is no upper limit on protected age in California. In other situations, federal laws predate state enactments and set the pattern for state laws. However,

---

[3]"Beyond Unions: A Revolution in Employee Rights Is in the Making," *Business Week* 2902 (July 8, 1985): 73.

when EEOC regulations conflict with state or local civil rights regulations, the legislation more favorable to the protected class will be followed.

COMPENSATION LAWS

Almost all states have minimum wage legislation and equal pay laws. Every state has some form of workers' compensation law. These laws vary greatly and are constantly changing. They typically provide benefits to workers or dependents in the case of job-related injuries, diseases, or death. Medical care and rehabilitation services are also usually provided. The total cost is borne by the employers, although the method of insuring may vary from state to state.

Each state also has an unemployment compensation law. These programs are financed by taxing employers according to the extent they have contributed to the unemployment rolls. Eligible unemployed workers receive an amount that varies by state. Compensation is provided for a limited number of weeks.

LABOR RELATIONS LAWS

A few states have enacted versions of the Wagner and Taft–Hartley Acts. Many have adopted legislation relating to other specific aspects of labor relations.

PRESIDENTIAL EXECUTIVE ORDERS

Executive Orders (EOs) are directives issued by the president and have the force and effect of laws enacted by Congress. Many executive orders affect private sector organizations doing business with the federal government. Executive orders having a major impact on human resource management are EO 10988 and EO 11246, as amended by EO 11375.

EXECUTIVE ORDER 10988

In the public sector, federal labor relations are also regulated by executive orders. Executive Order 10988, which President Kennedy signed in 1962, is a most significant one. This order resulted in greatly expanded unionism in the federal government. It was designed to permit collective bargaining in the public sector. However, in this EO a strong management-rights clause was included and strikes were banned. A major test of this ban occurred in 1981 when the Professional Air Traffic Controllers Organization (PATCO) was decertified as a bargaining agent. Approximately 11,500 striking controllers had previously been fired. In 1982, PATCO filed for bankruptcy.

Executive Order 10988 has subsequently been modified by EO 11491 (1969) and EO 11838 (1975). Executive Order 11491 established new procedures and agencies to oversee federal labor relations. It created the Federal Labor Relations Council, which reviews decisions of the Department of Labor and interprets the executive order implementation. Executive Order 11838 further extends and clarifies collective bargaining rules in the federal service. Federal agencies are required to bargain with employees on all issues unless the agency can show compelling reason not to negotiate.

EXECUTIVE ORDER 11246, AS AMENDED BY EO 11375

On September 24, 1965, President Lyndon B. Johnson signed EO 11246. This EO made it the policy of the government of the United States to provide equal opportunity in federal employment for all qualified persons. It prohibits discrimination in employment because of race, creed, color, or national origin. The EO also requires promoting the full realization of equal employment opportunity through a positive, continuing program in each executive department and agency. The policy of equal opportunity applies to every aspect of federal employment policy and practice.

A major provision of EO 11246 is that every executive department and agency that administers a program involving federal financial assistance will require adherence to a policy of nondiscrimination in employment as a condition for the approval of a grant, contract, loan, insurance, or guarantee. During the performance of a contract, contractors agree not to discriminate for employment because of race, creed, color, or national origin. Affirmative action is required to ensure that applicants are employed, and that employees are treated during employment, without regard to race, creed, color, or national origin. Personnel practices covered relate to employment; upgrading; demotion; transfer; recruitment or recruitment advertising; layoffs or termination; rates of pay or other forms of compensation; and selection for training, including apprenticeships. Employers are required to post notices to this effect in conspicuous places in the workplace. In the event of the contractor's noncompliance, contracts can be canceled, terminated, or suspended in whole or in part and the contractor may be declared ineligible for future government contracts. In 1968, EO 11246 was amended by EO 11375, which changed the word *creed* to *religion* and added *sex discrimination* to the other prohibited items. These EOs are enforced by the Department of Labor.

OFFICE OF FEDERAL CONTRACT COMPLIANCE PROGRAMS

The Secretary of Labor established the Office of Federal Contract Compliance Programs (OFCCP) and gave it the power and responsibility for implementing EO 11246. The degree of control the OFCCP will impose depends on the size of the contract. Contracts of $10,000 or less are not covered. The first level of control involves contracts that exceed $10,000 but are less than $50,000, which are subject to the equal opportunity clause. Under this clause, the contractor agrees to the specifications presented in Table 3–1.

The second level of control occurs if the contractor has 50 or more employees and (1) has a contract of $50,000 or more; (2) has contracts which, in any 12-month period total $50,000 or more, or reasonably may be expected to total $50,000 or more; or (3) is a financial institution that serves as a depository for government funds in any amount, acts as an issuing or redeeming agent for U.S. savings bonds and savings notes in any amount, or subscribes to federal deposit or share insurance. Contractors meeting these requirements must develop a written affirmative action program for each of its establishments and file an annual EEO–1 report (see Figure 3–1). The affirmative action program is the major focus of EO 11246. It requires specific steps to guarantee equal employment opportunity. A necessary prerequisite to the development of a satisfactory affirmative action program is the identification and analysis of problem areas inherent in employment of minorities and women and an evaluation of opportunities for utilization of minority and women employees.

The third level of control for contractors is when contracts exceed $1 million. All previously stated requirements must be met, and, in addition, the OFCCP is authorized to conduct preaward compliance reviews. The purpose of a compliance review is to determine whether the contractor is maintaining nondiscriminatory hiring and employment practices. The review also ensures that the contractor is taking affirmative action to guarantee that applicants are employed, placed, trained, upgraded, promoted, terminated, and otherwise treated during employment without regard to race, color, religion, sex, national origin, veteran status, or handicap.

In determining whether to conduct a preaward review, the OFCCP may consider, for example, the following:

1. The past EEO performance of the contractor, including its current EEO profile and indications of underutilization.
2. The volume and nature of complaints filed by employees or applicants against the contractor.
3. Whether the contractor is a growth industry.
4. The level of employment or promotional opportunities resulting from the expansion of or turnover in the contractor's work force.
5. The employment opportunities likely to result from the contract in issue.
6. Whether resources are available to conduct the review.

The OFCCP has taken action to enforce compliance of EO 11246. If an investigation indicates that a violation has occurred, a reasonable effort is first made to secure compliance through conciliation and persuasion. A conciliation agreement is a written agreement between the OFCCP and a contractor in which the contractor undertakes specific obligations to correct or remedy noncompliance with the EO.

Table 3–1. Equal opportunity clause—government contracts

1. The contractor will not discriminate against any employee or applicant for employment because of race, color, religion, sex, or national origin. The contractors will take affirmative action to ensure that applicants are employed, and that employees are treated during employment, without regard to their race, color, religion, sex, or national origin. Such action shall include, but not be limited to the following: Employment, upgrading, demotions, or transfer; recruitment or recruitment advertising, layoff or termination; rates of pay or other forms of compensation; and selection for training, including apprenticeship. The contractor agrees to post in conspicuous places, available to employees and applicants for employment, notices to be provided by the contracting officer setting forth the provisions for this nondiscrimination clause.

2. The contractor will in all solicitations or advertisements for employees placed by or on behalf of the contractor, state that all qualified applicants will receive consideration for employment without regard to race, color, religion, sex, or national origin.

3. The contractor will send to each labor union or representative of workers with which he has a collective bargaining agreement or other contract or understanding, a notice to be provided by the agency contracting officer, advising the labor union or workers' representative of the contractor's commitments under section 202 of Executive Order 11246 of September 24, 1965, and shall post copies of the notice in conspicuous places available to employees and applicants for employment.

4. The contractor will comply with all provisions of Executive Order 11246 of September 24, 1965, and of the rules, regulations, and relevant orders of the Secretary of Labor.

5. The contractor will furnish all information and reports required by Executive Order 11246 of September 24, 1965, and by the rules, regulations, and orders of the Secretary of Labor, or pursuant thereto, and will permit access to his books, records, and accounts by the contracting agency and the Secretary of Labor for purposes of investigation to ascertain compliance with such rules, regulations, and orders.

6. In the event of the contractor's noncompliance with the nondiscrimination clauses of this contract or with any of such rules, regulations, or orders, this contract may be canceled, terminated or suspended in whole or in part and the contractor may be declared ineligible for further Government contracts in accordance with procedures authorized in Executive Order 11246 of September 24, 1965, or by rule, regulation, or order of the Secretary of State, or as otherwise provided by law.

7. The contractor will include the provisions of paragraphs (1) through (7) in every subcontract or purchase order unless exempted by rules, regulations, or orders of the Secretary of Labor issued pursuant to section 204 of Executive Order 11246 of September 24, 1965, so that such provisions will be binding upon each subcontractor or vendor. The contractor will take such action with respect to any subcontract or purchase order as may be directed by the Secretary of Labor as a means of enforcing such provisions including sanctions for noncompliance: *Provided, however,* that in the event the contractor becomes involved in, or is threatened with litigation with a subcontractor or vendor as a result of such direction, the contractor may request the United States to enter into such litigation to protect the interests of the United States.

Source: *Federal Register,* Vol. 45, No. 251, Tuesday, December 30, 1980, p. 86230.

Standard Form 100
(Rev. 12/78)
O.M.B. No. 124-R0011
Approval Expires 12/79
100-210

EQUAL EMPLOYMENT OPPORTUNITY

EMPLOYER INFORMATION REPORT EEO-1

**Joint Reporting
Committee**

- Equal Employment Opportunity Commission
- Office of Federal Contract Compliance Programs

Section A — TYPE OF REPORT

Refer to Instructions for number and types of reports to be filed.

1. Indicate by marking in the appropriate box the type of reporting unit for which this copy of the form is submitted (MARK ONLY ONE BOX).

Multi-establishment Employer:

(1) ☐ Single-establishment Employer Report

(2) ☐ Consolidated Report

(3) ☐ Headquarters Unit Report

(4) ☐ Individual Establishment Report (submit one for each establishment with 25 or more employees)

(5) ☐ Special Report

2. Total number of reports being filed by this Company (Answer on Consolidated Report only)_____

Section B — COMPANY IDENTIFICATION *(To be answered by all employers)*

	OFFICE USE ONLY

1. Parent Company

  a. Name of parent company (owns or controls establishment in item 2) omit if same as label

a.

Name of receiving office | Address (Number and street)

b.

| City or town | County | State | ZIP code | b. Employer Identification No. |

2. Establishment for which this report is filed. (Omit if same as label)

  a. Name of establishment

c.

| Address (Number and street) | City or town | County | State | ZIP code |

d.

  b. Employer Identification No.   (If same as label, skip.)

3. Parent company affiliation

Multi-establishment Employers:
Answer on Consolidated Report only

  a. Name of parent—affiliated company   b. Employer Identification No.

| Address (Number and street) | City or town | County | State | ZIP code |

Section C — EMPLOYERS WHO ARE REQUIRED TO FILE *(To be answered by all employers)*

☐ Yes ☐ No 1. Does the entire company have at least 100 employees in the payroll period for which you are reporting?

☐ Yes ☐ No 2. Is your company affiliated through common ownership and/or centralized management with other entities in an enterprise with a total employment of 100 or more?

☐ Yes ☐ No 3. Does the company or any of its establishments (a) have 50 or more employees AND (b) is not exempt as provided by 41 CFR 60-1.5, AND either (1) is a prime government contractor or first-tier subcontractor, and has a contract, subcontract, or purchase order amounting to $50,000 or more, or (2) serves as a depository of Government funds in any amount or is a financial institution which is an issuing and paying agent for U.S. Savings Bonds and Savings Notes?

NOTE: If the answer is yes to ANY of these questions, complete the entire form; otherwise skip to Section G.

Figure 3–1. Equal employment opportunity employer information report (EEO-1).

Section D — EMPLOYMENT DATA

Employment at this establishment--Report all permanent, temporary, or part-time employees including apprentices and on-the-job trainees unless specifically excluded as set forth in the instructions. Enter the appropriate figures on all lines and in all columns. Blank spaces will be considered as zeros.

JOB CATEGORIES	OVERALL TOTALS (SUM OF COL B THRU K)	NUMBER OF EMPLOYEES									
		MALE					FEMALE				
	A	WHITE (NOT OF HISPANIC ORIGIN) B	BLACK (NOT OF HISPANIC ORIGIN) C	HISPANIC D	ASIAN OR PACIFIC ISLANDER E	AMERICAN INDIAN OR ALASKAN NATIVE F	WHITE (NOT OF HISPANIC ORIGIN) G	BLACK (NOT OF HISPANIC ORIGIN) H	HISPANIC I	ASIAN OR PACIFIC ISLANDER J	AMERICAN INDIAN OR ALASKAN NATIVE K
Officials and Managers											
Professionals											
Technicians											
Sales Workers											
Office and Clerical											
Craft Workers (Skilled)											
Operatives (Semi-Skilled)											
Laborers (Unskilled)											
Service Workers											
TOTAL											
Total employment reported in previous EEO-1 report											

(The trainees below should also be included in the figures for the appropriate occupational categories above)

| Formal On-the-job trainees | White collar | | | | | | | | | | |
| | Production | | | | | | | | | | |

1. NOTE: On consolidated report. skip questions 2-5 and Section E.
2. How was information as to race or ethnic group in Section D obtained?
   1 ☐ Visual Survey   3 ☐ Other — Specify ....
   2 ☐ Employment Record   ....
3. Dates of payroll period used –

4. Pay period of last report submitted for this establishment
_____
5. Does this establishment employ apprentices?
   This year? 1 ☐ Yes 2 ☐ No
   Last year? 1 ☐ Yes 2 ☐ No

Section E — ESTABLISHMENT INFORMATION

1. Is the location of the establishment the same as that reported last year?
   1 ☐ Yes 2 ☐ No 3 ☐ Did not report last year 4 ☐ Reported on combined basis
2. Is the major business activity at this establishment the same as that reported last year?
   1 ☐ Yes 2 ☐ No 3 ☐ No report last year 4 ☐ Reported on combined basis

OFFICE USE ONLY

3. What is the major activity of this establishment? (Be specific. i.e.. manufacturing steel castings. retail grocer. wholesale plumbing supplies. title insurance, etc. Include the specific type of product or type of service provided. as well as the principal business or industrial activity.)

e.

Section F — REMARKS

Use this item to give any identification data appearing on last report which differs from that given above. explain major changes in composition or reporting units. and other pertinent information.

Section G — CERTIFICATION (See instructions G)

Check one
1. ☐ All reports are accurate and were prepared in accordance with the instructions (check on consolidated only)
2. ☐ This report is accurate and was prepared in accordance with the instructions.

| Name of Certifying Official | Title | Signature | Date |
| | | | |

| Name of person to contact regarding this report (Type or print) | Address (Number and street) | | |

| Title | City and State | ZIP code | Telephone Area Code | Number | Extension |

All reports and information obtained from individual reports will be kept confidential as required by Section 709 (e) of Title VII
WILLFULLY FALSE STATEMENTS ON THIS REPORT ARE PUNISHABLE BY LAW, U.S. CODE, TITLE 18, SECTION 1001

When a complaint investigation indicates a violation of the EO and the matter has not been resolved, a notice to show cause or a notice of violation is served. A show cause notice contains a listing of the violations, a statement of how the OFCCP proposes that corrections be made, a request for a written response to the findings, and a suggested date for a conciliation conference. Thirty days are usually given for the firm to respond. Firms that do not correct violations can be passed over in the awarding of future contracts.

SIGNIFICANT U.S. SUPREME COURT DECISIONS

Knowledge of the law is obviously required by personnel practitioners. However, much more than the words in the law itself must be understood. The manner in which the courts interpret the law is also vitally important. And, interpretation continuously changes even though the law itself may not have been altered. Some of the more significant U.S. Supreme Court decisions will next be identified. A more indepth interpretation of some of these decisions will be made in appropriate chapters.

GRIGGS v. *DUKE POWER COMPANY*

A major decision affecting the field of personnel and human resource management was rendered on March 8, 1971. A group of black employees at Duke Power Company had charged job discrimination under Title VII of the Civil Rights Act of 1964. Prior to Title VII, Duke Power Company had two work forces separated by race—black and white. After Title VII a high school diploma and a paper-and-pencil test were required for certain jobs. The plaintiff was able to demonstrate that, in the relevant labor market, 34 percent of the white males had a high school education as opposed to only 12 percent of the black males. The plaintiff was also able to show that there were people in those jobs who were performing successfully even though they did not have a high school diploma. No business necessity could be shown for this educational requirement.

In an 8–0 vote, the Supreme Court ruled against Duke Power Company and stated, "If an employment practice which operates to exclude Negroes cannot be shown to be related to job performance the practice is prohibited." A major implication of the decision is that when personnel practices eliminate a higher percentage of minority applicants, or women, or any other member of a protected group, the burden of proof is on the employer to show that the practice is job related. This court decision significantly affected the personnel practices of many firms.

ALBERMARLE PAPER COMPANY v. *MOODY*

In August 1966, a class action suit was brought against Albermarle Paper Company and the plant employees' labor union. A permanent injunction was requested against any policy, practice, custom, or usage at the plant that violated Title VII. In 1975, the Supreme Court reaffirmed the idea that any test used in the selection process or in promotion decisions must be validated if it is found that its use has had an adverse impact on members of protected groups. The employer has the burden of proof for showing that the test is valid. Therefore the employer must be prepared to show that any selection or promotion device actually measures what it is supposed to measure.

WASHINGTON v. DAVIS

In 1970, two Washington, D.C. black police officers filed suit alleging that the promotion policies of the police department were racially discriminatory. To be accepted by the department and to enter an intensive seventeen-week training program, the police recruit was required to satisfy certain physical and character standards, to be a high school graduate or its equivalent, and to receive a grade of at least 40 on Test 21. **Test 21** was an examination that was used generally throughout the federal service and had been developed by the Civil Service Commission. The examination was designed to test verbal ability, vocabulary, reading, and comprehension.

The validity of Test 21 was in question. The test sampled material that the applicants would learn in the training program. Also, a positive relationship existed between success in the training program and success on the job. However, blacks and women failed the test at a much higher rate than white males. This was the basis for the discrimination charge. The Federal District Court noted that, since August 1969, 44 percent of new police force recruits had been black. That figure represented the proportion of blacks on the total force and was roughly equivalent to the proportion of 20–29-year-old blacks in the 50-mile recruiting radius. The District Court rejected the assertion that Test 21 was culturally slanted to favor whites and was satisfied that the undisputable facts proved the test to be reasonable and directly related to the requirements of the police recruit training program and that it is neither so designed nor operated to discriminate against blacks.

PHILLIPS v. MARTIN MARIETTA CORPORATION

In this 1971 case, the Court ruled that the company had discriminated against a woman because she had young children. The company had a rule of not hiring women with school-age children. The company argued that it did not preclude all women from job consideration; only those women with school-age children were not considered. Martin Marietta contended that this was a business requirement. Since the argument was obviously based on stereotypes, it was rejected. A major implication of this decision is that standards for employment cannot be imposed only on women and not men. For example, divorced women cannot be rejected for consideration if divorced men are also not rejected. Or, inquiries about what a woman's spouse does for a living should not be made if men are not asked the same question.

ESPINOZA v. FARAH MANUFACTURING COMPANY

In 1973, the Supreme Court ruled that Title VII does not prohibit discrimination on the basis of citizenship. By this ruling, the Supreme Court rejected a previous decision made by the EEOC. The EEOC had ruled that it was discriminatory to refuse to hire anyone on the basis of lack of citizenship, since this selection standard was likely to have an adverse impact on individuals of foreign national origin.

WEBER v. KAISER ALUMINUM AND CHEMICAL CORPORATION

In 1974, the United Steelworkers of America and Kaiser Aluminum and Chemical Corporation entered into a master collective bargaining agreement covering terms and conditions of employment at fifteen Kaiser plants. The agreement contained an affirmative action plan designed to eliminate conspicuous racial imbalances in Kaiser's then almost exclusively white craft work force. Black craft hiring goals equal to the percentage of blacks in the respective local labor forces were set for each Kaiser plant. To enable plants to meet these goals, on-the-job training programs were established to teach unskilled production workers—black and white—the skills necessary to become craft workers. The plan reserved 50 percent of the openings in these newly created in-plant training programs for black employees.

In 1974, only 1.83 percent (five out of 273) of the skilled craft workers at the Gramercy, Louisiana, plant were black, even though the work force in the Gramercy area was approximately 39 percent black. Thirteen craft trainees, of which seven were black and six were white, were selected from Gramercy's production work force. The most junior black selected for the program had less seniority than several white production workers whose bids for admission were rejected. Brian Weber subsequently instituted a class action suit alleging that the action by Kaiser and USWA discriminated against him and other similarly situated white employees in violation of Title VII. Although the lower courts ruled that Kaiser's actions were illegal because they fostered reverse discrimination, the Supreme Court reversed the decision, stating that Title VII does not prohibit race-conscious affirmative action plans. Since the affirmative action plan was voluntarily agreed to by the company and the union, it did not violate Title VII.

DOTHARD v. RAWLINGSON

At the time Rawlingson applied for a position as correctional counselor trainee, she was a 22-year-old college graduate whose major course of study had been correctional psychology. She was refused employment because she failed to meet the minimum height and weight requirements. In this 1977 case, the Supreme Court upheld the Federal District Court's decision that Alabama's statutory minimum height requirement of five feet two inches and minimum weight requirement of 120 pounds for the position of correctional counselor had a discriminatory impact on women applicants. The contention was that minimum height and weight requirements for the position of correctional counselor were job related. However, the Court stated that this does not rebut prima facie evidence showing that these requirements have a discriminatory impact on women, where no evidence was produced correlating these requirements with a requisite amount of strength thought essential to good job performance. The impact of the decision is that height and weight requirements must be job related.

UNIVERSITY OF CALIFORNIA REGENTS v. BAKKE

The University of California had reserved sixteen places in each beginning medical school class for minority persons. Allen Bakke, a white man, was denied admission even though he scored higher on the admission criteria than some minority applicants, who were admitted. The Supreme Court ruled 5–4 in Bakke's favor. As a result, Bakke was admitted to the university and received his degree in 1982. But, at the same time, the Court reaffirmed that race may be taken into account in admission decisions.

AMERICAN TOBACCO COMPANY v. PATTERSON

This 1982 Supreme Court decision allows seniority and promotion systems established since Title VII to stand, although they unintentionally hurt minority workers. Under *Griggs* v. *Duke Power Company*, a prima facie violation of Title VII may be established by policies or practices that are neutral on their face and in intent but that nonetheless discriminate against a particular group. A seniority system would fall under the Griggs rationale if it were not for Section 703(h) of the Civil Rights Act. That section provides:

> Notwithstanding any other provision of this subchapter, it shall not be an unlawful employment practice for an employer to apply different standards of compensation, or different terms, conditions, or privileges of employment pursuant to a bona fide seniority or merit system, . . . provided that such differences are not the result of an intention to discriminate because of race, color, religion, sex, or national origin, nor shall it be an unlawful employment practice for an employer to give and to act upon the results of any professionally developed ability test provided that such test, its administration or action upon the results is not designed, intended or used to discriminate because race, color, religion, sex, or national origin. . . ."

Thus the court ruled that a seniority system adopted after Title VII may stand, even though it has a discriminatory impact.

CONNECTICUT v. *TEAL*

In a 1982, 5–4 Supreme Court decision, the majority of the Court stated "that Connecticut's non-discriminatory 'bottom line' was no answer, under the terms of Title VII, to respondents' prima facie claim of employment discrimination." In this case, four black employees of the Department of Income Maintenance of the State of Connecticut had been promoted provisionally to the position of Welfare Eligibility Supervisor and had served in that capacity for almost two years. To attain permanent status as supervisors, however, these individuals had to participate in a selection process that required, as the first step, a passing score on a written examination. On the examination 54.17 percent of the black candidates passed, while 79.54 percent of the white candidates passed. The four blacks who had been promoted provisionally failed. In April 1979, these four filed suit alleging that Title VII had been violated by imposing, as an absolute condition for consideration for promotion, that applicants pass a written test that excluded blacks in disproportionate numbers and that the test was not job related.

More than a year after the suit was filed, and approximately one month before trial, promotions were made from the eligibility list generated by the written examination. In choosing persons for that list, past work performance, recommendations of the candidates' supervisors, and seniority were considered. After the selection process was completed, 22.9 percent of the blacks had been promoted and 13.5 percent of the whites had been promoted. Connecticut argued that it is this **bottom-line result** that should be considered. It is likely that this decision will not generally restrict the use of the bottom-line approach.

FIREFIGHTERS LOCAL UNION #1984 v. *CARL W. STOTTS*

The U.S. Supreme Court ruled on June 12, 1984, on the relationship between affirmative action and last-hired, first-fired seniority. Essentially, when seniority systems are involved, only individuals who can prove that they are victims of discrimination by an employer may benefit from affirmative action. In May 1981, the City of Memphis, Tennessee, had a budget deficit and had to lay off some employees. The city decided that the fairest policy was to use the last-hired, first-fired seniority system. Stotts appealed to the U.S. District Court for an order forbidding a layoff of any black employee. Both the District Court and the Appeals Court ruled in favor of Stotts, but the Supreme Court overturned the ruling.

UNIFORM GUIDELINES FOR EMPLOYEE SELECTION PROCEDURES

Prior to 1978, employers were faced with complying with several different selection guidelines. In 1978, the *Uniform Guidelines on Employee Selec-*

tion Procedures were adopted by the Equal Employment Opportunity Commission, the Civil Service Commission, the Department of Justice, and the Department of Labor. These *Guidelines* cover the major federal equal employment opportunity statutes and orders, including Title VII of the Civil Rights Act, EO 11246, and the Equal Pay Act. They do not apply to the Age Discrimination in Employment Act or the Rehabilitation Act.

The *Guidelines* provide a single set of principles that were designed to assist employers, labor organizations, employment agencies, and licensing and certification boards in complying with federal prohibitions against employment practices that discriminate on the basis of race, color, religion, sex, and national origin. The *Guidelines* provide a framework for making legal employment decisions about hiring, promotion, demotion, referral, retention, and licensing and certification, the proper use of tests and other selection procedures. Under the *Guidelines*, recruiting procedures *are not* considered selection procedures and therefore are not covered.

Regarding selection procedures, the *Guidelines* state that a test is:

> Any measure, combination of measures, or procedures used as a basis for any employment decision. Selection procedures include the full range of assessment techniques from traditional paper and pencil tests, performance tests, testing programs or probationary periods and physical, education, and work experience requirements through informal or casual interviews and unscored application forms.

Using this definition, virtually any factor used in the selection decision is considered a test.

Prior to issuance of the *Guidelines*, the only means for establishing job relatedness was through validation of each test. The *Guidelines* do not require validation in all cases. The fundamental principle underlying the *Guidelines* is that employer policies or practices that have an adverse impact on the employment opportunities of any race, sex, or ethnic group are illegal under Title VII and/or EO 11246 unless justified by business necessity. Adverse impact occurs when members of protected groups receive unequal consideration for employment. As specifically defined by the *Guidelines*, adverse impact occurs if protected groups are not hired at the rate of at least 80 percent of the best achieving group. This has also been called the four-fifths rule. The groups identified for analysis under the Uniform Guidelines are: (1) blacks; (2) American Indians (including Alaskan natives); (3) Asians; (4) Hispanics; (5) females; and (6) males.

Assuming that adverse impact is shown, employers have two avenues available to them if they still desire to use a particular standard. First, the employer may validate a selection device to show that it is indeed a predictor of success. When the device has proven to be a predictor of job performance, business necessity has been shown. In the event that the firm's selection tool has not been validated, business necessity may be demonstrated in another manner: The employer can show that there is a strong relationship between the selection device and job performance and that, without using this procedure, the firm's training costs would become prohibitive.

The second avenue available should adverse impact be shown is the bona fide occupational qualification (BFOQ) defense. The BFOQ defense means that only one group is capable of performing the job successfully. As might be expected, the BFOQ defense has been narrowly interpreted by the courts because it almost always relates to sex discrimination cases. For instance, courts have rejected the concept that since most women cannot lift fifty pounds that all women would be eliminated from consideration for a job requiring heavy lifting.

Creaters of the *Guidelines* adopted the bottom-line approach in assessing whether a firm's employment practices are discriminatory. For example, if a number of separate procedures are used in making a selection decision, the enforcement agencies will focus on the end result of these procedures to determine whether adverse impact has occurred. Essentially, the EEOC is concerned more with what is occurring than how it occurred. They admit that discriminatory employment practices may exist that cannot be validated. However, the net effect, or the bottom line, of the selection procedures is the focus of their attention.

ADDITIONAL GUIDELINES

Since the *Uniform Guidelines* were published in 1978, a number of modifications have been made. Some of these changes resulted from Supreme Court decisions, while others were made to clarify the implementation of the *Guidelines*. Three major changes—*Interpretative Guidelines on Sexual Harassment, Guidelines on Discrimination Because of National Origin,* and *Guidelines on Discrimination Because of Religion*—merit additional discussion.

INTERPRETATIVE GUIDELINES ON SEXUAL HARASSMENT

It is anticipated that in the 1980s one of the most fervently pursued civil rights issues will relate to sexual harassment. As previously mentioned, Title VII of the Civil Rights Act prohibits sex discrimination generally in employment. In 1980, the EEOC issued interpretative guidelines, which state that employers have an affirmative duty to maintain a workplace free from sexual harassment. The OFCCP issued similar guidelines in 1981. Managers in both profit and not-for-profit organizations should be particularly alert to the issue of sexual harassment. The EEOC issued the guidelines because of the belief that sexual harassment continues to be a widespread problem.[4] In a 1979 study, 59 percent of the women employees

[4]Michelle Hoyman and Ronda Robinson, "Interpreting the New Sexual Harassment Guidelines," *Personnel Journal* 59 (December 1980): 996.

interviewed reported experiencing one or more incidents of sexual harassment in their places of employment.[5]

The EEOC has defined sexual harassment as

Unwelcome sexual advances, requests for sexual favors, and other verbal
or physical conduct of a sexual nature that occur under any of the following
situations:

1. When submission to such contact is made either explicitly or
   implicitly a term or condition of an individual's employment.
2. When submission to or rejection of such conduct by an individual
   is used as the basis for employment decisions affecting such
   individual.
3. When such conduct has the purpose or effect of unreasonably
   interfering with an individual's work performance or creating an
   intimidating, hostile, or offensive working environment.[6]

According to these guidelines, employers are totally liable for the acts
of their supervisors regardless of whether the employer was aware of the
sexual harassment act. Where co-workers are concerned, the employer is
responsible for such acts if the employer knew, or should have known, of
the harassment conduct. This is true unless the employer can show that it
took immediate and appropriate action to correct the problem upon learning
of its existence.

Another important aspect of these guidelines is that employers may be
liable for acts committed by nonemployees in the workplace if the employer
knew, or should have known, of the conduct and failed to take appropriate
action. Firms are also responsible for developing programs to prevent sexual
harassment in the workplace. Also, firms must investigate all formal and
informal complaints alleging sexual harassment. After investigating, a firm
must take immediate and appropriate action to correct the situation. Failure
to do so constitutes a violation of Title VII, as interpreted by the EEOC.

There have been numerous test cases regarding sexual harassment. In
Miller v. Bank of America, the U.S. Court of Appeals for the Ninth Circuit
held an employer to be liable for the sexually harassing acts of its supervisors, even if the company had a policy prohibiting such conduct and
even if the victim did not formally notify the employer of the problem. The
U.S. Court of Appeals in Washington, D.C., ruled that sexual harassment
in and of itself is a violation of Title VII. The court ruled that the law does
not require the victim to prove that she resisted harassment and was penal-
ized for the resistance.

[5]Barbara Hagler, Testimony Before House Judiciary II Committee, State of Illinois, March 4,
1980, p. 5.
[6]Carolyn C. Dolecheck and Maynard M. Dolecheck, "Job-Related Sexual Harassment of
Women with College Degrees in Business: How Serious Is It?" *NABTE Review*, No. 9
(Spring 1982): 17.

GUIDELINES ON DISCRIMINATION BECAUSE OF NATIONAL ORIGIN

The EEOC has defined national origin discrimination broadly as the denial of equal employment opportunity because of an individual's ancestors or place of birth; or because an individual has the physical, cultural, or linguistic characteristics of a national origin group. Because height or weight requirements tend to exclude individuals on the basis of national origin, firms are expected to evaluate their selection procedures for adverse impact, regardless of whether the total selection process has an adverse impact based on national origin. Height and weight requirements are, therefore, exceptions to the bottom-line concept.

The EEOC has identified the following selection procedures which may be discriminatory:

1. *Fluency-in-English requirements:* One questionable practice involves denying employment opportunities because of an individual's foreign accent or inability to communicate well in English. When this practice is continually followed, the Commission will presume that such a rule violates Title VII and will closely study it. However, a firm may require that employees speak only in English at certain times if business necessity can be shown.
2. *Training or education requirements:* Denying employment opportunities to an individual because of his or her foreign training or education; or practices that require an individual to be foreign trained or educated may be discriminatory.

Harassment on the basis of national origin is a violation of Title VII. Employers have an affirmative duty to maintain a working environment free of harassment based on national origin. Ethnic slurs and other verbal or physical conduct relating to an individual's national origin constitute harassment when this conduct: (1) has the purpose or effect of creating an intimidating, hostile, or offensive working environment; (2) has the purpose or effect of unreasonably interfering with an individual's work performance; or (3) otherwise adversely affects an individual's employment opportunity.

GUIDELINES ON DISCRIMINATION BECAUSE OF RELIGION

Employers have an obligation to accommodate religious practices unless they can demonstrate that this would result in undue hardship. In determining whether an accommodation would constitute undue hardship, consideration is given to the identifiable costs in relation to the size and operating costs of the employer and the number of individuals who actually need the accommodation. These guidelines recognize that regular payment of premium wages would constitute undue hardship, whereas these payments on an infrequent or temporary basis do not. Undue hardship would also exist if an accommodation required a firm to vary from its bona fide seniority system.

These guidelines identify several means of accommodating religious practices that prohibit working on certain days. Some of the methods suggested include voluntary substitutes, flexible scheduling, lateral transfer, and change of job assignments. Some collective bargaining agreements include a provision that each employee must join the labor organization or pay the labor organization a sum equivalent to dues. When an employee's religious practices do not permit compliance with such a provision, the labor organization should accommodate the employee by permitting him or her, in lieu of union dues, to donate an equivalent amount of money to a charitable organization.

SUMMARY

The public often assumes that the major impact of laws and regulations on HRM began with the highly visible legislation of the 1960s. Although the legislation passed after 1960 is both extensive and important, previous enactments laid the groundwork for the government's increased intervention into business practices. Major legislation affecting human resource management passed prior to 1960 includes: the Civil Rights Acts of 1866 and 1871, the Railway Labor Act of 1926, the Davis–Bacon Act of 1931, the Anti-Injunction Act of 1932, the National Labor Relations Act of 1935, the Social Security Act of 1935, the Walsh–Healey Act of 1936, the Fair Labor Standards Act of 1938, the Labor–Management Relations Act of 1947, and the Labor–Management Reporting and Disclosure Act of 1959.

The laws passed prior to 1960 were important also because they initiated a new era of labor–management relations. These laws paved the way for a proliferation of legislation that had a significant effect on human resource management. Major human resource legislation passed after 1960 includes: the Equal Pay Act of 1963 — amended in 1972, Title VII of the Civil Rights Act of 1964 — amended in 1972, the Age Discrimination in Employment Act of 1967 — amended in 1978, the Occupational Safety and Health Act of 1970, the Rehabilitation Act of 1973, the Privacy Act of 1974, the Employee Retirement Income Security Act of 1974, the Pregnancy Discrimination Act of 1978, and the Civil Service Reform Act of 1978.

Executive Orders (EOs) are directives issued by the president and have the force and effect of laws enacted by Congress. Executive Order 11246 made it the policy of the government of the United States to provide equal opportunity in federal employment for all qualified persons. The Secretary of Labor established the Office of Federal Contract Compliance Programs and gave it the power and responsibility for implementing EO 11246.

The manner in which the courts interpret the law is vitally important. In *Albermarle Paper Company* v. *Moody,* the Supreme Court reaffirmed that organizations are required to prove that tests are related to contents of the job. A major conclusion of *Washington* v. *Davis* was that if a test is specifically job related, it is not illegal to discriminate against members of protected groups. In *Griggs* v. *Duke Power Company*, a major implication was that when personnel practices eliminate a higher percentage of minority applicants, the burden of proof is on the employer to show that the practice is job related. In *Phillips* v. *Martin Marietta Corporation*, a major implication was that standards cannot be imposed only on women and not on men. In *Espinoza* v. *Farah Manufacturing Company*, the Supreme Court ruled that Title VII does not prohibit discrimination on the basis of citizenship. The Supreme Court ruled in *Weber* v. *Kaiser Aluminum and Chemical Corporation* that Title VII does not prohibit race conscious affirmative action plans. The Supreme court in *Dothard* v. *Rawlingson* upheld a lower court ruling that Alabama's statutory minimum height and weight requirement had discriminatory impact on female applicants. In *University of California* v. *Bakke*, the Supreme Court ruled in Bakke's favor but reaffirmed that race may be taken into account in admission decisions. The Supreme Court decision in *American Tobacco Company* v. *Patterson* ruled that a seniority system adopted after Title VII may stand, even though it has a discriminatory impact.

In the *Connecticut* v. *Teal* decision, the majority of the court stated that "Connecticut's nondiscriminatory 'bottom line' was no answer, under terms of Title VII, to respondents' prima facie claim of employment discrimination." Finally, in *Firefighters Local Union #1984* v. *Carl W. Stotts*, the Supreme Court ruled that when seniority systems are involved, only individuals who can prove that they are victims of discrimination by an employer may benefit from affirmative action.

The *Uniform Guidelines on Employee Selection Procedures* provide a single set of principles that were designed to assist employers, labor organizations, employment agencies, and licensing and certification boards in complying with federal prohibitions against employment practices that discriminated on the basis of race, color, religion, sex, and national origin. Adverse impact occurs when members of protected groups receive unequal consideration for employment. As defined by *Guidelines*, adverse impact occurs if protected groups are not hired at the rate of at least 80 percent of the best achieving group. After the initial *Guidelines* were published in 1978, others regarding sexual harassment, national origin, and religion were published.

QUESTIONS FOR REVIEW

1. List and briefly describe the major federal legislation passed prior to 1960 that has had an impact on HRM.
2. Briefly describe the following laws:
   (a) Equal Pay Act of 1963 — amended in 1972.
   (b) Title VII of the Civil Rights Act of 1964 — amended in 1972.
   (c) Age Discrimination in Employment Act of 1967 — amended in 1972.
   (d) The Occupational Safety and Health Act of 1970.
   (e) Rehabilitation Act of 1973.
   (f) Privacy Act of 1974.
   (g) Employee Retirement Income Security Act of 1974.

(h) Pregnancy Discrimination Act of 1978.

(i) Civil Service Reform Act of 1978.

3. What impact have state and local laws had on human resource management?

4. What is a Presidential Executive Order? Describe the major provisions of EO 11246, as amended by EO 11375.

5. What is the purpose of the Office of Federal Contract Compliance Programs?

6. Discuss the significant Supreme Court decisions that have had an impact on human resource management.

7. What was the purpose of the *Uniform Guidelines on Employee Selection Procedures*?

8. How does the EEOC define *sexual harassment*?

TERMS FOR REVIEW

"Yellow-dog" contract
Protected groups
Executive Orders (EOs)
Plaintiff
Test 21

Incident 1

Until 1978, Supreme Construction Company was a relatively small organization located in Baytown, Texas. Its founder, Alex Boyd, had been satisfied with concentrating his efforts in the private home construction field. Known regionally for his reputation for building quality homes, his work force never exceeded fifteen employees.

It was in 1978 that his son, Michael, graduated from college with a degree in construction. Michael joined the company that year and Alex could immediately see that his son was really cut out for the construction business. After several years of proving himself to his father, he approached his father with a proposition, "Let's get into some of the bigger projects now. We have the capital to expand and I really believe we can do it."

Alex accepted the proposal and, when larger projects were bid on, Supreme Construction began to win its share. Supreme now had 75 full-time employees, and everything was going its way.

In 1984, Ellington Air Force Base, located south of Houston, released construc-

tion specifications for several new dormitories, a kitchen, and other miscellaneous small buildings. Although Supreme had never done any construction work for the government, the specifications appeared to have been tailored just for Supreme. Michael worked up the bid and submitted it to the appropriate agency. The bid was for approximately $500,000.

Several weeks later the bids were opened. Supreme had the low bid. However, the acceptance letter was contingent on submission of a satisfactory affirmative action program. As Alex read the letter, he did not know what to think. He had never been confronted with anything like this before.

QUESTIONS

1. Why does Supreme Construction Company have to submit an affirmative action plan?

2. What generally will Supreme have to agree to accomplish in its affirmative action plan?

Incident 2

Les Partain, supervisor of the training and development department for Gazelle Corporation, was sixty-four years old and had been with the firm for over 30 years. For the past twelve years he had served as Gazelle's training and development manager and felt that he had been doing a good job. This belief was supported by the fact that during the last five years he had received excellent performance reports from his boss, Bennie Helton, director of personnel.

Six months before Les's sixty-fifth birthday, he and Bennie were enjoying a cup of coffee together. "Les," said Bennie, "I know that you're pleased with the progress our T&D section has made under your leadership. We're really going to miss you when you retire this year. You'll certainly live the good life because you'll receive the maximum retirement benefits. If I can be of any assistance to you in developing the paperwork for your retirement, please let me know."

"Gee, Bennie, I really appreciate the good words, but I've never felt better in my life and although our retirement plan is excellent, I figure that I have at least five more good years. There are many other things I would like to do for the department before I retire. I have some excellent employees and we can get many things done within the next five years."

After finishing their coffee, both men returned to their work. As Bennie left, he was thinking, "My gosh, I had no idea that that character intended to hang on. The only reason I gave him those good performance appraisals was to make him feel better before he retired. He was actually only an average worker and I was anxious to move a more aggressive person into that key job. We stand to lose several good people in that department if Les doesn't leave. From what they tell me he's not doing much of a job."

QUESTIONS

1. From a legal viewpoint, what do you believe Bennie can do about this situation? Discuss.
2. What actions should Bennie have taken in the past to avoid his current predicament?

REFERENCES

Arvey, Richard D. *Fairness In Selecting Employees.* Reading, Mass.: Addison-Wesley, 1979.

Baroni, Barry J. "Age Discrimination in Employment: Some Guidelines for Employers." *Personnel Administrator* 26 (May 1981): 97–101.

Bell, James D., Castagnera, James, and Young, Jane Patterson. "Employment References: Do You Know the Law?" *Personnel Journal* 63 (February 1984): 32–36.

Belohlav, James A. and Ayton, Eugene. "Equal Opportunity Laws: Some Common Problems." *Personnel Journal* 61 (April 1982): 282–285.

Bergmann, B. R. and Darity, W., Jr. "Social Relations, Productivity, and Employer Discrimination." *Monthly Labor Review* 104 (April 1981): 47–49.

"Beyond Unions: A Revolution in Employee Rights Is in the Making." *Business Week* 2902 (July 8, 1985): 73.

Brandon, Fillie and Snyder, Robert A. "ADEA Update: Case Law and 'Cost' as a Defense." *Personnel Journal* 30 (February 1985): 116–119.

Britt, Louis P. III "Affirmative Action Is There Life After Stotts?" *Personnel Journal* 29 (September 1984): 96–100.

Carmel, Matthew M. and Dolan, Michael F. "An Introduction to Employee Right-to-Know Laws." *Personnel Journal* 29 (September 1984): 117–121.

Castagnera, James O. "Corporate Culpability in Work-Place Fatalities—A Growing Trend?" *Personnel Journal* 62 (September 1985): 8–12.

Copus, David A. and Lindsay, Ronald A. "Successfully Defending the Discriminatory/Wrongful Discharge Case." *Employee Relations Law Journal* 10 (Winter 1984/85): 456–467.

Denis, Martin D. "Race Harassment Discrimination: A Problem That Won't Go Away." *Employee Relations Law Journal* 10 (Winter 1984/85): 415–435.

Driscol, Jeanne Bosson. "Sexual Attraction and Harassment: Management's New Problems." *Personnel Journal* 60 (January 1981): 33 + .

Ellig, Bruce R. "The Impact of Legislation on the Personnel Function." *Personnel* 57 (September–October 1980): 49–53.

Engel, Paul G. "Preserving the Right to Fire." *Industry Week* 224 (March 18, 1985): 39–40.

Greenlaw, Paul S. "Affirmative Action or Reverse Discrimination?" *Personnel Journal* 64 (September 1985): 84–87.

Greenlaw, Paul S. and Kohn, John P. "Age Discrimination in Employment Guidelines." *Personnel Journal* 61 (March 1982): 224–228.

Hoyman, Michele and Robinson, Ronda. "Interpreting the New Sexual Harassment Guidelines." *Personnel Journal* 59 (December 1980): 996–1000.

Janner, Greville. "Implied Terms: The Unwritten Law of the Employment Contract." *Personnel Management* (September 1985): 44–45.

Linenberger, Patricia and Keaveny, Timothy J. "Performance Appraisal Standards Used by the Courts." *Personnel Administrator* 26 (May 1981) 89–94.

Loban, Lawrence. "The Handicapped—Sometimes Your Best Employee." *Supervision* 42 (February 1980): 3–7.

Lorber, Lawrence Z., Kirk, J. Robert, Samuels, Stephen L., and Spellman, David J. III. *Sex and Salary.* ASPA Foundation, 606 North Washington, Alexandria, Va., 1985.

McCulloch, Kenneth J. *Selecting Employees Safely Under the Law.* Englewood Cliffs, NJ: Prentice-Hall, 1981.

Murphy, B. S. "Supreme Court Explains Standard for Double Damages under ADEA." *Personnel Management* 64 (April 1985): 26 +

Myers, Donald W. "The Impact of a Selected Provision in the Federal Guidelines on Job Analysis and Training." *Personnel Administrator* 26 (July 1981): 41–45.

Nathanson, Robert B. and Lambert, Jeffrey. "Integrating Disabled Employees Into the Workforce." *Personnel Journal* 60 (February 1981): 103–113.

O'Meara, John Corbett. "The Emerging Law of Employees' Right to Privacy." *Personnel Administrator* 30 (June 1985): 159–165.

Pickens, Judy E. "Terms of Equality: A Guide To Bias-Free Language." *Personnel Journal* 64 (August 1985): 24–28.

Robertson, David E. "Quotas and the Courts." *Business Law Review* 13 (Winter 1980–81): 1–6.

Robertson, David E. and Johnson, Ron. "Reverse Discrimination: Did Weber Decide the Issue?" *Labor Law Journal* 31 (November 1980): 693–699.

Sheahan, Robert E. "Labor Relations: Age Discrimination Is a Growing Concern for Employers." *Personnel Journal* 61 (January 1982): 14–16.

Sovereign, Kenneth L. *Personnel Law.* Reston, 1984.

Stacy, Donald R. "A Case Against Extending the Adverse Impact Doctrine to ADEA." *Employee Relations Law Journal* 10 (Winter 1984/85): 437–455.

Steinberg, Harvey. "Where Law and Personnel Practice Collide: The At-Will Employment Crossroad." *Personnel* 62 (June 1985): 37–43.

Thurston, Kathryn A. "Sexual Harassment: An Organizational Perspective." *Personnel Administrator* 25 (December 1980): 59–64.

Trotter, Richard, Zacur, Susan Rawson, and Greenwood, Wallace. "The Pregnancy Disability Amendment: What the Law Provides, Part II." *Personnel Administrator* 27 (March 1982): 55–58.

William, Thomas H. "Employment-At-Will." *Personnel Journal* 64 (June 1985): 73–77.

Yoder, Dale and Staudohar, Paul D. "Testing and EEO: Getting Down to Cases." *Personnel Journal* 29 (February 1984): 67–74.

CHAPTER OBJECTIVES
1. Define *job analysis* and explain the reasons for conducting job analysis.
2. State the types of information required for job analysis and describe the various job analysis methods.
3. Explain the components of a well-designed job description and job specification.
4. Describe the newer methods available for conducting job analysis.
5. Describe how job analysis helps to satisfy various legal requirements.
6. Explain job design, job enrichment, and job enlargement.

Chapter 4

JOB ANALYSIS

"I'm having trouble figuring out what kind of machine operator you need, Mary," said John Anderson, the personnel director, "I've sent four people down who seem to meet the requirements of the job description and you have sent each of them back." "I haven't even read the job description, John," responded Mary Blackett, the supervisor. "What I'm concerned with is finding someone who can do the job, not just meet the requirements of the job description. I don't believe any of the people you have sent me can do the job."

John got the job description and went over it point by point with Mary. They discovered that either the job description never fit the job or the job had changed a great deal since the description was written. For example, the job description specified experience on an older model drill press while the one in use was a new digital machine. The new one really required less skill.

After going over the job description with Mary, John said, "I think you and I should work together to make sure that the job description actually describes the job." "Yes," said Mary, "We could have saved ourselves a lot of time if we had done this beforehand."

The situation just described reflects a very common problem in human resource management. The job description did not adequately indicate what duties and skills were needed to perform the job. Therefore it became virtually impossible for John Anderson, the personnel director, to do his job. Job analysis was critically needed if the problem were to be resolved. As will be stressed throughout the book, job analysis is the most basic function of human resource management.

The chapter begins with a definition of job analysis and a description of its importance to the performance of all personnel functions. Next, job analysis methods and the types of data gathered through the process are discussed. The use of job analysis in the preparation of job descriptions and job specifications is then explained. Newer methods for conducting job analysis are next described. Finally, the legal implications of a thorough job analysis are given.

JOB ANALYSIS: A BASIC HUMAN RESOURCE TOOL

A **job** *consists of a group of tasks that must be performed if an organization is to achieve its goals.* The job may require the services of one person, such as that of president, or the services of two hundred, as might be the case with clerk typists in a large firm.

In a work group consisting of a supervisor, two senior clerks, and four stenographers, there are three jobs and seven positions. A **position** is the *collection of tasks and responsibilities performed by one person;* there is a position for every individual in an organization. For instance, a small company might have 25 jobs for their 75 employees, whereas in a large company 2000 jobs may exist for 50,000 employees. In some firms, as few as 10 jobs constitute 90 percent of a work force.[1]

The systematic process of determining the duties and skills required for performing jobs in an organization is referred to as **job analysis.** The purpose of job analysis is to obtain answers to six major questions:

1. What physical and mental tasks does the worker accomplish?
2. When is the job to be completed?
3. Where is the job to be accomplished?
4. How does the worker do the job?
5. Why is the job done?
6. What qualifications are needed to perform the job?

Job analysis provides a summary of a job's duties and responsibilities, its relationship to other jobs, the knowledge and skills required, and working

---

[1]Donald W. Myers, "The Impact of a Selected Provision in the Federal Guidelines on Job Analysis and Training," *Personnel Administration* 26 (July 1981): 45.

conditions under which it is performed. Job facts are gathered, analyzed, and recorded as the job exists, not as the job should exist.[2] That function is most often assigned to industrial engineers, methods analysts, or others. Job analysis is conducted after the job has been designed, the worker has been trained, and the job is being performed.

Job analysis is performed on three occasions. First, it is needed when the organization is founded and a job analysis program is initiated for the first time. Second, it is performed when new jobs are created. Third, it is used when jobs are changed significantly as a result of new technology, methods, procedures, or systems. It is because of changes in the nature of jobs that the majority of job analyses are performed. Unless job analysis is properly conducted, it would be difficult, if not impossible, to satisfactorily perform staffing functions. Job analysis information is used to prepare both job descriptions and job specifications. Job descriptions specify the tasks, duties, and responsibilities associated with a job. Job specifications state the knowledge, skills, and abilities a person will need to perform the job. Both of these documents will be discussed in greater detail later in the chapter.

REASONS FOR CONDUCTING JOB ANALYSIS

Note in Figure 4–1 that data derived from job analysis have an impact on virtually every aspect of human resource management. A major use of job analysis data is in the area of human resource planning. Merely knowing that the firm will need 1000 new employees to produce products and/or services to satisfy sales demand is insufficient. Each job requires different knowledge, skills, and ability levels. Planning must take this into consideration. Employee recruitment and selection would be haphazard if the qualifications needed to perform the job were not known. Without up-to-date job descriptions and specifications, employees would have to be recruited and selected for a job with no more guidelines than the implication that the new employee should be warm and breathing. Such a practice is unheard of in the procurement of raw materials, supplies, or equipment. Using the same logic, establishing specifications for human resources is essential also.

Job specification information often proves beneficial in identifying training and development needs. If the specification suggests that the job requires a particular knowledge, skill, or ability, and the individual filling the position does not possess all of the qualifications required, training and development is likely in order. It should be directed at assisting workers to perform duties specified in their present job descriptions or prepare them for promotion to higher level jobs.

[2]John C. Crystal and Richard S. Deems, "Redesigning Jobs," *Training and Development Journal* 37 (February 1983): 45.

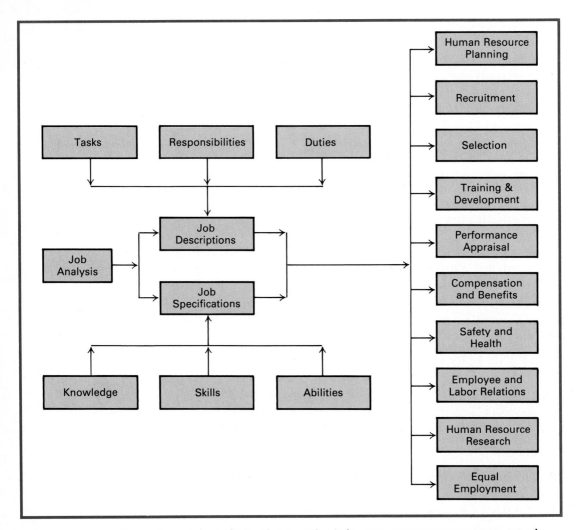

Figure 4–1. Job analysis: The most basic human resource management tool.

With regard to performance appraisal, employees should be evaluated in terms of how well they accomplish the duties specified in their job descriptions. An employer who evaluates an individual on factors not included in the job description is left wide open to allegations of discrimination.

In the area of compensation, we must know the relative value to the company of a particular job before a dollar value can be placed on it. The more significant the duties and responsibilities, the greater is the job's relative worth. In addition, jobs that require greater knowledge, skills, and abilities should be worth more to the firm. For example, if the specification called for a masters degree as opposed to a high school diploma, the relative value would likely be higher.

Information initially derived from job analysis is also valuable to the safety and health function. Employers are required to state whether a job is hazardous. The job description/specification should respond to this requirement. In addition, in certain hazardous jobs, workers may need specific information about the job in order to function safely in that environment.

Job analysis information is also important to employee and labor relations. When employees are considered for promotion, transfer, or demotion, the job description provides a standard for comparison of talent. Regardless of whether the firm is unionized, fair treatment is often based on information obtained through job analysis.

When human resource research is undertaken, job analysis information provides the researcher with a starting point. For example, if we are trying to identify factors that distinguish successful from less successful employees, we need to study only those employees who have similar job descriptions/specifications. Otherwise it would be like mixing apples and oranges in performing the research.

Finally, the significance of having properly accomplished job analysis is particularly important when the legality of employment practices is considered. As you will see in a later section of this chapter, job analysis data are needed in order to defend selection and promotion decisions. For this reason alone, job analysis is vital.

Thus far in our discussion we have described job analysis as it pertains to each function of human resource management. In practice, there is considerable interrelationship among these functions. Job analysis is the basis for tying the functional areas together. It is insufficient to use job analysis information for compensation decisions and not use it for selection decisions. Job analysis is the foundation for a sound personnel program.

TYPES OF JOB ANALYSIS INFORMATION

Considerable information is needed if job analysis is to be successfully accomplished. The job analyst identifies the actual duties and responsibilities associated with the job. Types of data gathered through job analysis are shown in Table 4–1. Notice that work activities and worker-oriented activities are important.

In addition, knowledge of the types of machines, tools, equipment, and work aids that are used in performing the job are also important. This information is useful in later determining the skills needed in order to

Table 4–1. Examples of the types of data gathered in job analysis

Summary of types of data collected through job analysis*

1. Work activities

   a. Work activities and processes.
   b. Activity records (in film form, for example).
   c. Procedures used.
   d. Personal responsibility.

2. Worker-oriented activities

   a. Human behaviors, such as physical actions and communicating on the job.
   b. Elemental motions for methods analysis.
   c. Personal job demands, such as energy expenditure.

3. Machines, tools, equipment and work aids used

4. Job-related tangibles and intangibles

   a. Knowledge dealt with or applied (as in accounting).
   b. Materials processed.
   c. Products made or services performed.

5. Work performance†

   a. Error analysis.
   b. Work standards.
   c. Work measurements, such as time taken for a task.

6. Job context

   a. Work schedule.
   b. Financial and nonfinancial incentives.
   c. Physical working conditions.
   d. Organizational and social contexts.

7. Personal requirements for the job

   a. Personal attributes such as personality, interests.
   b. Education and training required.
   c. Work experience.

*This information can be in the form of qualitative, verbal, narrative descriptions or quantitative measurements of each item, such as error rates per unit of time or noise level.
†All job analysis systems do not develop the work performance aspects.

Source: E. J. McCormick, ''Job and Task Analysis,'' in Marvin D. Dunnette (ed.), *Handbook of Industrial and Organizational Psychology*. New York: John Wiley & Sons. Copyright © 1976. Reprinted by permission of John Wiley & Sons, Inc.

perform the job. In addition, the job analyst looks for job-related tangibles and intangibles. For instance, what knowledge is needed and must be applied, what materials are processed, or what products are made or services performed?

Some job analysis systems identify the standards that are established for the job. Work measurement studies may be conducted to determine, for example, how long it takes for a task to be performed. With regard to job content, the analyst studies the work schedule, financial and nonfinancial incentives, and physical working conditions. Since jobs are often performed in conjunction with others, organizational and social contexts should also be noted. Also, specific education, training, and work experience pertinent to performing the job are identified.

JOB ANALYSIS METHODS

Job analysis has traditionally been conducted in a number of different ways. Also, firms differ in their needs and in the resources they have for conducting job analysis.[3] The selection of a specific method should be based on two primary factors: (1) the goals the information will serve (pay increases, development, etc.); and (2) the method that is most feasible for a particular organization. The most common methods of job analysis are described in the following sections.

QUESTIONNAIRES

Using questionnaires, the job analyst administers a structured questionnaire to employees who identify the tasks they perform in accomplishing the job. Questionnaires are typically quick and economical to use. However, in some cases employees may lack writing skills, which detracts from this method's usefulness. Also, some employees may tend to "build up" their jobs to suggest more responsibility than actually exists.

A portion of a job analysis questionnaire from First Interstate Bancorp is presented in Figure 4–2. Note that the total questionnaire consists of six sections. We have shown only Section III, which covers the skills and knowledge required to perform a job's tasks and activities.

OBSERVATION

When using the observation method, the job analyst usually watches the work being performed and records his or her observations. In this way the interrelationships of the physical and mental tasks are determined. This

[3]Ronald A. Ash and Edward L. Levine, "A Framework for Evaluating Job Analysis Method," *Personnel* 57 (November/December 1980): 53–54.

First Interstate Bancorp

Job Analysis Questionnaire

Name _____

Position Title _____

Affiliate _____

Division/Group/Unit _____

City and State _____

Immediate Manager _____

General Instructions

This questionnaire is designed to provide information about your current position. It is **not** intended to measure your performance or productivity. It is a tool for analyzing and describing your job.

The questionnaire consists of six sections.
- **Section I** deals with the tasks and activities that comprise your job.
- **Section II** asks you to compare various job dimensions, which are groupings of similar tasks.
- **Section III** covers the skills and knowledge required to perform the tasks and activities of your position.
- **Section IV** identifies specific scope measures of your position.
- **Section V** focuses on individual factors that you bring to your job.
- **Section VI** includes additional factors which may have an impact on your position.

Because this questionnaire covers a broad range of affiliates and jobs, a number of the questions may not apply to your position. However, **if you perform tasks that are not covered by the questionnaire, space has been provided for you to write them in.** Whether you perform a large number of tasks or only a few is not important. What is essential is that you respond to **all** of the questions (for example, you may perform certain financial management tasks, although you are in a marketing function), and in a manner which best describes your position as it is typically performed by you.

In responding to the questions, please use the following definitions:
- **affiliate** refers to an individual bank (e.g., First Interstate Bank of Arizona) or a nonbank subsidiary (e.g. First Interstate Services Company).
- **customer** means any individual or group, inside or outside the company, with which you deal on a client or customer basis. For example, an affiliate bank can be a customer for the data processing unit, a small business can be a customer for the venture capital group, and an individual or a corporation can be a customer for a bank.
- **unit** is the organizational group in which you report or for which you have responsibility. This could be a functional group, a department, or a division of a company. For example, for a Cashier position, the unit might be the Cashier's Department; for a VP Operations, the unit might be the Operations Department; for a VP Administration, the unit might be the Administration Division; or for a Chief Executive Officer, the unit would be the entire bank.

The questionnaires will be returned directly to Towers, Perrin, Forster & Crosby (TPF&C), so all responses on this form will remain confidential. However, to ensure that the information about your position is accurate and consistent, you and your immediate manager will review the results of TPF&C's analysis of the questionnaire.

Please follow the specific instructions at the beginning of each section. Read each section in full before attempting to complete it so that you can respond as accurately as possible.

Thank you for your efforts in participating in this study.

Figure 4–2. An example of a job analysis questionnaire. Source: Used with permission of First Interstate Bancorp.

Section III: Position Skills and Knowledge

This section focuses on the type and depth of skills and knowledge that are 1) required to perform your job, and 2) that you may possess.

For each of the skills listed, you are asked to rate two items: the **level required** and the **level you possess**. In the appropriate boxes, write the number that best describes the skill or knowledge level, according to the following scale:

0 = Job neither requires nor do I possess skill/knowledge.
1 = Familiarity with skill/knowledge.
2 = General working skill/knowledge.
3 = Advanced skill/knowledge.
4 = Unique expertise in skill/knowledge.

In the first column of boxes, identify the **level of skill/knowledge required** to successfully perform your present job.

In the second column of boxes, identify the **level of skill/knowledge** that **you possess**, regardless of whether the job requires it.

The third column identifies sources of skills and knowledge. To indicate where you acquired each skill or knowledge that is required for the performance of your current position, identify up to, but no more than, two sources. Mark 1 in the column that represents the primary source. Mark 2 in the column that represents the secondary source.

Column headers: Level required for position / Level you possess / On-the-job training / College/university / Formal banking program / Internal training program / External training program

A. Planning, Policies, Procedures

1 Organization design
2 Short-term planning (setting budgets, goals, etc.)
3 Strategic planning
4 Pricing/fee structuring

B. Business Development/Marketing

5 Market research (identifying markets, competitive analyses and evaluation)
6 Market analysis (client needs, trends, strategies, etc.)
7 Marketing tools (advertising, promotional campaigns, etc.)
8 Products/services (bank unit services, systems, etc.)
9 Marketing sales

C. Customer Relations

10 Customer industry (objectives, economics, trends, etc.)
11 Customer counsel/problem solving
12 Account management
13 Profit analysis

For every statement:
• If a task is not part of your job, mark X in the first box
• If a task is a part of your job, rate:

Relative Time Spent	Relative Importance
1 = Very small amount	A Unimportant
2 = Small amount	B Minor importance
3 = Moderate amount	C Important
4 = Large amount	D Very important
5 = Very large amount	E Crucial

Column headers: Not part of the job / Relative time spent / Relative importance

A. Planning

1 Develops business planning activities
2 Directs business planning activities
3 Develops annual unit goals and objectives
4 Approves annual unit goals and objectives
5 Develops longer-range strategic goals
6 Approves longer-range strategic goals
7 Develops specific strategy and action plans for unit
8 Approves specific strategy and action plans for unit
9 Reviews approves and monitors business plans
10 Prepares profit plans and updates
11 Approves profit plans and updates
12 Prepares operating budgets
13 Approves operating budgets
14 Approves requests for nonbudgeted items
15 Develops plans to improve administrative efficiency
16 Approves plans to improve administrative efficiency
17 Integrates the plans of other organizational units
18 Coordinates with other units to meet predetermined schedules
19 Proposes new or customized programs, services, products and research
20 Approves new or customized programs, services, products and research
21 Identifies impact of external conditions on unit
22 Coordinates units in the development of plans and programs
23 Monitors progress of specific projects
24 Recommends revisions to the unit organizational structure
25 Approves revisions to the unit organizational structure
26 Evaluates and recommends approval of affiliate facility projects
27 Recommends potential mergers, acquisitions or relocations
28 Approves potential mergers, acquisitions or relocations
29 Other: please list task(s) and check boxes
a
b
c

From the above list of Planning tasks, please mark the numbers of the three most important tasks in rank order
1
2

B. Policies and Procedures

30 Formulates and recommends policies or procedures for others to follow
31 Approves policies or procedures for others to follow
32 Reviews agreements or documentation for compliance with appropriate policies and standards
33 Directs the establishment of review or control procedures
34 Evaluates operating policies or procedures against desired objectives
35 Develops or maintains standards for service
36 Develops quality control programs and procedures
37 Approves quality control programs and procedures
38 Formulates or recommends pricing policies
39 Approves pricing policies
40 Develops methods and procedures to evaluate business strategies
41 Establishes planning guidelines and procedures
42 Directs creation, handling and disposition of records
43 Directs safeguarding of records and official records documents
44 Approves procedures for automating existing manual systems
45 Other: please list task(s) and check boxes
a
b
c

From the above list of Policies and Procedures tasks, please mark the numbers of the three most important tasks in rank order
1
2
3

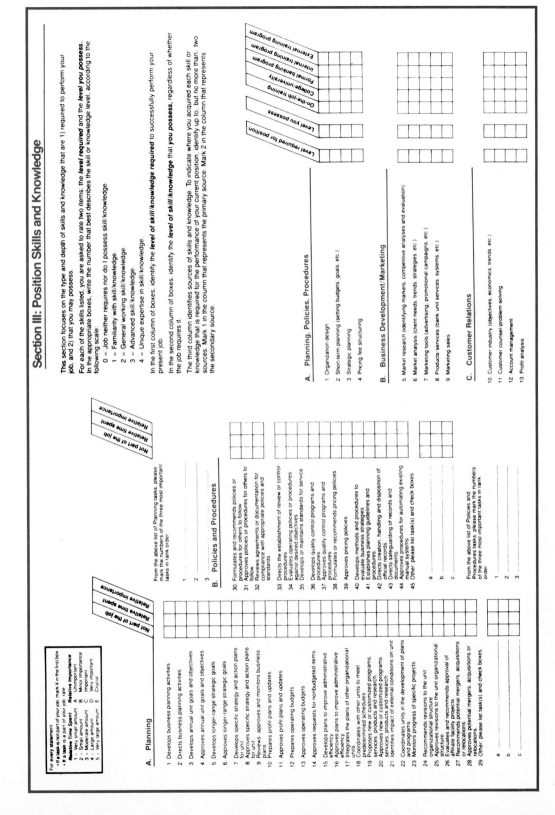

method is used primarily when manual skills are required, such as those of a machine operator. However, observation alone usually is insufficient as a sole means of job analysis. It is especially deficient when mental skills are dominant in a job. Try observing a computer programmer at work sometime and see what you can come up with.

INTERVIEW

An understanding of the job may also be gained through interviewing both the employee and the supervisor. Usually the employee is interviewed first, and the job analyst assists the worker in describing the duties performed. Once the worker has been interviewed, the supervisor is normally contacted for additional information to check the accuracy of information obtained and clarify certain points.

EMPLOYEE RECORDING

In some instances, job analysis information is gathered by having the employees describe their daily work activities in a diary or log. Again, the problem of employees exaggerating their jobs' importance may have to be overcome. For highly specialized jobs, however, valuable understanding of the job may be obtained through this method.

COMBINATION

It is likely that no one job analysis method will be used exclusively. Rather, a combination is often more appropriate. For instance, in analyzing clerical and administrative jobs, the analyst might use questionnaires supported by interviews and limited observation. In studying shop jobs, interviews supplemented by a greater degree of work observation may provide the needed data.

CONDUCTING JOB ANALYSIS

The person who conducts job analysis is interested in gathering data regarding what is involved in performing a particular job. The people who participate in job analysis should include the employee and the employee's immediate supervisor. In large organizations, there may be one or more job analysts. In smaller firms, line supervisors may have this responsibility. Outside consultants are often used if the organization itself lacks the expertise to perform the job analysis.

Before job analysis is conducted, the analyst (whatever the actual title) learns as much as possible about the job by such means as reviewing organizational charts and talking with individuals acquainted with the jobs to be studied. Before beginning, the analyst should be introduced to the employees by the supervisor, who should also explain the purpose of job analysis. Existing employee attitudes may be beyond the control of the job analyst. However, it is imperative that the analyst attempt to develop a feeling of mutual trust and confidence with those whose jobs are being analyzed. Failure in this area will stifle an otherwise technically sound job analysis. After job analysis has been conducted, two basic personnel documents — job descriptions and job specifications — may be prepared.

JOB DESCRIPTION

Information obtained through job analysis is crucial to the development of job descriptions. The **job description** is *a document that provides information regarding the tasks, duties, and responsibilities of the job.* The particular facts needed depend on how the job description is to be used. Job descriptions are accurate, concise statements of what employees are expected to do on their jobs. They should indicate what employees do, how they do it, and the conditions under which the duties are performed. Among the items often included in a job description are:

- Major duties performed.
- Percentage of time devoted to each duty.
- Performance standards to be achieved.
- Working conditions and possible hazards.
- Number of persons working on each job and their reporting relationships.
- The machines and equipment used on the job.

The sections typically placed in the job description vary somewhat with the purpose for which it will be used. The most common sections included on a job description are described next.

JOB IDENTIFICATION

This section includes the job title, department, reporting relationship, and a job number or code. A good title will closely approximate the nature of the work content and will distinguish that job from others. Job titles are often misleading. An "Executive Secretary" in one organization may be little more than a highly paid typist, while a person with the same title in another firm may practically run the company. For instance, a former student, after receiving a B.B.A. degree, took his first job with a major tire and rubber company as an "Assistant District Service Manager." Because the primary duties of the job were to unload tires from trucks, check the tread wear, and stack the tires in boxcars, a more appropriate title would have been "Tire Checker and Stacker."

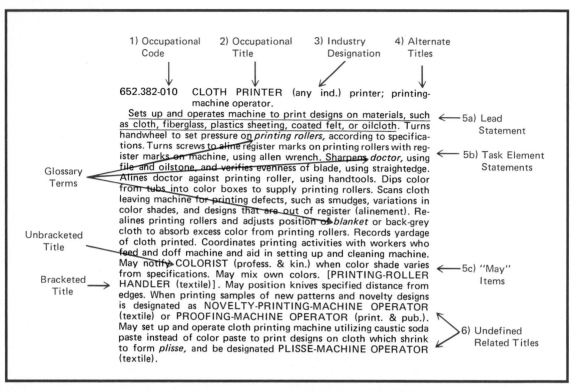

Figure 4–3. The parts of a DOT definition. Source: U.S. Department of Labor, *Dictionary of Occupational Titles.*

One information source that assists in standardizing job titles is the *Dictionary of Occupational Titles* (DOT).[4] The DOT includes standardized and comprehensive descriptions of job duties and related information for over 20,000 occupations. This permits improved uniformity in job titles and descriptions. Employers in different parts of the country are aided as they attempt to match job requirements with worker skills. The 1977 edition of DOT eliminated sex and age references.

An example of a DOT definition for a "Cloth Printer" — Occupational Code (652.382-010) — is provided in Figure 4–3. The first digit of the code identifies one of the following major job categories:

0/1   Professional, technical, and managerial occupations

2   Clerical and sales occupations

3   Service occupations

4   Farming, fishing, forestry, and related occupations

[4]U.S. Department of Labor, *Dictionary of Occupational Titles*, 4th ed. Washington, D.C.: U.S. Government Printing Office, 1977.

5	Processing occupations
6	Machine trade occupations
7	Bench work occupations
8	Structural work occupations
9	Miscellaneous occupations

In this instance, the major job classification would be "machine trade occupations." The next two digits represent further breakdowns of the specific job category.

Digits four through six describe the job's relationship to data, people, and things. For the "Cloth Printer" illustration, a code "3" for data would be "compiling," a code "8" for people would be "no significant relationship," and a code "2" for things would be "operating and controlling."

The final three digits of the occupational code indicate the alphabetical order of titles within the six-digit code group. These codes assist in distinguishing a specific occupation from other similar ones. The alphabetical order for "Cloth Printer" is indicated by the digits 010.

DATE OF THE JOB ANALYSIS

The job analysis date is placed on the job description to aid in identifying job changes that would make the description obsolete. Certain firms have found it useful to place an expiration date on the document to ensure that the job content is reviewed periodically and to minimize the number of obsolete job descriptions.

JOB SUMMARY

The job summary provides a concise overview of the job. It is generally a short paragraph that states the content of the job.

DUTIES PERFORMED

The body of the job description describes the major duties to be performed. Usually one sentence beginning with an action verb such as *receives, performs, establishes,* or *assembles* adequately explains each duty.

JOB SPECIFICATION

The minimum acceptable qualifications that a person should possess to perform a particular job is the **job specification.** Items typically included in the job specification are education requirements, experience, personality, and physical abilities.

In practice, job specifications are often included as a major section of

POSITION TITLE				POSITION NUMBER 217
SECRETARY II				APPROVAL RHS
DIVISION OR STAFF DEPARTMENT All	LOCATION All	REPORTS TO		EFFECTIVE DATE May 1987
DEPARTMENT OR ACTIVITY	SECTION	POINTS 165	GRADE 6	REVISES

JOB SUMMARY

Performs clerical, stenographic, and administrative duties for a manager and often one or more staff members of a major function.

NATURE OF WORK

Performs a wide variety of office duties including most of the following:

a. Typing correspondence, reports, manuscripts, graphs, charts, etc., from shorthand notes, dictating machine tapes, and/or hand written drafts proficiently and with minimum direction and instructions.
b. Receiving telephone calls and visitors skillfully and handling incoming mail efficiently.
c. Originating routine correspondence and handling inquiries, and routing non-routine inquiries and correspondence to proper persons.
d. Establishing and maintaining department files and records.
e. Assuming responsibility for arranging appointments and meetings, screening calls, and handling personal and confidential matters for superior.
f. Assembling, organizing, processing, and evaluating data and reports; operating office machines needed for accomplishing this.
g. Performing administrative duties and special projects as directed, such as collecting and compiling general reference materials and information pertaining to company, division, or department practices and procedures.

Works independently, receiving a minimum of supervision and guidance on established office procedures. Relieves supervisor of minor administrative details. May have some light work direction over others in department. Structure is light and most work is not checked.

QUALIFICATIONS

High school education or its equivalent plus three years of clerical and stenographic experience, including one year with the Company, and a typing skill of at least 60 WPM. Demonstrated proficiency in English grammar, punctuation, spelling, and proper word usage. Must be able to anticipate problems and use sound judgment and tact in handling confidential matters, screening telephone calls and visitors, and scheduling superior's time. Must have the ability to acquire a thorough knowledge of the organization's policies, procedures, and personnel in order to relieve superior of specified administrative duties. A shorthand skill of at least 80 WPM is necessary if required in a specific position. A basic figure aptitude and/or a working knowledge of certain business machines may be necessary depending on the specific job.

Figure 4–4. A nonexempt job description. Source: Used with permission of General Mills, Inc.

job descriptions. An example of this is the job description provided by General Mills, as shown in Figure 4–4. As you can see, the qualifications needed for the job of "Secretary II" include typing at least sixty words per minute and taking shorthand at the rate of at least eighty words per minute. This type of information is extremely valuable in the recruiting and selection process.

Ronald C. Pilenzo
President and Chief
Operating Officer,
American Society for
Personnel
Administration

During the early 1950s when Ronald C. Pilenzo was trying to decide upon a career, the personnel field was only beginning to emerge and make its presence felt. But, he says, "I wanted a career that offered personal growth and financial reward. I also wanted a career that offered wide scope and diversity, as opposed to a highly structured job that offered very narrow career ranges. Through Personnel I feel that I have achieved this goal."

After graduation from the University of Detroit, Pilenzo joined Ford Motor Company, where he progressed to the position of personnel director, Industrial and Chemical Products Division. Later, he became a principal consultant with the international consulting firm of Raymond E. Danto, where he was responsible for all personnel and organization consulting. He subsequently joined Allied Supermarkets, Inc., as director, corporate recruiting, compensation, and manpower planning. In this position he was responsible for 18,000 employees in eleven major divisions covering forty-three states. Pilenzo next served as director, manpower and organization development with Evans Products Company for five years before he joined International Multifoods as director, corporate compensation and management development, corporate human resource staff in 1975. In 1980, he was selected to become president and chief operating officer of the American Society for Personnel Administration (ASPA), the world's largest professional personnel organization.

When asked to identify some critical moments in his career, Pilenzo replied, "They involved making career decisions that related to the kind and type of organization where I was to be employed. For example, at least three times in my career I have been offered opportunities to create a professional organization where either one did not exist or one existed that was not performing satisfactorily." He accepted all three challenges, but says, "Interesting challenges present high risk situations." He did not fail and has become one of the most respected professionals in his field.

When asked about the qualities needed for success, he replies, "Personnel executives need to be tough-minded, intelligent, capable of working within and outside the personnel function, and not in a vacuum. They must be individuals who can work comfortably in a changing environment that involves complex problems with no readily available solutions. The successful personnel executive will probably have a personality profile that is comparable to an operating executive."

Asked to comment regarding the earning potential of personnel executives, Pilenzo stated, "It is interesting to note that in the past five years salaries for personnel executives have risen substantially faster than salaries for almost any other functional management group. It is not unusual today to find major corporations' top personnel executives earning salaries and bonuses in the six figure range."

He also believes that company loyalty is not the same as in the past. He says, "In today's changing world, and with people's obviously shifting value systems, loyalty to an organization is an interesting dilemma. The days of employees who dedicated their entire lives to the organization are probably at an end. This does not mean that, while people are employed in an organization, they should not give their best possible effort. What it does mean, however, is that people now place a different value on company loyalty. This means that younger people today generally consider loyalty to self above loyalty to company."

Finally, Pilenzo states, "It is no longer sufficient or desirable for organizations to employ personnel people who desire a career in personnel simply because they 'like people' and 'helping others.' In fact, people who see this as their primary role are usually unsuccessful as professional personnel managers."

After jobs have been analyzed and the descriptions written, the results should be reviewed with the supervisor and the worker to ensure that they are accurate, clear, and understandable. The courtesy of reviewing results with employees also assists in gaining their acceptance. This single factor may well determine the success of the entire project.

As previously stated, the job description and job specification are often combined into one form. Therefore, we will use the term *job description* to refer to both documents.

NEWER METHODS FOR CONDUCTING JOB ANALYSIS

In recent years, attempts have been made to provide more systematic methods of conducting job analysis. Several of these newer approaches will next be described.

DEPARTMENT OF LABOR JOB ANALYSIS SCHEDULE

The Department of Labor established a method of systematically studying jobs and occupations called Job Analysis Schedule (JAS). The basic thrust of the Job Analysis Schedule is illustrated in Figure 4–5. A major component of this schedule is the *Work Performed Ratings*. Here, what workers do in the performance of a job with regard to three categories (data, people, and things) is evaluated. Subdivisions of these categories are shown in Table 4–2. Each category is viewed as a hierarchy of functions, with those higher in the category being more difficult. The codes in the *Worker Functions* section represent the highest level of involvement in each of the three categories. The *Work Field* section states the characteristics of the machines,

Figure 4–5. A Department of Labor job analysis schedule. Source: U.S. Department of Labor, Manpower Administration. *Handbook for Analyzing Jobs.* Washington, D.C.: U.S. Government Printing Office, 1972, pp. 42–45.

JOB ANALYSIS SCHEDULE

1. Estab. Job Title   DOUGH MIXER

2. Ind. Assign.   (bake. prod.)

3. SIC Code(s) and Title(s)   2051 Bread and other bakery products

(Left margin: Code 520.782   Oper. Control p. 435   WTA Group   DOT Title   Ind. Desig.)

4. JOB SUMMARY:

Operates mixing machine to mix ingredients for straight and sponge (yeast) doughs according to established formulas, directs other workers in fermentation of dough, and cuts dough into pieces with hand cutter.

5. WORK PERFORMED RATINGS:

	D	P	(T)
Worker Functions	Data	People	Things
	5	6	2

Work Field   148 — Cooking, Food Preparing

M.P.S.M.S.   384 — Bakery Products

6. WORKER TRAITS RATINGS:

GED   1 (2) 3 4 5 6
SVP   1 2 3 (4) 5 6 7 8 9
Aptitudes   G 3 V 3 N 3 S 3 P 3 Q 4 K 3 F 3 M 3 E 4 C 4
Temperaments   D F I J (M) P R S (T) V
Interests   (1a) 1b 2a 2b 3a 3b 4a (4b) 5a (5b)
Phys. Demands   S L M (H) V 2 (3) (4) 5 (6)
Environ. Cond.   (I) O B 2 3 4 (5) 6 7

7. General Education
  a. Elementary   6   High School _____ Courses _____
  b. College   None   Courses _____

8. Vocational Preparation
  a. College   None   Courses _____

  b. Vocational Education   None   Courses _____

  c. Apprenticeship   None

Figure 4–5. A Department of Labor job analysis schedule. (continued)

> d. Inplant Training   None
>
> e. On-the-Job Training   Six months
>
> f. Performance on Other Jobs   DOUGH-MIXER HELPER—One year
>
> **9.** Experience   One year as DOUGH-MIXER HELPER
>
> **10.** Orientation   Four hours
>
> **11.** Licenses, etc.   Food Handlers Certificate issued by the Health Department
>
> **12.** Relation to Other Jobs and Workers
>
> Promotion: From   DOUGH-MIXER HELPER   To   BAKER
>
> Transfers: From   None   To   None
>
> Supervision Received   By BAKER
>
> Supervision Given   DOUGH-MIXER HELPER
>
>
> **13.** Machines, Tools, Equipment, and Work Aids—Dough-mixing machine;
> balance scales; hand scoops; measuring vessels; portable dough troughs.
>
> **14.** Materials and Products
>   Bread dough
>
> **15.** Description of Tasks:
>
>   1. Dumps ingredients into mixing machine: Examines production schedule to
>   determine type of bread to be produced, such as rye, whole wheat, or
>   white. Refers to formula card for quantities and types of ingredients
>   required, such as flour, water, milk, vitamin solutions, and shortening.
>   Weighs out, measures, and dumps ingredients into mixing machine. (20%)

tools, equipment, and work aids used in the performance of the job. It also specifies the techniques used in the performance of the job. The *M.P.S.M.S.* section identifies the machines, tools, equipment, and work aids used in performing the job.

The category *Worker Traits Ratings* is related primarily to job requirement data. Topics such as general education (GED), specific vocational preparation (SVP), aptitudes, temperaments, interests, physical demands, and environmental conditions are included.

The *Description of Tasks* section provides a specific description of the work performed. Both routine tasks and occasionally performed tasks should be included. When the JAS method is used, information is gathered by a trained analyst.

FUNCTIONAL JOB ANALYSIS

Functional job analysis (FJA) is *a comprehensive job analysis approach that concentrates on the interactions among the work, the worker, and the*

Figure 4–5. A Department of Labor job analysis schedule. (continued)

109

**Chapter 4
Job Analysis**

2. Operates mixing machine: Turns valves and other hand controls to set mixing time according to type of dough being mixed. Presses button to start agitator blades in machine. Observes gauges and dials on equipment continuously to verify temperature of dough and mixing time. Feels dough for desired consistency. Adds water or flour to mix measuring vessels and adjusts mixing time and controls to obtain desired elasticity in mix. (55%)

3. Directs other workers in fermentation of dough: Prepares fermentation schedule according to type of dough being raised. Sprays portable dough *Trough* with lubricant to prevent adherence of mixed dough to trough. Directs DOUGH-MIXER HELPER in positioning trough beneath door of mixer to catch dough when mixing cycle is complete. Pushes or directs other workers to push troughs of dough into fermentation room. (10%)

4. Cuts dough: Dumps fermentated dough onto worktable. Manually kneads dough to eliminate gases formed by yeast. Cuts dough into pieces with hand cutter. Places cut dough on proofing rack and covers with cloth. (10%)

5. Performs miscellaneous duties: Records on work sheet number of batches mixed during work shift. Informs BAKE SHOP FOREMAN when repairs or major adjustments are required for machines and equipment. (5%)

---

16. Definition of Terms
   Trough—A long, narrow, opened vessel used for kneading or washing ingredients.

17. General Comments
   None

---

18. Analyst Jane Smith Date 3/21/87 Editor John Rilley Date 3/30/87
   Reviewed By Alexandra Purcey Title, Org. Foreman, Bake Shop

Table 4–2 Worker function scale of functional job analysis

Data (4th digit)		People (5th digit)		Things (6th digit)	
0	Synthesizing	0	Monitoring	0	Setting-up
1	Coordinating	1	Negotiating	1	Precision working
2	Analyzing	2	Instructing	2	Operating–controlling
3	Compiling	3	Supervising	3	Driving–operating
4	Computing	4	Diverting	4	Manipulating
5	Copying	5	Persuading	5	Tending
6	Comparing	6	Speaking–signaling	6	Feeding–offbearing
7	No significant	7	Serving	7	Handling
8	relationship	8	No significant relationship	8	No significant relationship

work organization. It is a worker-oriented method of describing jobs that identify what a person actually does rather than for what he or she is responsible.[5] The fundamental elements of FJA are:

1. A major distinction is made between what gets done and what workers do to get things done. It is more important in job analysis to know the latter. For instance, a computer operator does not just keep the system running; there are a number of tasks that must be performed if his or her job is to be accomplished.
2. Each job is concerned with data, people, and things.
3. Workers function in unique ways relating to data, people, and things.
4. Each job requires the worker to relate to data, people, and things in some way.
5. Only a few definite and identifiable functions are involved with data, people and things (see Table 4–2).
6. These functions proceed from the simple to the complex. Referring again to Table 4–2, the least complex form of data would be *comparing* while the most complex would be *synthesizing.* In addition, it is assumed that, if an upper level function is required, all of the lower level functions are also required.
7. The three hierarchies for data, people, and things provide two measures for a job. First, there is a measure of relative complexity in relation to data, people, and things, in essence, the amount of interrelationship among the three functions. Second, there is a measure of proportional involvement for each function. For instance, 50 percent of a person's time may be spent in analyzing, 30 percent in supervising, and 20 percent in operating.[6]

One study determined that FJA was a useful technique for defining the work of heavy-equipment operators, so that the knowledge, skills, and abilities required can be easily communicated to the courts and the public.[7]

POSITION ANALYSIS QUESTIONNAIRE

The **Position Analysis Questionnaire (PAQ)** is *a structured job analysis questionnaire that distinguishes between job-oriented elements and worker-oriented elements.* There are 194 job descriptors, which are analyzed according to six activities: information input, mental processes, work output,

[5]Felix M. Lopez, Gerald A. Kesselman, and Felix E. Lopez, "An Empirical Test of a Trait-Oriented Job Analysis Technique," *Personnel Psychology* 35 (August 1981): 480.

[6]Ernest J. McCormick, "Job Information: Its Development and Application," in Dale Yoder and Herbert S. Heneman (eds.), *Staffing Policies and Strategies,* Washington, D.C.: The Bureau of National Affairs, 1979, pp. 4–58.

[7]Howard C. Olson, Sidney A. Fine, David C. Myers, and Margarette C. Jennings, "The Use of Functional Job Analysis in Establishing Performance Standards for Heavy Equipment Operators," *Personnel Psychology* 34 (Summer 1981): 351.

relationships with other persons, job context, and other job characteristics.

111

Chapter 4
Job Analysis

Each job description is evaluated on a specified scale such as *extent of use, amount of time, importance of job, possibility of occurrence,* and *applicability.*

Job descriptions can be prepared based on the relative importance and emphasis placed on the various job elements. In addition, a profile rating on 45 job dimensions can be determined. Proponents of the PAQ believe that the nature of the job descriptors makes it possible to use this approach for virtually any type of position or job.[8]

MANAGEMENT POSITION DESCRIPTION QUESTIONNAIRE

The **Management Position Description Questionnaire (MPDQ)** is *a form of job analysis designed for management positions and uses a checklist method to analyze jobs.* It contains 208 items that are related to the concerns and responsibilities of managers.[9] These 208 items have been reduced to 13 primary job factors:

1. Product, market, and financial planning
2. Coordination of other organizational units and personnel
3. Internal business control
4. Products and service responsibility
5. Public and customer relations
6. Advanced consulting
7. Autonomy of action
8. Approval of financial commitment
9. Staff service
10. Supervision
11. Complexity and stress
12. Advanced financial responsibility
13. Broad personnel responsibility

The MPDQ has been used to determine the training needs of individuals who are to move into managerial positions. It has also been used to evaluate and set compensation rates for managerial jobs, and assign these jobs to job families.

GUIDELINES ORIENTED JOB ANALYSIS

The **Guidelines Oriented Job Analysis (GOJA)** *responds to the growing amount of legislation affecting staffing and involves a step-by-step pro-*

---

[8]E. J. McCormick and J. Triffin, *Industrial Psychology,* 6th ed. Englewood Cliffs, N.J.: Prentice-Hall, 1974, p. 53.

[9]W. W. Tornow and P. R. Pinto, "The Development of Management Job Taxonomy: A System for Describing, Classifying and Evaluating Executive Positions," *Journal of Applied Psychology* 11 (1976): 410–418.

cedure for describing the work of a particular job classification.[10] It is also used for development of selection tools such as application blanks and is a way of documenting compliance with various legal requirements.

There are three versions of GOJA. The original method, *Full GOJA*, is very detailed and approximately twenty hours are required to analyze a job completely. Its use is most appropriate where there is a high probability of discrimination suits. Next, *Brief GOJA*, was developed after the *Uniform Guidelines* were published and reduces the amount of time taken to complete a job analysis. Because of the large amount of time still required, a third version, *Simplified GOJA*, was developed. Only about two to four hours are required to complete this job analysis form. The GOJA requests the following types of information: (1) machines, tools, and equipment; (2) supervision; (3) contacts; (4) duties; (5) knowledge, skills, and abilities; (6) physical and other requirements; and (7) differentiating requirements.

OCCUPATIONAL MEASUREMENT SYSTEM[11]

The Occupational Measurement System (OMS) enables organizations to collect, store, and analyze information pertinent to human resources through an electronic data base. Computers provide faster turnaround and more accurate job analysis, job descriptions, and evaluations, while multiple regression statistical techniques increase objectivity and hence responsiveness to potential discrimination claims.

OMS is designed to work with task-based information. Task-based job evaluation uses structured job analysis questionnaires covering work performed within the organization as the basic input document. The questionnaires are developed from a number of different sources, including a data base of industry job tasks, the organization's job descriptions, and job experts within the firm's work force. The questionnaires are composed of a basic text booklet with instructions and general information. Within the booklet are specific items tailored for the category of positions covered, with responses solicited in keypunch or optical scanning format. Sample items from a questionnaire are shown in Figure 4–6.

Job evaluation factors are determined through a policy-capturing approach using multiple regression analysis to identify the organization's current pay policy and practices. Selected compensable factors are then modified to reflect desired changes in the organization's pay policy and combined with a job content factor developed from the job analysis questionnaire. This forms the basis for a job evaluation program tailored to the organization's needs and objectives. Once the internal job evaluation model is developed, the results are integrated with the competitive analysis of the external marketplace into a series of salary ranges.

---

[10]Stephen E. Bemis, Ann Holt Belenky, and Dee Ann Soder, *Job Analysis: An Effective Management Tool*. Washington, D.C.: The Bureau of National Affairs, 1983, p. 42.

[11]Information for this section was furnished by First Interstate Bancorp.

For Every Statement:

- If a task is part of your job, mark X in the first box.
- If you PERFORM and/or SUPERVISE a task, rate it using the adjacent RELATIVE TIME SPENT scale:

1 = An extremely small amount of time.
2 = Between levels 1 and 3.
3 = A small amount of time.
4 = Between levels 3 and 5.
5 = A moderate amount of time.
6 = Between levels 5 and 7.
7 = A large amount of time.
8 = Between levels 7 and 9.
9 = An extremely large amount of time.

Relative time spent SUPERVISING _____
Relative time spent PERFORMING _____
Part of job _____

Relative time spent SUPERVISING _____
Relative time spent PERFORMING _____
Part of job _____

CREDIT ADMINISTRATION

1. Works with officers on national accounts to solve credit problems.

2. Responds to inquiries from branches regarding consumer regulations.

3. Establishes goals for delinquency ratios, charge-offs and recoveries.

4. Maintains annual forecasts for nonaccrual loans and other nonperforming assets.

5. Develops loan policy and procedures.

6. Recommends loan policy and procedures.

7. Maintains annual forecasts of commercial, consumer and real estate loan losses.

8. Prepares reports on branch compliance with consumer regulations.

9. Recommends interest rates for loans.

10. Reviews periodicals for changes to consumer protection laws.

11. Reviews analysis reports and financial statement spreads.

12. Performs commercial credit investigations.

13. Prepares credit memos.

14. Prepares loan write-ups.

15. Assembles and interprets debtor credit information.

16. Surveys collateral status for credit extension on potential and current customers.

17. Contacts credit agencies to secure credit reports and special services.

Figure 4–6. Job analysis questionnaire. Source: Used with the permission of First Interstate Bancorp.

The information obtained in the job analysis questionnaire is analyzed by the Occupational Measurement System (OMS), an integrated computer software system specifically designed to process, analyze, and display task-based information. This system provides large-scale storage and processing capabilities and integrates occupational data processing requirements. The following are illustrations of a few of the reports generated by OMS:

1. A computer-generated job description on a functional and detailed task level. The data include the overall job functions performed by each employee, job or job classification, the specific tasks covered by those functions, and the amount of time spent on the task and functions.
2. Identifies skills and knowledge and the level required to perform a function or job, those possessed by the incumbents, and the differences between the two where, for example, training needs can be identified.
3. Determines the costs involved to a company to have work produced, in terms of both performance and supervision of the work.

JOB ANALYSIS AND THE LAW

A good job analysis system is needed as a firm recruits, selects, and moves employees through the organization. Job analysis has become a focus of Personnel because of the need for selection methods to be job related.[12] Legislation requiring thorough job analysis includes:

- *Fair Labor Standards Act:* Employees are categorized as exempt or nonexempt. Job analysis is basic to this determination. Nonexempt personnel must be paid time and a half when they work over 40 hours per week. This is not required for exempt employees.
- *Equal Pay Act:* In the past, and to some extent today, men were often paid higher salaries than women, even though essentially the same job was being performed. If jobs are not substantially different, similar pay should be provided. When pay differences exist, job descriptions can be used to show whether jobs are substantially equal in terms of skill, effort, responsibility, or working conditions.
- *Civil Rights Act:* As with the Equal Pay Act, job descriptions may provide the basis for adequate defenses against unfair discrimination charges. When job analysis is not performed, it is usually difficult to defend a qualification established for the job. For instance, stating that a high school diploma is required without having determined its necessity through job analysis leaves the firm open to discrimination charges.

[12]Donald W. Myers, "The Impact of a Selected Provision in the Federal Guidelines on Job Analysis and Training," *Personnel Administration* 26 (July 1981): 41–45.

■ *Occupational Safety and Health Act:* Job descriptions are required to specify "elements of the job that endanger health, or are considered unsatisfactory or distasteful by the majority of the population." Showing the job description to the employee in advance is a good defense.

JOB DESIGN

Is it possible to increase employee motivation, improve job satisfaction, and raise production all at the same time? To do so is a significant challenge for managers. Increasingly, the work force is more highly educated. Workers expect more from the job than having it meet their financial needs only. They also want jobs that allow them to satisfy other needs, such as achievement, growth, recognition, and self-fulfillment. In other words, the challenge is to increase worker productivity by finding ways to "unlock the potential that exists in the overwhelming majority of our work force."[13]

J. Richard Hackman and Greg R. Oldham contend that the quality of work life can be improved, while at the same time increasing or maximizing worker productivity.[14] They challenge several long-held assumptions, such as:

■ The basic nature of work is fixed and cannot be changed.
■ Technology and work processes determine job design.
■ All that management can do is properly select and train personnel.

Job design is *the process of determining the specific tasks to be performed, the methods used in performing these tasks, and how the job relates to other work in the organization.* While the activity of job design is not usually assigned to Personnel, a good case can be made for it to be a function of the human resource manager. In their book, *Work Redesign*, Hackman and Oldham assert that if managers want to achieve a high level of motivation, reliable feedback on performance must be given to employees. Workers must also sense that they are accountable for specific results and feel that the job has meaning beyond pay.[15] Workers get more satisfaction from completing an entire task or an identifiable part of a process than from producing indistinguishable and seemingly unrelated pieces of work. Because of all this, job design is important in helping to motivate today's worker. In spite of its bright promise, however, a number of constraints exist.

---

[13]Robert H. Guest, "Review of Work Redesign," *Harvard Business Review* (January–February 1981): 46–47, 52.

[14]Ibid., p. 46.

[15]J. Richard Hackman and Greg R. Oldham, *Work Redesign*. Reading, Mass.: Addison-Wesley, 1980.

Technology has an impact on job design. The type of equipment and tools, as well as particular work layout and methods, used in producing a product or services tend to act as constraints. Technology may make job redesign, in particular, difficult and expensive, although not impossible. For example, adapting or redesigning the assembly-line production of automobiles or electronic components may not be technically or economically feasible.[16]

Economic factors also affect job design. If management believes that redesigning jobs can improve output and the level of worker satisfaction, the adequacy of the firm's other resources must be considered. Although job redesign may be desirable, its cost may be prohibitive. A manager must continually balance the benefits of job design with the costs.

Job design is also affected by laws and government regulations. Management may want to design a job in a way that might increase worker performance but in doing so would violate labor laws or environmental or safety standards.

If a company has a union, job design can be affected by the philosophy, policies, and strategies of the union. Typically, the contract between the company and the union specifies and defines the types of jobs and the duties and responsibilities of workers. Unions generally have opposed work redesign experiments. They have perceived them to be attempts by management to squeeze more work out of the worker without any increase in wages. Also, unions may view job redesign as a threat to their power and position with the workers. However, in recent years unions have become more flexible in order to maintain job security for their members.

Important considerations for job design are the abilities, attitudes, and motivation of the firm's employees. Obviously, the design of particular jobs depends on the ability or training of present or potential employees. It would not make sense to design a job that would be far more complex than the ability level of employees available to do it. The ability and willingness of employees to be trained can limit job redesign.

Finally, management philosophy and organizational objectives and strategies may determine the degree to which job redesign is possible. Top management must be committed to the concept of job redesign. Job redesign may let employees gain greater authority in determining how their jobs are performed and how workers are managed.

JOB ENRICHMENT

During the past twenty years or so, a great deal of interest has been shown in job enrichment. Strongly advocated by Frederick Herzberg, **job enrichment** refers to *basic changes in the content and level of responsibility of a job so as to provide greater challenge to the worker.* The worker is given

---

[16]John F. Runcie, "By Days I Make the Cars," *Harvard Business Review* (May–June 1980): 106–115.

a chance to experience greater achievement, recognition, responsibility, and personal growth in performing the job. Although job enrichment programs have not always been successful, many have produced improvements in job performance and in the level of employee satisfaction in a variety of organizations.

AT&T, Polaroid, Texas Instruments, Monsanto, Weyerhaeuser, General Motors, Corning Glass, and many other firms have achieved excellent results from job enrichment programs. In most of these cases, productivity and job satisfaction increased, and employee turnover and absenteeism decreased.[17]

According to Herzberg, job enrichment efforts should be based on the principles of:

1. *Increasing job demands:* Changing the job in such a way as to increase the level of difficulty and responsibility of the job.
2. *Increasing a worker's accountability:* Allowing more individual control and authority over the work while retaining the manager's accountability.
3. *Providing work scheduling freedom:* Within limits, allowing individual workers to schedule their own work.
4. *Providing feedback:* Making timely periodic reports on performance to employees (directly to the worker rather than to the supervisor).
5. *Providing new learning experiences:* Creating opportunities for new experiences and personal growth of the individual.[18]

JOB ENLARGEMENT

Many people have attempted to differentiate between job enrichment and job enlargement. **Job enlargement** *changes the scope of a job so as to provide greater variety to the worker.* Job enlargement provides a horizontal expansion of duties. For example, instead of knowing how to operate only one machine, a worker is taught to operate two or even three with the same level of responsibility. Job enrichment on the other hand, involves increased responsibility.

SUMMARY

A job consists of a group of tasks that must be performed if an organization is to achieve its goals. Every employee of an organization occupies a position. The systematic process of determining the duties and skills required

---

[17]See "Case Studies in the Humanization of Work," in *Work in America: Report of Special Task Force to the Secretary of Health, Education, and Welfare.* Cambridge, Mass.: MIT Press, 1973, appendix, pp. 188–200.

[18]Frederick Herzberg, "One More Time: How Do You Motivate Employees?" *Harvard Business Review* 22(2) (Winter 1979).

for performing the organization's jobs is referred to as job analysis. Job analysis is the most basic human resource management tool. Without properly conducted job analysis, it would be difficult, if not impossible, to perform the other personnel-related functions satisfactorily.

Job analysis information is used to prepare both job descriptions and job specifications. Job descriptions specify the tasks, duties, and responsibilities associated with a job. Job specifications state the knowledges, skills, and abilities a person must possess in order to perform the job.

Job analysis may be conducted in a number of ways. When using questionnaires, the job analyst has employees identify the tasks they perform in accomplishing the job. The job analyst actually witnesses the work being performed and records his or her observations when the observation method is used. The job analyst may also gain an understanding of the job by interviewing both the employee and the supervisor. In some instances, job analysis information is gathered by having employees describe their daily work activities in a diary or log. Finally, a combination of any of these methods may be used. The person who conducts job analysis is interested in gathering data about what is involved in performing a particular job.

The most common sections included on a job description are: (1) job identification; (2) date of the job analysis; (3) job summary; and (4) duties performed. Some of the items often included in the job specification section are requirements for education, experience, personality, and physical abilities.

In recent years, attempts have been made to provide more systematic methods for conducting job analysis. Several of these newer approaches include: (1) Department of Labor Job Analysis Schedule (JAS); (2) functional job analysis (FJA); (3) Position Analysis Questionnaire (PAQ); (4) Management Position Description Questionnaire (MPDQ); (5) Guidelines Oriented Job Analysis (GOJA); (6) Occupational Measurement System (OMS). Job analysis has become a focus of Personnel because of the need for selection methods to be job related.

Job design is the process of determining the specific tasks to be performed, the methods used in performing these tasks, and how the job relates to other work in the organization. Job enrichment refers to basic changes in the content and level of responsibility of a job so as to provide greater challenge to the worker. Job enlargement involves changes in the scope of a job so as to provide greater variety to the worker.

QUESTIONS FOR REVIEW

1. What is the distinction between a job and a position? Define *job analysis.*
2. Discuss what is meant by the statement, "Job analysis is the most basic human resource management tool."
3. Describe the traditional methods that are used in conducting job analysis.
4. List and briefly describe the types of data that are typically gathered when conducting job analysis.

5. What are the basic components of a job description? Briefly describe each.
6. What are the items typically included in the job specification?
7. Briefly describe each of the following: (a) Department of Labor job analysis schedule (JAS); (b) Functional job analysis (FJA); (c) Position analysis questionnaire (PAQ); (d) Management position description questionnaire (MPDQ); and (e) Guidelines oriented job analysis (GOJA).
8. How can effective job analysis be used to satisfy each of the following pieces of legislation: (a) Fair Labor Standards Act; (b) Equal Pay Act; (c) Civil Rights Act; and (d) Occupational Safety and Health Act?
9. Distinguish among job design, job enrichment, and job enlargement.

TERMS FOR REVIEW

Job position
Job analysis
Job description
Job specification
Functional job analysis (FJA)
Position Analysis Questionnaire (PAQ)

Management Position Description Questionnaire (MPDQ)
Guidelines Oriented Job Analysis (GOJA)
Job design
Job enrichment
Job enlargement

Incident 1

Richard Boudreaux was excited as he told his dad about his plan for developing job descriptions at their family-owned company, Boudreaux Gasket Company. Richard had been working with his father for some years after completing a stint in the Air Force. He was taking over more and more of the responsibilities for management because they both knew that it would not be long before Mr. Boudreaux retired. Richard had a degree in human resource management and had just completed a symposium on job analysis. "Dad," said Richard, "in two years the work force here has gone from 30 to over 50. I don't believe we can keep our finger on everything without a little more formality than we have had in the past." "I don't know son," said Mr. Boudreaux. "The way you describe it, creating job descriptions is pretty complicated. I don't know how to conduct job analysis. For my part, I wouldn't do it unless you can figure out how it can help us make rubber gaskets better, faster, or with fewer work hours than we use now."

Boudreaux Gasket Company is a small gasket maker near Gandeon, Louisiana. Most of the jobs involve operating punch presses. The operators place pieces of fiber-reinforced rubber sheeting into their machines, press the footpedals, and remove the gaskets that have been cut. Some of the workers make nonstandard gaskets. They cut these using various kinds of punches and cutters, which are hand operated. All workers are responsible for inspecting the items they make and packaging them for shipment. Even for standard items, a batch seldom exceeds 2,000 pieces in size. The gaskets are used throughout the country, primarily in the petrochemical industry.

QUESTIONS

1. Is Boudreaux Gasket Company big enough to justify formal job analysis? Explain your answer.
2. If you were Richard, what kind of arguments would you use to convince your father that formal job analysis is justified?
3. Which method of obtaining job analysis data would you use?
4. What steps would you follow to accomplish formal job analysis at Boudreaux Gasket Company?

Incident 2

As Professor Sharplin toured the Plymouth Tube Corporation plant in Pontiac, New Jersey, he became more and more impressed with his young guide, Jim Murdoch. Jim was the assistant personnel director at Plymouth Tube and was primarily responsible for job analysis. An industrial engineer was assigned full-time to the Personnel Department to assist Jim in job design. Professor Sharplin had been retained by the personnel director to study Plymouth Tube's job analysis system and to make recommendations for improvements. He had gone through the files of job descriptions in the personnel office with Jim and found them, in general, to be complete and directly related to the jobs to be performed.

One of the first stops on the tour was the office of the weld mill supervisor, a 10-foot by 10-foot room out on the factory floor with glass windows on all sides. As Jim approached, the supervisor, Roger Dishongh, was outside his office. "Hi, Jim," he said. "Hello, Roger," said Jim. "This is Professor Sharplin. Could we look at your job descriptions and chat with you for a moment?" "Sure, Jim," said Roger, opening the door. "Come on in and have a seat and I'll get them out." From their vantage point, the men in the office could see the workers in the weld mill area. As they reviewed each job description it was possible to ob-

serve the worker actually performing the work described. Roger Dishongh was familiar with each of the jobs. He was very knowledgeable about the job descriptions themselves, having contributed to preparing or revising each of them. "How are the job descriptions related to the performance evaluations here?" asked Professor Sharplin. "Well," answered Roger, "I only evaluate the workers on the items specified in the job descriptions. These were determined through careful job analysis. Limiting performance evaluations to those items helps to encourage me to correct the job descriptions when something changes and they don't accurately describe the job. Jim has conducted training sessions for all the supervisors so that we understand the relationship between job analysis, job descriptions, and performance evaluations. I think it's a pretty good system."

Jim and Professor Sharplin went on to several other areas of the plant and found similar situations. Jim seemed to have a good relationship with each of the supervisors as well as with the plant manager and the two or three mid-level managers they visited. As they headed back to the front office, Professor Sharplin was considering the comments that he would soon make to the plant manager.

QUESTIONS

1. What desirable attributes of job analysis do you see evident at Plymouth Tube Company?
2. What kind of report do you think Professor Sharplin should present to the plant manager?
3. Describe the relationship that might exist between the industrial engineer and the assistant personnel director regarding job analysis?

REFERENCES

Arvey, Richard D. *Fairness in Selecting Employees.* Reading, Mass.: Addison-Wesley, 1979.

Bemis, Stephen E., Belenky, Ann Hold, and Soder, Dee Ann. *Job Analysis: An Effective Management Tool.* Washington, D.C.: The Bureau of National Affairs, 1983.

Brennan, E. James. "Job Descriptions and Pay: The Inevitable Link." *Personnel Journal* 63 (July 1984): 18.

De Cotiis, Thomas A., and Morano, Richard A. "Applying Job Analysis to Training." *Training and Development Journal* 31 (July 1977): 20–24.

Ellig, Bruce R. "The Impact of Legislation on the Personnel Function." *Personnel* 57 (September–October 1980): 49–53.

Fleishman, E. A. "Systems for Linking Job Tasks to Personnel Requirements." *Public Personnel Management* 13 (Winter 1984): 395–408.

Foster, K. E. and Gimplin-Povis, S. "Job Evaluation: It's Time to Face the Facts." *Personnel Administrator* 29 (October 1984): 120–123+.

Gael, Sidney. *Job Analysis: A Guide to Assessing Work Activities.* San Francisco: Josey-Bass, 1983.

Hershey, Gerald L. "Determining Employee Training Needs," *Office Administration and Automation* 46 (January 1985): 82.

Hubbartt, William S. "Job Descriptions—An Important Aid to Office Automation." *Office Administration and Automation* 46 (February 1985): 49–51.

Linnen, Beth M. (ed.), "Job Descriptions: Revamping Clarifies Functions." *Savings Institutions* 106 (April 1985): 114.

Loftus, M. "Putting Action into Your Job Description." *Supervisory Management* 30 (January 1985): 25.

Myers, Donald W. "The Impact of a Selected Provision in the Federal Guidelines on Job Analysis and Training." *Personnel Administrator* 26 (July 1981): 41–45.

Owen, D. E. "Profile Analysis: Matching Positions and Personnel." *Supervisory Management* 29 (November 1984): 14–20.

Risher, Howard. "Job Evaluation: Problems and Prospects." *Personnel* 61 (January/February, 1984): 53–66.

Schnake, Mel E. and Dumler, Michael P. "Affective Response Bias in the Measurement of Perceived Task Characteristics." *Journal of Occupational Psychology* 58 (June 1985): 159–166.

Sims, Ronald R. and Veres, John G. III. "A Practical Program for Training Job Analysts." *Public Personnel Management* 14 (Summer 1985): 131–137.

Wright, Patrick M. and Wexley, Kenneth N. "How to Choose the Kind of Job Analysis You Really Need." *Personnel* 62 (May 1985): 51–55.

Yoder, Dale, and Heneman, Herbert G., Jr. (eds.), ASPA *Handbook of Personnel and Industrial Relations and Auditing PAIR,* Vol. 4. Washington, D.C.: The Bureau of National Affairs, 1976.

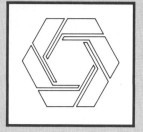

Parma Cycle Company of Parma, Ohio, a Cleveland suburb, is one of only three companies that actually manufacture complete bicycles in the United States. Most of Parma's competitors import parts from other countries and simply assemble bicycles here. Parma Cycle employs about 800 workers, mainly machine operators and assemblers. The factory is laid out, coincidentally, like a bicycle wheel, with component manufacturing departments representing the tire and spoke area and assembly being done in the center of the factory, representing the hub.

Parma Cycle makes a line of bicycles and markets them under the Parma name. However, most of the bicycles Parma manufactures are purchased by large national retailers and marketed under those retailers' house names. A few bicycles are exported to Europe and South America, but Parma has found it difficult to compete in the international market with Japanese and Italian manufacturers.

Parma Cycle Company, Inc. is a publicly held corporation, although 30 percent of its shares are controlled by a major recreational conglomerate corporation. There have been rumors of a take-over from time to time but none has materialized. Because of depressed earnings over the past two years, Parma's stock has declined from $27 per share to $13 per share. Interest rates have increased significantly during the same period. The company has found it costly, therefore, to raise funds to purchase the new machines that have been developed for bi-

cycle manufacture. Included in Parma's line of bicycles is a high performance racing cycle. A research and development program aimed at improving the performance of that bicycle was canceled because of the high cost of financing.

Jesse Heard is the personnel director. He has been with Parma Cycle for twenty-three years. His first job was as a painter, when painting was done with a hand-held spray gun. He was later promoted to supervisor and worked in several departments at the plant. Because the company paid for college tuition and fees, as well as books, to encourage supervisors to advance their education, Jesse had gone on to college. In 1970, he received his bachelor's degree in personnel administration from Case Western University in Cleveland. Jesse was immediately promoted to a job in the personnel department and three years later became the personnel director.

In May 1981, the Equal Employment Opportunity Commission received a complaint about employment practices at Parma. It was alleged that while the proportion of blacks in the Cleveland area approached 25 percent, only 8 percent of the Parma Cycle work force was black. There were only two black managers above the level of supervisor. Jesse Heard was advised of the complaint. He felt that the company was doing everything it should with regard to equal opportunity.

The company had an affirmative action plan and had a practice of encouraging managers to employ blacks and other minority group members as well as women. In fact, Jesse's efforts to encourage the employment of protected group members had provoked some managers to complain to the company president, his immediate supervisor.

In general, the working environment at Parma Cycle has been a good one. The company has a relatively flat organizational structure with few managerial levels, as shown in Figure I–1.

Most of Parma's workers are of European stock and are fairly acclimated to working in a factory environment. Since 1975, the company has had periodic management training seminars in which managers have been taught to be sensitive to workers and cooperative with one another. The management philosophy is one of decentralized authority. Managers, like Jesse Heard, are essentially responsible for their own operations.

As a result of an aggressive safety program, there has been only one fatal accident at Parma in the last ten years and work-related injuries are well below the industry average. Starting about 1965, the ventilation system in the factory was modernized. The lighting is good, by Cleveland area standards, and the health and safety officer once remarked that the air is cleaner inside the factory than outside. Gene Wilson, the corporate planner, has said that he believes the company has spent too much money on employee safety and working conditions and that this is one reason for Parma's declining profits. The company's mission has not been changed since 1960, when it was stated as: "To enhance the wealth of the common shareholder through efficient production and aggressive marketing of bicycles while contributing to the well-being of our workers and the stability of the Cleveland economy."

Parma's work force is unionized, with the local union being a member of the National Association of Machinists. Employee recruitment is done primarily through referrals from current workers. Selection is based on personal interviews, evaluation of job-related application forms and, for certain jobs, a basic skills test conducted by

Figure I–1. Parma Cycle Company: Organization chart.

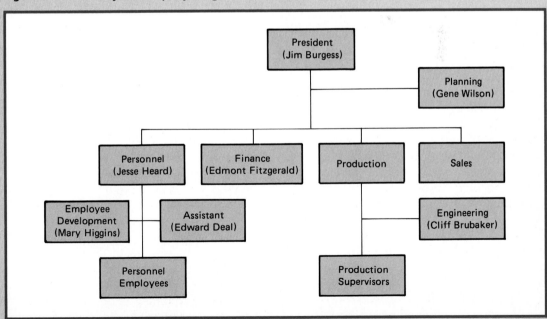

the supervisor. The supervisor makes the final hiring decision. Workers must join the union before the end of a three-month probationary period. Over the years, the union has won wages and benefits that are about average for the Cleveland area.

The factory work at Parma Cycle is neither especially difficult nor complicated. Cycle technology has changed very little over the years and most of the jobs have become standardized. However, growing foreign competition and the economic recession that began in 1981 have caused an increasing emphasis on productivity. Consequently, workers have been encouraged to put forth additional effort, and production standards have been raised to the point where many employees complain of the faster work pace. The productivity improvement program has been carried forward with the union's assistance. This was felt to be justified in order to save jobs. There hasn't been a strike at Parma in ten years and, with unemployment in the area very high due to auto industry and other layoffs, one is considered unlikely.

QUESTIONS

1. Discuss the external environment of Parma Cycle Company and its impact on human resource management.
2. Is the internal environment at Parma Cycle a good one? Explain.

Experiencing Human Resource Management

The Changing Labor Market

This is a role-playing exercise involving Jesse Heard, the personnel manager at Parma Cycle Company; Gene Wilson, the corporate planner; and Edmont Fitzgerald, the controller. Class members not assigned specific roles can be involved through participating in a question and answer session after the brief skit. The general background is provided in "Parma Cycle Company: An Overview" beginning on page 122. All participants should have studied that case thoroughly before reading the role descriptions below. The primary purpose of this exercise is to highlight a number of environmental concerns confronting personnel managers.

ROLE DESCRIPTIONS

Jesse Heard. As the personnel manager, you are faced with a dilemma. On the one hand, you know you must represent the company's economic interest. You purchase labor and as is true for other resources, you are obligated to find the best quality at the best available price. The company's competitive position is already tenuous so this is even more important now. On the other hand, you are concerned about the workers, some of whom have been with Parma Cycle for many years. Even though the highly favorable labor market allows you to replace many of them with lower paid workers, you hesitate to do so. Yesterday you received an angry call from the president, Mr. Burgess, who asked you to meet with the corporate planner and the controller and come up with a unified recom-

124

mendation for taking advantage of the improved labor market and cutting labor costs. As you head for the meeting, you think about how different your view of the situation is from that of the controller.

Edmont Fitzgerald. An Ohio State University graduate in finance, you feel that, above all, the corporation is an economic entity. You believe that market forces will take care of those workers who really wish to contribute to the economy and that the general welfare is served by companies aggressively competing on every conceivable basis and purchasing all resources, including labor, at the lowest possible price. You agree with Milton Friedman, your idol, that "The only social responsibility of business is to earn a profit, within the rules of the game." You have little time for those like Jesse Heard, who would waste company resources trying to fulfill some kind of paternalistic role with regard to employees. Moreover, you believe that the union has coerced management into accepting wages and working conditions that have increased Parma's personnel costs unreasonably. This is the reason, you believe, that Parma has trouble competing in the international market. You see the current situation as an opportunity to decrease costs radically. The union is weak, jobs are scarce, and there is a surplus of skilled workers in the Cleveland area. If some of the more senior workers can be provoked to leave or can be fired for some semilegitimate reason, they can be replaced with experienced workers who will have no seniority at Parma and who, consequently, will draw a much lower wage. It was at your recommendation that the president decided to call the meeting that you are about to attend.

Gene Wilson. You never really had much power at Parma Cycle, although your title sounds impressive enough. Primarily, you maintain a chart room and keep track of various trends, such as the cost of labor as a percent of total cost, fixed costs as opposed to variable costs in the plant, and trends in sales of the company's various products. You believe that a systematic corporate planning program, while always important, is now a critical necessity. You think that Parma Cycle Company is headed downhill because of depressed markets and an inability on the part of company managers to decrease unit costs. In your opinion the most important asset that Parma Cycle has is a trained and loyal work force. While many of the workers could be replaced with lower paid workers, you are afraid that this would destroy the team spirit that now exists. You believe that, with the insecurity the workers all feel because of the growing number of layoffs in the Cleveland area, they are more likely than ever to respond to financial incentives. Therefore you think it might be a good time to institute some kind of piece-rate program or suggestion and bonus system to encourage worker productivity. If such a system could be set up at Parma, you feel productivity would increase and labor costs decrease without any reduction in wages. The work force would be reduced over a period of time through attrition. If you could be instrumental in solving the company's problem it would be a feather in your cap, and perhaps you would become the respected power wielder in the company that you believe the corporate planner — and you personally — deserves to be.

QUESTIONS

1. Is labor a resource, "just like other resources?" Explain.
2. How might internal politics enter into the anticipated meeting?
3. How might the weak union and job scarcity in the Cleveland area affect the day-to-day function of personnel management?

Part Two

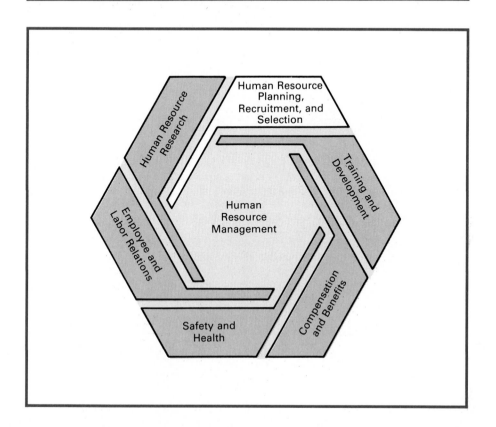

Human Resource Research

Human Resource Planning, Recruitment, and Selection

Training and Development

Human Resource Management

Employee and Labor Relations

Compensation and Benefits

Safety and Health

HUMAN RESOURCE PLANNING, RECRUITMENT, AND SELECTION

CHAPTER OBJECTIVES
1. Explain the human resource planning process.
2. Define the basic terms used in forecasting.
3. Describe some human resource forecasting techniques.
4. Explain how human resource requirements are forecasted.
5. State what a firm can do when a surplus of personnel exists.
6. Explain how human resource availability is forecasted.
7. Describe the important features of a human resource information system.

Chapter 5

HUMAN RESOURCE PLANNING

Mark Swann, the marketing director for a large manufacturing firm, commented at the weekly executive directors' meeting, "I have good news. We can get the large contract with Medord Corporation. All we have to do is complete the project in one year instead of two." Everyone was excited except one person, Linda Cane, vice president of personnel. She stunned the other members by saying, "There is no way we can meet that date, Mark. If we were going to bring on board the 200 extra workers who would be needed to complete the project, planning should have started nine months ago." Everyone sat back in shock because they realized that Linda's analysis was correct.

130

Part Two
Human
Resource
Planning,
Recruitment,
and Selection

While the situation described is not typical in all organizations, it exists in enough of them to prompt one corporate president to state: "The human resource is perhaps the last great cost that is relatively unmanaged."[1] While this may be an overstatement, it is true that human resource planning does not get the same amount of attention as other components of business planning. Indeed, people-planning is often considered after the fact. Neglecting human resources in the planning process can be very disruptive to a business venture if adequately trained people are not available when needed.[2]

Human resource planning (HRP) is *a management process that involves analyzing an organization's human resource needs under changing conditions and then developing policies and systems to satisfy those needs.*[3] HRP is the process of matching the internal and external supply of people with job openings the organization expects to have over a given period of time.[4] Although some organizations continue to provide only lip service to human resource planning, HRP is becoming increasingly recognized as an important company undertaking.[5] Human resource planning is a relatively new term and, unlike its predecessor — manpower planning — more accurately reflects the presence of both men and women in the work force.[6] The overall purpose of this chapter is to explain the role and nature of human resource planning in organizations today.

THE HUMAN RESOURCE PLANNING PROCESS

As defined in chapter 1, planning is determining in advance what should be accomplished and how it should be done. The human resource planning process is illustrated in Figure 5–1. Note that strategic planning — which requires consideration of the external and internal environments — precedes human resource planning. **Strategic plans** are *designed to help a firm achieve its primary objectives.*[7] The strategic plans developed to accomplish a firm's goals will affect every major department. In the past, the chief personnel officer often did not become involved in strategic planning. This

[1]Charles F. Russ, Jr., "Manpower Planning Systems: Part II," *Personnel Journal* 61 (February 1982): 123.

[2]Douglas B. Gehrman, "Objective Based Human Resources Planning," *Personnel Journal* 60 (December 1981): 942.

[3]James W. Walker, *Human Resources Planning.* New York: McGraw-Hill, 1980, p. 5.

[4]Charles F. Russ, Jr., "Manpower Planning Systems: Part I," *Personnel Journal* 61 (January 1982): 41.

[5]James W. Walker, "The New, More Substantive Approach to Manpower Planning," *Management Review* 66 (July 1977): 29.

[6]Lynda L. Moore, "From Manpower Planning to Human Resources Planning Through Career Development," *Personnel* 56 (May–June 1979): 9.

[7]George Steiner, *Top Management Planning.* New York: Macmillan, 1969, p. 34.

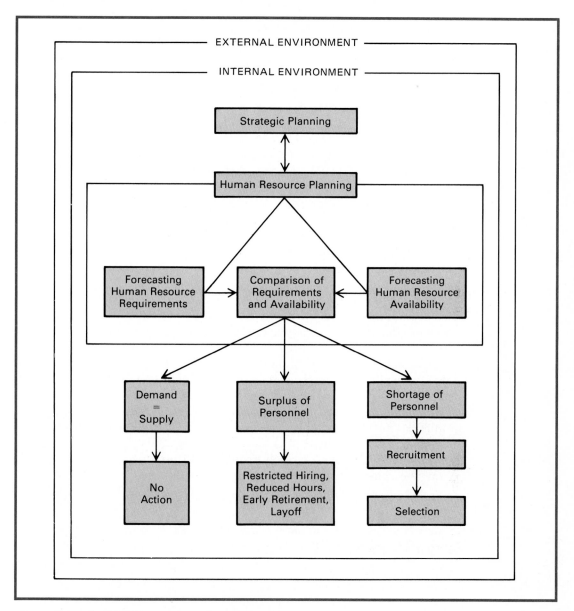

Figure 5–1. The human resource planning process.

practice has changed in some firms, and both practitioners and academics
have urged that the human resource function be involved in the formulation, as well as the implementation, of strategic plans.[8] Top management

[8]Kendrith M. Rowland and Scott L. Summers, "Human Resource Planning: A Second
Look," *Personnel Administrator* 26 (December 1981): 73.

132

Part Two
Human
Resource
Planning,
Recruitment,
and Selection

is beginning to recognize the necessity of including human resource professionals in the strategic planning process.

After strategic plans have been formulated, human resource planning can be undertaken. Organizational plans identified in the strategic planning process are reduced to specific quantitative and qualitative human resource plans. For example, note in Figure 5–1 that human resource planning has two sides: requirements and availability. Forecasting human resource requirements involves determining the number and type of employees needed, by skill level and location. These projections will be affected by various factors, such as production plans and changes in efficiency levels.[9] In order to forecast the availability of human resources, the organization looks to both internal sources (current employees) and external sources (the labor market).

When the requirements and availability of employees have been analyzed, the firm is in a position to determine whether there will be a surplus or shortage of employees. Ways must be found to reduce the number of employees if a surplus of workers is projected. Some of these methods include restricted hiring, reduced hours, early retirements, and layoffs. If a shortage is forecast, the firm must look to sources outside the organization to secure the proper quantity and quality of workers. External recruitment and selection is then required.

The human resource planning process is continuous. Conditions in either the external or internal environment can change in a short period of time. These changes could require extensive modification of forecasts. Planning enables managers to anticipate and prepare for changing conditions, and HRP affects every area of human resource management. For example, one of the keys to a good planning program is a fair and effective performance appraisal system.[10] Such a system can provide useful information about the characteristics of its successful employees. This will help the firm plan more effectively in meeting its personnel needs.

TERMINOLOGY OF FORECASTING

Four basic terms are used in forecasting. First, the **long-run trend** line *projects the demand for a firm's products, typically five years or more into the future.*[11] As you can see in Figure 5–2, the long-run trend is for increased sales: Sales are expected to double during the period shown. Early recognition of such a trend is critical. A firm may not be able to fill these positions quickly, as considerable training and development may be required. For

---

[9]Gehrman, "Objective Based Human Resources Planning," p. 944.

[10]Wendell W. Burton, "Manpower Planning in an Inflationary Period," *Personnel Administrator* 24 (August 1979): 38.

[11]Joseph E. Monks, *Operations Management: Theory and Problems.* New York: McGraw-Hill, 1977, p. 274.

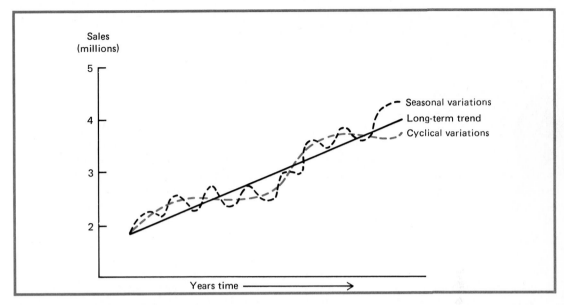

Figure 5–2. Seasonal demand.

instance, some employees may need several months or even years of training and development before they become capable of assuming new or added responsibilities.

Second, **cyclical variation** is *a reasonably predictable movement about the trend line that occurs over a period of more than a year.* Cyclical variations may be caused by such factors as war, political elections, economic conditions, changes in consumer demand, and sociological pressures.[12] These variations typically occur at intervals and last between one and five years. Knowledge of cyclical demand is important because of the potential for severe peaks and valleys. Additional people may be required to meet high cyclical demands, even though a stable long-run demand is forecast. And, although the long-run forecast may be upward, there may be a temporary recession that would require a temporary work force reduction.

Third, **seasonal variations** are *reasonably predictable changes that occur over a period of a year.* Seasonal variations follow cyclical variations but may fluctuate drastically (see Figure 5–2). These variations occur within a twelve-month period and are the most immediate concern of many firms. Electric shavers are sold primarily during the Christmas holiday season, whereas motor boats are sold primarily in the spring. Seasonal demand can

---

[12]Richard B. Chase and Nicholas J. Aquilano, *Production and Operations Management.* Homewood, Ill.: Richard D. Irwin, 1973, p. 183.

Executive Insights

Susan J. Marks
Vice President and Co-Owner,
ProStaff, Milwaukee, Wisconsin

Susan Marks, vice president and co-owner of ProStaff, Milwaukee, Wisconsin, a human resource consulting firm providing both permanent and temporary personnel services, is the current president of International Association for Personnel Women (IAPW). She is dedicated to IAPW and has plans to meet with many of the 2500-member organization and 25 affiliates across the United States. Her busy schedule includes meetings with affiliates on an individual basis to further the discussion of human resource issues, as well as issues that affect professional women.

Prior to the founding of ProStaff, Marks spent four years as manager and principal of a Milwaukee personnel firm. Today, as vice president of ProStaff, her many responsibilities include supervision of 12 direct and nondirect reports, management of both client development and service activities, and individual consulting and personnel search and placement in the human resource area. She was responsible for adding the Temporary Personnel Services division to ProStaff. In addition, she implemented the computer system to handle accounting functions. She also shares in the administrative responsibilities of the firm.

A graduate of Marquette University, Milwaukee, Wisconsin, Marks holds a B.S. degree in business administration with a major in human resource management. She was awarded the Senior Professional in Human Resources Designation in December 1984 from the Personnel Accreditation Institute and the Certified Personnel Consultants Designation in June 1978 from the National Association of Personnel Consultants.

Her many professional affiliations include the International Association for Personnel Women, of which she was the founder and president of the Milwaukee affiliate in 1980. She served as a conference co-director, secretary/treasurer, and president-elect prior to being named president in 1985.

Marks has also received a Service Award the past three years from the Personnel Industrial Relations Association of Wisconsin, an organization she has been involved with since 1981. She has also been elected to serve as a board member of the Personnel Accreditation Institute (PAI) for 1985–1987.

---

have a major impact on a firm as it attempts to stabilize its labor force but still meet production and inventory requirements.

Finally, **random variations** are *changes for which there are no patterns.* Even the most sophisticated forecasting techniques cannot anticipate these changes.[13]

[13]Elwood S. Buffa, *Modern Production Management*, 5th ed. New York: John Wiley & Sons, 1977, p. 314.

Several techniques of forecasting human resource requirements and availability are currently in use. Some of the techniques are qualitative in nature, while others are quantitative. Several of the better known methods will be described next.

ZERO-BASE FORECASTING

The **zero-base forecasting** approach *uses the organization's current level of employment as the starting point for determining future staffing needs.* If an employee retires, is terminated, or leaves the firm for any other reason, this position is not automatically filled. Instead, an analysis is made to determine whether the firm can justify filling the vacated position. Equal concern is shown for creating new positions when they appear to be needed. The key to zero-base forecasting is a thorough analysis of human resource needs to justify employment decisions.

BOTTOM-UP APPROACH

Some firms use what might be called the bottom-up approach to employment forecasting. It is based on the reasoning that the manager in each unit is the most knowledgeable about employment requirements. The **bottom-up approach** is *a forecasting method that forecasts progress upward in the organization from lower organizational units to ultimately provide an aggregate forecast of employment needs.* Each successive level in the organization forecasts its employment requirements. Effective human resource forecasting can result if managers forecast their personnel needs periodically, compare their current human resource needs with those anticipated, and give the personnel department adequate lead time to explore internal and external sources of personnel.[14] According to one practitioner, the most common approach to human resource forecasting is to rely most heavily on the judgments of unit managers, supplemented with basic statistical analysis.[15]

USE OF PREDICTOR VARIABLES

Another means of forecasting human resource requirements is to use past employment needs as a predictor of future requirements. Predictor variables that are known to have an impact on employment levels are identified. One of the most useful predictors of employment levels is sales volume. The relationship that tends to exist between demand and the number of employees needed is a positive one. As you can see in Figure 5–3, the firm's

[14]John F. DeSanto, "Work Force Planning and Corporate Strategy," *Personnel Administrator* 28 (October 1983): 34.
[15]Richard B. Frantzreb, "Human Resource Planning: Forecasting Manpower Needs," *Personnel Journal* 60 (November 1981): 854.

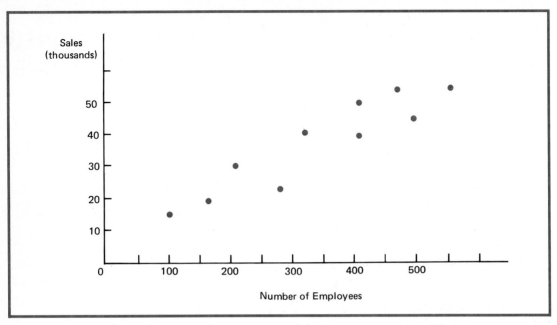

Figure 5–3. The relationship of sales volume to number of employees.

sales units are depicted on the vertical axis and the number of employees actually required is shown on the horizontal axis. In this illustration, as sales demand increases, so does the number of employees. Using this method, managers are able to approximate the number of employees required at different demand levels.

With the increased use of high speed computers and sophisticated statistical packages, personnel managers have at their disposal a most useful forecasting tool — regression analysis. **Regression analysis** is *used to predict one item (known as the dependent variable) through knowledge of other items (known as the independent variables).* When there is one dependent variable and one independent variable, the process is known as simple linear regression. When there is more than one independent variable, the technique is called multiple regression.

Because of the direct relationship between demand for a firm's products and/or services and employment level, regression analysis is often used to forecast employment levels. However, in most instances, the employment level is determined by several independent variables, and multiple regression is required. Instead of predicting employment levels strictly through knowledge of sales, other variables such as efficiency level of the work force might also be used. Multiple regression often produces superior results when compared to simple linear regression because it recognizes that a variety of factors may influence forecasted employment levels.

DELPHI TECHNIQUE

The **Delphi technique** is *a formal procedure for obtaining consensus among a number of experts through the use of a series of questionnaires.* Ideally, the experts do not know who else is involved. The steps in the Delphi technique are as follows:

1. The problem is presented to group members by means of a questionnaire that asks them to provide potential solutions.
2. Each expert completes and returns the questionnaire.
3. Results are compiled and provided to the experts, along with a revised and more specific questionnaire.
4. The experts complete the second questionnaire. The process continues until a consensus emerges.

Although the Delphi technique prevents the respondents from being influenced by the personalities of the other participants, it does make provision for the sharing of ideas. The end result is a consensus decision. This method was conceived by the Rand Corporation to forecast how severely a nuclear attack would affect the United States. It is expensive and time consuming and generally has been limited to consideration of important and futuristic ideas.

SIMULATION

In **simulation** *the computer is used to assist in analyzing a model of a real system.* A model is an abstraction of the real world. Thus a simulation model is an attempt to represent a real-world situation through mathematical logic in order to predict what will actually occur. Simulation assists the personnel manager by permitting him or her to ask many "What if . . ." questions without having to make the decision in the real world.

From a human resource management viewpoint, a simulation model might be developed to show the many interrelations that exist between employment level and a variety of other variables. "What if . . ." questions could then be asked, such as:

- What would happen if we put 10 percent of the present work force on overtime?
- What would happen if the plant went to two shifts? to three shifts?

Depending on the purpose of the model developed, the human resource manager can derive considerable insight into a particular problem before making an actual decision.

FORECASTING HUMAN RESOURCE REQUIREMENTS

In order to forecast human resource requirements, the need for the firm's products or services must first be forecasted. This forecast is then converted

138

Part Two
Human
Resource
Planning,
Recruitment,
and Selection

into person-hour requirements. Various work activities are stated in terms of what will be required to meet this demand. For instance, if the firm is manufacturing hand calculators, activities might be stated in terms of the number of units to be produced, number of sales calls to be made, number of vouchers to be processed, or a variety of other activities. These work activities are then translated into person-hours. For example, to manufacture 10,000 widgets each week might require 5000 hours of work by assemblers during a 40-hour week. If the 5000 hours are divided by the 40 hours in the work week, 125 assembly workers would be needed. Similar calculations are performed for the other jobs needed to produce and market the 10,000 widgets.

FORECASTING HUMAN RESOURCE AVAILABILITY

A large manufacturing firm on the West Coast was preparing to begin operations in a new plant. Analysts had already determined that there was a large long-term demand for the new product. Financing was available and equipment was in place. But production did not begin for three years! Management had made a critical mistake: They had studied the demand side of personnel but did not take the supply side into account. There were not enough qualified workers in the local labor market to operate the new plant. New workers had to receive extensive training before they would be capable of moving into the newly created jobs.

Forecasting of requirements provides the manager with the means of estimating how many and what kind of employees will be required. But there is another side of the coin. Management must also determine whether they will be able to secure employees with the necessary skills and from what sources these individuals may be obtained. As suggested by the preceding example, forecasting human resource availability results in determining the supply of needed employees. The supply of employees may be met by obtaining people from within the company, or the firm may have to go outside the organization to meet its needs.

INTERNAL SOURCES OF SUPPLY

Many of the workers that will be needed for future positions with a firm are already employed. If the firm is small, it is likely that management knows all the workers well enough so that their skills and aspirations can easily be matched. If, for instance, the company is establishing a new sales position, it may be common knowledge that Mary Garcia, a five-year employee with the company, has both the skills and desire to take over the new job. This unplanned process of matching demand with supply may be sufficient for smaller firms. As organizations grow, however, the matching process becomes increasingly difficult. Some of the tools available to identify internal sources of supply will be discussed next.

Management inventories. As its name implies, management inventory information relates specifically to managers. An inventory would likely include data such as:

- Work history.
- Strengths.
- Weaknesses — and identification of specific training that will be needed to possibly remove the weaknesses.
- Promotion potential.
- Career goals.
- Personal data.

A **management inventory** contains *detailed data regarding each manager to be used in identifying individuals possessing the potential to move into higher level positions.* In essence, the inventory provides information for preparing a management replacement chart. Detroit Edison calls their chart a Career Planning Inventory Organization Review Chart. As you can see in Figure 5–4, the chart shows a manager in the top box with immediate subordinates in the lower boxes. Information shown on the chart includes:

- *Position Box:* The position title and incumbent's name appear in each box. The symbol * preceding the name identifies incumbents retiring between 1981–1985 and indicates that short-range planning is required. If the symbol ** precedes the name, the incumbent is identified as one who will retire between 1986–1992. In these cases, long-range planning is required. If the word *Open* appears in the box, the position is unfilled; if *Future* appears, the position is anticipated but does not yet exist.
- *Dev Pgm:* Identifies the particular development program in which the employee participates.
- *Retire:* The month and year of the employee's planned retirement.
- *Est Prom:* Indicates the employee's estimated potential for promotion.
- *Lrp:* Indicates an estimate of the employee's long-range career potential in the Company.
- *Ppc:* Indicates the incumbent's current organizational level.
- *3 Developmental Needs:* Describes three priority developmental needs that have been identified.
- *Potential Positions:* The title of each position to which the incumbent is potentially promotable is shown along with codes that indicate an estimate of when the employee would be ready.
- *Possible Replacements:* The names of up to ten possible replacements for the incumbent are shown with codes indicating when the replacements would be ready for promotion to this position.

Skills inventories. While a management inventory includes information related specifically to managerial personnel, a **skills inventory** is an *internal*

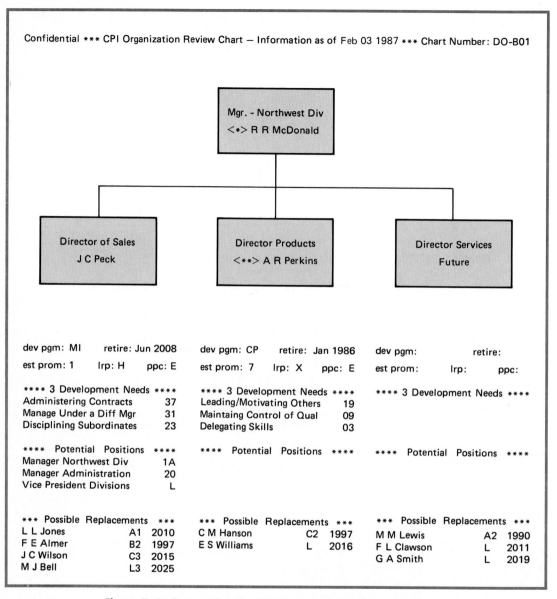

dev pgm: MI retire: Jun 2008	dev pgm: CP retire: Jan 1986	dev pgm: retire:
est prom: 1 lrp: H ppc: E	est prom: 7 lrp: X ppc: E	est prom: lrp: ppc:
**** 3 Development Needs ****	**** 3 Development Needs ****	**** 3 Development Needs ****
Administering Contracts 37	Leading/Motivating Others 19	
Manage Under a Diff Mgr 31	Maintaing Control of Qual 09	
Disciplining Subordinates 23	Delegating Skills 03	
**** Potential Positions ****	**** Potential Positions ****	**** Potential Positions ****
Manager Northwest Div 1A		
Manager Administration 20		
Vice President Divisions L		
*** Possible Replacements ***	*** Possible Replacements ***	*** Possible Replacements ***
L L Jones A1 2010	C M Hanson C2 1997	M M Lewis A2 1990
F E Almer B2 1997	E S Williams L 2016	F L Clawson L 2011
J C Wilson C3 2015		G A Smith L 2019
M J Bell L3 2025		

Figure 5–4. Career planning inventory organization review chart.

means of determining the skills of nonmanagerial employees. Although the process and the intent of the skills inventory is essentially the same as a management inventory, the information may differ somewhat. Information that might be included in a skills inventory is:

- Background and biographical data.
- Work experience.
- Specific skills and knowledge.
- Supervisory evaluations.
- Career goals.

A properly designed and updated skills inventory system permits management to readily identify employees with particular skills in order to satisfy the changing needs of the company.

EXTERNAL SUPPLY

Unless a firm is experiencing a declining demand, it may have to go outside the organization to obtain employees. By necessity, forecasting availability of employees is a continuous process and an important function of human resource management. Rapid employment of new employees is typically quite difficult. A firm must be capable of determining not only the number of employees required but also where they can be obtained. The best source of supply varies by industry, firms, and geographical location. Some organizations have found that their best sources of future employees are colleges and universities, while others achieve excellent results from vocational schools, competitors, or unsolicited applications.

If the company has information revealing where its employees were recruited, statistics regarding present and past employees may be used to project the best sources. For instance, a firm may discover that graduates from a particular college or university adapt well to the firm's environment. One large farm-equipment manufacturer has achieved excellent success in recruiting from schools located in rural areas. Managers in this firm believe that, since many students come from a farming environment, they can adapt more quickly to the firm's method of operation.

Other firms have identified their employees' residences. They may discover from past records that the majority of their more successful employees lived no more than twenty miles from their workplace. This information may suggest that recruiting efforts should be concentrated in that particular geographic area.

Forecasting can assist not only in identifying where the supply of employees may be located but also in predicting what type of individuals will likely succeed in the organization. When a regional medical center that was located a great distance from a large metropolitan area reviewed its personnel files of registered nurses, it discovered that registered nurses who were born and raised in smaller towns adapted better to the small-

142

Part Two
Human
Resource
Planning,
Recruitment,
and Selection

town environment than those who grew up in large metropolitan areas. After studying these statistics they modified their recruiting efforts.[16]

Examples of improper forecasting are numerous. Managers of one large convenience store chain were disturbed that their employee turnover rate was so high. When they analyzed their recruitment process, they discovered that the large majority of short-term employees had merely seen a sign in the store window announcing that a position was available. These individuals were often unemployed and highly transient. The source of supply had a built-in mechanism to ensure a high turnover rate. When this fact was discovered, new sources of supply were found, which significantly reduced turnover.

SURPLUS OF PERSONNEL

When analysis of requirements and availability indicates a personnel shortage, the firm must initiate recruitment efforts. Recruitment will be the focus of the next chapter. When the analysis shows a personnel surplus, restricted hiring, reduced hours, early retirements, or layoffs may be required.

RESTRICTED HIRING

When a firm implements a restricted hiring policy, a work force reduction is made by not replacing employees who leave the firm. New workers are hired only when overall performance of the organization may be affected. For instance, if a quality control department that consisted of four inspectors had one worker take a job with another firm, this individual would not likely be replaced. However, if the firm lost all of its inspectors, the firm would make an attempt to replace at least some of them to ensure continued operation.

REDUCED HOURS

Reaction to a declining demand can also be made by reducing the total number of hours worked. Instead of continuing a forty-hour work week, management may decide to cut each employee's time to thirty hours. This process normally applies to hourly employees because management and professional staff members are not typically paid on an hourly basis.

EARLY RETIREMENT

Early retirement of some present employees is another means of reducing the supply of personnel. Employees may be willing to accept early retirement if certain inducements are added to the total retirement package.

---

[16]Wayne Mondy and Harry N. Mills, "Choice Not Chance in Nurse Selection," *Supervisor Nurse* 9 (November 1978): 35–39.

LAYOFFS

143

**Chapter 5
Human
Resource
Planning**

At times, the firm has no other choice but to actually lay off a certain proportion of its work force. A layoff does not have the same connotation as being fired, but it has the same short-term effect — the worker is no longer employed. When the firm is unionized, the procedures affecting a layoff are usually stated quite clearly in the labor–management agreement. Typically, less senior members are laid off first. If the organization is nonunionized, a firm may lay off workers based on a combination of factors, such as their seniority and their productivity level. When managerial and professional employees are laid off, the decision of who is affected is very likely to be based on ability, although internal politics may be a factor.

HUMAN RESOURCE PLANNING: AN EXAMPLE

The human resource planning model presented in Figure 5–1 is a generalized one. Each firm must tailor human resource planning to fit its specific needs. The human resource planning process for Honeywell, Inc., is shown in Figure 5–5. Each element of the plan is discussed in the following sections.

ORGANIZATIONAL GOALS

To be relevant, a human resource planning system needs to be clearly tied to the organization's objectives. The plan must rest on a solid foundation of information about sales forecasts, market trends, technological advances, and major changes in processes or productivity. Considerable effort needs to be devoted to securing reliable data on business trends and needs as the basic input for the human resource plan in terms of quantity and quality of labor.

HUMAN RESOURCE NEEDS FORECAST

A second element in the planning process is the forecasting of human resource needs based on business objectives, production plans, and the various indicators of changes in technology or operating methods. This is usually accomplished utilizing historical data and reliable ratios (e.g., indirect/direct labor) and adjusting them for productivity trends. The result of this forecast is a spread sheet of employees needed to accomplish the organization's goals in terms of numbers, mix, cost, new skills, or job categories and numbers and levels of managers. Experience has shown that producing this forecast is the most challenging part of the planning process because it requires creative and highly participative approaches to dealing with business and technical uncertainties several years in the future.

144

Part Two
Human
Resource
Planning,
Recruitment,
and Selection

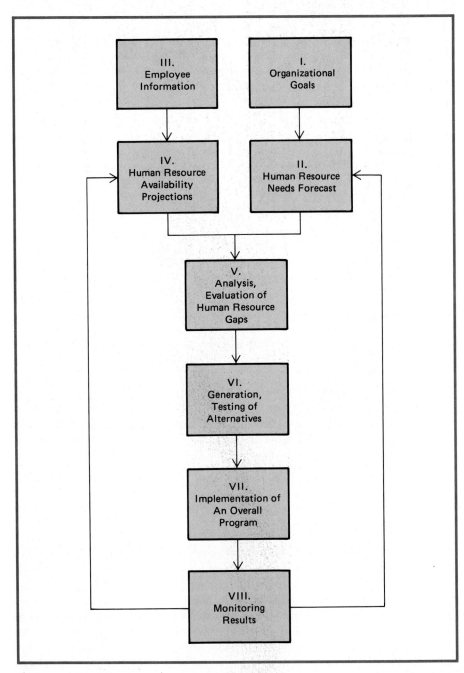

Figure 5–5. Elements of a human resource plan. Source: Used with the permission of Honeywell, Inc.

EMPLOYEE INFORMATION

A third element of the planning process is accurate information concerning the composition, configuration, and capabilities of the current work force. This includes information about job classifications, ages, sex, minority status, organization levels, salaries, and functions. Employee information may also include resume data such as skills, educational and training data, and career interests. Much of the data needed for human resource planning currently exists in other personnel systems (e.g., payroll, talent review, or professional development data).

HUMAN RESOURCE AVAILABILITY PROJECTIONS

The fourth element of the planning process is to estimate which of the current human resources could be or will be available in terms of skills, numbers, age, deployment, etc., in the future. By projecting past data about the size, configuration, and composition of the work force and data about the flows of the human resources (turnover, aging, hiring) probable availability at a specific future time can be determined. The result of this kind of activity is a picture of the human resources that an organization currently has and how they will evolve over time due to turnover, retirement, obsolescence, etc.

ANALYZING AND EVALUATING HUMAN RESOURCE GAPS

The fifth element of the planning process is to compare what is needed with what is available in terms of numbers, mix, skills, and technologies. This permits the personnel manager to determine gaps and to evaluate where the most serious mismatches occur. Such analysis should help the organization address issues such as:

- Are imbalances developing between human resource needs and projected availability?
- What is the effect of current productivity trends and pay levels on work-force levels and costs?
- Do turnover problems exist in certain jobs or age levels?
- Are there problems of career blockage and obsolescence?
- Are there sufficient high potential managers to fulfill future needs?
- Is there a shortage of any critical skills?

Such an analysis will lead to the development of specific plans on a long-range basis for recruiting, hiring, training, transferring, and retraining appropriate numbers and types of employees.

GENERATING AND TESTING ALTERNATIVES

The analysis of human resources should reveal much about a wide range of policies and practices, such as staffing plans, promotion practices and

146

Part Two
Human
Resource
Planning,
Recruitment,
and Selection

policies, EEO plans, organization design, training and development programs, salary planning, and career management. This phase of the process explores the implications of the analysis and generates alternatives to current practices and policies. Some of the more comprehensive human resource planning systems utilize modeling to simulate the configuration and composition of human resources that would result from specific changes in staffing strategies or other personnel policies. This allows evaluation and testing of alternatives. If testing of anticipated consequences is not performed by a computer model, an equivalent manual system should be utilized.

IMPLEMENTING AN OVERALL HUMAN RESOURCE PROGRAM

After the best alternatives for addressing the organization's human resource issues have been chosen, they need to become operational programs with specific plans, target dates, schedules, and resource commitments.

The analytical steps described should shape an organization's staffing plan, EEO plan, training and development activities, mobility plans, productivity programs, bargaining strategies, and compensation programs.

MONITORING RESULTS

The final element in any human resource planning process is to provide a means for management to monitor results of the overall program. This step should address such questions as:

- How well is the plan working?
- Is it cost effective?
- What is the actual versus planned impact on the work force?
- Where are the weak areas?
- What changes will be needed during the next cycle?

HUMAN RESOURCE INFORMATION SYSTEMS

Because of the many changes that are occurring that affect human resource management, personnel managers are beginning to use human resource information systems to help them meet new challenges.[17] A **human resource information system (HRIS)** is *any organized method for obtaining information on which to base human resource decisions.* The HRIS should be designed to provide information that is:

- Timely — when needed and up to date.
- Accurate — correct.

---

[17]Deborah Nikkel, "HRIS Implementation: A Systematic Approach," *Personnel* 62 (February 1985): 10.

- Concise — important data only.
- Relevant — what the manager needs to know.
- Complete — all that is needed to make a decision.

The absence of even one of these characteristics creates difficulty in decision making.

A problem that firms have historically confronted is the ability to generate information that meets these five requirements. For instance, suppose that the vice president of international operations of a firm employing 10,000 workers called the personnel manager with the following request: "Sam, this is Bill. I have a major problem. One of my managers was just killed in an automobile accident. I need someone immediately to take over that position. Hopefully, we can obtain someone from within the firm. The person I need must be able to speak Spanish fluently and be an electrical engineer with a working knowledge of electrical generators." If this type of search takes a month, Bill really has a problem. He needs the individual now! If the employee can be obtained in-house, the transition to this new position will likely be much faster than if the person must be brought in from outside the firm.

Although the benefits of an HRIS are numerous and can affect all personnel functions, it is mentioned here because human resource planning relates to and precedes all other areas of Personnel. The many changes that have occurred during the past twenty years have created a need for useful information regarding potential employees and workers who are currently employed with the firm.[18]

Since the advent of computers, management has been fascinated with the speed with which large amounts of data can be prepared. Large volumes of information can be stored in the computer and then be retrieved virtually instantly. However, an HRIS is not necessarily dependent on a computer. A firm without a computer can also have a very efficient system. The computer has merely made it possible for some larger firms to obtain human resources data with increased speed. Whether the HRIS is computerized or performed manually is not the point we are concerned with here. The procedure for designing useful human resource information systems is essentially the same. The general steps that should be followed in the development of a useful HRIS are:

1. Study of the present system.
2. Development of human resource information priorities.
3. Development of the new system.
4. Installation of a computer, if necessary.
5. Maintenance of the system.

[18]Alfred J. Walker, Jr., "Personnel Uses the Computer," *Personnel Journal* 51 (March 1972): 204–205.

148

Part Two
Human
Resource
Planning,
Recruitment,
and Selection

STUDY OF THE PRESENT SYSTEM

The first step in developing an effective HRIS is to identify and study the present system as it actually exists. This is important even if no formal system is currently in existence. An informal system may be used to obtain data, or each department or unit may even have developed separate systems to meet their needs. Whatever the situation, the future direction cannot be determined until the present system is thoroughly understood. Questions that may need to be answered are:

- What is the present flow of human resource data?
- How is the information used?
- How critical is the information that is available?
- What type of information is needed?
- Where is the information?
- How rapidly is the available information needed?

Art Bethke was employed as a consultant to develop a human resource information system for a national forest products firm. In studying the firm's existing system, Art was amazed to discover a large amount of duplication and wasted effort. Some weekly reports were essentially useless in the decision-making process. Two employees had to work a total of eight hours weekly to prepare one particular report. If the report was late, the vice president's secretary would send a strongly worded reprimand to the delinquent division chief. However, once the information arrived at headquarters, it was neatly filed and was never used. Numerous questions regarding this practice finally revealed that about five years ago this type of information was requested — as a one-time report. Preparation of the report had continued through the administrations of three vice presidents.

DEVELOPMENT OF HUMAN RESOURCE INFORMATION PRIORITIES

The next step in developing an HRIS is to rank information according to its importance. Certain data are critical to the successful accomplishment of the personnel function, while other information may merely be nice to have. A properly designed human resource information system will provide the high priority information required in decision making. Lower priority reports and information will be prepared only as time and cost permit. For instance, a report describing the specific abilities of the firm's employees would likely be ranked high, whereas the available parking spaces report might be ranked quite low. Through the development of this priority list, the manager begins to realize that some information is critical to the successful operation of the firm while other data provide only marginal benefits.

DEVELOPMENT OF THE NEW SYSTEM

After a priority has been assigned to specific reports and information, the human resource information system may be developed. The system should meet the overall human resource management needs of the company. Specific reports are designed to provide the required information.

Figure 5–6 presents an overview of a human resource information system that was prepared for one organization. Note that numerous types of input data are necessary. Information of these types is available from many sources. Through the HRIS, considerable output data then become available. These output reports have far-reaching value, ranging from personnel planning to operational uses. Some specific output reports will be described in a later section. The HRIS permits all areas related to human resource management to be tied together into a total information system. Data from several input sources are integrated to provide needed output data. Information critical to the firm's decision-making processes becomes available when the system is properly designed.

INSTALLATION OF A COMPUTER

One popular but mistaken assumption is that a human resource information system cannot function without a computer. A system should first be designed from the viewpoint of the optimum flow of data that will result in obtaining specific desired output. Many firms successfully use a manual system. A computer should be considered only when the speed and accuracy of a manual system are unacceptable. However, a computer should not be considered in the design phase but later, when actual system requirements are known.

MAINTENANCE OF THE SYSTEM

Workers in the data processing field have long had an expression called "GIGO," an acronym that means "Garbage-In-Garbage-Out." It certainly applies in maintaining an effective, timely, and accurate HRIS. It does not matter whether the system is manual or computerized. All sections and departments of the firm must be trained and made aware of the importance of forwarding documents that are accurate and timely. The importance of each document to the overall system must be clearly understood and appreciated. When this occurs, the HRIS can benefit everyone in the organization.

HRIS: AN ILLUSTRATION

Managers have desired reliable, fast, and useful human resource data for years. For a large number of firms this desire was relatively unfulfilled until the last ten or fifteen years. Computers capable of handling large data bases were quite expensive and software available to process the data was relatively unsophisticated. The use of computerized HRIS has become much more common because of the declining price of computers, the increasing

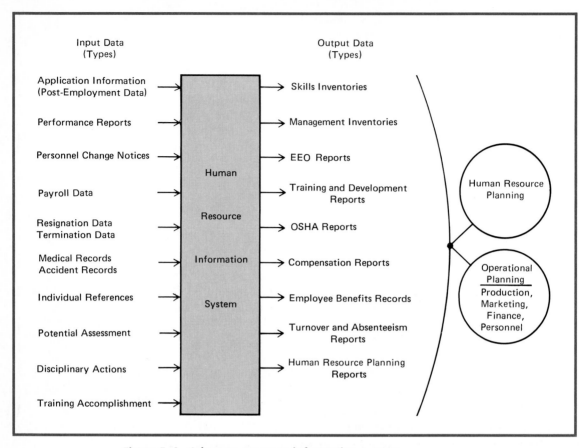

Figure 5–6. A human resource information system.

sophistication and availability of software, and the growing need for human resource data.[19]

One firm that has pioneered the development of personnel information systems is Information Science Incorporated (InSci). Founded in 1965, InSci was the first company to engage in the commercial development of computer-based personnel information systems. An overview of The Human Resource System developed by InSci is shown in Figure 5–7. As you can see, a large portion of the system is devoted to dealing with government requirements. The system also provides information that aids management in planning for the future.

Information available from the HRIS may be obtained through either "hard copy" or data display screens. An example of a hard copy of J. K. Robertson's career profile is shown in Figure 5–8. As you can see, consid-

[19]Ernest C. Miller and William H. Wagel, "Human Resources Has Its Own Computer," *Personnel* 55 (January–February 1978): 46.

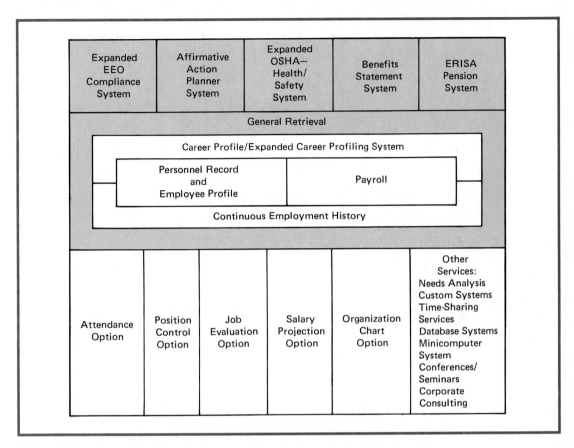

Figure 5–7. The human resource system developed by Information Science Incorporated. Source: Information Science Incorporated. Used with permission.

erable information is available, which should be beneficial in evaluating Robertson's career interests and capabilities. A sample of some of the types of information available on data display screens is shown in Figure 5–9. In this illustration, a person with access to the personnel file has requested a miniprofile of John Doe. When data display screens are used, files may be updated rapidly. These screens may be placed at critical areas in the firm to provide instant access to personnel information for individuals with a need to know. Decision-making information is available virtually immediately.

SUMMARY

Human resource planning (HRP) is a management process that involves analyzing an organization's human resource needs under changing con-

Profile Date	Employee's Name	Location Code		career profile	File Control Number	Date Change Made
05/01/76	J K ROBERTSON	NJ63409123			01 4311460731	

FOREIGN LANGUAGES

A	Description	Skill Code	Mod
	FRENCH	GA165	RW
	SPANISH	GA280	SP
	ITALIAN	GA200	ED

WORK PREFERENCES

Description	Skill Code	Mod
SALES FORCE ADMINISTRATION	EC110	PF
NEW PRODUCT PLANNING	ED150	PS
MARKETING, EC RESEARCH, GENERAL	EG100	PT

PROFESSIONAL LICENSES AND MEMBERSHIPS

B	Description	Skill Code	Mod
	INSTITUTE OF FOOD TECHNOLOGY	MB202	76
	BALTIMORE SALES EXECUTIVES	MB635	76
	HARVARD ALUMNI ASSOCIATION	MB982	74

WORK SPECIALTIES

Description	Skill Code	Mod
DIRECT VARIETY ACCOUNTS	EB215	FS
DIRECT DISCOUNT ACCOUNTS	EB220	SS
DEPARTMENT STORES	EB250	TS

FIRST CAREER OBJECTIVE / **FIRST CAREER DEVELOPMENT**

C	Code	Description	Date	Code	Description	Date
	SM400	DIST MGR	02/77	DA400	DIST ADM	12/76

SECOND CAREER OBJECTIVE / **SECOND CAREER DEVELOPMENT**

Code	Description	Date	Code	Description	Date
SM500	AREA MGR	02/79	DA500	AREA ADM	12/78

SKILLS/WORK EXPERIENCE

D	Description	Skill Code	Yrs Exp	Last Yr	Actn
	DISTRIBUTION DEVELOPMENT	EC160	1	76	
	INDUSTRY MEETINGS/CONVENTIONS	EC150	2	72	
	NEW PRODUCTS DEVELOPMENT	EG112	1	74	
	COMPETITIVE PRODUCT ANALYSIS	ED145	1	75	
	SPECIALITY SALES	EC125	3	63	
	SERVICE DISTRIBUTORS	EB225	2	63	
	DIRECT GROCERY ACCOUNTS	EB205	3	62	
	INSTITUTION SALES	EB260	3	62	
	REFINED FATS & OILS PRODUCTS	EB315	3	73	
	GROCERY PRODUCTS	EB310	3	72	

SKILLS/WORK EXPERIENCE

Description	Skill Code	Yrs Exp	Last Yr	Actn
FROZEN FOOD PACKERS	EA170	3	69	
FARMERS, FEEDERS, FEED MANUFACT.	EA160	2	66	
DEHYDRATED FOODS	EA145	2	62	
INDUSTRIAL COMPOUNDERS	EA320	2	60	
MONOMER/POLYMER	EA365	1	59	
PRODUCT EVALUATIONS	EH120	1	59	
CONSUMER INQUIRIES	EH110	1	58	
HOME ECONOMICS ACTIVITIES	EH130	1	57	

All changes and/or corrections to the information printed on this Career Profile, should be made on the reverse side.

To add one year experience, enter an 'X' in Action column.

To delete a skill, enter a 'D' in Action column.

To add a skill, use reverse side of form.

SIGNIFICANT ACHIEVEMENTS

E	Type	Date	Description
	P	04/74	PRESIDENT, BALT. SALES EXECUT.
	C	10/73	JC MAN OF THE YEAR AWARD
	S	06/73	SUGGEST. 56301 MAYONNAISE CAPS
	C	08/72	CHAIRMAN, TOWSON CANCER DRIVE

SIGNIFICANT ACHIEVEMENTS

Type	Date	Description
T	12/62	FOOD SALES, DISCOUNT DISPLAYS
E	06/53	DEAN'S LIST, MARKETING

Employee's and Manager's signatures must be entered below to authenticate changes on this and reverse side of form.

Employee's Signature	Date

Manager's Signature	Date

Figure 5–8. An example of the hard copy available from the InSci system. Source: Information Science Incorporated. Used with permission.

ditions and then developing policies and systems to satisfy those needs. Successful human resource planning is tied closely to organizational objectives and strategic planning. After organizational objectives and strategic plans have been formulated, human resource planning should occur. Forecasting human resource requirements involves determining the number and types of people needed for an organization to meet its objectives. To forecast the availability of human resources, the organization should look to both internal and external sources.

After the requirements for and availability of employees have been analyzed, the firm is in a position to determine whether there will be a balance, surplus, or shortage of employees. Means must be found to reduce the number of employees if a surplus of workers is projected. Some of these methods include restricted hiring, reduced hours, early retirements, and layoffs. If a shortage is forecast, the firm must look to sources outside the organization to secure the proper quantity and quality of workers. Recruitment and selection are then required.

Several forecasting techniques are currently being used to forecast human resource requirements and availability. The zero-base forecasting approach uses the organization's current level of employment as the starting point for determining future staffing needs. The bottom-up approach is a forecasting method in which forecasts are initially made at lower levels in the organization. Successively higher levels then make their forecasts to ultimately provide an aggregate forecast of human resource needs. Another means of forecasting human resource requirements is to use past employment as a predictor of future requirements. In simulation, a computer is used to assist in analyzing a model of a real system.

A human resource information system (HRIS) is any organized approach for obtaining information on which to base human resource decisions. The general steps that should be followed in the development of a useful HRIS are: (1) study the present system; (2) develop priorities for human resource information; (3) develop the new system; (4) install a computer, if necessary; and (5) maintain the system.

Figure 5–9. An example of the information available on data display screens from the InSci system. Source: Information Science Incorporated. Used with permission.

```
Employee Mini Profile as of 03/14/88    CO: 91    FCN:      T012345678
John Doe                                          AFCN:     A004610

Status: 102      Rehire·Full Time                 Hire Date    02/01/72
  Cat:   10      10/18/81                          Orig Hire    04/01/67
                                                   Birth Date   10/16/36

Loc:    6853431181    02/01/72    Promotion
        Fresno Int'l Sales 2                       Male
                                                   Race S
Job:    01487         02/01/72    Reason T         Married
        Dist Sales Mgr·Foreign
        Exempt        Officials & Managers         7-K Willybrook Ct
                                                   Selma        CA93662
Sal:    25,100.00     Per Year     Merit
        Effective 02/01/81                         408 394-5698
        Paid Bi-weekly

Grade/Level:          AN007                        Highest Ed   Year 1971
                                                   Level        Bach Law
Shift:   1                                         Subject      Law
                                                   School       Columbia Law
Action:
```

QUESTIONS FOR REVIEW

1. Describe the human resource planning process.
2. Identify and define the basic terms appropriate to an understanding of demand forecasting.
3. What are the means by which human resources may be forecasted? Briefly describe each.
4. Distinguish by definition and example between forecasting human resource requirements and forecasting human resource availability.
5. What actions could a firm take if it were experiencing a personnel surplus?
6. Distinguish between a management inventory and a skills inventory. What are the essential components of each?
7. What is the purpose of a human resource information system? What are the basic steps that should be considered in developing an HRIS?

TERMS FOR REVIEW

Human resource planning (HRP)
Strategic plans
Long-run trend
Cyclical variations
Seasonal variations
Random variations
Zero-base forecasting

Bottom-up approach
Regression analysis
Delphi technique
Simulation
Management inventory
Skills inventory
Human resource information system (HRIS)

Incident 1

Judy Anderson is the personnel recruiter for South Illinois Electric Company (SIE), a small supplier of natural gas and electricity for Cairo, Illinois, and the surrounding area. The company has grown rapidly over the five years that Judy has worked there and the growth is expected to continue. She just heard that SIE purchased the utilities system serving a neighboring county. The company work force increased by 30 percent the previous year and Judy found it a struggle to recruit enough qualified job applicants. She knows that the new expansion will intensify the problem.

Meter readers are an area of particular concern. The tasks required in meter read-

ing are relatively simple. A person drives to homes served by the company, finds the gas or electric meter, and records its current reading. If the meter has been tampered with, it is reported. The reader performs no calculations; there is no decision making of any consequence associated with the job. The pay is $10.00 per hour. Even so, Judy has been having considerable difficulty in keeping the 37 meter reader positions filled.

One day recently Judy was thinking about how to attract more job applicants when she received a call from the personnel director, Sam McCord. "Judy," Sam said, "I'm unhappy with the job specification calling for only a high school education for meter readers. In planning for the future we need more educated people in the company. I've decided to change the education requirement for the meter reader job from a high school diploma to a college degree." "But, Mr. McCord," protested Judy, "the company is growing rapidly. If we are to have sufficient people to fill those jobs we just can't insist on finding college applicants to perform such basic tasks. I don't see how we can meet our future needs for this job with such an unrealistic job qualification." Sam terminated the conversation abruptly by saying, "No, I don't agree. We need to upgrade all the people in our organization. This is just part of a general effort to do that. Anyway, I cleared this with the president before I decided to do it."

QUESTIONS

1. Should there be a minimum education requirement for the meter reader job? Discuss.
2. What is your opinion of Sam's effort to upgrade the people in the organization?
3. What legal ramifications, if any, should Sam have considered?

Incident 2

David Johnson, personnel manager for Eagle Aircraft, was a little anxious as he checked through his in-basket that morning. He had just returned from a long weekend at Cozumel, Mexico. His friend Carl Edwards, vice president of marketing, had called the night before to tell him about a meeting of the company's executive council. "It was a great meeting," Carl had said, "I don't think the future has ever looked brighter for Eagle."

Carl had gone on to tell about the president's decision to expand operations. He continued, "Everyone at the meeting seemed to be completely behind the president. Joe Davis, the controller, stressed our independent financial position; the production manager had done a complete work-up on the equipment we are going to need, including availability and cost information. And I have been pushing for this expansion for some time. So I was ready. I think it will be good for you too, David. The president said he expects employment to double in the next year."

David found nothing in his mail about the meeting. He decided not to worry about it. "I suppose they'll let me know when they need my help," he thought.

Just then he looked up to see Rex Schearer, a production supervisor, standing in the doorway. "David," said Rex, "the production manager jumped me Friday because maintenance doesn't have anybody qualified to work on the new digital lathe they are installing." "He's right," David replied, "we'd better get hot and see if we can find someone." David knew that it was going to be another busy Monday.

QUESTIONS

1. What deficiencies do you see in planning at Eagle Aircraft?
2. How might the planning situation at Eagle Aircraft be improved?
3. When should David start to work on finding the maintenance person for the digital lathe?

REFERENCES

Alpander, Guvenc G. and Boher, Constant H. "An Integrated Model of Strategic Human Resource Planning and Utilization." *Human Resource Planning* 4 (1981): 189–207.

Awad, E. M. "Using Computers as an EEO Compliance Tool." *Data Management* 20 (February 1982): 25–28.

Barnes, Anthony. "Manpower Planning for the 1990s: How Models Best Muddles." *Personnel Management* 16 (July 1984): 27–29.

"Computerized Personnel Systems." *Personnel Journal* 60 (November 1981): 826+.

Dyer, L. "Human Resource Planning at IBM." *Human Resource Planning* 7(3) (1984): 111–125.

English, J. W. "Human Resource Planning: The Ideal Versus the Real." *Human Resource Planning* 7(2) (1984): 67–72.

Ernest, Robert C. "Corporate Cultures and Effective Planning." *Personnel Journal* 30 (March 1985): 49–60.

Ferris, Gerald R. "Shaping Strategy: Tie Personnel Functions to Company Goals." *Management World* 14 (January 1985): 32–38.

Fiorito, J. "Factors Affecting Choice of Human Resource Forecasting Techniques." *Human Resource Planning* 8(1) (1985): 1–17.

Fitz-Enz, Jac. "HR Measurement: Formula for Success." *Personnel Journal* 64 (October 1985): 52–60.

Fottler, M. D. and Shuler, D. W. "Reducing the Economic and Human Cost of Layoffs." *Business Horizons* 27 (July–August 1984): 9–16.

Foxmoon, Loretta D. and Polsky, Walter L. "The Personnel Department During a Layoff." *Personnel Journal* 64 (October 1985): 18–21.

Frantzreb, Richard B. "Human Resource Planning: Forecasting Manpower Needs." *Personnel Journal* 60 (November 1981): 850–857.

Hestwood, T. M. "Human Resource Planning and Compensation: A Marriage of Convenience." *Human Resource Planning* 7(3) (1984): 141–150.

Jennings, Eugene E. "How to Develop Your Management Talent Internally." *Personnel Administrator* 26 (July 1981): 20–23.

Lederer, A. L. "Information Technology: Planning and Developing a Human Resources Information System." *Personnel* 61 (May–June 1984): 14–27.

Lederer, Albert L. "Planning and Developing a Human Resource Information System." *Personnel Journal* 29 (August 1984): 27–39.

Leshner, Martin. "The Case of the Missing HRP (and How to Solve It)." *Personnel Journal* 64 (April 1985): 57–64.

Lopez, Felix M. "Toward a Better System of Human Resource Planning." *S.A.M. Advanced Management Journal* 46 (Spring 1981): 4–14.

Mackey, Craig B. "Human Resource Planning: A Four-Phased Approach." *Management Review* 70 (May 1981): 17–22.

Nikkel, D. "HRIS Implementation: A Systematic Approach." *Personnel* 62 (February 1985): 10–15.

Odiorne, George S. "Developing a Human Resource Strategy." *Personnel Journal* 60 (July 1981): 534+.

Ondrack, Daniel A. and Nininger, James R. "Human Resource Strategies—The Corporate Perspective." *Business Quarterly* 49 (Winter 1984): 101–106.

Pursell, Donald E. "Planning for Tomorrow's Personnel Problems." *Personnel Journal* 60 (July 1981): 559–562.

Rowland, Kendrith M. and Summers, Scott L. "Human Resources Planning: A Second Look." *Personnel Administrator* 26 (December 1981): 73–80.

Russ, Charles F., Jr. "Manpower Planning Systems: Part I." *Personnel Journal* 61 (January 1982): 40–45.

Scarborough, Norman and Zimmerer, Thomas W. "Human Resources Forecasting: Why and Where to Begin." *Personnel Administrator* 27 (May 1982): 55–61.

Taguiri, Renato. "Planning: Desirable and Undesirable." *Human Resource Management* 19 (Spring, 1980): 11–14.

Walker, A. J. "The 10 Most Common Mistakes in Developing Computer-Based Personnel Systems." *Personnel Administrator* 25 (July 1980): 39–42.

Walker, A. J. "Management Selection Systems that Meet the Challenges of the 80s." *Personnel Journal* 60 (October 1981): 775–780.

Walker, Alfred J., Jr. "Personnel Uses the Computer." *Personnel Journal* 51 (March 1982): 204–207.

Walker, James W. *Human Resource Planning*. New York: McGraw-Hill, 1980.

Weiss, W. H. "Does Your Company Have an Abilities and Skills Record System?" *Supervision* 47 (March 1985): 7–8.

Wilson, Richard L. "A Worksheet for HRIS Management." *Personnel Journal* 64 (October 1985): 44–51.

Zippo, M. "Human Resources Data: Out of the Filing Cabinet, Into the Computer." *Personnel* 58 (November/December 1981): 51–53.

CHAPTER OBJECTIVES

1. Describe the recruitment process and explain why it is so closely related to human resource planning.
2. Identify actions that a firm might consider before trying outside recruitment.
3. Describe the external and internal factors that can influence the recruitment process.
4. Explain the methods that are often used in internal recruiting.
5. Identify the various sources and methods available to an organization for external recruiting.
6. State what is meant by adverse impact and the *Uniform Guidelines*.
7. Explain the impact of an affirmative action program on recruitment.
8. State what should be done to ensure that recruitment efforts are appropriate to meet legal requirements.

Chapter 6

RECRUITMENT

Joyce Sather, recruiting supervisor for the Pluto Manufacturing Company, had been promoted to her position after serving years as a production supervisor. One of Joyce's first major assignments was to recruit a general foreman for Pluto. After considering various alternatives, Joyce decided to place the following ad in a local newspaper with a circulation in excess of 1,000,000:

Employment Opportunity

Growing firm has position available for person with managerial experience. Contact Joyce Sather, Pluto Manufacturing Company.

More than 300 applications were received in the first week and Joyce was elated. However, when she reviewed the applications, it appeared that people with every conceivable type of work experience had applied. There were few if any good prospects in the group.

Mark Smith and Debra Coffee, two executives from competing firms, met at their annual product conference. They were discussing a hot topic, the effect of the government's civil rights activity in their firms. Mark said, "I don't think we have any difficulty at our company. I'm told that our employees are 35 percent minorities." "That's great," Debra replied, "How many of your minorities fill middle management positions?" After thinking a moment, Mark said, "I believe we have one over in maintenance." "Mark, you may have serious problems with EEO and not even realize it. I suggest that you do some checking."

160

Part Two
Human
Resource
Planning,
Recruitment,
and Selection

Recruitment is *the process of attracting individuals on a timely basis, in sufficient numbers and with appropriate qualifications, to apply for jobs with an organization.* Applicants with the highest qualifications may then be selected. According to the recruitment director of a leading energy company, "Recruitment today is like marketing breakfast cereals . . . tough and competitive."[1] Unless a sufficient number of qualified prospects apply, a firm cannot have a truly selective employment system.[2]

Joyce and Mark both are associated with the recruitment process. Joyce obviously did not tailor the recruitment message properly and obtained the wrong type of applicants. Mark may have difficulties because an insufficient number of minorities have progressed into management. Determining the proper means to encourage potential future employees to apply for employment is important to every firm, whether it is General Motors or Mr. Z's corner grocery store.

THE RECRUITMENT PROCESS

There is an old expression that states, "You can't turn down a job offer until one has been made." From the employer's side of this expression, it might be, "You can't make a job offer unless you have someone who wants the job." Obviously, personnel recruitment is an essential function of every firm. In most medium and large organizations, the personnel department is responsible for the recruitment process. In small firms recruiting will likely be conducted by individual managers.

The personnel recruitment process is shown in Figure 6–1. As you can see, both the internal and external environments continue to have an impact on personnel. When human resource planning indicates a need for employees, the firm may evaluate alternative ways to meet the demand for employees to produce its goods and services. When other alternatives are not appropriate, the recruitment process starts. Frequently, recruitment begins when a manager initiates an employee requisition. The **employee requisition** is *a document that specifies various details, including job title, department, and the date the employee is needed for work* (see Figure 6–2). With this information, personnel can refer to the appropriate job description to determine the qualifications needed by the person to be recruited. At times, firms continue their recruiting efforts even when vacancies do not exist. This practice permits them to maintain recruitment contacts and to identify and employ exceptional candidates.

[1]Murray J. Lubliner, "Developing Recruiting Literature That Pays Off," *Personnel Administrator* 26 (February 1981): 51.

[2]Edwin S. Stanton, "The Sequential Selection System®; The Key to Hiring Better People," *Training and Development Journal* 33 (March 1979): 61.

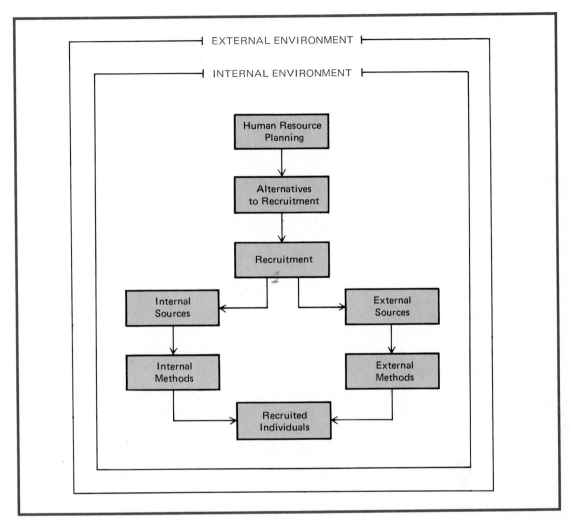

Figure 6–1. The recruitment process.

The next step in the recruitment process is to determine whether qualified employees are available within the firm (the internal source) or must be recruited externally from sources such as colleges, universities, and other companies. Recruitment methods are the specific means through which potential employees are attracted to the organization. Appropriate methods for either internal or external recruiting are then used.

Because of the high costs of recruiting, organizations must be assured that they are utilizing the most productive sources and methods. It may be discovered that one recruitment method is superior to another for a given company in locating executive talent. For instance, one large equipment

JOB NUMBER	JOB TITLE	DATE OF JOB VACANCY	DATE REPLACEMENT NEEDED

PLEASE CHECK	☐ Permanent ☐ Temporary ☐ Part-Time
	☐ Exempt ☐ Nonexempt If Nonexempt, Enter Job Class

REASON FOR REQUEST:
What management or employee action(s) caused the opening?

BRIEF DESCRIPTION OF MINIMUM QUALIFICATIONS FOR THE JOB CANDIDATES:

BRIEF DESCRIPTION OF JOB DUTIES:

LOCATION NAME

DATE	MANAGER'S SIGNATURE

Figure 6–2. Employee requisition.

manufacturer determined that medium-sized state-supported colleges and universities located in rural areas were good sources for potential managers.

ALTERNATIVES TO RECRUITMENT

Even when human resource planning indicates a need for additional or replacement employees, a firm may decide against engaging immediately in recruitment. Recruitment and selection costs are high. For example, it costs some hospitals as much as $12,000 just to recruit and orient one nurse.[3] Often included in the calculation of costs are factors such as the search process, interviewing, agency fee payment, and relocation and in-processing of the new employee. And, although decisions made in the selection process are not irreversible, once employees are placed on the payroll, they may be difficult to remove even if their performance is marginal. Therefore a firm should consider its alternatives carefully before engaging in recruitment.

OVERTIME

Perhaps the most common approach to meeting short-term fluctuations in work volume is through the use of overtime. Overtime can be useful to both employer and employee. The employer may benefit because the costs of recruitment, selection, and training are avoided. The employee benefits because higher pay is received.

While there are obvious advantages in using overtime, there are also potential problems. Many managers feel that when they are required to work their employees for unusually long periods of time, the company is paying more and receiving less in return. This condition may accelerate when excessive overtime is required. Employees may become fatigued and lack the energy to perform at a normal rate.

Two additional potential problems are related to prolonged overtime. Employees may, consciously or not, pace themselves so that their overtime will be assured. They may also become accustomed to the added income resulting from overtime payments. Employees may even elevate their standard of living to the level permitted by this additional income. Then, when overtime is no longer required, and the paycheck shrinks, the employees may become disgruntled.

SUBCONTRACTING

Even though an increased demand for its goods and/or services is anticipated, an organization may decide against expansion. Rather, the firm may decide to subcontract the work to another enterprise. This approach has great appeal when the increased demand is viewed as being of a short-term duration. Also, there are times when the subcontractor actually has greater expertise in producing a given product or providing a service. This arrangement may be mutually beneficial even for long periods of time.

TEMPORARY EMPLOYEES

When an anticipated increase in demand is only short term, another alternative to work-force expansion is the use of temporary help. In the past,

[3]"Re-entry Isn't Easy," *The Nurse Recruiter* 1 (February 1982): 1.

164

**Part Two
Human
Resource
Planning,
Recruitment,
and Selection**

as many as nine of ten companies in this country used temporary help services.[4] Temporary-help companies assist their clients by handling excess or special work loads. To accomplish this, they assign their own employees to their customers. The temporary-help firm fulfills all the obligations normally associated with an employer.[5] The expense of recruitment is avoided, as are absenteeism and turnover. Also, benefits are not normally provided. Suppose that the supervisor of the stenographic pool has an immediate, but short-term, need for six secretaries. Rather than recruit and hire additional employees, the supervisor calls a local organization that supplies temporary workers. This firm immediately sends the employees needed. These people remain on the payroll of the temporary help organization and the using firm is billed later for their services. Firms specializing in providing temporary employees now constitute a $2 billion industry.[6]

Not all aspects of temporary help are positive. Employees obtained in this manner are not on the client's payroll, so they may not feel as loyal as full-time employees. Also, temporary employees may lack required specialized training. Providing this training may take more time than can be justified.

EMPLOYEE LEASING

An alternative to recruiting that has been growing in popularity in recent years is employee leasing.[7] When employee leasing is used, a company obtains certain employees by contracting for the service of employees on the payroll of another company. Employee leasing is not the same as the services provided by temporary personnel services because leasing focuses on the permanent placement of employees. Since the passage of the Tax Equity and Fiscal Responsibility Act of 1982, employers who otherwise might be required to provide pension benefits can avoid this responsibility by leasing. Employee leasing is particularly attractive to small businesses because it avoids the expense and problems of personnel administration.

Another benefit of employee leasing is that it provides a way of avoiding union organizational activities or the requirement to recognize and bargain with an existing union. If the company that leases workers does not qualify as an "employer" under the National Labor Relations Act, employee leasing permits a firm to escape any requirement to recognize a representative of leased workers.[8]

---

[4]Charles J. Sigrist, "Nine Out of Ten Firms Use Temporary Help," *The Office* 87 (January 1978): 90.

[5]Charles W. L. Deale, "How to Choose a Temporary Help Service: A Guide to Quality Supplemental Staffing," *Personnel Administrator* (December 1980): 56.

[6]Howard Rudnitsky, "A Cushion for Business," *Forbes* 123 (February 5, 1979): 78.

[7]"Employee Leasing," *Newsweek*, May 14, 1984, p. 55.

[8]John V. Jansonius, "Use and Misuse of Employee Leasing," *Labor Law Journal* (January 1985): 35.

Barbara Sullivan
President and Co-
Owner, Quest
Personnel Services

Barbara Sullivan, President and co-owner of Quest Personnel Services in Los Angeles, was well on the road to becoming a social worker when she met her first personnel professional who inspired her to change her career goal. "Barbara, can you run the College Placement Service Office?" "Sure," was the answer of the naive second year graduate student at Tuskegee Institute in Alabama. Thus began a career in Personnel. While serving an internship in pupil personnel services at Tuskegee Institute, Sullivan was assigned to the Student Placement Office for her field project. When the director of the office became ill, she was given the responsibility of coordinating the recruitment program. She talked to the various recruiters who came to interview on campus about the work they performed. As a result of that experience, after graduation from college, Sullivan sought employment in the personnel field in Los Angeles, California.

However, she was surprised to discover that her master's degree in guidance and counseling and her related personnel experience did not eliminate the "need more experience" response from prospective employers. She wanted to be a recruiter, but in 1967, companies were not hiring many black female recruiters. After searching three months for a job, Sullivan finally accepted the only personnel-related position offered to her. She became an employment counselor for an employment agency. After working there for one year, she felt that her agency interviewing experience qualified her to apply for an interviewer's position in the personnel department of Cedars Sinai Medical Center, where she was hired. While employed there, she held the positions of employment manager, EEO coordinator, and employee counselor/trainer.

Sullivan was hired next as personnel director for a new medical facility, West Adams Community Hospital, where she organized and managed the personnel function. At West Adams, she and her staff of two employees were responsible for staffing, policy development, training, compensation, and benefits for over four hundred employees. She also found herself responsible for fighting a union organizational drive that prepared her with the experience needed to face the same situation later in her career.

Sullivan's career goals led her to seek an expanded work environment to further her personnel knowledge and experience. "I felt I was at the top of West Adams, yet I needed to learn more to sharpen my skills." She next joined Children's Hospital as assistant personnel director where she was mentored by two skilled, competent women in personnel and organizational development. "After three years at Children's Hospital, I knew I was professional-ready," states Sullivan, "and needed to move to the next challenge." She found that next challenge by responding to an advertisement in the *Los Angeles Times* for a personnel director for the City Attorney's Office, City of Los Angeles.

Sullivan says, "The personnel function, more than any other area in a company, provides the opportunity and exposure for developing executive skills. The combination of people (staffing), project, and financial tasks embodied in the daily duties of a personnel generalist are readily transferable to the executive suite." She is currently proving this as she and her partner, Elaine Wegener (president of the personnel consulting firm PACT), continue to build the highly praised temporary and permanent placement agency, Quest.

"Because we are personnel professionals, we conduct our offices as extensions of our clients' personnel operations," states Sullivan. She feels that there is a definite need for the services that agencies such as hers provide. She envisions more of a cooperative spirit developing in the future between personnel agencies and companies, as personnel agencies embrace a more professional posture of service to the companies.

EXTERNAL ENVIRONMENT OF RECRUITMENT

As with the other human resource functions, the recruitment process does not take place in a vacuum. Factors external to the organization can significantly affect the firm's recruitment efforts. Of particular importance is the supply and demand of specific skills in the labor market. If the demand for a particular skill is high relative to supply, an extraordinary recruiting effort may be required. For instance, the demand for computer programmers and accountants is likely to be greater than their supply, as opposed to the demand–supply relationship for nontechnical employees.

When the unemployment rate in a given area is high, the firm's recruitment process may be simpler. The number of unsolicited applicants is usually greater, and the increased size of the labor pool provides better opportunities for attracting qualified applicants. On the other hand, as the unemployment rate drops, recruiting efforts must be increased and new sources explored.

Labor market conditions in a local area are of primary importance in recruiting for most nonmanagerial, many supervisory, and even some middle-management positions. However, recruitment for executive and professional positions may be concerned more with the national market. Although the recruiter's day-to-day activities provide a feel for the labor market, accurate data regarding employment may be found in professional journals and Department of Labor reports.

Legal considerations also play a significant role in recruitment practices in the United States. The individual and the employer first make contact during the recruitment process. Therefore nondiscriminatory practices are absolutely essential at this stage of the employment relationship. Because many EEO practices begin with recruitment, this vital topic will be discussed in a later section of this chapter.

The firm's corporate image is another important factor that affects the recruitment process. If employees believe that their employer deals with them fairly, the positive word-of-mouth advertising they provide is of utmost value to the firm. It assists in establishing credibility with prospective employees. Good reputations earned in this manner can result in more and better qualified applicants seeking employment. Prospective employees are more inclined to respond positively to the organization's recruitment efforts. The firm with a healthy public image is one believed to be a "good place to work," and the recruitment efforts of such a firm are greatly enhanced.

INTERNAL ENVIRONMENT OF RECRUITMENT

While the labor market and the government exert powerful external influences on recruitment, the organization's own practices and policies also affect the recruitment effort. A major internal factor that can determine the success of a recruiting program is whether the firm engages in human resource planning. In most cases, a firm cannot attract prospective employees in sufficient numbers and with required skills overnight. It takes time to examine the alternatives regarding the appropriate sources of recruits and the most productive methods for obtaining them. Once the best alternatives have been identified, recruitment plans may be made. Effective human resource planning greatly facilitates the recruitment efforts.

An organization's promotion policy can also have a significant impact on its recruitment program. Basically, there are two approaches an organization can follow: (1) stressing a policy of promotion from within its own ranks; and (2) filling positions from outside the organization. There is a logical rationale for each approach.

Promotion from within is *the policy of filling vacancies above the entry-level positions with present employees.* When an organization emphasizes promotion from within, its workers have increased incentive to strive for advancement. When employees witness promotions occurring within their units, they become aware of their own opportunities. The motivation provided by this practice is often accompanied by a general improvement in employee morale. However, a strictly applied promotion from within policy is not always possible and practical because the firm may need fresh ideas that can only come from outsiders. In any event, a promotion policy that first considers insiders is great for employee morale and motivation.

Another advantage of recruiting internally is that the organization is usually aware of its employees' capabilities. An employee's past performance in a given job may not, by itself, be a reliable criterion for promotion.

168

Part Two
Human
Resource
Planning,
Recruitment,
and Selection

Nevertheless, many personal and job-related qualities may be known because the employee has established at least some track record as opposed to being an "unknown quantity." Also, the company's investment in the individual may be better utilized. Still another positive factor is the employee's knowledge of the firm, its policies, and its people.

Yet it is unlikely that a firm can or would even desire to adhere rigidly to a practice of promotion from within. The vice president of personnel and industrial relations for a major automobile manufacturer offers this advice: "A strictly applied 'PFW' policy eventually leads to inbreeding, a lack of cross-fertilization, and a lack of creativity. A good goal, in my opinion, is to fill 80 percent of openings above entry-level positions from within." Management may believe that new blood is badly needed to provide new ideas and innovation that must take place for firms to remain competitive. In such cases, even organizations with promotion from within policies may opt to look outside the organization for new talent.

Policies related to the employment of relatives may also affect a firm's recruitment efforts. The content of such policies varies greatly, but it is not uncommon for companies to have policies that discourage the employment of close relatives. This is often true when their assignments would be in the same chain of command.

METHODS USED IN INTERNAL RECRUITING

Management needs to be able to identify current employees who are capable of filling positions as they become available. Helpful tools used for internal recruitment include management and skills inventories, and job posting and bidding procedures. As mentioned in chapter 5, management and skills inventories permit organizations to determine whether current employees possess needed qualifications. As a recruitment device, these inventories have proved to be extremely valuable to organizations when they are maintained on a current basis. Inventories can be of tremendous value in locating internal talent. Also they support the concept of promotion from within.

Job posting is a procedure for communicating to company employees the fact that job openings exist. **Job bidding** is a technique that permits individuals in the organization who believe that they possess the required qualifications to apply for a posted job. A procedure that might be used in a medium-sized business firm is shown in Table 6–1. Larger firms, including Texas Instruments, often provide their employees with a weekly list of jobs available within the company. Any qualified employee is encouraged to apply for these job openings. You can see an example of this approach in Figure 6–3. The procedure followed by TI minimizes the complaint commonly heard in many companies that insiders never hear of a

Table 6–1. Job posting and bidding procedure	
Responsibility	**Action required**
Personnel Assistant	1. Upon receiving *Form PR-12, Personnel Requisition*, write a memo to each appropriate supervisor stating that a job vacancy exists. The memo should include job title, job number, pay grade, salary range, a summary of the basic duties performed, and the qualifications required for the job (data to be taken from job description/specification).
	2. Ensure that a copy of this memo is posted on all company bulletin boards.
Supervisors	3. Make certain that every employee who might qualify for the position is made aware of the job opening.
Interested Employee	4. Contact the Personnel Department.

job opening until it has been filled. A job posting and bidding system attempts to avoid this problem. It reflects a management practice of openness that is generally highly valued by employees. In addition, this system can assist in college recruitment efforts. A firm that offers freedom of choice and encourages career growth has a distinct advantage.[9]

There are some negative features of a job posting and bidding system. In order to have an effective system, considerable time and money may have to be devoted to the process. When bidders are unsuccessful, someone must explain to the unsuccessful candidates why they were not chosen. If care has not been taken to ensure that the most qualified applicant was chosen, the credibility of the system will be lost. It takes time and effort to ensure the success of such a system—and there will still be complaints.

EXTERNAL SOURCES OF RECRUITMENT

At times, a firm must look to the outside to find additional sources of recruits. This is particularly important if a firm is in the process of expanding its work force. The following circumstances require external recruitment: (1) to fill entry-level jobs; (2) to acquire skills not possessed by current employees; and (3) to obtain employees with different backgrounds to provide new ideas. As you can see in Figure 6–4, even when promotions

[9]J. Robert Garcia, "Job Posting for Professional Staff," *Personnel Journal* (March 1981): 192.

1. If you are interested in any of the opportunities listed below, please complete a "Job Opportunity Request" form and submit it to your Job Opportunity Office. Forms may be obtained from your personnel department.
2. Each opportunity will be held open for consideration of TIers for one week. To be considered, your Job Opportunity Request must be received in your site Job Opportunity Office by no later than seven days from the date of this bulletin.
3. To qualify for a job, you must satisfy all requirements of the job and you must list these qualifications on your Job Opportunity Request form. A resume or additional information may be attached if desired but the required qualifications as described in the job posting must be listed on the Job Opportunity Request form.
4. Each opportunity is coded to indicate payment of transfer expenses in accordance with Personnel Procedure PM 2-3-4 (Transfer Expenses of TI Personnel) as follows:
    CR—Candidates urgently needed. Transfer expenses including Home Guarantee Program paid.
    ER—Internal and external candidates are being sought locally and national. Transfer expenses paid as listed in PM 2-3-4.
    LR—Adequate local supply of qualified people. TIers in other locations may bid with understanding that no transfer expenses will be paid by TI.
    For details of transfer expenses paid for by each of the above classifications, see your personnel Administrator.
5. JOB GRADES—On jobs in locations other than your own, see your Personnel Adminstrator for comparison with your grading system.
6. If you do not receive an answer to your Job Opportunity Request by four weeks from the date of this Bulletin, call Job Opportunity at Dallas Expressway 5336. Remember the Job Number in requesting information about your Job Opportunity Request.

**NON-EXEMPT
ADMINISTRATIVE**

EQUIPMENT

CLK, GEN   (JPN)01DN2040
                           (JRC)0922723053
DUTIES: Prfm gen cler tasks; oper IBM key punch mach; oper calcul; some typg; maint logs, files, etc. MIN SKILL REQD: Prfm cler tasks. JG53:1-3 yrs expr. JG55: 3-5 yrs rel expr. SECURITY CLEARANCE REQD Grd 53/55 LR-CC922

CLK, GEN   (JPN)01DN2011
                           (JRC)0988723053
DUTIES: Oper various types of reprod/copy equip. Asst in oper of classified document contrl syst to include registration, transfer, filg % destruction of classified matl Typg ability reqd. Wrk hrs 10:30 a.m. - 7:00 p.m. MIN SKILL REQD: JG53: type 40-50 WPM, 1-5 yrs rel expr. JG55: type 50-60 WPM, 3-5 yrs rel expr. SECURITY CLEARANCE REQD. Grd 53/55 LR-CC988 s/lor Rotg

SECRETARY   (JPN)01DN2016
                           (JRC)0431731053
DUTIES: Sec duties f/Contract Admin includg hvy typg. filg, handlg classified documents, hvy phone liaison (cust/TI). JG53: over 1 yr dir rel expr. JG55: over 3 yrs dir rel expr MIN SKILL REQD: Typg 50-60 WPM. IBM Memory typg expr helpful. Abil to wrk under pressure & get along well w/others. Dependable, mature. Contracts or purchasing expr helpful. MIN EDUC REQD: Some bus sch &/or coll prefd. SECURITY CLEARANCE REQD. Grd 53/55 LR-CC431

WORD PROCESS   (JPN)01DN2032
OPER   (JRC)0713723053
DUTIES: Typg of draft copy, reprod copy & finished copy to meet contract data reqmts. Train on Word Procg Typg syst. Reqs attention to detail & sustained concentration f/long periods of time; abil to follow written, oral & mach-coded instructions. Prfm other rel duties as reqd. MIN SKILL REQD: JG53: 1-3 yrs rel expr & 40-50 WPM typg. JG55: 3-5 yrs rel expr & 60 WPM typg. SECURITY CLEARANCE REQD. Grd 53/55 LR-CC713

Figure 6–3. An example of Texas Instruments' job posting system. Source: Texas Instruments, Inc.

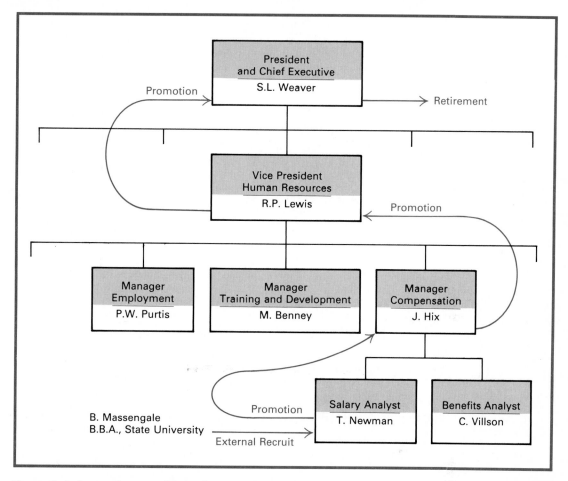

Figure 6–4. Internal promotion and external recruitment.

are made internally, entry-level jobs must be filled from the outside. In this example, after the president retires, a series of internal promotions are made. Ultimately, however, the firm resorts to external recruitment to fill the entry-level position of salary analyst. If the president's position had been filled from the outside, chain-reaction promotions from within would not have occurred. Depending on the qualifications desired, employees may be attracted from a number of outside sources.

HIGH SCHOOLS AND VOCATIONAL SCHOOLS

Organizations concerned with recruiting clerical and entry-level operative employees often depend heavily upon high schools and vocational schools.

172

Part Two
Human
Resource
Planning,
Recruitment,
and Selection

Many schools have designed outstanding training programs for specific occupational skills, such as home appliance repair and small-engine mechanics.

COMMUNITY COLLEGES

A number of community colleges are sensitive to the specific employment needs in their local labor markets and are graduating highly sought and marketable students. Typically, community colleges have two-year programs designed for both a terminal education and preparation for a four-year university degree program. Many community colleges have excellent mid-management programs combined with training for specific trades. In addition, career centers often provide a place for employers to contact students.

COLLEGES AND UNIVERSITIES

Colleges and universities represent a major source of recruitment for many organizations. Many professional, technical, and potential management employees are located in these institutions. Recruiters are commonly used to reach this important source.

Placement directors, faculty, and administrators are potentially helpful to organizations as they attempt to utilize this source of recruits. For instance, the large retailer, Bloomingdales, has improved its credibility on college campuses by making personal contacts with business professors and providing grants for studies and internships. The company has also used alumni to recruit and establish relationships with college placement offices.[10]

Since college recruitment is mutually beneficial, both employers and universities should take steps to develop and maintain close relationships. Once a recruiting program is established with educational institutions, it is important that programs be continued year after year and that an effective and sound relationship be established with each school involved. It is important that the business know the school and that the school know the business.

COMPETITORS AND OTHER FIRMS

Competitors and other firms in the area or industry may be the most important source of recruits for positions where recent experience is highly

[10]"Combing Colleges for Execs," *Chain Store Age Executive* 53 (July 1977): 27.

desired. The importance of these sources is emphasized by the fact that approximately 5 percent of the working population at any given time is either actively seeking or receptive to a change of position. Further, one of every three people — especially managers and professionals — change jobs every five years.[11]

Even organizations that have strong policies of promotion from within must occasionally look to the outside (which includes competitors) to fill important positions. Several years ago when Cessna Aircraft entered the business jet market, they needed a top sales executive with experience in this field. Cessna was able to lure a successful executive from Pan American World Airways to run their marketing operations.[12] Raiding other organizations for high quality talent often occurs.

Smaller firms, in particular, look for employees who have been trained by larger organizations which have the resources necessary to develop individuals.[13] For instance, one optical firm believes that its own operation is not large enough to provide extensive training and development programs. It is likely that a person recruited by this firm for a significant management role would have had at least two previous employers.

THE UNEMPLOYED

The ranks of the unemployed may also provide a valuable source of recruits. Qualified applicants are added to the unemployment rolls every day. Companies may close their doors, leaving qualified workers without jobs. Employees are fired sometimes merely because of personality differences with their bosses. Not infrequently, employees get fed up with their jobs and simply quit. Individuals who are unemployed, regardless of the reason, often provide a valuable source of recruitment.

SELF-EMPLOYED WORKERS

Finally, the self-employed worker may also be a good potential recruit. These individuals may provide a source of applicants to fill any number of jobs requiring technical, professional, administrative, or entrepreneurial expertise within a firm.

[11]Dan Lionel, "Dow Jones Tests Recruitment Weekly," *Editor & Publisher* 113 (May 24, 1980): 29.

[12]Richard R. Conarroe, *Executive Search: A Guide for Recruiting Outstanding Executives.* New York: Van Nostrand Reinhold, 1976, p. 8.

[13]Patrick Crow, "Industry Scrambling to Get Adequate Manpower," *The Oil and Gas Journal* 76 (December 11, 1978): 33.

174

**Part Two
Human
Resource
Planning,
Recruitment,
and Selection**

EXTERNAL METHODS OF RECRUITING

Through recruitment sources a firm is able to determine where the potential job applicants are located. Recruitment methods are the means by which job applicants may be enticed to seek employment with the firm. Recruitment methods such as advertising, employment agencies, and employee referrals may be effective in attracting virtually any type of person. The use of recruiters, special events, and internships are designed primarily for students, especially those attending colleges and universities. Also, executive search firms and professional organizations are particularly useful in the recruitment of managerial and professional employees.

ADVERTISING

Advertising is *a way of communicating the firm's employment needs to the public through media such as radio, newspaper, or industry publications.* In determining the content of an advertising message, a firm must decide on the corporate image it wants to project. Obviously, prospective employees should be given a clear and honest picture of the job and the organization. At the same time, an attempt should be made to determine what appeals to the self-interest of prospective employees, emphasizing the unique qualities of the job. The advertisement must communicate to them why they should be interested in the advertised job and organization. The message should also indicate how an applicant is to respond: apply in person, make a telephone response, or submit a resume.

Selection of the media to be used is purely an individual decision. The firm's previous experience with various media should suggest the approach to be taken for specific types of jobs. The least expensive form of advertising that provides the broadest coverage is probably the newspaper advertisement. Help-wanted advertising is being used by an increasing number of firms, and studies indicate that approximately 40 percent of all jobs are filled through recruitment advertising.[14] The greatest problem with its use stems from the large number of individuals who respond that are not really qualified. An effective ad avoids generalities and provides as much information as possible about the job, the organization, and possibilities for career mobility.[15] An examination of the Sunday edition of any major newspaper will reveal the extensive use of this medium for the recruitment of virtually every type of employee.

Advertisements placed in publications such as the *Wall Street Journal* are generally for managerial, professional, and technical positions. The reading audience generally is comprised of those individuals who may be

---

[14]James W. Schreier, "Deciphering Messages in Recruitment Ads," *Personnel Administrator* 28 (March 1983): 35.

[15]Van M. Evans, "Recruitment Advertising in the '80's," *Personnel Administrator* 23 (December 1978): 23.

qualified for the position. There is less likelihood of receiving marginally qualified or even totally unqualified applicants.

Virtually every professional group publishes a journal that is widely read by its members. When advertising for a personnel executive position, for example, *Personnel Administrator* would be an excellent medium.

Trade journals are widely utilized, but use of this medium is not without problems.[16] For example, regional editions are not offered, so trade journals may be useless to the employer who wants to avoid relocation expenses. Also, they lack scheduling flexibility. Their deadlines for black and white material are usually 30 days prior to the issue date and may be even further in advance for four-color material. Since staffing needs cannot always be anticipated far in advance, the use of trade journals for recruitment is obviously inappropriate at times.

Recruitment advertisers assume that qualified prospects read newspapers and trade journals and that they are dissatisfied with their present jobs to the extent that they peruse recruitment ads. This is not always the case, especially for those qualified individuals who are not actively considering a job change. Therefore, in high demand situations, the firm needs to consider all available media resources.[17]

Other media that can also be used include telephone, radio, billboards, and television. While these methods may be more expensive than newspapers or journals, they have been used with success in specific situations. For instance, a regional medical center used billboards successfully to attract registered nurses. One large manufacturing firm achieved considerable success in advertising for production trainees by means of radio spot advertisements. A large electronics firm used television to attract experienced engineers when it opened a new facility and needed more engineers immediately. In situations where hiring needs are urgent, television and radio may provide better results. However, the use of broadcasting alone may not be sufficient. It can alert people to the fact that an organization is seeking recruits. But it is limited in its ability to provide much more data than the general type of job available and company address and phone number. For this reason, broadcasting and print are often used together.[18]

EMPLOYMENT AGENCIES — PRIVATE AND PUBLIC

An **employment agency** is *an organization that assists firms in recruiting employees and, at the same time, aids individuals in their attempts to locate jobs.* They perform many recruitment and selection functions for the

---

[16]Jo Bredwell, "The Use of Broadcast Advertising for Recruitment," *Personnel Administrator* 26 (February 1981): 45.

[17]Dan Lionel, "Dow Jones Tests Recruitment Weekly," *Editor & Publisher* 113 (May 24, 1980): 29.

[18]Margaret M. Nemec, "Recruitment Advertising — It's More Than Just 'Help Wanted'," *Personnel Administrator* 26 (February 1981): 57.

176

**Part Two
Human
Resource
Planning,
Recruitment,
and Selection**

employer such as obtaining application blank data, holding screening interviews, and performing other selection functions for the employer.

Private agencies are utilized by firms for virtually every type of position. However, they are best known for their role in recruiting white-collar employees. Although the industry has gained a bad reputation in some areas, a number of highly reputable employment agencies have been in operation for decades. Difficulties that occasionally occur stem from a lack of industry standards. The quality of a particular agency depends on the professionalism of its management at each location. Even though problems may exist, private employment agencies present an important method of bringing qualified applicants and positions together. It is one that should not be overlooked by either the organization or the job applicant. Individuals are often turned off by agencies because of the fees they charge. However, the fee is often paid by the employer. An example of a typical employment agency fee schedule is shown in Table 6–2. Fee percentages are based on gross salary.

Table 6–2. Example of a typical employment agency fee schedule

Annual gross salary	Fee
$ 0–$9,999	10%
10,000–10,999	11%
11,000–11,999	12%
12,000–12,999	13%
13,000–13,999	14%
14,000–14,999	15%
15,000–15,999	16%
16,000–16,999	17%
17,000–17,999	18%
18,000–18,999	19%
19,000–19,999	20%
20,000–20,999	21%
21,000–21,999	22%
22,000–22,999	23%
23,000–23,999	24%
24,000–24,999	25%
25,000–25,999	26%
26,000–26,999	27%
27,000–27,999	28%
28,000–28,999	29%
29,000 +	30%

An example of successful use of private agencies is provided by the Fulton Supply Company of Atlanta. "Over the years," says Ira B. Abernathy, president, "we've gotten to know them and they've gotten to know us and our particular needs." Fulton employs more than 100 people, and most of them, he says, "came to us through agencies. When we first started using agencies, they would send over people with almost any kind of background. It was up to us to weed them out. Now that the agencies know our business well enough, they do the weeding."[19]

While public employment agencies are operated by each state, they receive overall policy direction from the U.S. Employment Service. Public employment agencies are best known for their efforts in recruiting and placing individuals in operative jobs. But recently they have been increasingly involved with technical, professional, and managerial positions. Some public agencies utilize computerized job matching systems to aid in the recruitment process. The services provided by public employment agencies are without charge to either the employer or prospective employee.

RECRUITERS

The most common use of recruiters is with technical and vocational schools, community colleges, colleges, and universities. The key contact for recruiters on college and university campuses is often the director of student placement. This administrator is in an excellent position to arrange interviews with students possessing the qualifications desired. Placement services make it feasible for organizations to utilize their recruiters efficiently. Qualified candidates are identified, interviews are scheduled, and suitable physical locations are provided for the interviews.

The company recruiter obviously plays a vital role in attracting applicants. The recruiter's actions will be viewed as those reflecting the character of the firm. If the recruiter is dull, the company represented may be considered dull; if he or she is apathetic, discourteous, or vulgar, all these negative characteristics may well be attributed to the recruiting firm. Recruiters should always be aware of the public relations aspect of the screening interview because it makes a lasting impression.

Recruiters determine which individuals possess the best qualifications and who are to be encouraged to continue their interest in the firm. In achieving this purpose, the recruiter becomes involved in a two-way communication process by providing information about the company, its products and/or services, its general organizational structure, its policies, and a description of the job to be filled. The organization's compensation and benefits program may also be mentioned. The recruiter will also ask the prospect numerous questions, which may range from, "What position do you want to occupy five years from now?" to, "How will your employment

---

[19]"The Scramble for Talent," *Industrial Distribution* 66 (August 1976): 32.

178

Part Two
Human
Resource
Planning,
Recruitment,
and Selection

benefit our firm?" Questions such as these may be difficult to answer. However, the prospect is expected to respond in some logical manner. Other questions may be more predictable, such as those relating to grades, extra-curricular activities, employment while attending school, and hobbies.

Considering the importance of the occasion, the interview between the prospect and recruiter is often short — about thirty minutes on the average. It is therefore imperative that:

- The interview begin on time.
- The recruiter be prepared, or at least have knowledge of the facts included on the prospect's data sheet.
- The interview take place in a quiet, private area without outside disturbance.[20]

The applicant must also prepare for the interview. If a good impression is to be made, the prospect must do some homework on the company. The school's placement service often has literature that describes the nature of the recruiting organization and gives other helpful information. In addition, library sources may provide data such as the company's sales volume, number of employees, products, and so forth. Prospects who possess facts such as these are in a good position to engage the recruiter in conversation and ask relevant questions. Other things being equal, an informed prospect has a competitive advantage.

By 1980, thirty college placement offices had installed the visual equiv-alent of a juke box to handle recruiting messages from companies. With the proliferation of video-disk equipment, it has been suggested that or-ganizations in need of critical skills may utilize playback machines and disks at college locations. It has also been suggested that the high cost of travel for screening interviews may be reduced through the use of cable and satellite communications.[21]

SPECIAL EVENTS

Special events is a recruiting method that involves an effort on the part of a single employer, or group of employers, to attract a large number of applicants for interviews. Job fairs, for example, are designed to bring to-gether applicants and a wide variety of company representatives. One con-vention held exclusively for women attracted 90 firms and about 4000 prospects from 16 states. The president of the sponsoring organization stated, "Employers want good women but often don't know how to get them. Women want good jobs and don't know how to go about it."[22]

A properly conducted open house attracts many people who might otherwise be unreachable: those who are undecided about changing posi-

[20]Richard A. Fear, *The Evaluation Interview*. New York: McGraw-Hill, 1973.

[21]Roy G. Foltz, "Recruiting Communications," *Personnel Administration* 26 (February 1981): 14.

[22]"Career Conventions Open Doors to Jobs," *Nation's Business* 69 (December 1981): 86.

tions. At the same time, the firm publicizes its continuing growth and success.

INTERNSHIPS

Internships are *special forms of recruiting that involve placing students in temporary jobs with no obligation either by the company to permanently hire the student or by the students to accept a permanent position with the firm.* Internships typically involve a temporary job for the summer months or a part-time job during the school year. In many instances, students alternate their schedule by working full-time one semester and becoming full-time students the next. In the course of the internship, students are given the opportunity to view first hand the practices of businesses. At the same time, they contribute to the firms by performing needed tasks. Through this relationship, a student can determine whether a company would be a desirable employer. Likewise, the business firm can make better judgments regarding the candidate's qualifications.[23] Internships provide opportunities for students to bridge the gap from management theory to practice.

Internships have also proved useful in moving minorities into the work force. Bob Edwards, formerly vice president for personnel, Southwestern Life Insurance Company, describes its program as follows:

The successful integration of our office work force after the Civil Rights legislation in 1964 required innovative approaches to selection as well as placement of minorities. The business leaders in Dallas were not yet confident that an acceptable solution could be found to answer the critics of integration or those advocates who did not want to weaken their companies' performance by active compliance. We elected to deal with this important issue by strengthening our high school internship program. Business-minded students in this program are provided full-time summer jobs in our home office prior to their senior year and are moved to part-time jobs through their final school term.

Our approach provides:

1. Summer employment to a predominantly minority population.
2. Part-time employment without giving any employment test.
3. Information to high school students that more accurately reflects the demands of an adult work environment.
4. Maximum discretion for the student as the company requires no commitment beyond the school term.
5. Maximum discretion for the company as full-time employment can be offered to those students who performed well on the internship jobs.
6. Up-to-date information for high school teachers and administrators on industry needs and hard data to motivate student development.

[23]H. Felix Kloman, "The Student Intern," *Risk Management* 26 (February 1979): 10.

180

Part Two
Human
Resource
Planning,
Recruitment,
and Selection

In summary, we integrated our work force with performers and min-imized management reluctance to enter an unknown and, in some situa-tions, a feared adventure with a population whose background is different from their own. Our success with this approach is evidenced by the size of our present employee minority population and their presence at all levels of responsibility.

EXECUTIVE SEARCH FIRMS

Executive search firms may be used by organizations in their recruitment efforts to locate experienced professionals and top level executives when other sources prove inadequate. **Executive search firms** are *organizations that are retained to search for the most qualified executive available for a specific position and are only on assignment from the company seeking a specific type of individual.*[24]

In the past ten years, the executive search industry has evolved from a basic recruitment service to a highly sophisticated profession serving a greatly expanded role. Search firms are now serving as sounding boards to assist organizations in determining their human resource needs, establish compensation ranges, and provide advice concerning organizational structure.[25]

Executive search firms differ from employment agencies and job ad-visory consultants in that they do not work for individuals. They are re-tained by corporations and governmental agencies, which pay the fees.[26] Korn/Ferry International, a prominent executive search firm, has thirty-one offices around the world, of which thirteen are in the United States. They concentrate on executives earning in excess of $60,000.[27]

Firms in this business often visit their clients' offices to interview com-pany management. This enables them to gain a clear understanding of the company's goals and the job qualifications required. After this information is obtained, potential candidates are contacted and interviewed, their ref-erences checked, and the best qualified are referred to the client for the selection decision. The search firm's fee is generally a percentage of the individual's first year's compensation. Expenses, as well as the fee, are paid by the client.

The key problem in executive searches is poor communication between the client and the search firm. Face-to-face meetings are highly desirable because they enable the parties to reach agreement on the specifications

---

[24]Richard J. Cronin, "Executive Recruiters: Are They Necessary?" *Personnel Administrator* (February 1981): 32.

[25]Ibid., p. 32.

[26]Beth Rosenthal, "Headhunters: Women's Division," *Across the Board* 14 (August 1977): 20.

[27]Interview with J. Alvin Wakefield, senior vice president and partner, Korn/Ferry International, August 9, 1982.

for the executive position. Competent executive search firms will be successful in their searches 70–80 percent of the time.[28]

PROFESSIONAL ASSOCIATIONS

Associations in many business professions such as finance, marketing, data processing, and Personnel provide recruitment and placement services for their members. The American Society for Personnel Administration is an example of an organization that operates a job referral service for members seeking new positions and employers with positions to fill.

EMPLOYEE REFERRALS

Many organizations have found that their employees can assist in the recruitment process. Employees may actively solicit applications from their friends and associates. In some organizations, especially where certain skills are scarce, this approach has proven quite effective. For example, a few years ago the demand for engineers was so great that firms such as Ampex Corporation and TRW, Inc., were offering a $1000 bonus to any employee who persuaded an engineer to join their organization.[29]

UNSOLICITED APPLICANTS

If an organization has the reputation of being a good place to work, it may be able to attract good prospective employees even without extensive recruitment efforts. Acting on their own initiative, high quality workers may seek out a specific company to apply for a job. Unsolicited applications often prove to be a valuable method of recruiting employees.

TAILORING METHODS TO SOURCES

Each organization is unique in many ways. Because of this, the types and qualifications of workers needed to fill various positions also vary. For recruitment efforts to be successful, they must be tailored to meet the needs of each firm. In addition, recruitment sources and methods of recruitment may vary according to the type of position being filled.

Figure 6–5 shows a matrix that depicts both methods and sources of recruitment. A personnel professional must first identify the source (where are they) before the methods (how to get them) can be chosen. Suppose, for example, that a large firm has an immediate need for a data processing manager with a minimum of five-years' experience. Considering the sources, it is most likely that this individual is employed by another firm, very

---

[28]Thomas A. Byrnes, "Why an Executive Search Fails," *Personnel Journal* 60 (December 1981): 922–923.

[29]"Engineering: Help Wanted," *Newsweek* 66 (January 1, 1979): 44.

182

**Part Two
Human
Resource
Planning,
Recruitment,
and Selection**

SOURCES OF RECRUITMENT	METHODS OF RECRUITING										
	Advertising	Private employment agencies	Public employment agencies	Recruiters	Special events	Internships	Executive search firms	Unsolicited applications	Professional associations	Employee referrals	Unsolicited applicants
High schools											
Vocational schools											
Community colleges											
Colleges and universities											
Competitors and other firms	X	X					X		X		
Unemployed											
Self-employed											

Figure 6–5. Methods and sources tailored to recruitment of a data processing manager.

possibly a competitor. Once the source of recruitment is identified, the recruiter must next choose the method or methods of recruitment that offer the best opportunity for attracting qualified candidates. Perhaps the job can be advertised in the classified section of the *Wall Street Journal*, the *National Employment Weekly*, or *Computerworld*. Or, an executive search firm may have to be employed to locate a qualified person. In addition, recruiters may want to attend meetings of professional associations, such as those of the Data Processing Management Association or the Association of Computing Machinery. In some instances, employment agencies that specialize in computer personnel may be effectively utilized. In all likelihood, methods such as public employment agencies, internships, and employee referral will be of only limited value in attracting an experienced professional.

Suppose now, for example, that a firm needs twenty entry-level machine operators, which the firm is willing to train. High schools and vocational schools would probably be productive recruitment sources. Methods of recruitment might include newspaper advertisements, public employment agencies, recruiters at vocational schools, and employee referrals.

The specific recruitment methods used will depend on external environmental factors, including market supply. Also, a certain method may prove to be satisfactory for one firm but be virtually useless for another. Each organization should maintain employment records and conduct its own research in order to determine which recruitment sources and methods are most appropriate for given circumstances.

UNIFORM GUIDELINES AND ADVERSE IMPACT

As discussed in chapter 3, prior to the issuance of the *Uniform Guidelines on Employee Selection Procedures* in 1978, the only way to prove job relatedness was through validation of each test. The new guidelines did not require validation in all cases. "It is essential only in instances where the test or other selection device produces an adverse impact on a minority group. Under the new guidelines, adverse impact has been defined in terms of selection rates, the selection rate being the number of applicants hired or promoted, divided by the total number of applicants."[30] **Adverse impact**, *a concept established by the Uniform Guidelines, occurs if protected groups are not hired at the rate of at least 80 percent of the best-achieving group.* This has also been called the four-fifths rule.

In computing adverse impact for hiring, the following formula may be used:

$$\frac{\text{Success rate for protected group applicants}}{\text{Success rate for best-achieving group applicants}} = \frac{\text{Determination of}}{\text{adverse impact}}$$

The success rate for protected group applicants is determined by dividing the number of members of a specific protected group *employed* in a period by the number of protected group member *applicants* in a period. The success rate for best-achieving group applicants is determined by dividing the number of people in the best-achieving group *employed* by the number of the best-achieving group *applicants* in a period.

Using the preceding formula, let us determine if there has been an adverse impact in a given organization. During 1987, 400 people were hired for a particular job. Of the total, 300 were white and 100 were black. There

---

[30]David E. Robertson, "New Directions in EEO Guidelines," *Personnel Journal* 57 (July 1978): 361.

184

Part Two
Human
Resource
Planning,
Recruitment,
and Selection

were 1500 applicants for these jobs, of whom 1000 were white and 500 were black. Using the adverse impact formula we have:

$$\frac{100 \div 500 \quad = .2}{300 \div 1000 \quad = .3} = 66.67 \text{ percent (adverse impact exists)}$$

Evidence of adverse impact is more than the total number of minority workers *employed*. The total number of *applicants* is also taken into consideration. For instance, assume that 300 blacks and 300 whites were hired. But there were 1500 black applicants and 1000 white applicants. Putting these figures into the adverse impact formula, we can see that adverse impact still exists:

$$\frac{300 \div 1500}{300 \div 1000} = \frac{.2}{.3} = 66.67 \text{ percent}$$

Thus it is clear that firms must monitor their recruitment efforts very carefully. Even though 300 blacks were hired, there were 1500 black applicants. Firms should recruit selectively because once individuals get into the applicant pool, they will be used in computing adverse impact.

AFFIRMATIVE ACTION

An **affirmative action program (AAP)** is a *program that an organization develops to demonstrate that protected group members are employed in proportion to their representation in the firm's recruitment area.* An affirmative action program may be voluntarily implemented by an organization. In such an event, goals are established and action is taken to hire and move members of protected groups upward in the organization. In other situations, an AAP may be mandatory. For example, if a firm has a federal procurement or federally assisted construction contract amounting to $50,000 or more, an affirmative action plan *must* be filed with the Office of Federal Contract Compliance Programs (OFCCP). Finally, an AAP may be required when a discrimination suit brought against a company by EEOC shows the existence of discrimination. The procedures for the development of affirmative action plans were published in the *Federal Register* of December 4, 1974. These regulations are referred to as Revised Order No. 4. The OFCCP guide for compliance officers, outlining what to cover in a compliance review, is known as Order No. 14.

The OFCCP is very specific about what should be included in an affirmative action program. A policy statement has to be developed that reflects the chief executive officer's attitude regarding EEO, assigns overall responsibility for preparing and implementing the AAP, and provides for reporting and monitoring procedures. The policy should state that the firm intends to recruit, hire, train, and promote persons in all job titles without regard to race, color, religion, sex, or national origin, except where sex is a bona fide occupational qualification (BFOQ). The policy should guarantee that all personnel actions involving such areas as compensation, benefits, transfers, layoffs, returns from layoff, company sponsored training, education, tuition assistance, and social and recreational programs will be administered without regard to race, color, religion, sex, or national origin.

Revised Order No. 4 is quite specific with regard to dissemination of a firm's EEO policy, both internally and externally. An executive should be appointed as director or manager of the firm's equal employment opportunity program. This individual should be given the necessary top management support to accomplish the assignment. Revised Order No. 4 specifies the minimum level of responsibility associated with the task of EEO manager.

An acceptable affirmative action program must include an analysis of areas where the firm is deficient in the utilization of minority groups and women. The first step in conducting utilization analysis is to complete a work-force analysis.

The second step involves an analysis of all major job groups at the firm's facility; an explanation of the situation is required if minorities or women are currently being underutilized. A job group is defined as one or more jobs having similar content, wage rates, and opportunities. Underutilization is defined as having fewer minorities or women in a particular job group than would reasonably be expected by their availability. The utilization analysis is important because the percentage calculated determines whether underutilization exists. For example, if the utilization analysis shows that the availability of blacks for a certain job group is 30 percent, the organization must have 30 percent black employment in that group. If less than 30 percent is present, underutilization exists, and the firm should set a goal of 30 percent black employment for that job group.

The primary focus of any affirmative action program is on goals and timetables: how many, by when. Goals and timetables developed by the firm should cover its entire affirmative action program, including correction of deficiencies. These goals and timetables should be attainable; that is, they should be based on results that the firm could reasonably expect from good-faith efforts to make its overall affirmative action program work.

In the goal setting process, both personnel managers and line managers should be involved. Goals should be significant, measurable, and attainable. Two goals must be established regarding underutilization: annual and ultimate. The annual goal is to move toward elimination of underutilization, whereas the ultimate goal is to correct any underutilization. Goals should be specific in terms of planned results with timetables for completion. However, goals should not be so rigid as to establish inflexible quotas that must be met. Rather, they should be targets that are reasonably attainable.

Employers should conduct a detailed analysis of job descriptions to ensure that they accurately reflect job content. In addition, job specifications should be validated, with special attention given to academic, experience, and skills requirements. If a job specification screens out a disproportionate number of minorities or women, the requirements must be

186

Part Two
Human
Resource
Planning,
Recruitment,
and Selection

professionally validated in terms of job performance. Thus, a comprehensive job analysis program is required.

When an opening occurs, all of the managers who are involved in personnel recruiting, screening, selection, and promotion should be aware of the opening. In addition, the firm should evaluate the entire selection process to ensure freedom from bias. And, individuals involved in the process should be carefully selected and trained in order to eliminate bias in all personnel actions.

Firms should observe the requirements of the *Uniform Guidelines*. Selection techniques other than tests can also be used improperly and thus discriminate against minority groups and women. Such techniques include unscored interviews, unscored or casual application forms, arrest records, credit checks, consideration of marital status, dependency, and minor children. Where data suggest that discrimination or unfair exclusion of minorities and women exists, the firm should analyze its unscored procedures and eliminate them if they are not objective and valid. Some techniques that can be used to improve recruitment and increase the flow of minority and women applicants are shown in Table 6–3.

Table 6–3. Techniques to improve recruitment of minorities and women

- Identify referral organizations for minorities and women.
- Hold formal briefing sessions with representatives of referral organizations.
- Encourage minority and women employees to refer applicants to the firm.
- Include minorities and women on the Personnel Relations staff.
- Permit minorities and women to participate in Career Days, Youth Motivation Programs and related activities in their community.
- Actively participate in job fairs and give company representatives the authority to make on-the-spot commitments.
- Actively recruit at schools having predominant minority or female enrollments.
- Recruiting efforts at all schools should use special efforts to reach minorities and women.
- Special employment programs should be undertaken whenever possible for women and minorities. These might include technical and nontechnical co-op programs, "after school" and/or work-study jobs, summer jobs for underprivileged, summer work-study programs, and motivation, training and employment programs for the hardcore unemployed.
- Pictorially present minorities and females in recruiting brochures.
- Help wanted advertising should be expanded to include the minority news media and women's interest media.

Source: *Federal Register*, Vol. 45, No. 251, Tuesday, December 30, 1980, p. 86243.

In spite of existing equal opportunity laws, many past personnel practices are deeply embedded in some organizations. These practices continue to have an unequal impact on protected groups. This has been the case even when the organization has not consciously discriminated. In the anecdote at the beginning of this chapter, Mark Smith may have some serious problems with EEO and not even realize it. Some traditional employment systems perpetuate the effects of past discrimination even after the original practices have been discontinued. The result is a continuation of what has been labeled *systemic discrimination*. Courts have found that some employment practices, regardless of intent, have resulted in discrimination against members of protected groups.

To offset the momentum of past discrimination in employment, firms may need to resort to additional recruitment approaches. Members of protected groups, because of a lifetime of unequal opportunity, may not respond to traditional recruitment methods or be a part of typical recruitment sources. Therefore a recruitment program that is designed specifically to attract members of protected groups should be implemented.

ANALYSIS OF RECRUITMENT PROCEDURES

To ensure that an organization's recruitment program is nondiscriminatory, the firm must analyze its recruitment procedures. For example, it might be unwise to use employee referral or unsolicited applicants as main recruitment methods. These actions may perpetuate the present composition of an organization's membership. And, where minorities and females are not well represented at all levels, the courts have ruled that reliance on these practices is discriminatory.

In identifying sources of continuing discrimination, it may be helpful to develop a record of applicant flow. This record would include personal and job-related data concerning each applicant. It would also indicate whether a job offer was extended; if no job offer was made, an explanation should be provided. These records would enable the organization to analyze its recruitment and selection practices related to minority and women candidates and to take corrective action when necessary.

UTILIZATION OF MINORITIES AND WOMEN

Each individual who engages in recruitment should be trained in the use of objective, job-related standards. These recruiters are in critical positions to either encourage or discourage protected group members in applying for jobs. Qualified minorities and women may be effectively utilized in key recruitment activities such as visiting schools and colleges and participating in career days. They are in an excellent position to provide valuable

188

Part Two
Human
Resource
Planning,
Recruitment,
and Selection

inputs for recruitment planning. And they may effectively serve as referral sources. Pictures of minority and women employees in help-wanted advertisements and company brochures may assist in conveying the message, "We are an equal employment opportunity employer."

ADVERTISING

With few exceptions, jobs must be open to all individuals. Therefore, sex-segregated advertisements, for example, cannot be used unless sex is a bonafide occupational qualification. The BFOQ exception provided in Title VII of the Civil Rights Act requires that the qualifications be job-related. This definition is narrowly interpreted by EEOC and the courts. The burden of proof is on the employer to establish that job requirements are essential for successful performance of the job.

Other recruitment practices designed to provide equal opportunity include:

1. Ensuring that the content of advertisements does not indicate preference for any race, sex, or age or that these factors are a qualification for the job. For "A Want Ad That'll Kill You," see Figure 6–6.
2. Utilizing media that are directed toward minorities, such as appropriate radio stations.

Figure 6–6. A want ad that'll kill you. Source: Vivian C. Pospisil, "What Can You Ask a Job Applicant?" *Industry Week,* March 1, 1976, p. 25. Used with permission.

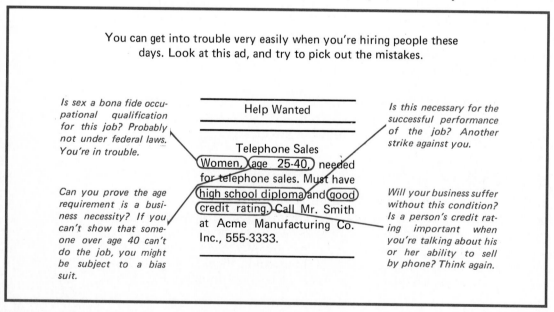

You can get into trouble very easily when you're hiring people these days. Look at this ad, and try to pick out the mistakes.

Is sex a bona fide occupational qualification for this job? Probably not under federal laws. You're in trouble.

Can you prove the age requirement is a business necessity? If you can't show that someone over age 40 can't do the job, you might be subject to a bias suit.

Help Wanted

Telephone Sales
Women, age 25-40, needed for telephone sales. Must have high school diploma and good credit rating. Call Mr. Smith at Acme Manufacturing Co. Inc., 555-3333.

Is this necessary for the successful performance of the job? Another strike against you.

Will your business suffer without this condition? Is a person's credit rating important when you're talking about his or her ability to sell by phone? Think again.

```
┌─────────────────────────────────────────────┐
│                                             │
│           CORPORATE CONTROLLER              │
│                                             │
│      Sureway  Development  Company  offers  an │
│      outstanding  opportunity  for  an  individual │
│      with a degree in accounting and a minimum │
│      of 4 years experience. Background should │
│      include  financial  analysis  and  budgeting. │
│      Real  estate  development  experience  pre- │
│      ferred  and/or  CPA.  Please  contact  Bill │
│      Smith 318/255-1656.                     │
│                                             │
│         Equal Opportunity Employer M/F      │
│                                             │
└─────────────────────────────────────────────┘
```

Figure 6–7. A newspaper ad stressing equal employment opportunity for males and females.

3. Emphasizing the intent to recruit both sexes by including the phrase "Equal Employment Opportunity Employer, M/F" where jobs have traditionally been held by either males or females (see Figure 6–7). To many, EEO suggests only racial nondiscrimination.

EMPLOYMENT AGENCIES

An organization should emphasize its nondiscriminatory recruitment practices when placing job orders with employment agencies. While private agencies may be successfully utilized, jobs at all levels should be listed with the local public employment agency. State employment agencies can provide valuable assistance to organizations seeking to fulfill affirmative action goals.[31] In addition, agencies and consultant firms that specialize in minority and women applicants should be contacted.

OTHER SUGGESTED AFFIRMATIVE RECRUITMENT APPROACHES

Personal contacts should be made with counselors and administrators at high schools, vocational schools, and colleges with large minority and/or women enrollments. These counselors and administrators should be made aware that the organization is actively seeking minorities and women for jobs that they have not traditionally held. Also, they should be familiar with the types of jobs available and the training and education needed to perform these jobs successfully. The possibilities for developing internships and summer employment for minorities and women should be carefully investigated.

[31]William S. Hubbartt, "The State Employment Service: An Aid to Affirmative Action Implementation," *Personnel Journal* 56 (June 1977): 289.

190

Part Two
Human
Resource
Planning,
Recruitment,
and Selection

Organizations should develop contact with minority, women's, and other community organizations. While the most productive sources may vary in each locality, some helpful organizations may include: National Association for the Advancement of Colored People, National Urban League, American Association of University Women, Federation of Business and Professional Women's Talent Bank, National Council of Negro Women, and the local Veteran's Administration. The EEOC's regional offices will assist employers in locating appropriate agencies.

SUMMARY

Recruitment involves attracting individuals on a timely basis, in sufficient numbers and with appropriate qualifications, to apply for jobs. Unless a sufficient number of qualified prospects apply for a job, the company cannot have a truly selective employment system. When human resource planning indicates a need for new employees, the firm may evaluate the possibility of using alternatives to hiring in order to meet the demand for its goods and/or services. Some alternatives include: overtime, subcontracting, temporary help, and employee leasing. The recruitment process must also consider the internal and external environments.

Frequently, recruitment begins when a manager initiates an employee requisition. The requisition specifies job title, department, the date the employee is needed, and other details. The next step in the recruitment process is to determine whether qualified employees are available within the firm or must be recruited externally. External recruitment sources include: high schools and vocational schools, community colleges, colleges and universities, competitors and other firms, and unemployed and self-employed workers.

Recruitment methods are the specific means by which potential employees are attracted to the firm. Internal methods include job posting and bidding. External methods include: advertising, employment agencies, recruiters, special events, internships, executive search firms, professional associations, and employee referrals.

Adverse impact occurs when members of protected groups receive unequal consideration for employment. It occurs if protected groups are not hired at the rate of at least 80 percent of the best-achieving group. Certain organizations must develop an affirmative action program (AAP) to show that they hire members of protected groups in proportion to their representation in the firm's area of recruitment. The Office of Federal Contract Compliance Programs is very specific about what should be included in an AAP. A policy statement should be developed that reflects the chief executive officer's attitude regarding equal employment opportunity (EEO), assigns overall responsibility for the AAP, and provides for reporting and monitoring procedures. An executive should be appointed as director of the firm's equal opportunity program. An AAP must include an analysis of areas where the firm is deficient in the utilization of minority groups and women. The primary focus of any AAP is on goals and timetables.

QUESTIONS FOR REVIEW

1. Describe the components of the basic recruiting process.
2. What are some of the actions that could be taken prior to engaging in recruitment?
3. List and discuss the various external and internal factors that could affect the recruitment process.
4. What is meant by the term internal recruitment? Describe the advantages and disadvantages of internal recruitment.
5. Describe the methods often used in internal recruitment. Briefly define each.
6. Discuss the rationale for an external recruitment program.
7. Distinguish between sources and methods of external recruitment. Identify various sources and methods of external recruitment.
8. Distinguish between an executive search firm and an employment agency.
9. How is adverse impact computed? Give an example.
10. What situations can occur that would cause a firm to have an affirmative action program?
11. How can a firm improve its recruiting efforts under the law?

TERMS FOR REVIEW

Recruitment
Employee requisition
Promotion from within
Job posting
Job bidding
Advertising

Employment agencies
Special events
Internships
Executive search firms
Adverse impact
Affirmative action program (AAP)

Incident 1

From the president on down, the management at Epler Manufacturing Company in Greenfield, Wisconsin, is committed to equal employment opportunity. According to Robert Key, the personnel manager, the commitment goes much deeper than posting the usual placards and filing an "affirmative action program" with the federal government. Still, the percentage of black employees at Epler is only 7 percent, while the surrounding community is 22 percent black.

Epler pays high wages and has a good training program. The main need is for machine operator trainees, who require training on Epler's specialized machines. The machines are not difficult to operate and there is no educational requirement for the jobs.

Robert was thinking of the problem of recruiting qualified blacks when Betty Alexander walked into his office, "Got a minute?" said Betty, "I need to talk to you about the recruiting trip to Michigan State next week." "Sure," said Robert, "but, first I need your advice about something. How can we get more qualified black people to apply for work here. We are running ads on WBEZ along with the classified ads in the *Tribune*. I think I've had you and John make recruiting trips to every community college within 200 miles. We've encouraged employee referral, too, and I still think that's the most reliable source of new workers we have. But we just aren't getting any black applicants."

QUESTIONS

1. What is the basic problem associated with the low employment rate for blacks at Epler Manufacturing Company?
2. What do you believe would be the most effective way for Epler to recruit blacks?

Incident 2

Five years ago when Bobby Bret joined Crystal Productions as a junior accountant, he felt that he was on his way up. He had just graduated from college with a B+ average and was well-liked both by his peers and by the faculty. He had been an officer in several student organizations. Bobby had shown a natural ability to get along with people as well as to get things done. He remembered what Roger Friedman, the controller at Crystal, had told him when he was hired, "I think you will do well here, Bobby. You've come highly recommended. You are the kind of guy that can expect to move right on up the ladder."

Bobby felt that he had done a good job at Crystal and everybody seemed to like him. In addition, his performance appraisals had been excellent. However, after five years he was still a junior accountant. He had applied for two senior accountant positions that had come open, but they were both filled by people hired from outside the firm. When the accounting supervisor's job came open two years ago, Bobby had not applied. He was surprised when his new boss turned out to be a hot shot graduate of State University whose only experience was three years with a "Big Eight" accounting firm. Bobby had hoped that Ron Greene, a senior accountant he particularly respected, would get the job.

On the fifth anniversary of his employment at Crystal, Bobby decided it was time to do something. He made an appointment with the controller. At that meeting Bobby explained to Mr. Friedman that he had worked hard to obtain a promotion and shared his frustration about having stayed in the same job for so long. "Well," said Mr. Friedman, "you don't think that you were all that much better qualified than the people that we have hired, do you?" "No," said Bobby, "but, I think I could have handled the senior accountant job. Of course, the people you have hired are doing a great job too." The controller responded, "We just look at the qualifications of all of the applicants for each job and, considering everything, try to make a reasonable decision."

QUESTIONS

1. Explain the impact of a promotion from within policy on outside recruitment.
2. Do you believe that Bobby has a legitimate complaint? Explain.

REFERENCES

Arvey, Richard D. *Fairness in Selecting Employees.* Reading, Mass.: Addison-Wesley, 1979.

Baier, L. O. "Job Searching and the Advertising Dilemma." *Personnel Administrator* 29 (April 1984): 22–24.

Baldwin, Wren. "I am a Professional Temp. . . ." *Personnel Journal* 64 (October 1985): 32–39.

Bjerregaard, Wayne J. and Gold, Mark E. "Employment Agencies and Executive Recruiters: A Practical Approach." *Personnel Administrator* 26 (May 1981): 127–135.

Bredwell, Jo. "The Use of Broadcast Advertising for Recruitment." *Personnel Administrator* 26 (February 1981): 45–49.

Britt, Louis P. III. "Affirmative Action: Is There Life After Stotts?" *Personnel Journal* 29 (September 1984): 96–100.

Byrne, John A. "Punch Me Up a Future." *Forbes* 134 (October 22, 1984): 216–220.

Cronin, Richard J. "Executive Recruiters: Are They Necessary?" *Personnel Administrator* 26 (February 1981): 31–34.

Dennis, Donn L. "Evaluating Corporate Recruitment Efforts." *Personnel Administrator* 30 (January 1985): 21–26.

"Employee Leasing." *Newsweek,* May 14, 1984, p. 55.

Fader, Shirley Sloan. "Fielding Tough Questions." *Working Woman* (October 1984): 64–68.

Feuer, Dale. "Adverse Impact: Can Your Hiring System Pass the Test?" *Training* 22 (March 1985): 111–112.

Foxmoon, Loretta D. and Polsky, Walter L. "Recruitment on a Budget." *Personnel Journal* 64 (September 1985): 26–28.

Garcia, J. Robert. "Job Posting for Professional Staff." *Personnel Journal* (March 1981): 189.

Gest, Ted. "Why Drive on Job Bias Is Still Going Strong." *U.S. News & World Report* 98 (June 17, 1985): 67–68.

Halcrow, Allan. "Anatomy of a Recruitment Ad." *Personnel Journal* 64 (August 1985): 64–65.

Hansen, Thomas J. "Recruitment." *Personnel Journal* 64 (June 1985): 114–121.

Hutton, Thomas J. "Recruiting the Entrepreneurial Executive." *Personnel Journal* 30 (January 1985): 35–41.

Huxtable, Fulton L. "Executive Hiring Deserves More Than Spare-Time Treatment." *Personnel Administrator* 27 (March 1982): 35–38.

Ingber, Dina. "Omigod, I've Hired a Turkey: How to Pick Winners and Avoid Personnel Disasters." *Success* (June 1985): 22–29.

Jansonius, John V. "Use and Misuse of Employee Leasing." *Labor Law Journal* (January 1985): 35–41.

Kelley, Robert E. "The Gold-Collar Worker." *Success* (June 1985): 38–41.

Kenney, Robert M. "The Open House Complements Recruitment Strategies." *Personnel Administrator* 27 (March 1982): 27–32.

Ledvinka, James. *Federal Regulation of Personnel and Human Resource Management.* Boston: Kent, 1982.

Lorber, Lawrence Z. "Employers Should Not Take Precipitous Action in Affirmative Action Cases." *Personnel Journal* 29 (September 1984): 101–102.

Lubliner, Murray J. "Developing Recruiting Literature That Pays Off." *Personnel Administrator* 26 (February 1981): 51–54.

Magnus, Margaret. "Recruitment Ads at Work." *Personnel Journal* 64 (August 1985): 42–63.

Mangum, Stephen L. "Recruitment and Job Search: The Recruitment Tactics of Employers." *Personnel Administrator* 27 (June 1982): 96–102.

Marr, Richard and Schneider, Joseph. "Self-Assessment Test for the 1978 Uniform Guidelines on Employee Selection Procedures."

Personnel Administrator 26 (May 1981): 103–108.

McCreary, Charles. "Recruitment: Don't Assume Anything about Executive Search Firms." *Personnel Journal* 64 (October 1985): 92–94.

McCulloch, Kenneth J. *Selecting Employees Safely Under the Law*. Englewood Cliffs, NJ: Prentice-Hall, 1981.

McKendrick, J. "The Employee as Entrepreneur." *Management World* 14 (January 1985): 12–13.

Myers, D. C. and Fine, S. A. "Development of a Methodology to Obtain and Assess Applicant Experiences for Employment." *Public Personnel Management* 14 (Spring 1985): 51–64.

Nemei, Margaret McClure. "Recruitment Advertising — It's More Than Just 'Help Wanted'." *Personnel Administrator* 26 (February 1981): 57–60.

———. "Personnel: Hiring Recovery Maintains Life." *Industry Week* 223 (October 1984): 33 + .

Powell, G. N. "Effects of Job Attributes and Recruiting Practices on Applicant Decisions: A Comparison." *Personnel Psychology* 37 (Winter 1984): 721–732.

A Professional and Legal Analysis of the Uniform Guidelines on Employee Selection Procedures. Day, Virgil B., Erwin, Frank, and Koral, Alan M. (eds.). Berea, Ohio: The American Society for Personnel Administration, 1981.

Rohan, Thomas M. "Loaded Questions . . . Help to Hire the Right People." *Industry Week* 224 (January 21, 1985): 43–44.

Schweitzer, Nancy J. and Deely, John. "Interviewing the Disabled Job Applicant." *Personnel Journal* (March 1982): 205–209.

———. "Sexual Harassment." *Supervision* 46 (August 1984): 20.

Skeegan, Sam. "Six Steps to Hiring Success." *Management World* 14 (May 1985): 11–13.

Soothill, Keith. "The Extent of Risk in Employing Ex-Prisoners." *Personnel Management* 13 (April 1981): 35–37 + .

Stacy, Donald R. "A Case Against Extending the Adverse Impact Doctrine to ADEA." *Employee Relations Law Journal* 10 (Winter 1984–85): 437–455.

———. "Star Tracks." *Forbes* 134 (October 8, 1984): 228.

Stoops, Rick. "Recruitment." *Personnel Journal* 60(10) (October 1981): 768–769.

———. "Recruitment: The Supply and Demand of College Recruiting." *Personnel Journal* 64 (April 1985): 84, 86.

Wallrapp, Gary G. "Job Posting for Nonexempt Employees: A Sample Program." *Personnel Journal* (October 1981): 796–798.

Webb, Susan L. "Sexual Harassment: Court Costs Rise for a Persistent Problem." *Management Review* (December 1984): 25–28.

CHAPTER OBJECTIVES

1. Explain how environmental factors affect the selection process.
2. Describe the importance of the preliminary interview and the application blank to the selection process.
3. State the role of tests in the selection process.
4. Explain the importance of interviewing in the selection process.
5. State why reference checks and background investigations are conducted.
6. Describe the factors related to the use of physical examinations and explain the factors related to acceptance or rejection of job applicants.

Chapter 7

SELECTION

Judy Thompson, the data processing manager for Ampex Manufacturing, called her friend, Bill Alexander in Personnel, to ask a favor. "Bill, I have a friend I'd like you to consider for the new sales manager's position. I really like the fellow and would appreciate anything you could do." "That's fine, Judy. Send me his resume and we'll look it over." A week later Bill called Judy with some bad news. "Judy, there's just no match between your friend's qualifications and our company's needs. After looking at the requirements of the new position and comparing them with your friend's background and experience, I'm certain that it would be a very poor match. It would be like putting you in charge of the production department where you've had no experience."

Jack Johnson, personnel manager for Zoomer Electronics, was speaking to the production manager, Phillip Lewis, regarding who should be hired to fill a newly created position. Jack started the conversation by saying, "Of all the applicants, Betty Jones scored highest on the tests. Her previous work experience is right in line with our needs, and her references check out great. What do you think, Phillip?" Phillip replied, "I don't know. We've never had a woman in that position, and I don't know if she could handle the job. It's a demanding one and you know that women don't always react well under pressure." Jack immediately interrupted Phillip by saying, "You should have a better reason than that if you reject Ms. Jones. We're already under pressure because we don't employ enough women. I hope that you'll reevaluate your thinking."

When Bobby Edwards applied for a job as an engineer with More Oil Company, he used Frank Edee as one of his references. Because More Oil's policy required that all references be checked prior to making a selection decision, a personnel specialist, Janet Adams, called Mr. Edee about Bobby's qualifications. After hearing the purpose of her call, Frank said, "You bet I know that worthless character. He worked for me for a time and was always coming in late and making some excuse to leave early. Still owes me $100. Can't believe he put my name down as a reference. He must have thought you didn't check references." Janet thanked Frank and completed her report, thinking, "We're going to have to check some more on Bobby before he's employed."

198

**Part Two
Human
Resource
Planning,
Recruitment,
and Selection**

When Bill Alexander evaluated Judy Thompson's friend against the job description, there was no way he could justify selecting Judy's buddy for the position. Phillip Lewis is resisting hiring a woman to fill a position, an action that has serious legal implications. If Bobby Edwards is rejected, it may occur to him that many firms do conduct reference checks on prospective employees. These examples depict only a few aspects of the tasks that need to be accomplished in the selection process. The recruitment process encourages individuals to seek employment opportunities with the firm. The purpose of the selection process is to identify the best qualified workers who apply.

THE SELECTION PROCESS

Selection is *the process of choosing from a group of applicants those individuals best suited for a particular position.* As you might expect, a firm's recruitment efforts exert a significant impact on the efficiency of the selection process. The organization may be forced to employ marginally acceptable workers if there are only a few applicants.

The effectiveness of the selection process can significantly affect, and is also affected by, the other functional areas of Personnel. For instance, if the selection process only provides the firm with marginally qualified workers, the organization may have to develop an extensive training program. If the compensation package is inferior to those provided by the firm's competition, it may be difficult to attract the best qualified applicants.

A generalized selection model is provided in Figure 7–1. The selection process typically begins with the preliminary interview where obviously unqualified candidates are rejected. Next, applicants complete the firm's application blank, then progress through a series of selection tests. This is followed by the employment interview and the reference and background checks. When the selection decision has been made, the prospective employee is given a company physical examination. Naturally, there continue to be external and internal factors that have an impact on the selection process.

ENVIRONMENTAL FACTORS AFFECTING THE SELECTION PROCESS

The selection process would be greatly simplified if a standardized screening process could be developed that would never change. However, deviations from this precise sequence are often made to conform to the needs of a particular situation. As one personnel manager expressed it, "The only thing certain is that exceptions will be made."

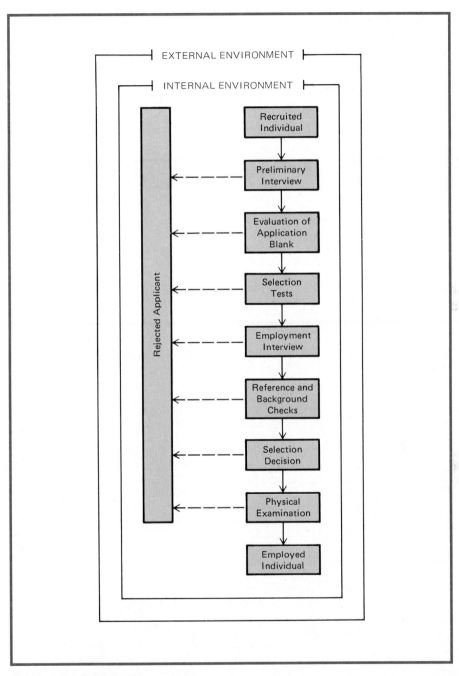

Figure 7–1. The selection process.

200

**Part Two
Human
Resource
Planning,
Recruitment,
and Selection**

LEGAL CONSIDERATIONS

As we described in chapter 3, legislation, Executive Orders, and court decisions have had a major impact on human resource management. However, merely having knowledge of legal facts affecting selection is often insufficient. Table 7–1 identifies selection criteria that obviously should not be used. It also identifies selection standards that should be avoided because of their discriminatory potential.

Table 7–1. Hiring criteria and standards to avoid

Gender

Hiring persons based on whether they are men or women is unlawful. The only exception is where sex is a bona fide occupational qualification (BFOQ). However, the use of BFOQs has been narrowly interpreted by EEOC and the courts. The specification of a man versus a woman must be made in view of whether gender is absolutely job related. For example, if the job in question is for an attendant for a women's restroom, gender can legitimately be specified.

Presuming that a particular job is physically too demanding for a woman to perform is also ill-advised. Instead, women applicants must be given the opportunity to prove that they can perform the job. For example, if a job requires frequent lifting of a fifty-pound object, an employer may require applicants to demonstrate that they—both men and women—can regularly lift the required weight.

National origin

Information regarding an applicant's national origin should not be sought. In addition, other data that might be used to determine national origin should not be requested. Questions regarding an applicant's place of birth and the place of birth of parents, grandparents, or spouse fall into this category.

Marital status

This is a difficult selection standard to defend and should be avoided. Although asking marital status is not by itself illegal under federal law, the standard has often been applied differently to women than to men.

Physical handicap

The key factor in determining whether an applicant's physical handicap should be used in the selection decision is job relatedness. This standard applies to those employers with federal contracts of $2500 or more and in the states that have passed nondiscrimination laws on behalf of the handicapped.

Religion

Discrimination based on religious beliefs is generally unlawful. The only exception is when the employer is a religious corporation, association, educational institution, or society. Questions regarding the applicant's religious denomination, religious affiliation, church, parish, or religious holidays observed are generally ill-advised. Another form of discrimination occurs when individuals' religious beliefs cause them to be away from work before sundown, on Saturdays, or at other times. When this occurs, these practices should be reasonably accommodated unless undue hardships are imposed on the employer.

Table 7–1. Hiring criteria and standards to avoid (continued)

Race

Race is very rarely a legal employment requirement. Therefore selection decisions must be made without regard to this factor.

Age

Questions asked about an applicant's age or date of birth may be ill-advised in light of the Age Discrimination in Employment Act. However, a firm may ask for age information to comply with the child labor law. For example, the question could be asked, "Are you under the age of 18?" With this exception, an applicant should not be asked his or her age or date of birth. Also, questions about the ages of children, if any, could be potentially discriminatory because a close approximation of the applicant's age often is obtained through knowledge of the ages of the children.

Pregnancy

Discrimination in employment based on pregnancy, childbirth, or complications arising from either is illegal. Questions regarding a woman's family and child-bearing plans should not be asked. Similarly, questions relating to family plans, birth control techniques, and the like may be viewed as discriminatory because they are not also asked of men.

Physical requirements

Specifications that set a minimum height or weight should be used only when these characteristics are necessary for performing a particular job. Women, Hispanics, Asians, and Pacific Islanders are generally shorter and smaller than others. Therefore nonjob-related physical requirements would tend to reject a disproportionate number of individuals in those groups.

Standards relating to the ability to lift a certain amount of weight also should not be used unless they are clearly job related. At times, it may be feasible for the employer to redesign the job to overcome a weight-lifting requirement.

Credit record

An individual's poor credit rating has been found to be an improper standard for rejecting applicants where this has a disproportionate negative effect on protected groups. Members of certain protected groups are more likely to have credit problems than others. Therefore the standard should not be used unless the employer has a business necessity for obtaining this information. Inquiries about charge accounts, credit references, home, or car ownership should not be made unless they are job related.

Background of spouse

Basing employment decisions on the background of a spouse is very difficult, if not impossible, to support. Some employers believe that they need to know what the spouse does for a living in making selection decisions. Merely asking this type of question may be interpreted as sex discrimination. In certain instances, women have been turned down for employment because the employer believed that a woman with a working husband would be denying an unemployed man the opportunity for a job.

202

**Part Two
Human
Resource
Planning,
Recruitment,
and Selection**

Table 7–1. Hiring criteria and standards to avoid (continued)

Care of children

Employers have, at times, denied employment to women who have nonschool-age children. If this standard is imposed on women and not on men, it amounts to sex discrimination. While it may be true that some women find it difficult to work and take care of children at the same time, the same can be said for men. A person should be evaluated on his or her ability to perform a particular job. The U.S. Supreme Court has clearly decided this issue.

Arrest record

In our system of justice, the fact of an arrest is not an indication of guilt. Standards related to arrest records have been found to constitute race or national origin discrimination because the arrest rate for minority group members tends to be higher than that for nonminorities. Therefore this selection criterion can rarely be used as a justification for rejecting applicants from certain minority groups.

Conviction record

Unlike an arrest record, a conviction record is an indication of guilt. Even though some minorities have a greater conviction rate than nonminorities, this standard may be used if it is job related. It would be quite acceptable to reject a job applicant who had been convicted of robbery if the job required handling of large sums of money. On the other hand, it would be difficult to justify rejecting an applicant for a laborer job if that individual had only been convicted for failure to pay alimony.

Work experience requirements

Experience requirements should be reviewed to ensure that they are actually job related. Many protected group members have not been in the work force long enough to gain extensive work experience. Requiring that a person have, for example, ten-years' work experience may tend to eliminate a large proportion of members of protected groups and would be discriminatory if this experience is not actually needed to perform the job.

Garnishment record

As with arrest and conviction records, members of certain minority groups have had their wages garnished more than nonminorities. Therefore, if knowledge of this information cannot be shown to be job related, it should not be used as an employment standard.

Dress and appearance

Employers have the right to establish standards relating to dress and appearance. This is especially true in situations where the applicant is dealing directly with the public. Requiring hair to be a certain length has been found by the courts to be nondiscriminatory except when standards have varied by gender. Care should be taken when rejecting applicants strictly on their appearance. A person's appearance may be related to a special dress and style typical of a protected group. Rejecting a black for wearing afros and dashikis, for example, may appear to be race related.

Table 7–1. Hiring criteria and standards to avoid (continued)

Education requirements

Nonjob-related educational standards should not be used because of their potential for discrimination. A disproportionate number of certain minorities have not graduated from high school or college. Stating that a job requires a college degree when it could be accomplished effectively by a high school graduate can potentially be discriminatory.

Any educational standard may be difficult to defend. Therefore it may be advisable to state such a standard in terms like "High school diploma or equivalent required."

Relatives working for the company (Antinepotism Rule)

Standards established about an applicant's relatives working for the company may be discriminatory if they result in reducing employment opportunities for members of protected groups. Some firms have rules that prohibit hiring the spouse of a current employee. On the surface, this rule appears to affect men and women similarly. In reality, because men have normally been in the work force longer, the rule reduces employment opportunities much more for women. Therefore antinepotism rules should be avoided unless they can be shown to be a business necessity.

SPEED OF DECISION MAKING

The time available to make the selection decision can have a major effect on the selection process. Suppose, for instance, that Bobby Noles, the production foreman for a manufacturing firm, comes to the personnel manager's office and says, "My only quality control inspectors just had a fight and both quit. I can't operate until those positions are filled." Speed becomes a critical factor in this instance, and two interviews, a few phone calls, and a prayer may comprise the entire selection process. On the other hand, selecting a university dean may take an entire year, with considerable attention being devoted to careful study of resumes, intensive reference checking, and hours of interviews. And, still, mistakes are made.

ORGANIZATIONAL HIERARCHY

Different approaches to selection are particularly appropriate when filling positions at different levels in the organization. For instance, consider the differences that would exist in hiring a top level executive as opposed to hiring a person to fill a clerical position. Extensive background checks and interviewing would be conducted to verify the character and capabilities of the applicant for a high level position. However, an applicant for a clerical position would most likely take only a typing test and perhaps have a relatively short employment interview.

204

Part Two
Human
Resource
Planning,
Recruitment,
and Selection

APPLICANT POOL

The number of applicants for a particular job can also affect the selection process. The process can be truly selective only if there are many applicants for a particular position. On the other hand, few applicants with highly demanded skills may be available. The selection process then becomes a matter of choosing whomever is available. Expansion and contraction of the labor market exert considerable influence on availability and thus the selection process.

The number of people hired for a particular job compared to the individuals in the applicant pool is often expressed as a **selection ratio.** The ratio is expressed as follows:

$$\text{Selection ratio} = \frac{\text{Number of individuals hired to fill a particular job}}{\text{Number of available applicants}}$$

A selection ratio of 1.00 would indicate that there is one applicant for each job. It is difficult to have an effective selection process if this situation exists. People who might otherwise be rejected are often hired. The lower the ratio falls below 1.00, the more alternatives the manager has in making a selection decision. For example, a selection ratio of .10 would indicate that there are ten applicants for the position.

TYPE OF ORGANIZATION

The sector of the economy for which individuals are to be employed — private, governmental, or not-for-profit — can also affect the selection process. A business in the private sector is heavily profit-oriented. Prospective employees are screened with regard to how they can help achieve this goal. Consideration of the total individual, including personality factors, is involved in the selection of future employees for this sector.[1]

The government's civil service system typically identifies qualified applicants through competitive examinations. Often, a manager can select only from the top three applicants for a given position. A manager in this sector frequently does not have the prerogative to interview other applicants. On the other hand, individuals who are applying for positions in not-for-profit organizations (such as the Scouts or YMCA or YWCA) confront a different situation. The salary level may not be competitive with private and governmental organizations. Therefore a person who fills one of these positions must not only be qualified but also dedicated toward this type of work.

PROBATIONARY PERIOD

Many firms use a probationary period, which provides for the evaluation of an employee's ability based on performance. This may be either a substitute for or a supplement to the use of tests. The rationale is that if an individual can successfully perform the job during the probationary period, tests may not be needed.

[1]"Why Employers Turn Down Some Job Applicants," *The Office* 85 (May 1977): 151.

Even though a firm may be unionized, a new employee typically is not protected by the union–management agreement until after a certain, probationary period. This period may be a month or longer. During this time, employee termination may occur with little or no justification. When the probationary period is over, it may prove quite difficult to terminate a marginal employee. When a firm has a union, it becomes especially important for the selection process to be efficient in identifying the most productive workers. Once they fall under the union–management agreement, the power of the union must be considered in changing the status of a firm's union member.

PRELIMINARY INTERVIEW

The selection process often begins with an initial screening of applicants to remove individuals who obviously do not fulfill the position requirements. At this stage, a few straightforward questions are asked. For instance, a position may require a degree in petroleum engineering and considerable work experience. If an applicant has no experience and a degree in an unrelated field, any further discussion regarding this particular position will prove useless for both the firm and the applicant.

In addition to eliminating obviously unqualified job applicants quickly, a preliminary interview may produce other positive benefits for the firm. It is likely that the position for which the applicant applied is not the only one available. A skilled interviewer who is up to date regarding other vacancies in the firm may be able to identify prospective employees who could fill other positions. The fact that a person does not qualify for one position does not mean that he or she would not be capable of performing well in another. For instance, the applicant may obviously be unqualified to fill the advertised position of senior programming analyst. But the individual might well be qualified to work as a computer operator. This type of interviewing not only builds goodwill for the firm but also can maximize recruitment and selection efforts.

REVIEW OF APPLICATION BLANKS

The next step in the selection process involves having the prospective employee complete an application blank. The employer evaluates it to see whether there may be a match between the individual and the position. The specific type of information requested on an application blank may vary from firm to firm and even by job types within an organization. Sections of an application typically include name, address, telephone number, physical condition, military service, education, work experience, and specific job qualifications.

An employment application blank must reflect not only the firm's informational needs but also EEO requirements. An excellent illustration of a properly designed application form is provided in Figure 7–2. Potentially

GENERAL ⊗ ELECTRIC

An Equal Opportunity Employer

Application For Employment

It is the policy of the General Electric Company to provide employment, training, compensation, promotion and other conditions of employment based on qualifications, without regard to race, color, religion, national origin, sex, age, veteran status or handicap.

Print
Name _____ _____ _____
          Last   First   Middle

Date of Application _____

Address _____
          Number and Street

_____ _____ _____
          City   State   Zip Code

Telephone _____   Social Security No. _____
            Area Code/Number

Job Interest

Position Desired _____

Wages or Salary Expected $ _____   Per Hr. ☐   Week ☐   Month ☐
                                                    (Please Check One)

Other Positions for Which you are Qualified _____

Date Available for Employment _____

Were you Ever Employed by GE?   Yes ☐   No ☐

If Yes, Where? _____   Dates _____
                                                 From   To

Education and Training

Circle Highest Grade Completed in Each School Category

	Grade School	High School	Tech School	College	Grad School
	1 2 3 4 5 6 7 8	9 10 11 12	1 2	1 2 3 4	1 2 3 4

	Name	Location	Course/Degree	Class Standing
Grade School				
High School				
College				
Graduate School				
Apprentice, Business, Technical, Military or Vocational School				

Other Training or Skills (Factory or Office Machines Operated, Special Courses, Military Training, etc.) _____

Other Job-Related Activities

List professional, trade, business or civic activities and offices held (exclude groups which indicate race, color, religion, sex or national origin). _____

To Be Detached By Employee Relations

Personal Data

Print
Name _____ _____ _____
          Last   First   Middle

Address _____
          Number and Street

_____ _____ _____
          City   State   Zip Code

Telephone _____   Social Security No. _____
            Area Code/Number

Is Your Age: Under 18 ? .... Yes ☐   No ☐
                                                (Please Check One)
               Over 70 ? .... Yes ☐   No ☐
                                                (Please Check One)

Are you a citizen of USA? .... Yes ☐   No ☐
                                                (Please Check One)

If you are not a U.S. Citizen, have you a legal right to remain permanently in the U.S.? ...... Yes ☐   No ☐
                                                (Please Check One)

Military

Were you in the U.S. Armed Forces? ...... Yes ☐   No ☐
                                                (Please Check One)
If yes, what branch? _____

Date Entered _____   Date Discharged _____

Final Rank _____   Type of Discharge _____

Military experience should have been included in Employment History section on Page 2.

Convictions

Have you ever been convicted of a felony? ...... Yes ☐   No ☐
                                                (Please Check One)

Have you been convicted of a misdemeanor committed within the past five years, or were you imprisoned for a misdemeanor which occurred more than five years ago? ...... Yes ☐   No ☐
                                                (Please Check One)

If Yes to either of above questions, please explain fully. **This information will not necessarily bar an applicant from employment.**

_____
_____
_____

Additional Information

State any additional information you feel may be helpful to us in considering your application:

_____
_____

Figure 7–2. An employment application. Source: General Electric Company.

Employment History

Please read carefully before starting. List all employment starting with the **present** or **most recent** employer. Account for all periods, including unemployment and **service with the Armed Forces**. Also include relevant voluntary and/or part-time work experience. Use additional sheet if necessary.

Employer	Dates		Hourly Rate/Salary	
	From	Month Year	Starting $	per
Address	To	Month Year	Final $	per
Job Title	Describe Major Duties			
Department				
Supervisor	Reason For Leaving			

Employer	Dates		Hourly Rate/Salary	
	From	Month Year	Starting $	per
Address	To	Month Year	Final $	per
Job Title	Describe Major Duties			
Department				
Supervisor	Reason For Leaving			

Employer	Dates		Hourly Rate/Salary	
	From	Month Year	Starting $	per
Address	To	Month Year	Final $	per
Job Title	Describe Major Duties			
Department				
Supervisor	Reason For Leaving			

Employer	Dates		Hourly Rate/Salary	
	From	Month Year	Starting $	per
Address	To	Month Year	Final $	per
Job Title	Describe Major Duties			
Department				
Supervisor	Reason For Leaving			

Interviewer's Comments:

Interviewed By: _____ Date: _____

Continue on Next Page

Affirmative Action

Special Employment Notice To Disabled Veterans, Vietnam Era Veterans And Individuals With Physical Or Mental Handicaps:

Government contractors are subject to Section 402 of the Vietnam Era Veterans Readjustment Act of 1974 which requires that they take affirmative action to employ and advance in employment qualified disabled veterans and veterans of the Vietnam Era (i.e., served more than 180 days between August 5, 1964 and May 7, 1975), and Section 503 of the Rehabilitation Act of 1973, as amended, which requires government contractors to take affirmative action to employ and advance in employment qualified handicapped individuals.

Please Check Below If You Are A:

☐ Vietnam Era Veteran

☐ Disabled Veteran

☐ Handicapped Individual

And wish to be considered under our Affirmative Action Program(s) **Submission of this information is voluntary.**

Please read this carefully before signing:

Employee Release and Privacy Statement

I understand that the General Electric Company requires certain information about me to evaluate my qualifications for employment and to conduct its business if I become an employee. Therefore, I authorize the Company to investigate my past employment, educational credentials and other employment-related activities. I agree to cooperate in such investigations, and release those parties supplying such information to the Company from all liability or responsibility with respect to information supplied.

I agree that the Company may use the information it obtains concerning me in the conduct of its business. I understand that such use may include disclosure outside the Company in those cases where its agents and contractors need such information to perform their functions, where the Company's legal interests and/or obligations are involved, or where there is a medical emergency involving me. I understand, however, that the Company intends to protect the confidentiality of personal information it obtains concerning me. Consequently, personal information in Company record-keeping systems, other than the fact and location of past or present Company employment, the dates of employment, or the job name or description of general duties, will not otherwise be disclosed outside the Company with a personal identifier without my consent. Further, the Company will require its agents and contractors to safeguard personal information disclosed to them by the Company.

I understand that any employment with the Company would not be for any fixed period of time and that, if employed, I may resign at any time for any reason or the Company may terminate my employment at any time for any reason in the absence of a specific written agreement to the contrary.

I understand that any false answers or statements made by me on this application or any supplement thereto or in connection with the above-mentioned investigations will be sufficient grounds for immediate discharge, if I am employed.

Applicant's Signature: _____   Date: _____

208

Part Two
Human
Resource
Planning,
Recruitment,
and Selection

discriminatory questions such as sex, race, age, and number of children living at home have been eliminated from the form.

The information contained in a completed application blank is compared to the job description to determine whether a potential match exists between the firm and the applicant. As you might expect, this is often a difficult task. Applicants may attempt to present themselves in a positive light. Also, it is difficult to compare past duties and responsibilities with those needed for the job the applicant is seeking. A person with the title of "manager" in one firm may actually perform few managerial tasks, whereas a person with the same title in another firm may have a great deal of managerial experience.

Over the years considerable effort has been devoted to using application blank data to assist in differentiating between individuals who will be successful and those who will be less successful. Research during the past fifty years has suggested that the application blank can be a valuable predictive device in selection for certain types of positions. Personal factors such as number of dependents, hobbies (if not related to sex, race, religion, national origin, or age), years of education, and work experience have been found to be predictive of length of service and success on the job.[2] One large firm found that class standing was the primary factor related to the successful performance of its managerial jobs. Neither prestige of the university nor extracurricular activities was found to be significant in job success in this particular firm.

One technique for identifying factors that differentiate between successful and less successful employees is the **Weighted Application Blank (WAB)**. The WAB is *an approach that attempts to identify factors on the application blank that differentiate between such criteria variables as long- and short-term employees, productive and less productive employees, and satisfied and less satisfied employees.* You can see one variable, *years on the last job,* in Figure 7–3. The percentage difference between short- and long-term workers is first computed. Then a weight is assigned, based on the percentage difference.[3] After the weights for all variables on the application blank have been computed, applicants can be screened on the basis of the point total they receive on the WAB. Using the WAB, applicants with the highest point total are considered to have the highest potential for success.

At times, the WAB has proven to be quite accurate. Yet, in spite of the WAB's ability to determine which personal history factors of job applicants are important for predicting tenure and job success, the overwhelming majority of U.S. firms continue to use traditional application blanks.[4] Also,

---

[2]C. Harold Stone and Floyd L. Ruch, "Selection, Interviewing and Testing," in *ASPA Handbook of Personnel and Industrial Relations: Staffing Policies and Strategies.* Washington, D.C., The Bureau of National Affairs, 1974, pp. 4–131.

[3]Stanley R. Novack, "Developing an Effective Application Blank," *Personnel Journal* (May 1970): 422.

[4]Daniel G. Lawrence, Barbara L. Salsburg, John G. Dawson, and Zachary D. Fashman, "Design and Use of Weighted Application Blanks," *Personnel Administrator* 27 (March 1982): 47.

Item	Percentage Responding		Difference	Weight
	Short-term	Long-term		
Years on the Last Job				
No response	4	12	+ 8	0
Less than 1	50	0	−50	−5
1–1 1/2	7	35	+28	+2
1 1/2–2 1/2	37	12	−25	−2
2 1/2–3	0	6	+ 6	0
More than 3	2	35	+33	+3

Figure 7–3. An example of a weighted application blank question. Source: Stanley R. Novack, "Developing an Effective Application Blank." Reprinted with permission, *Personnel Journal*, copyright May 1970, p. 422.

in other instances, the WAB's benefits have been marginal. Because the WAB approach has produced some unsatisfactory results, many personnel researchers have turned to other quantitative techniques for evaluating application form data, such as regression analysis and discriminant analysis (discussed in chapter 19).

ADMINISTRATION OF SELECTION TESTS

Selection tests are often used to assist in assessing an applicant's qualifications and potential for success with the organization. The popularity of selection tests declined sharply following enactment of the Civil Rights Act and subsequent court decisions. For instance, in *Griggs, et al.* v. *Duke Power Company*, the U.S. Supreme Court ruled that preemployment requirements, including tests, must be related to job performance. In *Albermarle Paper* v. *Moody*, the Supreme Court ruled that any test used in the selection process or in promotion decisions must be validated if it is found that its use had an adverse impact on members of protected groups. For a selection test to be considered nondiscriminatory, it must conform to the *Uniform Guidelines*. The general standard is that if the use of a test results in an adverse impact on a protected group, the employer will be required to show that it is job related; that is, the employer must validate the test.

By curtailing test usage, some employers apparently felt that they would be immune from legal requirements for valid instruments. It is quite clear, however, that all the tools used in making selection and other employment decisions are subject to the same validity requirements. While many individuals distrust tests, they may well be the most valid instrument available. Recognition of this — and increased awareness of the interview's

Robert E. Edwards,
AEP
Senior Vice President,
Drake Beam Morin, Inc.

Bob Edwards is presently a Senior Vice President in the Dallas office of Drake Beam Morin, Inc. He has full responsibility for the management of the office and for the development and delivery of consulting services. Prior to choosing his present position in 1984, Edwards held a key human resource management position in the life insurance operations of Tenneco, Inc. Previous business affiliations included a national retailer, a bank, and a manufacturer of sports clothing.

Edwards's first job was as a caddie at the Ohio State University golf course at age eleven. He then worked at a variety of jobs, such as bundle boy in a textile mill, bank clerk, warehouseman, and newspaper route salesman. Because of his father's failing health and the economic hardships of a depressed era, Bob frequently moved with his family to areas that offered better economic opportunities. In order to boost family income and obtain some financial independence, he found jobs in each new location.

He reentered college after serving a four-year military commitment in the U.S. Air Force, where he was trained as an airborne communications specialist and as a fighter pilot. He completed his undergraduate degree while working a part-time job in the credit department of a large retailer, where he became involved with the extension of credit and repossession of unpaid-for goods, which was one of the few tasks he disliked.

His breadth of work experience at an early age had given him an understanding of jobs, people, and organizations. This knowledge proved invaluable as his career progressed.

Edwards joined Southwestern Life Insurance Company in 1957, after graduating from college with a degree in personnel and industrial relations. Subsequently, he earned an M.S. degree in communications and industrial psychology. Although he began his professional career in a general management training program, he soon accepted an opportunity to head up a major staff function. He was transferred to the personnel department in 1962. In 1965, he was promoted to assistant personnel manager and in 1969 to personnel director with responsibility for two life insurance companies, a real estate development company, and a mutual fund company. In 1971, he was promoted to vice president for personnel for

Southwestern Life Corporation, with full accountability for contributing to the profitability of the company through human resource leadership.

When asked why he left sales work, Edwards replies simply, "I haven't." He explains, "A good personnel executive must sell — he or she must have all the sales tools to deliver." To reinforce this point, he tells a story about two of his top assistants who left Personnel to become Southwestern sales representatives. In their first year, both individuals received their company's top sales award.

Edwards says, "As a top personnel executive, you view the organization as much like the chief executive as any other person. In top management you don't miss a corner of it. You are in a unique position to shape the organization because you deal with both its people and its structure in a primary way. This challenge — if met — results in a tremendous amount of intrinsic satisfaction."

He believes that knowledge gained from continuing academic curiosity and a searching examination of company operations determine the quality of the human resource department's contribution to the success of the company. He suggests that managers should strive for an organizational climate that motivates individuals to perform to the best of their abilities. In explaining how this can be accomplished, he identifies one of the major areas, saying, "Training and development should be on a continuous basis. This permits employees to know that we care about them and that we are vitally concerned about their performance and mobility within that company."

Currently, Edwards is a member of the American Society for Personnel Administration, Dallas Personnel Association, American Management Association, and Life Office Management Association. He is a past executive director of the North Texas Personnel Conference and past president of the Dallas Personnel Association. He has served as chairman of the National Chapter Awards Committee, district director of the American Society for Personnel Administration, and as national chairman of the Personnel Accreditation Institute Management Practices Committee. He has also served as a member of the Executive Committee and Secretary of PAI. He has earned the SPHR designation and an FLMA (fellowship in the Life Office Management Association) with a specialization in personnel administration.

212

**Part Two
Human
Resource
Planning,
Recruitment,
and Selection**

vulnerability — has recently led to a resurgence of test usage in the selection process.[5]

Evidence suggests that tests are more widespread in the public sector than in the private sector, that medium and large companies are more likely than small companies to use tests, and that larger firms are more likely to have trained specialists to run their testing programs.[6] A survey of companies that use selection tests revealed that more than 80 percent use them for filling office positions, 20 percent for filling production positions, and only 10 percent for filling sales and service positions.[7]

ADVANTAGES OF SELECTION TESTS

Selection tests used in the overall selection process are valuable because they help the employer make better selection decisions. One example of the contribution of effective selection tests to productivity is provided by the Philadelphia Police Department. Labor savings in this 5000-member organization stemming from the use of cognitive ability tests to select officers has been estimated to be $18 million for each year's hires.[8]

Another study, using a computer programming test as an example, suggested that if all 18,498 programmers employed by the federal government had been selected by the use of a specific test, the productivity gain would have been $1.2 billion. If use of this procedure were to include all programmers employed in the public and private sectors, the productivity gain would have been $10.78 billion.[9] Remember that this increase is for computer programmers only!

DISADVANTAGES OF SELECTION TESTS

Individual performance on jobs is related primarily to two factors: ability to do the job and motivation. Selection tests may accurately predict an applicant's ability to perform the job but be less successful in indicating the extent to which an individual will want to perform it. For one reason or another, many employees with high potential never seem to reach it. The factors related to success on the job are so numerous and complex that selection may always be more of an art than a science.

---

[5]"Employee Selection Tests: Upping the Odds for Success," *Personnel* 57 (November/December 1980): 48.

[6]"Ability Tests: They Can Provide Useful Information about the Probability of an Applicant's Performing Successfully on the Job," *Across the Board* 19 (July/August 1982): 27.

[7]Ibid.

[8]John E. Hunter and Frank L. Schmidt, "Ability Tests: Economic Benefits versus the Issue of Fairness," *Industrial Relations* 21 (Fall 1982): 293.

[9]Frank L. Schmidt, John E. Hunter, Robert C. McKenzie, and Tressie W. Muldrow, "Impact of Valid Selection Procedures on Work-Force Productivity," *Journal of Applied Psychology* 64 (1979): 624.

Another potential problem related primarily to personality tests and interest inventories has to do with the applicant's honesty. There may be a strong motivation for an applicant to respond to questions untruthfully or provide the answers that he or she believes the firm expects. To prevent this occurrence, some tests have built-in lie detection scales.

A problem not unique to tests, but one that is commonly present, is test anxiety. Individuals seeking employment may become quite anxious when confronting another hurdle that might eliminate them from consideration. People vary greatly with regard to anxiety levels. The test administrator's display of a reassuring manner and a well-organized testing operation should serve to reduce the threat. Actually, while a large amount of anxiety is detrimental to test performance, a slight amount is helpful.[10]

The dual problems of hiring unqualified candidates and rejecting qualified candidates will continue. Organizations can minimize such errors through the use of well-developed tests administered by competent professionals. Nevertheless, selection tests rarely, if ever, are perfect predictors. Using even the best test, errors will be made in predicting success. For this reason, tests alone should not be used in the selection process but rather in conjunction with other tools.

CHARACTERISTICS OF PROPERLY DESIGNED SELECTION TESTS

Properly designed selection tests are standardized, objective, based on sound norms, reliable and, of utmost importance, valid. These concepts are discussed next.

Standardization.   **Standardization** refers to *the uniformity of the procedures and conditions related to administering tests.* In order to compare the performance of several applicants on the same test, it is necessary for all of them to take the test under conditions that are as close to identical as possible. For example, the content of instructions provided and the time allowed must be the same, and the physical environment must be similar. If one person takes a test in a noisy room and another takes the exam in a quiet one, differences in test results are likely to occur. Deviations in any of these factors may produce a change in an applicant's performance. While procedures for test administration may be specified by its developers, it is the responsibility of test administrators to ensure standardized conditions.

Objectivity.   **Objectivity** *in testing is achieved when all individuals scoring a given test obtain the same results.* Multiple-choice and true–false tests are said to be objective. Persons either choose the correct answer or they do not. Scoring them is a highly clerical process, which can be accomplished with little or no training. Such tests also lend themselves to machine grading.

[10]Anne Anastasi, *Psychological Testing*, 5th ed. New York: Macmillan, 1982, pp. 36–37.

214

**Part Two
Human
Resource
Planning,
Recruitment,
and Selection**

Norms. Norms provide a frame of reference for comparing applicants' performance with that of other similar individuals. Specifically, **norms** reflect the *distribution of many scores obtained by people similar to the applicants being tested*. The scores will be distributed according to the normal probability curve presented in Figure 7–4. Standard deviations measure the amount of dispersion of the data. A normalized test will have approximately 68.3 percent of the scores with ±1 standard deviation from the mean. Individuals achieving scores in this range would be considered average for the population studied. Individuals achieving scores outside the range of ±2 standard deviations would likely be projected to be highly unsuccessful or highly successful, based on the particular criteria chosen.

When a sufficient number of employees are performing the same or similar work, employers can standardize their own tests. Typically, this is not the case, and national norms for a particular test must be used. When national norms are used, a prospective employee takes the test, the score obtained is compared to national scores, and the significance of the test score is determined.

Figure 7–4. A normal probability curve. Source: John Neter, William Wasserman, and G. A. Whitmore, *Fundamental Statistics for Business and Economics,* 4th ed., Boston: Allyn and Bacon, Inc., 1973, p. 136.

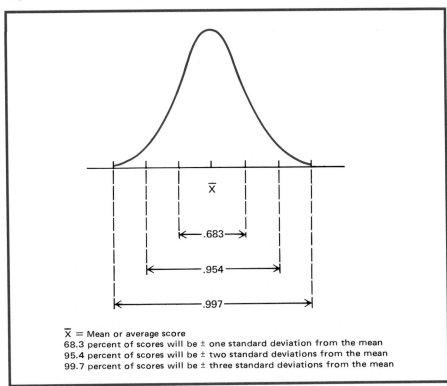

$\overline{X}$ = Mean or average score
68.3 percent of scores will be ± one standard deviation from the mean
95.4 percent of scores will be ± two standard deviations from the mean
99.7 percent of scores will be ± three standard deviations from the mean

Reliability. **Reliability** is *the extent to which a selection test provides consistent results.* Reliability data reveal the degree of confidence that can be placed in a test. Ideally, the reliability coefficient will exceed $+0.801$.[11] If a test has low reliability, its validity as a predictor will also be low. But the existence of reliability does not in itself guarantee validity.[12]

To ensure its usefulness, the test's reliability must be verified. The **test–retest method** is *a method of determining selection test reliability by giving the test twice to the same group of individuals and correlating the two sets of scores.* A perfect positive correlation is $+1.00$. The closer the reliability coefficient is to perfection, the more consistent the results, and therefore the more reliable is the test. Problems with this method for determining reliability include the cost of administering the test twice, employees recalling test questions, and the learning that may take place between test administrations. Similar to the test–retest method, **equivalent forms** involves *a method of testing selection test reliability by correlating the results of tests that are similar but not identical.* While some of the difficulties encountered with the test–retest method are overcome, developing two forms of a test can be expensive. The **split-halves method** *tests reliability by dividing the results of a test into two parts and then correlating the results of the two parts.* The one-time administration of the test has the obvious advantage of minimizing costs. Also, there is no opportunity for learning or recall, which would distort the second score.

Validity. The basic requirement for a selection test is that it be valid. **Validity** is *the extent to which a test measures what it purports to measure.* If a test cannot indicate ability to perform the job, it has no value as a predictor. For this reason, validity has always been a proper concern of organizations that use tests. Because our society is committed to equal employment opportunity, greater emphasis has been given in recent years to the validation process.

Validity is commonly reported as a correlation coefficient, which summarizes the relationship between two variables. For example, these variables may be the score on a selection test and some measure of employee performance. A coefficient of 0 shows no relationship, while coefficients of either $+1.0$ or -1.0 indicate a perfect relationship, one positive and the other negative. Naturally, no test will be 100 percent accurate. Yet organizations strive for the highest feasible coefficient. If a test is designed to predict job performance and validity studies of the test indicate a high correlation coefficient, most prospective employees who score high on the

---

[11]Duane P. Schultz, *Psychology and Industry Today*, 2nd ed. New York: Macmillan, 1978, p. 122.
[12]C. Harold Stone and Floyd L. Ruch, "Selection Interviewing and Testing," in Dale Yoder and Herbert G. Heneman (eds.), *Staffing Policies and Strategies, ASPA Handbook of Personnel and Industrial Relations, Vol. I.* Washington, D.C., The Bureau of National Affairs, 1979, pp. 4–135.

216

**Part Two
Human
Resource
Planning,
Recruitment,
and Selection**

test will probably later prove to be high performers. The ability to select better qualified individuals will help increase the firm's productivity.

Employers are not required to automatically validate their selection tests. Generally speaking, validation is required only when the selection process as a whole results in an adverse impact on any protected group.[13] Validation of selection tests is expensive. However, an organization cannot know whether the test is actually measuring the qualities and abilities being sought without this information.

TYPES OF VALIDATION STUDIES

The *Uniform Guidelines* established three approaches that may be followed to validate selection tests: criterion-related validity, content validity, and construct validity.[14]

CRITERION-RELATED VALIDITY

Criterion-related validity is *determined by comparing the scores on selection tests to some aspect of job performance as determined, for example, by performance appraisal.* Performance measures might include quantity and quality of work, turnover, and absenteeism. A high relationship between the score on the test and job performance suggests that the test is valid.

There are two basic forms of criterion-related validity: concurrent and predictive validity. With **concurrent validity,** *the test scores and the criterion data are obtained at essentially the same time.* For instance, all currently employed machine operators may be given a test. Company records contain current information about each operator's job performance. If the test is able to identify the productive and the less productive workers, it is said to be valid. A potential problem in using this validation procedure results from changes that may have occurred within the work group. For example, the less productive workers may have been fired and the more productive ones may have been promoted out of the group.

Predictive validity involves *administering a test and later obtaining the criterion information.* For instance, a test might be administered to all applicants. However, the results of the test are not used in the selection decision. After employees' performance has been observed, the test results are analyzed to determine whether they distinguish between the successful and less successful employees. Predictive validity is considered a techni-

---

[13]Charles F. Schanie and William L. Holley, "An Interpretive Review of Federal Uniform Guidelines on Employee Selection Procedures," *Personnel Administrator* 25 (June 1980): 45.

[14]Dwight R. Norris and James A. Buford, Jr., "A Content Valid Writing Test: A Case Study," *Personnel Administrator* 25 (January 1980): 40.

cally sound procedure. However, because of the time and cost involved, its use is often not feasible.

CONTENT VALIDITY

Although it is less statistically oriented, many personnel practitioners believe that content validity provides a more sensible approach to validating the selection process. **Content validity** is *a test validation method whereby a person performs certain tasks that are actual samples of the kind of work the job requires or completes a paper-and-pencil test that measures relevant job knowledge.* Thorough job analysis and carefully prepared job descriptions are needed when this form of validation is used.

The classic example of the use of content validity is giving a typing test to an applicant whose primary job would be to type. In *Washington v. Davis,* the Supreme Court gave support to the use of content validity. Its use will likely grow in the future.

CONSTRUCT VALIDITY

Construct validity is *a test validation method to determine whether a test measures certain traits or qualities that have been identified as important in performing the job.* For instance, if the job requires a large amount of persistence, such as in some forms of life insurance sales, a test would be used to measure persistence. However, traits or qualities needed on the job must first be identified through job analysis.

CUT-OFF SCORES

After a test has been shown to be valid, an appropriate cut-off score must be established. A **cut-off score** is *the score below which an applicant will not be selected.* Cut-off scores will vary over time because they are directly related to the selection ratio. The more individuals applying for a job, the higher the cut-off score, and the more selective the firm can be. Cut-off scores should normally be set to reflect a reasonable expectation of acceptable proficiency.

An example of what would likely occur when a validated test is administered to prospective employees is shown in Figure 7–5. The firm's experience indicates that individuals who score 40 and above on the test will be successful. Those who score below 40 will be less successful. Note that test results do not precisely predict performance. A small number of individuals who scored below the cut-off score of 40 proved to be good workers. Also, some applicants scoring above 40 proved to be less successful. However, the test appears to be a good predictor a large portion of the time. It is because of this gray area that test results should serve as only one of several criteria in the selection decision.

218

**Part Two
Human
Resource
Planning,
Recruitment,
and Selection**

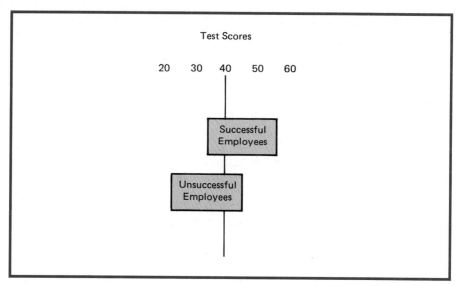

Figure 7–5. An example of the results of a validated test.

The setting of a cut-off score to determine who will be screened out may have adverse impact. If so, the *Uniform Guidelines* requires an employer to justify the initial cut-off score used.

TYPES OF PSYCHOLOGICAL TESTS

Individuals differ in characteristics related to job performance. These differences, which are measurable, relate to cognitive abilities, psychomotor abilities, job knowledge, interests, and personality. Tests to measure these characteristics are discussed next.[15]

COGNITIVE APTITUDE TESTS

Cognitive aptitude tests are *tests to measure an individual's ability to learn, as well as to perform a job.* This type of test is particularly appropriate for making a selection from a group of inexperienced candidates. Abilities may be broken down into factors most often found to be job related, such as verbal, numerical, perceptual speed, spatial, and reasoning.

PSYCHOMOTOR ABILITIES TESTS

Psychomotor abilities tests *measure strength, coordination, and dexterity.* The development of tests to determine these abilities has been accelerated

[15]Stone and Ruch, "Selection Interviewing and Testing," pp. 4-138—4-142.

by miniaturization in assembly operations. Much of this work is so delicate that magnifying lenses must be used, and the psychomotor abilities required to perform the tasks are critical. While standardized tests are not available to cover all of these abilities, it is feasible to measure those that are involved in many routine production jobs and some office jobs. **Finger dexterity** is *the ability to make precise, coordinated finger movements, such as those performed by an electronics assembler or a watchmaker.* **Manual dexterity** involves *the coordinated movements of both hands and arms, such as those required by large assembly jobs.* **Wrist–finger speed** is *the ability to make rapid wrist and finger movements,* such as those required in inspector-packers and assembly operations jobs. **Aiming** is *the ability to move the hands quickly and accurately from one spot to another,* which is important in jobs such as electronic parts assembly.

JOB KNOWLEDGE TESTS

Job knowledge tests are *tests designed to measure a candidate's knowledge of the duties of the position for which he or she is applying.* Such tests are commercially available, but they may be specifically designed for any job, based on the data derived from job analysis. While such tests frequently involve written responses, they may be administered orally. Regardless of the form, they often are comprised of key questions that serve to distinguish experienced, skilled workers from those with less experience or skill.

When jobs within firms are unique to the organization, job knowledge tests must be specifically designed for that job, based on job analysis information. When in-house specialists are not available, consultants are often utilized.

Job knowledge tests are by definition job related. However, they do present some problems. For example, heavy equipment may not easily be moved to a testing site. Untrained applicants may injure themselves or damage expensive equipment. In addition, the economy of group testing is not always possible.

WORK-SAMPLE TESTS

Work sample tests *identify a task or set of tasks that are representative of the job and use these tasks for selection testing.*[16] The evidence to date about these tests is that they can produce high predictive validities, reduce adverse impact, and be more acceptable to applicants.[17]

[16]I. T. Robertson and R. M. Mindel, "A Study of Trainability Testing," *Journal of Occupational Psychology* 53 (June 1980): 131.

[17]I. T. Robertson and R. S. Kandola, "Work Sample Tests: Validity, Adverse Impact, and Applicant Reaction," *Journal of Occupational Psychology* 55 (1982): 180.

220

Part Two
Human
Resource
Planning,
Recruitment,
and Selection

VOCATIONAL INTEREST TESTS

Vocational interest tests are *tests to indicate the occupation in which a person has the greatest interest and is most likely to receive satisfaction.* These tests compare the individual's interest pattern with those of successful employees in a specific job.

While interests appear to be stable over a long period of time and have been related to success in some fields, they must not be confused with aptitude or abilities. Tests for these characteristics should accompany the administration of an interest test. Also, it should be noted that answers to interest test questions can easily be faked. Although interest tests may possibly have some application in employee selection, their primary use has been in counseling and vocational guidance.

PERSONALITY TESTS

As selection tools, personality tests have not been as useful as other types of tests. They are often characterized by low reliability and low validity. Because some personality tests emphasize subjective interpretation, the services of a qualified psychologist are required. Additional research is needed before personality tests can be used with confidence as a selection tool.

THE EMPLOYMENT INTERVIEW

An **employment interview** is defined as *a goal-oriented conversation in which the interviewer and applicant exchange information.* Although the employment interview is but one step in the selection process, it is *the basic* selection tool.[18] It is used by virtually every company in the United States.[19] The employment interview is especially significant because applicants who reach this stage are obviously the most promising candidates.[20] They have survived the preliminary interview, made satisfactory scores on selection tests, and fared well in reference and background checks. At this point, the candidates appear to be qualified, at least on paper. Every seasoned manager knows, however, that appearances can be quite misleading. Additional information is needed to indicate whether the individual is willing to work and can adapt to the particular environment of the organization.[21]

---

[18]Thomas L. Moffatt, *Selection Interviewing for Managers.* New York: Harper & Row, 1979, p. 2.

[19]Gary P. Latham, Lise M. Saari, Elliott D. Pursell, and Michael A. Campion, "The Situational Interview," *Journal of Applied Psychology* 65 (1980): 422.

[20]Richard A. Fear and James F. Ross, *Jobs, Dollars — and EEO: How to Hire More Productive Entry-Level Workers.* New York: McGraw-Hill, 1983, p. 113.

[21]Ibid.

For a number of years following the enactment of the Civil Rights Act, many employers abandoned the use of tests and relied even more heavily on the employment interview as a selection tool. This change in practice was based on the false assumption that legal validity requirements applied only to tests.[22] But the definition of a test in the *Uniform Guidelines* included "physical, education and work experience requirements from informal or casual interviews." Since the interview is clearly a test, it is therefore subject to the same validity requirements as any other step in the selection process, should adverse impact be shown. For the interview, this presents special difficulties. To begin with, few firms are willing to pay the cost of validating interviews. They can be validated only by a long-term follow up — a method that requires collecting much data over a long period of time.[23] Also, for any instrument to be valid, it must be reliable. However, significant evidence indicates that, if two managers in a firm interview the same applicant at different times, the outcomes will differ.[24]

The interview is perhaps more vulnerable to charges of discrimination than any other tool used in the selection process. In a large number of instances, there is little or no documentation of the questions asked or the answers received. There may also be a tendency to ask irrelevant questions in the interview that would never appear on an application blank. But, since an interview is a test, all questions must be job related.

Some interviewers are inclined to ask questions that are not job related but which reflect their personal biases. They probably reason that this practice will go uncriticized because there is no written or verbal record of the interview. Nevertheless, interviewing in this manner is risky and can lead to charges of discrimination. The appendix to this chapter provides a further discussion of potential interviewing problems.

OBJECTIVES OF THE INTERVIEW

Employment interviews have several basic objectives. It is important that at least the following objectives be successfully achieved.

Obtain additional information from the applicant. It is essential that additional information be obtained about the applicant to complement the data provided by other selection tools. The interview is the step in the selection process that permits clarification of certain points, the uncovering

---

[22]James G. Goodale, *The Fine Art of Interviewing.* Englewood Cliffs, N.J.: Prentice-Hall, 1982, p. 41.

[23]Robert L. Decker, "The Employment Interview: Are We Seeing the Demise of Another Management Prerogative?" *Personnel Administrator* 27 (November 1981): 71.

[24]James G. Goodale, "The Neglected Art of Interviewing," *Supervisory Management* 26 (July 1981): 2.

222

**Part Two
Human
Resource
Planning,
Recruitment,
and Selection**

of additional information, and the elaboration of data that is needed to make a sound selection decision.

Provide information regarding the firm.   General information about the job, company policies, its products, and its services should be communicated to the applicant during the interview. If the interviewee is adequately prepared, all of the information will not come as a surprise.

Sell the company.   The employment interview provides an excellent opportunity for selling the company to the applicant. This should be accomplished in a realistic manner, and the organization should not be presented by an interviewer who appears to view the firm through rose-colored glasses. Describing the company as a virtual utopia may well result in a disappointed employee or even an ex-employee.

Make new friends.   The applicant should leave the interview with a positive attitude about the company. Hopefully this attitude will not change regardless of whether a job offer is made. The interview should never serve to make the applicant feel inadequate.

CONTENT OF THE INTERVIEW

The specific content of employment interviews varies greatly by organization and the level of the job concerned. However, the following general topics are frequently included: academic achievement, personal qualities, occupational experience, interpersonal competence, and career orientation.[25] The interviewer should deal only with the information in these categories that represents bona fide occupational qualifications (BFOQ).

Academic achievement.   An employment interviewer might attempt to obtain additional insight into application blank data. At times, the applicant fails to record positive events that could affect employment decisions. The interviewer should attempt to discover any underlying factors related to academic performance. For example, a student who earned only a 2.28/4.0 GPA may turn out to be a very bright individual who, because of financial difficulties, might have worked virtually full time while still participating in a variety of activities. On the other hand, a student who received a 3.8/4.0 GPA may not be a well-rounded individual and may be a weak candidate for many jobs.

Personal qualities.   Personal qualities normally observed during the interview include physical appearance, speaking ability, vocabulary, poise, and assertiveness. Even though the "halo effect" occurs at times, efforts

---

[25]Felix M. Lopez, "The Employment Interview," in Joseph J. Famularo (ed.), *Handbook of Modern Personnel Administration.* New York: McGraw-Hill, 1972, pp. 134–135.

should be made to keep nonjob-related personal qualities from biasing the selection process.[26]

Because of legal ramifications, it would obviously be unwise to permit personal qualities to influence the selection decision unless they were BFOQs. Physical appearance might very well be an occupational qualification if the job being filled were that of an actress who was to portray the early career of Brooke Shields. Speaking ability, vocabulary, and poise may be job-related qualifications if the job is that of a sportscaster. Assertiveness may be required for the successful performance of a credit collector's job.

Occupational experience.   Exploring an individual's occupational experience provides an indication of the applicant's skills, abilities, and willingness to handle assigned responsibilities. Job titles in one organization do not necessarily represent the same job content in another. And good performance in one job does not guarantee that the individual will succeed in another. At the same time, past performance does provide some indication of the employee's ability and willingness to work.

Interpersonal competence.   To a degree an interviewer may observe an applicant's interpersonal competence. However, the interviewer may be witnessing an academy award performance by the candidate displaying an "I like people" nature. For this reason, the interview may need to consist of questions regarding the applicant's interpersonal relationships with family and friends and how he or she behaves in other social and civic situations. The primary cause of failure in performing jobs is not due to the lack of technical ability but rather to shortcomings in interpersonal competence. Even though an individual may be a highly skilled worker, if he or she cannot work well with other employees, the chances for success are diminished.

Career orientation.   Questions about a candidate's career objectives may aid the interviewer in determining the degree to which an applicant's aspirations are realistic. The odds are rather great that a recent college graduate who expects to become a senior vice president within six months will become quickly dissatisfied with the company.

In addition to determining an applicant's career goals, the interviewer should present an honest and accurate description of career prospects in the organization. Deception on this point may prove counterproductive in that the applicant, if employed, may well become dissatisfied later as the truth unfolds. The firm may lose a substantial investment in the form of recruitment, selection, and training.

---

[26]Ray Jeffery, "Taking the Guesswork Out of Selection," *Personnel Management* 9 (October 1977): 40.

224

Part Two
Human
Resource
Planning,
Recruitment,
and Selection

TYPES OF INTERVIEWS

Interviews may be classified by the degree to which they are structured. At one extreme, interviews may be highly structured, and, at the other, they may have virtually no structure. In practice, interviews fall between these extremes, with tendencies toward one or the other. Generally speaking, interview questions should solicit the following types of information from applicants: (1) ability to perform the job; (2) motivation to stay on the job; and (3) adaptability to the job situation.[27]

The Unstructured (Nondirective) Interview. The **unstructured interview** is *an interview where probing, open-ended questions are asked.* This type of interview is comprehensive in nature, and the applicant is encouraged to do much of the talking. The nondirective interview is often more time-consuming than those with more structure, yet some interviewers believe that it is more effective in obtaining significant information. The nature of the nondirective interview requires a highly trained and skillful interviewer who asks open-ended questions such as:

- What do you believe are your primary strengths? Your main weaknesses?
- How will our company benefit by having you as an employee?
- Where do you want to be in this firm five years from now?
- What was your most significant contribution in your last job?

The answers to the questions may not be as important to the interviewer as how the questions are answered and the thought process leading to the response.

The nondirective interview consists of a highly subjective appraisal of the candidate. Research conducted on traditional selection interviews has indicated very low reliability and little or no validity.[28] Various types of errors have contributed to this poor performance (see Appendix).

The Structured (Directive or Patterned) Interview. The **structured interview** is *an interview consisting of a series of job-related questions that are consistently asked of each applicant for a particular job.*[29] Use of structured interviews increases reliability and accuracy by reducing the subjectivity and inconsistency of unstructured (traditional) interviews.[30] The advantages of structure are diminished, however, if the interviewer asks each of the questions in a perfunctory manner. This approach could easily result

---

[27]Barbara Felton and Sue Ries Lamb, "A Model for Systematic Selection Interviewing," *Personnel* 59 (January/February 1982): 43.

[28]Elliott D. Pursell, Michael A. Campion, and Sarah R. Gaylord, "Structured Interviewing: Avoiding Selection Problems," *Personnel Journal* 59 (November 1980): 908.

[29]Ibid.

[30]Herbert G. Heneman, Donald P. Schwab, D. L. Huett, and J. J. Ford, "Interviewer Validity as a Function of Interview Structure, Biographical Data, and Interviewer Order," *Journal of Applied Psychology* 60 (1975): 752.

in an overly formal environment and severely impair the candidate's ability or desire to respond.

A structured job interview typically contains four types of questions.[31] **Situational questions** are *questions that pose a hypothetical job situation to determine what the applicant would do in such a situation.* **Job knowledge questions** are *questions that assess the knowledge required for performing the job, which must be possessed prior to filling the job.* These questions may relate to basic educational skills or complex scientific or managerial skills. **Job-sample simulation questions** are *situations in which an applicant may be required to actually perform a sample task from the job.* When this is not feasible, a simulation of critical job aspects may be utilized. As suggested, these kinds of questions may require physical activity.

The last type of question used in structured interviews deal with worker requirements. **Worker requirements questions** are *questions that seek to determine the applicant's willingness to conform to the requirements of the job.* For example, the applicant may be asked about his or her willingness to perform repetitive work or to relocate. The nature of these questions serves as a realistic job preview and may aid in self-selection.

A properly designed patterned interview will contain only those questions that are job related. An illustration of a patterned interview guide for discussing work experience is provided in Table 7–2. Note that each question is asked for a specific purpose.

METHODS OF INTERVIEWING

Interviews may be conducted in several ways. A majority of employment interviews consist of the applicant meeting with an interviewer in a one-to-one situation. Since the interview itself may represent a highly emotional situation to the applicant, the one-to-one interview is often less threatening.

Unlike a one-to-one interview, a **group interview** is *an interview consisting of several applicants interacting in the presence of one or more company representatives.* This approach, while not mutually exclusive of the other types, may provide useful insights into the candidates' interpersonal competence as they engage in group discussion. The technique is often used because it saves the time of busy professionals and executives.

A **board interview** is *an interview where one candidate is quizzed by several interviewers.* While a thorough examination of the applicant would likely result from this approach, the interviewee's anxiety level is often quite high. L. C. Barry, vice president of industrial relations for Gates Learjet said, "We use a three-person board to screen each applicant, asking a series of questions designed to ferret out the individual's attitudes toward former employers, jobs, etc. Then, a week later, we bring successful applicants and their spouses in for a family night meeting with top management and their

[31]Pursell, Campion, and Gaylord, "Structured Interviewing," p. 909.

226

Part Two
Human
Resource
Planning,
Recruitment,
and Selection

Table 7–2. Portion of a patterned interview guide

Work Experience

Cover:	Look for:
Earliest jobs: part-time, temporary	Relevance of work
Military assignments	Sufficiency of work
Full-time positions	Skill and competence
Ask:	Adaptability
Things done best? Done less well?	Productivity
Things liked best? Liked less well?	Motivation
Major accomplishments? How achieved?	Interpersonal relations
Most difficult problems faced? How handled?	Leadership
Ways most effective with people?	Growth and development
Ways less effective?	
Level of earnings?	
Reasons for changing jobs?	
What learned from work experience?	
What looking for in job? In career?	

Source: Reproduced from *The Interviewer's Manual* by special permission. Copyright © 1980, by Drake Beam Morin, Inc. All rights reserved.

spouses, where we further screen them while discussing the company and employee benefits." Naturally, the amount of time devoted to a board interview will differ depending on the type and level of job.

Most interview sessions are designed to minimize stress on the part of the candidate. The **stress interview** is *a form of interview that intentionally creates anxiety to determine how an applicant will react in certain types of situations.* The stress interview should be attempted only by highly trained and skilled interviewers. Interviewers for some types of sales jobs subject applicants to stress situations in order to determine how they will react under pressure. For instance, on the first interview, everything might progress extremely smoothly. The applicant is led to believe that all he or she has to do is come back for the second interview and the job offer will be made. However, on the second interview, events progress a bit differently. The individual might have to wait in the outer office for a considerable period of time before the interview begins. This tactic allows the candidate's anxiety level to build up. Then the interviewer might begin with a statement such as, "Mr. Noles, I appreciate your interest, but we just don't believe there is any need to continue this interview. Your qualifications just don't appear to match our needs." The purpose of this approach is to see how the applicant will react when confronted with an unexpected situation.

The company has discovered that individuals who are able to turn this situation around will become successful sales representatives.

Another point of view relative to stress interviews relies on evidence that indicates that the stress interview is not only inconsiderate but is also ineffective. Proponents of this view feel that information exchange in a stressful environment is often distorted and misinterpreted. The data obtained, these critics maintain, is not the type of information upon which to base a selection decision.[32] In any event, it seems clear that the stress interview is not appropriate for the majority of situations.

THE INTERVIEWER, INTERVIEW PLANNING, AND THE INTERVIEW PROCESS

The interviewer should possess a pleasant personality, empathy, and the ability to listen and communicate effectively. He or she should have a healthy respect for individuals who are different in terms of personal attributes and backgrounds. It is essential that interviewers be free from stereotyped views concerning the capabilities of women and minorities. Instead, they must be able to recognize the ability and potential possessed by individual candidates. Interviewers should also have a solid knowledge of actual job requirements so that they can properly assess the applicant's qualifications.

In addition, interview planning is essential for conducting effective employment interviews.[33] The physical location of the interview should be both pleasant and private. This type of environment provides for a minimum of interruptions. The interviewer should become familiar with the applicant's record by reviewing data provided by other selection tools.

The interview process should begin with a warm and sincere welcome for the candidate, and rapport should be quickly developed. Since people can often talk most easily about themselves, it is a good practice for the interview to begin in this manner. After this initial ice breaking, the interviewer can proceed to ask relevant, job-related questions. It is important that the interviewer avoid asking leading questions such as, "You didn't do too well in statistics, did you?" Rather, questions should be posed in a manner that permits the applicant some flexibility in answering the question.

When the necessary information has been obtained and the applicant's questions answered, the interview should be brought to a conclusion. At this point, the applicant should be told that he or she will receive notification of the selection decision shortly. In reality this promise is often broken. Unfortunately, if this commitment is not kept, a positive relationship between the applicant and the organization can quickly break down.

[32]Susan Gribben, "A Guide to the Hiring Process," *CA Magazine* 115 (September 1982): 85.
[33]"How Good Is Your Interviewing Style?" *International Management* 32 (December 1977): 56.

228

Part Two
Human
Resource
Planning,
Recruitment,
and Selection

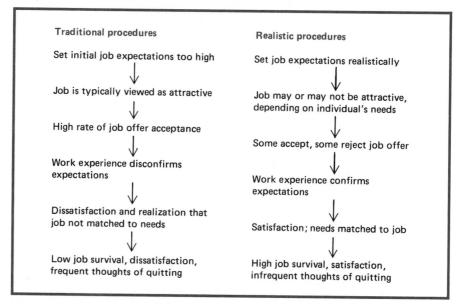

Figure 7–6. Typical consequences of job preview procedures. Source: Reprinted by permission of the publisher, from "Tell It Like It Is at Realistic Job Previews," by John Wanous, *Personnel,* p. 54 July–August 1975, © 1975 AMACOM, a division of American Management Associations, New York. All rights reserved.

REALISTIC JOB PREVIEWS[34]

Many recruits have unrealistic expectations about the prospective job and employer. This inaccurate perception, which may have negative consequences, is often encouraged by firms that present themselves in overly attractive terms. To correct this situation, we suggest that a realistic job preview be given to applicants early in the selection process and definitely before a job offer is made.

A **realistic job preview (RJP)** *conveys job information to the applicant in an unbiased manner, including both positive and negative factors.* This approach assists applicants in developing a more accurate perception of the job and the firm. Research studies suggest that newly hired employees who received RJPs have a greater rate of job survival and higher job satisfaction. At the same time, use of this technique does not reduce the flow of qualified applicants. A comparison of the results of traditional preview procedures as opposed to realistic preview procedures is in Figure 7–6. Note that traditional procedures result in low job survival and dissatisfaction, whereas RJPs overcome these difficulties.

[34]John P. Wanous, "Tell It Like It Is at Realistic Job Previews," in Kendrith M. Rowland, Manual London, Gerald R. Ferris, and Jay L. Sherman (eds.), *Current Issues in Personnel Management.* Boston: Allyn & Bacon, 1980, pp. 41–50.

REFERENCE CHECKS

Information contained in the completed application blank is at times incorrect or colored to present a favorable image of the applicant. **Reference checks** are *means of providing additional insight into the information provided by the applicant and to verify the accuracy of the information provided.* It is likely that if you have ever applied for a job you have had to provide a list of references. Reference checks are normally made by letter or phone, or a combination of the two methods. When reference letters are used, the writer typically describes the nature of the job for which the applicant is being considered. Reference information is typically limited to dates of employment, job title, absentee record, promotions and demotions, compensation, and reasons for termination.[35] As you might expect, there are numerous problems associated with written reference checks.

Since passage of the Federal Privacy Act of 1974, a person who has been employed by the federal government has the legal right to review reference checks that have been made regarding his or her employment unless the individual waives this right. There have been instances where applicants have sued and won court cases when it was proven that the reference was biased. Because of the possible expansion of the Privacy Act, many people are reluctant to provide negative reference information.[36] Often, a firm responding to a written reference check will provide only objective facts, such as duration of employment, title of position when the individual left the firm, and his or her ending salary. Comments regarding the reason for termination and job performance are often not included in a letter.

Another difficulty of a letter of reference is that the job applicant provides the names of his or her references. Applicants will carefully select their references in order to present a favorable image. For instance, it is unlikely that an applicant would choose a reference who would give an unfavorable report. Therefore the majority of references are biased in a positive manner.

Perhaps because of the bias associated with a written reference letter, many firms use the telephone to obtain information about applicants. They reason that a more objective appraisal will result if there is no documentation of the conversation. Still, managers must be careful of the type of questions they ask. However, if the respondent desires to elaborate on a particular topic, the reference checker should certainly encourage further discussion. For instance, the question might be asked, "How long was Bill with your firm? A response such as, "He was here ten years, but we should have fired him years ago," may reveal more information than a written reference. The reference checker should always remember that comments from a reference can be biased.

---

[35]G. Bruce Knecht, "Screening Out Thieves Before They're Hired," *Dun's Business Month* 120 (October 1982): 70.

[36]J. David Jackson and Bruce W. Taylor, "A Scientific Approach to Management Selection," *CA Magazine* 110 (August 1977): 41.

230

**Part Two
Human
Resource
Planning,
Recruitment,
and Selection**

BACKGROUND INVESTIGATION

Although a reference check often provides sufficient information with which to verify certain statements on the application blank, there are many times when it does not. Often it is important to perform a background investigation of the applicant's past employment history. This background investigation may be helpful in determining whether past work experience is related to the qualifications needed for the new position. For instance, job titles are quite deceptive in terms of past work experience. A person with the title of "manager" in one firm may have been only an overpaid clerk, while in another firm a person with the same title may have been in the mainstream of decision making.

Another reason for background investigations is that credential fraud has increased in recent years.[37] It has been found that 7–10 percent of job applicants are not what they present themselves to be.[38] Some applicants are not even who they say they are. Although background checks are expensive, costing approximately $250, properly conducted background investigations can confirm or disprove claims made by job applicants.[39]

POLYGRAPH TESTS

Another means used to verify background information is the polygraph, or lie detector test. One purpose of the polygraph is to confirm or refute the information contained in the application blank. The polygraph measures changes in a person's breathing, blood pressure, and pulse rate. Supposedly, if an individual tells a lie, a detectable change will occur, although, actually, the polygraph can only measure tension and cannot measure honesty.

The person who is administering the polygraph test will typically ask a series of questions that are known to be true and then ask questions relevant to the selection decision. For instance, questions such as, "Is your name Bobby Halmes? Do you live at 1401 Malloy Street? Are you married?" might be followed by the question, "Have you ever stolen anything from your employer?" If there was a major change on the polygraph when a "No" response was given, further probing would be needed. It could indicate that five years ago Bobby took a pencil home and did not return it, or it could mean that the prospective employee stole from his employer on a regular basis.

It has been estimated that 60–70 percent of all firms use polygraph tests when a fiduciary position is involved or when an employee would have access to drugs or consumer items with resale value.[40] Despite wide-

---

[37]Kenneth C. Cooper, "Those 'Qualified' Applicants and Their Phony Credentials," *Administrative Management* 38 (August 1977): 44.

[38]Scott T. Rickard, "Effective Staff Selection," *Personnel Journal* (June 1981): 477.

[39]Ibid.

[40]Donald H. Dunn, Editor, "When a Lie Detector Is Part of the Job Interview," *Business Week*, July 27, 1981, p. 85.

spread use, the polygraph has received considerable criticism from a variety of sources. In fact, twenty states and the District of Columbia prohibit or restrict the use of polygraphs in preemployment screening.[41] However, it continues to be used as a screening device in some organizations.

While statistics are not available, an approach similar to the polygraph may be used by literally thousands of firms. Here, *stress evaluators* are used to assess the responses of applicants while they are being interviewed. They are used without the person's knowledge and supposedly detect when a person is lying. It is obvious that this approach should be subjected to scientific study that specifically addresses the relationship between high stress levels and lying.[42]

THE SELECTION DECISION

After information has been obtained from the preceding steps, the most critical of all of the steps — the actual hiring decision — must be taken. The other stages in the selection process have been used to narrow the number of candidates. The final decision will be made from among the individuals who are still being considered after reference checks, selection tests, background investigations and interview information have been evaluated. The individual with the best overall qualifications may not be hired. Rather, the person whose qualifications most closely conform to the requirements of the open position should be selected.[43]

Personnel has been heavily involved in all phases leading up to the final employment decision. However, the person who normally makes the final selection is the manager who will be responsible for the performance of the new employee.[44] In making this decision, the operating manager may or may not solicit the advice of the personnel manager. The role of Personnel in this process is to provide service and counsel to the operating manager to facilitate the selection decision. The rationale for permitting the supervisor to make the final selection is simple: Managers should be allowed the prerogative to select those individuals for whom they will be responsible.

There are instances, however, in which the personnel manager serves in a strong advisory capacity. For example, if the organization is under pressure from the federal government to employ more individuals in a certain protected group, a recommendation by Personnel as to who should be employed may have the same impact as a directive from the president of the firm. However, the personnel manager should realize the dangers

[41]"Prehire Tests Cut Chain's Theft by 28 Percent," *Chain Store Age Executive* 59 (June 1983): 25.

[42]"Polygraphs — Useful or Useless?" *CPA Journal* 50 (December 1980): 94–95.

[43]Hall A. Acuff, "Quality Control in Employee Selection," *Personnel Journal* 60 (July 1981): 563.

[44]A. Peter Fredrickson, "The Hiring Process: How It Works," *Supervisory Management* 20 (October 1975): 4.

232

**Part Two
Human
Resource
Planning,
Recruitment,
and Selection**

involved in this practice. The operating manager's authority may be severely undermined.

PHYSICAL EXAMINATION

After the decision has been made to extend a job offer, the next phase of the selection process involves the successful completion of a physical examination. Typically, a job offer is contingent on successful passing of this physical examination. The purposes of this examination are several. Obviously, one reason for requiring a physical is to screen out individuals who have a contagious disease. The exam also assists in determining whether an applicant is physically capable of performing the work. For instance, if the work is very demanding and a physical examination uncovers a heart problem, the individual will likely be rejected. Finally, the physical examination information may be used to determine whether there are certain physical capabilities that differentiate between successful and less successful employees.

Personnel managers should be aware of the legal liabilities related to physical examinations. The *Uniform Guidelines* state that examinations should only be used to reject applicants when the exam results show that job performance would be adversely affected.

The Rehabilitation Act of 1973 does not prohibit employers from requiring physical examinations. However, it has encouraged covered employers to consider carefully each job's physical requirements. The act requires employers to take affirmative action to hire qualified handicapped persons who, with reasonable accommodation, can perform the essential components of a job.

ACCEPTANCE OF JOB APPLICANTS

Assuming that no medical problems were discovered in the physical examination, the applicant can now be employed. The starting date of the job is typically based on the needs of both the firm and the individual. If the individual is currently employed by another firm, it is customary for him or her to give between two and four weeks notice. Even after this notice, the individual may need some personal time to prepare for the new job. This is particularly important if the new job requires a move to another city. The transition time before the individual can join the firm is often considerable.

The firm may also want the individual to delay the date of employment. If the new employee's first job upon joining the firm is to go to a training school, the organization may request that the individual delay joining the firm until perhaps a week before the school. This would keep the new employee from having nothing to do until school begins. This practice should not be abused, especially if the individual is unemployed and does not have money to live on in the meantime.

233

Chapter 7
Selection

REJECTION OF JOB APPLICANTS

Applicants may be rejected at any phase of the selection process. This section focuses on the individuals who for various reasons were not offered employment with the firm.

When an individual makes application for employment, he or she is essentially saying, "I think I am qualified for the job. Why don't you hire me?" Tension builds as the applicant progresses through the selection process. If the preliminary interview shows that he or she is obviously not qualified, there is likely to be only a minimum amount of damaged ego. The company may even be able to smooth this over by informing the individual of other jobs in the firm that better match his or her qualifications.

For most people, the employment interview is not one of the most enjoyable of experiences. Taking a test that could affect your career often causes hands to become moist and perspiration to break out on the forehead. Suffering through all of this only to be told, "There does not appear to be a proper match between your qualifications and our needs" can be a painful experience. Most firms recognize this fact and attempt to let the individual down as easily as possible. But it is often difficult to tell people that they will not be employed. Where considerable time has been spent with the individual in the selection process, a company representative often sits down with the applicant and explains why another person was offered the job. On the other hand, if there were many applicants, time constraints may force the firm to notify individuals by letter that they were not chosen. A letter informing an applicant of his or her rejection can be personalized. A personal touch will often reduce the stigma of a rejection and reduce the chance that the applicant will have bad feelings about the company, which a depersonalized letter could elicit. If the selection was made objectively, most individuals can, with time, understand why they were not chosen.

SELECTION AND UTILITY ANALYSIS

The determination of the ratio of benefits to costs for any selection technique is referred to as **utility analysis.** Each step in the selection process has a cost associated with it. If tests are to be used, they need to be validated. Professionals are required to administer the tests, interpret the results, and explain the results to management. In addition, application blanks that are job related for particular job classes need to be developed. This takes time, effort, and money. Properly conducted reference checks and background investigations also have a cost associated with them. Even the preliminary

234

Part Two
Human
Resource
Planning,
Recruitment,
and Selection

interview requires that an individual be trained and time provided to perform the task properly.

Even though substantial costs are involved in developing, implementing, and using a job-related selection process, the benefits are likely to outweigh the costs. If individuals are placed in positions for which they are not suited, dissatisfaction is inevitable.[45] There are also numerous hidden costs involved. For example, before discovering that the individual was wrong for the job, considerable supervisory effort may be involved. The quality and quantity of work in the department may suffer. And the selected individual may have a negative impact on the other workers. When a worker leaves the firm, a replacement must be found. If training has been provided, it is wasted and must be performed once again when a replacement is hired. Turnover costs associated with a poor selection process can be substantial.

When formal utility analysis is used, an attempt is made to assign dollar values to the various selection activities.[46] Managers are first asked to estimate the dollar value of hypothetical performance levels. They are then expected to estimate the performance level that is expected to be achieved by the selection activities. As might be expected, formal utility analysis is rarely accomplished. However, informal utility analysis is performed every day as managers evaluate the costs and benefits of employing a particular applicant.[47]

SUMMARY

Selection is the process of choosing from a group of applicants those individuals best suited for a particular position. External and internal factors continue to influence the selection process — legal considerations, in particular. Managers must be keenly aware of the effect of legislation, regulations, and court decisions as they engage in selecting new employees. Other factors that affect the selection process include: (1) the time available to make the decision; (2) the organizational hierarchy; (3) the number of people in the applicant pool; (4) the type of organization; and (5) the use of probationary periods.

The effectiveness of the selection process can significantly influence, and is itself affected by, the other functional areas of Personnel. The selection process begins with an initial screening of applicants to remove

---

[45]John C. Hafer and C. C. Hoth, "Selection Characteristics: Your Priorities and How Students Perceive Them," *Personnel Administrator* 28 (March 1983): 25.

[46]Frank L. Schmidt, John E. Hunter, and Kenneth Pearlman, "Assessing the Economic Impact of Personnel Programs on Workforce Productivity," *Personnel Psychology* 35 (1982): 333–347.

[47]Kendrith M. Rowland and Gerald R. Ferris, *Personnel Management*. Boston: Allyn & Bacon, 1982, p. 134.

individuals who obviously do not fulfill the position requirements. The next step in the selection process involves having the prospective employee complete an application blank. The employer evaluates it to determine whether there appears to be a match between the individual and the position.

Selection tests may next be administered to assist in assessing the applicant's potential for success with the organization. When tests are used as selection tools they should be reliable, valid, objective, and standardized. The employment interview is next considered. Interviews may be distinguished by the amount of structure or preplanned format they possess.

The purpose of the reference check is to provide additional insight into the information in the application blank and to verify its accuracy. A background investigation may be helpful in determining whether past work experience is related to the qualifications needed for the new position. After information has been obtained from the preceding steps, the actual hiring decision must be made. The person whose qualifications most closely conform to the requirements of the open position should be selected. When a decision has been made to extend a job offer, the next phase of the selection process involves the successful passing of a physical examination. Assuming that no medical problems are discovered in the physical examination, the applicant can then be employed.

QUESTIONS FOR REVIEW

1. What are the basic steps that are normally followed in the selection process?

2. Identify and describe the various factors outside the control of the personnel manager that could affect the selection process.

3. What would be the selection ratio if there were fifteen applicants to choose from and only one position to fill? Interpret the meaning of this selection ratio.

4. If a firm desires to use selection tests, what major points should be considered in their use to avoid discriminatory practices?

5. What is the general purpose of the preliminary interview?

6. What types of questions should be included in an application blank?

7. What basic conditions should be met if selection tests are to be used in the screening process? Briefly describe each.

8. Briefly describe each of the basic objectives of the employment interview.

9. Define briefly each of the following types of interviews: (a) nondirective interview; (b) structured interview; (c) group interview; (d) board interview; and (e) stress interview.

10. What is the purpose of reference checks and background investigations?

11. What are the reasons for administering a physical examination?

TERMS FOR REVIEW

Selection
Selection ratio
Weighted application blank (WAB)
Standardization
Objectivity
Norms
Reliability
Test–retest method
Equivalent forms
Split-halves method
Validity
Criterion-related validity
Concurrent validity
Predictive validity
Content validity
Construct validity
Cut-off score
Cognitive aptitude tests
Psychomotor abilities tests
Finger dexterity

Manual dexterity
Wrist–finger speed
Aiming
Job knowledge tests
Work-sample tests
Vocational interest tests
Employment interview
Unstructured (nondirective) interview
Structured (directive or patterned) interview
Situational questions
Job knowledge questions
Job-sample simulation questions
Worker requirements questions
Group interview
Board interview
Stress interview
Realistic job preview (RJP)
Reference checks
Utility analysis

Incident 1

As production manager for Thompson Manufacturing, Jack Stephens has the final authority to approve the hiring of any new supervisors who work for him. The personnel manager performs the initial screening of all prospective supervisors and then sends the most likely candidates to Jack for interviews.

One day recently, Jack received a call from Pete, the personnel manager. "Jack, I've just spoken to a young man who may be just who you're looking for to fill that final line supervisor position. He has some good work experience and it appears as if his head is screwed on straight. He's here right now and available if you could possibly see him." Jack hesitated a moment before answering. "Gee Pete," he said, "I'm certainly busy today but I'll try to squeeze him in. Send him on down."

A moment later Allen Guthrie, the new applicant, arrived at Jack's office and introduced himself. "Come on in, Allen," said Jack. "I'll be right with you after I make a few phone calls." Fifteen minutes later Jack finished the calls and began talking with Allen. Jack was quite impressed. After a few minutes Jack's door opened and a supervisor yelled, "We have a small problem on line number one and need your help." "Sure," Jack replied, "Excuse me a minute, Allen." Ten minutes later Jack returned and the conversation continued for at least ten more minutes before a series of phone calls again interrupted them.

This same pattern of interruptions continued for the next hour. Finally Allen looked at his watch and said, "I'm sorry, Mr. Stephens, but I have to pick up my wife." "Sure thing, Allen," Jack said as the phone rang again. "Call me later today."

QUESTIONS

1. What specific policies might a company follow to avoid interviews like this one?
2. Explain why Jack and not Pete should make the selection decision.

Incident 2

"Mrs. Peacock, I've decided that we should quit using selection tests altogether," said John Barnes, the personnel manager. "I'm not sure there are any that could be defended if we ever got a discrimination complaint." John had just read a report of a court decision finding a large company nearby guilty of discriminatory employment practices. Essentially, the company had been using tests designed to measure general intelligence as a screening device for all kinds of employees. The court held that the tests caused certain protected groups to be eliminated from employment consideration.

The tests that John's firm, Miller Chemical Company, used were aptitude tests, carefully designed to apply to the specific job for which the applicant was applying. For example, the test for a certain mechanical mixer operator job included questions about the relative weights of various liquids and solids, the ways in which emulsions were formed, and the dangers involved in working with rotating machinery. No study had been done, however, to determine the relationship between performance on the test and success on the job. Most of the managers felt that the interviews and references were more valuable than the tests anyway.

Besides, John thought that validation of the tests would be too expensive and time-consuming.

As John was thinking about all of this, Nancy Peacock called back. "Mr. Barnes," she said, "I've been thinking about your decision to eliminate our tests. Do we still have enough to go on in making an employment decision?" "Not really," said John, "but I don't know what else we can do to be safe. A discrimination suit could tie us up for months. The tests may not be any more discriminatory than interviews, but I don't think that interviews can get us into trouble. The same thing is true of application blanks and reference checks. It would just be harder for the EEOC to attack us on those points." "Then I suppose the decision is final?" asked Nancy. "I've thought about it a lot, Mrs. Peacock," said John, "and I suppose it is."

QUESTIONS

1. Do you agree with the rationale for Mr. Barnes's decision? Explain.
2. Under what circumstances might Miller Chemical have been required to validate the tests?

REFERENCES

Acuff, Hall A. "Quality Control in Employee Selection." *Personnel Journal* 60 (July 1981): 562–565.

"Adverse Impact: Can Your Hiring System Pass the Test?" *Training* 22 (March 1985): 111–112.

Ayers, J. and Heineman, R. E. "The Most Cost Effective Part of the Hiring Process (Preemployment Screening)." *Security Management* 29 (March 1985): 55–56.

Barrett, G. V. et al. "The Concept of Dynamic Criteria: A Critical Reanalysis." *Personnel Psychology* 38 (Spring 1985): 41–56.

Bekiroglu, H. and Gonen, H. "Labor Turnover: Roots, Costs, and Some Potential Solutions." *Personnel Administrator* 26 (July 1981): 67–72.

"Companies Move Cautiously into 1985 with Employment Plans for Marketers." *Marketing News* 19 (January 18, 1985): 1 +.

Cronin, Richard J., APD. "Executive Recruiters: Are They Necessary?" *Personnel Administrator* (February 1981): 31–34.

Davey, B. W. "Personnel Testing and the Search for Alternatives (Selection Procedures)." *Public Personnel Management* 13 (Winter 1984): 361–374.

Decker, Robert L. "The Employment Interview." *Personnel Administrator* 26 (November 1981): 71–73.

Ely, E. S. "How to Unmask Bogus Job Seekers." *Computer Decisions* 17 (January 29, 1985): 100–104 +.

Frew, David R. "Diagnosing and Dealing With Task Complexity." *Personnel Administrator* 26 (November 1981): 87–92.

Huxtable, Fulton L. "Executive Hiring Deserves More Than Spare-Time Treatment." *Personnel Administrator* 27 (March 1982): 35–38.

Jablin, Fredric M. "Use of Discriminatory Questions in Screening Interviews." *Personnel Administrator* 27 (March 1982): 41–43.

Kravetz, Dennis J. "Selection Systems for Clerical Positions." *Personnel Administrator* 26 (February 1981): 39–42.

Langer, Steven. "Budgets and Staffing: A Survey." *Personnel Journal* 60 (June 1981): 464–468.

Lawrence, Daniel G., Salsburg, Barbara L., Dawson, John G., and Fasman, Zachary D. "Design and Use of Weighted Application Blanks." *Personnel Administrator* 27 (March 1982): 47–53.

Levesque, J. D. "Selecting and Managing Competent Managers." *Personnel Administrator* 30 (March 1985): 63–64 +.

Malinowski, Frank A. "Job Selection Using Task Analysis." *Personnel Journal* (April 1981): 288.

McCulloch, Kenneth J. *Selecting Employees Safely Under the Law.* Englewood Cliffs, N.J.: Prentice-Hall, 1981.

Meyers, Donald W. "The Impact of a Selected Provision in the Federal Guidelines on Job Analysis and Training." *Personnel Administrator* 26 (July 1981): 41–45.

Mullins, Terry W. and Davis, Ronald H. "A Strategy for Managing the Selection Interview Process." *Personnel Administrator* 26 (March 1981): 65–67 +.

Perham, J. C. "How Recruiters Get the Low Down (Confidential Information about Executives Is Easy to Obtain)." *Dun's Business Month* 125 (May 1985): 60–61.

Pursell, Elliott D., Campion, Michael A. and Gaylord, Sarah R. "Structured Interviewing: Avoiding Selection Problems." *Personnel Journal* 59 (November 1980): 907–912.

Rehfuso, John. "Management Development and the Selection of Overseas Executives." *Personnel Administrator* 27 (July 1982): 35–43.

Rickard, Scott T. "Effective Staff Selection." *Personnel Journal* 60 (June 1981): 475–478.

Schneider-Jenkins, C. and Carr-Ruffino, N. "Smart Selection: Three Steps to Choosing New Employees." *Management World* 14 (March 1985): 38–39.

Schultz, C. B. "Saving Millions Through Judicious Selection of Employees (Valid Tests)." *Public Personnel Management* 13 (Winter 1984): 409–415.

Scott, R. A. et al. "On-Campus Recruiting: The Students Speak Up (CPA Firms)." *Journal of Accounting* 159 (January 1985): 60–62 +.

Sewell, C. "Be Prepared — The Overriding Concern in Personnel Screening for Data Processing Positions." *Security Management* 29 (March 1985): 57–59.

Sewell, Carole, "Pre-Employment Investigations: The Key to Security in Hiring." *Personnel Journal* 60 (May 1981): 376–379.

Sleveking, Nicholas, Anchor, Kenneth, and Marston, Ronald C. "Selecting and Preparing Expatriate Employees." *Personnel Journal* (March 1981): 197.

Von der Embse, T. J. and Wyse, R. E. "Those Reference Letters: How Useful Are They? (Family Educational Rights Privacy Act of 1974)." *Personnel* 62 (January 1985): 42–46.

Williams, J. "The Baby Bust Hits the Job Market." *Fortune* 111 (May 27, 1985): 122–126 +.

Appendix: *Potential Interviewing Problems*

One source alone lists almost a dozen serious problems especially associated with unstructured interviews.[1] Although each of the following potential interviewing problems can be satisfactorily dealt with, they nevertheless threaten the success of employment interviews.

LACK OF GOALS

It is an axiom in management that clearly stated goals are essential if meaningful activity is to take place. The requirement for goals, or objectives, is no less essential for the interviewing process. Goals for the selection interview are tied to both the job to be filled and the qualifications of the applicant. Unfortunately, individuals are often selected on the basis of whim, with less consideration for specifications (skills, knowledge, and abilities) than is typically given to the acquisition of a typewriter or other type of nonhuman asset.

In order to effectively conduct an interview, the interviewer must have a good knowledge of the job content and the human requirements for satisfactory performance of the job. As previously discussed, these data are determined from job analysis. Without them, the interviewer is not in a position to set goals, ask pertinent questions, or make rational judgments about candidates.

PREMATURE JUDGMENTS (FIRST IMPRESSION BIAS)

One researcher established that the first four minutes of personal meetings typically provide the most lasting impressions of ourselves to others.[2] This being the case, an interviewer should consciously resist the temptation to make quick decisions about applicants. When this does occur, the interviewer will likely spend the remaining interview time searching for information to support the decision already made. This practice represents not only wasted time but a foolhardy approach to selection. A more appropriate technique is to objectively gather all needed data, analyze it, and then make an evaluation.

INTERVIEWER DOMINATION

When interviewers dominate the conversation, the collection of job-related information about the candidate is hindered. In successful interviews, rel-

---

[1]Terry W. Mullins and Ronald H. Davis, "A Strategy for Managing the Selection Interview Process," *Personnel Administrator* 26 (March 1981): 66–67.
[2]Leonard Zunin, *Contact: The First Four Minutes.* New York: Ballantine Books, 1974, p. 6.

240

Part Two
Human
Resource
Planning,
Recruitment,
and Selection

evant information must flow both ways; thus interviewers must develop listening skills. Listening is essential for effective communication, but studies have shown that only about 10 percent of us listen properly.[3] One of the most common errors made by an interviewer is talking too much. The applicant should be permitted to talk about 75 percent of the time during a job interview.[4] People listen in different ways, but all do not provide satisfactory results. We can engage in marginal listening, giving the speaker only part of our attention. When we do this, we may understand only a part of what is said. But what about the remainder? We may not even have heard the most essential part of what was said, in which case we obviously will not understand it.

A second type of listening is referred to as evaluative. In this case, while the speaker is talking, the listener starts formulating his or her response or rebuttal to what has been said. Once again, parts of the speaker's message are not even received. The portions that were received are often misunderstood.

A third type of listening is called empathic. Here, the listener makes an effort to enter the mind of the speaker. The listener attempts to put aside personal biases and his or her own frame of reference. While all transmissions must ultimately be evaluated, the evaluation is not made prematurely; it is delayed until the entire message has been received and a sincere effort has been made to understand what the speaker means. Empathic listening is difficult to perform. Yet, it is this approach that permits understanding, therefore communication, to take place.

From the firm's viewpoint, the objective of the employment interview is to acquire sufficient information for making an informed choice. If the interviewer dominates the conversation, dispenses facts, or merely outlines the parameters of the position, he or she will not succeed. A primary interviewing goal is to gather information. To do so, interviewers must question and listen.

INCONSISTENT QUESTIONS

Various applicants may be asked different questions by the same or different interviewers. In these instances, all the applicants are not judged on the same basis and charges of discrimination may result. If interviewers ask applicants essentially the same questions and in the same sequence, a better basis is provided for comparing the qualifications of the applicants, and higher interrater reliability should occur.[5]

---

[3]Eugene Raudsepp, "The Art of Listening," *Supervision* 41 (November 1979): 14.

[4]Charles Denova, "The Job Interview and the Supervisor," *Supervision* XLV (September 1983): 26.

[5]Paul S. Greenlaw and John P. Kohl, "Selection Interviewing and the New Uniform Federal Guidelines," *Personnel Administrator* 25 (August 1980): 78.

CENTRAL TENDENCY

The central tendency error occurs when an interviewer rates virtually all candidates as average. In this instance, the interviewer is refusing to differentiate between strong and weak candidates.

HALO ERROR

The type of bias known as the halo error is manifested when an interviewer is overly impressed with one or more personal characteristics and permits this bias to unduly affect his or her opinion of the applicant. For example, an interviewer who places a high value on neatness and communication skill may automatically favor candidates who rate high on these attributes, without due regard for other abilities that may relate more directly to job requirements.

CONTRAST EFFECTS

An error in judgment may occur when, for example, an interviewer meets with several poorly qualified applicants and then confronts a mediocre candidate. By comparison, the last applicant may appear to be better qualified than he or she actually is and, as a result, receive a higher rating than deserved.

INTERVIEWER BIAS

All individuals, through their experiences, have acquired certain biases. These biases, however, can totally disrupt the interviewing process, which should be as objective as possible. It is necessary, then, for interviewers to know themselves, acknowledge and understand their own prejudices, and learn to deal with them. If this does not occur, the interviewer's attitude — perhaps at the unconscious level — can lead to unfair treatment of candidates. For example, research has indicated that interviewers terminate interviews with physically handicapped applicants sooner than they do with nonhandicapped candidates.[6]

Another example of such bias is *stereotyping*, where the interviewer has a preconception of the ideal candidate. Some interviewers may not believe that women or blacks, for example, are qualified to handle executive positions because they do not match the interviewers' stereotypes. They may view such individuals as best suited to secretarial, clerical, or more menial jobs. While actions taken based on these stereotyped views are

[6]Robert L. Dipboye, "Self-Fulfilling Prophecies in the Selection-Recruitment Interview," *The Academy of Management Review* 7 (October 1982): 52.

242

**Part Two
Human
Resource
Planning,
Recruitment,
and Selection**

illogical and clearly illegal, they do occur and, as a result, qualified candidates may be eliminated from the selection process.

LACK OF INTERVIEWER TRAINING

Employment interviews are often conducted by line managers who interview infrequently. They are typically not well-trained in interviewing techniques. This deficiency is compounded by the fact that they also have the pressures of performing full-time jobs. As a result, interview goals may not be clearly formulated, and these interviewers may not be prepared to answer questions posed by the candidate.

BEHAVIOR SAMPLE

It has been suggested that, even if an interviewer spent a week with an applicant, the sample of behavior would be too small to properly assess the candidate's qualifications. Furthermore, not only is the sample of behavior too small, but the candidate's behavior during an interview also is seldom typical or natural.[7]

NONVERBAL COMMUNICATION

While the tendency is to dwell on potential verbal problems, nonverbal communication often has a greater impact on the interview.[8] Facial expressions and body movements can often convey meaning very effectively. An interviewer should be aware of his or her nonverbal behavior, which might transmit unintended signals. For example, the interviewer may glance at the clock to determine how much time is left for the interview. The applicant may interpret this action as meaning "the interview is over." Other actions during the interview and common interpretations of them by applicants are shown in Table A–1.

Often, interviewers are not fully aware of their nonverbal behavior. Actually, they should make a conscious effort to view themselves as applicants will view them in order to avoid sending inappropriate or unintended signals.

INTERPRETATION OF BEHAVIOR

An additional problem in assessing an applicant is that of interpreting his or her behavior. Suppose, for example, that during a stress interview, in

[7]Robert L. Decker, "The Employment Interview: Are We Seeing the Demise of Another Management Prerogative?" *Personnel Administrator* 27 (November 1981): 72.

[8]Thomas L. Moffatt, *Selection Interviewing for Managers.* New York: Harper & Row, 1979, p. 25.

Table A–1. Nonverbal communication	
Behavior	**Possible interpretation**
Sitting stiffly behind desk	*This is a very formal meeting. I'd better not reveal too much of myself.*
Reading the application blank	*This interviewer doesn't even know who I am.*
Nodding head	*You understand what I'm saying.*
Frequent glancing out the window	*This person would rather be someplace else.*
Receiving telephone calls	*This manager is too busy to see me.*
Frowning	*My answer to that question didn't go over very well.*

which the interviewer makes insulting remarks, the candidate simply gets up and walks out or decides to sue. Should this be interpreted as: (1) as an indication that the candidate is well-informed, i.e., knows his or her rights; (2) an indication of immaturity and insecurity; or (3) as an indication of stupidity, in that the candidate has lost a chance of a job? No one, including the "experts" has satisfactorily solved this problem.[9]

INAPPROPRIATE QUESTIONS

A basic requirement in employee selection is that the data asked for be job related. During an interview, it is very easy for an interviewer to innocently ask questions that may reveal irrelevant information about members of protected groups. Employers must be extremely cautious in asking those questions that are generally considered risky from a legal point of view.

At this point, litigation has revolved around two basic themes. First, do questions give the impression of a discriminatory attitude? For example, is reference made to "girls" and are women asked about marital status, child care, etc.? And, second, does the question have the effect of creating an adverse impact on members of protected groups?[10] A 1981 study revealed that discriminatory questions were still being asked in the screening interview by firms interviewing at college placement offices.[11]

[9]Decker, "Employment Interview," p. 72.

[10]Richard D. Arvey and James E. Campion, "The Employment Interview: A Summary and Review of Recent Research," *Personnel Psychology* 35 (1982): 289.

[11]Frederick M. Jablin, "Use of Discriminatory Questions in Screening Interviews," *Personnel Administrator* 27 (March 1982): 41–42.

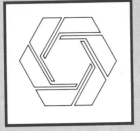

Gene Wilson, the corporate planner at Parma Cycle Company, was ecstatic as he talked with the personnel director, Jesse Heard, on Tuesday morning. He had just received word that the board of directors had approved the plan for Parma's new southern plant. "I really appreciate your help on this, Jesse," he said. "Without the research you did on the personnel needs for the new plant, I don't think that it would have been approved." "We still have a long way to go," said Jesse. "There's no doubt that we can construct the building and install the machinery, but getting skilled workers in Clarksdale, Mississippi, may not be so easy." "Well," said Gene, "the results of the labor survey that you did in Clarksdale last year indicate that we'll be able to get by. Anyway, some of the people here at Parma will surely agree to transfer." "When is the new plant scheduled to open?" asked Jesse. Gene replied, "The building will be finished in February 1987; the machinery will be in by May; and the goal is to be in production by September 1987." "Gosh," said Jesse, "I'd better get to work."

A few minutes later, back in his office, Jesse considered what the future held at Parma Cycle. The company had been located in Parma, Ohio, a Cleveland suburb, since its founding. It had grown over the years to become the nation's fourth largest bicycle manufacturer. The decision to open the Clarksdale, Mississippi, plant had been made in hopes of cutting production costs through lower wages. Although no one ever came right out and said it, it was assumed that the southern plant would be nonunion. The elimination of union work rules was expected to be a benefit.

The state of Mississippi had offered a ten-year exemption from all property taxes. This was a significant advantage because tax rates for Cleveland area industries were extremely high. Jesse was pleased that he had been involved in the discussions from the time that the new plant was first suggested. Even with all the advanced preparation he had done, he knew that the coming months would be extremely difficult for him and his staff.

At that moment Jesse's assistant, Ed Deal, walked in with a bundle of papers. "Hi, Ed," said Jesse, "I'm glad you're here. The Clarksdale plant is definitely on the way and you and I need to get our act together." "That's great," said Ed. "It's quite a coincidence, too, because I was just going over this stack of job descriptions, identifying which ones might be eliminated as we scale back at this plant." Jesse said, "Remember, Ed, we are not going to cut back very much here. Some jobs will be deleted and others added. But out of the 800 positions here, I'll bet that not more than forty will actually be eliminated." "So, what you are saying is that we basically have to staff the plant with people we hire from the Clarksdale area?" Ed asked. Jesse replied, "No, Ed, we will have some people here who are willing to transfer even though their jobs are not being eliminated. We will then replace them with others we hire in the Cleveland area. Most of the workers at Clarksdale, though, will be recruited from that area."

"What about the management team?" asked Ed. "Well," said Jesse, "I think the boss already knows who the main people will be down there. They are managers we currently have on board plus a fellow we located at a defunct three-wheeler plant in Mound Bayou, Mississippi."

"Who will be the personnel director down there?" asked Ed. "Well," replied Jesse, "I don't think I'm talking out of school by telling you that I've recommended you for the job." After letting that soak in for a minute, Ed said, "It's no secret that I was hoping for that. When will we know for sure?" "There's really not much doubt," said Jesse, "I'm so sure that I've decided to put you in charge of personnel matters for that whole project. During the next two weeks I'd like you to put together a comprehensive plan. I want a detailed report of the people we will need, including their qualifications. Secondly, we will need a more complete knowledge of the labor supply in Clarks-

dale. Finally, I'd like you to come up with a general idea of who might be willing to transfer from this plant. They are really going to be the backbone of our work force at Clarksdale." "Okay, Jesse, but I'll need a lot of help," said Ed as he gathered his papers and left. As Jesse watched Ed leave he thought he noticed a certain snappiness about Ed's movements that had not been there before.

QUESTIONS

1. What procedures do you feel should be followed in determining the personnel needs at the new plant?
2. How might Jesse and Ed go about recruiting workers in Clarksdale? Managers?

Experiencing Human Resource Management

Writing a Job Description

During this exercise each participant will have an opportunity to prepare a rough draft of a job description from job analysis data. In addition to helping the student develop personnel skills, this exercise will help students make the connection between what is learned in the classroom and what is actually done in the workplace.

YOUR ROLE

As a senior personnel specialist at Parma Cycle Company you have been involved in

job analysis planning for the new plant in Clarksdale, Mississippi. Most of the job analysis data have been gathered and now it is time to prepare specific job descriptions. You have been given a stack of job analysis information sheets and assigned responsibility for writing job descriptions for each of them. When the assistant personnel director, Ed Deal, handed you the data sheets, he said, "I'd like for you to do the first one, then bring it to me and we'll go over it together."

Figure II–1 shows the first job analysis sheet. Figure II–2 is a copy of the job description form that Parma uses. You are to complete the job description before Mr. Deal returns, thirty minutes from now.

Job Title: Marquette Spotwelder Operator

Work Activities:

Weld parts together as assigned by supervisor. All parts consist of thin steel pieces weighing less than two pounds each. The preformed pieces to be welded together are taken from numbered bins surrounding the spotwelder and placed in position on the machine. Then, the foot pedal is depressed to weld the pieces together. Completed pieces are next placed in a container for movement to another work station. The operator is responsible for ensuring that the settings on the machine are correct for the part being welded.

Relationship With Other Workers:

Job is located on the factory floor. Other machine operators running similar machines are within view, twenty to thirty feet away. The crane operator moves the parts bins to this work station and away as required, placing them where specified by the operator. There is little time for social interaction on the job.

Degree of Supervision:

The Spotwelder Supervisor supervises twelve operators, all doing essentially the same job. Operators are expected to do their jobs essentially without supervision, consulting with the supervisor only infrequently. Along with each job, the operator is provided a specification sheet showing the machine settings and describing the welding procedure. A sample prewelded part is also provided for each job and kept on a display board at the work station. The job instruction sheet shows the standard time that each job should take and the total time for each batch.

Records and Reports:

None.

Skill and Dexterity Requirements:

In order to meet the standard times, the worker must be able to take two parts from separate bins, place them together in the correct position, insert them into the machine against a prearranged jig, press the foot pedal, and put the completed part into the completed parts bin within 3.2 seconds.

Working Conditions:

The work station is relatively crowded because the parts bins have to be placed within armreach of the operator. Lighting is excellent. The operator is required to wear safety goggles because of the emission of an occasional hot spark from the welding machine. Ambient temperature varies from 60° F. in winter to 80° F. in summer. The noise level is about 60 decibels, distracting but safe.

Figure II–1. Parma Cycle Company's job analysis sheet.

Position Title		Position Number
		Approval

Division or Staff Department	Location	Reports To	Effective Date
Department or Activity	Section	Point	Grade	Revises

Job Summary

Nature of Work

Qualifications

Figure II–2. Parma Cycle Company's job description form.

Part Three

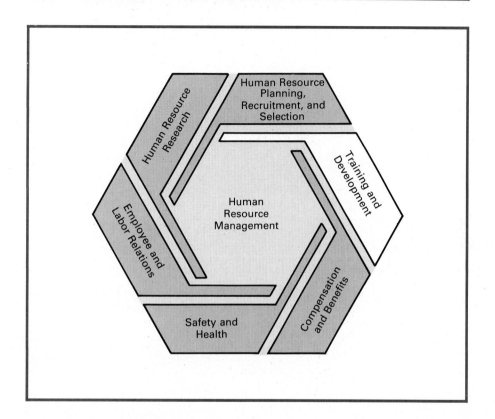

HUMAN
RESOURCE DEVELOPMENT

CHAPTER OBJECTIVES
1. Describe the organization change sequence, accompanying difficulties, and means of reducing resistance to change.
2. Define *training and development* (T&D), list the general purposes of T&D, and describe factors influencing T&D.
3. Explain the training and development process.
4. Describe the importance of employee orientation.
5. Describe the various management development methods.
6. Explain the T&D methods specifically available for operative employees.
7. Describe problems associated with the implementation of T&D programs and explain the importance of evaluation of T&D.

Chapter 8

ORGANIZATION CHANGE AND TRAINING AND DEVELOPMENT

Marian Lillie recently graduated from high school and wants to work for Sweeny Manufacturing as a machine operator. Marian has neither the training nor the experience to perform this job. Because the firm currently has vacancies for machine operators, and it is difficult to recruit skilled operators, Sweeny Manufacturing decides to hire Marian and train her to become a machine operator.

Brit Swain, a recently retired Marine officer, has begun his second career. He is employed by the Texoma Corporation as a production supervisor. Brit's military record was excellent and he was shocked when John Hicks, the plant superintendent, told him, "Brit, you have the potential to become a good manager, but your people resent your high-handed methods." Brit replied, "John, I have been successful for twenty years managing people and using these exact methods." Before John turned to leave, he said, "I know, but you're not in the military now and times are changing. I think you should make plans to enroll in our basic supervisory management development seminar."

In the first instance, it is evident that Marian lacks the skills necessary to perform efficiently as a machine operator. Through training, her skill level will be changed to that of a qualified operator. Brit has been a good manager in the military, but obviously has not adjusted to his new working environment. A development program that could provide him with new leadership and motivation concepts might assist him in becoming a good manager with Texoma.

Training and development (T&D) permits individuals and groups to learn something of value relative to their present or future performance. Training and development also helps and encourages members of the organization to change and to perform their jobs more effectively. This chapter focuses on T&D as a planned effort by management to effectively deal with change and as a means to improve productivity and the firm's profitability.

ORGANIZATION CHANGE

The instances involving Marian Lillie and Brit Swain concern the implementation of change. Change involves moving from one condition to another and it may affect individuals, groups, or an entire organization. Therefore those who desire to gain a better appreciation of training and development must understand the change sequence, accompanying difficulties, and means of reducing resistance to change.

THE CHANGE SEQUENCE

Change for the sake of change is seldom justified. Some degree of stability is needed to allow employees to accomplish assigned tasks. Even too many rational changes over a short period of time may leave workers bewildered and confused.[1] Of course, circumstances in the internal or external environments may make change desirable or even necessary (see Figure 8–1). Basically, the impetus for change comes from a belief that the organization and its human resources can be more productive and successful. But, if change is to be successfully implemented, it must be approached systematically. Many managers tend to feel that "We have always done it this way, so why argue with success?" However, a firm's past success does not guarantee future success nor does it indicate that further success is not possible. Once we have recognized that change is needed, we must then select a T&D method based upon the needs of the particular situation.

A critical phase of the change process involves reducing resistance to change. At times, this may be an extremely difficult process because it usually requires a change in attitude. Although a Marian Lillie is not likely

---

[1]H. Kent Baker and Stevan R. Holmberg, "Stepping Up to Supervision: Coping with Change," *Supervisory Management* 27 (March 1982): 23.

253

**Chapter 8
Organization
Change and
Training and
Development**

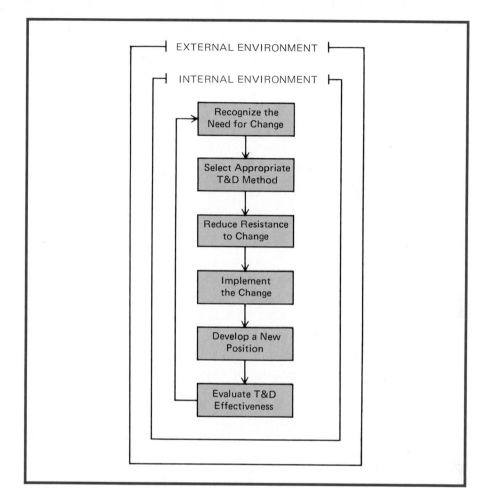

Figure 8–1. The organization change sequence.

to resist a change that will permit her to get a job, many times resistance to change is substantial. Consider, for instance, a machine operator who has been operating one piece of equipment for a long period of time and has just been told that another skill will have to be learned. In this situation, the individual concerned may become quite anxious and vigorously oppose any proposed changes in the work routine.

However, if resistance can be reduced, change can then be more effectively implemented. Change may stem from an order or a suggestion, or it may be undertaken voluntarily. The change will be accomplished more satisfactorily if the person involved in it desires the change and feels that it is needed. The most successful approach to attitude change requires that a close relationship exists between the person attempting to implement the change and the individual(s) to be changed.

The change sequence does not end when the change is implemented. A new and flexible position must be developed. The new position must be capable of dealing with present requirements and of adapting to further change. The final phase of the change sequence involves evaluating the effectiveness of the specific T&D method chosen. As previously mentioned, one primary measure of effectiveness is how the program impacted the firm's "bottom line." T&D is an on-going process because both internal and external conditions affecting the organization are never constant and are always changing.

REASONS FOR RESISTANCE TO CHANGE

In business circles, there has been much discussion of employees' "natural" resistance to change. We cannot deny that change is often resisted, sometimes quite vigorously.[2] This opposition, however, is not due to employees' innate characteristics. Rather, the resistance may be explained in terms of their expectations and past experiences. Individuals may resist change when they feel that it will result in their being denied satisfaction of their basic needs. For instance, one of the most frightening prospects for many people is the threat of being deprived of their employment. At times, methods and systems changes do result in the elimination of some jobs. They may also involve a drastic upgrading or downgrading of skills. Many employees believe that they lack the flexibility to adjust. Since most adults derive their primary income from their jobs, if they become unemployed they would be economically unable to obtain the basic necessities of life.

Many changes in organizations are perceived as disrupting established social groups. There may also be a fear that change will disturb established friendships. Because numerous social needs are satisfied on the job, any threat to these relationships may be resisted.

The potential threat to a person's status in the organization may also be a powerful reason for resisting change. Many workers have literally invested their lives in their jobs. They are likely to resist any change effort that they perceive as disrupting their standing in the organization or their sense of importance. For instance, the master machinist, when faced with new automation in his firm, may fear that his high level skill will no longer be needed and that his prestige will be lowered.

A classic example of resisting change has been repeated countless times in organizations planning computer installations. In some instances, many employees learned of the firm's plans through the grapevine. Employees may easily envision how the computer could accomplish all or a part of their work. They may fear unemployment, dispersion of their work group, or loss of status. The prospect of change can conceivably threaten every

---

[2]Rensis Likert and Jane Gibson Likert, *New Ways of Managing Conflict*. New York: McGraw-Hill, 1976, p. 245.

level of human need. This feeling often results in employees resisting change. The resistance is not "natural" but is based on reasons that seem quite logical to the employee.

255

**Chapter 8
Organization
Change and
Training and
Development**

REDUCING RESISTANCE TO CHANGE

If a firm is going to achieve wide acceptance of a needed change, management needs to be aware of the means by which resistance can be reduced. However, a firm cannot expect attitudes that cause resistance to be overcome overnight.

Building trust and confidence. The degree to which employees trust and have confidence in management relates directly to their past experiences. If they have suffered in the past as a result of change, they may well attempt to avoid future changes. When management has misrepresented the results of changes, by failing to level with employees, the resistance tends to become even greater. For instance, when faced with the prospect of having to reduce the work force, management may assure employees that layoffs will be based on productivity. However, if previous layoffs appeared to be determined by favoritism or some other factor, employees may not believe that current actions will be different.

On the other hand, trust builds if management deals with employees in an open and straightforward manner. Workers who are told that they need additional training will accept the idea much more readily if they believe their manager. The desired level of trust and confidence cannot be achieved overnight. Rather, it results from a long period of fair-dealing by the firm's management.

Developing open communication. It has been estimated that 90 percent of "confidential" information in most organizations is not truly confidential. It is withheld from employees because of an unwillingness to share information.[3] Managers who possess this attitude are likely to create a climate that breeds distrust and fear. In such an environment any rumor of planned changes may become extremely distorted, and the firm's employees will often fear the worst.

By sharing information with employees, organizations can take a giant step toward developing open communications. In speaking to this point, Louis Lunborg once stated:

> People want to know several things. They want to know what their own job is all about, why they are doing what we ask them to do, what good it does anybody, and above all, how well they are doing it. And then they want to know what's going on — if they see strange things happening or

[3]Justin G. Longenecker, *Principles of Management and Organizational Behavior*, 3rd ed. Columbus, Ohio: Charles E. Merrill, 1973, p. 479.

hear rumors that something new is about to happen, they want to know about it.

> If you don't tell them, you're saying, "It's none of your business," and that in turn means, "I just don't think you are important enough." It is the deadliest thing you can do to people.[4]

Managers must recognize that subordinates are human beings and deal with them accordingly. Their needs should be recognized and reasonably met, if possible.

Employee participation.

> Margaret Thomson is an experienced accountant. She competently handled the administrative tasks for an automobile agency for more than ten years and really knew the business. Two months ago the agency was sold to a young man with a background in data processing. He immediately leased a personal computer and automated every conceivable administrative function. Margaret was not consulted at any point in this process. She was, however, presented with an "Operating Manual" when the project was completed.

Margaret may well show considerable resistance to this change because she was not consulted. People are more inclined to accept changes if they have had an opportunity to participate in planning for them. For instance, suppose that it has been determined that a department's operating budget must be cut by 25 percent. The department's manager may more readily accept this change if permitted to help determine where the cuts should be made. Participation is also more effective when permitted in the early planning stages. For example, an employee might not feel too involved if brought in on a change the day before it is to be implemented.

Through participation, resistance to change can be minimized and in some cases eliminated. It is possible to develop a participative climate within which employees aggressively seek change. In order to achieve such an atmosphere, it is necessary to remove, or at least minimize, the fear that employees may have concerning their ability to satisfy their needs. Managers must be convinced that their own actions — not their employees' inherent nature — are most often responsible for attitudes about change. Only then can training and development programs take place efficiently.

TRAINING AND DEVELOPMENT: IMPORTANCE AND SCOPE

Training and Development (T&D) is *planned continuous effort by management to improve employee competency levels and organizational per-*

---

[4]Louis B. Lunborg, "Managing for Tomorrow," *Information and Records Management*, April 1971, p. 72. Reprinted by permission.

formance. The emphasis is on increased productivity. Developing human resources has become even more critical as a result of our current obsession with technology. "High tech" has made the need for "high touch" quite apparent.[5] Recent plant shutdowns coupled with increases in the amount of imported goods have also made an impression on U.S. workers. The connection between survival and efficiency has been made, with the result that productivity is no longer considered a bad word.[6]

257

Chapter 8
Organization
Change and
Training and
Development

In order to improve productivity, change must occur. Training and development programs should be designed to accomplish needed change. The change may include new approaches to managing people or it may simply involve upgrading the skill levels that are required to operate a machine. It may focus on individuals, groups, or the entire firm. Training and development is responsible for much of the planned change that occurs in a company. When management recognizes that change is needed for the entire firm, organization-wide approaches to T&D are required. Approaches of this magnitude are the focus of chapter 9. The methods used to respond to change with a narrower scope (as with Marian Lillie or Brit Swain) are discussed in the following sections.

GENERAL PURPOSES OF T&D

The primary purpose of T&D is to improve worker productivity and the firm's profitability. Another major goal of T&D is to prevent obsolescence of skills at all levels in the company. Few employees operate anywhere near their full potential. In fact, there are estimates that most of us achieve only five percent of our total potential.[7] As Frederick Herzberg stated, "Resurrection is more difficult than giving birth."[8] While he was emphasizing the role of enriched jobs, effective T&D programs can also play a vital role in avoiding obsolescence.

Another purpose of T&D is to upgrade employees' skills in anticipation of their achieving higher positions in the organization. The organization is responsible for assisting employees in upgrading their skills based on their aptitudes and interests, in addition to the needs of the company. Training and development costs should be viewed as an investment in human resources.

[5]Benjamin B. Tregoe and John W. Zimmerman, "Needed: A Strategy for Human Resource Development," *Training and Development Journal* 38 (May 1984): 78.

[6]George J. McManus, "Team Concept Stressed in Productivity Confab," *Iron Age* 224 (December 7, 1981): 47.

[7]Herbert A. Otts, "New Light on the Human Potential," in Jong S. Jun and William B. Storm (eds.), *Tomorrow's Organization*. Glenview, Ill.: Scott, Foresman, 1973, p. 112.

[8]*Motivation Through Job Enrichment*, BNA Films. Washington, D.C.: The Bureau of National Affairs, Inc., 1967.

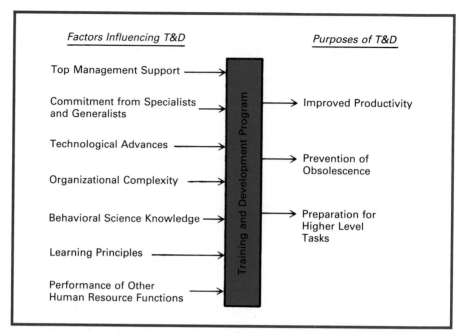

Figure 8–2. Factors influencing training and development.

FACTORS INFLUENCING T&D

As with all human resource functions, both external and internal factors can affect a T&D program. Several of the most important factors that can influence a training and development program's effectiveness are shown in Figure 8–2. These factors often determine the success in achieving T&D objectives.

First and foremost, training and development programs must have top management's full support. The support must be real — not merely lip service — and it should be communicated to all concerned in the organization. True support becomes evident when the executive group provides the resources needed for the T&D function. The support is further strengthened when top executives actually take part in the training. These actions tend to convince employees of the significance of training and development programs.[9]

In addition to support from top management, T&D programs must also have the commitment of other executives, both generalists and T&D specialists. It is highly desirable for all managers to become involved in the training and development process. Views of some practitioners concerning

---

[9]Dan R. Paxton, "Employment Development: A Lifelong Learning Approach," *Training and Development Journal* 30 (December 1976): 24–26.

the T&D manager's role are presented in Table 8–1. Some important conclusions regarding Personnel's responsibility in T&D can be drawn from these comments.

In the first place, the T&D manager operates essentially in a staff or advisory capacity. Milton R. Scheiber, director of corporate management development for Lone Star Industries, Inc., has said, "The primary responsibility for training and development lies with line managers, from the President and Chairman of the Board on down. T&D management merely provides the technical expertise, plus blood, sweat, and tears."

In order to ensure effective programs, T&D managers must show management that there will be a tangible payoff if resources are expended toward this end. Merely stating, "I think this program will be beneficial"

259

**Chapter 8
Organization
Change and
Training and
Development**

Table 8–1. Today's role of the training and development manager	
Personnel executive	**Comments**
Barry N. Lastra, Senior Advisor, Personnel Development, Chevron Corporation	Principal role is to be a consultant to managers to help identify: (1) operating problems or potential problems; (2) scenarios or alternative courses of action to solve these problems or prevent them from occurring; and (3) feedback processes to see that on-job results are consistent with stated management goals.
Raymond Lee, Director of Personnel, Fotomat Corporation	The role varies greatly, depending on the industry and the individual in the job. My perception is that the role is becoming more important and is expanding into nontraditional training and development functions.
T. M. Fabek, District Manager, Training, Ohio Bell Telephone Company	The role of the training/development manager is a staff function that must prove to the line organization and users that the services provided are job relevant, and will improve productivity, lower costs, and increase profits.
Henry L. Dahl, Jr., Manager, Employee Development and Planning, The Upjohn Company	Plan, develop, and administer programs that meet the needs of line managers in assisting their people to obtain the knowledge and skills they need to perform their present job satisfactorily, prepare employees for future jobs in the company, and assist them in achieving their personal goals.

is not sufficient because "training for training's sake doesn't work."[10] Some form of cost-benefit analysis must be made prior to implementing any program. The program should be job related, improve productivity, lower costs, and increase profits.

> This is the era of "pursuit of excellence," "high performance," and "the right stuff." When quality is returning to popularity, it is important to review, rethink and perhaps reshape the building blocks of our corporate reputation for training effectiveness. It is helpful to examine anew the trail between training effectiveness and our reputation for being/for doing (what we are and what we achieve).[11]

A major role of the T&D manager is to assist people in obtaining the knowledge and skills they need for present and future jobs and to assist them in attaining personal goals. Learning is a self-activity, and all development is self-development. The T&D manager explains the type of training available, shows how it can be accomplished, and provides encouragement to ensure its successful accomplishment.

In recent years, changes in products, systems, and methods have occurred at increasingly rapid rates. These changes have had a significant impact on jobs that are required by business organizations. Employees must constantly update their skills. Also, they need to develop an attitude that permits them not only to adapt to change, but also to accept and even seek it.

Organizations have grown to gigantic proportions in terms of the number of employees, sales volume, and diversity of products. This growth has also resulted in complex organizational structures. The resulting high degree of specialization necessitates greater interdependence of people operating in organizations. Individuals must interact with peers, subordinates, and superiors in groups to perform their jobs successfully.

During the past several decades, a vast amount of new knowledge has emerged from the behavioral sciences. A large portion of this information relates directly to human resource management. Today's managers must be aware of and capable of utilizing this new knowledge. The T&D activity has a substantial task in keeping pace with behavioral science developments and in informing members of the organization about these developments.

Training and development specialists must know more than the topic to be presented. There must be some understanding of basic learning principles. The purpose of training is to effect change in employee behavior. And information must be learned if change is to take place. While there is still much to be discovered about the learning process, several generalizations may be helpful in understanding this phenomenon. Some general concepts — fundamentals related to learning — are shown in Table 8–2.

---

[10]Martin M. Broadwell, *The Supervisor as an Instructor*, 3rd ed. Reading, Mass.: Addison-Wesley, 1978, p. 85.

[11]Chip R. Bell, "Building a Reputation for Training Effectiveness," *Training and Development Journal* 38 (May 1984): 50.

261

**Chapter 8
Organization
Change and
Training and
Development**

Table 8–2. General learning principles

- Behavior that is rewarded (reinforced) is more likely to recur.
- This reinforcement, to be most effective, must immediately follow the desired behavior and be clearly connected with that behavior.
- Mere repetition, without reinforcement, is an ineffective approach to learning.
- Threats and punishment have variable and uncertain effects on learning. Punishment may disturb the learning process.
- The sense of satisfaction that stems from achievement is the type of reward that has the greatest transfer value to other situations.
- The value of any external reward depends on who dispenses the reward. If the reward giver is highly respected, the extrinsic reward may be of great value; if not, it may be without value.
- Learners progress in an area of learning only as far as they need to in order to achieve their purposes.
- Individuals are more likely to be enthusiastic about a learning situation if they themselves have participated in the planning of the project.
- Autocratic leadership has been found to make members more dependent on the leader and to generate resentment in the group.
- Overstrict discipline tends to be associated with greater conformity, anxiety, shyness, and acquiescence; greater permissiveness is associated with more initiative and creativity.
- Many people experience so much criticism, failure, and discouragement that their self-confidence, level of aspiration, and sense of worth are damaged.
- When people experience too much frustration, their behavior ceases to be integrated, purposeful, and rational.
- People who have met with little success and continual failure are not apt to be in the mood to learn.
- Individuals tend to think whenever they encounter an obstacle or intellectual challenge which is of interest to them.
- The best way to help people form a general concept is to present an idea in numerous and varied situations.
- Learning from reading is aided more by time spent recalling what has been read than by rereading.
- Individuals remember new information that confirms their previous attitudes better than they remember new information that does not confirm their previous attitudes.
- What is learned is more likely to be available for use if it is learned in a situation much like that in which it is to be used, and immediately preceding the time when it is needed.
- The best time to learn is when the learning can be useful. Motivation is then at its strongest peak.

Source: Adapted from Goodwin Watson, "What Do We Know About Learning?" *N.E.A. Journal* 52 (March 1963): 20–22. (Reprinted by permission.)

Executive Insights

Rosemarie Ramirez
Organization Planning
and Development
Officer, The St. Paul
Property and Liability
Insurance Company

After graduating from the University of Minnesota and Minnesota School of Business in 1963, Rosemarie Ramirez was employed by 3M Company as a secretary in sales development. After several promotions — including working for twenty different people during the first two years — she was promoted from executive secretary to a division head. Because of her firsthand knowledge of the product line, she accepted the opportunity to train customers in the use of 3M Brand Overhead Projector and Transparencies. While traveling 60–80 percent of the time from 1967–1969, she discovered that industrial adult education training was exciting and fulfilling for herself and beneficial to others.

Ramirez proposed to the corporate education department that they expand their program and curriculum for 3M employees. They agreed, and she joined the Education, Training, and Development Department as a trainer in June 1970. She said, "It didn't take me long to understand that I needed to expand the job for continued self-growth." Within a short time she was promoted to supervisor and in 1975 became manager. During this time, she developed total training programs in office skills, affirmative action, interpersonal communications, group dynamics, time management, problem solving, decision making, women in management, minority in the corporate world, career development, and handling conflicts. Again this came about by her continuing to take on more responsibility to show others

what she was capable of doing. While developing program content, Ramirez expanded her administrative management skills by managing the corporate tuition refund program, an office staff of fifteen, the training facility, and the budget for the total department of sixty people.

Knowing that practical experience alone would not be sufficient to further her career, she became active in the International Association for Personnel Women (IAPW) to broaden her "personnel" expertise, and returned to school to complete her B.A. in personnel management in 1978. She knew this had paid off when St. Paul Companies (property and casualty insurance company) recruited her as their employment development officer. Ramirez joined the organization in 1980 to manage career and management development units, library, underwriting-marketing, and claims training units. Also in 1980, Ramirez was selected as the Outstanding Woman in Business by the St. Paul YWCA. In May 1985, she became Organization Planning and Development Officer responsible for organization design and development consultative services.

When asked to describe a major problem she had overcome, Ramirez replied, "While at 3M for seventeen years, I had to overcome the image of being female and a secretary. I had to demonstrate that I was capable and interested in assuming greater responsibility and that what my unit performed was adding to the bottom line by helping employees (management and nonmanagement) be more productive. My way of handling this was to constantly look for opportunities, i.e., turning problem areas into challenges, especially those no one else thought of or wanted to tackle or solve."

Most of these concepts relate to the management and development of human resources. For example, behavior that is rewarded (reinforced) is more likely to recur. In applying this concept to managing people, management would want to ensure that the firm's pay system rewards good producers. Training and development specialists need to keep trainees advised of their performance. Failure to provide the desired feedback on their performance — according to this concept — would not encourage learning.

263

**Chapter 8
Organization
Change and
Training and
Development**

From the personnel manager's viewpoint, the successful accomplishment of other personnel functions can have a significant impact on training and development. For instance, if recruitment and selection efforts produce only unskilled workers, an extensive T&D program may be needed to train entry level workers. Training and development efforts may also be influenced by the firm's compensation package. A firm with a competitive program may find it easier to attract qualified workers, which substantially influences the type of training required. Also, a competitive compensation plan may help decrease the turnover rate, thereby reducing the need to train new workers.

A firm's employee relations efforts can also influence the T&D program. Workers want to feel that the company is interested in them. One way to express this interest is through management's support of good T&D programs. These programs can also train managers to deal more effectively with employees and their problems. Managers can be taught to treat employees as individuals and not merely as numbers.

The emphasis a firm places on its employees' health and safety can also impact a T&D program. Heavy emphasis in this area can pave the way for extensive training programs throughout the firm. Providing a healthy and safe work environment can affect all other personnel functions as the firm gains a reputation as a healthful and safe place to work. Hence, you can see how T&D affects, and is affected by, other human resource functions.

THE T&D PROCESS

The broad scope of the training function is reflected by its three components: training, education, and development.[12] The term *training* describes those activities that serve to improve an individual's performance on a currently held job or one related to it.[13] Training a worker to operate a lathe or a supervisor to schedule daily production are examples. *Education* consists of activities that are conducted to improve the overall competence of an individual in a specific direction and beyond the current job.[14] Seminars designed to develop communication or leadership skills are in this category.

[12]Leonard Nadler, *Developing Human Resources*, 2nd ed. Austin, Texas: Learning Concepts, 1979, p. 40.
[13]Ibid., p. 60.
[14]Ibid., p. 88.

Training and education both focus on either currently held jobs or predetermined different jobs within the firm. *Development*, on the other hand, includes activities that are designed to prepare employees to continuously keep pace with the organization as it changes and grows.[15] University courses providing new insights for executives illustrate this T&D component.

The general training and development process is shown in Figure 8–3. Alterations in the external and internal environments necessitate change and training may be the appropriate response.[16] Recognition that a change is needed may come from a variety of sources. For instance, Brit Swain's supervisor noticed that Brit's management style was not appropriate for the situation.

The next phase of the process entails determining training needs and objectives. Essentially two questions must be asked. The first is "What are our training needs?" Second, "What do we want to accomplish through our T&D efforts?" The objectives might be quite narrow if limited to the supervisory ability of a Brit Swain. Or, they might be so broad as to include improving the management skills of all first-line supervisors.

After objectives have been stated, the appropriate methods and media that will be used to accomplish them can be determined. As you will see later in this chapter, there are a variety from which to choose. Naturally, T&D must be continuously evaluated to determine whether training and development needs are being met. George Odiorne has stated that training directors must move more toward economic evaluation of their training efforts.[17] Because numerous external and internal factors continuously affect training requirements, any effective training and development program must be a dynamic, ongoing process.

DETERMINING T&D NEEDS

The first step in the training and development process is to determine training needs. In our competitive environment, bona fide needs must be addressed.

A traditional approach to determining training needs has included organizational analysis, operational analysis, and individual analysis.[18] In conducting an organizational analysis, the firm's goals and plans should be studied along with the results of human resource planning. Training

---

[15]Dugan Laird, *Approaches to Training and Development*. Reading, Mass.: Addison-Wesley, 1978, p. 9.

[16]Chip R. Bell, "Criteria for Selecting Instructional Strategies," *Training and Development Journal* 31 (October 1977): 5.

[17]George Odiorne, *Training by Objectives*. London: Macmillan, 1970, p. 14.

[18]W. McGeehee and P. W. Thayer, *Training in Business and Industry*. New York: John Wiley & Sons, 1961.

265

Chapter 8
Organization
Change and
Training and
Development

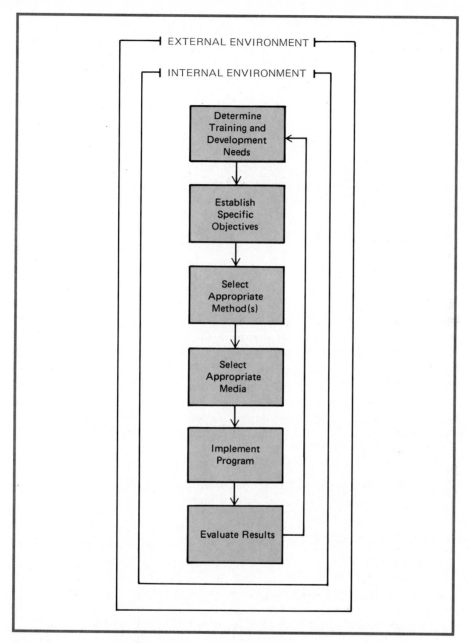

Figure 8–3. The training and development process.

needs may be indicated by information about new positions, retirements, turnover, absenteeism, grievances, quality control, accidents, and customer complaints. The results of an organization's MBO system might also reveal areas where the need for training is indicated.

Operational analysis relies largely on the results of job analysis. Specific ability needs are reflected in job descriptions and specifications. Training managers may also refer to job performance standards as they observe work group performance. In addition, managers and operative employees may be interviewed or surveyed to obtain suggestions.

Individual analysis may be carried out by comparing actual employee performance against established standards. Training managers may utilize surveys, interviews, or observation in making these determinations. In addition, tests, role playing, and assessment centers may yield helpful information. Also, the results of career planning programs and performance appraisal systems may be quite revealing.

ESTABLISHING T&D OBJECTIVES

Objectives are desired end results. In training and development, clear and concise objectives must be formulated. Without them, we could not design a T&D program nor, after it had been accomplished, would we have an important means for evaluating its effectiveness. The purposes and objectives of a segment of a training program designed by the Chevron Corporation for "Employment Compliance" is provided below:

Employment Compliance

Purpose: To provide supervisor with:

1. Knowledge and value of consistent personnel practices.
2. The intent of EEO legal requirements.
3. The skills to apply them.

Objectives: Be able to:

1. Cite the supervisory areas affected by EEO laws on discrimination.
2. Identify acceptable and nonacceptable actions, according to EEO laws.
3. State how to get help on EEO and Affirmative Action matters.
4. Describe why we have discipline and grievance procedures.
5. Describe our discipline and grievance procedures including who is covered.

As you can see, the purpose is first clearly established. Managers would have little difficulty in determining whether this is the type of training a subordinate needs. The specific learning objectives have little doubt of the knowledge that should be obtained from the course. Action words such as *cite*, *identify*, *state*, and *describe* are used to tell the specific content of the program. With these types of objectives, evaluation of whether a person has achieved the necessary knowledge may be made. For instance, a trainee either can or cannot state how to get help on EEO and Affirmative Action matters.

267

Chapter 8
Organization
Change and
Training and
Development

ORIENTATION

The initial T&D effort aimed at employees is orientation. **Orientation** involves *the guided adjustment of new employees to the company, job, and work group.* Essentially, orientation paves the way for successful implementation of many of the other tasks associated with human resource management.

Requirements for promotion will likely be explained. Rules, the infraction of which may lead to potential disciplinary action, will be stated. The mechanics of promotion, demotion, transfer, resignation, discharge, layoff, and retirement should be spelled out in policy handbooks and given to each new employee.

PURPOSES OF ORIENTATION

When an applicant has been selected and has joined the firm, his or her initial days may be spent in orientation. The three primary purposes of orientation are discussed next.

Easing the new employee's adjustment to the organization. Orientation helps ease the new employee's adjustment to the organization, both formally and informally. From a formal standpoint, the organization wants the employee to become productive as rapidly as possible. In order to facilitate this process, the employee needs to know what is involved in doing the job. Explanations concerning the job by the supervisor can do much to speed the process.

Many of the benefits attached to orientation are associated with the informal organization. New employees are not automatically greeted with open arms. There may be a certain amount of hazing and kidding. Older workers may want to make sure that the new employee knows his or her place. A mistake or a lack of speed in accomplishing tasks may bring joking comments such as, "The last person who messed up like that was fired the next day," or "If you can't produce any more than that, there's no need to stay here." Anxiety builds up as the new employee takes these comments seriously and wonders whether he or she made the proper decision in taking this job.

In order to reduce the anxiety that new employees are sure to have, attempts should be made to integrate the new hire into the informal organization. Perhaps a senior employee, as opposed to the supervisor, can be assigned the task of showing the new person the "ropes." High turnover is often associated with the failure to have informal acceptance of new employees. It is a lonely feeling to be on a job when you feel unwanted by peers.

Members of protected groups may also experience rejection from the informal work group, especially when the group consists primarily of white men. Women, blacks, and other minorities often have a lonely experience as they seek acceptance into the work group. Initial job turnover may be higher among members of protected groups than for those in the more traditional work group.

Providing information concerning tasks and performance expectations. Another purpose of orientation is to provide specific information concerning the task and performance expectations. Employees want and need to know precisely what is expected of them. Not knowing, they may establish some unrealistic performance standards. New employees should be informed of the standards that must be met in order to qualify for raises and the criteria that must be met for promotion. Rules of the company and of the particular department to which the individual is assigned should be explained.

Creating a favorable impression. A final purpose of orientation is to create a favorable impression on new employees of the organization and its work. Doubts may arise after they begin their new jobs. The new employee may begin to wonder, "Did I make the right decision?" The orientation process can do much to make the employee believe that he or she made the proper decision.

Orientation programs are designed basically for new employees. Here in itself is a problem. It has been estimated that 60–80 percent of the current work force in an organization is new not only to the job but also to the job market. This new work force includes either late entries or reentries of women, men and women who were self-employed, recent graduates, and people who have made radical career changes.[19] Many of these inexperienced individuals have anxieties about entering the organization. An effective orientation program can do much to reduce these anxieties.

STAGES IN EFFECTIVE ORIENTATION

There are essentially three different stages in an effective orientation program.[20] During the first stage, general information about the organization

---

[19]Mark S. Tauber, "New Employee Orientation: A Comprehensive Systems Approach," *Personnel Administrator* 26 (January 1981): 65.

[20]Diana Reed-Mendenhall and C. W. Millard, "Orientation: A Training and Development Tool," *Personnel Administrator* 25 (August 1980): 42–44.

is provided. Matters that relate to all employees, such as a company overview, review of company policies and procedures, and salary, are given. A new-employee checklist is often used to ensure that certain information is provided the new hire. One such checklist is shown in Figure 8–4. It is also helpful for the new employee to know how his or her department fits

269

Chapter 8
Organization
Change and
Training and
Development

Figure 8–4. New employee checklist.

NEW EMPLOYEE CHECKLIST

NAME _____ EMPLOYMENT DATE _____

POSITION TITLE _____ DEPARTMENT _____

PAY GRADE _____ APPOINTMENT TYPE: PT ___ FT ___ SUPERVISOR _____

PROBATIONARY PERIOD ENDS _____

FIVE MONTH PERFORMANCE APPRAISAL DUE _____

INFORMATION PROVIDED:

_____ Orientation packet   By:_____Date_____

_____ I.D. card   By:_____Date_____

_____ Staff handbook   By:_____Date_____

_____ Grievance guide   By:_____Date_____

_____ Retirement information   By:_____Date_____

_____ Life insurance   By:_____Date_____

_____ Disability insurance   By:_____Date_____

_____ Health insurance   By:_____Date_____

I understand that an exit interview with a Personnel Department representative is required of all terminating employees receiving benefits.

I have received the information checked above, understand my employment status, and have been fully informed about my insurance options and benefits.

I have chosen not to enroll in HEALTH, LIFE, DISABILITY insurance (Circle those you are not enrolling in.)

_____   _____
Employee Signature   Date

_____   _____
Personnel Representative   Date

Effective Date_____

into the overall scheme of the company's operations. Orientation programs should provide information about how the products or the services of the company benefit society. Another purpose of this stage is anxiety reduction. New employees are informed of some of the possible hazing games that older employees may play. The personnel department may be heavily involved in this stage.

In the second stage, the employee's immediate supervisor is responsible for the orientation program. Topics and events covered include an overview of the department, job requirements, safety, a tour of the department, a question and answer session, and introductions to other employees. It is crucial that performance expectations and specific work rules be clearly understood by the new hire at this point. It is also important for the supervisor to strive to ensure that the newly hired individual gains social acceptance as quickly as possible.

The third stage involves evaluation and follow up, which are conducted by the personnel department in conjunction with the immediate supervisor. The new employee does not simply go through the orientation program and then is forgotten. During the first week or so, the supervisor works with the new employee to clarify misunderstandings and make sure that he or she has been properly integrated into the work group. Personnel works with the supervisor to ensure that this vital third step is accomplished.

TRAINING THE SUPERVISOR

One of the most vital aspects of an orientation program is ensuring that supervisors are properly trained to conduct orientation. Personnel can provide the new hire with organizational information, but the supervisor must successfully integrate the employee into the work environment.

In order to achieve the highest probability for making the new hire an integral part of the work group, supervisors need training in how to conduct a thorough orientation.[21] In the first place, new employees should be assured that the supervisor is confident that they are going to do well on the job. Often new hires enter a job not fully convinced that they are capable of performing expected tasks successfully. Supervisors need to be able to communicate to these individuals that they would not have been hired if the company did not believe that they could do the job.

Second, supervisors need to be trained to tell both the good and bad points of the job. Often during the orientation period, managers spend most of their time speaking about the positive aspects of the job, leaving the employees to find out the negative aspects on their own. It has been proven that when employees have a more complete understanding of the job lower turnover results.

---

[21]Loi Dene Williams, "Off to a Good Beginning," *Supervision* 44 (October 1982): 4–5.

Third, the new hire should be informed of what supervisors like and dislike in job performance. Every manager has particular preferences — usually small things that they react to favorably or unfavorably. Knowing these preferences, the employees are in a much better position to adapt to a particular work environment. For example, if a supervisor is a stickler for neatness, this fact should be communicated to the new hire. Throughout the orientation process, the supervisor should attempt to reduce the number of "surprises" that the new employee will encounter.

Fourth, the supervisor should describe both the standards set by the company and any particular customs of a particular work group. All company rules and, in particular, those pertaining to the new hire's section should be explained.

Finally, the supervisor should introduce the new employee to members of the work group. If an informal leader exists, this person should be identified. Here again, an attempt should be made to reduce the number of surprises that the employee will encounter. Starting off on the wrong foot with significant members of the informal organization can interfere with a new employee's acceptance into the work group. In jobs that require considerable interaction among group members, group acceptance is especially important.

TRAINING AND DEVELOPMENT METHODS

When a person is working on a car, some tools are more appropriate in performing certain functions than others. The same logic applies when considering the many T&D methods. Note the various methods shown in Table 8–3. Some apply strictly to managers, others to operative employees, and several can be used in the training and development of both managers and operative employees. We will discuss these methods as they apply to management development training for entry-level professional employees, and training of operative employees. Methods that apply to both management and operative training will be included under management development.

Again referring to Table 8–3, you can see that T&D methods are used both on and off the job. Often it is not feasible to learn while doing. Therefore, while a large portion of training and development takes place on the job, many T&D programs occur away from the job.

MANAGEMENT DEVELOPMENT

A firm's future lies primarily in the hands of its management. This group performs the essential functions necessary for the organization to survive and prosper. Managers of an organization must make the right choices in

271

**Chapter 8
Organization
Change and
Training and
Development**

Table 8–3. Training and development methods

Method	Utilized for			Conducted	
	Managers and entry-level professionals	Operative employees	Both	On the job	Off the job
Coaching			X	X	
Business games	X				X
Case study	X				X
Conference/discussion	X				X
Behavior modeling	X				X
In-basket training	X				X
Internships	X			X	
Role playing	X				X
Job rotation			X	X	
Programmed instruction			X		X
Computer-assisted instruction			X		X
Classroom lecture			X		X
On-the-job training		X		X	
Apprenticeship training		X		X	
Simulators		X			X
Vestibule training		X			X

most of the numerous decisions they make. Otherwise, the firm will not grow and may even succumb to competitive pressures. For these reasons, it is imperative that managers continue to be developed. They must remain attuned to the latest developments in their various fields and be capable of managing an ever-changing work force within a dynamic environment. To assist in this process, many organizations emphasize training and development programs for managers. **Management development** consists of *all learning experiences provided by an organization for the purpose of providing and upgrading skills and knowledge required in current and future managerial positions.* First-line supervisors, middle managers, and executives may all be expected to participate in management development programs. These programs are offered in-house, through professional organizations, and by colleges and universities. In-house programs are those that are planned and presented by a firm's own members, who are often assigned to a T&D unit within Personnel. Line managers are also frequently utilized to conduct segments of a program.

Outside the company, professional organizations and universities are additional sources of management development programs. Organizations such as the American Society for Personnel Administration and the American Management Association are active in conducting conferences, seminars, and other programs. The American Management Association offers courses in a number of areas including supervisory development. One such program covers a number of topics, such as the nature of management and the managerial functions of planning, organizing, directing, and controlling. Communication, leadership, motivation, and decision making are also featured.[22]

273

**Chapter 8
Organization
Change and
Training and
Development**

Numerous universities provide management training and development programs for industry, as they are often staffed with capable faculty and have adequate facilities. At times, colleges and universities possess expertise not available within organizations. Another possible advantage of college programs is that T&D programs may be provided at less expense than in-house programs. In some cases, it is advantageous for academicians and management practitioners to jointly present T&D programs.

Regardless of whether programs are presented in-house or by an outside source, a number of methods are utilized in imparting knowledge to managers. A discussion of these methods follow.

COACHING

Coaching is an on-the-job approach to management development in which the manager is given an opportunity to teach on a one-to-one basis. Some firms create "assistant to" positions for this purpose. An individual placed in this type of staff position becomes an understudy to his or her boss. In addition to having the opportunity to observe, the subordinate will also be assigned significant tasks requiring decision-making skills. To be productive, coach-counselor managers must have a thorough knowledge of the job as it relates to the firm's goals. They should also have a strong desire to share information with the understudy and be willing to take the time — which can be considerable — for this endeavor. The relationship between the supervisor and subordinate should be based on mutual trust and confidence.

BUSINESS GAMES

Simulations that represent actual business situations are referred to as **business games**. These simulations attempt to duplicate selected factors in a particular situation, which are then manipulated by the participants.[23] Business games involve two or more hypothetical organizations competing in a given product market. The participants are assigned such roles as

---

[22]Debra Gottheimer, "A Manager's Training Film Festival," *Administrative Management* 38(7) (July 1977): 25.

[23]Larry C. Coppard, "Gaming Simulation and the Training Process," in Robert L. Craig (ed.), *Training and Development Handbook: A Guide to Human Resources Development*, 2nd ed. New York: McGraw-Hill, 1976, pp. 40–2, 40–3.

president, controller, and marketing vice president. They make decisions affecting price levels, production volume, and inventory levels. The results of their decisions are manipulated by a computer program, with the results simulating those of an actual business situation. Participants are able to see how their decisions affect other groups and vice versa. The best part about learning in this environment is that if you make a decision that costs the company $1 million, you won't lose your job.

CASE STUDY

The **case study** is *a training method that utilizes simulated business problems for trainees to solve*. The individual is expected to study the information given in the case and make decisions based on the situation. If the student is provided a case involving an actual company, he or she would be expected to research the firm to gain a better appreciation of its financial condition and environment. Typically, the case study method is used in the classroom with an instructor who serves as a facilitator.

CONFERENCE METHOD

The **conference method**, or discussion method, is *a widely used instructional approach that brings together individuals with common interests to discuss and attempt to solve problems*. Often the leader of the group is the supervisor. The group leader's role is to keep the discussion on course and avoid some people's tendency to get off the subject. As problems are discussed, he or she listens and tries to permit group members to solve their own problems. When this is not possible, the group leader may serve as a facilitator of learning. Individuals engaged in the conference method may not even perceive that they are in training. They are working to solve problems that are occurring in their everyday activities.

BEHAVIOR MODELING[24]

Behavior modeling *utilizes videotapes prepared specifically to illustrate how managers function in various situations and to develop interpersonal skills*. The trainees observe the "model's" actions. For example, a supervisor may act out his or her role in disciplining an employee who has been consistently late in reporting to work. Since the situations presented are typical of their firm's problems, the participants are able to relate the behavior to their own jobs.

The most important characteristic of high performance managers is that they set high standards for themselves and others. This is the heart of

---

[24]Bernard L. Rosenbaum, "Common Misconceptions about Behavior Modeling and Supervisory Skill Training (SST)," *Training and Development Journal* 33 (August 1979): 40–44.

behavior modeling.[25] Although it is a relatively new approach, behavior modeling seems to have outstanding potential as a training and development method. In fact, more than 300 companies — including such giants as Exxon, Westinghouse, Union Carbide, and Federated Department Stores — now use this method.

275

Chapter 8
Organization
Change and
Training and
Development

IN-BASKET TRAINING

In-basket training is *a simulation in which the participant is given a number of business papers such as memoranda, reports, and telephone messages that would typically come across a manager's desk.* The papers, presented in no particular order, call for actions ranging from urgent to routine handling. The participant is required to act on the information contained in these papers. Assigning a priority to each particular matter is initially required.

INTERNSHIPS

An **internship** program is *a training approach whereby university students divide their time between attending classes and working for an organization.* From the employer's point of view, the internship provides an excellent means of viewing a potential permanent employee at work. The internship normally provides much more information than can be obtained in an employment interview. Management is then in a better position to make selection and placement decisions.

Internships also provide advantages for students. The experience they obtain through working enables them to integrate theory learned in the classroom with the practice of management. At the same time, interns may gain knowledge of the organization that will help them determine whether the firm would be a good place to work.

ROLE PLAYING

Role playing is *a technique in which some problem — real or imaginary — involving human interaction is presented and then spontaneously acted out.*[26] Participants may assume the roles of specific organizational members in a given situation and then act out their roles. For example, a trainee might be assigned the role of a supervisor who is required to discipline an employee for excessive absences. Another participant would assume the role of the employee. The individual in the supervisory role would then

---

[25]Kenneth H. Blanchard and Alice S. Sargent, "The One Minute Manager Is an Androgynous Manager," *Training and Development Journal* 38 (May 1984): 83.

[26]Wallace Wohlking, "Role Playing," in Robert L. Craig (ed.), *Training and Development Handbook: A Guide to Human Resources Development*, 2nd ed. New York: McGraw-Hill, 1976, p. 36–1.

proceed to take whatever action is deemed appropriate. This action then provides the basis for discussion and comments by the group. Role reversal — an exchange of roles by the participants — is an effective version of role playing. This exchange provides trainees with a different perspective of the problem. It helps them to develop empathy, a quality vitally needed by managers.

JOB ROTATION

Job rotation involves *moving employees from one job to another for the purpose of providing them with broader experience.* This added knowledge may be needed for performing higher level tasks. Considering this example:

> Roy Jackson's firm is grooming him to fill the position of plant controller at the company's new branch plant. Roy is expected to assume his new responsibilities within the next six months. In preparing Roy for his new job, the vice president for finance and the personnel director have decided that he needs additional experience in credit operations and accounts receivable. They have scheduled him to spend three months in each of these departments prior to his move to the new plant.

As might be expected, Roy's temporary assignment will not make him an expert in either area. He will, however, gain an overview of these functions, which will assist him in his new position.

There are several potential problems related to job rotation. Individuals are often not permitted to remain on a job long enough to really learn its essential elements. Because these assignments are temporary, individuals may not be very productive during this time. In fact, they may even be detrimental to the productivity of the work group. In addition, department employees who witness an individual coming aboard on a job rotation basis may jealously resent the so-called fair-haired employee.

PROGRAMMED INSTRUCTION

A teaching method that provides instruction without the intervention of an instructor is called **programmed instruction (PI).**[27] In PI, information is broken down into small portions (frames). The learner reads each frame in sequence and responds to questions, receiving immediate feedback on response accuracy. If correct, the learner proceeds to the next frame. If not, the learner repeats the frame. Primary features of this approach are immediate reinforcement and the ability of learners to proceed at their own pace. Programmed instruction material may be presented in a book or in more sophisticated forms, such as teaching machines that mechanically advance frames.

[27]Leonard Silvern, "Training: Man–Man and Man–Machine Communications," in Kenyon De Greene (ed.), *Systems Psychology.* New York: McGraw-Hill, 1970, p. 383.

COMPUTER-ASSISTED INSTRUCTION

277

**Chapter 8
Organization
Change and
Training and
Development**

Computer-assisted instruction (CAI) is *an extension of PI that takes advantage of the speed, memory, and data manipulation capabilities of the computer for greater flexibility*. For example, a student's response may determine the difficulty level of the next frame, which can be selected and displayed almost instantaneously.

The increased speed of presentation and less dependence on an instructor are advantages of both PI and CAI. However, some students object to the absence of a human facilitator. Another primary disadvantage is the cost of developing programs. One source estimated that up to 200 hours of preparation time is required for each hour of CAI student instruction.[28] However, if there is a sufficient number of trainees, the cost may quickly reach an acceptable level. It appears that CAI is much more than a fad. A recent survey indicated that more than 20 percent of training departments use it.[29]

CLASSROOM LECTURE

The classroom lecture provides effective employee training in certain areas. A great deal of information may be transmitted in a relatively short time. The lecture seems to be most appropriate when new information is to be presented.

The passive role of students is perhaps the major disadvantage of the typical lecture. Lecture effectiveness can be improved when groups are small enough to permit discussion. The instructor's ability to capture the imagination of the class is another significant factor. Also, lectures can be assisted through timely and appropriate use of audiovisual equipment.

MANAGEMENT DEVELOPMENT PROGRAMS AT IBM

At IBM, formal management development programs are conducted for three groups of individuals: new managers, middle managers, and executives. These groups are described as follows:

- New managers — those appointed to their first level of management responsibility.
- Middle managers — those whose responsibility it is to manage managers.
- Executives — those who have reached executive level positions and those who are considered to have potential for such responsibility.

---

[28]Walter Goodman and Thomas F. Gould, *New York State Conference on Instructional Uses of the Computer: Final Report*. Yorktown Heights, N.Y., U.S. Educational Resources Information Center, ERIC Document ED 035 291, 1968.

[29]William R. Neher and Leopold Hauser III, "How Computers Can Help Adults Overcome the Fear of Learning," *Training: The Magazine of Human Resources Development* 19 (February 1982): 49.

An overview of the programs provided for these management groups is provided in Figure 8–5. In addition to providing training early in the manager's career, IBM emphasizes regular and continuous development. Annual training programs have been initiated to ensure that managers at all levels have an opportunity to receive at least one week of formal training each year.

SUPERVISORY MANAGEMENT TRAINING PROGRAMS: AN ILLUSTRATION

Numerous firms conduct supervisory training programs. They view this training as necessary if their first-line managers are to perform to their maximum potential. An overview of a supervisory training program developed by Chevron Corporation for their first-line managers is shown in

Figure 8–5. IBM's management development programs. Source: Used with the permission of International Business Machines Corporation.

New Manager School

All individuals appointed to the initial level of management responsibility, after receiving basic orientation to their job by their immediate managers, are enrolled, usually within one month, in a one-week basic training program.

The objectives of this training are:

Developing a deeper awareness of the basic policies and practices by which the company is managed.

Learning the practical application of these policies and practices.

Acquiring the basic management concepts, skills and techniques.

Included in the program are such subjects as A Business and Its Beliefs, Performance Planning, Counseling and Evaluation, and Managing Individuals.

Middle Management Training

Individuals newly appointed to the responsibility of managing managers attend, usually within ninety days, a week-long program.

The objectives of such training are:

Defining the role of the manager of managers.

Learning the organization, delegation, and control skills required of this level of management.

Understanding the interrelationship of the various business functions within the company.

Acquiring a knowledge of, and appreciation for, the issues and challenges of the business environment.

Included in the program are such subjects as Transition to Middle Management, Business Management Issues, People Management, and Leadership Styles.

279

Chapter 8
Organization
Change and
Training and
Development

Executive Development

Managers who have been appointed to executive-level positions, and those identified as having potential to be promoted to such positions, receive formal training at internally conducted programs as well as out-company programs.

The earliest of this series of company-conducted internal programs is scheduled within a year of the individual being included in the executive resource category. These classes, usually of three to four weeks duration, have objectives related to these areas:

The IBM Company: its organization, missions, management system; its policies, practices, and strategies; and its current issues and challenges.

Management Practices: leadership and decision making, general management concepts, functional integration, and management of change.

External Environment: international economic, political, and social changes; the current relationship of business, government, and other institutions.

Included in the programs are such courses as Finance, Marketing, Personnel, Environmental Analysis and Strategic Thinking, Goals and Means of Our Economy, and Business Ethics.

In addition, individuals attend external training programs conducted by colleges, universities, and other institutions. Such programs include concentration on general management, leadership, government relations, and the humanities. Attendance at such internal and external executive development programs is scheduled at intervals to complement on-the-job experiences.

Figure 8–6. This program is designed to provide new supervisors with the skills and knowledge they need in order to manage people effectively. The training program is also available to supervisors with long service to update their knowledge. The program has three phases: presession activities; a five-day, live-in session; and postsession activities.

Several weeks prior to the live-in session, participants are asked to engage in the following activities, which will prepare them for program involvement:

1. Identify their productive and nonproductive activities.
2. Discuss the basic elements of their jobs with their bosses.
3. Select a major opportunity or problem that both the participant and the boss are committed to deal with (this becomes an action plan).
4. Send a sample of an employee evaluation to the training program coordinator.

The five-day live-in session comprises the heart of the program. It begins on a Sunday night with a social get-together, dinner, and business meeting. Participants are asked to tell briefly about their jobs and discuss their action plan. A top management representative meets with the group during this initial meeting to discuss the role of the supervisor, the purpose of the program, and the expected on-job results.

| Presession Activities | Five-Day, Live-In Session Activities | | | Postsession Activities |
	Support Subjects	Key Course Subjects	Program Evaluation	
Time Analysis	Why We Are Here	Performance Planning and Review Documentation Skills	Formulate an Action Plan Project	Approval and Implementation of an Action Plan Project
Work Analysis	Analyzing Performance Problems			
Performance Planning Discussion	Training	Employee Ranking	Rank Session's Topics	Possible Performance Planning and Review Discussions
Selecting an Action Plan Project	Special Health Services	Salary Administration	Evaluate Program	Follow-up Questionnaire to Participant and Boss
Writing a Performance Evaluation	Time Management	Employee Development		
Interview with Coordinator	Employment Compliance			
Time:	*Time:*	*Time:*	*Time:*	*Time:*
Completed Prior to Start of Program	1 1/2 days	2 1/2 days	1 day	2–4 months after program

Figure 8–6. An overview of Chevron Corporation's supervisory training program. Source: Used with the permission of the Chevron Corporation.

During this main session, a number of support subjects and key course subjects are presented. At the same time, information is provided concerning laws, company policies and practices, and situations that affect typical discussions. A brief description of the purposes of support subjects and key course subjects are presented in Table 8–4. Action plan projects are worked with during the program evaluation. The results of these projects are used to measure the program's value.

281

**Chapter 8
Organization
Change and
Training and
Development**

Table 8–4. Chevron Corporation's supervisory training program's purpose for a five-day live-in session	
Support subjects	**Key course subjects**
Why we are here	*Performance planning and review*
To orient participants with top management views of the role of a supervisor, the purpose of this program, and what on-job results are expected to occur.	To increase supervisory productivity and efficiency by creating better: ■ Communications ■ Understanding of the job ■ Planning and allocation of time ■ Data for evaluating employees' work performance
Analyzing performance problems	*Documentation skills*
To provide supervisors with the skills necessary to analyze a performance discrepancy so that they can determine the best solution.	To improve writing skills of supervisors in order that they may better manage their human resources.
Training	*Employee ranking*
To provide supervisors with the skill and knowledge to effectively train others.	To provide supervisors with the skill and knowledge needed to objectively evaluate employee performance on the job.
Special health services	*Salary administration*
To provide supervisors with an expanded awareness of their responsibilities in the area of Special Health Services and with information and skills to deal with the troubled employee.	To review the basics of salary administration so that supervisors can provide meaningful inputs to higher management and provide feedback to employees about salary decisions.
Time management	*Employee development*
To provide skills in how to better manage and use time.	To assist supervisors in their role of developing employees both within their current jobs and for future jobs as appropriate.
Employment compliance	
To teach supervisors the value of consistent personnel practices and the skills to apply them, as well as the intent of EEO legal requirements.	

Source: Used with the permission of the Chevron Corporation.

The postsession phase of Chevron's supervisory training program consists of implementing the action plan. Further attempts are also made to relate the program's impact to the supervisor's job performance. At this point, training needs that are not being met are emphasized. Appropriate changes are made to ensure that the training program maintains practical worth to both the employee and the company.

TRAINING FOR ENTRY-LEVEL PROFESSIONAL EMPLOYEES

Firms have a special interest in college-trained employees hired for entry-level professional positions, including management trainees. As an example, the General Electric Company has programs that are conducted for new employees in numerous fields. One such program is their information systems manufacturing program (ISMP). This is a two-year program combining rotational work assignments with graduate level seminars. It prepares employees to design, program, and implement integrated computerized and manual information systems.

General Electric's ISMP emphasizes challenging work assignments in such areas as programming, systems analysis and design, computer center operation, project management, and functional work. The length of these assignments varies and individual progress is determined by employee performance and demonstrated potential.

Candidates for ISMP must have taken at least two computer science courses in college and have bachelor's degrees in one of the following majors or related fields: computer science, industrial engineering, accounting, mathematics, business administration, industrial management, or management information systems. Selection for the ISMP is based on a careful review of the employee's course curriculum, academic records, leadership in extracurricular activities, and work experience.

Other training programs for college graduates may have more or less structure than GE's ISMP. However, most other programs also emphasize training provided on the job. "Hands on" experience, alone or in combination with other methods, appears to be an essential component of these programs.

TRAINING FOR OPERATIVE EMPLOYEES

Unlike managers, operative employees do not make their contributions to the firm through the efforts of other people. They are, always, the "other people." Their contributions are direct and, collectively, of utmost significance to any organization. Organizations rely heavily on their executive secretaries, senior clerks, leadpersons, and other individuals occupying operative positions. Every position in an organization is necessary or it would not (or should not) exist. Therefore training and development for operative employees must also be given high priority by firms.

283

Chapter 8
Organization
Change and
Training and
Development

In this section we will present T&D methods that apply to the training of operative employees. However, these are not the only available methods. You may recall that Table 8–3 listed methods that are available to both management and operative employees.

ON-THE-JOB TRAINING

A supervisor once told a young applicant that "We have the best training program in our industry. Our company emphasizes OJT." This reply led the applicant to believe the firm had a formal training program. Actually, **on-the-job training (OJT)** is an *informal approach to training in which the person learns job tasks by actually performing them.*

Although some may not consider OJT a separate method, it is the most commonly used approach to T&D. With OJT, there is no problem in later transferring what has been learned to the task. Individuals may also be more highly motivated to learn because they are acquiring knowledge needed to perform their jobs. At times, however, the emphasis on production may tend to detract from the training process. The trainee may feel pressure to perform to the point where learning is negatively affected. To improve the effectiveness of OJT, three requirements must be kept in mind:

1. OJT is a joint effort involving both the superior and the subordinate.
2. The superior is responsible for creating a climate of trust.
3. The superior must be a good listener.[30]

APPRENTICESHIP TRAINING

One approach to operative training is apprenticeship training. **Apprenticeship training** is *a method that combines classroom and on-the-job training.* Such training is traditionally used in craft jobs such as those of plumber, barber, carpenter, machinist, and printer. While in training, the employee earns less than the master craftsperson who is the instructor. The training period varies according to the craft, as shown in Table 8–5. For instance, the apprenticeship training for barbers is two years; for machinists, four years; and for pattern makers, five years.

SIMULATORS

Simulators are *training devices of varying degrees of complexity that duplicate the real world.* They range from simple paper mock-ups of mechanical devices to computerized simulations of total environments. Train-

---

[30]Delbert W. Fisher, "Educational Psychology Involved in On-the-Job Training," *Personnel Journal* 56 (October 1977): 519.

Table 8–5. Selected apprenticeable occupations classified by length of apprenticeship			
Two years	Barber Cosmetician	Four years	Boilermaker Carpenter Machinist Printing pressman Tailor
Two to three years	Brewer Butcher Roofer		
Two to four years	Bindery worker	Four to five years	Electrical worker Lithographer Mailer
Three years	Baker Bricklayer Photographer	Four to eight years	Die sinker
Three to four years	Airplane mechanic Leatherworker Operating engineer Sheet-metal worker	Five years	Lead burner Pattern maker
		Five to six years	Electrotyper Photoengraver Stereotyper
Three to five years	Draftsman–designer		

Source: U.S. Department of Labor. *The National Apprenticeship Program*. Washington, D.C.: U.S. Government Printing Office, 1972, pp. 9–27.

ing and development specialists often prepare simulated sales counters, automobiles, and airplanes.[31] While simulator training may be less valuable than on-the-job training for some purposes, it provides certain advantages. A prime example is the training of airline pilots; simulated training crashes neither take lives nor deplete the firm's fleet of jets.

VESTIBULE TRAINING

Vestibule training is *training that takes place away from the production area on equipment that closely resembles the actual equipment used on the job.* For example, a group of lathes may be located in a training center where the trainees will be instructed in their use. A primary advantage of vestibule training is that it removes the employee from the pressure of having to produce while learning. The emphasis is on learning the skills required by the job.

USE AND SUCCESS OF VARIOUS T&D METHODS

Selecting an appropriate method is a crucial step in developing any training program. Results of a study of training directors' perceptions provides some insights about the effectiveness of various training methods. These specialists were employed by the 200 U.S. firms identified by *Forbes* as having

---

[31]Dugan Laird, *Approaches to Training and Development*. Reading, Mass.: Addison-Wesley, 1978, pp. 206–207.

the largest number of employees. The results of this study are shown in Table 8–6.

285

**Chapter 8
Organization
Change and
Training and
Development**

The case study was ranked highest for both *problem-solving skills* and *participant acceptance*. The conference (discussion) method topped the list for *knowledge acquisition*. Programmed instruction was rated best for *knowledge retention*. Role playing was ranked highest for *interpersonal skills* and was perceived as being the best overall method. Sensitivity training, while no longer a popular training method, topped the list for *changing attitudes*. The most-criticized method — lecture — generally did not fare well. However, it was ranked a respectable third for *knowledge retention*, following only programmed instruction and the conference method for this training goal. The television lecture was rated the poorest overall method. Generally, methods requiring participant involvement were rated higher than those requiring less participation.

Another study revealed the frequency of use of instructional methods (see Table 8–7). Comparing the results of this study to the one previously mentioned, the lecture method (rated low for most training objectives) is apparently one of the most frequently used instructional methods. On the other hand, the highly rated methods of role playing and case study are used much less frequently. (It is assumed that role playing is included as part of experiential exercises.)

Table 8–6. Training directors' ratings of effectiveness of alternative training methods for various training objectives

Training method	Knowledge acquisition Mean rank	Changing attitudes Mean rank	Problem-solving skills Mean rank	Inter-personal skills Mean rank	Participant acceptance Mean rank	Knowledge retention Mean rank
Case study	4	5	1	5	1	4
Conference (discussion) method	1	3	5	4	5	2
Lecture (with questions)	8	7	7	8	8	3
Business games	5	4	2	3	2	7
Movie films	6	6	9	6	4	5
Programmed instruction	3	8	6	7	9	1
Role playing	2	2	3	1	3	5
Sensitivity training (T-group)	7	1	4	2	6	9
Television lecture	9	9	8	9	7	8

Note: 1 = highest rank.

Source: Adapted from John W. Newstrom, "Evaluating the Effectiveness of Training Methods," from the January 1980 issue of *Personnel Administrator*, copyright 1980, The American Society for Personnel Administration, 606 North Washington Street, Alexandria, VA 22314.

Table 8–7. Frequency of use of instructional methods		
	Number of using firms	Percent of firms in study
Lectures	99	73
Discussions	98	73
Reading books	39	29
Textbooks	108	80
Films/audio-visual materials	15	11
Cases	54	40
Incidents	36	27
Experiential exercises	46	34
Guest speakers	7	5
Internships/co-op programs	7	5

Source: Adapted from "Newsletter of Personnel/Human Resources Division," *Academy of Management,* Volume 3, Issue 1 (December, 1978), p. 3. (Reprinted by permission.)

TRAINING AND DEVELOPMENT MEDIA

Many organizations have found it beneficial to utilize various forms of media to enhance training program effectiveness. As used in this context, **media** are *special methods of communicating ideas and concepts in training and development.* These media include videotapes, films, closed-circuit television, slide projectors, overhead and opaque projectors, flip charts, chalkboards, and slap boards.

Some critics have referred to audiovisual aids as "gadgetry for its own sake," but these devices have filled a useful role in training and development programs.[32] Criticism of the use of audiovisual aids is placed in proper perspective when you realize that approximately 75 percent of what you learn is by sight, whereas about 75 percent of what you hear is forgotten within two days.[33] These facts underlie the importance of using visual aids in training programs. Consider, for instance, the impact a film might have in dramatizing the role of informal groups as they affect the formal organization.

An overview of the various forms and uses of audiovisual media are shown in Table 8–8. Audiovisual aids are valuable supplements to training methods. For example, a lecture might be greatly enhanced by use of an overhead projector or a short film. These media can assist in gaining and

[32]Max H. Forster, "Training and Development Programs, Methods, and Facilities," in Dale Yoder and Herbert G. Heneman, Jr. (eds.), *ASPA Handbook of Personnel and Industrial Relations: Training and Development.* Washington, D.C.: The Bureau of National Affairs, Inc., 1977, pp. 5–53.

[33]Martin M. Broadwell, *The Supervisor as an Instructor,* 3rd ed. Reading, Mass.: Addison-Wesley, 1978, p. 85.

maintaining trainee interest and attention. Various applications of audiovisual media are not mutually exclusive. The use of more than one type of audiovisual aid (multimedia) may be appropriate for many training sessions. An example would be the use of a slide-tape presentation.

287

Chapter 8
Organization
Change and
Training and
Development

Table 8–8. Audiovisual media

Films

Films are heavily relied on because of their versatility. Films can combine many elements such as color, motion, action, plot, and musical scoring. Films provide a wide range of topics available for rental at a relatively low cost but are very expensive for an organization to produce.

Filmstrips

A series of still pictures, usually 35 mm, on a strip of film may be accompanied by a sound program using records, cassette tapes, etc. Each picture may be advanced manually or automatically, depending on the projector and the system. The production cost is much less than for films.

Slide projectors

Slide projectors are commonly used, with slide–tape presentations becoming more popular. In these programs, the projector may be advanced automatically by an inaudible signal from one stereo channel.

Overhead and opaque projectors

An overhead projector, providing an image on a screen by passing light through a transparency, can be used to provide colorful visual presentations. The trainer can maintain eye contact in an undarkened room and the trainees may take notes.

An opaque projector does not require transparencies but can project from opaques such as organizational charts or pages from a book.

Audio tapes

While there are several types of audio tape systems on the market, the compact cassette is becoming increasingly popular. The running time varies from sixty minutes (thirty minutes per side) to two hours.

Video

The instant-replay capability of video makes it a potentially valuable medium for use in training programs. Most of the advantages of film are inherent in video. However, as with film, costs may be a factor, especially the secondary costs associated with production, maintenance, operating personnel, etc.

Flip charts, chalkboards, and slap boards

These relatively inexpensive pieces of equipment can assist the trainer in emphasizing major points. A new type of chalkboard permits the use of a colored ink pen, and the ink may be easily erased.

Source: Adapted from O'Sullivan, Devin, "Audiovisuals and the Training Process." In Robert L. Craig (ed.), *Training and Development Handbook, A Guide to Human Resource Development*. 2nd ed. New York: McGraw-Hill, 1976. (Reprinted by permission.)

IMPLEMENTATION OF T&D PROGRAMS

A perfectly conceived training program can fail if the participants are not sold on its merits. They must be convinced that the program has value and that it will assist them in achieving their personal and professional goals. The credibility of T&D specialists may come only after a series of successful programs.

The implementation of T&D programs is often difficult. One of the reasons is that many managers are action oriented and frequently say they are too busy to engage in training efforts. As one management development executive stated, "Most busy executives are too involved chopping down the proverbial tree to stop for the purpose of sharpening their axes. . . ." Another difficulty in program implementation is that qualified trainers must be available. In addition to possessing communication skills, the trainers must know the company's philosophy, its objectives, its formal and informal organization, and the training program's goals. Training and development requires a higher degree of creativity than perhaps any other human resource specialty.

In implementing a new program it is very important that it be monitored carefully, especially during the initial phases. Training implies change, which, as we know, is often vigorously resisted. There are some who may even sit back waiting, perhaps even hoping, that the program will fail. Participant feedback is vital at this stage because there will be "bugs" in any new program. The sooner these problems are solved, the better the chances for success.

The T&D manager has specific problems associated with implementation. For example, it is often difficult to schedule the training around present work requirements. Unless the employee is new to the firm, he or she undoubtedly has prescribed duties to perform. Although it is the line manager's job to have positions covered while an employee is in training, the T&D manager must assist with this problem.

Another difficulty in implementing T&D programs is record keeping. For instance, records need to be maintained as to how well the trainee performed in the training. This information may prove beneficial as the trainee progresses in the company.

When training is conducted outside the organization, considerable coordination is required. Consider the magnitude of the problem if managers are coming from all parts of the country to participate in a T&D program in Bangor, Maine. The logistics and costs involved in this type of undertaking can be significant.

In order to deal with these factors, a relatively new approach has been developed. **Teletraining** is *a training method that may be used for training people more efficiently and more effectively utilizing teleconferencing.* This approach can complement existing professional development training programs and, in many instances, make it possible economically to reach individuals who would not otherwise have access to training.[34]

---

[34]Mary E. Boone and Susan Schulman, "Teletraining: A High Tech Alternative," *Personnel* 62 (May 1985): 4.

EVALUATION OF T&D

289

Chapter 8
Organization
Change and
Training and
Development

The credibility of T&D is greatly enhanced when it can be shown that the organization has benefited tangibly. Thus effective training directors will attempt to evaluate all their training efforts.[35] Organizations have taken several approaches in attempting to determine the worth of specific programs. These involve evaluations of: (1) the participants' opinion of the program; (2) the extent to which they have learned the material; (3) their ability to apply the new knowledge; and (4) whether the stated training goals have been achieved.

PARTICIPANTS' OPINIONS

Evaluation of training programs is often attempted by determining how well the participants enjoyed training sessions. Measuring reaction to training can be especially useful when its basic purpose is to justify the use of training in the firm. This approach provides an immediate response and suggestions for improvements. It is also inexpensive to conduct. The basic problem is that this type of evaluation is based on opinion rather than fact; in truth, the trainee may have learned nothing.[36] For example, Charlie Dixon has just completed a three-day executive seminar in Honolulu. At the conclusion of the program, Charlie was given a brief questionnaire that, in essence, asked him whether the seminar was beneficial. It is difficult to imagine Charlie or any of his fellow participants downgrading this training program. Even if it had been conducted in a less exotic location, a brief break from the hectic pace of an executive's job can be a welcome relief. Participants' perceptions of the value of such programs should be viewed in proper perspective.

EXTENT OF LEARNING

Some organizations resort to administering tests in an attempt to determine what the participants in a training program have learned. The most widely accepted evaluation procedure is referred to as the *pretest/posttest, control group design*.[37] This procedure requires that the same test be used before and after training. It also calls for both a control group (which does not receive the training) and an experimental group (which does). Trainees are randomly assigned to each group. Differences that are shown to exist between pretest and posttest results and between groups are then attributed to the training provided.

---

[35]Donald L. Kirkpatrick, "Evaluation of Training," in Robert L. Craig, (ed.), *Training and Development Handbook: A Guide to Human Resources Development*, 2nd ed. New York: McGraw-Hill, 1976, p. 18-1.

[36]John Dopyera and Louise Pitone, "Decision Points in Planning the Evaluation of Training," *Training and Development Journal* 37 (May 1983): 67.

[37]John H. Zenger and Kenneth Hargis, "Assessing Training Results: It's Time to Take the Plunge!" *Training and Development Journal* 36 (January 1982): 13–14.

BEHAVIORAL CHANGE

Tests may provide fairly accurate indications of what has been learned, but they give little insight into desired behavioral changes. For example, it is one thing for a manager to learn about motivational techniques. It is quite another matter for this same individual to apply the new knowledge.

> Max Johnson sat in the front row at the supervisory training seminar his company sponsored. The primary topic of the program was delegation of authority. As the lecturer made each point regarding effective delegation techniques, Max would nod his head in agreement. He thoroughly understood what was being said over the three-day period of the seminar. At the end of the program, Max returned to his department and continued the management style he had followed for ten years — a style that involved little delegation of authority. Max had learned the material presented in the seminar, but the learning of the material in this instance was of little value to the organization.

ACCOMPLISHMENT OF TRAINING GOALS

Still another approach to the evaluation of T&D programs involves determining the extent to which stated training goals have been achieved. For instance, if the goal of an accident prevention program is to reduce the number and severity of accidents by 15 percent, a comparison of accident rates before and after training provides useful evaluation data. However, many programs dealing with broader topics are somewhat more difficult to evaluate. A group of executives may, for example, be sent to a state university for a one-week course in management and leadership development. "Before" and "after" performance appraisals of the participants may be available. Yet, a number of other factors could affect the managers' performance following the training. The managers may actually be better prepared to perform their jobs, but other variables may distort the picture. For instance, a mild recession forces the layoff of several key employees; a competing firm is successful in luring away one of the department's top engineers; or the company president could pressure the employment director to hire an incompetent relative. These and many other factors could cause the performance level of the group to decline, even though the managers had benefited from the training.

In evaluating training programs, a past president of the American Society for Training and Development suggested that a manager should strive for proof that the program is effective. But, at times, evidence of a sound program is insufficient and proof is not possible.[38] Nevertheless, in spite of problems associated with evaluation, the human resource manager must continue to strive for solid evidence of T&D's contributions in achieving organizational goals.

---

[38]Donald L. Kirkpatrick, "Evaluating Training Programs: Evidence vs. Proof," *Training and Development Journal* 31(11) (November 1977): 12.

SUMMARY

291

**Chapter 8
Organization
Change and
Training and
Development**

A person who desires to gain a better appreciation of training and development must understand the change sequence, accompanying difficulties, and means of reducing resistance to change. Training and development (T&D) is a planned, continuous effort by management to improve competency levels and the organization work environment. The primary purpose of T&D is to improve productivity and the firm's profitability. As with all human resource functions, both external and internal factors can affect a T&D program. The training and development process involves the following steps: (1) determine training and development needs; (2) establish specific objectives; (3) select appropriate method(s); (4) select appropriate media; (5) implement the program; and (6) evaluate results. Orientation is the initial training and development that employees receive.

Management development is defined as all learning experiences provided by an organization for the purpose of providing and upgrading skills and knowledge required in current and future managerial positions. Coaching is an on-the-job approach to management development in which the manager — on a one-to-one basis — is given an opportunity to teach by example. Other management development techniques include: business games, case study, conference method, behavior modeling, in-basket training, internships, role playing, job rotation, programmed instruction, computer-assisted instruction, and classroom lecture.

Unlike managers, operative employees do not make their contributions to the firm through the efforts of other people. Their contributions are direct, and collectively, of utmost significance to any organization. Training and development methods that apply primarily to the training of operative employees include: on-the-job training, apprenticeship training, simulators, and vestibule training.

Many organizations have found it beneficial to utilize various forms of media to enhance training program effectiveness. As used in this context, media are special methods of communicating ideas and concepts. The media often used include videotapes, films, closed-circuit television, slide projectors, overhead and opaque projectors, flip charts, chalkboards, and slap boards.

When implementing a new program, it is important that it be monitored carefully, especially during the initial phases. The T&D manager has specific problems associated with implementation. It is often difficult to schedule the training around present work requirements. Another difficulty is record keeping.

The credibility of T&D is greatly enhanced when it can be shown that the organization has benefited tangibly. Organizations have taken several approaches in attempting to determine the worth of specific programs. These involve evaluation of: (1) participants' opinion of the program; (2) the extent to which they learned the material; (3) their ability to apply the new knowledge; and (4) whether the stated training goals have been achieved.

QUESTIONS FOR REVIEW

1. Explain the importance of the following statement: "A person who desires to gain a better appreciation of training and development must understand the change sequence, accompanying difficulties, and means of reducing resistance to change."
2. What are the general purposes of T&D?
3. What are the major external and internal factors influencing T&D?
4. Describe the training and development process.
5. Define *orientation* and explain the importance of employee orientation to a firm.
6. Define *management development.* Why is it important to a firm?
7. List and define the primary methods used in management development.
8. What training methods are used primarily to train operative employees?
9. Describe the major factors that should be considered in the implementation of training and development programs.
10. What are some of the means by which training and development programs are evaluated? Discuss.

TERMS FOR REVIEW

Training and development (T&D)
Orientation
Management development
Coaching
Business games
Case study
Conference method
Behavior modeling
In-basket training
Internship

Role playing
Job rotation
Programmed instruction (PI)
Computer-assisted instruction (CAI)
On-the-job training (OJT)
Apprenticeship training
Simulators
Vestibule training
Media
Teletraining

Incident 1

"I'm a little discouraged," said Susan Matthews to the training officer. "I keep making mistakes running the new printing press. It's a lot more complicated than the one I operated before, and I just can't seem to get the hang of it." "Well, Susan," responded George Duncan, "Maybe you're just not cut out for the job. You know that we sent you to the two-week refresher course in Atlanta to get you more familiar with the new equipment." "Yes," said Susan. "They had modern equip- ment at the school, but it wasn't anything like this machine." "What about the factory rep," asked George. "Didn't he spend some time with you?" "No, I was on vacation at that time," said Susan. "Have you asked your boss to get him back for a day or two?" "I asked him," said Susan, "but he said training was your responsibility. That's why I'm here." After she was gone, George got a yellow legal pad and began to write a letter to the printing press manufacturer.

1. What steps in the training and development process had the company neglected?
2. Is George taking the proper action?

What would you do?
3. Who should have primary responsibility for training and development? Why is this true?

Incident 2

As the initial training session began, John Robertson, the hospital administrator, spoke of the tremendous benefits he expected from the management development program the hospital was starting. He also complimented Brenda Short, the personnel director, for her efforts in arranging the program. As he finished his five-minute talk, he said, "I'm not sure what Brenda has in store for you, but I know that management development is important, and I'll expect each of you to put forth your best efforts to make it work." Mr. Robertson then excused himself from the meeting and turned the program over to Brenda.

For several years Brenda had been trying to convince Mr. Robertson that the supervisors could benefit from a management development program. She believed that many problems within the hospital were management related. Reluctantly, Mr. Robertson had agreed to authorize funds to employ a consultant. Through employee interviews and a self-administered questionnaire completed by the supervisors, the consultant attempted to identify development needs. The consultant recommended twelve four-hour sessions emphasizing communication, leadership, and motivation. Each session was to be repeated once so that supervisors who missed the first session could attend the second.

Mr. Robertson had signed the memo that Brenda had prepared, directing all supervisors to support the management development program. There was considerable grumbling, but all the supervisors agreed to attend. As Brenda replaced Mr. Robertson on the podium, she could sense the lack of interest in the room.

QUESTIONS

1. Have there been any serious errors up to this point in the management development program? What would you have done differently?
2. What advice do you have for Brenda at this point to help make the program more effective?

REFERENCES

Argyris, Chris. *Management and Organizational Development.* New York: McGraw-Hill, 1971.

Baird, John E., Jr. "Supervisor and Managerial Training Through Communication by Objectives." *Personnel Administrator* 26 (July 1981): 28–32.

Bell, Chip R. "Building a Reputation for Training Effectiveness." *Training and Development Journal* 38 (May 1984): 50.

Bennis, Warren G. *Changing Organizations.* New York: McGraw-Hill, 1966.

Blanchard, Kenneth H. and Hersey, Paul. "The Management of Change." *Training and Development Journal* 34 (June 1980): 80–98.

Blanchard, Kenneth H. and Sargent, Alice S. "The One Minute Manager Is an Androgynous Manager." *Training and Development Journal* 38 (May 1984): 83.

Boone, Mary E. and Schulman, Susan. "Teletraining: A High Tech Alternative." *Personnel* 62 (May 1985): 4.

Bowen, Donald D. and Hall, Douglas T. "Career Planning for Employee Development: A Primer for Managers." *California Management Review* 20 (Winter 1977): 23–35.

Bownas, D. A. et al. "A Quantitative Approach to Evaluating Training Curriculum Content Sampling Adequacy (Fit Between Training Curriculum Content and Job Task Performance Requirements)." *Personnel Psychology* 38 (Spring 1985): 117–131.

Braun, Alexander. "Assessing Supervisory Training Needs and Evaluating Effectiveness." *Training and Development Journal* 33 (February 1979): 3–10.

Caffarella, R. S., "A Checklist for Planning Successful Training Programs." *Training and Development Journal* 39 (March 1985): 81–83.

Connelly, Sharon L. "Career Development: Are We Asking the Right Questions?" *Training and Development Journal* 33 (March 1979): 8–11.

Craig, Robert L. (ed.). *Training and Development Handbook: A Guide to Human Resource Development.* New York: McGraw-Hill, 1976.

Decotiis, Thomas A. and Morano, Richard A. "Applying Job Analysis to Training." *Training and Development Journal* 31 (July 1977): 20–24.

Dethlefs, Dennis and Sellentin, Jerry L. "How to Be a 'Houdini' in Training." *Personnel Administrator* 24 (January 1979): 66–67.

Dickey, John D. "Training With a Focus on the Individual." *Personnel Administrator* 27 (June 1982): 35–38.

Elsbree, Asia Rial and Howe, Christine. "An Evaluation of Training in Three Acts." *Training and Development Journal* 31 (July 1977): 10–14.

Eng, Jo Ellen E. and Gottsdanker, Josephine S. "Positive Changes from a Career Development Program." *Training and Development Journal* 33 (January 1979): 3–7.

Ezzell, William W. "Orientation: Tell Them What They Need to Know!" *Training and Development Journal* 33 (January 1979): 54–56.

Fiedler, F. E. and Garcia, J. E. "Comparing Organization Development and Management Training." *Personnel Administrator* 30 (March 1985): 35–37 +.

"First Ask What You Want Training to Achieve." *Human Resources: Journal of the International Association for Personnel Women* 2(3) (Summer 1985): 3–5.

Frank, Frederic D. and Preston, James R. "The Validity of the Assessment Center Approach and Related Issues." *Personnel Administrator* 27 (June 1982): 87–95.

Gottheimer, Debra. "A Manager's Training Film Festival." *Administrative Management* 38 (July 1977): 24–27 +.

Guyot, James F. "Management Training and Post-Industrial Apologetics." *California Management Review* 20 (Summer 1978): 84–93.

Hance, Marjorie Mathison and Campbell, Sam. "Management Development: It's More Than Just Training." *Human Resources: Journal of the International Association for Personnel Women* 2(3) (Summer 1985): 6–7.

Hays, Richard D. "The Myth and Reality of Supervisory Development." *Business Horizons* 28 (January-February 1985): 75–79.

Huber, V. L. "Training and Development: Not Always the Best Medicine." *Personnel* 62 (January 1985): 12–15.

Jamieson, David W. "Developing the Profession and the Professional." *Training and Development Journal* 36 (May 1982): 118–121.

Jobe, Ernest D., Boxx, W. Randy and Howell, D. L. "A Customized Approach to Management Development." *Personnel Journal* 58 (March 1979): 150–153.

Kempfer, Homer. "Getting Your Money's Worth from Outside Training?" *Training and Development Journal* 34 (May 1980): 116–118.

Kronenberger, George K. and Banker, David L. "Effective Training and the Elimination of Sexual Harassment." *Personnel Journal* 60 (November 1981): 879–933.

Kuzmits, Frank E. "Train Your New Managers with CCI." *Personnel* 62 (April 1985): 69–72.

Lambert, L. L. "Nine Reasons That Most Training Programs Fail." *Personnel Journal* 64 (January 1985): 62 +.

Langford, Harry. "Needs Analysis in the Training Directors." *Training and Development Journal* 23 (August 1978): 18–25.

Leifer, M. "Things People Never Tell You about Corporate Training." *Personnel Administrator* 30 (February 1985): 19 +.

Levine, Hermine Zagat. "Consensus: Employee Training Programs." *Personnel* 58 (July-August 1981): 4–11.

Mangrum, S. L. "On-The-Job Versus Classroom Training: Some Deciding Factors." *Training* 22 (February 1985): 75–77.

McLagan, Patricia A. "The ASTD Training & Development Competency Study: A Model

Building Challenge." *Training and Development Journal* 36 (May 1982): 18–24.

Milbrath, Mona A. "Professional Accreditation Training Programs: An Overlooked Resource?" *Training: The Magazine of Human Resources Development* 19 (June 1982): 52–53.

Miles, Wilford G. and Briggs, William D. "Common, Recurring and Avoidable Errors in Management Development." *Training and Development Journal* 33 (February 1979): 32–35.

Mirabile, Richard J. "A Model for Competency-Based Career Development." *Personnel* 62 (April 1985): 30–38.

Monat, Jonathan S. "A Perspective on the Evaluation of Training and Development Programs." *Personnel Administrator* 26 (July 1981): 47–52.

Newstrom, John W. "Evaluating the Effectiveness of Training Methods." *Personnel Administrator* 25 (January 1980): 55–60.

Niehoff, Marilee S. and Romans, M. Jay. "Needs Assessment as Step One Toward Enhancing Productivity." *Personnel Administrator* 27 (May 1982): 35–39.

Ponthieu, J. F. "Gaining Mutual Independence Through Training." *Supervisory Management* 27 (April 1982): 16–19.

Roman, D. "Laughter Leavens Learning." *Computer Decisions* 17 (January 29, 1985): 70 + .

Schrader, Albert W. "How Companies Use University-Based Executive Development Programs." *Business Horizons* 28 (March-April, 1985): 53–62.

Smith, Judson. "A Trainer's Guide to Successful Productivity Improvement Planning." *Training: The Magazine of Human Resources Development* 19 (March 1982): 41–44.

Smith, Peter. "Coming to Terms with Job Crises." *Personnel Management* 10 (January 1978): 32–35.

Swierczek, F. W. and Carmichael, L. "The Quantity and Quality of Evaluating Training." *Training and Development Journal* 39 (January 1985): 95–99.

Tregoe, Benjamin B. and Zimmerman, John W. "Needed: A Strategy for Human Resource Development." *Training and Development Journal* 38 (May 1984): 78.

Trost, A. "They May Love It But Will They Use It?" *Training and Development Journal* 39 (January 1985): 78–81.

Truskie, Stanley D. "Getting the Most from Management Development Programs." *Personnel Journal* 61 (January 1982): 66–68.

———. "Guidelines for Conducting In-House Management Development." *Personnel Administrator* 26 (July 1981): 25–27.

Urban, T. F. et al. "Management Training: Justify Costs or Say Good-bye." *Training and Development Journal* 39 (March 1985): 68–71.

Yeomans, William N. "How to Get Top Management Support." *Training and Development Journal* 36 (June 1982): 38–40.

Zemke, Ron. "Job Competencies: Can They Help You Design Better Training?" *Training: The Magazine of Human Resources Development* 19 (May 1982): 28–31.

Zenger, John H. and Hargis, Kenneth. "Assessing Training Results: It's Time to Take the Plunge." *Training and Development Journal* (January 1982): 11–16.

CHAPTER OBJECTIVES
1. Define *corporate culture* and describe the factors that interact to affect corporate culture.
2. Explain *participative climate*.
3. Define *organization development* (OD) and explain the techniques for implementing OD.
4. State means whereby OD programs can be evaluated.

Chapter 9

CORPORATE CULTURE AND ORGANIZATION DEVELOPMENT

International Motor Corporation profits have declined over the past four years. Alyson Munson, the president, is especially concerned about several areas: the number of product recalls due to poor quality, unreasonably high sales costs, and excessive turnover in the firm. The problems do not appear to be limited to only a few of her departments. The general attitude of people throughout the firm seems to have declined. Alyson recognizes that if productivity is to be improved, changes must be made throughout the organization.

The International Motor Corporation experience depicts a firm that needs to undertake human resource development on an organizationwide basis. Virtually every individual in the firm will need to become involved in what is called organizational development, which is the focus of this chapter. The results sought from this degree of change effort will modify the corporate culture, or climate. This concept will be dealt with in the following section.

CORPORATE CULTURE

Corporate culture is *the system of shared values, beliefs, and habits within an organization that interacts with the formal structure to produce behavioral norms.*[1] It stems from the firm's mission, setting, and requirements for success. Important factors include high quality, efficiency, reliable products and customer service, innovation, hard work, and loyalty. The firm's reward systems, policies, and procedures imply the types of behavior and attitudes that are important for success.[2] According to Howard M. Schwartz, vice president of Management Analysis Center, Inc., a leader in corporate culture consulting, "Culture gives people a sense of how to behave and what they ought to be doing."[3]

Corporate culture is similar in concept to meteorological climate. Just as the weather is described by variables such as temperature, humidity, and precipitation, corporate culture is composed of factors such as friendliness, supportiveness, and risk taking. Perceptions of the job and organization are gradually formed by each individual over a period of time as a person performs assigned tasks under the general guidance of a superior and a set of organizational policies. A firm's culture has an impact on employee satisfaction with the job, as well as on the level and quality of employee performance. Assessment of the quality of an organization's culture may differ for each employee. One person may perceive the culture negatively, and another may view it positively. An employee may actually leave an organization in the hope of finding a more compatible culture.

Writing in 1967, Anthony Jay stated, "It has been known for some time that corporations are social institutions with customs and taboos, status groups and pecking orders, and many sociologists and social scientists have studied and written about them as such. But they are also political institutions, autocratic and democratic, peaceful and warlike, liberal and paternalistic."[4] What Jay was writing about, although the term had not then

[1]Arthur Sharplin, *Strategic Management*. New York: McGraw-Hill, 1985, p. 102.

[2]Ralph H. Kilmann, "Corporate Culture: Managing the Intangible Style of Corporate Life May Be the Key to Avoiding Stagnation," *Psychology Today*, April 1985, p. 64.

[3]"Corporate Culture: The Hard to Change Values that Spell Success or Failure," *Business Week*, October 27, 1980, pp. 148–160.

[4]Antony Jay, *Management and Machiavelli*. New York: Holt, Rinehart and Winston, 1967, 231.

achieved broad usage, was corporate culture. In the early 1980s, several best-selling books on corporate culture appeared, including *In Search of Excellence, Theory Z: How American Business Can Meet the Japanese Challenge,* and *Corporate Cultures.*[5] In 1981, Harvard University introduced its first course on corporate culture.

299

**Chapter 9
Corporate
Culture and
Organization
Development**

FACTORS THAT DETERMINE CORPORATE CULTURE

Numerous factors can interact to determine the culture of a firm. Three of them — communication, motivation, and leadership — will be discussed first because of the special impact they have on a firm's psychological environment. Other factors that can interact to determine corporate culture include organizational characteristics, administrative processes, organizational structure, and management style.

COMMUNICATION

Effective communication involves transmitting a message or idea in such a manner that it will be accurately understood and acted on by the receiver. All managers must communicate effectively if they are to be successful. In fact, it has been estimated that 80 percent of poor management decisions occur because of ineffective communication.[6] Effective organizational communication has a positive influence on organizational climate. In addition, good communication within the organization enhances management's ability to accomplish its objectives successfully, helping to ensure the firm's growth and profits. John Kasper, president of Elco Industries, stated that "We have our communication department, with a full-time group working to refine communication with our people. They're going out on the plant floor to ask questions and get opinions."[7] To reinforce successful communication throughout the firm, Elco Industries has created a position of corporate director of communication, which reports directly to the president.

Many companies, including Elco Industries, recognize that communication can break down in many different ways. Fortunately, the ability to communicate effectively can be learned. Individuals who are willing to exert the effort to improve their ability to communicate can benefit from aids that are readily available.

[5]Thomas J. Peters and Robert H. Waterman, Jr., *In Search of Excellence: Lessons from America's Best Run Companies.* New York: Harper & Row, 1982; William G. Ouchi, *Theory Z: How American Business Can Meet the Japanese Challenge.* New York: Avon Books, 1982; and Terrence E. Deal and Allan A. Kennedy, *Corporate Culture.* Reading, Mass.: Addison-Wesley, 1981.

[6]"If They Just Don't Seem to Get the Message," *Changing Times* 24 (June 1970): 39.

[7]Keith W. Bennett, "Communication and Costs Can Alter the Bottom Line," *Iron Age* 221 (June 26, 1978): 28.

MOTIVATION

Motivation refers to *the willingness to put forth effort in the pursuit of goals.* Management's job is to provide an organizational climate in which employee behavior can be constructively oriented toward task performance.

In the late 1800s and early 1900s, management believed that employees were motivated entirely by money. This simplistic version of motivation seemed valid at the time, and the idea is by no means dead today. However, managers of human resources in the 1980s must also consider other motivational factors. Employee needs and values have changed dramatically during the past 80–100 years. Individuals no longer work for pay alone. They expect the employment relationship to result in more than merely a paycheck.

Managers do not actually motivate their employees. Motivation is internal to the individual and stems from perceived needs, which serve as motivators. These motivators activate behavior that may result in the satisfaction of perceived needs. Motivation cannot be viewed directly; as with the wind, only the results are observable.

People in our society have a multitude of needs, many of which may be satisfied (or thwarted) on the job. Management has traditionally relied on motivational theory for help in understanding human motivation in general. Recently, however, greater attention has been directed toward understanding the wants and needs of individuals. What generally serves to motivate one person effectively may not be successful with another. Today's human resource management professionals recognize that, in order to achieve an organizational culture conducive to improved productivity, employees' personal needs must be reasonably well satisfied. For example, the concept of flexible compensation, discussed in chapter 13, allows workers, essentially, to select a pay package from numerous options.

LEADERSHIP

Leadership is the ability of getting others to do what the leader wants them to do. Managers have different personalities, backgrounds, goals, and experience. Therefore the manner in which they attempt to influence their employees may be quite different and can affect the organization's culture in different ways.

Many experts suggest that a "situational approach" to leadership is needed to cope with today's changing business environment. This means that the specific situation — comprising primarily the interrelationships between the manager, subordinate, and task to be performed — dictates the best approach to leadership. Those who hold this view believe that the most effective leadership style is one that is best adapted to the particular situation (see Figure 9–1).

The Leader. Because leaders differ in many ways, they develop different approaches to accomplishing tasks. They will likely continue to use a par-

301

**Chapter 9
Corporate
Culture and
Organization
Development**

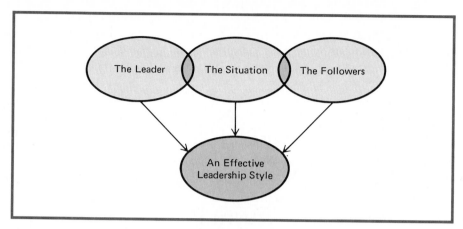

Figure 9–1. A situational approach to leadership.

ticular approach in the future if their experience indicates that it was successful in the past. For example, a person who has been successful in utilizing the ideas of subordinates will tend to continue this leadership approach. Leaders should also adapt their style to meet the needs of the followers and the situation.

The Followers. Followers also have different abilities, personalities, experience, and expectations. They do not automatically obey orders given by supervisors. Followers accept direction when they believe it to be in their best interests. For example, as a student, you will likely follow a teacher's instructions if you believe that they will assist you in preparing for the next exam.

The type of subordinates can affect a person's leadership style. If the followers are inexperienced and do not want more responsibility, an autocratic leadership style may be the most effective. Followers who are better educated and experienced and who seek responsibility will likely respond more readily to a participative leadership style. A manager must consider the needs, goals, capabilities, and experience of subordinates in order to lead the group effectively.

The Situation. The situation that managers confront can also have a significant effect on the type of leadership style that will prove most effective. Many factors in the external and internal environments may cause a leader to alter his or her style. For instance, a firm's policies may encourage an autocratic style among its managers.

Leadership styles may vary within a firm for a number of reasons. An organization's overall leadership approach must of necessity be stated in broad terms. Thus, in a firm that generally exhibits autocratic leadership, there may be some managers whose leadership style is highly participative.

At the same time, when describing an individual manager's leadership style, we should refer to a *dominant* style. A manager may, for example, normally stress employee participation. However, when the building is on fire, he or she may issue an order, "Get out of here *now* through exit number 2!" The leader does not consult anyone about this decision, and no committees are formed to study the problem. The leader has simply reverted to a more autocratic style. The situation required that the leader quickly respond to it. In organizations, there are many "fires." Leaders who develop a high degree of mutual trust and confidence within their work group will be able to adjust their leadership styles to differing situations and have them more readily accepted.

ORGANIZATIONAL CHARACTERISTICS

Organizational characteristics also affect corporate culture. Organizations vary in terms of size and complexity. Large organizations tend toward higher degrees of specialization and greater impersonalization. Labor unions often find that large firms are easier to organize than smaller ones because smaller firms tend to have closer and more informal relationships between employees and management. Complex organizations tend to employ a greater number of professionals and specialists, which alters the general approach to solving problems. Organizations vary in the degree to which communications are written and attempts are made to program behavior through rules, procedures, and regulations. Organizations also differ in the degree of decentralization of their decision-making authority, which affects the amount of autonomy and freedom of personnel within the organization.

ADMINISTRATIVE PROCESSES

Corporate culture can also be affected by administrative processes. Firms that can develop a direct link between performance and rewards tend to create climates conducive to achievement. Communication systems that are open and free-flowing tend to promote participation and creative atmospheres. General attitudes about the handling of risk and the tolerance of conflict will, in turn, have considerable impact on the type and amount of teamwork, organizational innovation, and creativity generated.

ORGANIZATIONAL STRUCTURE

Organizational structure is *the purposeful way in which the human resources of the firm are related or arranged.* An organization's structure may be rigid or flexible, depending on how rapidly its environment is changing. Another important aspect of structure is the determination of where major decisions are made. In some companies, all important decisions are made by top managers. In other firms, lower level managers are permitted to make significant decisions. Lincoln Electric Company, a highly successful weld-

303

**Chapter 9
Corporate
Culture and
Organization
Development**

ing products maker, is one such company. Richard Sabo, an executive with Lincoln says, "Around here we give a high school graduate more authority than some companies give their mid-level managers." Yet another important characteristic of organizational structure is the number of managerial levels — whether the structure is tall (many managerial levels) or flat (few managerial levels). The manager's job is very different in a flexible and flat organization from that in an inflexible and tall organization.

MANAGEMENT STYLE OF THE BOSS

The attitudes and preferences of middle and top management constrain first-line managers in much the same way that the attitudes and preferences of stockholders constrain top managers. This is why it is important for organizations to have a consistent policy about an appropriate degree of openness and participation.

At times, the managerial style of the boss is different from that of a subordinate manager. For example, a middle manager may believe in simply giving orders and having them followed. A supervisor who works for that manager may prefer to involve employees in decision making and give them a larger amount of freedom. This may create conflict, especially if the boss thinks that the supervisor's approach indicates a lack of toughness or decisiveness.

TYPES OF CULTURES

At times an organization must alter its culture in order to optimize success or influence events to survive. *Fortune* magazine concluded that this was necessary at IBM when the computer industry changed so drastically in the early 1980s.

What are the types of corporate culture that a firm may wish to emulate, and why should one particular culture prove superior to another? In terms of the openness and the degree of participation allowed, most behavioralists advocate an open and participative culture. Some behavioralists contend that such a culture is the best one for all situations. This type of culture is characterized by:

- Trust in subordinates.
- Openness in communication.
- Considerate and supportive leadership.
- Group problem solving.
- Worker autonomy.
- Information sharing.
- High output goals.

The opposite of the open and participative culture is a closed and autocratic one. It, too, may be characterized by high output goals. But such goals are more likely to be declared and imposed on the organization by autocratic and threatening leaders. There is greater rigidity in this culture, resulting from strict adherence to the formal chain of command, shorter spans of management, and stricter individual accountability. The emphasis is on the individual rather than on teamwork. Employee reactions are often characterized by their simply going through the motions and doing as they are told.

Despite criticism of traditional cultures by behavioralists, a more participative philosophy may not always work. In one instance involving the packaging of low-priced chinaware, low productivity of the work group was caused by excessive and unnecessary interaction among employees during working hours. Management found that the threat of termination did not prevent the unproductive talking because these low skilled and low paid employees were eligible for government subsidy programs. Management resolved the problem by redesigning the space allocated to the packaging process. Individual cubicles constructed of soundproof material were built for each worker. The cubicles virtually eliminated the unproductive conversation between workers. As a result, productivity increased substantially, and employee turnover was reduced. The total cost was $3200, which was recovered during the first three weeks.[8] While the executives involved were pleased with the results of their decision, the same type of action in another situation might well backfire. Many employees have strong social needs; when their attempts to satisfy these needs on the job are thwarted, negative behavioral consequences may result.

THE PARTICIPATIVE CULTURE

The prevailing managerial approach in most organizations has been characterized as being highly structured. Consequently, most attempts to alter organizational culture have been directed toward creating a culture that is more open and participative. The theme of participation developed by McGregor, Herzberg, and Maslow, among others, relates primarily to self-actualization, consultative and democratic leadership, job enrichment, and management by objectives. All of the companies identified by Peters and Waterman in their book *In Search of Excellence* as having favorable corporate cultures also had participative environments.

VALUES OF PARTICIPATION

The possible values of involving more people in the decision-making process within a firm relate primarily to productivity and morale. Increased

[8]H. Kenneth Bobele and Peter J. Buchanan, "Building a More Productive Environment," *Management World* 1 (January 1979): 8.

Paul A. Banas, Ph.D., APD
Chief Consultant and Manager, Corporate Personnel Research, Ford Motor Company

Paul A. Banas brings a unique set of experiences to his position, which makes him an invaluable asset to his company. Under his direction, the Personnel Research Section has grown steadily to become a unit that deals with a broad array of human resource management issues, including productivity, quality of work life, and organizational change and development. His major contributions have been in the areas of conceptual development, strategy formulation, consultation, and training.

Banas believes that individual and organizational improvement requires accurate information and the involvement of management, employees, and — where appropriate — union leadership. He says, "Too often managers act on perceptions rather than actual data, treating the symptoms rather than the causes of the problem." Also, he feels that in the past too few managers saw the employee as a valuable resource in problem identification and resolution. He goes on to state, "At Ford, there are indications that the management climate is changing. For example, over the last six years, a process called employee involvement (EI) has been implemented at most Ford facilities. This is a joint effort of the United Auto Workers and the Ford Motor Company. Also, managers at all levels have received special training in participative techniques and skills to support the EI processes for both salaried and hourly people. As a result, there have been significant improvements in product quality, efficiency, and the quality of work life."

Banas acknowledges that the kinds of changes needed in the workplace cannot be dictated from the top of the company. Action planning requires involvement of both management and employees at all levels if the actions are to be on target and implemented effectively. He says, "The results I've seen from our hourly and salaried EI efforts show commitment, creativity, and hard work. The recommendations that are being put into effect represent a significant and meaningful investment in the company's human resources. Over the years, this investment should reinforce the link between satisfying employee needs and attaining company goals."

According to Banas, "The personnel research consultant of the future will be the person with a broad knowledge of human resource management and a thorough understanding of individual differences, group dynamics, and management processes."

Banas originally intended to pursue a career in the physical sciences, graduating with a bachelor's degree in chemistry. During subsequent service in the U.S. Navy, he was assigned as the safety officer at a rocket and explosive producing plant that employed about 5000 people. As safety officer, he investigated industrial accidents to determine their probable causes. Inevitably, he recalls, they resulted from human action.

As a result of this assignment with the Navy, he was determined to learn more about human behavior in industry, so he earned a Ph.D. in industrial psychology from the University of Minnesota. While pursuing the degree, he was head of the undergraduate psychology office and was elected president of the local chapter of Psi Chi, an honorary psychology society.

After receiving his doctorate, Banas worked as a research psychologist for the U.S. Army Personnel Research Office. Subsequently, he became a research scientist and consultant for Human Sciences Research, Inc. While with Human Sciences Research, he was asked to join Ford Motor Company's Personnel Research Section.

Banas has produced more than twenty-five publications and participates actively in several professional organizations, including Division Fourteen of the American Psychological Association and the Personnel/Human Resources Division of the Academy of Management, which he has chaired. He has been a member of the editorial boards of *Personnel Psychology* and *Human Resources Planning*. He is an advisor to the Ball Foundation and Department of Organization and Human Resources at the State University of New York (Buffalo), and a member of the board of trustees of the Michigan Quality of Worklife Council. In addition, he maintains contact with the academic world through his teaching. He has taught courses in organizational behavior, human resource management, industrial psychology, and survey research.

productivity can result from the stimulation of ideas and from the encouragement of greater effort and cooperation. Psychologically involved employees will often respond to shared problems with innovative suggestions and unusually productive effort.

Open and participative cultures are often used to improve employee morale and satisfaction. Specific benefits to be derived include:

- Increased acceptability of management's ideas.
- Increased cooperation with members of management and staff.
- Reduced turnover.
- Reduced absenteeism.
- Reduced complaints and grievances.
- Greater acceptance of changes.
- Improved attitudes toward the job and the organization.

In general, the development of greater employee participation seems to have a direct and immediate effect on employee morale. Employees take a greater interest in the job and the organization. They tend to accept, and sometimes initiate, change not only because they understand the necessity for change, but also because they are more secure, knowing more about the change. Most experience and research indicates a positive relationship between employee participation and measures of morale, turnover, and absenteeism. However, little evidence has been presented that suggests a positive relationship between job satisfaction and productivity. Therefore, if productivity is not adversely affected by participation, the supplementary benefits alone may make participation worthwhile. On the other hand, if productivity were actually lowered, management's philosophy of organizational and human values would have to be carefully scrutinized.

307

Chapter 9
Corporate
Culture and
Organization
Development

LIMITATIONS OF PARTICIPATION

Despite the benefits of a participative approach, there are certain prerequisites to and limitations on greater employee participation in decision making. The requirements for greater participation in decision making are: (1) sufficient time; (2) adequate ability and interest on the part of the participants; and (3) restrictions generated by the present structure and system.

If immediate decisions are required, time cannot be spared for group participation. The manager decides what to do and issues directives accordingly. Also, if management should decide to switch from autocratic leadership to increased participation, some time for adjustment on the part of both manager and subordinate would be required. Participation calls for some measure of ability to govern oneself instead of leaning on others. In addition, it requires time for the subordinate to learn to handle this new-found freedom and time for the supervisor to learn to trust the subordinate.

Whether greater involvement in decision making can be developed depends largely on the abilities and interests of the participants, both subordinates and managers. Obviously, if the subordinate has neither knowledge of nor interest in a subject, there is little need to consult. As organizations and technology become increasingly complex, and as management becomes more professionalized, it is likely that employee participation will involve more cooperation seeking or information gathering. It should also be noted that not all employees are equally desirous of participation. Managers must face the fact that some workers do not seek more responsibility and greater involvement in their jobs.

QUALITY OF WORK LIFE

During the past decade, a concept that has many implications for employee participation has emerged and received much attention. This concept, called **quality of work life (QWL),** is *the extent to which employees satisfy significant personal needs through their organizational experiences.* The basic philosophy underlying many such programs is that improvements in the quality of work life stem from efforts at every organizational level to seek greater effectiveness by enhancing human dignity and growth.[9]

Firms that want to develop QWL programs must first determine the goals they wish to achieve. Therefore it is difficult to cite a list of appropriate

---

[9]Lee M. Ozley and Judith S. Ball, "Quality of Work Life: Initiating Successful Efforts in Labor–Management Organizations," *Personnel Administrator* 27 (May 1982): 27.

activities as with, for example, management by objectives (MBO) programs. The goals and actions undertaken are the joint responsibility of management, the union, and members of the organization.

Certain guidelines may be helpful in initiating QWL efforts. These guidelines include:

- QWL improvement efforts are not short-term, quick-fix programs that should be undertaken lightly.
- Organizations must forge new definitions of "how we work in this organization" when initiating QWL efforts.
- QWL improvement efforts require the willing participation and involvement of people at all levels of the organization.
- QWL improvement efforts require the commitment of organization leaders. This goes beyond the rhetoric of endorsement and support and must be demonstrated daily.
- QWL improvement efforts enable organizations to communicate and integrate their strategic goals into the day-to-day operations of the business.
- QWL improvement efforts are most effective when management and labor leaders work with their constituencies to examine and resolve internal issues before moving to cooperative problem solving in joint committees. Management's demonstrated commitment in addressing its own issues and barriers contributes substantially to supportive and responsible behaviors and actions on the part of others within the organization.
- QWL improvement efforts represent new approaches and processes in most organizations. These processes are never static and require constant attentiveness and responsiveness to developments as they occur.[10]

Thus a multitude of activities might be considered appropriate for a specific QWL program. These activities might include everything from emphasizing performance appraisal systems to initiating counseling programs to developing a more open approach to internal communication.

ORGANIZATION DEVELOPMENT

In the preceding discussion, we examined various factors within a firm that affect employee behavior on the job. To bring about desired changes in these factors and behaviors, some firms utilize **organization development (OD),** which is *an organization-wide application of behavioral science knowledge to the planned development and reinforcement of a firm's strategies, structures, and processes for improving its effectiveness.*[11]

[10]Ibid.
[11]Edgar F. Huse and Thomas G. Cummings, *Organization Development and Change,* 3rd ed. St. Paul, Minn.: West, 1985, p. 2.

309

Chapter 9
Corporate
Culture and
Organization
Development

Organization development applies to an entire system, such as a company or a plant. Based on behavioral science knowledge, OD does not neglect personal needs. It does not provide a blueprint for how things should be done, but rather an adaptive strategy for planning and implementing change. In addition, OD ensures a long-term reinforcement of change. Organization development involves both changes in the grouping of people (structure) and changes in the methods of communication (process).[12]

In order for the International Motor Company (referred to at the beginning of the chapter) to overcome substantial problems, its corporate culture must be altered significantly. A special T&D program here and a management development session there may not be sufficient. In fact, some advocates of OD view traditional management development as an antiquated idea. The essential problem with T&D is that it usually addresses organizational change in an environment away from the job. Individual managers are often provided with a good educational experience, but when the development program ends and they return to their firms, they find it very difficult to apply their new skills and knowledge. To avoid this problem, OD practitioners focus on changing organizational conditions that regulate individual behavior.[13]

Some common OD techniques, which will be discussed in the next section, include team building, quality circles, management by objectives, job enrichment, survey feedback, transactional analysis, and sensitivity training. From a practical standpoint, some of these techniques may be combined to provide a strategic approach to organization development.[14]

TEAM BUILDING

A conscious effort to develop effective work groups throughout the organization is referred to as **team building.** Although some activities may be more efficiently pursued by an individual, many problems are too broad and complex for one person to handle. In these instances, management teams may be more effective. A task-focused approach to team building may be more beneficial than an approach that views harmony and cooperation as end products in themselves. A work unit's attention is given to actual organizational tasks, with harmony and cooperation being by-products of the problem-solving process. This approach has been effectively used by both business organizations and government agencies.[15]

---

[12]Ibid.

[13]Harvey A. Hornstein and Fred T. Mackenzie, "Consultraining: Merging Management Education with Organization Development," *Training and Personnel Journal* 38 (January 1984): 52.

[14]Thomas H. Patten, Jr. and Peter B. Vaill, "Organization Development," in Robert L. Craig (ed.), *Training and Development Handbook,* 2nd ed. New York: McGraw-Hill, 1976, pp. 20-10–20-16.

[15]Jeffrey P. Davidson, "A Task-Focused Approach to Team Building," *Personnel* 62 (March 1985): 16.

Douglas McGregor has identified several characteristics of effective management teams (see Table 9–1). His version of an effective group emphasizes an informal organizational climate that is relatively free from tension. The group's decision-making process involves much discussion and broad participation. Communications are open, and listening to the views of others is emphasized. Members feel free to disagree but do so in an atmosphere of acceptance. The effective group works as a team in pursuing goals that are understood and accepted.

Effective work groups focus on solving actual problems while building efficient management teams. The team-building process begins when the team leader defines a problem that requires organizational change (see Figure 9–2). The group diagnoses the problem to determine the underlying factors. These factors may be related to such areas as breakdowns in communication, inappropriate leadership styles, or deficiencies in the organizational structure. The group then considers alternative solutions and selects the most appropriate alternative. As a result of open and frank discussions, the participants are likely to be committed to the proposed course of action. The overall improvement in the interpersonal relations of group members enhances implementation of the change.[16]

QUALITY CIRCLES

One approach to teamwork is the use of quality circles. **Quality circles are** *groups of employees who meet regularly with their supervisors to identify production problems and recommend actions for solutions.* These recommendations are then presented to higher level management for review, and the approved actions are implemented with employee participation.[17]

It is reported that in Japan more than 10 million workers participate in quality circles, which results in annual savings of 20–25 billion dollars per year.[18] Even though the culture in the United States is different, an increasing number of firms are finding that the quality circle concept can be adapted to our society. To illustrate, according to the International Association of Quality Circles, more than 100 U.S. firms are now using quality circles, including 30 of the 50 largest companies. Westinghouse alone has over 700 circles.[19]

---

[16]Michael A. Hitt, R. Dennis Middlemist, and Robert L. Mathis, *Management: Concepts and Effective Practice.* St. Paul, Minn.: West, 1983, p. 394.

[17]Robert J. Shaw, "From Skepticism to Support: Middle Management's Role in Quality Circles," *Peat Marwick/Management Focus* 29 (May–June 1982): 35.

[18]Sud Ingle, "How to Avoid Quality Circle Failure in Your Company," *Training and Development Journal* 36 (June 1982): 59.

[19]Roy G. Folz, "QWL's Effect on Productivity," *Personnel Administrator* 27 (May 1982): 20.

311

**Chapter 9
Corporate
Culture and
Organization
Development**

| **Table 9–1. Characteristics of effective groups** |

1. The atmosphere, which can be sensed in a few minutes of observation, tends to be informal, comfortable, relaxed. There are no obvious tensions.

2. There is a lot of discussion in which virtually everyone participates, but it remains pertinent to the task of the group.

3. The task or the objective of the group is well understood and accepted by the members.

4. The members listen to each other! The discussion does not have the quality of jumping from one idea to another unrelated one. Every idea is given a hearing. People are not afraid of seeming foolish by putting forth a creative thought even if it seems fairly extreme.

5. There is disagreement. The group is comfortable with this and shows no signs of having to avoid conflict or to keep everything on a plane of sweetness and light. Disagreements are not suppressed or overridden by premature group action. Individuals who disagree do not appear to be trying to dominate the group or to express hostility. Their disagreement is an expression of a genuine difference of opinion, and they expect a hearing in order to find a solution.

6. Most decisions are reached by a kind of consensus in which it is clear that everybody is in general agreement and willing to go along.

7. Criticism is frequent, frank, and relatively comfortable. There is little evidence of personal attack, either openly or in a hidden fashion. The criticism has a constructive flavor in that it is oriented toward removing an obstacle that prevents the group from getting the job done.

8. People are free in expressing their feelings as well as their ideas on both the problem and the group's operation. There is little pussyfooting, there are few hidden agendas. Everybody appears to know quite well how everybody else feels about any matter under discussion.

9. When action is taken, clear assignments are made and accepted.

10. The chairman of the group does not dominate it, or, on the contrary, does the group defer unduly to him or her. In fact, as one observes the activity, it is clear that the leadership shifts from time to time, depending on the circumstances. At various times different members, because of their knowledge or experience, are in a position to act as "resources" for the group. The members utilize them in this fashion and they occupy leadership roles while they are thus being used. There is little evidence of a struggle for power as the group operates. The issue is not who controls but how to get the job done.

11. The group is self-conscious about its own operations. Frequently, it will stop to examine how well it is doing or what may be interfering with its operation. The problem may be a matter of procedure, or it may be that an individual whose behavior is interfering with the accomplishment of the group's objectives. Whatever the problem is, it receives open discussion until a solution is found.

Source: Adapted from Douglas McGregor, *The Human Side of Management*. New York: McGraw-Hill, 1960, pp. 232–235. Copyright © 1960, McGraw-Hill Book Company. Reprinted by permission.

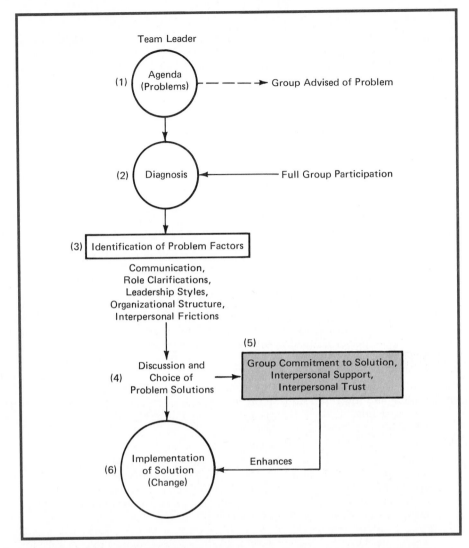

Figure 9–2. The team building process. Source: Reproduced by permission from Michael A. Hitt, R. Dennis Middlemist, and Robert L. Mathis, *Management: Concepts and Effective Practice.* St. Paul, Minn.: West, 1983, p. 393. Copyright © 1983 by West Publishing Company. All rights reserved.

Quality circles are not a panacea for T&D and productivity problems. In fact, the concept has not worked for some firms.[20] In order to implement a successful program, the following actions should be taken:

■ Establish clear goals for the program.
■ Obtain top management support.

[20]Ingle, "Quality Circle Failure," p. 54.

- Create an organizational climate that accepts the idea of participative management.
- Select an enthusiastic and capable manager for the program.
- Communicate the goals and nature of the program to all employees.
- For the initial effort, select an area of the firm where cooperation and enthusiasm from participants can be expected.
- Keep the program strictly on a voluntary basis.
- Ensure that the participants receive adequate training in the operation of quality circles.
- Start the program slowly and then let it proceed gradually but steadily.[21]

313

**Chapter 9
Corporate
Culture and
Organization
Development**

MANAGEMENT BY OBJECTIVES

> Eileen Murphy, personnel manager for Red River Wholesale Company, stopped by Michael Wills's office to discuss a vacancy in her department. While she was waiting for Michael to return from lunch, she noticed that one of his employees appeared to be very busy at his desk. His desk was cluttered and he was filling out forms and talking on the phone at the same time. When Michael returned, Eileen mentioned this extremely busy person. "Yes," said Michael, "He's always very active. The only problem is that he's one of my least effective employees. He has so many projects going at one time that nothing seems to get accomplished. He's active, yes. But productive, no!"

Michael Wills is keenly aware that activity is not necessarily a measure of productivity. **Management by objectives (MBO)** is *a philosophy of management that emphasizes the setting of agreed-on objectives by superior and subordinate managers and the use of these objectives as the primary basis of motivation, evaluation, and control efforts.* It facilitates achievement of results by directing efforts toward attainable goals. It is a management approach that encourages managers to anticipate and plan for the future. It deemphasizes guessing or making decisions based on hunches. Knowledge of MBO is especially important to the personnel manager as Personnel is often responsible for overseeing the entire company MBO program.

Because MBO emphasizes participative management approaches, it has been called a philosophy of management. Within this broader context, MBO becomes an important method of organization development. It focuses on the achievement of individual and organizational goals. The participation of individuals in setting goals and the emphasis on self-control promote not only development of individuals but also development of the entire organization.

Management by objectives as a means of organization development is a dynamic process. It must be continuously reviewed, modified, and up-

[21]Ibid., pp. 57–59.

dated. Top management's support is essential for its success.[22] It is top management that initiates the MBO process by establishing long-range goals (see Figure 9–3). For example, the president and vice president of personnel (superior–subordinate) jointly establish the firm's long-range goals regarding minority employment. When long-range goals have been formulated, it is then possible to determine intermediate and short-range objectives. After individual performance goals have been formulated, intermediate and short-range objectives may be established. At this point, the subordinate's goals are mutually agreed upon. Action plans, which outline how the objectives will be achieved, are then established and the subordinate proceeds to work toward his or her goals. At the end of the appraisal period, both superior and subordinate review the subordinate's performance and determine what can be done to overcome any problems that were encountered. Goals are then established for the next period and the process is repeated.

From an organization development standpoint, MBO offers numerous potential benefits. Some of the more prominent ones are:

- MBO provides a golden opportunity for development for managers and employees.
- It facilitates the firm's ability to change.
- It provides a more objective and tangible basis for performance appraisal and salary decisions.
- It results in better overall management and the achievement of higher performance levels.
- It provides an effective overall planning system.
- It forces managers to establish priorities and measurable targets or standards of performance.
- It clarifies the specific roles, responsibilities, and authority of employees.
- It encourages the participation of individual employees and managers in establishing objectives.
- It facilitates the process of control.
- It lets individuals know what is expected of them.
- It improves communications within the organization.
- It helps identify promotable managers and employees.
- MBO increases motivation and commitment of employees.

As you can imagine, if these benefits are achieved, the entire organization will be positively affected. Viewed from this standpoint, MBO truly becomes a means of organization development.

But certain problems have been associated with MBO. Without total support and commitment from top management, it is bound to fail. In addition, goals are at times difficult to establish, and the system can create a seemingly insurmountable paper mill if it is not closely monitored. An-

[22]Jack Bucalo, "Personnel Directors . . . What You Should Know Before Recommending MBO," *Personnel Journal* 56 (April 1977): 476.

315

**Chapter 9
Corporate
Culture and
Organization
Development**

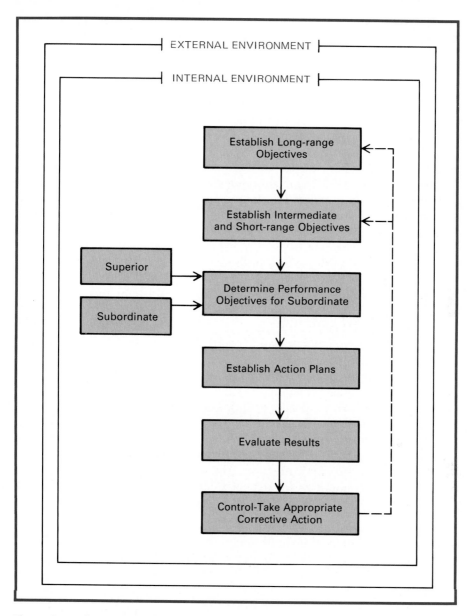

Figure 9–3. The MBO process.

other potential weakness is that there is a tendency to concentrate too much on the short-run at the expense of long-range planning. Short-term goals may be achieved while long-term goals are sacrificed. Finally, some managers believe that MBO programs are excessively time-consuming. Management by objectives forces people to think ahead and be capable of seeing how their goals fit into the overall picture. This is not an easy task for some managers.

USE OF THE MBO CONCEPT AT MONSANTO COMPANY

Utilizing many MBO concepts, the Monsanto Company has implemented its management by results (MBR) program throughout the company. While the initial direction came from top level management, program implementation has since been decentralized and has become part of the fabric of the management process.

At Monsanto, MBR is one component of the management style used to accomplish corporate objectives. Its purpose is to motivate people, assist them in setting personal and unit directions, evaluate performance, provide equitable compensation, and ensure development for employees throughout the firm. Management by results ensures that plans of individuals are properly integrated with those of their reporting unit and that involvement and cooperation are encouraged as the unit seeks to achieve group goals. In addition, Monsanto's MBR system permits flexibility by focusing not on subordinates' specific and immediate activities, but rather on their progress on a broader and longer term basis. By emphasizing results for one year or longer, employees are encouraged to avoid short-term gains at the expense of longer-term results.

One mechanism for achieving these ends is the job results analysis/goals form — the basic document in the direction-setting phase of Monsanto's MBR system. The corporate guidelines for preparing this document are broad and flexible and emphasize that managers and units should use their best judgment as to the use of the form and its various sections. The first four sections constitute the job results analysis and center on the job's longer-term definition and direction. The last five sections, the goals document, deal with coming-year expectations and performance (see Figure 9–4). The following is a brief description of each section:

1. *General conditions.* In this section, employees state their assumptions about the environment in which they plan to operate for the coming year. For example, a salesperson would consider the growth rate of industries to be served and make projections about the health of the economy. If those assumptions later turn out to be off the mark, supervisor and subordinate are encouraged to review the document for possible change in overall direction or level of expectation.
2. *Principal thrust.* The most important thing to be done during the next year is stated in this section. It serves as a good check on the goals set later.
3. *Results sought.* Here, employees identify the areas of longer-term accomplishment which are important to the job and the unit.
4. *Major results.* An X is placed in this column to identify the most important results; this helps to establish priorities.

Monsanto	COMPANY CONFIDENTIAL	JOB RESULTS ANALYSIS — GOALS 19

Principal Thrust ②

Location _____ Name _____
JRA — Date _____ Goals Date _____ Title _____

General Conditions Premises ①

Results To Be Worked Toward	Major Results	Goals	Joint Account Ability	Range		Weight
				Basic	Outstanding	
relates to Principal Thrust ③	④	⑤	⑥	⑦		⑧

JRA Approved By _____

Date _____

Goals Approved By _____

Date _____

⑨ Goals represent _____ % of total performance

Figure 9–4. Monsanto's job results analysis/goals form.

5. *Goals.* Here, the most important accomplishments for the coming year are set forth. Goals are considered milestones toward longer-term results. Normally, a Monsanto employee has from three to five goals for the year.

6. *Joint accountability.* The purpose of this section is to identify and gain commitment from those individuals — other than the supervisor or subordinates — who give or receive help in achieving each goal. Employees are encouraged to discuss their goals with others from whom support is required.

7. *Basic/Outstanding.* The range of performance for each goal is established and stated in this portion of the form. As an example, suppose a goal was established "to achieve new customer sales of $1,000,000 (expected)." In this case, $500,000 would be entered in the Basic Column and perhaps $2,000,000 in the Outstanding Column.

8. *Weight.* The entries in this column establish goal priorities for the coming year. The weight established indicates priority — not the amount of time to be spent on each goal. To accomplish this ranking

process, 100 points may be allocated among the goals or the goals may be numerically ranked.

9. *Goals represent* —— *% of your performance.* The purpose of this entry is to show the relative importance of the stated goals to the entire job.

The MBR program at Monsanto provides a means for ensuring that employee training and development is accomplished on a continuous basis. This approach integrates training and development into the overall Monsanto management process.

JOB ENRICHMENT

Job enrichment is *the deliberate restructuring of a job to make it more challenging, meaningful, and interesting.* It emphasizes the accomplishment of significant tasks so that the employee can receive a sense of achievement. Job enrichment takes an optimistic view of employee capabilities. Its use presumes that individuals have the ability to perform more difficult and responsible tasks. Further, it assumes that most people will respond favorably if they are given the opportunity to perform challenging tasks. They will also be motivated to produce at higher efficiency levels. When job enrichment is applied on a broad scale, it becomes an important OD method.

An illustration of the implementation of job enrichment is provided by a department in which employees assembled a variety of hot plates. In this work unit, employees assembled hot plates in a normal assembly-line operation. Although management was satisfied with productivity, the supervisor and an engineer applied job enrichment principles that radically changed work methods. Each employee was given responsibility for assembling the entire hot plate. Their reaction to this change was quite positive and controllable rejects decreased from 23 percent to 1 percent within six months. During the same period of time, absenteeism dropped from 8 percent to less than 1 percent. During the last six months of the year, productivity increased by 84 percent. The routine final inspection was later delegated to the assembly-line workers — a change that eliminated the need for a full-time quality control job.[23]

One of the more publicized experiences with job enrichment involves Sweden's leading car manufacturer, A. B. Volvo. Pehr Gyllenhammar introduced a drastic alternative to the traditional assembly line soon after assuming the presidency in 1971. Work at the new Kalmar plant was arranged in such a manner that groups of about twenty employees could assemble complete car components. This work arrangement permitted them to personally identify with their product. Gyllenhammar wanted his production employees to see a Volvo being driven down the street and say, "I made that car."[24]

---

[23]Edgar F. Huse and Michael Beer, "Eclectic Approach to Organizational Development," *Harvard Business Review* 49 (September–October 1971): 107.

[24]"Lessons from the Volvo Experience," *International Management* 33 (February 1978): 42.

319

**Chapter 9
Corporate
Culture and
Organization
Development**

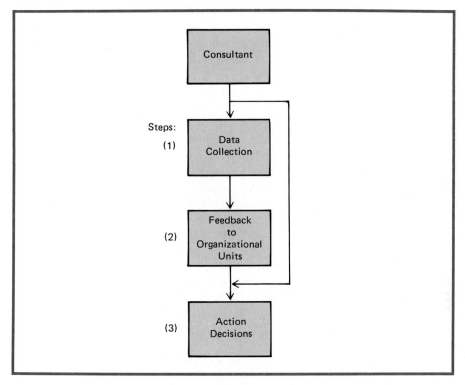

Steps:

(1) Data Collection

(2) Feedback to Organizational Units

(3) Action Decisions

Figure 9–5. The survey feedback method. Reprinted, by permission of the publisher, from ORGANIZATION DEVELOPMENT FOR OPERATING MANAGERS, by Michael E. McGill, p. 66 © 1977 AMACOM, a division of American Management Associations, New York. All rights reserved.

When jobs within an organization are restructured to increase their responsibility and challenge, the employees continually develop while performing them. The nature of these jobs actually requires that employees keep their skills updated.

SURVEY FEEDBACK

The method of basing organizational change efforts on the systematic collection and measurement of subordinate attitudes by anonymous questionnaires is **survey feedback.** It has been estimated that in the 1960s survey feedback was used more frequently than all other methods combined — and its popularity continues.[25]

Survey feedback is comprised of three essential steps, as you can see in Figure 9–5. In the first step, a consultant collects data from members of

[25]Michael E. McGill, *Organization Development for Operating Managers.* New York: AMACOM, A Division of American Management Association, 1977, pp. 62–63.

the organization. Normally, questionnaires are used and they are answered anonymously. It has been suggested that the survey include only those areas in which management is willing to make changes. Otherwise, the expectations of participating employees may not be realistic.[26]

The second step involves presenting the results of the study in the form of feedback to concerned organizational units. In the third step, the data are analyzed and action decisions are made. The decisions are directed at improving relationships in the organization. This is accomplished by revealing problem areas and dealing with them through straightforward discussions. Consultants facilitate this process by providing counsel.

An example of a survey feedback instrument is provided in Figure 9–6. This management diagnosis chart is widely used to analyze management performance in critical areas such as leadership, motivation, communication, decisions, goals, and controls. Employees are asked to check, along a continuum, the point that best describes their organization. They are also requested to indicate their views of a desired state. An organizational profile is then prepared by averaging the responses and charting them. Referring again to Figure 9–6, you can see that the present state of leadership is perceived as being quite negative. The employees surveyed apparently feel that leadership in their firm is condescending. The consensus is that the leader should show "substantial" confidence in subordinates (the desired state).

TRANSACTIONAL ANALYSIS[27]

The use of transactional analysis as an OD method is a relatively recent development.[28] It has been used, however, for a number of years as a technique for teaching behavioral principles to individuals and small groups in training and development programs. **Transactional analysis (TA) is an OD method that considers the three ego states of the Parent, the Adult, and the Child in helping people understand interpersonal relations and thus assists in improving an organization's effectiveness.**

The Parent ego state stores all the attitudes, beliefs, and values learned from authority figures early in our lives. Everything seen or heard is recorded, as on tape, and these messages influence our current behavior. The Parent ego state may reflect nuturing behavior that is sympathetic, protective, and instructive or critical behavior that is punitive, prejudicial, and judgmental. The boss who comes on as a critical parent tends to find fault excessively and to punish rather than to guide and develop subordinates.

---

[26]Don Hellriegel, John W. Slocum, Jr., and Richard W. Woodman, *Organizational Behavior,* 4th ed. St. Paul, Minn.: West, 1986, p. 610.

[27]The material on transactional analysis in this section is abridged and adapted from Thomas A. Harris, M.D., *I'm O.K. — You're O.K.* Copyright © 1967, 1968, and 1969 by Thomas A. Harris, M.D. Reprinted by permission of Harper & Row Publishers, Inc.

[28]McGill, "Organization Development," p. 106.

		Present State		Desired State	
LEADERSHIP	How much confidence is shown in subordinates?	None	Condescending	Substantial	Complete
	How free do they feel to talk to superiors about job?	Not at All	Not Very	Rather	Fully
	Are subordinates' ideas sought and used, if worthy?	Seldom	Sometimes	Usually	Always
MOTIVATION	Is predominant use made of (1) fear, (2) threats, (3) punishment, (4) rewards, (5) involvement?	1, 2, 3, Occasionally 4	4, Some 3	4, Some 3 and 5	5, 4, based on group-set goals
	Where is responsibility felt for achieving organization's goals?	Mostly at Top	Top and Middle	Fairly General	All Levels
COMMUNICATION	How much communication is aimed at achieving organization's objectives?	Very Little	Little	Quite a Bit	A Great Deal
	What is the direction of information flow?	Downward	Mostly Downward	Down and Up	Down, Up and Sideways
	How is downward communication accepted?	With Suspicion	Possibly with Suspicion	With Caution	With an Open Mind
	How accurate is upward communication?	Often Wrong	Censored for the Boss	Limited Accuracy	Accurate
	How well do superiors know problems faced by subordinates?	Know Little	Some Knowledge	Quite Well	Very Well
DECISIONS	At what level are decisions formally made?	Mostly at Top	Policy at Top, Some Delegation	Broad Policy at Top, More Delegation	Throughout but well integrated
	What is the origin of technical and professional knowledge used in decision making?	Top Management	Upper and Middle	To a Certain Extent Throughout	To a Great Extent Throughout
	Are subordinates involved in decisions related to their work?	Not at all	Occasionally Consulted	Generally Consulted	Fully Involved
	What does decision making process contribute to motivation?	Nothing, Often Weakens it	Relatively Little	Some Contribution	Substantial Contribution
GOALS	How are organizational goals established?	Orders Issued	Orders, Some Comment Invited	After Discussion, by Orders	By Group Action (Except in Crisis)
	How much covert resistance to goals is present?	Strong Resistance	Moderate Resistance	Some Resistance at Times	Little or None
CONTROL	How concentrated are review and control functions?	Highly at Top	Relatively Highly at Top	Moderate Delegation to Lower Levels	Quite Widely Shared
	Is there an informal organization resisting the formal one?	Yes	Usually	Sometimes	No—Same Goals as Formal
	What are cost, productivity and other control data used for?	Policing, Punishment	Reward and Punishment	Reward, Some Self-guidance	Self-guidance Problem Solving

Figure 9–6. An example of a survey feedback questionnaire. Reprinted, by permission of the publisher, from ORGANIZATION DEVELOPMENT FOR OPERATING MANAGERS, by Michael E. McGill © 1977 AMACOM, a division of American Management Associations, New York. All rights reserved.

The Adult ego state, on the other hand, is the objective part of us. Through our Adult, we analyze data and make independent, logical judgments. The Adult serves as our internal computer, and behavioral changes occur through this ego state.

The emotional side of individual behavior stems from the Child ego state. This state may take on different qualities — the Natural Child, the Little Professor, or the Adaptive Child. When the Natural Child dominates, the individual is expressive, self-centered, impulsive, and curious. The ego state of the Little Professor centers around being intuitive, manipulative, and creative. The manner in which the Adaptive Child behaves is determined by the parental figures with whom the individual was associated.

The interaction of ego states can have a significant impact on behavior in organizations. If organizational members know which ego state a person is in at a given time, they may be able to determine the best way to communicate. Various situations that a person may confront are presented in Figures 9–7 through 9–9. In Figure 9–7, Frank's three ego states are shown on the left and John's on the right. The two have engaged in an adult-to-adult transaction. It is a *complementary transaction* because Frank's mes-

Figure 9–7. A complementary transaction. Source: Used with the permission of Bristol-Myers Products, A Division of Bristol-Myers Company.

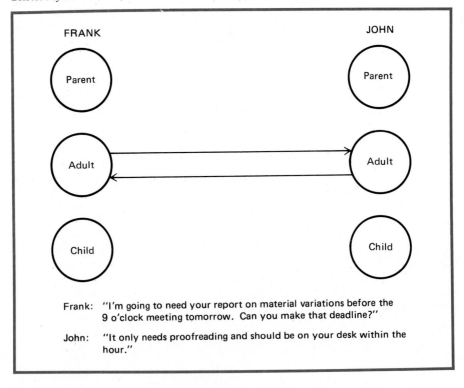

323

Chapter 9
Corporate
Culture and
Organization
Development

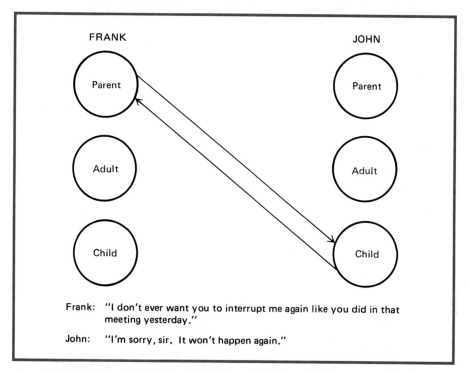

FRANK   JOHN

Parent   Parent

Adult   Adult

Child   Child

Frank: "I don't ever want you to interrupt me again like you did in that
        meeting yesterday."

John: "I'm sorry, sir. It won't happen again."

Figure 9–8. A complementary transaction involving parent and child ego states. Source: Used with the permission of Bristol-Myers Products, A Division of Bristol-Myers Company.

sage gets the expected response. When this occurs, communication remains open and there is no conflict or difficulty between the two.

A different situation is presented in Figure 9–8. Here, Frank speaks from his parent ego state to John's child state. This also illustrates a complementary transaction. However, while the lines of communication are open for the present, condescending behavior of this sort may have negative long-term consequences.

Crossed transactions occur when the message sent gets an unexpected response. Note that in Figure 9–9 Frank delivers a message from his parent ego state intended for John's child state, "I never want you to interrupt me again like you did in that meeting yesterday." Instead, John replies from his parent state, "Who the hell are you to hog the whole conversation?" Frank expected an apologetic response but instead received one that was unexpected. Here, the transaction was crossed. These types of transactions are generally unproductive and represent a breakdown in communication. While individuals should use all their ego states, the adult should remain in charge. As previously mentioned, it is through this state that behavioral changes occur.

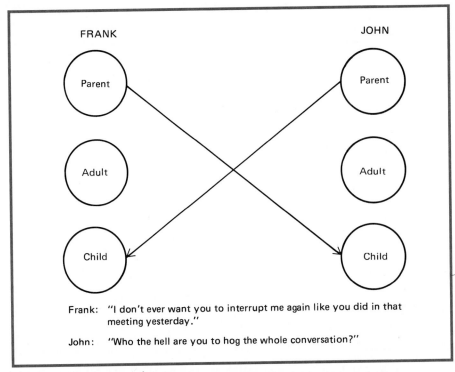

FRANK   JOHN

Parent   Parent

Adult   Adult

Child   Child

Frank: "I don't ever want you to interrupt me again like you did in that
        meeting yesterday."

John: "Who the hell are you to hog the whole conversation?"

Figure 9–9. An unexpected response results in a crossed transaction. Source: Used with the permission of Bristol-Myers Products, A Division of Bristol-Myers Company.

At Bristol-Meyers Products, a development program uses transactional analysis as the model. Since its inception in 1975, this program has involved over 1000 managers, supervisors, professionals, and sales representatives. As Richard Crosbee, vice president, personnel, puts it, "The model is unique in that it teaches basic behavioral principles and does so in a down-to-earth, practical manner, using words that all people know and understand. It can be successfully employed at all levels in the organization." Mr. Crosbee developed the program because, he states, "It was clear to me, as a personnel executive, that the poor handling of people (self and others) was the primary reason for the failure of managers."

Applying TA concepts in OD efforts on a broad basis may prove valuable in producing desired organizational change. As individuals in a firm learn to analyze their own social interactions, better communication and greater organizational effectiveness can follow.

SENSITIVITY TRAINING

An organization development technique that is designed to make us aware of ourselves and our impact on others is referred to as **sensitivity training.**

It is quite different from traditional forms of training, which stress the learning of a predetermined set of concepts.[29]

325

**Chapter 9
Corporate
Culture and
Organization
Development**

Sensitivity training features a group — often called a training group or T-group — in which there is no preestablished agenda or focus. The trainer's purpose is merely to serve as a facilitator in this unstructured environment. Participants are encouraged to learn about themselves and others in the group. Some objectives of sensitivity training are to:

1. Increase self-insight and self-awareness concerning the participant's behavior and its meaning in a social context.
2. Increase sensitivity to the behavior of others.
3. Increase awareness and understanding of the types of processes that facilitate or inhibit group functioning and the interactions between different groups.
4. Heighten diagnostic skill in social, interpersonal, and intergroup situations.
5. Increase the participant's ability to intervene successfully in intergroup or intragroup situations so as to increase member satisfaction, effectiveness, and output.
6. Increase the participant's ability to analyze continually his or her own interpersonal behavior in order to help himself or herself and others achieve more effective and satisfying interpersonal relationships.[30]

When sensitivity training begins, there is no agenda — and there are no leaders and no authority or power positions. Essentially, a vacuum exists until participants begin to talk. Through dialogue people begin to learn about themselves and others. Participants are encouraged to look at themselves as others see them. Then, if they want to change, they can.

Although the purpose of sensitivity training (to assist individuals to learn more about how they relate to other people) cannot be questioned, the technique has received considerable criticism in recent years. Individuals may be encouraged to be more open and supportive in the T-group. Then when they return to their jobs, the environment there has not changed. In addition, there has been criticism of the emotional stress that participants often undergo. And finally, there are mixed results concerning whether sensitivity training leads to improved organizational effectiveness.[31]

[29]James L. Gibson and John M. Ivancevich, *Organizations: Behavior, Structure, Processes,* 4th ed. Plano, Texas: Business Publications, 1982, pp. 580–581.

[30]John P. Campbell and Marvin D. Dunnette, "Effectiveness of T-Group Experiences in Managerial Training and Development," *Psychological Bulletin* 70(2) (August 1968): 23–104. Copyright © 1968 by the American Psychological Association. Reprinted by permission.

[31]William J. Kearney and Desmond D. Martin, "Sensitivity Training: An Established Management Development Tool," *Academy of Management Journal* 17 (December 1974): 755–760.

ORGANIZATIONAL CHANGE: AN EXAMPLE

Ronald C. Pilenzo, president of the American Society for Personnel Administration, tells of a major change he was involved with at International Multifoods Corporation. In 1979, the company was confronted with the challenge of how to integrate women into its management ranks. The organization was very conservative and did not wish to create special opportunities (jobs) for women. It was seeking a way to (1) sensitize men holding managerial positions; (2) create an awareness in women employees of job opportunities and their individual responsibilities for self-determination and self-development; and (3) achieve affirmative action goals.

After conducting extensive research on the subject, discussing the challenge with consultants and women who were experts in the field, and reviewing existing programs, Pilenzo made the following proposal to top management:

1. Design a program to fit the "organizational personality" of the company and its unique needs.
2. Offer the program on a voluntary basis to *all* women, regardless of position and rank, and on a mandatory basis to men holding managerial positions.
3. Obtain full top management support and participation.
4. Design and install a skills inventory system to identify available skills of both men and women employees nationwide to support the program.

The program was accepted by top management. Over a two-year period, more than 700 women employees and 250 executives attended sessions designed for each group. The president of the company personally introduced the first four meetings for the men to emphasize the company's commitment and goals. During the course of the program, fifteen to twenty high potential women candidates were identified for top management positions. An additional group of women began self-development programs. The financial cost of the program was significantly less than comparable programs in other companies fundamentally because of the use of existing company resources and available talent.

CONSULTANTS

Organization development efforts rely heavily on the use of qualified consultants who work with teams from the firm's management and work groups. These teams are located throughout the organization, from top management to the shop floor.[32] The consultant — a facilitator — assists both types of groups in identifying goals and solving problems that interfere with goal

[32]Fred E. Fiedler and Joseph E. Garcia, "Comparing Organization Development and Management Training," *Personnel Administrator* 30 (March 1985): 35.

achievement. The consultant is also responsible for helping guide implementation of planned change.

A consultant may come from within the organization or from the outside. The role of the consultant is to utilize his or her specialized knowledge in the area of T&D and OD in making proposals for intervention in the activities of the organization.[33] They assist managers in bringing about change in areas such as communication, leadership styles, and motivational techniques.

Management frequently believes that an outside expert brings objectivity to a situation and obtains acceptance and trust from organizational members. However, another school of thought seems to be developing. Lately, internal consultants (employees of the firm) have been serving as effective change agents. Proponents of this approach believe that the internal consultant, who knows both the formal and informal nature of the organization, can often produce desired results at a lower cost.

ORGANIZATION DEVELOPMENT PROGRAM EVALUATION

When an OD effort has been implemented, the following question must be asked: "Did anything happen as a result of this experience?" All too often the answer is "We don't know." Evaluation of an OD effort is more difficult than determining whether an employee has learned to operate a particular piece of equipment. Nevertheless, the evaluation should be done. The company has likely invested a considerable amount of time and money on the program and deserves to know whether it has produced tangible benefits.

One means of measuring program effectiveness is by assessing changes in meeting performance criteria.[34] Some of the factors to be measured might include: (1) productivity; (2) absenteeism rate; (3) turnover rate; (4) accident rate; (5) costs; and (6) scrappage. An improvement in these and other areas may mean that improvement has resulted from the OD method. For instance, if the turnover rate has declined, this might mean that workers are more satisfied with the work environment and have chosen to remain with the firm. If costs per unit produced have been reduced, it may suggest that workers are paying more attention to their work as a result of the OD program. Although this form of evaluative data is useful, it probably will not provide the entire answer as to program effectiveness.

An excellent means of determining the extent of change in worker attitudes is through the use of a survey questionnaire. This survey is administered to employees prior to OD efforts and after implementation of the change program. A measurable difference in total employee satisfaction may well suggest the effectiveness of the effort.

[33]Patten and Vaill, *Training and Development Handbook*, pp. 20-5–20-6.
[34]Gibson and Ivancevich, *Organizations*, pp. 547–548.

327

Chapter 9
Corporate
Culture and
Organization
Development

Measurement of effectiveness should not be limited to immediately after the program has been completed. It is necessary to continue to administer questionnaires on a periodic basis over an extended period of time. Evaluation is not a one-time event. And, in viewing the survey results, performance criteria should be considered in order to gain a good appreciation of the effect of the change effort.

As early as the 1950s, OD was identified as a promising and effective approach to organizational change. This appraisal has proved accurate, with the successful utilization of OD by many organizations.[35]

SUMMARY

Corporate culture is the system of shared values, beliefs, and habits within an organization that interacts with the formal structure to produce behavioral norms. Numerous factors can interact to determine the corporate culture of a firm. Communication, motivation, and leadership have an impact on a firm's psychological environment. Other factors interacting to determine corporate culture include organizational characteristics, administrative processes, organizational structure, and management style.

The prevailing management approach in most organizations has been one characterized as being highly structured. Consequently, most attempts to alter organizational culture have been directed toward creating a more open and participative culture. The possible values of involving more people in the decision-making process within a firm relate primarily to productivity and morale. Increased productivity can result from the stimulation of ideas and from the encouragement of greater effort and cooperation.

Organization development (OD) is an organization-wide application of behavioral science knowledge to the planned development and reinforcement of a firm's strategies, structures, and processes for improving its effectiveness. OD techniques include team building, quality circles, management by objectives (MBO), job enrichment, survey feedback, transactional analysis (TA), and sensitivity training. A conscious effort to develop effective work groups throughout the organization is referred to as team building. Quality circles are groups of employees who meet regularly with their supervisors to identify production problems and recommend actions for solutions. Management by objectives is a philosophy of management that emphasizes the setting of agreed-on objectives by superior and subordinate managers and the use of these objectives as the primary basis of motivation, evaluation, and control efforts. The deliberate restructuring of a job to make it more challenging, meaningful, and interesting is called job enrichment. The method of basing organizational change efforts on the systematic collection and measurement of subordinate attitudes by anonymous questionnaires is called survey feedback. Transactional analysis is

---

[35]Fiedler and Garcia, "Comparing Organization Development," p. 36.

an OD method that considers the three ego states of the "Parent," the "Adult," and the "Child" involved in interpersonal relations and assists in improving an organization's effectiveness. Sensitivity training uses leaderless discussion groups and is designed to make people aware of themselves and their impact on others.

329

Chapter 9
Corporate
Culture and
Organization
Development

QUESTIONS FOR REVIEW

1. Define *corporate culture*. What factors determine corporate culture?
2. Does a participative culture improve productivity? Defend your answer.
3. What are the values of an open and participative culture?
4. What are the limitations of participation?
5. Define each of the following terms:
   (a) Organization development
   (b) Team building
   (c) Quality circles
   (d) Job enrichment
   (e) Survey feedback
   (f) Transactional analysis
   (g) Sensitivity training
6. How can organization development programs be evaluated?
7. What is meant by the term "quality of work life?"

TERMS FOR REVIEW

Corporate culture
Motivation
Leadership
Organizational structure
Quality of work life (QWL)
Organization development (OD)
Team building

Quality circles
Management by objectives (MBO)
Job enrichment
Survey feedback
Transactional analysis (TA)
Sensitivity training

Incident 1

Burt MacDaniel was president and owner of the MacDaniel Corporation for thirty years prior to his retirement. Burt had guided the growth of the firm from a three-person operation to an organization with over 500 employees. He was hard-working, often being at his office for fifteen hours a day. Although Burt had made all major decisions, his pleasant personality had kept the firm's other managers from feeling alienated; they had accepted this arrangement.

When Burt retired, his son Jim became president. Jim had received an M.B.A. degree and was eager to take over his father's business. He believed that his college training had prepared him well for this. One of the first things Jim wanted to do was to give decision-making authority to the managers. This would permit him to look at the big picture while the day-to-day problems were solved lower in the organization.

Jim called a meeting to tell the managers

that the firm was going to implement an MBO program and that they would have more responsibility over their areas. They would not have to come to him for every decision. He spent over an hour that day describing how the MBO program would work. Over the following week he spent an additional thirty minutes or so with each manager establishing objectives.

Incident 2

For the past few years, sales at Glenco Manufacturing had been falling. The decline was industry wide. In fact, Glenco had actually been able to increase its share of the market slightly. Although forecasts indicated that demand for the products would improve in the future, Joe Goddard, the company president, believed that something needed to be done immediately to help the firm to survive this temporary slump. As a first step he employed a consulting firm to determine whether a reorganization might be helpful.

A team of five consultants arrived at the firm. They told Mr. Goddard that they first had to gain a thorough understanding of the current situation before they could make any recommendations. Mr. Goddard told them that the company was open to them. They could ask any questions that they thought were necessary.

The grapevine was full of rumors virtually from the day the consulting group arrived. One employee was heard to say, "If they shut down the company, I don't know if I could take care of my family." Another worker said, "If they move me away from my friends I'm going to quit."

When workers questioned their supervisors, they received no explanations. No one had told the supervisors what was going on either. The climate began to change to one of fear. Rather than being concerned about their daily work, employees worried about what was going to happen to the company and their jobs. Productivity dropped drastically as a result.

A month after the consultants departed, an informational memorandum was circulated throughout the company. It stated that the consultants had recommended a slight modification in the top levels of the organization to achieve greater efficiency. No one would be terminated. Any reductions would be the result of normal attrition. By this time, however, some of the best workers had already found other jobs and company operations were severely disrupted for several months.

QUESTIONS

1. Why do you believe that the employees tended to assume the worst about what was happening?
2. How could this difficulty have been avoided?

REFERENCES

Alber, Antone F. "Making Job Enrichment Pay Off." *Supervisory Management* 27 (January 1982): 30–33.

Allen, Robert F. and Silverzweig, Stanley. "Changing Community and Organizational Cultures." *Training and Development Journal* 31 (July 1977): 28–34.

Aluise, J. J. et al. "Organizational Development in Academic Medicine: An Educational Approach." *Health Care Management Review* 10 (Winter 1985): 37–43.

Bennigson, L. A. "Managing Corporate Cultures." *Management Review* 74 (February 1985): 30–32.

Cohen, Michael H. and Ross, Mary E. "Team Building: A Strategy for Unit Cohesiveness." *The Journal of Nursing Administration* XII (January 1982): 29–34.

Cowan, J. "Is Organization Development Out of Date?" *Training and Development Journal* 39 (May 1985): 18+.

Cox, Martha Glenn and Brown, Jane Covey. "Quality of Worklife: Another Fad or Real Benefit?" *Personnel Administrator* 27 (May 1982): 99–153.

Craig, Robert L. (ed.), *Training and Development Handbook: A Guide to Human Resource Development.* New York: McGraw-Hill, 1976.

Davis, Philip A. "Building a Workable Participative Management System." *Management Review* 70 (March 1981): 26–28+.

"Developing HRD and OD: The Profession and the Professional." *Training and Development Journal* 36 (January 1982): 18–30.

Donegan, Priscilla. "Quality Circles — New Productivity Power Source." *Progressive Grocer* 61 (January 1982): 105–110.

Drucker, P. F. "A Prescription for Entrepreneurial Management." *Industry Week* 225 (April 29, 1985): 33–34+.

Ernest, R. C. "Corporate Culture and Effective Planning (Organizational Culture Grid)." *Personnel Administrator* 30 (March 1985): 49–50+.

Frank, Frederic, Struth, Michael, and Donovan, Jim. "Practitioner Certification: The Time Has Come." *Training and Development Journal* 34 (October 1980): 80–83.

Franke, Arnold G., Harrick, Edward J., and Klein, Andrew J. "The Role of Personnel in Improving Productivity." *Personnel Administrator* 27 (March 1982): 83–88.

Franklin, Jerome L. "Improving the Effectiveness of Survey Feedback." *Personnel* 55 (May/June 1978): 11–17.

Gardner, M. P. "Creating a Corporate Culture for the Eighties." *Business Horizons* 28 (January–February 1985): 59–63.

George, William W. "Task Teams for Rapid Growth." *Harvard Business Review* 55 (March/April 1977): 71–80.

Grahn, John L. "White Collar Productivity: Misunderstandings and Some Progress." *Personnel Administrator* 26 (August 1981): 27–31.

Greenwood, Ronald G. "Management by Objectives: As Developed by Peter Drucker, Assisted by Harold Smiddy." *Academy of Management Review* 6 (April 1981): 225–230.

Herzberg, Frederick and Zautra, Alex. "Orthodox Job Enrichment: Measuring True Quality in Job Satisfaction." *Personnel* 53 (September/October 1976): 54–68.

Jamieson, D. W. "Improving Organizations Is Not for Lone Rangers." *Training and Development Journal* 39 (May 1985): 83.

Johnston, Robert W. "Seven Steps to Whole Organization Development." *Training and Development Journal* 33 (January 1979): 12–22.

Kanarick, Arnold. "The Far Side of Quality Circles." *Management Review* 70 (October 1981): 16–17.

Kanter, R. M. "Growth Through Cultural Change." *Management World* 14 (April 1985): 21.

Kanter, Rosabeth Moss and Stein, Barry A. "Ungluing the Stuck Motivation Performance and Productivity Through Expanding Opportunity." *Management Review* 70 (July 1981): 45–49.

"Lessons from the Volvo Experience." *International Management* 33 (February 1978): 42–46.

Littlejohn, Robert F. "Team Management: A How-to Approach to Improved Productivity, Higher Morale, and Lasting Job Satisfaction." *Management Review* 71 (January 1982): 23–28.

Mahoney, Francis X. "Team Development, Part 2: How to Select the Appropriate TD Approach." *Personnel* 58 (November–December 1981): 21–38.

Marchington, Mick. "Employee Participation — Consensus or Confusion?" *Personnel Management* 13 (April 1981): 38–41.

Myers, Donald W. "The Impact of a Selected Provision in the Federal Guidelines on Job Analysis and Training." *Personnel Administrator* 26 (July 1981): 41–45.

Niehoff, Marilee and Romans, M. Jay. "Needs Assessment as One Step Toward Enhancing Productivity." *Personnel Administrator* 27 (May 1982): 35–39.

O'Toole, James. "How Management Hinders Productivity," *Industry Week* 210 (August 10, 1981): 55–58.

Ozley, Lee M. and Ball, Judith S. "Quality of Work Life: Initiating Successful Efforts in Labor-Management Organizations." *Personnel Administrator* 27 (May 1982): 27–33.

Pascale, R. "The Paradox of Corporate Culture: Reconciling Ourselves to Socialization." *California Management Review* 27 (Winter 1985): 26–41.

Patten, Thomas M., Jr. "The Productivity of Human Resources in Government: Making Human Effort and Energy Count for More." *Human Resource Management* 19 (Spring 1980): 2–10.

Rowlandson, P. "The Oddity of Organizational Development." *Management Today* (November 1984): 90–92.

Shrivastava, P. "Integrating Strategy Formulation with Organizational Culture." *Journal of Business Strategy* 5 (Winter 1985): 103–111.

Snyder, Robert A. "A Model for the Systematic Evaluation of Human Resource Development Programs." *Academy of Management Review* 5 (July 1980): 431–443.

Strauss, Nan and Castino, Anthony. "Human Resource Development: Promise or Platitude?" *Personnel Administrator* (November 1981): 25–27.

"Three Faces of Organizational Change." *Training* 22 (March 1985): 108–109.

CHAPTER OBJECTIVES
1. Define *career planning and development* and describe factors affecting career planning.
2. Explain the importance of individual career planning and how a thorough self-assessment is crucial to career planning.
3. Explain the nature of career planning and why organizational career planning is important.
4. Discuss career paths and identify methods of organization career planning and development.
5. Describe career development.

Chapter 10

CAREER PLANNING AND DEVELOPMENT

Bob Allen and Thelma Gowen, both supervisors at Sharpco Industries, were speaking to each other one day last week. Bob said, "I'm really frustrated. I spoke with the boss last week about career opportunities at Sharpco and all he kept saying was, 'there are all kinds of opportunities.' I need more than that. I'm not sure if I want to spend my life in production or if there are better career opportunities." Thelma replied, "I'm having the same trouble. He told me that 'the sky's the limit.' I'd like to know where I might end up if I decide to stay with Sharpco."

It seems obvious from the preceding discussion that Sharpco Industries has no career planning and development program. Bob is frustrated, and Thelma wants to know what career avenues are available to her. Lacking this knowledge, they may decide not to remain with Sharpco. Career planning and development is important to both the individual and the company to ensure that people with the necessary skills and experience will be available when needed. According to a recent American Management Association study, promoting career development is the hallmark of a superior manager.[1]

In this chapter we first introduce the concept of career planning and development. Next, we identify some factors affecting career planning. Then we describe the nature of career planning. This is followed by a discussion of individual career planning and a section on the reasons why organizations get involved in career planning. Types of career planning that organizations conduct are then described, followed by a section on methods used in career planning and development. Finally, we discuss how a person might begin a career in Personnel.

CAREER PLANNING AND DEVELOPMENT DEFINED

A **career** is *a general course of action a person chooses to pursue throughout his or her working life.* **Career planning** is *a process whereby an individual sets career goals and identifies the means to achieve them.* The major focus of career planning should be on helping the employees achieve a better match between personal goals and the opportunities that are realistically available in the organization. Career programs should not concentrate only on advancement opportunities. From a practical standpoint, there are not enough high level positions to make upward mobility a reality for a large number of employees. Career planning needs to focus on providing psychological successes that do not necessarily entail promotions.[2]

Individual and organizational careers are not separate and distinct. A person whose individual career plan cannot be carried out within the organization will probably leave the firm sooner or later. Thus organizations should assist employees in career planning so that both can satisfy their needs. **Career paths** are *flexible lines of progression through which employees typically move.* Following established career paths, the employee can undertake career development with the firm's assistance. **Career development** is *a formal approach taken by the organization to ensure that people with the proper qualifications and experience are available when*

---

[1]Robert W. Goddard, "Building Careers for Your Employees," *Management World* 14 (June 1985): 13.

[2]Marilyn A. Morgan, Douglas T. Hall, and Alison Martier, "Career Development Strategies in Industry: Where Are We and Where Should We Be?" *Personnel* (March/April 1979): 14.

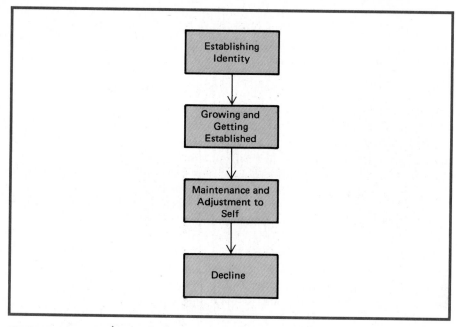

Figure 10–1. Life stages. Source: Adapted from James W. Walker, *Human Resource Planning*. Copyright © 1980 by McGraw-Hill Book Company. Used with the permission of McGraw-Hill Book Company.

needed. Individual career planning and human resource planning are highly interrelated.

Career planning and development benefits both the individual and the organization. For example, a large bank estimated that it saved $1.95 million in one year through its career counseling program. Turnover was reduced by 65 percent. Performance improved by 85 percent, productivity increased by 25 percent, and opportunity for promotion increased by 75 percent.[3]

FACTORS AFFECTING CAREER PLANNING

Several factors affect a person's view of a career. Two of these, life stages and career anchors, are described in this section.

LIFE STAGES

People change constantly and thus view their careers differently at various stages of their lives. Some of these changes are caused by the aging process, but others result from factors such as the opportunity for growth and status. The basic life stages are shown in Figure 10–1.

[3]Milan Moravec, "A Cost-Effective Career Planning Program Requires a Strategy," *Personnel Administrator* 27 (January 1982): 28.

The first stage is that of establishing identity. This stage is typically reached between the ages of ten and twenty. In this stage, career alternatives are explored and an attempt is made to move into the adult world. Stage two involves growing and getting established in a career. It typically lasts from ages twenty to forty. During this stage a person chooses an occupation and establishes a career path. The third stage, self-maintenance and self-adjustment, generally lasts to age fifty and beyond. A person either accepts life as it is or makes adjustments. Career change and divorce often occur at this stage when people have serious questions about the quality of their lives. The final stage is that of decline. Diminishing physical and mental capabilities may bring on this stage. Aspiration and motivation may be lowered. In some instances, this stage is induced by forced retirement.

Individuals have different career development needs at different stages in their careers.[4] However, most development activities are directed at new, younger workers. Because of the change in the mandatory retirement age in the Age Discrimination in Employment Act (from age sixty-five to age seventy), the maintenance and adjustment stage is likely to be extended.[5] Therefore career development in the future may be needed in more than the initial years of an employee's work life.

CAREER ANCHORS

All of us have different aspirations, backgrounds, and experiences. Our personalities are molded, to a certain extent, by the results of our interactions with our environments. Edgar Schein's research identified *five different motives that account for the way people select and prepare for a career*, and he called them **career anchors**.[6] These five career anchors are:

1. *Managerial Competence.* The career goal of managers is to develop qualities of interpersonal, analytical, and emotional competence. People using this anchor want to manage people.
2. *Technical/Functional Competence.* The anchor for technicians is the continuous development of technical talent. These individuals do not seek managerial positions.
3. *Security.* The anchor for security-conscious individuals is to stabilize their career situations. They often see themselves tied to a particular organization or geographical location.
4. *Creativity.* Creative individuals are somewhat entrepreneurial in their attitude. They want to create or build something that is entirely their own.
5. *Autonomy and Independence.* The career anchor for independent people is a desire to be free from organizational constraints. They

---

[4]Morgan, Hall and Martier, "Career Development Strategies," p. 14.
[5]James W. Walker, *Human Resource Planning.* New York: McGraw-Hill, 1980, pp. 331–332.
[6]Edgar Schein, "How 'Career Anchors' Hold Executives to Their Career Paths," *Personnel* (May–June 1975): 11–24.

value autonomy and want to be on their own and work at their own pace.

One of the implications of these career anchors is that companies must be flexible enough to provide alternative paths to satisfy people's varying needs. Firms must recognize that not everyone is motivated by the need for managerial competence. Individuals may be valued employees even if they do not have managerial aspirations.

INDIVIDUAL CAREER PLANNING

The primary responsibility for career planning rests with the individual. Career planning begins with gaining a realistic understanding of oneself. Better self-understanding will help a person to see which career anchor may be predominant. Then a person is in a position to establish realistic goals and to determine what must be done if these goals are to be achieved. This action also lets the person know whether his or her goals are realistic.

Getting to know oneself is not a one-time occurrence. As we progress through life, our priorities change. You may know yourself at one stage of your life and later begin to see yourself differently. Gaining self-insight involves conducting a thorough self-assessment. Some tools that have been proven useful in this endeavor include preparing a strengths/weaknesses balance sheet and a likes and dislikes analysis.

STRENGTHS/WEAKNESSES BALANCE SHEET

Each person is unique. This creates problems in decision making. Individuals have different strengths and weaknesses, which may change somewhat as they grow older. In making career decisions, it is critical for people to understand their strengths and weaknesses. By recognizing strengths, a person may be encouraged to pursue a particular career path. Awareness of weaknesses may discourage a certain career path or encourage training or development to remove deficiencies.

The **strengths/weaknesses balance sheet (SWBS)** is *a technique that was developed to assist people in making career path decisions.* Many have found this procedure beneficial when confronting career decisions. The procedure involves identifying both strengths and weaknesses as they are perceived. If people believe that they have a certain strength or weakness, whether real or not, it may affect their choice of a career.

The first step in preparing an SWBS is to draw a line down the middle of a sheet of paper. One side is headed *Strengths* and the other, *Weaknesses*. Perceived strengths and weaknesses are then listed. The process is not complete after only one attempt, however; it must be repeated several times. For most people, the first listing will probably produce more weaknesses than strengths. As people understand themselves better, perceived weaknesses may be seen in a different light as strengths. For example, a perceived weakness such as, "I cannot bear to look inactive," may also be viewed as a strength if considered from a different perspective. An illustration of an actual SWBS is presented in Figure 10–2. The most important consideration in completing the SWBS is that a person be totally honest. No one except the person completing the SWBS should have access to the information. It should be used strictly as a means of gaining a better understanding of factors that could affect career path decisions. Remember also that items on the SWBS can change at different life stages.

LIKES AND DISLIKES ANALYSIS

Similar to the SWBS, the **likes and dislikes analysis** provides a person with *a tool for assessing certain factors that could have an impact on the development of a career path.* An illustration of a likes and dislikes analysis is shown in Figure 10–3. Dislikes should be considered as self-imposed restrictions. For instance, if an individual is unwilling to relocate outside a certain region, this preference should be listed as a dislike. Likewise, a disdain for a desk job should be placed in the same category. On the other hand, likes are things that a person has discovered to be enjoyable. An example of a "like" might be enjoyment of working for a large company, a medium-sized company, or even a small company. There are advantages and disadvantages associated with any of the choices. It is a matter of personal preference as to which size firm should be placed in the likes category.

As with a person's strengths and weaknesses, likes and dislikes can also change over time. People might enjoy extensive traveling at one stage of a career and at a later phase find it quite distasteful. In any event, likes and dislikes should certainly be taken into consideration in establishing individual career paths.

The self-assessment helps a person understand his or her basic motives or career anchors. Understanding oneself may set the stage for progressing into management or seeking further technical competence. A person with no desire to progress into management would be foolish to accept such a promotion. People who know themselves can make the needed rational decisions that are necessary for successful career planning. Many people get sidetracked because they choose careers based strictly on the wishes of others and not on what is best for them personally.

THE NATURE OF CAREER PLANNING

The process by which individuals plan their life's work is referred to as career planning.[7] Through career planning, a person evaluates his or her

---

[7]James W. Walker, "Does Career Planning Rock the Boat?" *Human Resource Management* 17 (Spring 1978): 2.

STRENGTHS	WEAKNESSES
Hard worker	Tend to be close-minded
Responsible	Inefficient time manager
Honest	Tend to nitpick
Religious	Hot tempered (sometimes)
High morals	Nervous in unfamiliar places
Take criticism well	Can't stay put in one place very long (i.e. desk, class-room, etc.)
Give constructive criticism	
Patient	Very opinionated
Very prompt	Put things off until last minute
Dependable	Bog down on detail in interesting subjects and over-look detail in less interesting subjects
Conservative	
Enjoy people	Poor in mathematics
Active	Allow friendship to affect decisions and judgment at times
Like to work	
Work well under pressure	Too serious at times
Good jugdment	Possessive
Slow to anger	Bored easily
High degree of empathy	Tend to preach at times
Help others	Stubborn
Go an extra mile	Daydream
Kind	Judgmental
Very neat and orderly	Quick to speak out before rationally analyzing facts
Confident	Open mouth without engaging brain
Persistent	Have hard time remembering names
Like to read	Tend to overemphasize and exaggerate
Like to work with hands	Spelling
Like to travel	On occasion make snap judgments about situations and people's characters
Like to make friends	
Do things my own way	Tend to downgrade myself
Write well	Like to spend money
Don't smoke, drink, etc.	Quick to correct people (even superiors) when they are wrong
Don't hold grudges	
	Impatient reading technical material; skim through, missing important detail
	Clock watcher

Figure 10–2. A strengths/weaknesses balance sheet.

LIKES	DISLIKES
Like to travel	Do not want to work for a large firm
Would like to live in California	Will not work in the North
Like to be my own boss	Do not like to work behind a desk all day
Would like to live in a large city	Do not like to wear suits all the time
Enjoy watching football and baseball	
Enjoy playing golf and tennis	

Figure 10–3. A likes and dislikes analysis.

own abilities and interests, considers alternative career opportunities, establishes career goals, and plans practical development activities.

A person should gain insight into his or her personal values and goals as part of individual career planning. However, an individual should also conduct a corporate opportunity assessment, asking questions such as the following:

1. What are the prospects for promotion or transfer from my present job?
2. What percentage of employees reach a certain target level within this organization?
3. What are the pay ranges for various job levels?
4. Where is the fastest growth and therefore the best promotion opportunity in the company?
5. If I have reached a dead end, what are paths for moving down so I can move up faster somewhere else?[8]

Although the primary responsibility for career planning rests with the individual, organizations can do much to assist in the process. Firms should recognize this and should be actively interested in career planning. From the organization's viewpoint, career planning involves a conscious attempt to maximize a person's potential contribution. Firms that actively assist in career planning programs for their employees reap many benefits. As Hendy Stewart MacKenzie Burns, an internationally known Shell Oil Company executive, said, "Good managers are people who aren't worried about their own careers, but rather the careers of those who work for them. My advice: Don't worry about yourself. Take care of those who work for you, and you'll float to greatness on their achievements."[9]

The career planning process is depicted in Figure 10–4. It is a continuous endeavor, which begins with a person's placement in an entry-level

[8]Morgan, Hall, and Martier, "Career Development Strategies," pp. 14–30.
[9]Goddard, "Building Careers," p. 12.

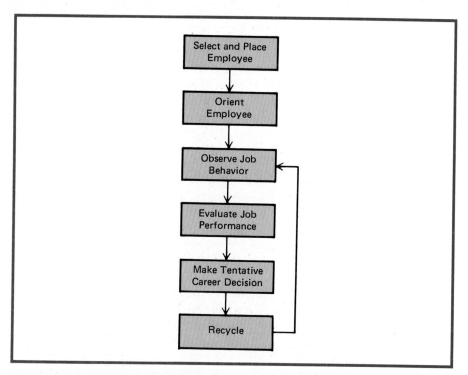

Figure 10–4. The career planning process. Source: Adapted from John E. McMahon and Joseph C. Yeager, "Manpower and Career Planning," in (ed.), Robert L. Craig, *Training and Development Handbook*. Copyright © 1976 by McGraw-Hill Book Company. Used with permission of McGraw-Hill Book Company.

job and initial orientation. Job performance will then be observed and compared with the job standards. At this stage, strengths and weaknesses will be noted, which will enable management to assist the employee in making a tentative career decision. Naturally, this decision can be altered at a later date as the process continues. This tentative career decision is based on a number of factors, including personal needs, abilities, and aspirations, as well as the needs of the organization. Management can then schedule training and development programs that relate to the employee's specific needs. For instance, a person who desires to progress upward in the field of labor relations may require additional legal training.

Note again in Figure 10–4 that career planning is an ongoing process. It takes into consideration the changes that occur in people and organizations. This type of flexibility is absolutely necessary in today's dynamic organizational environment.[10] Not only do the firm's requirements change,

[10]John E. McMahon and Joseph C. Yeager, "Manpower and Career Planning," in Robert L. Craig (ed.), *Training and Development Handbook*. New York: McGraw-Hill, 1976, pp. 11–18.

Gayla S. Godfrey,
SPHR
Personnel/Industrial
Relations Manager,
Pneumotive, A Division
of FL Industries, Inc.

When Gayla S. Godfrey first entered college in 1966, she jokingly referred to her major as "fun." Godfrey says, "It was several years before I recognized the true value of a formal education and returned to earn a degree from Northeast Louisiana University." Because the personnel field is dynamic, she believes that professionals working in this area must keep abreast of expanding knowledge and current laws through a continuing process of career growth and development. In view of this, she has attended and completed more than sixty personnel-related courses and seminars. She is accredited by the Personnel Accreditation Institute as a Senior Professional in Human Resources (SPHR).

Godfrey has a varied work history that includes experience in government, private industry, service organizations, and direct selling. Oddly enough, her first job was in personnel. She was fresh out of college (the first time) and went to an employment agency, which could not place her because of lack of work experience — so they hired her. Later, she worked in several secretarial positions in the banking industry. Being highly motivated by the challenge and reward of sales, she joined Home Interiors & Gifts, Inc., and rose to the top 1 percent of 16,000 saleswomen nationwide for three consecutive years. "Mary Crowley, founder of Home Interiors, inspired me with her famous quotation, 'Be somebody. God doesn't have time to make a nobody.'"

Godfrey goes on to say, "I've been extremely fortunate to have worked for people who expressed confidence in me and who gave me the opportunity to grow professionally. I set my goals high and was promoted through the ranks to the position of personnel director for the Ouachita Parish Police Jury (local government)." In that position, she directed all activities of the Per-

but individuals may choose to revise their career progression. An employee might believe, for instance, that he or she could be more productive in Personnel than in marketing or vice versa. Rather than lose a valued employee, the firm may attempt to facilitate this change.

WHY ORGANIZATIONAL CAREER PLANNING?

If an organization is to be successful, it must be capable of ensuring that properly qualified people are available when vacancies occur. We have already discussed recruitment and selection as means of accomplishing this goal. However, if a company stresses promotion from within, a pro-

sonnel Department, including planning, organizing, developing, and coordinating the functions of recruitment, selection, evaluation, classification, administration of compensation and benefits, EEO compliance, grievance, training and development. She also developed the personnel management system for the Ouachita Parish Public Libraries, which included conducting a job analysis; writing all job descriptions, the policy manual, and the employee handbook; and developing the classification and compensation plan.

Next, as personnel director for G. B. Cooley Hospital, Godfrey met the challenge of developing the first personnel department for the hospital.

In 1981, she accepted an opportunity to join ITT Pneumotive, a unit of ITT Corporation, as personnel specialist/EEO coordinator. She said, "During my first interview with ITT I was asked if I considered this position a step backward in my career from my current position as director. I told my future boss it's difficult to consider working

for one of the world's largest corporations as anything but a step forward, and besides, my intentions were to do such an outstanding job that he would be promoted and I would be in line for his position." Three years later this goal was achieved and she was promoted to personnel/industrial relations manager. Within six months of her promotion, the company was acquired by FL Industries, Inc. Today, she is responsible for employee relations policies and practices, as well as for the functional areas of personnel services, union negotiations and labor relations, and safety and security.

Godfey believes that the personnel professional must be active in professional, civic, and community organizations. She is past president of the local chapter of the American Society for Personnel Administration (ASPA), served on the Intergovernmental Personnel Advisory Board to the Governor of Louisiana, and is active in the Chamber of Commerce and United Way.

cedure is needed that will identify job progression possibilities and establish the required qualifications for each position. The process of establishing career paths within a firm is referred to as organizational career planning.

Career planning programs should be implemented only when they contribute to the accomplishment of basic organizational goals. Therefore the rationale for career planning programs varies among firms. In most organizations, career planning programs are expected to achieve one or more of the following goals:

- *More effective development of available talent.* Individuals are more likely to be committed to development that is directed toward a specific career plan. The purpose of the development can then be better understood.

- *Self-appraisal opportunities for employees considering new or nontraditional career paths.* Some excellent workers do not view the traditional upward mobility progression as their optimum career path. Other workers see themselves in dead-end jobs and seek relief. Rather than lose these workers, a firm can offer career planning to help them identify new and different career paths.
- *More efficient development of human resources within and among divisions and/or geographic locations.* If the traditional progression of workers was upward mobility in a division, career paths should be developed that cut across division and geographic location lines.
- *A demonstration of a tangible commitment to EEO and affirmative action.* Adverse impact can occur at virtually any level in an organization. In many instances firms that are totally committed to reducing adverse impact cannot find qualified members of protected groups to fill vacant positions. One means of overcoming this problem is to have an effective career planning and development program. Frequently, AAPs require companies to set up career development programs for protected groups.
- *Satisfaction of employees' personal development needs.* Individuals who see their personal development needs being met tend to be more satisfied with their jobs and the organization.
- *Improvement of performance through on-the-job training experiences provided by horizontal and vertical career moves.* The job itself is the most important influence on career development. Each job can provide different challenges and experiences.
- *Increased employee loyalty and motivation, leading to decreased turnover.* Individuals who see that the firm is interested in their career planning will be more likely to remain with the organization.
- *A method of determining training and development needs.* If a person desires a certain career path and does not presently have the proper qualifications, this focuses attention on the training and development needs that should be stressed.[11]

All of these goals may be desirable. But successful career planning depends on a firm's ability to satisfy the goals that it considers to be most crucial.

As shown in Figure 10–5, a career planning program may prompt some employees to develop more realistic expectations. This ultimately leads to enhanced performance, improved retention, and better utilization of talent. Although certain benefits are associated with career planning, risks are also involved. Difficulties occur when the career planning program raises employee expectations to unrealistic levels. When this occurs, organizational disruption, diminished performance, and turnover may result. Therefore the focus of a career planning program should be on developing realistic

---

[11]Moravec, "Cost-Effective Career Planning," p. 29.

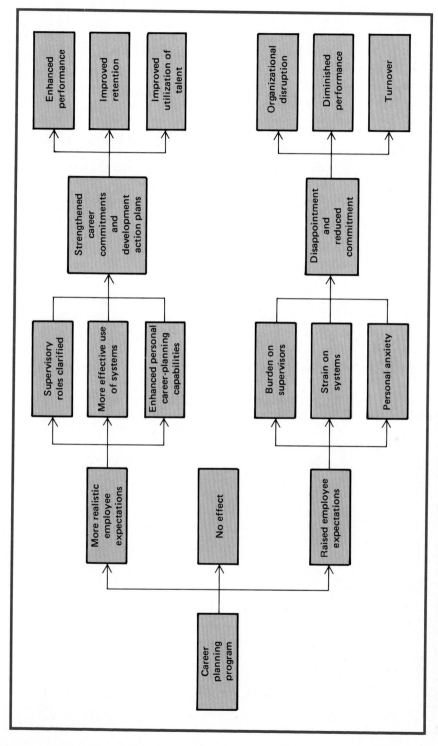

Figure 10–5. The effects of career planning. Source: James W. Walker, "Does Career Planning Rock the Boat?" *Human Resource Management* 17 (Spring 1978): 3. Used with permission of Human Resource Management, University of Michigan, Ann Arbor, Mich.

Table 10–1. Job title samples with related career guidance information

Conventional investigative job family		Prerequisites			Career path	
Job title	Division	Supervisory	Educational level	Years of experience	From	To
Senior Staff Accountant	Accounting	No	B.A. or B.S.	3–4	Staff Accountant Supervisor—Accounts Receivable Provider Auditor	Cost Analysis Coordinator Credit and Collection Coordinator Supervising Senior Staff Accountant
Cost Production Supervisor	Accounting	Yes	Some College	2–3	Supervisor—Cash Receipts Staff Accountant—Payroll	Supervisor—Government Reporting Assistant Manager—Payroll Accounts Payable Cost Production Coordinator
Cost Analyst	Controller	Yes	B.A. or B.S.	4–5	Senior Financial Analyst Cost Analyst Senior Staff Accountant	Manager—Cost Management and Investments Manager—Budget Administration Manager—Corporate Reporting and Business Analysis
Reports Analyst	Accounting	No	Some College	1–2	Payroll Processor Statistical Clerk IV Report Specialist	Management Information Coordinator Staff Accountant—Payroll

Source: Dennis J. Kravetz and Stephanie E. Derderian, "Developing a Career Guidance Program Through the Job Family Concept," reprinted from the October 1980 issue of *Personnel Administrator*, copyright 1980, the American Society for Personnel Administration, 606 North Washington Street, Alexandria, VA 22314.

expectations.[12] If employees believe that they have better opportunities than actually exist, disappointments are inevitable.

CAREER PATHS

As previously mentioned, career paths are flexible lines of progression through which employees typically move. Information regarding career options and opportunities must be available before individuals can begin to set realistic career goals. One means of accomplishing this task is to develop career path information for each job. This information may be based on historical trends within the organization, or it may be based on similarities to other jobs in the same job family.[13] A small sample of job titles with related career guidance information is shown in Table 10–1. Information such as this can be developed from job descriptions. The career path information is particularly useful because it:

1. Shows each employee how his or her job relates to other jobs.
2. Presents career alternatives.
3. Describes educational and experience requirements for a career change.
4. Points out the orientations associated with other jobs.[14]

Traditionally, career paths have focused on upward mobility within a particular occupation. Several paths might lead to a high level position in that occupation. A career path chart showing progression steps from an entry-level personnel position to corporate personnel director is shown in Figure 10–6. As you can see, a person may choose from among many avenues if his or her ultimate goal is to be the corporate personnel director. Through studying job descriptions, a person should be able to determine the developmental needs required to achieve a higher level position.

Some enlightened firms have recognized that not everyone wants to follow traditional vertical career movements within specific functions. Career paths have been developed that take into consideration lateral, diagonal, and even downward career progression. Not all employees want promotions. Some, after analyzing their career goals, may prefer to try something new and make a lateral move. Others may want to change career fields. Still others have reached a stage in their lives where they desire less responsibility and more personal time. These individuals may seek a downward career progression.[15] Although the needs of the organization must first

---

[12]Walker, "Career Planning," p. 3.

[13]Dennis J. Kravetz and Stephanie E. Derderian, "Developing a Career Guidance Program Through the Job Family Concept," *Personnel Administrator* 29 (October 1980): 41.

[14]Ibid., p. 42.

[15]Richard D. Conner and Robert L. Fjerstad, "Internal Personnel Maintenance," in Dale Yoder and Herbert G. Heneman (eds.), *Staffing Policies and Strategies: ASPA Handbook of Personnel and Industrial Relations*, Vol. I. Washington, D.C.: The Bureau of National Affairs, 1979, pp. 4-226–4-227.

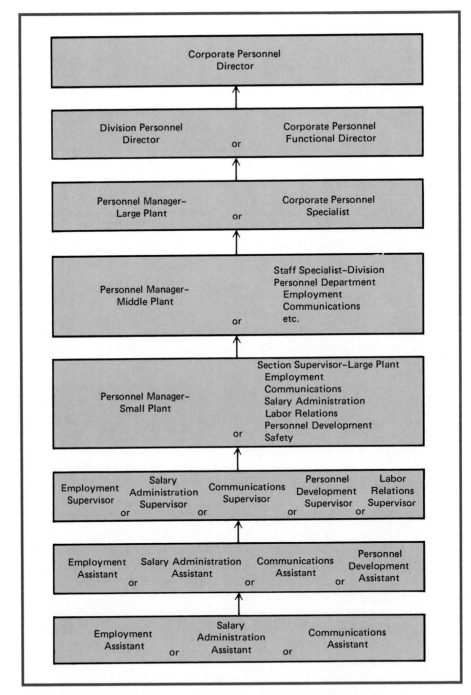

Figure 10–6. From entry level position to corporate personnel director. Source: Howard M. Mitchell, "Selecting and Developing Personnel Professionals." Reprinted with permission *Personnel Journal*, copyright © July 1970.

be taken into consideration, it is often possible to retain and motivate valued employees by making available these forms of career paths.

Another problem related to traditional career paths is plateauing. Plateauing is a career condition that occurs when job functions and work content remain the same.[16] Between 1950 and 1976, there were extraordinary opportunities for promotions in many companies. However, quite a different picture exists today as a large number of people in the work force with similar educational backgrounds compete for fewer promotions. In a society where promotions have always been an important measure of success, plateauing will present new challenges for those involved with career planning and development. Alternative means of rewarding employees must be found and used. Importantly, employees must be convinced that their worth is not measured solely in terms of promotion. This topic is dealt with further in chapter 12.

METHODS OF ORGANIZATION CAREER PLANNING AND DEVELOPMENT

Career planning and development is becoming increasingly necessary in order for firms to maintain their effectiveness. There are numerous means by which individuals can be assisted in career planning and development. Some currently used methods, most of which are used in various combinations, are:

- *Management by Objectives (MBO)*. MBO provides an excellent means of assisting in career planning. Recall from our previous discussion of MBO that the superior and subordinate jointly agree on goals that can be accomplished during a certain period of time. Also, you may recall that needed resources are made available. These resources may well include developmental programs. In addition, when goals are not achieved, future developmental needs may be identified.
- *Career Counseling*. Persons either inside or outside the organization may counsel employees as to the most beneficial career paths for them. Personnel professionals are often called on for assistance. Psychologists or guidance counselors are also used. Colleges and universities may be sources of counseling help.
- *Company Material*. Some firms provide material specifically developed to assist their workers in career planning. Such material is tailored to the firm's special needs.
- *Performance Appraisal System*. The firm's appraisal system can also be a valuable tool in career planning. Because strengths and weaknesses are typically noted, development needs may be discovered during this process. At times it may be difficult or even

---

[16]Geraldine Spruell, "Say So Long to Promotions," *Training and Development Journal* 39 (May 1985): 70–74.

impossible to overcome a particular weakness, and an alternate career path may have to be chosen.

- *Workshops.* Some organizations conduct workshops lasting two or three days for the purpose of helping workers develop careers within the company. It helps them to match their specific career goals with the needs of the company.

CAREER DEVELOPMENT

Career development includes any and all activities that prepare a person for progression along a designated career path. Thus career development may involve both formal and informal means. Career development programs may be conducted in-house or by outside sources, such as professional organizations or colleges and universities.

In-house programs are usually planned and implemented by a training and development unit within the firm's personnel department. Line managers are also frequently utilized to conduct program segments. Outside the company, organizations such as the American Society for Personnel Administration and the American Management Association are active in conducting conferences, seminars, and other types of career development programs.

Numerous colleges and universities provide management training and development programs for industry. They are often staffed with capable faculty, usually have adequate facilities, and may be able to provide programs less expensively. At times, these institutions possess expertise not available within business organizations. In some cases, it is advantageous for academicians and management practitioners to jointly present such programs.

Certain principles should be observed with regard to career development.[17] First, the job itself has the most important influence on career development. Each day may present a different challenge. What is learned on the job has much more influence on development than formally planned development activities. Second, the type of development skills that will be needed is determined by the specific type of job demands. The skills needed to become a first-line supervisor will likely be different from those needed to become middle manager. Third, development will occur only when a person has not yet obtained the skills demanded by a particular job. If the purpose of a transfer is to further develop an employee, and this individual already possesses the necessary skills for the new job, little or no learning will take place. Finally, the time required to develop the necessary skills can be reduced by identifying a rational sequence of job assignments for a

[17]Harry L. Wellbank, Douglas T. Hall, Marilyn A. Morgan, and W. Clay Hammer, "Planning Job Progression for Effective Career Development and Human Resources Management," *Personnel* (March–April 1978): 12.

person. Prior planning is necessary to ensure that individuals are developed in a timely manner.

353

**Chapter 10
Career Planning
and
Development**

RESPONSIBILITY FOR CAREER DEVELOPMENT

Many key individuals must work together if an organization is to have an effective career development program. Management must first make a commitment to support the program. Policy decisions must be made and resources must be committed to the program. Personnel professionals are then responsible for coordinating the career development program. These individuals provide the information, tools, and guidance that permit employees to plan and implement development of their careers. They also provide program liaison with top management. The worker's immediate supervisor is responsible for providing support, advice, and feedback. Through the supervisor, a worker can find out how supportive of career development the organization actually is. Finally, individual employees are responsible for becoming personally involved in the development of their own careers. "You can lead a horse to water but you can't make him drink" is an appropriate analogy when considering career development. The employee is ultimately responsible for undertaking the training and development necessary to progress along his or her chosen career path.

Unrealistic expectations on the part of participants are a major problem associated with a career development program. Employees often see the opportunity for promotion as the major outcome after participating in career development. If no positions are available, individuals often become disappointed and frustrated.

CAREER DEVELOPMENT PROGRAM: AN EXAMPLE

Realizing that highly skilled employees hold the key to corporate growth, Detroit Edison designed an initial professional development program (IPDP). The program helps build individual careers and, in so doing, assures the development of employees required to satisfy future personnel needs.

Detroit Edison's program is available to most entry-level professionals who possess a bachelor's degree and have less than three years experience related to their major field of study. If selected for the program, participants assume the primary responsibility for their professional growth and are expected to take advantage of various opportunities provided.

The IPDP takes place over a three-year period and involves a number of specific developmental activities (see Figure 10–7). The major activities include rotational work assignments and participation in company seminars. Work assignments involve the participants in stimulating and productive projects. Assistance is given by seasoned professionals who answer questions and provide guidance. Attendance at three formal seminars gives

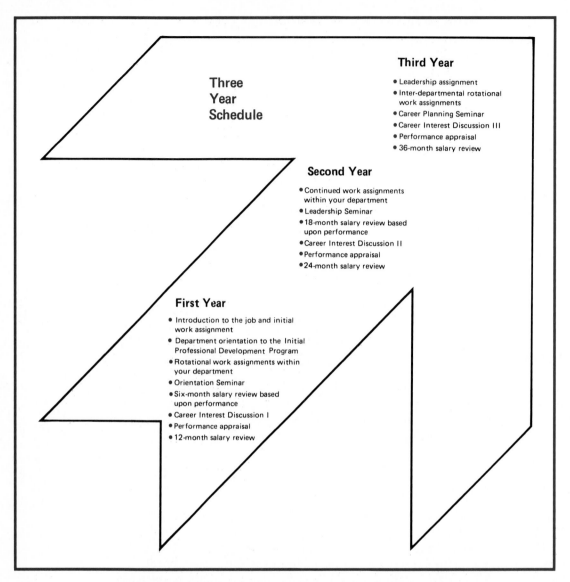

Three Year Schedule

Third Year
- Leadership assignment
- Inter-departmental rotational work assignments
- Career Planning Seminar
- Career Interest Discussion III
- Performance appraisal
- 36-month salary review

Second Year
- Continued work assignments within your department
- Leadership Seminar
- 18-month salary review based upon performance
- Career Interest Discussion II
- Performance appraisal
- 24-month salary review

First Year
- Introduction to the job and initial work assignment
- Department orientation to the Initial Professional Development Program
- Rotational work assignments within your department
- Orientation Seminar
- Six-month salary review based upon performance
- Career Interest Discussion I
- Performance appraisal
- 12-month salary review

Figure 10–7. Detroit Edison's professional development program. Source: Used with the permission of Detroit Edison.

trainees the opportunity to expand skills and interact with employees from other functional areas of the company.

Additional development opportunities are provided in-house through courses covering such subjects as communication skills, power systems engineering, economic analysis, and problems and challenges faced by public utilities. Also, although not required, program participants are encouraged to take advantage of educational opportunities at local colleges and universities. Many employees have earned advanced degrees with the aid of the Detroit Edison educational assistance program.

BEGINNING A CAREER IN PERSONNEL

For individuals desiring a career in Personnel there are two basic ways of entering the field. They may enter the firm of their choice in another department and later transfer to Personnel. Or, they may secure a beginning position in Personnel. There appears to be no uniform agreement as to the best means to obtain an entry-level personnel position. However, the second approach is often the more difficult. In order to assist us in solving this dilemma, personnel practitioners from a wide variety of firms were asked the following questions:

1. Which entry-level position in your firm would be most helpful if a person desires to progress into Personnel?
2. What types of education or experience are most desirable for these entry-level positions?
3. Which Personnel entry-level position would best assist a person's career progression in your firm?

As you can see in Table 10–2, there is no consistency in the responses to these questions. However, it is clear that some firms stress work in other functional areas before moving into Personnel, while others believe in direct entry into Personnel.

ENTRY-LEVEL POSITIONS IN OTHER FUNCTIONAL AREAS

Executives in some firms believe that experience should be gained in positions other than Personnel before moving into the human resource function. They reason that future personnel professionals need wide company exposure to be effective in personnel positions. This exposure can increase their credibility in dealing with other managers.

Numerous firms have this philosophy. For instance, Trans World Airlines selects personnel staffing specialists from among their experienced reservation sales agents. The best route for an individual to move into Personnel with the Chicago, Rock Island and Pacific Railroad Company is from the position of "trainman." Experience in this job permits an individual to learn the operations from the ground up.

ENTRY-LEVEL POSITIONS IN PERSONNEL

Not all firms require broad-based experience prior to entering Personnel. In fact, the number of individuals entering Personnel directly appears to be increasing. Perhaps this trend is due to the high degree of specialized

Table 10–2. Careers in personnel management

Company	Entry-level position	Education/experience
A. B. Dick Company	*Assistant Hourly Employment Manager Shop Foreman Assistant Salary Administrator	Bachelor's degree for all positions
Bristol-Myers Products	Personnel Assistant	Bachelor's degree with two or three years experience in general personnel work
Chicago, Rock Island and Pacific Railroad Company	*Trainman Operations Analyst Cost/Engineering	Bachelor's degree for all positions
Conoco, Inc.	*Personnel Trainee Any position with Conoco	Bachelor's or master's degree in personnel administration, industrial relations, organizational development, business, or engineering
Denny's Inc.	*Interviewer	Bachelor's degree in business or two years in personnel interviewing
	Wage and Salary Analyst	Bachelor's degree and one year experience in personnel, preferably with compensation experience
	Personnel Administrator	Bachelor's degree and/or two years experience in personnel
GAF Corporation	*Production Supervisor Industrial Engineer Wage and Salary Analyst Safety Specialist	B.S.I.E., B.S.M.E., B.B.A. B.A. with relevant coursework B.S. with relevant coursework
General Cable Technologies	Assistant Plant Industrial Relations Manager Compensation Analyst	B.S. in industrial relations
Gerber Products Company	*Supervisor Trainee *Administrative Trainee	Four years of college Four years of college
Grumman Corporation	*Salary Analyst Employment Interviewer Career Development Analyst	Bachelor's degree in any of a variety of concentrations including psychology, business, and data processing
Hartmarx	Personnel Assistant Compensation Assistant Employee Relations Assistant Personnel Director (small plant or store)	Bachelor's or master's degree in business, personnel, or employee relations

356

Company	Position	Requirements
International Paper Company	*Supervisor—Employee Relations Administrator—Industrial Relations	B.S. or B.A. in personnel or industrial management B.S. or B.A. in industrial or labor relations, or B.S. in industrial management
	Entry level specialist assigned to the Corporate Human Resources Department	
Manville Corporation	*Employee Relations Supervisor *Plant Supervisor *Benefits Clerk	Bachelor's degree and some plant experience desirable
Motorola, Inc.	*Employment Interviewer	B.S. or B.A.; no experience
Nabisco Brands, Inc.	*Personnel Assistant (Field)	Bachelor's degree in such fields as business or psychology
Rockwell International Corporation	Supervisory Trainee (Field) Personnel/Industrial Relations Trainee	M.B.A. in personnel or industrial relations
Shell Oil Company	Employee Relations Analyst	Bachelor's or master's degree in personnel or industrial relations preferred
Squibb Corporation	Personnel Assistant (nonexempt recruiting)	Two or three years experience of personnel related activities preferred
Standard Oil Company of California	Employee Relations Trainee	M.B.A. (industrial relations) with up to two years experience
Stokely-Van Camp, Inc.	Employee Relations—Management Trainee	Master's degree (preferably in personnel)
Teledyne, Inc.	*Wage and Salary Representative Labor Relations Representative	B.A. or personnel or financial administrative experience B.A. or general plant or personnel administrative experience
Trans World Airlines	Reservation Sales Agent	High school diploma, customer contact, and sales experience
United States Steel Corporation	Labor Relations Trainee Employee Relations Trainee Line Operations Management Trainee	Law degree Master's degree, accreditation, experience Technical degree plus leadership
Walt Disney Productions	*Personnel Interviewer	People skills; B.A. and/or equivalent People skills; B.A. and/or equivalent
	Personnel Assistant Wage and Salary Analyst	Salaried experience and statistical orientation

*Indicates best entry-level position.

357

knowledge currently expected. Some firms need people who can produce very quickly after being placed in Personnel. These organizations apparently do not feel that time is available to provide basic training.

Several firms believe that the compensation specialty provides excellent entry-level positions. For example, the Grumman Corporation identifies salary administration as the best entry-level position "because it affects almost every aspect of personnel work and company operations." Teledyne, Inc., believes that "starting in wage and salary provides an individual with exposure to relationships of job classifications throughout the company," and that this background is helpful to the personnel practitioner.

The nature of the firm's business may also affect the best personnel entry-level position. Labor intensive organizations — those that have high labor costs relative to total operating costs — appear to emphasize staffing and recruitment positions where interviewing skills are quite important. For instance, Denny's, Inc., lists the "interviewer" as being the best personnel entry-level position. Walt Disney Productions also identifies the "personnel interviewer" position as one of the best.

ENTRY-LEVEL POSITIONS: AN OVERVIEW

Practitioners do not agree as to the most appropriate entry-level position for individuals aspiring to a job in Personnel. A position considered best by one firm may not be viewed in the same way by another. The nature of the firm's business or its management's personnel philosophy may account for these differences. Some firms stress the need for operating experience before entering Personnel. Others believe that direct entry into Personnel provides a more suitable beginning. People with ability who truly desire to obtain a position in Personnel will likely be given the opportunity.

SUMMARY

A career is a general course of action a person chooses to pursue throughout his or her working life. Career planning is a process whereby individual goals are set and the means to achieve them are established. Career paths are flexible lines of progression along which employees typically move through an organization. Career development is a formal approach taken by the organization to ensure that people with the proper qualifications and experience are available when needed.

Several factors affect a person's view of a career, such as life stages and career anchors. The basic life stages are: (1) establishing identity; (2) growing and getting established; (3) maintenance and adjustment to self; and (4) decline. The five career anchors are: (1) managerial competence; (2) technical/functional competence; (3) security; (4) creativity; and (5) autonomy and independence.

The primary responsibility for career planning rests with the individual. Career planning begins with gaining a realistic understanding of oneself. Gaining insight involves conducting a thorough self-assessment.

Career planning does not end when an individual obtains his or her first job. In fact, it is just beginning for many people. Firms should be vitally interested in career planning. From the organization's viewpoint, career planning involves a conscious attempt to maximize employees' potential ability. Career planning programs should be implemented only when they contribute to the accomplishment of basic organizational goals.

Traditionally, career paths have focused on upward mobility within a particular occupation. Some firms have recognized that not everyone wants to follow traditional vertical career movements within specific functions. Career paths have been developed that take into consideration lateral, diagonal, and even downward career progression.

There are numerous means by which individuals can be assisted in their career planning and development. Some of these means include: Management by objectives, career counseling, company material, performance appraisal systems, and workshops. Most of these methods are used in combination with each other.

There are two basic means for entering Personnel. A person may be required to enter the firm of his or her choice in another department and later transfer to Personnel. Or, a beginning position in Personnel may be secured. There appears to be no uniform agreement as to the best means of obtaining an entry-level Personnel position.

QUESTIONS FOR REVIEW

1. Define the following terms:
   (a) Career
   (b) Career planning
   (c) Career paths
   (d) Career development
2. Identify the basic life stages that people pass through.
3. List and briefly define the five types of career anchors.
4. How should a strengths/weaknesses balance sheet and a likes and dislikes analysis be prepared?
5. What type of questions does a person involved in career planning attempt to answer?
6. Describe in your own words the stages in the organizational career planning process.
7. Why is it important for firms to engage in organizational career planning?
8. What are the reasons for establishing career paths?
9. Identify and describe some of the methods of organizational career planning.
10. What are the two basic means for entering Personnel? Why do you think firms might favor one means over the other?

Career

Career planning

Career paths

Career development

Career anchors

Strengths/weaknesses balance sheet (SWBS)

Likes and dislikes analysis

Incident 1

"Could you come to my office for a minute, Bob?" asked Terry Geech, the plant manager. "Sure, be right there," said Bob Glemson. Bob was the plant's quality control director. He had been with the company for four years. After completing his degree in mechanical engineering, he worked as a production supervisor and then as maintenance manager, prior to promotion to his present job. Bob thought he knew what the call was about.

"Your letter of resignation catches me by surprise," began Terry. "I know that Wilson Products will be getting a good man, but we sure need you here, too." "I thought about it a lot," said Bob, "but there just doesn't seem to be a future for me here." "Why do you say that," asked Terry. "Well," replied Bob, "the next position above mine is yours. With you only 39 I don't think it's likely that you'll be leaving soon." "The fact is that I am leaving soon," said Terry. "That's why it's even more of a shock to know that you are resigning. I think I'll be moving to the corporate offices in June of next year.

Besides, the company has several plants that are larger than this one and we need good people in those plants from time to time. Both in quality control and in general management." "Well, I heard about an opening in the Cincinnati plant last year," said Bob, "but by the time I checked, the job had already been filled. We never know about job opportunities in the other plants until we read about the incumbent in the company paper."

"All this is beside the point now. What would it take to get you to change your mind?" asked Terry. "I don't think I can change my mind now," replied Bob, "I've already signed a contract with Wilson."

QUESTIONS

1. Evaluate the career planning and development program at this company.
2. What actions might have prevented Bob's resignation?

Incident 2

It was a nervous Jerry Fox who was ushered into the company president's office by the secretary. In the office he encountered Allen Anderson, the vice president of personnel, and Vince Gorman, the president. Jerry was flattered when the president stood to shake his hand. "I'll make this short and sweet," Mr. Gorman said. "You probably have heard

Taylor, Harold. "Personal Goal Setting." *Supervision* XLII (September 1981): 3.

VanCleve, Roy R. "Human Resources Administration: Curriculum for a Profession." *Personnel Administrator* 27 (March 1982): 61–67.

Veiga, J. F. "Do Managers on the Move Get Anywhere?" *Harvard Business Review* 59 (March–April 1981): 20–22+.

Walker, James W. *Human Resource Planning*. New York: McGraw-Hill, 1980.

Wolf, James F. and Bacher, Robert N. "Career Negotiation: Trading Off Employee and Organizational Needs." *Personnel* 58 (March–April 1981): 53–59.

Zenger, John H. "Career Planning: Coming in from the Cold." *Training and Development Journal* 35 (July 1981): 47–52.

CHAPTER OBJECTIVES
1. Define *performance appraisal* and identify its basic objectives.
2. Describe the performance appraisal process.
3. Identify who may typically be responsible for performance appraisal and identify typical appraisal periods.
4. Identify the various methods that have been used in the appraisal process.
5. Explain when the various appraisal methods are actually used in business.
6. List the problems that have been associated with performance appraisal.
7. Describe the importance of the appraisal interview.
8. Explain the characteristics of an effective performance appraisal system.
9. Describe how assessment centers are used to assess an employee's management potential.

Chapter 11

PERFORMANCE APPRAISAL

"Tim, we've got to get more production out of the people in this plant," exclaimed Doug Parsley, vice president of production. "Our productivity is declining while our costs are skyrocketing." Tim Overbeck, production superintendent, nodded his head in agreement and replied, "I agree with you, Doug. What these people need is a good swift kick." "I don't think so," Doug countered, "we've tried that approach before. I think you'd better talk with the personnel office first thing tomorrow and see if we can come up with a reasonable system of evaluating employee performance. If so, we can then reward employees for what they do. Maybe that would give them some incentive to work harder."

Doug Parsley was beginning to realize a need for identifying his top producers. All managers need to be able to recognize differences in job performance. Employees can then be rewarded on the basis of their contributions toward organizational goals. The appraisal method used must be perceived as being fair and equitable and it should also serve to identify employee development needs. The overall purpose of this chapter is to emphasize the importance of performance appraisal as it relates to human resource management and its special implications for training and development of the firm's human resources.

PERFORMANCE APPRAISAL DEFINED

Nothing is more discouraging for a top producer in a work group than to receive the same pay increase as a marginal employee. In such a situation, the incentive to do superior work certainly declines. While employees at all levels, management and nonmanagement alike, are informally appraised continuously, it is desirable to formally summarize these evaluations periodically. The process that leads to formal evaluation is often referred to as performance appraisal. **Performance appraisal (PA)** is *a system that provides a periodic review and evaluation of an individual's job performance.*[1]

A survey of 3500 organizations revealed that management's major human resource concern was the PA system used in their firms.[2] Considerable evidence exists to suggest that many managers are not pleased with the results of their appraisal efforts. For example, a Conference Board study of more than 290 organizations found widespread dissatisfaction with appraisal systems. This attitude was prevalent despite the fact that over one-half of the responding firms had developed new systems within the three years preceding the study.[3] The primary reasons for disappointment in performance appraisal systems include the inability of a single plan to achieve multiple purposes, lack of management support, impracticality of the system, subjectivity, and lack of job relatedness.[4]

---

[1]Thomas N. Baylie, Carl J. Kujawski, and Drew M. Young, "Appraisals of 'People' Resources," in Dale Yoder and Herbert G. Heneman, Jr. (eds.), *ASPA Handbook of Personnel and Industrial Relations, Staffing Policies and Strategies,* Vol. 1. Washington, D.C.: The Bureau of National Affairs, 1974, pp. 4–168.

[2]Douglas B. Gehrman, "Beyond Today's Compensation and Performance Appraisal Systems," *Personnel Administrator* 29 (March 1984): 21.

[3]William M. Fox, "Consentient Merit Rating: A Critical Incident Approach," *Personnel* 58 (July–August 1981): 70.

[4]Robert L. Lazer, "Performance Appraisal: What Does the Future Hold?" *Personnel Administrator* 25 (July 1980): 70.

The overall goal of performance appraisal systems is to improve the organization's effectiveness by developing and communicating vital information about the firm's human resources. This necessitates providing feedback to employees on their performance. In order to accomplish this purpose, a number of specific objectives need to be attained. There is no universal agreement as to the precise objectives to be pursued. There are, however, several human resource management areas within which objectives may be achieved. It is unlikely that a single system can effectively serve all of these purposes. As we will show later, some appraisal systems are more appropriate for achieving certain objectives than others.

HUMAN RESOURCE PLANNING

In assessing a firm's internal supply of human resources, data must be available that describe the promotability and potential of all employees, especially key executives. Management succession planning is a key concern for all firms, and PA yields essential data for this activity. A well-designed appraisal system provides a profile of the organization in terms of its human resource strengths and weaknesses.[5]

RECRUITMENT AND SELECTION

Performance evaluation ratings may be helpful in predicting the future performance of job applicants. For example, it may be found that a significant number of successful managers received their training from certain schools or majored in particular fields. This type of knowledge could certainly influence a firm's approach to recruitment. Also, in validating selection tests, employee ratings may be used as the variable against which test scores are compared. In this instance, the selection test's validity would depend largely on the accuracy of appraisal results.

TRAINING AND DEVELOPMENT

A completed appraisal form should point out employees' specific needs for training and development, which can lead to improved performance.[6] For instance, if Mary Jones receives a marginal evaluation with regard to her written communication abilities, additional training in this area is suggested. If the personnel manager detects that a number of first-line supervisors were rated low in communication skills, communication improvement sessions for all first-line supervisors may be needed. By iden-

---

[5]Charles J. Fombrun and Robert J. Laud, "Strategic Issues in Performance Appraisal: Theory and Practice," *Personnel* 60 (November–December 1983): 24.

[6]Baylie, Kujawski, and Young, "Appraisals," pp. 4–168.

tifying these deficiencies, Personnel is able to develop T&D programs that permit individuals to build on their strengths and minimize their deficiencies. The existence of an appraisal system does not guarantee that employees will be properly trained and developed. However, the task of determining training and development needs is simplified when appraisal data are available.

CAREER PLANNING AND DEVELOPMENT

Career planning and development may be viewed from either an individual or organizational viewpoint. In either case, PA data are essential in assessing an employee's strengths and weaknesses and in determining potential. Managers may use such information to counsel with subordinates and assist them in developing and implementing their career plans.

COMPENSATION

The results from performance appraisal provide the basis for decisions regarding pay increases. Most managers feel that outstanding job performance should be rewarded tangibly through increased financial compensation. They believe that "what you reward is what you get." This may be the difficulty with the compensation practice described at the beginning of the chapter by Doug Parsley, the production vice president. He has discovered that a good swift kick does not encourage people to produce at their highest level of efficiency over the long run. And, when poor performers are given the same pay increases as top producers, chances are good that the organization will begin to receive marginal performance even from its previously productive employees. To encourage good performance, a firm should design and implement a fair performance appraisal system and then reward the most productive workers.

INTERNAL EMPLOYEE RELATIONS

Performance appraisal data are also frequently used for decisions in several areas of internal employee relations including promotion, demotion, termination, layoff and transfer. Although an individual's performance in one position may not serve as an accurate predictor of job success in another, PA data may nevertheless be useful. For example, an employee's mastery of certain tasks may become apparent, as may those areas in which development is required.

An employee's performance record in one job may be useful in determining his or her ability to perform in another job at the same level, as is required in the consideration of transfers. Or, when the performance level is unacceptable, demotion or termination may be indicated.

When employees working under a labor agreement are involved, layoff of employees is typically determined on the basis of seniority. However, when management has more flexibility, an employee's performance record may be considered a more rational and effective approach to layoff decisions.

ASSESSMENT OF EMPLOYEE POTENTIAL

Some organizations attempt to assess employee potential as they appraise job performance. It has been said that the best predictors of future behavior are past behaviors.[7] However, an employee's past performance in a given job may not accurately indicate future behavior in a higher level position. The best salesperson in the company may not become a successful district sales manager. The best computer programmer may, if promoted, be a disaster as a data processing manager. Overemphasizing technical skills and ignoring other equally important skills is a common error in promoting employees into management jobs. Recognition of this problem has led some firms to separate performance appraisals from the assessment of potential. These firms have established "assessment centers," which will be discussed in a later section.

PERFORMANCE APPRAISAL USE

As indicated in the previous sections, performance appraisal data are potentially useful in a variety of ways. A recent study identified the areas in which businesses are actually using appraisal information. In Table 11–1 you can see that at least 50 percent of those who responded to the survey use the appraisal process in areas related to compensation (merit pay increases), communication (feedback), human resources planning (performance potential, succession planning), career planning and internal employee administration.

THE PERFORMANCE APPRAISAL PROCESS

Many of the external and internal environmental factors discussed in chapter 2 can influence the appraisal process. Legislation, for example, requires that appraisal systems be nondiscriminatory. In the 1977 case of *Mistretta* v. *Sandia Corporation* (a subsidiary of Western Electric Company, Inc.), a Federal District Court judge ruled against the company, stating that "There is sufficient circumstantial evidence to indicate that age bias and age based policies appear throughout the performance rating process to the detriment of the protected age group.[8] The *Albermarle Paper* v. *Moody* case supported validation requirements for performance appraisals in addition to selection

---

[7]L. L. Cummings and Donald P. Schwab, "Designing Appraisal Systems for Information Yield," *California Management Review* 20 (Summer 1978): 22.

[8]James W. Walker and Daniel E. Lupton, "Performance Appraisal Programs and Age Discrimination Law," *Aging and Work* 2 (Spring 1978): 73–83.

Table 11–1. Uses of performance appraisal systems

Rank	Function for which appraisal is used	Percentage
1	Merit increases	91
2	Performance results/feedback/job counseling	90
3	Promotion	82
4	Termination or layoff	64
5	Performance potential	62
6	Succession planning	57
7	Career planning	52
8	Transfer	50
9	Human resource planning	38
10	Bonuses	32
11	Development and evaluation of training programs	29
12	Internal communication	25
13	Criteria for selection procedure validation	16
14	Expense control	7

Source: Adapted, by permission of the publisher, from "Strategic Issues in Performance Appraisal: Theory and Practice," by Charles J. Fombrun and Robert J. Laud, *Personnel* November–December 1983, pp. 26, 28 © 1983 Periodicals Division, American Management Associations, New York. All rights reserved.

tests. Organizations must avoid any appraisal method that results in discriminatory decisions related to training opportunities, pay increases, promotions, or other areas of employment.[9]

The labor union is another external factor that might affect a firm's appraisal process. Unions have traditionally stressed seniority as the basis for promotions and pay increases. They may vigorously oppose the use of a management designed performance appraisal system that would be used for these purposes.

Factors within the internal environment can also affect the performance appraisal process. For instance, the type of organizational culture can serve to assist or hinder the process. In today's highly complex organizations, employees must often rely on co-workers in performing their tasks. A closed, nontrusting culture may discourage the cooperation that is so often needed to successfully complete a job. In such an environment, performance may suffer even though the worker would like to do a good job. It may also be quite difficult to recognize the true contributions of an individual worker.

Identification of specific goals is the starting point for the PA process (see Figure 11–1). An appraisal system may be unable to effectively serve all the purposes desired, so a firm should select those specific goals it

[9]Dena B. Schneir, "The Impact of EEO Legislation on Performance Appraisals," *Personnel* 55 (July–August 1978): 24.

desires to achieve with PA. For example, some firms may want to stress employee development goals, whereas other organizations may wish to focus on administrative decisions such as pay adjustments. Too many performance appraisal systems are poorly designed and implemented because clear objectives have not been established. In these instances, managers do

Figure 11–1. The performance appraisal process.

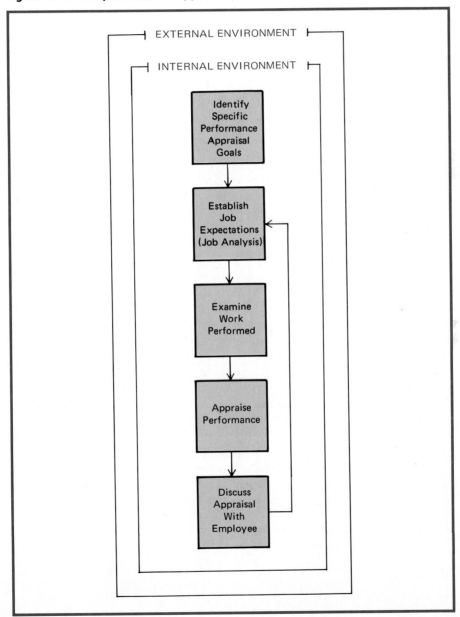

not determine specifically what they want the system to accomplish. They often expect too much from one system.[10] It is entirely possible that a firm may require more than one system if the achievement of multiple goals is desired.

After specific appraisal goals have been established, workers must then understand what is expected from them in their jobs. This normally takes the form of discussions with their supervisors to review the major duties determined through job analysis and contained in the job description.

When the work has been performed, the results are examined and performance is then evaluated, based on previously established job performance standards. The results of evaluation are then communicated to the worker. The performance evaluation discussion serves to reestablish job requirements in the employee's mind.

RESPONSIBILITY FOR APPRAISAL

In most organizations, the personnel department is responsible for designing and overseeing appraisal programs. Responsibility for conducting performance appraisals varies from company to company. However, direct participation by line management in the operation of the program is necessary for success.[11] Several possibilities exist as to who will actually rate the employee.

IMMEDIATE SUPERVISOR

An employee's immediate supervisor is the most common choice for evaluating performance. In fact, in one study, 96 percent of the respondents revealed that in their firms appraisals were conducted by immediate supervisors.[12] There are several valid reasons for this approach. In the first place, the supervisor is usually in an excellent position to observe the employee's job behavior. Another reason is that the supervisor has the responsibility for managing a particular unit. When the task of evaluating subordinates is given to someone else, the supervisor's authority may be seriously undermined. Finally, training and development of subordinates is an important element in every manager's job and — as previously mentioned — appraisal programs and development are often closely related.

On the negative side, immediate supervisors may emphasize certain aspects of employee performance to the neglect of others. Also, managers have been known to manipulate evaluations to justify their decisions on

---

[10]Ed Yager, "A Critique of Performance Appraisal Systems," *Personnel Journal* (February 1981): 129.

[11]William F. Lloyd, Jr., "Performance Appraisal: A Shortsighted Approach for Installing a Workable Program," *Personnel Journal* 56 (September 1977): 446–450.

[12]Fombrun and Laud, "Strategic Issues," p. 27.

Nina E. Woodard
Vice President —
Human Resource
Management, First
Interstate Bank of
Casper, N.A.

Nina E. Woodard, the 1984–1985 ASPA Region 16 vice president, feels that human resource management issues are the cornerstone of future business success. She recently expanded on her view of the changing role of the personnel executive by comparing it to a clock maker. She indicated in one of her speeches, "On the Future Direction of the Profession," that the challenge of operating as a human resource executive today is like that of bringing the telling of time from use of the sun dial to use of the digital, fully automated clock. It is a difficult mission because the sun dial still works, and the digital, fully automated clock, with the mass of information it can provide, can sometimes be confusing to read.

Woodard's background includes participation in the American Bankers Association Personnel School and Graduate Personnel School. In order to maintain her skills, she continually reads and is involved in extensive networking activities through ASPA and other professional organizations.

Her entrance into banking occurred quite by accident when she sought employment to help pass the time while her husband served a tour of duty in Vietnam. She spent several years working in various operational positions and eventually landed a position in the newly formed personnel department at what was then the First National Bank of Casper in 1975. Since that time, she has taken advantage of every available opportunity to enhance and develop her expertise in human resources and has grown into the top human resource management position at the bank: manager of human resources. During the 1985 National ASPA Conference, she sat for and passed the accreditation exam as a Senior Professional in Human Resources (SPHR). She is currently attending Pacific Coast School of Banking and was honored in 1984 as one of only six National Association of Bank Women national scholarship winners.

Woodard has utilized volunteer leadership as a valuable tool to develop management skills. She lends her expertise to community and state activities, as well as applying it to her position at First Interstate.

The Woodards have two "young adults." Nina and her husband, John, feel that Wyoming is their home. They moved their family there from southern California in 1971 and now feel "rooted."

She has served as an instructor at Casper Community College, conducting courses in both human resources and marketing management. She feels that effective time management is a busy manager's best ally. Goal setting and an orientation to achievement are her strengths, and she applies those strengths to human resource management. Woodard feels that the profession must provide the environment for change; that human resource professionals, of necessity, have to be effective change agents, and, therefore, artful managers of creative conflict.

pay increases and promotions. The immediate supervisor will probably continue to be the person most likely to evaluate employee performance. Organizations will seek alternatives, however, because of the weaknesses mentioned and a desire to broaden the perspective of the appraisal.

SUBORDINATES

Managers in a few firms have concluded that evaluation of managers by subordinates is feasible. They reason that subordinates are in a good position to view their superior's managerial effectiveness. Advocates of this approach believe that supervisors will become especially conscious of the work group's needs and will do a better job of managing. Others argue that evaluation by subordinates may cause the supervisor to become excessively concerned with popularity.

PEERS

Another possible practice is to have employees evaluated by their peers. Proponents of this approach believe that peer evaluation need not result in popularity contests. Peer appraisal, they feel, may be reliable if the work group is stable over a reasonably long period of time and performs tasks that require interaction. However, little research has been conducted to determine how peers establish standards for evaluating others or the overall effect of peer appraisal on the group's attitude.[13]

GROUP APPRAISAL

Group appraisal involves *the use of two or more managers who are familiar with the employee's performance, and, as a team, they appraise his or her performance.* For instance, if a person regularly works with the data processing manager and the financial manager, these two individuals might participate in the evaluation. An advantage of this approach is that it maintains as much objectivity as possible. A disadvantage is that it diminishes the role of the immediate supervisor. Also, it may be difficult to get managers together for a group appraisal because of other demands on their time and differing schedules.

SELF-APPRAISAL

If individuals understand the objectives they are expected to achieve and the standards by which they are to be evaluated, they are — to a great extent — in the best position to appraise their own performance.[14] Also, since

---

[13]Angelo S. DeNisi and Jimmy L. Mitchell, "An Analysis of Peer Ratings as Predictors and Criterion Measures and a Proposed New Application," *Academy of Management Review* 3 (April 1978): 369–374.

[14]Margaret A. Bogerty, "How to Prepare for Your Performance Review," *S.A.M. Journal* 47 (Autumn 1982): 12.

employee development is self-development, employees who appraise their own performance may become more highly motivated. Self-appraisal has great appeal to managers who are primarily concerned with employee participation and training and development.

COMBINATIONS

In seeking an answer to the question, "Who shall evaluate?" we should recognize that the approaches previously cited are not mutually exclusive. Many are used in combination. For example, "RCA Corporation tries to minimize subjectivity by having each RCA manager rated separately by a group of fellow workers, generally including his immediate superior, two or three higher level managers, two or three peers and one or two workers in lower positions. This multiple assessment, RCA feels, gives a better-rounded indication of a manager's performance."[15] This unique approach illustrates the importance that some organizations place on the appraisal process. The combined use of several methods may provide greater insight into an individual's actual performance.

THE APPRAISAL PERIOD

Performance evaluations typically are written up at specific intervals. In most organizations, this is done either annually or semiannually.[16] Evaluations are often made just before the end of an individual's probationary period, and it is also a common practice to evaluate new employees several times during their first year of employment. The following are examples of the evaluation periods for three companies:

- The New York Times Company evaluates all its guild and nonunion employees annually. Craft unions are not included in this process.
- Cessna Aircraft Company appraises all monthly salaried employees and all weekly salaried supervisors approximately once a year.
- General Mills, Inc., evaluates all employees on an annual basis except for operative, nonexempt employees, who are evaluated each six months.

The appraisal period may begin with the employee's hiring-in date, or all employees may be evaluated at the same time. While there are advantages to both practices, the staggered appraisal period seems to have greater merit. There may not be sufficient time to evaluate each employee adequately if all evaluations are conducted at the same time. The problem would be especially acute in large departments.

---

[15]"The Rating Game," *The Wall Street Journal*, May 23, 1978, p. 1. Reprinted by permission of *The Wall Street Journal*. Copyright Dow Jones & Company, Inc. (1978). All rights reserved.

[16]Robert C. Ford and Kenneth M. Jennings, "How to Make Performance Appraisals More Effective," *Personnel* 54 (April 1977): 51.

PERFORMANCE APPRAISAL METHODS

There are a number of appraisal methods from which to choose. The best type of performance appraisal system depends on its purpose. If the major emphasis is on selecting people for promotion, training, and merit pay increases, then some traditional method such as rating scales may be the most appropriate. On the other hand, collaborative methods, such as MBO, are designed to assist employees in developing and becoming more effective.[17] A discussion of various appraisal methods follows.

RATING SCALES

A widely used appraisal method, which rates employees according to defined factors, is called the **rating scales method**. Using this approach, judgments about performance are recorded on a scale.[18] The scale is divided into degrees — normally 5–7 in number — which are often defined by adjectives such as *outstanding, average,* or *unsatisfactory*. While a global rating may be provided, the method generally allows for more than one performance criterion. One reason for the popularity of the rating scales method is its simplicity, which permits many employees to be quickly evaluated.[19]

The factors chosen for evaluation are typically of two types: job-related and personal characteristics (see Figure 11–2).[20] Note that job-related factors include quantity and quality of work, whereas personal factors are comprised of such attributes as dependability, initiative, adaptability, and cooperation. The rater (evaluator) completes the form by indicating the degree of each factor that is most descriptive of the employee and his or her performance.

Some firms provide space for the rater to comment on the evaluation given for each factor. This practice may be especially encouraged, or even required, when either the highest or lowest rating is given. For instance, if an employee is rated *unsatisfactory* on initiative, the rater might have to provide written justification for this low evaluation. The purpose of this type of requirement is to avoid arbitrary and hastily made judgments.

Refer again to Figure 11–2 and note that each factor and each degree have been defined. In order to receive an *exceptional* rating for the factor *quality of work,* a person must consistently exceed the prescribed work requirements. The more precisely the various factors and degrees are de-

[17]Robert L. Taylor and Robert A. Zawaki, "Trends in Performance Appraisal: Guidelines for Managers," *Personnel Administrator* 29 (March 1984): 71.

[18]J. Peter Graves, "Let's Put Appraisal Back in Performance Appraisal: Part I," *Personnel Journal* 61 (November 1982): 848.

[19]Stuart Murray, "A Comparison of Results-Oriented and Trait-Based Performance Appraisals," *Personnel Administrator* (June 1983): 100.

[20]Because the system depicted makes liberal use of personal factors that may not be job related, it has been described by a reviewer as "a good example of a poor method."

Employee's Name _____

Job Title _____

Department _____

Supervisor _____

Evaluation Period:
From _____ to _____

Instructions for Evaluation:
1. Consider only one factor at a time. Do not permit rating given for one factor to affect decision for others.
2. Consider performance for entire evaluation period. Avoid concentration on recent events or isolated incidents.
3. Remember that the average employee performs duties in a satisfactory manner. An above average or exceptional rating indicates that the employee has clearly distinguished himself or herself from the average employee.

EVALUATION FACTORS	Unsatisfactory. Does not meet requirements.	Below average. Needs improvement. Requirements occasionally not met.	Average. Consistently meets requirements.	Good. Frequently exceeds requirements.	Exceptional. Consistently exceeds requirements.
QUANTITY OF WORK: Consider the volume of work achieved. Is productivity at an acceptable level?					
QUALITY OF WORK: Consider accuracy, precision, neatness, and completeness in handling assigned duties.					
DEPENDABILITY: Consider degree to which employee can be relied on to meet work commitments.					
INITIATIVE: Consider self-reliance, resourcefulness, and willingness to accept responsibility.					
ADAPTABILITY: Consider ability to respond to changing requirements and conditions.					
COOPERATION: Consider ability to work for and with others. Are assignments, including overtime, willingly accepted?					

POTENTIAL FOR FUTURE GROWTH AND DEVELOPMENT:

☐ Now at or near maximum performance in present job.

☐ Now at or near maximum performance in this job, but has potential for improvement in another job, such as:
_____

☐ Capable of progressing after further training and experience.

☐ No apparent limitations.

EMPLOYEE STATEMENT: I agree ☐   Disagree ☐   with this evaluation
Comments:
_____

Employee _____	Date _____
Supervisor _____	Date _____
Reviewing Manager _____	Date _____

Figure 11–2. Rating scales method of performance appraisal.

fined, the better the rater can evaluate worker performance. Evaluation consistency throughout the organization is achieved when each rater interprets the factors and degrees — and rates employees — in the same way.

Many rating scale performance appraisal forms also provide for an assessment of the employee's growth potential. The rating scale form shown in Figure 11–2 contains four categories relating to a person's potential for future growth and development. They range from "Now at or near maximum performance in present job" to "No apparent limitations." Although there are drawbacks to attempting to evaluate both past performance and future potential at the same time, this practice is often followed.

THE USE OF RATING SCALES AT THE SOUTHLAND CORPORATION

At The Southland Corporation, immediate supervisors are required to conduct a written performance review of nonexempt and exempt employees at least annually. An example of the form used to appraise nonexempt employees is shown in Figure 11–3. The appraisal system involves seven steps:

■ Select key job parts.
■ Describe employee performance.
■ Rate employee performance.
■ Determine overall efficiency.
■ Prepare for the performance appraisal discussion.
■ Present results and (an optional step) prepare a performance development plan.
■ Obtain necessary signatures.

Key job parts are aspects of the job such as duties, responsibilities, and assignments that are so important that their performance affects overall success or failure. Key job parts are determined by job analysis for each job family. The rating supervisor selects those that are most relevant to the job of the employee being evaluated. Normally, 6–8 job parts are utilized. Again referring to Figure 11–3, you can see that the supervisor evaluates performance on a five-point scale. The factors used, however, are not nebulous personality traits, which are so often used. Rather, they are those that are job related. This version not only conforms to requirements of the *Uniform Guidelines*, but the rating supervisor's task of evaluating performance is placed on a more solid foundation.

CRITICAL INCIDENTS

The **critical incident method** is a *performance appraisal technique that requires written records be kept of highly favorable and highly unfavorable actions occurring in an employee's work.* When an employee's action has a significant impact on the department's effectiveness — either positively or negatively — the manager writes it down. This is a critical incident. At

Figure 11–3. Performance appraisal system nonexempt personnel. Used by permission of the Southland Corporation Personnel Research Department.

Location _____

Period of Evaluation ___2/86___ to ___2/87___

Date of Last Review ___2/85___

Employee Name ___John Jacobs___

Employee Title ___MIS Supply Clerk___

Supervisor's Name ___Harry Hines___

Supervisor's Title ___MIS Supply Supervisor___

Employee Social Security Number ___450-30-2641___

Type of Review _____

Refer to the *Performance Appraisal System Reference Guide* before completing this form.

KEY JOB PARTS	PERFORMANCE DESCRIPTION	PERFORMANCE RATING*
1. Typing ■ Typing from handwritten draft ■ Typing information on forms ■ Statistical or financial typing ■ Typing from recorded dictation		N/A 1 2 3 4 5
2. Maintaining and ordering supplies ■ Checking supply levels ■ Ordering and picking up supplies	Employee needs to work with forms order and inventories more to gain more experience in this area. Make sure letters are prepared for checks taken from area.	N/A 1 2 ③ 4 5
3. Copying and recording information ■ Making routine entries in files, books, or on forms ■ Keeping tallies or lists	Employee does well making entries in check logs and on transmittals.	N/A 1 2 ③ 4 5
4. Making job-related decisions ■ Setting priorities for own work ■ Deciding the best way to complete an assignment ■ Reading and interpreting policies, rules, and procedures ■ Doing limited research (calling, looking things up in manuals, etc.) to resolve a problem or question ■ Conducting research or analyzing information	Employee has improved in limited research and writing Request for Assistance. Still needs to review all possibilities when researching missing reports.	N/A 1 2 ③ 4 5

*Ratings are defined in *Reference Guide* and range from "well below performance requirements (1)" to "well above performance requirements (5)."

Figure 11–3. Performance appraisal system nonexempt personnel. (continued)

KEY JOB PARTS	PERFORMANCE DESCRIPTION	PERFORMANCE RATING*
5. Processing requests ■ Receiving and reviewing incoming correspondence, telephone calls, or other requests ■ Deciding what the problem or inquiry is ■ Preparing responses to inquiries ■ Persuading others to take action or change their opinions ■ Responding to telephone inquiries		N/A 1 2 3 4 5
6. Proofreading and checking work ■ Reviewing forms, reports, correspondence for completeness and accuracy ■ Checking material for errors in typing, spelling, punctuation, grammar, capitalization or word usage ■ Checking work done by others to make sure procedures and/or instructions have been followed	Employee does well in checking the completeness of production output. Has improved in locating one-page reports attached to multipage reports.	N/A 1 2 3 (4) 5
7. Performing routine calculations ■ Adding, subtracting, multiplying, or dividing ■ Computing wages, taxes, commissions, etc. ■ Determining rates, discounts, etc. by referring to tables		N/A 1 2 3 4 5
8. Sorting, filing, or retrieving information ■ Sorting information ■ Filing or retrieving information (in an existing filing system) ■ Developing new filing or cross-index systems ■ Searching for missing files, forms, orders, etc.		N/A 1 2 3 4 5
9. Preparing written reports ■ Writing reports which summarize available information ■ Writing short, routine reports ■ Writing long or complicated reports ■ Preparing financial statements or numerical or statistical reports ■ Composing or initiating correspondence	Prepares precise transmittals and Request for Assistance.	N/A 1 2 (3) 4 5

	Rating
10. Performing receptionist duties ■ Answering and routing telephone calls ■ Taking and distributing messages ■ Greeting visitors	N/A 1 2 3 4 5
11. Scheduling ■ Contacting individuals to schedule meetings ■ Making travel arrangements ■ Reserving meeting facilities	N/A 1 2 3 4 5
12. Performing data entry and retrieval tasks ■ Operating a key punch, data entry terminal, or verifier ■ Look up information using CRT	N/A 1 2 3 4 5
13. Performing accounting functions ■ Posting to ledgers ■ Receiving, counting, or paying out checks or cash ■ Balancing receipts ■ Debiting/crediting accounts	N/A 1 2 3 4 5
14. Operating and maintaining office machines (such as an offset press) ■ Setting up and adjusting machines (such as an offset press) ■ Cleaning or performing simple repairs on office machines ■ Operating simple office machines such as copying machines Continues to do a good job operating all machines in distribution. He is an excellent operator of the burster.	N/A 1 2 3 ④ 5
1 istributing material ■ Picking up or distributing materials ■ Preparing materials for mailing or shipping Does well at preparing materials for mailing or shipping.	N/A 1 2 3 ④ 5
16. Performing supervisory duties ■ Making work assignments ■ Conducting employee evaluations ■ Coordinating activities of assigned employees ■ Resolving conflicts or problems among assigned employees	N/A 1 2 3 4 5
17. Computer operations ■ Operating Central Processing Unit ■ Operating a high-speed printer (on-line to CPU) ■ Operating tape drives	N/A 1 2 3 4 5

*Ratings are defined in *Reference Guide*

Figure 11–3. Performance appraisal system nonexempt personnel. (continued)

KEY JOB PARTS	PERFORMANCE DESCRIPTION	PERFORMANCE RATING*
18. Word Processing ■ Operating a word processor using a terminal or printer ■ Inputting and manipulating statistical data ■ Inputting and formatting text		N/A 1 2 3 4 5
19. Operating a Personal Computer ■ Creating simple programs ■ Performing sort, math and merge functions		N/A 1 2 3 4 5
20. Computer Knowledge ■ Input Documents	Employee has a good knowledge of distribution area. Needs to expand his knowledge of Data Control—Input, UCC7, Schedule.	N/A 1 2 ③ 4 5
21. General ■ Quality Control ■ Unsupervised Work ■ Attendance	Employee is very dependable and has an excellent attitude. He is very responsible and needs very little supervision. Employee continues to improve.	N/A 1 2 3 ④ 5
22. Attitude		N/A 1 2 3 4 5

*Ratings are defined in *Reference Guide*.

OVERALL PERFORMANCE DESCRIPTION

Well below performance requirements. 1	Below performance requirements. 2	Meets performance requirements. 3	Above performance requirements. ④	Well above performance requirements. 5

Refer to the *Guide to Developing Goals* before completing this section.

PERFORMANCE GOALS/RESULTS DESIRED	ACTION SUPERVISOR WILL TAKE TO HELP EMPLOYEE ACHIEVE GOALS	ACTION EMPLOYEE WILL TAKE TO ACHIEVE GOALS	TARGET DATE
1. Work with forms orders and inventories to gain more experience in this area. 2. Ensure that checks are accounted for with letters. 3. Improve research techniques. 4. Expand knowledge of UCC7 and scheduling.			

382

EMPLOYEE COMMENTS:

_____

Employee Signature

Date   8/19/87

NOTE: Your signature does not necessarily signify your agreement with the appraisal; it simply means that the appraisal was discussed with you.

_____

Reviewer's Signature

Date   8/15/87

_____

Second Level Reviewer's Signature

Date   8/15/87

the end of the appraisal period, the rater has relevant data to use in evaluating employee performance. With this method, the appraisal is more likely to include the entire evaluation period and not, for example, focus on the last few weeks or months. However, if a supervisor has many employees to rate, the time required for recording behaviors may become excessive.

ESSAY

The **essay method** is *a performance appraisal method whereby the rater simply writes a brief narrative describing the employee's performance*. This method tends to focus on extreme behavior in the employee's work rather than routine day-to-day performance. Ratings of this type depend heavily upon the evaluator's writing ability. As the evaluations are reviewed, a positive evaluation may be negatively received if the evaluator misspells words or cannot write a good paragraph. Some supervisors, because of their excellent writing ability, can make even a marginal worker appear to be excellent. There might also be difficulty in comparing evaluations. However, some managers believe that the essay method is the best approach to employee evaluation.

WORK STANDARDS

The **work standards method** is *a performance appraisal method that compares each employee's performance to a predetermined standard, or expected level of output*. Standards reflect the normal output of an average worker operating at a normal pace. Work standards may be applied to virtually all types of jobs, but they are most frequently used for those related to production. Several methods may be utilized in determining work standards, including time study and work sampling.

An obvious advantage of using standards as the criterion for appraisal is objectivity. However, in order to ensure that employees perceive that the standards are objective, employees should have a clear understanding of how the standards were set. It follows that the rationale for any changes to the standards must also be carefully explained.

RANKING

In using the **ranking method** of performance appraisal, *the rater simply places all employees in a given group in rank order on the basis of their overall performance*. For example, the best employee in the department will be ranked highest, and the poorest employee will be ranked lowest. A major difficulty occurs when individuals to be evaluated have performed at comparable levels.

Paired comparison is *a variation of the ranking method that involves comparing the performance of each employee with every other employee* in the group. The comparison is often based on a single criterion, such as overall performance. The employee who receives the greatest number of favorable comparisons is ranked highest.

It has been argued that some comparative approach — such as ranking — is used whenever personnel decisions are made. For example, the point is often made that employees are not promoted because they achieve their goals but rather because they achieve their goals better than the others being considered. Decisions of this type do not involve a single individual.[21]

FORCED DISTRIBUTION

The **forced distribution method** is *an appraisal approach where the rater is required to assign individuals in the work group to a limited number of categories similar to a normal frequency distribution.* As an example, employees in the top 10 percent are placed in the highest group; the next 20 percent in the next highest group, the next 40 percent in the middle group, the next 20 percent in the next group, and the remaining 10 percent in the lowest category. This approach is based on the rather questionable assumption that all groups of employees will have the same distribution of excellent, average, and poor performers. If one department has all outstanding workers, the supervisor would likely be hard pressed to decide who should be placed in the lower categories.

FORCED-CHOICE AND WEIGHTED CHECKLIST PERFORMANCE REPORTS

The **forced-choice performance report** is *a technique in which the appraiser is given a series of statements about an individual and the rater indicates which items are most or least descriptive of the employee.* A difficulty often arises because the statements may appear to be virtually identical in describing the employee.

The **weighted checklist performance report** is *a technique whereby the rater completes a form similar to the forced-choice performance report, but the various responses have been assigned different weights.* The form includes questions related to the employee's behavior and the evaluator answers each question either positively or negatively. The evaluator is not aware of how each question is weighted.

As with forced-choice performance reports, the weighted checklist is expensive to design. While both methods strive for objectivity, they have the mutual problem of the evaluator not knowing the items which contribute most to successful performance.

[21]J. Peter Graves, "Let's Put Appraisal Back in Performance Appraisal: Part II," *Personnel Journal* 61 (December 1982): 918.

BEHAVIORALLY ANCHORED RATING SCALES

The **Behaviorally Anchored Rating Scale (BARS) method** is *a performance appraisal method that combines elements of the traditional rating scales and critical incidents methods.* Using BARS, job behaviors derived from critical incidents — effective and ineffective behavior — are described more objectively. The method uses individuals who are familiar with a particular job to identify its major components. They then rank and validate specific behaviors for each of the components.[22] Because BARS typically requires considerable employee participation, its acceptance by both supervisors and their subordinates may be greater. Behaviorally anchored rating scales are potentially more reliable than graphic rating scales and therefore more defensible from a legal point of view.[23]

In BARS, various performance levels are shown along a scale and described in terms of an employee's specific job behavior. Table 11–2 illustrates a portion of a BARS system that was developed to evaluate interviewers and claims deputies for the employment service of a state department of labor. Note that the factor *ability to absorb and interpret policies* is job related and carefully defined. Instead of using adjectives at each scale point, BARS uses behavioral anchors related to the criterion being measured. This modification clarifies the meaning of each point on the scale. For example, instead of dealing with *outstanding performance*, an actual example of such behavior is provided. This approach facilitates discussion of the rating since specific behaviors can be addressed.[24] This method was developed to overcome weaknesses in other evaluation methods. While the results of research on the effectiveness of BARS are mixed, BARS has not been shown to be superior to other methods in overcoming rater errors or in achieving psychometric soundness.[25] A specific deficiency is that the behaviors used are activity oriented rather than results oriented. This poses a potential problem for supervisors doing the rating, who may be forced to deal with employees who are performing the activity but not accomplishing the desired goals.[26]

MANAGEMENT BY OBJECTIVES (MBO)

Although the concept of management by objectives was set forth in Peter F. Drucker's *The Practice of Management*,[27] published in 1954, it was described only a few years ago as the "latest rage" in performance appraisal.[28]

---

[22]Roger J. Plachy, "Appraisal Scales that Measure Performance Outcomes and Job Results," *Personnel* 60 (May–June 1983): 59.

[23]Ronald G. Wells, "Guidelines for Effective and Defensible Performance Appraisal Systems," *Personnel Journal* 61 (October 1982): 777.

[24]Graves, "Part I," pp. 848–849.

[25]Stephen J. Carroll and Craig E. Schneier, *Performance Appraisal and Review Systems: The Identification, Measurement, and Development of Performance in Organizations.* Glenview, Ill.: Scott, Foresman and Company, 1982, p. 117.

[26]Plachy, "Appraisal Scales," p. 59.

[27]Peter F. Drucker, *The Practice of Management.* New York: Harper & Row, 1954.

[28]"The Rating Game," p. 1.

Table 11–2. BARS for factor: "Ability to absorb and interpret policies"

Interviewers and claims deputies must keep abreast of current changes and interpret and apply new information. Some can absorb and interpret new policy guides and procedures quickly with a minimum of explanation. Others seem unable to learn even after repeated explanations and practice. They have difficulty learning and following new policies. When making this rating, disregard job knowledge and experience and evaluate ability to learn on the job.

Very Positive	9	This interviewer could be expected to serve as an information source concerning new and changed policies for others in the office.
	8	Could be expected to be aware quickly of program changes and explain these changes to employers.
	7	Could be expected to reconcile conflicting policies and procedures correctly to meet immediate job needs.
	6	Could be expected to recognize the need for additional information to gain better understanding of policy changes.
Neutral	5	After receiving instruction on completing ESAR forms, this interviewer could be expected to complete the forms correctly.
	4	Could be expected to require some help and practice in mastering new policies and procedures.
	3	Could be expected to know that there is a problem, but might go down many blind alleys before realizing they are wrong.
	2	Could be expected to incorrectly interpret program guidelines, thereby referring an unqualified person.
Very Negative	1	Even after repeated explanations, this interviewer could be expected to be unable to learn new procedures.

Source: Adapted from Cheedle W. Millard, Fred Luthans, and Robert L. Ottemann, "A New Breakthrough for Performance Appraisal," *Business Horizons* 19 (August 1976): 69. Copyright 1976 by the Foundation for the School of Business at Indiana University. Reprinted by permission.

As previously discussed, the MBO concept reflects a management philosophy that values and utilizes employee contributions. It is also an effective method of evaluating an employee's performance and we now discuss it in this context.

In traditional approaches to performance appraisal, personal traits of employees are often used as criteria for evaluating performance. In addition, the role of the evaluating supervisor is similar to that of a judge. With MBO, the focus of the appraisal process shifts from the worker's personal attributes to job performance. The supervisor's role changes from that of an umpire to that of a counselor and facilitator. Also, the employee's function evolves from that of passive bystander to that of active participant. Individuals jointly establish goals with their superiors and then are given some latitude in the means used to achieve their objectives.

At the end of the appraisal period, the employee and supervisor meet for an appraisal interview. They review first the extent to which the goals have been achieved and second, the actions needed to solve remaining problems. Under MBO, the supervisor keeps communication channels open throughout the appraisal period. The problem-solving discussion during the appraisal interview is merely another conversation designed to assist the worker in progressing according to plan. At this time, goals are established for the next evaluation period and the process is repeated.

It should be obvious that not all leadership styles are compatible with the participative concept of MBO. It probably would not be successful in an organization run by highly autocratic managers. An attempt to implement an MBO appraisal system in such a firm would likely result in top management believing that, "MBO is okay in theory but no good in practice." In this case, the theory is quite sound. Implementation problems often stem from the incompatibility of the theory with the organization's culture.

ACTUAL USE OF VARIOUS APPRAISAL METHODS

A recent study of 1000 industrial and 300 nonindustrial firms that comprise the "*Fortune* 1300" revealed how these organizations use performance appraisal systems by job level.[29] Definitions of appraisal approaches used in the study were generally the same as those provided in this chapter. One exception was a second variation of management by objectives which was identical to MBO except that action plans are not established. For our purposes, we have combined these systems into one: objectives-based approach — MBO.

As you can see in Table 11–3, a large number of firms (29 percent) do not evaluate hourly workers using a formal system. This may reflect philosophical differences that exist between union and management. None of the firms in this study utilized MBO for this group of employees. However, a work standards approach is prominent for hourly workers and for the nonexempt group, being used by 29 percent and 33 percent, respectively, of the firms.

In the remaining categories, some form of MBO dominates: exempt (73 percent); professional (75 percent); supervisory (75 percent); middle management (86 percent); and top management (82 percent). The use of essay, work standards, and behaviorally anchored ratings is also significant. Conspicuously missing from the listings are graphic rating scales, which appear only in the hourly and nonexempt categories. It should be noted that multiple responses indicate that more than one appraisal system is used in some companies.

Another major study of performance appraisal systems provided results that are significantly different from those just discussed. This study of 200

[29]Fombrun and Laud, "Strategic Issues," p. 28.

Table 11–3. Rank order of performance appraisal system use by job level*

Hourly (N = 160)	Percent	Nonexempt† (N = 237)	Percent
No system	29	Work standards approach	33
Work standards approach	29	Essay	30
Graphic rating scales	23	Behaviorally anchored ratings	28
Essay	14	Graphic rating scales	26
Behaviorally anchored ratings	14	Objectives-based approach—MBO	19
Exempt† (N = 247)		**Professional (nonmanagerial) (N = 234)**	
Objectives-based approach—MBO	73	Objectives-based approach—MBO	75
Essay	36	Essay	36
Work standards approach	32	Work standards approach	33
Behaviorally anchored ratings	24	Behaviorally anchored ratings	24
Supervisory (N = 235)		**Middle Management (N = 238)**	
Objectives-based approach—MBO	75	Objectives-based approach—MBO	86
Essay	36	Essay	37
Work standards approach	32	Work standards approach	27
Behaviorally anchored ratings	25	Behaviorally anchored ratings	24
Top Management (N = 217)			
Objectives-based approach—MBO	82		
Essay	33		
Work standards approach	24		
Behaviorally anchored ratings	18		

*Multiple responses to some questions result in percentages greater than 100.
N = number of responses.
†The terms *exempt* and *nonexempt* refer to whether a job so classified is subject to provisions of the Fair Labor Standards Act. They are more fully discussed in chapter 12.

Source: Adapted, by permission of the publisher, from "Strategic Issues in Performance Appraisal: Theory and Practice," by Charles J. Fombrun and Robert J. Laud, *Personnel* November–December 1983, p. 24 © 1983 Periodicals Division, American Management Associations, New York. All rights reserved.

randomly selected "*Fortune* 500" and "Second 500" firms revealed significant changes in the use of appraisal systems over a five-year period.[30] The 1981 study — a replication of one conducted in 1976 — indicated that the use of collaborative systems (MBO and BARS) relative to other systems for evaluating managers declined from 57 percent in 1976 to 47 percent in 1981 (see Table 11–4). An increase in the popularity of traditional methods is reflected by their increased use: from 43 percent in 1976 to 53 percent in 1981.

[30]Taylor and Zawaki, "Trends," pp. 71–80.

Table 11–4. Performance appraisal systems used for evaluating managers 1976–1981		
Year of Survey	Percent of responding firms reporting system type	
	Traditional	Collaborative
1976	43	57
1981	53	47

Source: Adapted from Robert L. Taylor and Robert A. Zawacki, "Trends in Performance Appraisal: Guidelines for Managers," reprinted from the March 1984 issue of *Personnel Administrator*, copyright 1984, the American Society for Personnel Administration, 606 North Washington Street, Alexandria, VA 22314.

PROBLEMS IN PERFORMANCE APPRAISAL

Many performance appraisal approaches have received considerable criticism. The rating scales method seems to have received the greatest attention. In all fairness, many of the problems commonly mentioned are not inherent in the method but, rather, reflect improper use. For example, raters may be inadequately trained, or the appraisal device actually used may not be job related.

LACK OF OBJECTIVITY

A potential weakness of traditional methods of performance appraisal is that they lack objectivity. In the rating scales method, for example, commonly used factors such as attitude, loyalty, and personality are difficult to measure accurately. In addition, these factors may have little to do with an employee's performance.

A degree of subjectivity will probably exist in any appraisal method. However, to emphasize objectivity, job related factors should be stressed. Employee appraisal based primarily on personal characteristics may place the evaluator and the company in untenable positions relative to both the employee and EEO guidelines. They may have to show that the factors used are job related.

HALO ERROR

Halo error *occurs when the evaluator perceives one factor as being of paramount importance and gives a good overall rating to an employee who rates high on this factor.* Of course, this type of error could work in the opposite direction as well. For example, David Edwards, accounting supervisor, placed a high value on "neatness," which was a factor used in the company's performance appraisal system. As David was evaluating the performance of his senior accounting clerk, Carl Curtis, he noted that Carl was not a very neat individual and gave him a low ranking on this factor. David also permitted, consciously or unconsciously, the low ranking on neatness to carry over to other factors with the effect that Carl received undeserved low ratings on all factors.

LENIENCY

The giving of undeserved high ratings is referred to as **leniency**. Thomas M. Jordan, vice president of personnel for Sea-Land Service, Inc., stated that one of the major problems encountered in his company's appraisal system is "getting managers to be objective and honest, especially where poor performance is involved." Research tends to support the belief that evaluations will be inflated if a supervisor is required to discuss them with employees.[31] In many situations the evaluating supervisor simply gives the employee the benefit of the doubt. One study revealed that over 50 percent of the employees in one organization were rated in the most favorable category, *excellent*.[32] These actions are often motivated out of a desire to avoid controversy over the appraisal. This practice is more prevalent where highly subjective factors are used as performance criteria.

CENTRAL TENDENCY

Central tendency *is a common error that occurs when employees are incorrectly rated near the average or middle of the scale.* Some rating scale systems require the evaluator to justify in writing extremely high or extremely low ratings. In these instances, the rater may avoid possible controversy or criticism by giving only average ratings.[33]

RECENT BEHAVIOR BIAS

Anyone who has observed the behavior of young children several weeks before Christmas can readily identify with the problem of recent behavior bias. All of a sudden, it seems, the wildest hellions in the neighborhood develop angelic personalities in anticipation of the rewards they expect to receive.

Individuals in the work force are not children, but they are human. Almost every employee will be able to tell you the exact time he or she is

---

[31]Hubert S. Field and William H. Holley, "Subordinates' Characteristics, Supervisors' Ratings, and Decisions to Discuss Appraisal Results," *Academy of Management Journal* 20 (June 1977): 315–321.

[32]William H. Holley, Hubert S. Field, and Nona J. Barnett, "Analyzing Performance Appraisal Systems: An Empirical Study," *Personnel Journal* 55 (September 1976): 458.

[33]Marion G. Haynes, "Developing an Appraisal Program: Part I," *Personnel Journal* 57 (January 1978): 17.

scheduled for a performance review. The employees' actions may not be conscious. But behavior often improves, and productivity tends to rise several days or weeks before the scheduled evaluation. It is only natural to remember recent behavior more clearly than actions from the more distant past. However, performance appraisals generally cover a specified period of time. Therefore an individual's performance should be considered for the entire period.

PERSONAL BIAS

Supervisors doing performance appraisals may have biases related to their employees' personal characteristics such as race, religion, gender, or age group. While federal legislation protects employees in these groups, discrimination continues to be an appraisal problem.

Discrimination in appraisal can be based on many factors in addition to race, creed, gender, age, marital status, or national origin. For example, mild-mannered people may be appraised more harshly simply because they do not raise serious objections to the results. This type of behavior is a sharp contrast to the "hell raisers" who confirm the adage, "The squeaking wheel gets the grease."

JUDGMENTAL ROLE OF EVALUATOR

Supervisors conducting performance evaluations have at times been accused of "playing God" with their employees. In some instances they control virtually every aspect of the process. Manipulation of evaluations by managers to justify their pay increase and promotion decisions is one example of how supervisors abuse the system. They make decisions about the ratings and typically try to tell or sell their version to their employees. The highly judgmental role of some evaluators often places employees on the defensive. The results of such a relationship are hardly conducive to employee development.

CHARACTERISTICS OF AN EFFECTIVE APPRAISAL SYSTEM[34]

Validation studies of an appraisal system may be the most direct and certain approach to determining whether the system is satisfactory. However, validation studies can be costly and time-consuming. Also, many smaller firms will simply not have a sufficient number of jobs to meet technical validation requirements.

It is unlikely that any appraisal system will be totally immune to legal challenge. However, systems that possess certain characteristics may be

[34]Portions of this section were adapted from Ronald G. Wells, "Guidelines for Effective and Defensible Performance Appraisal Systems," *Personnel Journal* 61 (October 1982): 776–782.

more defensible legally. And, at the same time, they can provide a more effective means for achieving performance appraisal goals.

JOB RELATED CRITERIA

The criteria used for appraising employee performance must be job related. The *Uniform Guidelines* and court decisions are quite clear on this point. More specifically, job information must be determined through job analysis. Subjective factors, such as initiative, enthusiasm, loyalty, and cooperation, are obviously important. However, they virtually defy definition and measurement. Unless factors such as these can be clearly shown to be job related, they should not be used.

PERFORMANCE EXPECTATIONS

Managers must clearly explain their performance expectations to their subordinates in advance of the appraisal period. Otherwise, it is not reasonable to evaluate employees using yardsticks that they know nothing about.

The establishment of highly objective work standards is relatively simple in many areas such as manufacturing, assembly and sales. However, for many other types of jobs this task is more difficult. Still, evaluation must take place and performance expectations, however elusive, must be defined in understandable terms.

STANDARDIZATION

Employees in the same job categories under a given supervisor should be appraised using the same evaluation instrument. In addition, the appraisals should cover similar periods of time. Feedback sessions and appraisal interviews should be regularly scheduled for all employees.

Another aspect of standardization is formal documentation. Records should include a description of employees' responsibilities, expected performance results, and the way these data will be viewed in making appraisal decisions. However, smaller firms are not expected to maintain performance appraisal systems that are as formal as those used by larger organizations. The courts reason that objective criteria are not as important in firms with fewer than 30 employees because a smaller firm's top managers are more familiar with their employees' work.[35]

QUALIFIED APPRAISERS

Responsibility for evaluating employee performance must be assigned to the individual or individuals who have an opportunity to observe directly a representative sample of job performance. Most commonly this is the

---

[35]Barry J. Baroni, "The Legal Ramifications of Appraisal Systems," *Supervisory Management* (1982): 41–42.

employee's immediate supervisor, who usually is assigned the responsibility. In other instances, multiple raters may be used.

Other situations that detract from the immediate supervisor's ability to appraise performance objectively include those found in matrix organizations, where certain employees may be technically assigned to a supervisor but actually work under various project managers. Also, a supervisor who is in a new position may have insufficient knowledge of employee performance.

In order to ensure consistency, appraisers must be well-trained. The training should emphasize the importance of performance appraisal as a significant component of every manager's job. The training should also stress that a primary task of the supervisor is to ensure that subordinates understand performance expectations.[36] In addition, the training itself is an ongoing process. It responds to changes in the appraisal system and to the fact that supervisors, for various reasons, may deviate from established procedures. The training should include information on how to rate employees and conduct appraisal interviews. Written instructions should be provided to all individuals who will be performing appraisals. These instructions should be rather detailed and include the need for raters to be objective and unbiased.

It has been suggested that nonsupervisory employees should also receive a set of the performance appraisal instructions. The major benefits cited for this approach are not only the provision of a performance management and planning tool, but also a legal safeguard to deal with potentially disgruntled employees.[37]

OPEN COMMUNICATION

Most employees have a strong need to know how well they are performing. A good appraisal system provides highly desired feedback on a continuing basis. A worthwhile goal would be to avoid surprises during the appraisal interview. While the interview presents an excellent opportunity for both parties to exchange ideas, it should not serve as a substitute for day-to-day communication.

EMPLOYEE ACCESS TO RESULTS

Now, let's imagine you are in a bowling alley where drapes are hanging midway down the alley. You can't see the pins and you never know how many pins your ball knocked over. Your coach is standing behind you saying, "You're doing fine, just keep bowling." You keep rolling the balls and the coach keeps encouraging you. But, you don't know the score. You

---

[36]Milan Moravec, "How Performance Appraisal Can Tie Communication to Productivity," *Personnel Administration* 26 (January 1981): 52.

[37]Beverly L. Kaye and Shelley Krantz, "Preparing Employees: The Missing Link in Performance Appraisal Training," *Personnel* 59 (May–June 1982): 24.

don't really know how well you are doing. At the end of the game, the
scorekeeper informs you that you have set a new record — for low score.
You are flabbergasted and disappointed. You're out. You are off the team.
Tough luck.[38]

Obviously, this anecdote does not describe the best way to manage a
bowling team or, for that matter, any other type of organization. Yet, in too
many instances the same kind of mistakes are made when employees do
not fully know the rules of the game and are not provided adequate feedback
on their performance. Such a situation is uncomfortable at best and, at
worst, totally demoralizing and defeating.

As a result of the Federal Privacy Act of 1973, employees of the federal
government and federal contractors must be provided access to their personnel files, which may include performance appraisal data. While this
requirement does not currently apply to all employees in the private sector,
there are a number of good reasons — aside from the threat of broader
legislative coverage — for allowing such access. Most importantly, employees will not trust a system they don't understand. Secrecy will invar-
iably breed suspicion and thereby thwart efforts to obtain employee
participation.

For the many appraisal systems that are designed to improve performance, withholding appraisal results would be unthinkable. Employees simply could not perform better without having access to this information. Also,
permitting employees to review the results of their appraisal allows them to
detect any errors that may have been made. Or, the employee may simply
disagree with the evaluation and may wish to formally challenge it.

DUE PROCESS

In connection with the last point, it is vitally important that due process
be ensured. A formal procedure should be developed — if one does not
exist — to permit employees the means for appealing appraisal results that
they do not consider accurate or fair. They must have the means for pursuing
their grievances and having them addressed objectively.

From a review of court cases, it is clear that perfect appraisals are not
expected from employers. Nor is it anticipated that supervisory discretion
should be removed from the process. However, the courts normally require
the following:

- Either the absence of adverse impact on protected groups or
  validation of the process.
- A review process that prevents one manager from directing or
  controlling a subordinate's career.

---

[38]Largent Parks, Jr., "Appraising Personnel Appraisals," *National Underwriters* (Life, Health
. . .) 87 (August 27, 1983): 13.

- The rater having personal knowledge and contact with the appraisee's job performance.
- The use of formal appraisal criteria that limit the manager's discretion.[39]

LEGAL IMPLICATIONS

It has been estimated that more than 30 million workers had their performance formally appraised during 1980. Thus appraisals have been and are still widely used in industry and government. Yet, the process contains many potential sources for error.[40] Mistakes in appraising performance can have serious repercussions in various areas of human resource management, such as the improper allocation of money for merit increases. In addition, mistakes can result in costly legal action being taken against a firm. In settling cases, courts have held employers liable for back pay, court costs, and other costs related to training and promoting protected group members. The four most common forms of personnel actions that lead to Age Discrimination in Employment Act complaints are promotions, layoffs, retirements, and discharges. In a study that analyzed 26 ADEA cases decided in federal courts where employee appraisal had been a determinative factor, it was found that employers with formal appraisal systems were successful 73 percent of the time. However, employers who did not use a formal system were successful defendants only 40 percent of the time.[41]

Despite the *Uniform Guidelines*, one survey indicated that fewer than 50 percent of the companies responding considered these guidelines when designing their appraisal systems.[42] While it is unlikely that any appraisal system will be totally immune to legal challenge, systems that possess the characteristics previously discussed are apparently more legally defensible. At the same time, they can provide a more effective means for achieving performance appraisal goals.

THE APPRAISAL INTERVIEW

The Achilles' heel of the entire evaluation process is the appraisal interview itself. It is the central source of difficulty.[43] However, regardless of the

---

[39]Patricia Linenberger and Timothy J. Keaveny, "Performance Appraisal Standards Used by the Courts," *Personnel Administrator* 26 (May 1981): 94.

[40]N. B. Winstanley, William H. Holley, and Hubert S. Field, "Will Your Performance Appraisal System Hold Up in Court?" *Personnel* (January–February 1982): 59–64.

[41]Michael H. Schuster and Christopher S. Miller, "Performance Appraisal and the Age Discrimination in Employment Act," *Personnel Adminstrator* 29 (March 1984): 48–57.

[42]Fombrun and Laud, "Strategic Issues," p. 27.

[43]C. O. Colvin, "Everything You Always Wanted to Know About Appraisal Discrimination," *Personnel Journal* 60 (October 1981): 758–759.

problems involved, it is common practice for supervisors to conduct a formal appraisal interview at the end of an employee's appraisal period. This interview is essential if employee development is to be achieved. At the same time, it should be noted that effective performance appraisal systems require more than this single interview. Rather, a series of continuing discussions must be held to emphasize the employee's responsibility for development and improvement and to emphasize the supportive role of the manager.[44]

The key to a successful appraisal interview is to structure it so that both the manager and the subordinate will view the interview as a problem-solving rather than a fault-finding session.[45] Three basic purposes should be considered when planning for the appraisal interview: discussing the employee's performance, assisting the employee in setting goals, and suggesting means for achieving these goals.[46]

The interview should be scheduled soon after the end of the appraisal period. Employees usually know when their interview should take place, and their anxiety tends to increase when it is delayed. Interviews with top performers are often pleasant experiences. However, many supervisors are reluctant to meet face-to-face with poor performers. They tend to postpone these anxiety-provoking interviews.

The amount of time devoted to an appraisal interview varies considerably with company policy and the position of the evaluated employee. While interviewing costs must be considered, there is merit in conducting separate interviews for discussing: (1) employee performance and development; and (2) pay increases. Many managers have learned that as soon as pay is mentioned in an interview it tends to dominate the conversation. For this reason, it is now a rather common practice to defer pay discussions. A brief interview for this purpose should be held within one or two weeks after the first interview.

Conducting an appraisal interview requires tact and patience on the part of the supervisor. It is often one of management's more difficult tasks. Praise should be provided when warranted, but it can have only limited value if not clearly deserved.

Criticism is especially difficult to apply. So-called constructive criticism is often not perceived as such by the employee. Yet, it is difficult for a manager at any level to avoid criticism when conducting appraisal interviews. The supervisor should realize that all individuals have some deficiencies that may not be changed easily, if at all. Continued criticism may lead to frustration and have a damaging effect on employee development. Again, this does not mean that undesirable employee behavior should be ignored. However, discussions of sensitive issues should focus on the

[44]John F. Kikoshi and Joseph A. Litterer, "Effective Communication in the Performance Appraisal Interview," *Public Personnel Management Journal* 12 (Spring 1983): 33.

[45]Randall Brett and Alan J. Fredian, "Performance Appraisal: The System Is Not the Solution," *Personnel Administrator* 26 (December 1981): 61.

[46]Ibid., p. 62.

deficiency and not the person. Threats to the employee's self-esteem should be minimized.[47]

A serious error that is sometimes committed is for the supervisor to surprise the subordinate by bringing up some past mistake or problem. For example, if an incident had not been previously discussed, it would be most inappropriate for the supervisor to state, "Two months ago, you failed to properly coordinate your plans for implementing the new accounts receivable procedure." Good management practices and common sense dictate that this type of situation should be dealt with as it occurs and not be saved for the appraisal interview.

The entire performance appraisal process should be a positive experience for employees. In practice, however, it often is not. Negative feelings can often be traced to the appraisal interview and the manner in which it is conducted by the supervisor.[48] Ideally, appraised employees will leave the interview with positive feelings about the supervisor, the company, the job, and themselves. The prospects for improved performance will be bleak if the employee's ego is deflated. While past behavior cannot be changed, future performance can. Specific plans for the employee's development should be clearly outlined and mutually agreed on. Cessna Aircraft Company has developed several hints for supervisors, which have been found helpful in conducting appraisal interviews (see Figure 11–4).

ASSESSMENT CENTERS

Many employee performance appraisal systems evaluate an individual's past performance and at the same time attempt to assess his or her potential for advancement. Other organizations have developed a separate approach for assessing potential. This process often takes place in what is appropriately referred to as an assessment center.

The **assessment center method** is *an appraisal approach that requires employees to participate in a series of activities similar to what they might be expected to do in an actual job.* The situational activities exercises are developed as a result of thorough job analysis.[49] Such activities include in-basket exercises, management games, leaderless group discussions, mock interviews, and tests. The assessors observe the employees in a secluded environment, usually separate from the work place, over a certain period of time. The assessors selected are typically experienced managers who participate in the exercises and evaluate the performance of the candidate.

---

[47]Don Caruth, Bill Middlebrook, and Frank Rachel, "Performance Appraisals: Much More Than a Once-a-Year Task," *Supervisory Management* (September 1982): 33.

[48]Herbert H. Meyer, "The Annual Performance Review Discussion — Making It Constructive," *Personnel Journal* 56 (October 1977): 508–511.

[49]Cabot L. Jaffee and Joseph T. Sefcik, Jr., "What Is an Assessment Center?" *Personnel Administrator* 25 (February 1980): 40–43.

Figure 11–4. Suggestions for conducting appraisal interviews. Source: Used with the permission of Cessna Aircraft Company.

1. Give the employee a few days notice of the discussion and its purpose. Encourage the employee to give some preparatory thought to his or her job performance and development plans. In some cases, have employees read their written performance evaluation prior to the meeting.

2. Prepare notes and use the completed performance appraisal form as a discussion guide so that each important topic will be covered. Be ready to answer questions employees may ask about why you appraised them as you did. Encourage your employees to ask questions.

3. Be ready to suggest specific developmental activities suitable to each employee's needs. When there are specific performance problems, remember to "attack the problem, not the person."

4. Establish a friendly, helpful and purposeful tone at the outset of the discussion. Recognize that it is not unusual for you and your employee to be nervous about the discussion and use suitable techniques to put you both more at ease.

5. Assure your employee that everyone on Cessna's management team is being evaluated so that opportunities for improvement and development will not be overlooked and each person's performance will be fully recognized.

6. Make sure that the session is truly a discussion. Encourage employees to talk about how they feel they are doing on the job, how they might improve, and what developmental activities they might undertake. Often an employee's viewpoints on these matters will be quite close to your own.

7. When your appraisal differs from the employee's, discuss these differences. Sometimes employees have hidden reasons for performing in a certain manner or using certain methods. This is an opportunity to find out if such reasons exist.

8. These discussions should contain both constructive compliments and constructive criticism. Be sure to discuss the employee's strengths as well as weaknesses. Your employees should have clear pictures of how you view their performance when the discussions are concluded.

9. Occasionally the appraisal interview will uncover strong emotions. This is one of the values of regular appraisals; they can bring out bothersome feelings so they can be dealt with honestly. The emotional dimension of managing is very important. Ignoring it can lead to poor performance. Deal with emotional issues when they arise because they block a person's ability to concentrate on other issues. Consult Personnel for help when especially strong emotions are uncovered.

10. Make certain that your employees fully understand your appraisal of their performance. Sometimes it helps to have an employee orally summarize the appraisal as he or she understands it. If there are any misunderstandings they can be cleared up on the spot. Ask questions to make sure you have been fully understood.

11. Discuss the future as well as the past. Plan with the employee specific changes in performance or specific developmental activities that will allow fuller use of potential. Ask what you can do to help.

12. End the discussion on a positive, future-improvement-oriented note. You and your employee are a team, working toward the development of everyone involved.

Table 11–5. General Electric Company's supervisory assessment center's (SAC) typical schedule

Day 1

Approximately four hours per candidate are required for the background interview and an in-basket exercise. The interview covers such traditional areas as work experience, educational background, and leadership experience. The in-basket exercise provides an opportunity for the individual to demonstrate how he or she would handle administrative problems including day-to-day "fire-fighting." All Day 1 activities are scheduled on an individual basis and are typically administered by persons in Employee Relations.

Day 2

An additional four hours are devoted to group and individual exercises. Group exercises related to reallocation of resources allow an individual's performance to be observed as the candidate solves problems in peer group situations. In the individual exercises each candidate assumes the role of a supervisor to handle four typical work-related problems. Six operating managers serve as the SAC staff for Day 2 activities. They observe and evaluate the performance of six candidates. The staff completes structured rating forms on each candidate's performance immediately following each exercise. After all exercises have been completed and the candidates dismissed, the staff conducts an overall evaluation of each individual's potential for a supervisory position. Over fifty pieces of data from each candidate's performance are reviewed along with information obtained from the interview. The staff then arrives at a consensus decision and a recommended course of action for each candidate.

Source: Used with permission of the General Electric Company.

Assessment centers are used increasingly for purposes of: (1) identifying employees who have higher level management potential; (2) selecting first level supervisors; and (3) determining employees' developmental needs. Assessment centers are used by more than 1000 organizations,[50] including small firms and large corporations such as General Electric Company, J. C. Penney Company, Ford Motor Company, and AT&T. A typical schedule for General Electric's supervisory assessment center (SAC) is shown in Table 11–5. The SAC program is used for selecting new employees and assessing current employees' management potential. Note the number of exercises that are utilized in evaluating a participant's behavior.

An evaluation of the General Electric SAC process revealed that:

- The SAC was based on a job analysis of a supervisor's job and is considered to have content validity.[51]
- The SAC provides all candidates an equal opportunity to demonstrate their skills and does not discriminate against any

[50]*General Electric Assessment Center Manual*, General Electric Company.

[51]Content validity is inherent in the assessment center process when the exercises developed are based on job analysis. This type of validity is acceptable according to the *Guidelines*.

employee group. For example, a study of more than 1000 candidates from fourteen company locations shows the following success ratios in the SAC:

Caucasian	39%
Minority	43%
Female	46%

- Those individuals who scored highest in the SAC are the same individuals who have subsequently received the greatest number of job promotions. Thus one area of predictive validity of the SAC was demonstrated.

There often are as many as a half-dozen assessors evaluating each participant, as is the case at General Electric. The participant's position in the organization often determines the amount of time spent in the center. First-line supervisory candidates may only spend a day or two, while more time may be needed for those being considered for middle management and executive jobs. The participants return to their jobs after the session is completed. The assessors then prepare their evaluation. Interestingly, because the assessors are often not full-time members of the training and development staff, they also often gain improved insights as to how managers in their organization should function. Also, while the primary purpose of assessment centers is to identify management potential, J. C. Penney's experience indicates that the "participants gain valuable insights into their own strengths, weaknesses and interests." This permits the organization and the individual to make plans for the employee's development.

SUMMARY

Performance appraisal is defined as a system that provides a periodic review and evaluation of an individual's job performance. The overriding purpose of any performance appraisal system is to improve the overall effectiveness of the organization. The performance appraisal process begins by considering the external and internal environment. Legislation and labor unions are prime external factors.

Identification of specific goals provides the starting point for the performance appraisal process. Because an appraisal system cannot serve all purposes, a firm must select those specific goals it desires to achieve. Once specific goals have been established, workers must then understand what is expected from them in their jobs. This normally takes the form of discussions with their supervisors to review the major duties contained in the job description.

After the work has been performed, the results are examined and performance is then periodically evaluated, based on previously established job performance standards. The results of the evaluation are then communicated to workers. The performance evaluation discussion serves to reestablish job requirements in the employee's mind. The process is dynamic and ongoing; each appraisal discussion results in reestablishing job performance standards.

Personnel is responsible for designing and overseeing the appraisal program. The person who conducts performance appraisals varies from company to company. Direct participation by line management in the operation of the program is necessary for success. Several possibilities exist as to who will actually rate the employee, including: immediate supervisor, subordinates, peers, group appraisal, self-appraisal, and combinations of these methods.

There are a number of appraisal methods from which to choose. These methods include: (1) rating scales; (2) critical incidents; (3) essay; (4) work standards; (5) ranking; (6) forced distribution; (7) forced choice and weighted checklist performance reports; (8) behaviorally anchored rating scales, and (9) management by objectives.

A number of problems are associated with the various performance appraisal methods. These include: lack of objectivity, halo error, leniency, central tendency, recent behavior bias, personal bias, and the judgmental role of the evaluator ("playing God").

At the end of an employee appraisal period it is a common practice for the evaluating supervisor to conduct a formal appraisal interview. This interview is essential for achieving employee development. The key to a successful interview is to structure it so that both the manager and subordinate will approach it as a problem-solving rather than a fault-finding session.

Certain practices have been found to be associated with the successful legal defense of employers' appraisal systems. Mistakes can result in costly legal action being taken against a firm.

The assessment center method requires employees to participate in a series of activities similar to those that they might be expected to perform in an actual job. Assessment centers are being used increasingly for the purpose of: (1) identifying employees who have higher level management potential; (2) selecting first-line supervisors; and (3) determining employees' developmental needs.

QUESTIONS FOR REVIEW

1. Define and state the basic purposes of performance appraisal. Briefly discuss.
2. What are the basic steps involved in the performance appraisal process?
3. Briefly describe the various alternatives as to who should conduct performance appraisal.

4. Briefly describe each of the following methods of performance appraisal:
   (a) rating scales
   (b) critical incidents
   (c) essay
   (d) work standards
   (e) ranking
   (f) forced distribution

(g) forced-choice and weighted checklists

(h) behaviorally anchored rating scales

(i) management by objectives

5. What are the various problems associated with performance appraisal? Briefly describe each.

6. What is the purpose of an appraisal interview? Discuss.

7. Describe how an assessment center could be used as a means for performance appraisal.

8. What are the characteristics of an effective appraisal system?

TERMS FOR REVIEW

Performance appraisal (PA)
Group appraisal
Rating scales method
Critical incident method
Essay method
Work standards method
Ranking method
Paired comparison

Forced distribution method
Forced-choice performance report
Weighted checklist performance report
Behaviorally anchored rating scale (BARS) method
Halo error
Leniency
Central tendency
Assessment center method

Incident 1

It was performance appraisal time again and Alex Funderburk knew that he would receive a low evaluation this time. Janet Stevens, Alex's boss, opened the appraisal interview with this comment, "The sales department had a good increase this quarter. Also, departmental expenses are down a good bit. But, we nowhere near accomplished the ambitious goals you and I set last quarter." "I know," said Alex. "I thought we were going to make it, though. We would have, too, if we had received that big Simpson order and if I could have gotten us on the computer a little earlier in the quarter."

"I agree with you, Alex," said Janet. "Do you think we were just too ambitious or do you think there was some way we could have made the Simpson sale and speeded up the computerization process?" "Yes," replied Alex, "we could have gotten the Simp-

son order this quarter. I just made a couple of concessions to Simpson and their purchasing manager tells me he can issue the order next week. The delay with the computer was caused by a thoughtless mistake I made. I won't let that happen again."

The discussion continued for about thirty minutes longer. Alex discovered that Janet was going to mark him very high in all areas despite his failure to accomplish the goals that they had set.

Prior to the meeting, Janet had planned to suggest that the unattained goals for last period be set as the new goals for the coming quarter. After she and Alex had discussed matters, however, they both decided to establish new, somewhat higher goals. As he was about to leave the meeting, Alex said, "Janet, I feel good about these objectives, but I don't believe we have more than a 50 percent chance of accomplishing them." "I believe you can do it," replied Janet. "If you knew for sure, though, the goals wouldn't be high enough." "I see what you mean," said Alex, as he left the office.

QUESTIONS

1. What was wrong or right with Janet's appraisal of Alex's performance?
2. Should the new objectives be higher or lower than they are? Explain.

Incident 2

As the production supervisor for Sweeney Electronics, Mike Mahoney was generally well thought of by most of his subordinates. Mike was an easygoing individual who tried to help his employees any way he could. If a worker needed a small loan until payday, he would dig into his pocket with no questions asked. Should an employee need some time off to attend to a personal problem, he would not dock the individual's pay; rather, he would take up the slack himself until the worker returned.

Everything had been going smoothly, at least until the last performance appraisal period. One of Mike's workers, Bill Overstreet, had been experiencing a large number of personal problems for the past year. Bill's wife had been sick much of the time and her medical expenses were high. Bill's son had a speech impediment and the doctors had recommended a special clinic. Bill, who had already borrowed the limit the bank would loan, had become upset and despondent over his general circumstances.

When it was time for Bill's annual performance appraisal, Mike decided he was going to do as much as possible to help him. Although Bill could not be considered more than an average worker, Mike rated him outstanding in virtually every category. Because the firm's compensation system was tied heavily to the performance appraisal, Bill would be eligible for a merit increase of 10 percent in addition to the regular cost of living raise he would receive as an average worker.

Mike explained to Bill why he was giving him such high ratings and Bill acknowledged that his performance had really been no better than average. Bill was very grateful and expressed this to Mike. As Bill left the office he was excitedly looking forward to telling his friends about what a wonderful boss he had. Seeing Bill smile as he left gave Mike a warm feeling.

QUESTIONS

1. From Sweeney Electronic's standpoint, what difficulties might Mike Mahoney's performance appraisal practices create?
2. What can Mike do now to diminish the negative impact of his evaluation of Bill?

REFERENCES

Baird, Lloyd S., Beatty, Richard W., and Schneier, Craig Eric. *The Performance Appraisal Sourcebook*. Amherst, Mass.: Human Resource Development Press, 1982.

Banks, C. G. and Roberson, L. "Performance Appraisers as Test Developers." *Academy of Management Review* 10 (January 1985): 128–142.

Brett, Randall and Fredian, Alan J. "Performance Appraisal: The System Is Not the Solution." *Personnel Administrator* 26 (December 1981): 61–68.

Bucalo, Jack. "Personnel Directors . . . What You Should Know Before Recommending MBO." *Personnel Journal* 56 (April 1977): 176–178.

Carroll, Stephen J. and Schneier, Craig E. *Performance Appraisal and Review Systems.* Glenview, Ill.: Scott, Foresman and Company, 1982.

Catalanello, Ralph E. and Hooper, John A. "Managerial Appraisal." *Personnel Administrator* 26 (September 1981): 75–81.

Cummings, L. L. and Schwab, Donald P. "Designing Appraisal Systems for Information Yield." *California Management Review* 20 (Summer 1978): 18–25.

Dipboye, R. L. "Some Neglected Variables in Research on Discrimination in Appraisals." *Academy of Management Review* 10 (January 1985): 116–127.

Edwards, M. R. and Sproull, J. R. "Making Performance Appraisals Perform: The Use of Team Evaluation." *Personnel* 62 (March 1985): 28–32.

Gehrman, Douglas B. "Beyond Today's Compensation and Performance Appraisal Systems." *Personnel Administrator* 29 (March 1984): 21.

Gordon, R. F. "Does Your Performance Appraisal System Really Work?" *Supervisory Management* 30 (February 1985): 37–41.

Grant, Philip C. "How to Manage Employee Job Performance." *Personnel Administrator* 26 (August 1981): 59–65.

Henderson, Richard. *Performance Appraisal: Theory and Practice.* Reston, Va.: Reston, 1980.

Holley, William H. and Field, Hubert S. "Will Your Performance Appraisal System Hold Up in Court?" *Personnel* (January–February 1982): 59–64.

Ilgen, D. R. and Favero, J. L. "Limits in Generalization from Psychological Research to Performance Appraisal Processes." *Academy of Management Review* 10 (April 1985): 311–321.

Jacobs, R. and Kozlowski, S. W. J. "A Closer Look at Halo Error in Performance Ratings." *Academy of Management Journal* 28 (March 1985): 201–212.

Lanza, P. "Team Appraisals." *Personnel Journal* 64 (March 1985): 46–51.

Lee, C. "Increasing Performance Appraisal Effectiveness: Matching Task Types, Appraisal Process, and Rater Training." *Academy of Management Review* 10 (April 1985): 322–331.

Lotham, Gary P. and Wexley, Kenneth N. *Increasing Productivity Through Performance Appraisal.* Reading, Mass.: Addison-Wesley, 1981.

Maravec, Milan, "Performance Appraisal: A Human Resource Management System with Productivity Payoffs." *Management Review* 70 (June 1981): 51–54.

Nathan, B. R. and Alexander, R. A. "The Role of Inferential Accuracy in Performance Rating." *Academy of Management Review* 10 (January 1985): 109–115.

Schuster, D. V. "Performance Recognition: The Power of Positive Feedback." *Training* 22 (January 1985): 69+.

Schuster, Michael H. and Miller, Christopher S. "Performance Appraisal and the Age Discrimination in Employment Act." *Personnel Administrator* 29 (March 1984): 48–57.

Slattery, P. D. "Performance Appraisal Without Stress." *Personnel Journal* 64 (February 1985): 49–50+.

Taylor, Robert L. and Zawaki, Robert A. "Trends in Performance Appraisal: Guidelines for Managers." *Personnel Administrator* 29 (March 1984): 71.

Umapathy, S. "Teaching Behavioral Aspects of Performance Evaluation: An Experiential Approach (Teaching Behavioral Aspects of Accounting)." *The Accounting Review* 60: (January 1985): 97–108.

White, R. N. "Corrective Action: A Treatment Plan for Problem Performers." *Personnel* 62 (February 1985): 7–9.

Winstanley, N. B. "Legal and Ethical Issues in Performance Appraisals." *Harvard Business Review* 58 (November–December 1980): 186.

Woods, J. G. and Dillion, T. "The Performance Review Approach to Improving Productivity." *Personnel* 62 (March 1985): 20–27.

Yager, Ed. "A Critique of Performance Appraisal Systems." *Personnel Journal* 60 (February 1981): 129–133.

Yoder, Dale and Heneman, Herbert G., Jr. (eds.), *ASPA Handbook of Personnel and Industrial Relations: Staffing Policies and Strategies,* Vol 1. Washington, D.C.: The Bureau of National Affairs, 1974.

Parma Cycle Company: Training the Work Force

As the date for the new plant opening drew near, Mary Higgins, director of employee development at Parma Cycle Company in Parma, Ohio, grew increasingly nervous. With only six months to train the work force for the new Clarksdale, Mississippi plant, Mary knew that there was little room for error.

Mary had already arranged to lease a building near the factory site, and some of the machinery for the new plant was being installed in that building for training purposes. Most of the machinery was similar to that being used at Parma, and Mary had selected trainers from among the supervisory staff at the Parma plant. One machine, however, a robotized frame assembler, was entirely new. The assembler was being purchased from a Japanese firm. Mary had arranged to have two operators trained in the Japanese factory.

In connection with all of this activity, Mary had personally made two trips to Clarksdale. She had also retained a training consultant, a management professor from the University of Mississippi. The training consultant had agreed to help Mary plan the training program and to evaluate the program as it went along. It was at the consultant's suggestion that Mary decided to use a combination of vestibule training and classroom lectures in developing a trained work force prior to factory start-up time. In the past, Parma Cycle had used on-the-job training almost exclusively. This was not feasible, she felt, at the new plant.

As Mary was thinking about how short the time was, the phone rang. It was the personnel director, Jesse Heard, telling her that he was ready for their meeting. When she got to his office she found him studying a training report she had prepared a few days earlier. "Mary," said Jesse, "It looks like you have things well under control for the Clarksdale plant. But I don't see anything here about training the workers who are going to be transferred down from this plant." "Well," said Mary, "they have all been working in bicycle manufacture for quite a while. I thought it might not be necessary to have any formal training for them." "That's true," said Jesse, "but most of them will be taking different jobs when they move to Clarksdale." "I'll get on it right away," said Mary.

"What are we going to do about supervisory training at the Clarksdale plant?" asked Jesse. Mary replied, "I think we'll use the same system we use here for the long haul. We'll bring our supervisors up through the ranks and have quarterly off-site seminars. To start, the supervisors who move down from Parma can help train the others." Jesse asked, "What do you think about bringing the supervisors hired in Clarksdale up here for a few days to help them learn how we do things?" "That's a good idea," said Mary. "We can pair them off with some of our better people at Parma."

"That won't help us with performance evaluations, Mary," said Jesse. "You know we're going to use a different system down there. We've decided to use management by objectives down to the supervisory level and a new three-item rating scale for the workers." "I know," answered Mary. "I'd planned classroom training on that beginning the month after start-up at the Clarksdale plant. I'm going to conduct those sessions myself. Because the performance scores will be used to allocate incentive bonuses, I want to make sure that they are consistently assigned."

"Mary," said Jesse, "I'm really impressed with the way you are taking charge of our training effort for the Clarksdale plant. Just keep up the good work." "Thank you, Jesse," said Mary. "I'll get back to you next week on the training I recommend for the workers who will transfer down from Parma."

QUESTIONS

1. Describe how an untrained person hired in Clarksdale could become a competent machine operator by the time the new plant opens.
2. Do you think Mary needed the training consultant? Why or why not?
3. What do you think of Jesse's idea to have the supervisors for the new plant trained by those transferred from Ohio? Explain your answer.

Experiencing Human Resource Management

An In-Basket Exercise

In-basket exercises are becoming increasingly popular, both as a selection tool and for training managers at several levels. Essentially the exercise consists of prioritizing pieces of correspondence and determining how to respond to them. The way the present or prospective manager handles various items gives some insight into that manager's competence and helps to prepare managers for situations that may arise.

YOUR ROLE

You are Jesse Heard, personnel director at Parma Cycle Company, and you have been away for four days attending a seminar on "New Developments in Personnel Management" at Northeast Louisiana University. It is Friday morning and you have come in at 7 o'clock so that you can go through your in-basket and plan for the busy day you expect. The basket is piled high with correspondence, forms, reports, computer printouts, etc. After laying aside a number of the voluminous reports, which you always receive but never read, you place the remainder of the items on your desk and begin to go through them. Your objective is to prioritize them according to when you will take action and then determine what action to take on each. You have decided to sort them into four stacks: "Immediate Action Required," "Action Required Sometime Today," "Delay Until Next Week," and "Ignore." The first three items selected are on pages 408–409.

QUESTIONS

1. In the long run, what should you do about the reports you "always receive but never read"?
2. Was it ethical for Jim Burgess's friend to call Jim about Edward Deal's job-seeking efforts?
3. What information would you normally provide a prospective employer about a previous employee?

CONFIDENTIAL

MEMORANDUM

TO: Jesse Heard
FROM: Jim Burgess
DATE: December 16, 19--
SUBJECT: Edward Deal

I had a call from a friend the other day who said that Edward Deal is on the job market. I thought he was excited about the job down in Clarksdale. If he's not, we'd better start scrambling. Check it out and get with me Monday or Tuesday. I'll be out of town until Sunday afternoon. I would have waited to talk with you personally but I didn't think this should wait.

Figure III–1.

Figure III–2.

To _Jesse Heard_
Date _12/16_   Time _3:00_

WHILE YOU WERE OUT

M _Mary Diggins_
of _Training_

Phone _____

Area Code		Number	Extension
TELEPHONED	✓	PLEASE CALL	✓
CALLED TO SEE YOU		WILL CALL AGAIN	
WANTS TO SEE YOU		URGENT	✓
	RETURNED YOUR CALL		

Message _____
_____
_____
_____

                    Operator

December 16, 19--

Parma Cycle Company
301 West 31st Street
Parma, OH 40127

Dear Mr. Heard:

I have tried to call you several times, but could never get through to you. Since I have
been traveling, I did not leave a message. Perhaps you will kindly respond to this letter
right away.

Mr. Claude L. Simpson, who used to work in your office as a personnel specialist, has
applied for a job with us as Assistant Personnel Manager. Could you please provide the
following information about Mr. Simpson. For your convenience just fill it in on this
letter and return it in the enclosed envelope.

Length of time employed by Parma. _____

How would you evaluate his ability to get along with others? _____

_____

Rate of pay at time of discharge. _____

Reason discharged. _____

Record of disciplinary offenses, if any. _____

_____

Your overall recommendation as to whether Mr. Simpson would make a reliable
employee. _____

I assure you that the information which you provide will be held in strictest confidence.
I must make a decision on Mr. Simpson's employment within a few days, so if you could
do this while you have it before you, I would appreciate it.

Sincerely,

Ryan Chappell,
Plant Manager

RC:ds

Enclosure

Figure III–3.

Part Four

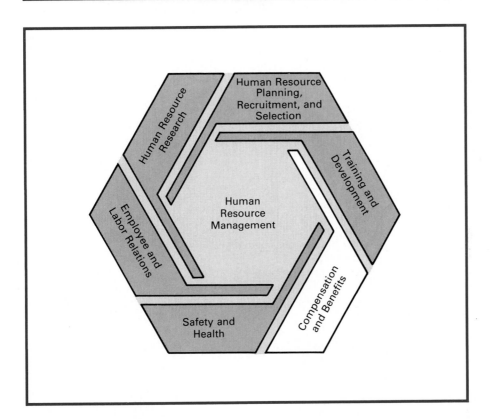

Human Resource Research

Human Resource Planning, Recruitment, and Selection

Training and Development

Human Resource Management

Employee and Labor Relations

Compensation and Benefits

Safety and Health

COMPENSATION AND BENEFITS

CHAPTER OBJECTIVES
1. Define *compensation* and explain the concept of equity as related to compensation.
2. Describe the determinants of financial compensation.
3. Define *job evaluation* and describe the basic job evaluation methods.
4. Describe how employee-related factors assist in determining pay and employee equity.
5. Explain the factors associated with job pricing and describe pay secrecy and pay compression.

Chapter 12

FINANCIAL COMPENSATION

Earl Lewis and his wife are full of excitement and anticipation as they leave their home for a shopping trip. Earl had recently found a job after several weeks of unemployment, and the paycheck he received today will enable them to make a down payment on a much-needed refrigerator.

Inez Scoggin's anxiety over scheduled minor surgery was somewhat relieved. Her supervisor has assured her that 90 percent of her medical and hospitalization costs will be covered by her firm's health insurance plan.

Trig Ekeland, executive director of the local YMCA, returns home dead tired from his job each evening no earlier than six o'clock. His salary is small compared with the salaries of many other managers in the local area who have similar responsibilities. Yet, Trig is an exceptionally happy person who feels that his work with youth, civic leaders, and other members of the community is extremely important and worthwhile.

Joanne Abrahamson has been employed by a large manufacturing firm for eight years. Although her salary is not what she would like it to be, her job in the accounts payable department enables her to have contact with some of her best friends. She likes her supervisor and considers the overall working environment to be great. Joanne would not trade jobs with anyone she knows.

As suggested by the anecdotes involving Trig and Joanne, a total compensation package includes more than pay. Because it has many components, compensation administration is one of the most difficult and challenging areas confronting managers of human resources.

This chapter emphasizes direct financial compensation. Other financial compensation considerations such as incentives, as well as the unique aspects of managerial, professional, and sales compensation, will be discussed in chapter 13. Benefits and nonfinancial compensation will also be described in that chapter.

COMPENSATION: AN OVERVIEW

Compensation refers to *every type of reward that individuals receive in return for performing organizational tasks*. The components of a total compensation program are shown in Figure 12–1. Earl Lewis has just received his paycheck and wants to purchase a needed item for his family. **Direct financial compensation** consists of *the pay that a person receives in the form of wages, salary, bonuses, and commissions*. Inez Scoggin is receiving indirect financial compensation because her company pays 90 percent of all medical and hospitalization costs. **Indirect financial compensation** (benefits) includes *all financial rewards that are not included in direct compensation*. As you can see in Figure 12–1, this form of compensation includes a wide variety of rewards that are normally received indirectly by the employee.

Nonfinancial compensation consists of *the satisfaction that a person receives by performing meaningful job tasks or from the psychological and/or physical environment in which the job is performed*. Trig Ekeland and Joanne Abrahamson are receiving important forms of nonfinancial compensation. Trig is extremely satisfied with the job he performs. This type of nonfinancial compensation consists of the satisfaction that a person receives by performing meaningful job-related tasks. On the other hand, Joanne's job permits her to have contacts with her best friends. This form of nonfinancial compensation involves the psychological and/or physical environment in which the job is performed.

All these types of compensation comprise a total compensation program. People have different reasons for working. When people are responsible for providing food and clothing for their families, money may well be the most important reward. Yet, why is it that some people work many hours each day, receive little pay, and yet love their work? To a large degree, adequate compensation is in the mind of the receiver. It is often more than the financial compensation that a person receives in the form of a paycheck.

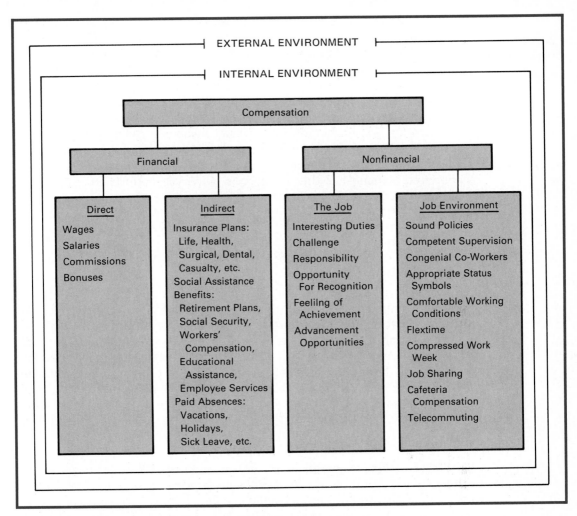

Figure 12–1. The components of a total compensation program.

COMPENSATION EQUITY

Organizations must attract, motivate, and retain competent employees. In pursuing these goals, firms strive for equity in their compensation systems. The primary concerns are for fairness to both employee and employer and equity both within and outside the organization.[1]

Organizational equity is *achieved by balancing the needs of operative employees, managers, and shareholders.* Compensation policies, which

[1]George T. Milkovich and Jerry M. Newman, *Compensation.* Plano, Texas: Business Publications, 1984, pp. 8–9.

reflect top management's philosophy and the firm's financial condition, should be established to guide action toward this end.

External equity exists *when employees performing jobs within a firm are paid at levels comparable to those paid for similar jobs in other firms.* Compensation surveys enable organizations to determine the extent to which external equity is present. On the other hand, **internal equity** exists *when employees are paid according to the relative value of their jobs within that organization.* Job evaluation is a primary means for determining internal equity. Finally, **employee equity** exists *when individuals performing similar jobs for the same firm are paid commensurate with factors unique to the employee.* Foremost is this category is employee performance, as determined by performance appraisal.

DETERMINANTS OF INDIVIDUAL FINANCIAL COMPENSATION

As emphasized throughout this book, many factors interact with and affect human resource management. Again, external and internal environmental factors exert considerable influence — this time in determining the financial compensation a person will receive. The primary determinants of compensation are shown in Figure 12–2. The organization, the labor market, the job, and the employee all have an impact on job pricing and the ultimate determination of the individual's financial compensation.

THE ORGANIZATION

Managers tend to view financial compensation as both an expense and an asset. In service industries, the fastest growing segment of the U.S. economy, labor costs account for more than 50 percent of all costs. At the same time, however, compensation programs have the potential to influence employee work behavior, encouraging workers to be more productive.[2] Improved performance and increased productivity are sought by all managers, so compensation programs warrant serious attention by top management.

Corporate culture has a major influence on an individual's financial compensation. An organization often establishes — formally or informally — compensation policies that determine whether it will be a pay leader or a pay follower, or strive for an average position in the labor market. The leaders pay higher wages and salaries than competing firms. Organizations with this leadership philosophy expect to have lower per unit labor costs. They feel that they will be able to attract high quality employees who will be very productive. Higher paying firms usually attract not only more ap-

[2]Ibid., p. 3.

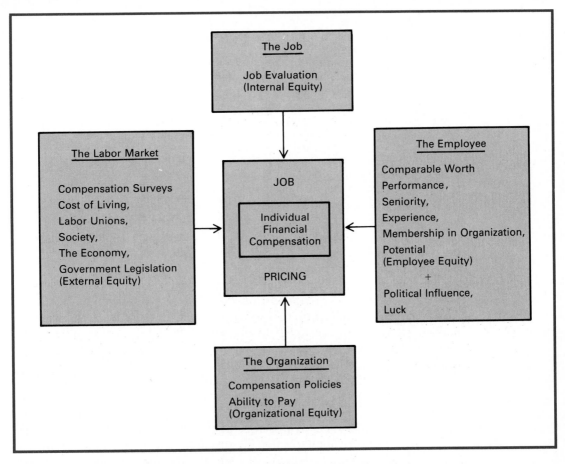

Figure 12–2. Primary determinants of individual financial compensation.

plicants, but more *qualified* applicants, than do lower paying companies in the same industry.[3]

A person who is paid the **going rate** receives *the average wage that most employers pay for the same job in a particular area or industry.* Most organizations have a policy that calls for paying the going rate. Management in these firms believes that it will be able to employ qualified people and still remain competitive by not having to raise the price of goods and/or services. Employers with this policy may be overlooking the possibility of hiring more proficient workers. Yet, there are a number of firms with jobs that require only average qualifications on the part of their employees. An assembly-line worker who is assigned the job of tightening four bolts every

[3]Gene Milbourn, Jr., "The Relationship of Money and Motivation," *Compensation Review* 12 (Second Quarter 1980): 33.

minute and a half is an example. In this situation, an excellent employee may not be much more productive than one with only average ability.

> Charlie Davis managed a large but financially strapped farming operation in the southwest. Although no formal policies had been established, Charlie had a tendency to pay the lowest wage possible. One of his farm hands, Ron Poole, was paid the minimum wage. During a period of three weeks, Ron wrecked a tractor, severely damaged a combine, and stripped the gears in a new pickup truck. Ron's actions prompted Charlie to remark, "Ron is the most expensive darned employee I've ever had."

Some companies choose to pay below the going rate because of a poor financial condition (as with Charlie's farm) or a belief that they simply do not require highly capable employees. These firms may experience a high turnover rate as their most qualified employees leave to join organizations offering higher pay. Regardless of their reasons for paying below the going rate, such firms will most likely experience a lower productivity level in addition to a higher turnover rate.

The organizational level where compensation decisions are made can also have an impact. Compensation decisions are often made at a high management level to ensure consistency. However, there are advantages to making pay decisions at lower levels where more information may exist regarding employee performance. Top level executives could make major errors if they made decisions that should be handled at lower levels.

An organization's assessment of its ability to pay is also an important factor in determining pay levels. Financially successful firms are often under pressure from both employees and the union to pay higher wages. In fact these firms tend to provide higher than average compensation.[4] However, an organization's financial strength establishes only the upper limit of what it will pay. To arrive at a specific pay level, other factors must be considered.

THE LABOR MARKET

The geographical area from which employees are recruited for a particular job is referred to as the **labor market.** Labor markets for some jobs may extend far beyond a local area. Human resource management of an aerospace firm in Orlando, for example, may be concerned about the labor market for engineers in Wichita or Seattle. Managerial and professional employees are often recruited from a wide geographical area. In fact, recruitment on a national basis is not unusual for certain skills.[5]

---

[4]David W. Belcher, *Compensation Administration.* Englewood Cliffs, N.J.: Prentice-Hall, 1974, p. 487.
[5]R. E. Hollerbach, in Milton L. Rock (ed.), in "Determining Wage and Salary Policy," *Handbook of Wage and Salary Administration.* New York: McGraw-Hill, 1972, pp. 4–12.

Executive Insights

Richard G. Jamison,
APD
Director of
Compensation,
Rockwell International
Corporation

Richard G. Jamison joined the Vick Chemical Division of Richardson-Merrell as a co-op student from Drexel University. Upon graduation in 1953, he was asked, "Would you mind working in Personnel for a while?" Jamison remembers that he was not terribly enthusiastic about this proposal because his major in college had been statistics. He accepted the position of assistant employment manager, however, and quickly discovered the reason for the request. His boss was terminated almost before Jamison was shown to his desk, and he soon became personnel supervisor for the entire plant. This was the turning point in his career. Looking back, he has no regrets about his career, and his record provides the evidence of his success. In 1956, he was promoted to the position of personnel director of the National Drug Division of Richardson-Merrell. Eight years later, he was named director of compensation and benefits for General Mills.

Jamison joined Rockwell International in 1974 as director of compensation, the position he holds today. In this capacity, he is responsible for compensation throughout the company, including executive compensation. In connection with this specialized area, Jamison says, "Executives know when they perform well. And, when they do, they expect to be rewarded. If your compensation system does this, fine. If not, you will lose your best people."

He believes that the field of compensation is extremely exciting and says, "It has a direct and important impact on the bottom line of company results." When asked what difficulties a compensation manager might face, he said, "It's managing compensation practices in a multi-industry corporation where the economy is having an adverse affect on one business unit while another is growing. Although internal consistency is desirable, salaries cannot be overmanaged to the point of forcing all units to ignore the competitive demands of their particular business."

Jamison believes that Personnel is broadening its scope and that to be a successful practitioner, one needs a good understanding of the total operations of the business. "We need to avoid becoming so enthralled with our specialty that we lose sight of the total business picture," Jamison says.

Jamison is past president of the Pittsburgh Personnel Association, Philadelphia Chapter of ASPA, and the Twin Cities Personnel Association. He has held several leadership positions within ASPA, including regional vice president, national treasurer, and national vice president. He also served as treasurer of the Personnel Accreditation Institute and is the past chairman of the steering committee for the Conference Board Council on Compensation. He is a member of the American Compensation Association. In 1979, Jamison received the Distinguished Service Award at West Virginia University, and, in 1984, he was given the William W. Winter Memorial Publications Award. He has been elected to Who's Who in Finance and Industry each year since 1977.

Moreover, pay for jobs within these markets may vary considerably. The job "executive secretary," for example, may carry an average salary of $20,000 per year in a large, urban community but only $12,000 in a small, rural town. Compensation managers must be aware of these differences in order to compete successfully for employees. The going wage, or prevailing rate, is an important guide in determining pay, and many employees view it as the standard for judging the fairness of their firm's compensation practices.

COMPENSATION SURVEY

Large organizations routinely conduct compensation surveys to determine prevailing pay rates within labor markets. These studies provide information for establishing both direct and indirect compensation. The decisions that must be made prior to conducting a compensation survey include determining (1) the geographic area of the survey; (2) the specific firms to contact; and (3) the jobs to include. The geographic area to be included in the survey is often determined from personnel records. Data from this source may indicate maximum distance or time employees are willing to travel to work. Also, the firms that are to be contacted for the survey are often from the same industry. But they also include those that compete for the same type of skills. Because it may not be feasible to obtain data on all jobs in the organization, Personnel often surveys only key jobs. A **key job** is *a job that is well known in the company and industry and one that can be easily defined.*

The primary difficulty in conducting a compensation survey involves determining comparable jobs. There are many different ways of organizing work and designing jobs. A job in one company may only roughly resemble a comparable job in another. For this reason, job titles are of little value in making surveys. Instead, well-written job descriptions must be used when requesting compensation data.

There are alternatives for obtaining compensation data in a given labor market. Some professional organizations periodically conduct surveys. The Bureau of Labor Statistics makes yearly surveys and provides data by area, industry, and job type. A number of journals, such as *Compensation Review* and *Hospital Administration,* also produce periodic compensation information. Some organizations choose to use other sources, even though they are large enough to afford a survey. Southwestern Life Insurance Company, for example, uses compensation data provided by the Life Office Management Association, along with survey data supplied by A. S. Hansen, Hay Associates, the American Society for Personnel Administration, and American Management Associations.

COST OF LIVING

The logic for using cost of living as a pay determinant is simple: When prices rise over a period of time and pay does not, "real pay" is actually lowered. A pay increase must be roughly the equivalent to the cost of living increase if a person is to maintain a previous level of real wages. If John Findley earns $24,000 during a year in which the average rate of inflation is 10 percent, a $200 per month salary increase will be necessary merely to maintain his standard of living.

People living on fixed incomes (primarily the old and the poor) are especially hard hit by inflation. But they are not alone; most employees also suffer financially. In recognition of this problem, some organizations grant pay increases indexed to the inflation rate. Some firms will sacrifice "merit money" to provide across-the-board increases designed to offset the results of inflation.

LABOR UNIONS

An excerpt from the Wagner Act prescribes the areas of mandatory collective bargaining between management and unions as "wages, hours, and other terms and conditions of employment." These broad bargaining areas obviously have great potential impact on compensation decisions. The words of Samuel Gompers, the first president of the American Federation of Labor (AFL), "more, more, now!" still ring in the ears of company representatives sitting at bargaining tables as they try to stem the tide of union demands. The union affects company compensation policies in three important areas. It influences the standards used in making compensation decisions, wage differentials, and wage payment methods.[6]

When a union uses comparable pay as a standard for making compensation demands, the employer must obtain accurate labor market data. When cost of living is emphasized, management may be persuaded to include a **cost-of-living allowance (COLA),** which is *an escalator clause in the labor agreement that automatically increases wages as the Bureau of Labor Statistics cost of living index rises.*

Unions may also attempt to create, preserve, or even destroy pay differentials between wages for craft workers and unskilled workers. The politics of a given situation will determine the direction taken. For instance, if the unskilled workers have the strongest membership, an attempt may be made to eliminate pay differentials.

Incentive plans may be desired by management as a means of providing greater employee motivation. However, decisions to implement such plans may be scrapped if the union strongly opposes this approach. Employee acceptance of such plans is essential for successful implementation, and union opposition may make a plan unworkable.

SOCIETY

Compensation paid to employees often affects a firm's pricing of its goods and/or services. For this reason, the consuming public is also interested in

---

[6]Cyril Curtis Ling, *The Management of Personnel Relations.* Homewood, Ill.: Richard D. Irwin, 1965, pp. 146–151.

compensation decisions. Public sentiments are often reflected in legislation. At times, the government responds to public opinion and steps in to encourage business to keep wages in line. The process of "jawboning" (as initiated by President John F. Kennedy in the early 1960s) involves using the prestige of the presidency to informally pressure large companies to hold wages and prices down.

Businesses in a given labor market are also concerned with the pay practices of competitors. For instance, when the management of a large electronics firm announced plans to locate a branch plant in a relatively small community, it was confronted by local civic leaders. Their questions largely concerned the wage and salary rates that would be paid. Subtle pressure was applied to keep the company's wages in line with other wages in the community. The electronics firm agreed to begin operations with initial compensation at a lower level than it usually paid. But the firm's management made it clear that a series of pay increases would be given over a period of two years to maintain its own "pay leader" policy.

THE ECONOMY

Although it is possible for some firms to thrive in a recession, there is no question that the economy affects compensation decisions. For example, a depressed economy will probably increase the labor supply. This, in turn, should serve to lower the going wage rate.

In most cases, the cost of living will rise in an expanding economy. Because the cost of living is commonly used as a pay standard, the economy's health exerts a major impact on pay decisions. Labor unions, government, and society are all less likely to press for pay increases in a depressed economy.

LEGISLATION

The amount of compensation a person receives can also be affected by certain federal and state legislation. Four of the more significant pieces of federal legislation in this area are described in the following paragraphs.

Fair Labor Standards Act of 1938. The most significant law affecting compensation is the Fair Labor Standards Act of 1938 (FLSA), as amended. This act is also called the Wage and Hour Law. It establishes a minimum wage, requires overtime pay, and provides standards for child labor. This act is administered by the Wage and Hour Division of the Department of Labor. The basic requirements of the act apply to employees engaged in interstate commerce.[7]

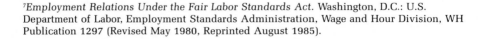

[7]*Employment Relations Under the Fair Labor Standards Act.* Washington, D.C.: U.S. Department of Labor, Employment Standards Administration, Wage and Hour Division, WH Publication 1297 (Revised May 1980, Reprinted August 1985).

As of January 1986, the Act provided for a minimum wage of not less than $3.35 an hour. It also required overtime payment at the rate of one and one-half times the employee's regular rate after forty hours of work in the work week. Although most organizations and employees are covered by the act, certain classes of employees are specifically exempt from the minimum wage and overtime provisions. On the other hand, nonexempt employees, many of whom are paid salaries, must receive overtime pay.

Exempt employees are *categorized as executive, administrative, professional employees, and outside salespersons.* An executive employee is essentially a manager (such as a production manager) with broad authority over subordinates. An administrative employee, while not a manager, occupies an important staff position in an organization and might have a title such as systems analyst or assistant to the president. A professional employee performs work requiring advanced knowledge in a field of learning normally acquired through a prolonged course of specialized instruction. This type of employee might have a title such as company physician, legal counsel, or senior statistician. Outside salespeople sell tangible or intangible items, away from the employer's place of business. Employees in jobs not conforming to these definitions are considered nonexempt.

During fiscal year 1981, the Wage and Hour Division received over 46,000 wage complaints and conducted more than 68,000 investigations. The agency recovered $745 million in unpaid overtime wages owed to 291,000 employees. An employer must be aware of the minimum wage level, maintain accurate payroll records, and accurately identify workers covered by the Act.[8]

Equal Pay Act of 1963. The Equal Pay Act of 1963 (an amendment to the FLSA) has also influenced the field of compensation. The purpose of this legislation is to prohibit discrimination on the basis of sex. As evidence that the act does have teeth, women employees have received millions of dollars to compensate for past discrimination in pay policies.

The act applies to all organizations and employees covered by the FLSA, including the exempt categories. The act requires equal pay for equal work for both sexes. Equal work is defined as work requiring equal skill, effort, and responsibility, which is performed under similar working conditions. This act does not prohibit the establishment of different wage rates based on seniority or merit systems. Also permitted are pay systems that are based on the quantity or quality of production and differentials based on any factor other than sex.

Davis–Bacon Act of 1931. The Davis–Bacon Act of 1931 was the first national law to deal with minimum wages. It requires federal construction contractors with projects valued in excess of $2000 to pay at least the

[8]William S. Hubbartt, "The Ten Commandments of Salary Administration," *Administrative Management* 4 (April 1982): 60.

prevailing wages in the area. The Secretary of Labor has the authority to make this determination, and the prevailing wage is often the average local union rate. Davis–Bacon has been under fire because critics claimed that it has resulted in construction cost overruns approaching 20 percent. Charges have also been made that the act is inflationary and obstructs minority hiring because of its limitation of one apprentice for every three full-time journeymen on a job.[9]

Walsh–Healy Act of 1936. The Walsh–Healy Act of 1936 requires companies with federal supply contracts exceeding $10,000 to pay prevailing wages. The act differs from the Fair Labor Standards Act in that overtime payment is required for hours worked over forty per week *or* eight per day.

THE JOB

The jobs people are given to do are a major determinant of the amount of financial compensation they will receive.[10] Organizations pay for the value they attach to certain duties, responsibilities, and other job-related factors (such as working conditions). Factors that must be considered in the process of determining a job's relative worth include job analysis, job descriptions, and job evaluation.

Before a company can determine the relative difficulty or value of its jobs, it must first define their content. This is normally achieved through job analysis. Recall that job analysis involves gathering, analyzing, and recording job facts in the form of job descriptions. The job description is the primary by-product of job analysis and consists of a written document describing the duties and responsibilities associated with a job. Job descriptions are used for many different purposes, including job evaluation. They are essential to all job evaluation methods, with the success of a job evaluation program depending largely on their accuracy and clarity.

JOB EVALUATION

Job evaluation is *that part of a compensation system in which a firm determines the relative value of one job compared with that of another.*[11] The basic purpose of job evaluation is to eliminate internal pay inequities that exist because of illogical pay structures. For example, a pay inequity

[9]George Fowler, "Davis–Bacon Needs a Decent Burial," *Nation's Business* 67 (March 1979): 57.

[10]"Is Inflation Wrecking Salary Structures?" *Industry Week* 199 (October 30, 1978), p. 55.

[11]Richard I. Henderson, *Compensation Management*, 4th ed. Reston, Va.: Reston Publishing, 1985, p. 231.

exists if the person who delivers the mail earns more money than the accounting supervisor.

The concept of internal pay equity is closely related to the purposes of job evaluation. It refers to the relationship between what employees believe they should receive and what they actually receive. Although individuals may be concerned with external equity, they believe that their pay should be related to their contributions to the firm. They quickly become unhappy when they perceive that someone in their organization receives more pay for performing the same or lower level work.

Within the Bendix Corporation, the precise method of implementing job evaluation programs is left to the discretion of individual business groups and divisions. However, corporate philosophy serves as a basic guide to these operating units. This philosophy includes the belief that the job evaluation process is the foundation of a sound compensation system. The job evaluation process must in turn satisfy these requirements:

- Provide a consistent measure of job worth that can be easily understood by everyone concerned.
- Involve managers from its inception through its administration and subsequent revision.
- Protect employees from favoritism, bias, and resultant internal pay inequities.
- Measure the job and not the performance of the employee doing the job.
- Apply to broad job clusters within functional groups.

The personnel department is usually responsible for the administration of job evaluation programs. However, the evaluation of jobs is typically accomplished through a committee. The committee is often comprised of managers from different functional areas. A typical committee might include the personnel director as chairperson and the vice presidents for finance, production, and marketing. The composition of the committee usually depends on the type and level of the jobs that are being evaluated. In all instances, it is important for the committee to keep personalities out of the evaluation process. As the Bendix approach indicates, it is the job which should be evaluated, not the person(s) performing the job.

Small- and medium-sized organizations often lack job evaluation expertise. Therefore they may elect to use an outside consultant. Many qualified consultants are available, but management should require that they develop an internal job evaluation program and train company employees so that they will be able to administer the system successfully.

Four basic job evaluation methods are used in organizations: the ranking method, the classification method, the factor comparison method, and the point method.[12] In selecting a method, firms should choose one and modify it to fit their particular needs. The ranking and classification methods are

[12]Milkovich and Newman, p. 98.

nonquantitative, whereas the factor comparison and point methods are quantitative approaches.

THE RANKING METHOD

The simplest of the four job evaluation methods is the ranking method. The **ranking method** is *a job evaluation method in which the raters examine the description of each job being evaluated and arrange the jobs in order according to their value to the company.* The procedure is essentially the same as that discussed in chapter 11 regarding the ranking method for performance evaluation. The only difference is that jobs, not people, are being evaluated. The first step in this method — as with all the methods — is conducting job analysis and writing job descriptions.

CLASSIFICATION METHOD

The **classification method** is *a job evaluation method by which a number of classes or grades are defined to describe a group of jobs.* The best-known example of this method is the federal government's classic Civil Service System. In this system, there are eighteen grades (GS-1 to GS-18). At the bottom of the scale (GS-1), the nature and typical duties of the job are very simple and routine. Jobs become progressively more difficult up through GS-18, where high level executive tasks are required.

In evaluating jobs by the classification method, the job description is compared with the class description. The class description that most closely agrees with the job description determines the classification for that job. For example, in evaluating the job of clerk-typist, the description might include these duties:

1. Type letters from prepared drafts.
2. Address envelopes.
3. Deliver completed correspondence to unit supervisor.

Assuming that the remainder of the job description includes similar routine work, this job would most likely be classified as a GS-1 job. The description of that job class best matches the job description.

It is difficult to clearly define grade descriptions for many diverse jobs. For this reason, the federal government has now implemented a new system called Factor Evaluation System (FES). This system combines three methods of job evaluation: the ranking method (which has previously been discussed); and the factor comparison method and the point method (which are covered next).[13] It will likely be the late 1980s before all GS jobs are evaluated under this system.[14]

---

[13]Arch S. Ramsay, "The New Factor Evaluating System of Position Classification," *Civil Service Journal* 16 (January–March 1976): 15–19.

[14]Henderson, *Compensation Management*, p. 311.

The basic version of the factor comparison method was developed by Eugene Benge and is somewhat more complex than the two previously discussed qualitative methods. The **factor comparison method** is *a job evaluation method in which: (1) raters need not keep the entire job in mind as they evaluate; (2) raters make decisions on separate aspects, or factors, of the job; and (3) the method assumes the existence of five universal job factors.* These factors are:

- *Mental requirements.* Reflect mental traits such as intelligence, reasoning, and imagination.
- *Skill.* Pertains to facility in muscular coordination and training in the interpretation of sensory impressions.
- *Physical requirements.* Involved in such activities as sitting, standing, walking, lifting, etc.
- *Responsibilities.* In such areas as raw materials, money, records, and supervision.
- *Working conditions.* Reflect the environmental influences of noise, illumination, ventilation, hazards, and hours.[15]

The first step requires that selected key jobs be ranked by the five factors according to their difficulty. The job description serves as a basis for making these decisions. An example of this initial ranking is shown in Table 12–1. Note that the jobs are first ranked according to mental requirements. It was determined that the systems analyst job ranked highest, followed by the jobs of programmer (2), console operator (3), and data entry clerk (4). The same ranking procedure was used for the other four factors.

The committee must next allocate pay rates for each job to each factor. This allocation is based on the importance of the respective factor to the job. An example of allocating the systems analyst's average pay rate ($12.00

Table 12–1. Average ranks of key jobs by difficulty

| Job | Factor | | | | |
	Mental	Skill	Physical	Responsibility	Working Conditions*
Systems analyst	1	4	2	1	3
Data entry clerk	4	1	1	4	1
Programmer	2	3	3	2	4
Console operator	3	2	4	3	2

*The poorer the working conditions, the higher the rating. (The highest rating is 1.)

[15]John A. Patton, C. L. Littlefield, and Stanley Allen Self, *Job Evaluation: Text and Cases,* 3rd ed. Homewood, Ill.: Richard D. Irwin, 1964, p. 115.

per hour) to each of the five factors is shown in Table 12–2. This step is probably the most difficult to explain satisfactorily to employees because the decision is highly subjective.

After pay rates have been assigned to each factor for each job, the results may be placed in a format similar to the one shown in Table 12–3. This procedure results in a ranking of jobs within each factor on the basis of pay rates. (Rank order is shown in parentheses.)

By comparing the first ranking of jobs on the basis of difficulty (DR) with the last ranking achieved on the basis of pay (PR), the committee's consistency in making judgments may be determined. A side-by-side comparison of the two separate rankings is shown in Table 12–4. You can see

Table 12–2. Allocation of pay to factors

Job: Systems analyst	Mental	$4.00
Average pay per hour: $12.00	Skill	2.00
	Physical	0.80
	Responsibility	4.00
	Working conditions	1.20

Table 12–3. Average ranks of key jobs by pay rates

Job	Mental	Skill	Physical	Responsibility	Working conditions	Pay rate
Systems analyst	$4.00(1)	$2.00(4)	$0.80(2)	$4.00(1)	$1.20(3)	$12.00
Data entry clerk	1.50(4)	2.70(1)	1.00(1)	1.30(4)	1.40(1)	7.90
Programmer	3.40(2)	2.50(3)	0.70(3)	3.00(2)	1.00(4)	10.60
Console operator	2.30(3)	2.60(2)	0.60(4)	1.80(3)	1.30(2)	8.60

Table 12–4. Comparison of difficulty ranking (DR) and pay ranking (PR) by factor

	Factor									
	Mental		Skill		Physical		Responsibility		Working conditions	
Job	DR	PR	DR	PR	DR	PR	DR	PR	DR	PR
Systems analyst	1	1	4	4	2	2	1	1	3	3
Data entry clerk	4	4	1	1	1	1	4	4	1	1
Programmer	2	2	3	3	3	3	2	2	4	4
Console operator	3	3	2	2	4	4	3	3	2	2

that no differences exist. If there had been a ranking inconsistency, the jobs affected would not be used in the next step.

A job comparison scale consisting of the five universal factors is constructed next (see Figure 12–3). This scale is used to rate other jobs in the group being evaluated. The raters compare each job, factor by factor, with those appearing on the job comparison scale. They then place them on the chart in an appropriate position. For example, assume that the committee is evaluating the job of programmer analyst (which was not used as a key job). It determines that this job requires fewer mental requirements than that of systems analyst and more than that of programmer. The job would then be plotted on this chart between these two jobs at a point agreed on by the committee. In this example, the mental requirements factor was evaluated at $3.80. This procedure would be repeated for the remaining four factors and for all jobs to be evaluated.

Figure 12–3. A job comparison scale.

	Mental	Skill	Physical	Responsibility	Working Conditions
$4.00	Systems Analyst (Programmer Analyst)			Systems Analyst	
3.80					
3.50	Programmer				
3.00		Data Entry Clerk Console Operator Programmer		Programmer	
2.50	Console Operator				
2.00		Systems Analyst		Console Operator	
1.50	Data Entry Clerk			Data Entry Clerk	Data Entry Clerk Console Operator Systems Analyst
1.00			Data Entry Clerk Systems Analyst Programmer		Programmer
.50			Console Operator		
.00					

The factor comparison method provides a systematic approach to job evaluation. However, there are some problems that should be recognized. The assumption that the five factors are universal has been questioned. Certain factors may be more appropriate to some job groups than others. Finally, while the steps are not overly complicated, they are somewhat detailed and may be difficult to explain.

POINT METHOD

Most job evaluation plans in use today are some variation of the **point method**.[16] This is *a job evaluation method that requires that job factors be selected according to the nature of the specific group of jobs being evaluated.* Point method plans are used by both large and small companies. Their use has been encouraged by associations such as the National Electrical Manufacturers' Association, the Life Office Management Association, and the Administrative Management Society.

Normally, organizations develop a separate plan for each group of similar jobs (job clusters) in the company. Shop jobs, clerical jobs, and sales jobs are examples of job clusters. The procedure for establishing a point method is illustrated in Figure 12–4. The first activity that takes place — after determining the group of jobs to be studied — is conducting job analysis and writing job descriptions. The job evaluation committee will later use these descriptions as the basis for making evaluation decisions.

The next activity entails selecting and defining the job factors to be used in measuring job value. These factors become the standards used for the evaluation of jobs. They can best be identified by individuals who are thoroughly familiar with the content of the jobs under consideration. Education, experience, job knowledge, mental effort, physical effort, responsibility, and working conditions are examples of factors typically used. Each factor should be significant in helping to distinguish among jobs. Factors that exist in equal amounts in all jobs obviously would not serve this purpose. As an example, in evaluating clerical jobs in a company, the factor *working conditions* would be of little value in distinguishing among jobs if all jobs in the cluster had approximately the same working conditions. The number of factors used varies, with the average being approximately eleven.[17]

Factor weights must next be established according to their relative importance in the jobs to be evaluated. For example, if experience is considered quite important for a particular job cluster, this factor might be weighted as much as 35 percent. Physical effort (if used at all as a factor in an office cluster) would likely be low, perhaps less than 10 percent.

---

[16]Leonard R. Burgess, *Wage and Salary Administration.* Columbus, Ohio: Charles E. Merrill, 1984, p. 93.

[17]See Belcher, *Compensation Administration,* for a detailed discussion of job factors and compensable factors.

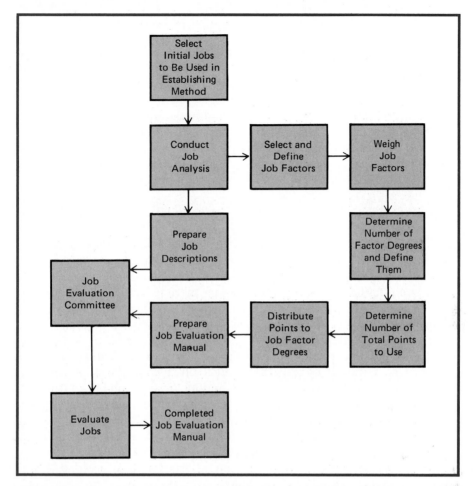

Figure 12–4. The procedure for establishing the point method of job evaluation.

The next consideration is to determine the number of degrees for each job factor and providing each degree with a definition. Degrees represent the number of distinct levels associated with a particular factor. The number of degrees needed for each factor depends on job requirements. If a particular cluster required virtually the same level of formal education (a high school diploma, for example), fewer degrees would be appropriate than if some jobs in the cluster required advanced degrees.

The number of total points to be used in the plan is next determined. The exact number may vary, but typically 500 or 1000 points are used. The use of a smaller number of points (for example, 50) would not likely provide the proper distinctions among jobs, whereas a larger number (such as 50,000) would be unnecessarily cumbersome. The total number of points in a plan indicates the maximum points any job could receive.

The next step in the point method is to distribute point values to job factor degrees (see Table 12–5). As you can see, factor number 1 has five degrees; factor 2 has four; factor 3 has five; and factor 4 has three. The maximum number of points is easily calculated by multiplying the maximum points in the system by the assigned weights. For education, the maximum points would be 250 (50 percent weight multiplied by 500 points). The points for the minimum degree could take the percentage weight assigned to the factor (50 points). The degree interval may be calculated by subtracting the minimum number of points (50) from the maximum number (250) and dividing by the number of degrees used minus one. For example, the interval for factor 1 (education) was calculated as follows:

$$\text{Interval} = \frac{250 - 50}{5 - 1} = 50$$

This approach to determining the number of points for each degree is referred to as arithmetic progression. An arithmetic progression is simple to understand and to explain to employees. It makes sense when the factors have been defined in such a manner that there is equal distance between the degrees.[18] In other instances, the firm may choose to use a geometric or even an irregular progression in order to conform to the manner in which degrees have been defined.

The next step involves preparing a job evaluation manual. Although there is no standard format, the manual often contains an introductory section, factor and degree definitions, and job descriptions. As a final step, the job evaluation committee then evaluates jobs in each cluster by comparing each job description with the factors in the job evaluation manual. A portion of a large appliance manufacturer's job evaluation manual is shown in Figure 12–5. Assume that the job of personnel interviewer is being evaluated. After studying the job description, it is decided that the job requirements closely match degree IV of the factor *contacts*. The job receives 79 points for this factor. After the point values of all factors have

Table 12–5. Overview of the point system (500 point system)

Job factors	Weight	Degrees of factors				
		1	2	3	4	5
1. Education	50%	50	100	150	200	250
2. Responsibility	30%	30	70	110	150	
3. Physical effort	12%	12	24	36	48	60
4. Working conditions	8%	8	24	40		

[18]Other alternatives, such as geometric progression and irregular progression, exist. For a detailed discussion of methods of progression, see Patton et al., *Job Evaluation*, pp. 153–154.

been determined, they are totaled and the numerical value of the job is obtained. Values of all other jobs in each cluster are determined in this manner.

Considerable time and effort are required to design a point plan. A redeeming feature of the method is that, once it is developed, the plan may be useful over a long period of time. The procedure for using an established point method is presented in Figure 12–6. As new jobs are created and the contents of old jobs substantially changed, job analysis must be conducted and job descriptions rewritten. The job evaluation committee evaluates the jobs and updates the manual. Only when job factors change, or for some reason the weights assigned become inappropriate, does the plan become obsolete.

Figure 12–5. The point method as used in a job evaluation manual.

FACTOR: CONTACTS

This factor considers the responsibility for working with other people to get results, either interdepartmental or outside the plant. In the lower degrees, it is largely a matter of giving or getting information or instructions. In the higher degrees, the factor involves dealing with or influencing other persons. In rating this factor, consider how the contacts are made, the duration of the contacts, and their purposes.

Level (Degree)		Points
IV	Usual purposes of the contacts are to discuss problems and possible solutions, to secure cooperation or coordination of efforts, and to get agreement and action; more than ordinary tact and persuasiveness required.	79
III	Usual purposes of the contacts are to exchange information or settle specific problems encountered in the course of daily work.	46
II	Contacts may be repetitive but usually are brief and with little or no continuity.	27
I	Contacts normally extend to persons in the immediate work unit only.	16

FACTOR: COMPLEXITY OF DUTIES

This factor considers the complexity of duties in terms of the character of the tasks to be performed, the scope of independent action allowed, and the exercise of perception and judgment required.

Level (Degree)		Points
IV	Performs work where only general methods are available. Independent action and judgment are required regularly to analyze facts, evaluate situations, draw conclusions, make decisions, and take or recommend action.	91
III	Performs duties working from standard procedures or generally understood methods. Some independent action and judgment are required to decide what to do, determine permissible variations from standard procedures, review facts in situations, and determine action to be taken, within limits prescribed.	53
II	Standard procedure limits independent action and judgment to decisions not difficult to make since choices are limited. Duties require deciding when to ask for assistance.	31
I	Little or no independent action or judgment. Duties are so standardized and simple as to involve little choice as to how to do them.	18

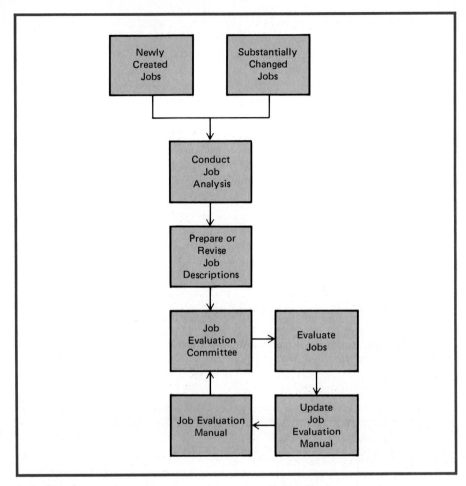

Figure 12–6. The procedure for using an established point method of job evaluation.

THE EMPLOYEE

In addition to the organization, the labor market, and the job, factors related to the employee are also essential in determining pay and employee equity. Each of these will be discussed in this section. The concept of comparable worth, called by some the "issue of the 1980s," will be presented first.

COMPARABLE WORTH

The comparable worth theory extends the concept of the Equal Pay Act, and it has become an extremely important political and social issue.[19] The

[19]John F. Sullivan, "Comparable Worth and the Statistical Audit of Pay Programs for Illegal Systematic Discrimination," *Personnel Administrator* 30 (March 1985): 102.

issue became somewhat heated after Clarence Pendleton, Chairman of the U.S. Commission on Civil Rights, stated that comparable worth amounts to "Looney Tunes," which would skew the free-market system.[20] The Equal Pay Act requires equal pay for equal work, but advocates of comparable worth prefer a broader interpretation, requiring equal pay for comparable worth. **Comparable worth (CW)** requires *the value of dissimilar jobs (e.g., company nurse and welder) to be compared under some form of job evaluation and pay rates to be assigned according to their evaluated values.* Because of the great amount of support for this theory, it is not one that will likely fade quickly.[21]

Underlying the comparable worth concept is the concern about the significant earnings gap that exists between women and men workers. Specifically, for the first quarter of 1984, the median weekly earnings of full-time women employees was 65 percent of that of men.[22] Jobs that have historically been filled by women pay less, and, when employers use market data for establishing pay rates, the pay differentials are perpetuated. Many business managers and business groups oppose comparable worth, but some human resource executives believe that pay systems based on the comparable worth concept are fairer than those that rely on market pricing.[23]

Opponents of comparable worth are equally vocal in their disapproval of the idea. They contend that the earnings gap reflects an overall statistic and does not compare the earnings of two people performing the same job. They state that the gender difference is explainable by the large number of young women who have recently entered the work force at entry-level pay rates. It is also pointed out that a substantial number of women are employed in low paying industries. Another point frequently made is that women often voluntarily leave the work force to raise a family, while men continue with the job and receive promotions and pay increases.

Comparable worth detractors often state that the real problem in the pay gap is gender segregation in jobs rather than either the underpayment of jobs traditionally filled by women or the overpayment of jobs traditionally filled by men.[24] Furthermore, they note that existing law prohibits employers from paying women at a lower rate than a man for doing the same work. A more effective solution, they suggest, would be to continue to enforce equal opportunity and equal pay laws. In addition, women should be encouraged to enter nontraditional occupations and be provided with equal access to education, training programs, and employment. Also, efforts

---

[20]"Oakar, Pendleton Trade Barbs over Comparable Worth Argument," *Resource,* American Society for Personnel Administration, May 1985, p. 1.

[21]Lawrence Z. Lorber, J. Robert Kirk, Stephen L. Samuels, and David J. Spellman III, *Sex and Salary: A Legal and Personnel Analysis of Comparable Worth.* Alexandria, Va.: The ASPA Foundation, 1985, p. 51.

[22]"Twenty Questions on Comparable Worth," The Equal Employment Advisory Council, 1984. Reprinted in *Personnel Administrator* 30 (April 1985): 65.

[23]Daniel Seligman, " 'Pay Equity' Is a Bad Idea," *Fortune* 14 (May 1984): 140.

[24]Sullivan, "Comparable Worth," p. 103.

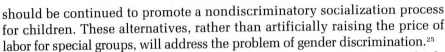

should be continued to promote a nondiscriminatory socialization process for children. These alternatives, rather than artificially raising the price of labor for special groups, will address the problem of gender discrimination.[25]

Perhaps the greatest fear of implementing comparable worth standards is the cost of replacing market forces of supply and demand with a government-imposed system of job evaluation. One source estimated that closing the earnings gap would cost $320 billion a year.[26]

The Washington state case is perhaps the best known example of comparable worth in action. In 1982, the state was sued by the American Federation of State, County, and Municipal Employees (AFSCME). The union charged that women employees of the state were being discriminated against. In fact, some jobs traditionally filled by women had been evaluated at a higher level under the state's job evaluation plan, but the pay rates were less than for jobs traditionally filled by men. The discrimination charge was upheld in U.S. District Court and the District Judge's order required the state to immediately bring all workers in the job categories filled predominately with women up to their evaluated rates. In 1985, the U.S. Court of Appeals for the Ninth Circuit overturned this decision, which could have cost the State of Washington $1 billion if not overturned.[27] The issue will probably be decided finally by the U.S. Supreme Court.

In addition to Washington, a number of other states are obviously taking comparable worth seriously. For example, Minnesota has been giving average raises of $1600 to more than 8000 employees in job categories filled predominantly with women.[28]

The goal of nondiscriminatory pay practices is one that every organization should seek to achieve for ethical and legal reasons. Whether comparable worth is an appropriate solution remains to be seen.

PERFORMANCE

Nothing is more demoralizing to outstanding employees than to be paid the same as less productive workers. Therefore management generally prefers a pay system based on employee performance. Such an approach rewards individuals according to their productivity. Further, such a system allows pay to serve as a motivator of performance. It gives employees an incentive to give their best efforts.

A prerequisite to a merit system is a sound performance appraisal program. If pay is to be related to performance, an organization must have a valid means of determining varying performance levels. Across-the-board

[25]Julie M. Buchanan, "Comparable Worth: Where Is It Headed?" *Human Resources: Journal of the International Association for Personnel Women* 2 (Summer 1985): 12.

[26]"Twenty Questions on Comparable Worth."

[27]Carrie Dolan and Leonard M. Apcar, "Washington State Union to Fight Ruling That Hurts Equal Pay–Equal Jobs Drive," *The Wall Street Journal*, September 6, 1985, p. 6.

[28]Seligman, "Pay Equity," pp. 136–137.

dollar or percentage pay increases are still common, but this approach is slowly losing ground. Pay increases are to a greater extent now being based on the achievement of performance goals.[29]

SENIORITY

The length of time an employee has been associated with the company, division, department, or job is referred to as seniority. Management prefers performance as the primary basis for compensation changes; labor unions tend to favor seniority, which they believe provides an objective and fair basis for pay increases. Many union leaders believe performance evaluation systems are too subjective and permit management to reward favorite employees arbitrarily.

An acceptable performance–seniority compromise might be to permit employees to receive pay increases to the midpoints of their pay grades on the basis of seniority. The rationale is that workers performing at an acceptable level should eventually receive the average wage or salary of their pay grades. However, progression beyond the midpoint should be based on performance. This practice would permit only the outstanding performers to reach the maximum rate for the grade and reflects the initial rationale for rate ranges.

EXPERIENCE

"Experience has taught our best racquetball players how to really play the game," the director of a state university's recreational facility recently exclaimed. This statement, no doubt, was true. But, as someone else put it, "Experience has also taught our worst racquetball players how to play." The point is that, while experience is invaluable, not all experience is good experience. You can play golf for ten years (without lessons from a pro, of course), have a hook that almost returns to the tee box, and be further away from being a good golfer than you were before you started playing. Although not always realized in business circles, the same is true of management experience. How much ahead of the game is the manager who has been a poor manager for two decades? Managers who comment, with considerable confidence and pleasure, that they have had twenty years of management experience may actually have (because of the duplication involved) only ten years of experience two times, or five years of experience four times. Heaven forbid the possibility of having six months of experience forty times!

Experience is truly indispensable. And, in many cases, management does compensate employees on this basis. Sometimes the practice is justified because of the invaluable insights that can only be acquired through experience on the job. Occasionally, experience may still be rewarded even though it is irrelevant.

[29]"Compensation Currents," *Compensation Review* 17 (First Quarter 1985): 2.

MEMBERSHIP IN THE ORGANIZATION

Some components of individual financial compensation are given to employees without regard to the particular job they perform or their level of productivity. These rewards are provided because employees are members of the organization. As an example, an average performer occupying a job in pay grade 1 may receive the same number of vacation days, the same amount of group life insurance, and the same reimbursement for educational expenses as a superior employee working in a job classified in pay grade 10. In fact, the worker in pay grade 1 may get more vacation time if he or she has been with the firm longer. Rewards based on organizational membership are intended to maintain a high degree of stability in the work force and recognize loyalty.

POTENTIAL

Potential is useless if it is never realized. Yet, organizations do pay some individuals based on their potential. In order to attract talented young people to the firm, the overall compensation program must appeal to the person with no experience or any immediate ability to perform difficult tasks. Many young employees are paid because they possess the potential to become a first-line supervisor, manager of compensation, vice president of marketing, or possibly even the chief executive officer.

College graduates typically do not have significant business experience for employment managers to examine. Lacking such a record, organizations turn elsewhere for factors to predict the success of the graduate. Grades in college are often considered. Although there is controversy about the relationship between grades and performance on the job, personnel recruiters and line managers often have no alternative but to emphasize a student's academic success. Of course, there are other factors that might indicate potential. Some questions commonly asked of college prospects are:

- What percentage of your school expenses did you pay?
- What class offices did you hold?
- To what professional student associations did you belong, such as American Society for Personnel Administration, Society for Advancement of Management, Pi Sigma Epsilon, Delta Sigma Pi, or Alpha Kappa Psi? Did you hold offices in these organizations?
- Were you a member of a social sorority or fraternity? What leadership positions did you occupy?

These and many other questions may or may not be job related but are nevertheless asked as organizations attempt to identify individuals who will provide the future leadership of their firm. The people sought are those with potential.

Political influence is a factor that definitely should not be considered a bona fide determinant of financial compensation. However, to deny that it exists would be unrealistic. It is disheartening to hear someone say, "It's not what you know, it's who you know." Yet, there is an unfortunate element of truth in that statement. To varying degrees in business, government, and not-for-profit organizations, a person's pull or political influence may influence pay and promotion decisions. It may be natural for a manager to favor a friend or relative in granting a pay increase or promotion. Whether it is natural or not, if the person receiving the reward is not truly deserving, this fact will become known by the peer group. This practice can have a devastating impact on employee morale. Employees want, and are beginning to demand, fair and equitable treatment. There is nothing either fair or equitable about a person receiving a promotion and/or pay increase based strictly on politics.

LUCK

We have all heard people say, "It certainly helps to be in the right place at the right time." There is more than a smattering of truth in this statement as it relates to the determination of a person's compensation; it might be termed sheer luck. Positions are continually opening up in firms. Realistically, there is no way for managers to foresee many of the changes that occur. For instance, who could have known that the purchasing agent, Joe Flynch, an apparently happily married man, would suddenly quit his job, take off with his neighbor's wife, and never be heard from again? Although the company may have been grooming several managers for Joe's position, none may be capable of immediately assuming the increased responsibility. The most experienced person, Tommy Foy, has been with the company only six months. Tommy had been an assistant buyer for a competitor for four years. Because of his experience, Tommy receives the promotion and the increased financial compensation. Tommy Foy was in the right place at the right time.

When asked to explain their most important reasons for success and effectiveness as managers, two chief executives responded candidly. One said, "Success is being at the right place at the right time and being recognized as having the ability to make timely decisions. It also depends on having good rapport with people, a good operating background, and the knowledge of how to develop people." The other replied, "My present position was attained by being in the right place at the right time with a history of getting the job done." Both executives recognize the significance of luck combined with the ability to perform. Their experiences lend support to the idea that luck works primarily for the efficient.

In determining individual compensation, other factors may be unique to specific organizations. Although there is currently no perfect system, human resource managers should constantly strive to improve their financial compensation systems.

JOB PRICING

The primary considerations in pricing jobs are the organization's policies, the labor market, and the job itself. If allowances are to be made for individual factors, they, too, must be considered. Recall that the process of job evaluation results in a job hierarchy. It might reveal, for example, that the job of senior accountant is more valuable than the job of computer operator, which, in turn, is more valuable than the job of senior invoice biller. At this point, the relative value of these jobs to the company is known but not their absolute value. *Placing a dollar value on the worth of a job* is referred to as **job pricing.** It may take place once the job has been evaluated and the relative value of each job in the organization has been determined. However, as you observed in Figure 12–2, additional factors should be considered in determining the job's absolute value. Firms often use pay grades and pay ranges in the job pricing process. These topics along with problems associated with pay rate adjustments are discussed next.

PAY GRADES

A **pay grade** is *the grouping of similar jobs together to simplify the job pricing process.* It is much more convenient for organizations to price fifteen pay grades rather than 200 separate jobs. The point plan readily lends itself to this practice.

Plotting jobs on a scatter diagram is often useful in determining the appropriate number of pay grades. In Figure 12–7, each dot on the scatter diagram represents one job as it relates to pay and the evaluated points, which reflect its difficulty. By following this procedure, it will likely be found that a certain point spread will work satisfactorily (100 points are used in this illustration). Each dot represents one job but may involve dozens of individuals who fill that one job. The large dot at the lower left corner of the diagram represents the job of data entry clerk, which was evaluated at 75 points. The data entry clerk's hourly rate of $7.90 represents either the average wage currently being paid the job or its market rate. This decision depends on how the organization wants to price its jobs.

A **wage curve** is *the fitting of plotted points in order to create a smooth progression between pay grades.* The line that is drawn to minimize the distance between all dots and the line — a line of best fit — may be straight or curved. However, when the point system is used (normally considering only one job cluster), a straight line is the usual result, as in Figure 12–7. Two approaches used in drawing this wage line are the least squares line

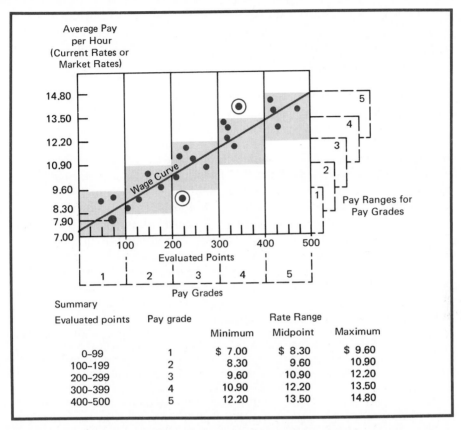

Figure 12–7. A scatter diagram of evaluated jobs illustrating the wage curve, pay grades, and rate ranges.

Summary				
Evaluated points	Pay grade	Rate Range		
		Minimum	Midpoint	Maximum
0–99	1	$ 7.00	$ 8.30	$ 9.60
100–199	2	8.30	9.60	10.90
200–299	3	9.60	10.90	12.20
300–399	4	10.90	12.20	13.50
400–500	5	12.20	13.50	14.80

(a statistical version) and the less sophisticated "eyeball" approach.[30] Some compensation specialists use the latter because of its simplicity.

RATE OR PAY RANGES

A decision must next be made as to whether all individuals performing the same job will receive equal pay or whether pay ranges will be used. A **pay range** includes *a minimum and maximum pay rate with enough variance between the two to allow some significant pay difference.* Pay ranges are generally preferred because they allow employees to be paid according to experience and performance levels. Pay can then serve as a positive incentive. When pay ranges are used, some method must be employed to advance individuals through the range. Although many organizations grant

[30]For a discussion of the least squares method, see Morris Hamburg, *Statistical Analysis for Decision Makers.* New York: Harcourt, Brace and World, 1970.

pay increases based on seniority, others hold the view that only outstanding performers have an automatic right to advance to the top of their pay ranges. This philosophy also dictates that any discrepancy between where a person is in the pay range and where he or she should be — based on performance — should be corrected within a reasonable amount of time. This would necessitate larger pay increases for outstanding performers who are being paid at or near the bottom of their pay ranges.[31]

Refer again to Figure 12–7. You can readily determine the minimum, midpoint, and maximum pay rates per hour for each of the five pay grades. For example, for pay grade 5, the minimum rate is $12.20, the midpoint, $13.50, and the maximum, $14.80. The minimum rate is normally the "hiring in" rate that a person receives when joining the firm.[32] The maximum pay rate represents the most that an employee can receive for that job, regardless of how well the job is performed. A person who is at the tops of a pay grade will have to be promoted to a job in a higher pay grade in order to receive a pay increase unless (1) an across-the-board adjustment is made; or (2) the job is reevaluated and placed in a higher pay grade. This situation has caused numerous managers anguish as they attempt to explain the pay system to an employee who is doing a tremendous job but is at the top of a pay grade. Consider this situation:

> Everyone in the department realized that Beth Smith was the best secretary in the company. At times she appeared to do the job of three secretaries. Bill Merideth, Beth's supervisor, was especially impressed. Recently he had a discussion with the personnel manager to see what could be done to get a raise for Beth. After Bill described the situation, the personnel manager's only reply was, "Sorry, Bill. Beth is already at the top of her pay grade. There is nothing you can do unless you can have her job upgraded or promote her to another position."

Situations such as Beth's present personnel managers with a perplexing problem. Many would be inclined to make an exception to the system and give Beth a salary increase. However, this action would be contrary to a basic principle that holds that there is a maximum value for every job in the organization, regardless of how well it is performed. In addition, making exceptions to the compensation plan could soon result in pay inequities.

The rate ranges established should be large enough to provide an incentive to do a better job. At times, pay differentials may need to be greater to be meaningful, especially at higher levels. There may be logic in having the rate range become increasingly wide at each consecutive level (see Figure 12–8). Consider, for example, what a $50 per month salary increase would mean to a file clerk earning $600 per month (an 8.3 percent increase) and to a senior cost accountant earning $1500 per month (a 3.3 percent

---

[31]Graef S. Crystal, "Outlook on Compensation and Benefits: To the Rescue of Pay for Performance," *Personnel* 62 (January 1985): 9.

[32]Howard Risher, "Inflation and Salary Administration," *Personnel Administrator* 26 (May 1981): 36.

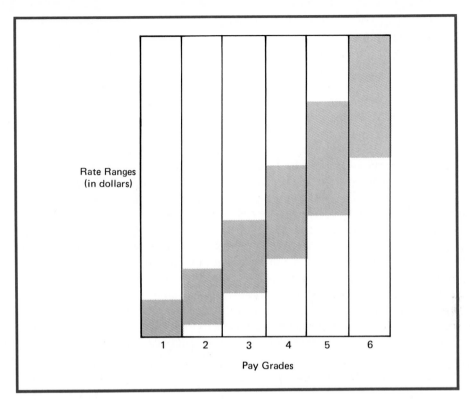

Figure 12–8. Rate ranges based on a percentage spread.

increase). Assuming an inflationary rate of 8 percent, the file clerk would be able to retain his or her real pay while the cost accountant would obviously fall behind.

Some workplace conditions do not favor pay ranges. For instance, in a situation where all or most jobs are routine, with little opportunity for employees to vary their productivity, a single rate, or fixed rate, system may be more appropriate. When single rates are used, everyone on the same job receives the same pay regardless of seniority or productivity.[33]

ADJUSTMENTS IN PAY RATES

When pay rate ranges have been determined and jobs assigned to pay grades, it may become obvious that some jobs are overpaid and others underpaid. Underpaid jobs are normally brought to the minimum of the pay range as soon as possible. Refer again to Figure 12–7. A job evaluated at about 225

[33]Robert J. Greene, "Which Pay Delivery System Is Best for Your Organization?" *Personnel* 58 (May–June 1981): 52.

points and having a rate of $9.00 per hour is represented by a circled dot immediately below pay grade 3. The job was determined to be difficult enough to fall in pay grade 3 (200–299 points). However, employees working in the job are being paid 60 cents per hour less than the minimum for the pay grade ($9.60 per hour). Some jobs in pay grade 2 and even in pay grade 1 are paid more. A good management practice would be to correct this inequity as rapidly as possible by placing the job in the proper pay grade and increasing the pay of those who work that job.

Overpaid jobs present more of a problem. An illustration of an overpaid job for pay grade 4 is provided in Figure 12–7 (note the circled dot above pay grade 4). Employees in this job earn $14.00 per hour, or 50 cents more than the maximum for the grade. This type of overpayment (and underpayment as well) is referred to as *red circle* rates.[34]

An ideal solution to the problem of an overpaid job is to promote the employee. This might be a reasonable approach if he or she is qualified for a higher rated job and a job opening is available. Another possibility would be to bring the job rate and employee pay into line through a pay cut. This type of action may appear logical, but it is not consistent with good management practice. This action would punish employees for a situation they did not create. Somewhere between these two possible solutions is a third: to freeze the rate until across-the-board pay increases bring it into line. If the past thirty years are an indication of the future, rising pay levels will eventually solve this problem.

PAY SECRECY

Organizations tend to keep their pay rates secret for various reasons. If a firm's compensation plan is illogical, secrecy may indeed be appropriate. Only a well-designed pay system can stand the light of full disclosure.[35] An open system would almost certainly require managers to provide many explanations to subordinates.

Secrecy has curious results, however. For example, managers who are unaware of pay rates in their firm tend to overestimate the pay of managers around them and to underestimate what higher level employees make. Such perceptions destroy much of the motivation intended in a differential pay system and indirectly contribute to turnover.[36]

Ideally, a firm will strive to develop a logical pay system, which reflects both internal and external equity. In the process, employee participation

---

[34]J. D. Dunn and Frank M. Rachel, *Wage and Salary Administration: Total Compensation Systems.* New York: McGraw-Hill, 1971, p. 228.

[35]Roy G. Goltz, "Compensation Communications," *Personnel Administrator* 25 (May 1980): 22.

[36]Edward E. Lawler, III, *Pay and Organizational Effectiveness: A Psychological View.* New York: McGraw-Hill, 1971, pp. 174–175, 196–197.

should be fully utilized. Compensation managers should then take necessary action to ensure that employees understand the basis for their pay. Obviously, happiness for all employees cannot be guaranteed. The dissatisfaction and costs associated with a secret pay system, however, seem to make that approach highly questionable.

PAY COMPRESSION

As previously mentioned, organizations normally strive for both internal and external pay equity. In practice, however, this is often difficult or even impossible to accomplish. For example, in order to attract an engineer to a firm, an unusually high salary may have to be paid. Individuals possessing the skills needed to perform this job are in short supply relative to the demand for their services. Therefore these workers, and others in similar situations, are able to command high salaries (and in the process experience external pay equity).[37]

But how does the hiring of this type of employee affect internal equity? Other jobs within the firm may have greater value to the firm — as determined by job evaluation — but are now paid less than that of engineers. In this instance, internal equity has been sacrificed for external equity and the firm, assuming that it had to have the engineer job filled, had little choice in the matter.

Situations of this type may result in somewhat less serious consequences and still affect internal pay equity. One troublesome problem is called pay compression. **Pay compression** *occurs when workers perceive that the pay differential between their pay and that of employees in jobs above or below them is too small.*[38] It can be created in several ways, including the hiring of new employees at pay rates comparable to those of current employees who may have been with the firm for several years. Pay adjustments made at the lower end of the job hierarchy without commensurate adjustments at the top are common causes of pay compression.

Pay compression can also result from the granting of pay increases on a flat cents-per-hour basis over a long period of time. Percentage increases, on the other hand, maintain relative differences in pay rates. The result of compression is dissatisfaction on the part of employees in higher level jobs. With the slope of the pay curve flattened, there is less incentive for employees to strive for promotion.[39]

[37]Hubbartt, "Ten Commandments," p. 24.
[38]Thomas J. Bergmann, Frederick S. Hills, and Laurel Priefert, "Pay Comparison: Causes, Results and Possible Solutions," *Compensation Review* 15 (Second Quarter 1983): 17–18.
[39]Bruce R. Ellig, "Pay Inequities: How Many Exist within Your Organization?" *Compensation Review* 12 (Third Quarter 1980): 42.

PLATEAUING

As previously mentioned, promotions in the future may not be as available as in the past. For one thing, many organizations are reducing the number of management positions and are developing a "lean, mean" management staff. International competition has also slowed the growth of firms that might otherwise have needed more management positions. Too, women and minority members are now competing for positions that once were not available to them. The effect of these changes is that more people will be striving for fewer promotional opportunities. Consequently, organizations must look for ways other than promotion to reward deserving employees. The problem of plateauing, previously discussed in chapter 10, clearly suggests the need for new compensation strategies, both financial and non-financial. **Plateauing** is *a career condition that occurs when job functions and work content remain the same.*

Several approaches have been suggested to deal with this problem.[40] One possibility is to move individuals laterally within the organization. Although the employee's status or pay may remain unchanged, he or she is given the opportunity to adapt and to develop new skills. Firms that want to encourage lateral movements may choose to pay a transfer bonus or utilize a skill-based pay system that rewards individuals for the type and number of skills they possess.

Another means of rewarding without promoting an employee is to increase the challenge of the job by redesigning it to provide more meaning and a greater sense of accomplishment for the employee. This approach — previously described as job enrichment — is frequently written about but often overlooked by organizations.

Exploratory career development is still another way of dealing with the problem of plateauing. It provides an employee the opportunity to test out ideas in another field without committing to an actual move. Demotions have long been associated with failure, but limited promotional opportunities in the future may make them more legitimate career options. If the stigma of demotion can be removed, it is possible that more employees — especially older workers — would choose such a move. In certain instances this approach might open up a clogged promotional path and, at the same time, permit a senior employee to relieve himself or herself of unwanted stress without loss of face.

TWO-TIER WAGE SYSTEM

In an attempt to remain competitive in national and international markets, the General Motors Packard Electric Division devised a radically new compensation approach.[41] This approach — a **two-tier wage system** — is *a wage structure that reflects lower pay rates for newly hired employees than those*

[40]Beverly Kaye and Kathryn McKee, "New Compensation Strategies for New Career Patterns," *Personnel Administrator* 31 (March 1986): 61–68.
[41]"The Double Standard That's Setting Worker Against Worker," *Business Week*, April 8, 1985, p. 70.

received by established employees performing similar jobs. The benefits provided to these new hires may also be less than those given current employees. In addition, the employment conditions for those recently hired may include a lower level of job security and, at the same time, broader job descriptions.

The two-tier system seriously damages a firm's ability to achieve internal pay equity. It may result in employee resentment and negatively affect product quality, cooperation, and loyalty to the company.[42] In spite of the potential disadvantages, however, numerous organizations, including United Airlines, Phelps Dodge, the U.S. Postal Service, and McDonnell Douglas, have adopted this system. Provisions that reduce entry-level rates for new hires by as much as $4–$5 per hour have been negotiated in the airline, copper, trucking, auto, and aerospace industries. Because unions have typically been heavily involved in the development and negotiation of this innovative and controversial concept, it will be discussed further in chapter 16.

SUMMARY

Compensation refers to every type of reward that individuals receive in return for performing organizational tasks. Direct financial compensation consists of the pay a person receives in the form of wages, salary, bonuses, and commissions. Indirect financial compensation includes all financial rewards that are not direct. Nonfinancial compensation consists of the satisfaction that a person receives by performing meaningful job tasks or from the psychological and physical environments in which the job is performed.

Firms should strive for equity, or fairness, in their compensation systems. Organizational equity is achieved when the needs of operative employees, managers, and shareholders are balanced. External equity exists when employees performing jobs within a firm are paid at levels comparable to those paid for similar jobs in other firms. Internal equity exists when employees performing jobs for a company are paid according to their job's relative value within that organization. Employee equity exists when employees performing similar jobs for the same firm are paid commensurate with factors unique to that employee.

Determinants of financial compensation include: the organization, the labor market, the job, and the employee. A person who is paid the going rate receives the average wage that most employers pay for the same job in a particular area or industry. The geographical area from which employees are recruited for a particular job is referred to as a labor market. Pricing of jobs within a labor market are affected by the cost of living, labor unions, government legislation, society, and the economy.

The job that a person is hired to do is a major determinant of the amount of financial compensation he or she will receive. Organizations pay for the

[42]Ibid.

value they attach to certain duties, responsibilities, and other job-related factors (such as working conditions). Job evaluation is that part of a compensation system by which management determines the relative value of one job compared to others. Four basic job evaluation methods are used in organizations: (1) the ranking method; (2) the classification method; (3) the factor comparison method; (4) and the point method. When selecting a method, many firms choose one and modify it to fit their particular needs. The ranking and classification methods are qualitative, and the factor comparison and point methods are quantitative approaches.

Placing a dollar value on a job's worth is referred to as job pricing. Many organizations group similar jobs into pay grades to simplify the pricing process. A pay range includes a minimum and a maximum rate with enough variance between the two to allow some significant pay difference. Even after the job has been priced, other factors determine how much pay a specific employee will receive. These factors range from sheer luck to the manner in which he or she actually performs the job.

QUESTIONS FOR REVIEW

1. Define each of the following terms: (a) compensation (b) direct financial compensation (c) indirect financial compensation (d) nonfinancial compensation.
2. Distinguish among organizational equity, external equity, internal equity, and employee equity.
3. What are the primary determinants of financial compensation? Briefly describe each.
4. Distinguish among a pay follower, a pay leader, and a going rate organization.
5. How has government legislation affected compensation?
6. Give the primary purpose of job evaluation.

7. Distinguish among the four basic methods of job evaluation: the ranking method, the classification method, the factor comparison method, and the point method.
8. What is the purpose of job pricing? Discuss briefly.
9. What is the basic procedure for determining pay grades?
10. What is the purpose for establishing pay ranges for jobs?
11. List and describe the various factors concerning the individual employee as they relate to the determination of pay and benefits.

TERMS FOR REVIEW

Compensation
Direct financial compensation
Indirect financial compensation
Nonfinancial compensation
Organizational equity
External equity

Internal equity
Employee equity
Going rate
Labor market
Key job
Cost-of-living allowance (COLA)

Job evaluation
Ranking method
Classification method
Factor comparison method
Point method
Comparable worth (CW)
Exempt employees

Job pricing
Pay grade
Wage curve
Pay range
Pay compression
Plateauing
Two-tier wage system

Incident 1

David Rhine, compensation manager for Farrington Lingerie Company, was generally a relaxed and good natured individual. Although he was a no-nonsense, competent executive, David was one of the most popular managers in the company. This Friday morning, however, David was not his usual self. As chairperson of the company's job evaluation committee, he had called a late morning meeting at which several jobs were to be considered for reevaluation. The jobs had already been rated and assigned to pay grade 3. But the office manager, Ben Butler, was upset that one was not rated higher. To press the issue, Ben had taken his case to two executives who were also members of the job evaluation committee. The two executives (production manager Bill Nelson and general marketing manager Betty Anderson) then requested that the job ratings be reviewed. Bill and Betty supported Ben's side of the dispute and David was not looking forward to the confrontation that was almost certain to occur.

The controversial job was that of receptionist. There was only one receptionist position in the company and it was held by Beth Smithers. Beth had been with the firm twelve years, longer than any of the committee members. She performed her tasks in an unusually efficient manner and her outstanding work was noticed by virtually all the executives in the company, including the president. Bill Nelson and Betty Anderson were particularly pleased with Beth because of the cordial manner in which she greeted and accommodated Farrington's customers and vendors, who frequently visited the plant. They felt that Beth's professionalism projected a positive image of the company.

When the meeting began, David said, "Good morning. I know that you are busy so let's get the show on the road. We have several jobs to evaluate this morning and I suggest we begin . . ." Before he could finish his sentence, Bill interrupted, "I suggest we start with Beth." Betty nodded in agreement. When David regained his composure, he quietly but firmly asserted, "Bill, we are *not* here today to evaluate Beth. Her supervisor does that at performance appraisal time. We're meeting to evaluate jobs based on job content. In order to do this fairly with regard to other jobs in the company, we must leave personalities out of our evaluation." David then proceeded to pass out copies of the receptionist job description while Bill and Betty appeared to be most irritated.

QUESTIONS

1. Do you feel that David was justified in insisting that the job, not the person, be evaluated? Discuss.

2. Do you believe that there is a maximum rate of pay for every job in an organization, regardless of how well the job is being performed? Justify your position.

3. Assuming that Beth is earning the maximum of the range for her pay grade, in what ways can she obtain a salary increase?

Incident 2

Harry Neal had been employed with Trimark Data Systems, Inc. (TDS) for five years and had progressed to the position of senior programmer analyst. He was generally pleased with the company and thoroughly enjoyed the creative demands of his job.

One Saturday afternoon during a golf game with his friend and co-worker Randy Dean, Harry discovered that his department had hired a recent university graduate as a programmer analyst. Harry really became upset when he learned that the new man's starting salary was only $30 a month less than his own. Although Harry was a good-natured fellow, he was bewildered and upset because he felt that he was being treated unfairly.

The following Monday morning Harry confronted Dave Edwards, the personnel director, and asked if what he had heard was true. Dave apologetically admitted that it was and attempted to explain the compa-ny's situation: "Harry, the market for programmer analysts is very tight and in order for the company to attract qualified prospects, we have to offer a premium starting salary. We desperately needed another analyst and this was the only way we could get one." Harry asked Dave if his salary would be adjusted accordingly. Dave answered, "Your salary will be reevaluated at the regular time. You're doing a great job, though, and I'm sure the boss will recommend a raise." Harry thanked Dave for his time but left the office shaking his head and wondering about his future.

QUESTIONS

1. Do you think that Dave's explanation was satisfactory? Discuss.
2. What action do you believe the company should have taken with regard to Harry?

References

"Are Companies Alienating the Great Middle?" *Management Review* 74 (May 1985): 5.

Ash, Ronald A. "Job Elements for Task Clusters: Arguments for Using Multi-Methodological Approaches to Job Analysis and a Demonstration of Their Utility." *Public Personnel Management* 11 (Spring 1982): 80–90.

Baxter, D. "Why Does a Company Need Salary Ranges?" *Personnel Administrator* 30 (April 1985): 12.

Burgess, Leonard R. *Wage and Salary Administration.* Columbus, Ohio: Charles E. Merrill, 1984, p. 93.

"Compensation Currents." *Compensation Review* 17 (First Quarter 1985): 2.

Crystal, Graef S. "Outlook on Compensation and Benefits: To the Rescue of Pay for Performance." *Personnel* 62 (January 1985): 9.

Davis, K. R., Jr., et al. "What College Graduates Want in a Compensation Package (Survey of

Preferences)." *Compensation Review* 17(1) (1985): 42–53.

Dunn, J. D. and Rachel, Frank M. *Wage and Salary Administration: Total Compensation Systems.* New York: McGraw-Hill, 1971.

Ellig, B. R. "Compensation Management: Its Past and Its Future." *Personnel* 54 (May 1977): 30–40.

Feeney, Edward J. "Developing the High Performance Edge," *S.A.M. Advanced Management Journal* 46 (Autumn 1981): 29–30 +.

Finegan, T. A. "Discouraged Workers and Economic Fluctuations." *Industrial and Labor Relations Review* 35 (October 1981): 88–102.

Henderson, R. I. "Changing Role of Wage and Salary Administrator." *Personnel* 53 (November 1976): 53–63.

Kaye, Beverly and McKee, Kathryn. "New Compensation Strategies for New Career Patterns." *Personnel Administrator* 31 (March 1986): 61–68.

Kien, J. M. "Keeping Up with the Jones's." *Pulp and Paper* 59 (May 1985): 5.

Kuhne, R. J. and Toyne, B. "Who Manages the International Compensation and Benefit Program?" *Compensation Review* 17(1) (1985): 34–41.

"Latin America Poses Challenges to Executive Remuneration Plans." *Employee Benefit Plan Review* 39 (January 1985): 60–61.

Lawler, Edward E., III. *Pay and Organizational Effectiveness: A Psychological View.* New York: McGraw-Hill, 1971.

Lee, J. A. and Mendoza, J. L. "Comparison of Techniques Which Test for Job Differences." *Personnel Psychology* 34 (Winter 1981): 731–748.

Lorber, Lawrence Z., Kirk, J. Robert, Samuels, Stephen L., and Spellman, David J. III, *Sex and Salary: A Legal and Personnel Analysis of Comparable Worth.* Alexandria, Va.: The ASPA Foundation, 1985, p. 51.

Metzger, M. "Year End Compensation Accruals." *The CPA Journal* 55 (April 1985): 64–66.

Milkovich, George T. and Newman, Jerry M. *Compensation.* Plano, Texas: Business Publications, 1984, pp. 8–9.

Morjaes, R. "Pay Policy: No Company Should Be Without One." *Accountancy* 96 (March 1985): 148–151.

Murphy, B. S., et al. "Pay Raises to Match Competing Bids Do Not Violate the Equal Pay Act." *Personnel Journal* 64 (February 1985): 14.

Nasar, S. "Why Wages Won't Take Off." *Fortune* 111 (April 20, 1985): 62–64 +.

"Oakar, Pendleton Trade Barbs over Comparable Worth Argument." *Resource,* American Society for Personnel Administration, May 1985, p. 1.

"Outlook on Compensation and Benefits." *Personnel* 62 (February 1985): 72–74.

Pierce, Jon L. "Job Design in Perspective." *Personnel Administrator* 25 (December 1980): 67–74.

Pine, S. R. and Wright, P. B. "Treasury Indicates a Future Interest in P/C Insurers: IRS Considers Taxibility of Deferred Compensation Plan Payments." *Risk Management* 31 (December 1984): 18 +.

Piso, E. "Task Analysis for Process-Control Tasks: The Method of Annett et al. Applied," *Journal of Occupational Psychology* 54 (1981): 247–254.

Sears, D. "Make Employee Pay a Strategic Issue." *Compensation Review* 17(1) (1985): 55–60.

Sibson, Robert E. *Compensation.* New York: AMACOM, A Division of American Management Associations, 1974.

Stull, G. J. "Effective Compensation: Cafeteria Plans." *Taxes* 63 (March 1985): 10–20.

Stull, G. J. "Effective Compensation: Qualified Cash or Deferred Arrangements." *Taxes* 63 (April 1985): 267–277.

Sullivan, J. F. "Comparable Worth and the Statistical Audit of Pay Programs for Illegal Systematic Discrimination." *Personnel Administrator* 30 (March 1985): 102–111.

"Ten Terrific Employers (For Working Parents' Money)." *Money* 14 (May 1985): 144.

"The Double Standard That's Setting Worker Against Worker." *Business Week,* April 8, 1985, p. 70.

"Twenty Questions on Comparable Worth." The Equal Employment Advisory Council, 1984. Reprinted in *Personnel Administrator* 30 (April 1985): 65.

"Women at Work." *Business Week,* January 28, 1985), 85.

CHAPTER OBJECTIVES
1. Define *benefits* and describe the importance of benefits to the total compensation program.
2. Explain the various incentive compensation programs that are available in many organizations.
3. Describe how compensation for managers, professionals and sales personnel is determined.
4. Explain the many forms of nonfinancial compensation that members of organizations are beginning to expect.

Chapter 13

BENEFITS AND OTHER COMPENSATION ISSUES

Mac Lewis — a college dropout — was a senior credit clerk at Ajax Manufacturing Company. A bright young man, Mac had been with Ajax for four years. He had received excellent performance ratings in each of several positions he had held with the firm. However, during his last appraisal interview, Mac's supervisor implied that promotion to a higher level job would require additional formal education. Because Mac appeared to be receptive to the idea, his supervisor suggested that he check with Personnel to learn the details of Ajax's educational assistance policy.

Arnold Thompson, Joe Minnis, and Randy Anderson are all employed as shipping clerks for Mainstreet Furniture Company. Arnold and Joe are energetic young people who consistently work hard each day. Both earn about $6.50 per hour. Randy is a "good ole boy" who spends most of his time flipping quarters with dock workers and talking with the department secretary. Yesterday, work was piling up in the department and Arnold and Joe were working furiously to keep up. Randy was nowhere to be found. "Arnold," Joe said disgustedly, "the pay here just isn't fair. We do twice as much work as Randy yet he makes as much as we do." "I know," Joe acknowledged, "but he punches in and out at the same time we do."

Liz Brown was a divorcee and the mother of three elementary school children. She worked as an illustrator for Busiform Company to support her family. Her normal working hours were from 8:00 A.M. to 5:00 P.M., Monday through Friday. The children's school began each weekday morning at 9:00 A.M. and ended at 3:30 P.M. Satisfactory arrangements had been made for the children after school. However, she faced an almost impossible task of transporting them to school in the morning and arriving at her job on time. The school's principal permitted the children to enter the building at 7:45 each morning to wait until classes began, but Liz was afraid she could not count on this practice to continue indefinitely. When Busiform management announced implementation of a new system of flexible working hours, Liz was delighted.

While these anecdotes may seem to have little in common, each relates to the broad area of compensation. Mac is investigating the possibility of continuing his education through his company's educational assistance program. Arnold and Joe are not on an incentive system and are angry because they do more work than Randy. Liz's primary concern is the well-being of her children. She believes that the new flexible working hours will solve her most difficult problem.

The overall purpose of this chapter is to emphasize the increasing significance of benefits in a total compensation system and provide an overview of other important issues associated with compensation programs. The chapter begins with a discussion of mandated and voluntary benefits. Next, various types of incentive compensation systems are presented, followed with a discussion of special pay considerations that are required for managers, professionals, and sales personnel. The final section covers nonfinancial compensation that stems from the job and the environmental factors that surround the job.

BENEFITS (INDIRECT FINANCIAL COMPENSATION)

Most organizations recognize a responsibility to their employees by providing benefits for their health, safety, security, and general welfare (see Figure 13–1). **Benefits** include *all financial rewards that generally are not paid directly to the employee.* Benefits cost the firm money, but employees usually receive them indirectly. For example, an organization may spend $1,500 a year to pay the health insurance premiums for each nonexempt employee. The employee does not receive money but does obtain the benefit of health insurance coverage. This type of compensation has two distinct advantages. First, it is generally nontaxable to the employee. Second, in the case of insurance, the premium rates are much less for large groups of employees than for individual policies.

Generally speaking, benefits are provided to employees because of their membership in the organization. They are typically not related to employee productivity and therefore do not serve as motivation for improved performance. However, an attractive benefit package can assist in the recruitment and retention of a qualified work force.

The cost of benefits is high and is growing rapidly. Benefits cost employers approximately $350 billion a year. A recent survey showed that the average responding firm provides benefits amounting to 36.6 percent of payroll costs. The range varied from 18 percent to more than 65 percent of the payroll.[1] A typical worker who earns $24,000 per year receives ap-

---

[1]J. H. Foegen, "Update on Benefits: Health, Home, Help, Fun, Taxes," *Personnel Administrator* 30 (November 1985): 87.

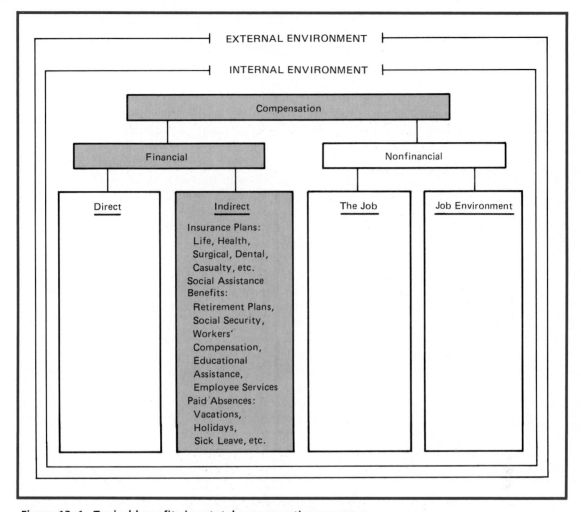

Figure 13–1. Typical benefits in a total compensation program.

proximately $12,000 more, indirectly, in the form of benefits. These facts no doubt account for the less frequent use of the term *fringe benefits*. In fact, this term "... has become a misnomer in most organizations."[2]

BENEFITS REQUIRED BY LAW

Some organizations would probably provide mandated benefits regardless of legal requirements. However, most firms have no choice in the matter and must provide certain benefits to their employees. Some might say, "If

[2]Richard C. Huseman, John D. Hatfield, and Russell W. Driver, "Getting Your Benefit Programs Understood and Appreciated," *Personnel Journal* 57 (October 1978): 560.

it is required by law, then it is not a benefit." Nevertheless, in these instances the firm is contributing additional money on behalf of the employee because he or she is a member of the organization. For this reason, we will consider these items to be benefits. These legally required benefits are social security, unemployment compensation, and workers' compensation.

Social security. The Social Security Act of 1935 created a system that provided retirement benefits only. Subsequent amendments to the act added other forms of protection, such as disability insurance, survivors benefits, and, most recently, Medicare. Today, approximately nine out of ten employees in the United States are covered by social security. Disability insurance protects employees against loss of earnings due to total disability. Survivors benefits are provided to certain members of an employee's family when he or she dies. These benefits are paid to the widow, widower, and unmarried children of the deceased employee. Unmarried children may be eligible for survivors benefits until they are eighteen years of age. In some cases, students retain eligibility until they are nineteen. Medicare provides hospital and medical insurance protection for individuals sixty-five years of age and older or those who have become disabled.

While employees must pay a portion of the cost, the employer makes an equal contribution for Social Security coverage. It is this part that is considered a benefit. As you can see in Table 13–1, the tax rate paid by both employee and employers and the maximum wage taxable have increased sharply. Between 1977 and 1985, the maximum social security tax almost tripled. This dramatic increase, coupled with a continuing debate over the fiscal soundness of the system, leaves many employees and employers with mixed feelings about its desirability.

Table 13–1. Social security taxes, 1977–1990 and after

Year	Tax rate for employees and employers (each)			Maximum taxable wage	Maximum tax
	For cash benefits	For hospitalization insurance	Total		
1977	—	—	5.85%	$16,500	$ 965.25
1984	5.70%	1.30%	7.00	37,800	2,646.00
1985	5.70	1.35	7.05	39,600	2,791.80
1986	5.70	1.45	7.15	42,000	3,003.00
1987	5.70	1.30	7.15	*	*
1988–89	6.06	1.45	7.51	*	*
1990 and after	6.20	1.45	7.65	*	*

*The maximum will rise automatically as earnings levels increase.

Source: *Your Social Security*, January 1986 ed. Washington, D.C.: U.S. Government Printing Office, 1986, pp. 31–32.

457

Chapter 13
Benefits and
Other
Compensation
Issues

The normal retirement age under Social Security will be increased after the turn of the century. Beginning with employees who reach age sixty-two in the year 2000, the retirement age will be increased gradually until 2009 when it reaches age sixty-six. After stabilizing at this age for a period of time, it will again increase slowly until 2027 when it reaches age sixty-seven. These changes will not affect Medicare, and full eligibility under this program will remain at age sixty-five.[3]

Unemployment compensation   If an individual is laid off by an organization covered by the Social Security Act, he or she may receive unemployment compensation for up to twenty-six weeks. While the federal government provides certain guidelines, unemployment compensation programs are administered by the states. As you might expect, the benefits vary by state. A payroll tax paid by the employer furnishes the funds for unemployment compensation.

Workers' compensation.   Workers' compensation benefits provide a degree of financial protection for employees who incur expenses resulting from job-related accidents or illnesses. As with unemployment compensation, the various states administer individual programs subject to federal regulations. Employers pay the entire cost of workers' compensation insurance. Their premium expense is directly tied to their past experience with job-related accidents and illnesses. This situation should encourage employers to actively pursue health and safety programs — topics we will discuss in chapter 14.

VOLUNTARY BENEFITS

There seems to be an endless number of benefits provided voluntarily by organizations. These benefits may be classified as follows: (1) payment for time not worked; (2) employee health and security benefits; (3) services to employees; and (4) premium pay. Generally speaking, benefits provided within these categories are not legally required. While they are provided voluntarily by some firms, they no doubt have resulted from union–management negotiations in many organizations.

Payment for time not worked.   In providing payment for time not worked, employers recognize employees' need for some time away from the job. For instance, paid vacations provide workers with time to rest and become rejuvenated, while also encouraging them to remain with the firm. A person in an operative job will normally receive two weeks of annual vacation. Paid vacation time typically increases with seniority. For example, employees with six months service may receive one week of vacation; em-

[3]"Compensation Currents," *Compensation Review* 15 (Third Quarter 1983): 4.

ployees with one year service, two weeks; ten years service, three weeks, and fifteen years service, four weeks.

A senior executive with a month of vacation and an annual salary of $96,000 would receive approximately $8000 each year while not working. A junior employee earning $24,000 a year might receive two weeks of vacation time worth about $1000.

Each year many firms allocate employees a certain number of days of sick leave, which can be used when they are ill. The employees continue to receive their pay up to a maximum number of days if they cannot report to work. As with vacation pay, the number of sick leave days typically depends on seniority. Some sick leave programs have been severely criticized. At times they have been abused by individuals calling in sick when all they really wanted was additional paid vacation. In order to counter this situation, some firms require a doctor's statement after a certain number of sick leave days have been taken.

There are other occasions on which employees are paid, though they are not working. Holidays, coffee breaks, rest periods, jury duty service, voting time, clean-up time, and bereavement time are in this category.

Employee welfare. Benefits that provide for general employee welfare may be of several kinds. Health insurance typically includes hospital room and board costs, service charges, and surgical fees. This increasingly costly benefit is often paid in part, or totally, by the employer. Many plans provide for major medical benefits to cover extraordinary expenses. The use of "deductibles" is a common feature of major medical benefits. For example, the employee may pay the first $100 of the health care cost before the insurance becomes effective.

Health insurance premiums alone in some firms amount to almost 10 percent of the total payroll. In an attempt to control medical costs, as many as 30 percent of businesses that provide medical benefits now use some type of utilization review service. **Utilization review** is *a process that scrutinizes medical diagnoses, hospitalization, surgery, and other medical treatment and care prescribed by doctors.* The reviewer, often a registered nurse, explores alternatives to the treatment provided, such as outpatient treatment or admission on the day of surgery. The objective of this process is, of course, to hold the line on businesses' portion of the nearly $400 billion Americans spend annually on medical care.[4]

Wellness is *a concept that focuses on the prevention of illness and diseases.* It is also an approach to health care that offers great promise in stemming the tide of increasing treatment costs. Heavy smoking, poor nutrition, and undue stress are lifestyle and habit patterns of individuals that wellness programs challenge. These patterns are also the underlying contributors to diseases that account for a large share of health care expenditures.

[4]Ellen Paris, "Hold That Scalpel?" *Forbes* 135 (May 6, 1985): 35–36.

Executive Insights

Beverly J. Mason
Corporate Manager,
Human Resources,
DynaCor, Inc.

Beverly J. Mason is vice president of the Compensation and Benefit Committee of the American Society for Personnel Administration. She is an active member of her profession and has served as vice president, Region 17, for ASPA (Arizona, Colorado, Utah, and New Mexico), lecturer and member of the American Compensation Association, past president of Phoenix Personnel Management Association, and member of the Arizona Hospital Personnel Association.

Her extensive background in the health care field has included jobs at all levels in personnel. "Human resource managers must be able to relate to employees and managers at every level. I have worked at every level and understand the problems and concerns of both employees and supervisors," says Mason. "If you can't communicate, you can't make it in our field."

While still in college, she began her career in personnel. "As a personnel file clerk at age 17, I wasn't giving too much thought to a career," says Mason. This proved, however, to be the beginning of a long and rewarding career.

From the file clerk position at Good Samaritan Hospital in Phoenix, she was promoted to personnel assistant. Still attending school at night, Mason began developing career objectives and, within three years, assumed responsibility for the Personnel Records Department of the hospital.

"Good Samaritan Hospital was a large, 650-bed, teaching hospital. We had about 2000 employees at that time. Age was the biggest obstacle I had to face in working with a professional team more than twice my years. I made up for my lack of experience with a lot of hard work and solid career goals," says Mason.

Her next opportunity arose when an opening occurred for a personnel technician in the Salary Administration Department of the hospital. For the next year, she researched salary administration plans, techniques, and laws and became a resource to other local health care professionals on salary administration matters. She moved up and assumed full responsibility for salary administration, remaining there through a series of mergers and acquisitions. When the dust settled, she was corporate manager of salary administration for Samaritan Health Service. Samaritan is a large, nonprofit, health care corporation that owns and operates hospitals, clinics, and related services throughout Arizona and Utah.

Mason headed the Salary Administration Department at Samaritan until July 1977. She recalls, "I learned a great deal from 1975 to 1977. The health care field was beginning to be treated as big business and management was expected to evolve with it. There was a lot of turmoil, a few union attempts, and 'fallout' from the management ranks because they couldn't keep up. Human resource managers had their hands full with labor shortages, salary increases running 15 percent annually, and the community screaming about rising health care costs."

All the attention the health care field was getting was a boost to Mason's career. Valley National Bank sought her out to head their salary administration program in July 1977. "I was misquoted on the front page of our local paper concerning salary increases for county employees the morning the bank board of directors voted on bringing me in as an officer. I was serving on a special task force reviewing proposed salary increases for county employees; the subject was very controversial because their wages had been frozen. Although they voted me in, I think they were a little worried about my press following!" she reports.

She stayed at Valley for two years. She feels this experience broadened her knowledge base and provided insight into another specialized field. They never quite made her a banker, though, and on August 1, 1979 the senior vice president for Samaritan lured her back to that company.

Mason's career took a slightly different turn in December 1980, when she was asked to assume responsibility for benefits in addition to her responsibilities for salary administration. "Samaritan had grown to over 7000 employees, was self-insured, and self-administered almost all of its benefit plans. It was a real challenge for an individual who had limited exposure to benefits administration," she says. Mason spent three years designing and implementing benefit plans, conducting benefit fairs, and improving the overall understanding of employee benefits and their costs.

Her latest career opportunity came in January 1984. The president of DynaCor, Inc., asked her to join his executive staff as corporate manager of human resources. Her people skills and ability to get things done were what they were looking for. DynaCor specializes in providing services to the health care market. They also own and operate long-term care facilities in Arizona and South Dakota. "This has been my most challenging position yet. We've gone through the phases of rapid growth, cutbacks, and reorganization. I've had to draw on my own experience as well as that of my fellow professionals."

There is considerable evidence that wellness programs work. For example, New York Telephone estimates annual savings of more than $2 million in reduced absenteeism and lowered medical costs from its stop-smoking program. Kennecott Corporation has reduced its medical care costs by more than 50 percent for the 12,000 employees participating in its wellness program.[5] Topics related to wellness, such as stress and physical fitness, are discussed in chapter 14.

Group life insurance is a common benefit provided to protect the employee's family in the event of his or her death. The cost of group life insurance is low, even when the employee must contribute toward payment of the premium. Some plans call for a flat amount of coverage, say $10,000.

[5]Robert D. Kilpatrick, "Increasing the Wellness Effort," Industry Week 224(3) (February 4, 1985): 14.

461

Chapter 13
Benefits and
Other
Compensation
Issues

Other plans base the coverage on the employee's annual earnings. For example, a worker earning $12,000 per year may have $24,000 worth of group life coverage. Typically, members of group plans do not have to show evidence of insurability. This provision is especially important to older employees and those with physical problems. Many of these employees may find the cost of insurance on an individual base to be prohibitive.

Private retirement plans provide income for employees who retire after reaching a certain age or having served the firm for a specific period of time. Pension plans are vitally important to employees because Social Security was not designed to provide complete retirement income. The Employee Retirement Income Security Act of 1974 (ERISA) was passed to strengthen existing and future retirement programs. The act also ensures that retired employees will receive deserved pensions.

In 1984, ten years after ERISA was enacted, a major amendment, Retirement Equity Act (REACT), was signed into law by President Reagan. The purpose of this act is to provide greater equity in private pension plans for covered workers and their spouses. Changes were made in some of ERISA's rules, which originally tended to penalize working women, to increase the likelihood that women will actually receive benefits on the basis of their participation in the work force or as a surviving spouse.[6] Key features of REACT include:

- Pension plans must pay benefits as a qualified joint-and-survivor annuity when a participant retires, unless the employee's spouse cosigns the benefit election form in which some other option is chosen.
- The qualified joint-and-survivor annuity requirement now also applies to defined-contribution pension plans other than Employee Stock Ownership Plans (ESOPs).
- Pension and profit-sharing plans must pay a survivor benefit to the widow or widower of any vested participant who dies before retirement, not just those of active employees who are fifty-five and older.
- Plans are allowed to honor state law alimony awards and other support orders if the order meets uniform basic standards, which may include an order to pay a benefit to the ex-spouse even if the covered employee has not retired.
- Employees who are absent from work because of pregnancy, childbirth, adoption, or infant care are protected against break-in-service penalties for up to a year.
- A nonvested employee who leaves the employer's service and then comes back within five years will be entitled to credit for that earlier service, even if it was for less than five years.

---

[6]Jack H. Schechter, "The Retirement Equity Act: Meeting Women's Pension Needs," *Compensation Review* 17 (First Quarter 1985): 13–21.

- The minimum age for plan participation and benefit accrual cannot be higher than twenty-one, and the minimum age for vesting service cannot be higher than eighteen.
- Service pensions and other subsidized retirement benefits — as well as optional payment forms — can only be dropped from a plan with respect to benefits that are earned after the plan is amended to make the change.
- Plans can cash out benefits worth up to $3500 without the recipient's consent (it used to be $1,750).[7]

Supplemental unemployment benefits (SUB) first appeared in automobile labor agreements in 1955.[8] They are designed to provide additional income for employees receiving unemployment insurance benefits. These plans have spread to many other industries and are usually financed by the company. They tend to benefit newer employees because layoffs are normally determined by seniority. For this reason, employees with considerable seniority are often not enthusiastic about SUB.

Employee services.   Organizations offer a variety of benefits that are classified under employee services. These include company subsidized food services, financial assistance for employee operated credit unions, legal and income tax aid, club memberships, athletic and recreational programs, discounts on company products, moving expenses, parking spaces, and tuition rebates for educational expenses. These benefits have the potential for greatly enhancing the employment relationship.

Premium pay.   **Premium pay** is *compensation given employees for working long periods of time or working under dangerous or undesirable conditions.* As mentioned in chapter 12, payment for overtime is required for nonexempt employees who work beyond forty hours in a given week. However, some firms pay overtime for hours worked beyond eight in a given day and pay double time — or even more — for work on Sundays and holidays.

Additional pay provided to employees who work under extremely dangerous conditions is called **hazard pay.** A window washer on skyscrapers in New York City might well be given extra compensation because of dangerous working conditions. Military pilots receive extra money in the form of flight pay because of the hazards associated with flying.

Shift differentials are paid to reward employees for the inconvenience of working undesirable hours. This type of pay may be provided on the basis of additional cents-per-hour. For example, employees who work the

[7]Judith F. Mazo, "Another Compliance Challenge for Employers: The Retirement Equity Act," *Personnel* 62 (February 1985): 43.

[8]David W. Belcher, *Compensation Administration.* Englewood Cliffs, N.J.: Prentice-Hall, 1974, p. 315.

second shift ("swing" shift) from 4:30 P.M. until midnight might receive $.25 per hour above the base rate. The third shift ("graveyard" shift) often warrants an even greater differential. For example, an extra $.32 per hour may be given. Shift differentials are sometimes based on a percentage of the employee's base rate.

463

Chapter 13
Benefits and
Other
Compensation
Issues

A COMPREHENSIVE VOLUNTARY BENEFITS PROGRAM

International Business Machines Corporation offers a comprehensive voluntary benefits program. The program is noncontributory; that is, the company bears the full cost of the benefits. The growth of the IBM benefits program is shown in Figure 13–2. Note that since its inception the program has been improved and enlarged to meet changing employee needs. Two of the most recent additions are particularly interesting: the adoption assistance plan and the retirement education assistance plan.

Under the adoption assistance plan, IBM will reimburse employees for 80 percent of eligible charges up to a maximum of $1000 for each adoption. Eligible charges include:

- Adoption agency fees.
- Placement fees.
- Lawyers' fees and other required legal fees.
- Maternity fees (child's natural mother).
- Temporary foster care charges (immediately preceding placement of the child with the adopting family).

The IBM retirement education assistance plan is designed to help employees and their spouses prepare for activities and personal fulfillment in their retirement years. Under this plan, IBM will reimburse tuition costs for retirement courses — up to $2500 per individual — upon evidence of course completion. This plan covers any course offered by nationally accredited colleges and postsecondary schools, as well as adult continuing education courses conducted by state certified schools or educational organizations. Other courses that appear to meet the intent of the plan are also considered for reimbursement. An employee's eligibility in this plan continues until two years after the actual date of retirement.

NEW BENEFITS

Several new benefits have recently appeared on the scene in addition to those included in IBM's innovative plan. One such benefit is subsidized day care centers; the firm provides facilities for young children of employees for a modest fee. Parents typically transport the children to and from the center. While there, the children engage in supervised play and receive meals. This benefit is a good recruitment aid and helps to reduce absenteeism. The need for such programs is emphasized by the fact that in 1980 almost half of the American women with children under six years of

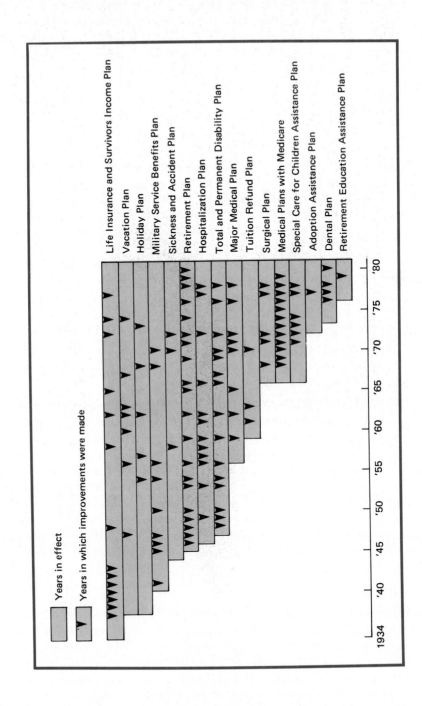

Figure 13–2. IBM benefits: A history of growth.

age were in the work force.[9] Although relatively few companies provide substantial child care assistance, the number is growing rapidly. According to the U.S. Department of Health and Human Services, almost 600 firms provided this type of benefit in 1983, compared to only 100 five years earlier.[10]

465

Chapter 13
Benefits and
Other
Compensation
Issues

In an attempt to conserve energy and relieve traffic congestion some firms have begun transporting workers to and from work. In these programs, participating employees pay a portion of the cost and ride in company vans or buses. Some employees find this benefit very convenient and a means to avoid heavy commuter traffic.

Massachusetts Mutual Life Insurance Company has initiated two new benefits in the health care area.[11] One of these programs serves to detect and treat high blood pressure. Once each year, all employees are offered a physical examination. When a case of high blood pressure is detected, the employee is referred to his or her own physician for further diagnosis and treatment. The company pays all medical costs for this treatment. The company and employees believe that this program literally saves lives and, for this reason, it is a very popular benefit.

Another Mass Mutual program encourages employees to stop smoking. The company will reimburse any person on the payroll who consults a hypnotist for treatment. Although the program is new, about half of the employees in the program have stopped smoking cigarettes.

COMMUNICATING INFORMATION ABOUT THE BENEFITS PACKAGE

Employee benefits can help a firm recruit and retain a quality work force. Management depends on an upward flow of information from employees in order to know when benefit changes are needed.[12] In addition, because employee awareness of benefits is often severely limited, the essential aspects of programs must be communicated downward.[13] Regardless of a benefits program's technical soundness, a firm simply cannot get its money's worth if its employees do not know what they are receiving. It has been suggested that workers may even become resentful if they are not frequently reminded of a benefits plan values. They may resent their obligation to pay for a portion of some benefits while overlooking the larger picture of what they receive and the substantially greater costs borne by their employer.[14]

---

[9]"The New Corporate Goodies," *Dun's Review* 18 (July 1981): 49.

[10]Carol Dilks, "Employers Who Help With the Kids," *Nation's Business,* February 1984, p. 59.

[11]"The New Corporate Goodies," p. 49.

[12]Huseman, Hatfield and Driver, "Benefit Programs," p. 564.

[13]Jeffery C. Claypool and Joseph P. Cangemi, "The Annual Employee Earnings and Benefits Letter," *Personnel Journal* (July 1980): 563.

[14]Robert M. McCaffery, "Employee Benefits: Beyond the Fringe?" *Personnel Administrator* 26 (May 1981): 30.

The Employee Retirement Income Security Act provides still another reason for communicating information about a firm's benefits program. This act requires organizations with a pension or profit-sharing plan to provide employees with specific data at specified times. The act further mandates that the information be presented in an understandable manner and include:

- The kind of plan.
- Eligibility requirements.
- Amount of benefits due at specific times and payment options.
- Surviving dependents' benefits.
- How the pension trust is invested.
- Who is responsible for managing the plan.[15]

Naturally, organizations can go beyond what is legally required. In fact many firms, such as the Southland Corporation, did so before ERISA's enactment. As you can see in Figure 13–3, Southland's report provides each employee with a compensation and benefits profile. A summary of this type helps employees to become aware of their total rewards package and assists the firm in achieving its compensation and benefits objectives.

INCENTIVE COMPENSATION

One of the most significant economic problems of recent years in the United States has been the slowdown in the rate of growth in productivity. There is evidence that this productivity problem, which affects both the public and private sectors of the economy, has become increasingly serious over the past few years.[16] Compensation is most often determined by how much time an employee spends at work. *Compensation programs that relate pay to productivity* are referred to as **incentive compensation.** A primary purpose of an incentive plan is to encourage greater productivity from individuals and work groups. The assumption made by management is that money will motivate performance. It is likely that the more productive workers such as Arnold Thompson and Joe Minnis, mentioned at the beginning of the chapter, would prefer to be paid on the basis of their output.

Money can serve as an important motivator for those who value it, which most of us do. However, a clear relationship must exist between performance and pay if money is to serve as an effective motivator.

Output standards must be established before any type of incentive system can be applied. This standard is a measure of work that an average, well-trained employee, working at a normal pace, should be able to accomplish in a given period of time. For example, a firm may determine that

---

[15]Robert Krogman, "Is Your Company Getting the Most Out of Its Benefits Program?" *Personnel Administrator* 25 (May 1980): 45–46.

[16]Edward M. Glaser, "Productivity Gains Through Worklife Improvement," *Personnel* 57 (January–February 1980): 71.

Figure 13–3. The Southland Corporation individual employee compensation and benefits profile. Source: Used with the permission of The Southland Corporation.

Prepared for: John Doe
2828 N. Haskell Ave.
Dallas, TX 75204

Hire Date: 01/05/82
Employee #: 987654321

COMPENSATION

Listed below is a schedule of compensation and benefits which Southland provided you either directly or indirectly for 1984:

Regular Earnings		$22,326.20
Profit Sharing Deferral	$1,665.90	
Earned Bonus		$ 2,679.14
F.I.C.A. — Social Security		$ 1,662.83
Medical Expense Reimbursement		$ 282.71
Company Paid Medical Insurance Premium		$ 2,133.69
Profit Sharing Company Contribution		$ 883.01
Educational Reimbursement		$ 629.57
Vacation Days	10	
		$30,597.15

This Year 1985

Compensation:
Based on Your Present Annual Salary of $25,260.00
and Including:
  Normal Bonus .... $ 3,031.20
Your Estimated Compensation for 1985 Will Be $28,291.20

Benefits

This benefits statement has been prepared for you based on information in Southland's records as of 02/19/85. Every effort has been made to assure the accuracy of the information reported, however, errors can occur. In all cases, actual benefits will be paid in accordance with the governing plan documents or insurance contracts. For more details on any of your benefits, refer to your plan booklets.

Benefits Package:
Protection for Today and Tomorrow . . .

Health Care

Hospital and Medical Benefits are provided for you by the Southland Corporation at no cost to you.

You have extended this benefit for 2 or more dependents at the cost of $14 per week. This premium is deducted from your check on a pre-tax basis.

Your medical plan reimburses 70% of all eligible hospital expenses after a $150 in-patient deductible (maximum $450 per year). With pre-admission certification the hospital deductible is waived and hospital room and board charges are paid at 80%. Your medical plan reimburses 70% of eligible non-hospital expenses after a $200 deductible per year. After your out-of-pocket expenses in 1985 have reached $3,000 (not including hospital deductible) you will be reimbursed 100% for eligible medical expenses for the remainder of the year. The lifetime maximum for reimbursement per covered individual is $1,000,000

Dental Benefits

Your medical plan reimburses 70% of eligible dental expenses. Dental expenses are subject to the annual deductible. The maximum reimbursement for 1985 for each insured individual is .... $ 1,000

Figure 13–3. The Southland Corporation individual employee compensation and benefits profile (continued).

Disability Benefits

Your disability benefits are based on your average weekly earnings at the time this statement was prepared and are subject to change.

		Benefits Period	
	Monthly	Annual	Total

Disability benefits are provided for you after 90 days of employment at no cost. Benefits are based on 75% of your weekly earnings for the first 26 weeks of disability—65% thereafter during the remainder of the disability, before applicable deductions. Your benefits for the first 26 weeks

would be $384.67

Per week, benefits thereafter would be $333.38

Per week, and could be payable for a total of 51 weeks.

Life Insurance Benefits

Your life insurance benefits are based on your average weekly earnings at the time this statement was prepared and are subject to change.

At no cost to you, The Southland Corporation has provided term life insurance to your beneficiary or estate in the amount of $13,335.62

You have elected to increase the amount of your term life insurance by selecting:

  Additional life insurance payable to your beneficiary as a lump sum in the amount of $40,006.86

  Survivor's life insurance payable to your beneficiary as a lump sum in the amount of $40,006.86

The total life insurance benefit payable to your beneficiary in the event of your natural death is $80,013.72

Through the election of additional life insurance and survivor's life insurance, you have added:

  AD&D on yourself in the amount of $80,013.72

  Life insurance on your eligible spouse in the amount of $6,667.81

  Life insurance on each of your eligible dependent children in the amount of $3,333.90

The total life insurance benefit payable to your beneficiary in the event of your accidental death is $160,027.44

For more detailed information regarding other life insurance coverage, contact your division personnel manager or the group insurance department.

Employee Stock Ownership Plan

The employee stock ownership plan (ESOP) allows eligible employees to receive shares of the Southland Corporation common stock and participate in the growth of the company. If you were employed for one year or more on December 31, 1984, you will receive share allocations. These shares will be allocated to an account in your behalf. For 1984, Southland contributed in excess of $3,000,000

This amount was used to purchase shares of stock on behalf of eligible employees. Your account is paid to you if you retire or leave the company, or to your beneficiary in the event of your death. ESOP participants will receive their individual statements at the annual profit sharing meeting.

Profit Sharing

The 1984 company contribution was in excess of $18,000,000

Your profit sharing account balance is payable to you at retirement. Payment may be made in a lump sum or on an installment schedule, whichever you select. Your account is payable to Jane Doe in the event of your death. Payment may be made in a lump sum or on an installment schedule, whichever your beneficiary elects. Your individual statement will be available to you at the annual profit sharing meeting.

The foundation of your retirement income will be your Southland profit sharing account along with social security. An individual retirement account (IRA) is another way to plan for your future and also provide tax advantages. IRA accounts are available through profit sharing, The Southland Credit Union, or other financial institutions. Consult with a savings/investment specialist to determine an approach that best suits your own savings ability and retirement income goals.

Other Benefits

Social Security:

Southland Matches your FICA payment for social security benefits. These benefits are provided to you by the United States government at age 65 or as early as age 62 at a reduced basis. Your spouse, age 65 or older, can receive additional social security payments equal to 40 to 50% of your benefit. In the event of your death or disability, benefits may be payable to your eligible dependents. For more detailed information, contact the Social Security Administration.

Credit Union:

You and your family members may join the credit union at any time after your employment. Secured and unsecured (signature) loans are available to credit union members at competitive rates. The credit union offers you the convenience of payroll deductions for savings, making loan payments and for the direct deposit of your paycheck for those with checking accounts. The credit union also offers you many savings plans including regular shares (savings), checking (share draft) accounts, certificate accounts, individual retirement accounts (IRA) and an insured money management star account.

Workers' Compensation and Unemployment Compensation:

The Southland Corporation pays the required cost of federal and state mandated benefits such as workers' compensation, unemployment compensation and disability benefits in some states.

Paid Time off for:

Vacation:
During 1984, you accrued 10 days of vacation time to be taken during 1985. This time may be adjusted if you were on a leave of absence during 1984.

Jury Duty:
Full pay for time served on jury duty.

Sick days:
Sick days vary by division as does eligibility.

Holidays:
Holidays vary by division as does eligibility.

Death in Family:
Full pay up to three days if there is a death in your immediate family.

In addition to all of the above, Southland provides numerous other valuable benefits which are significant and important to you:

Service Awards	Scholarships	Matching Gifts
Pre-Retirement Publications	Company Publications	Monthly Stock Investment
Leave of Absence	United States Auto Club	Holiday Gift Program
Discount Buying Service	Educational Reimbursement	Employee Assistance Program

employees in a particular department should be able to produce five finished parts per hour. The standard then becomes five. Time study specialists (who generally report to industrial engineering or methods departments) are often responsible for establishing work standards. A more direct approach to balancing pay and performance is to pay incentive compensation, which can be offered on an individual, group, or companywide basis.

INDIVIDUAL INCENTIVE PLANS

Many individual incentive plans have been used in an attempt to improve worker productivity and firms' profitability. If Arnold Thompson produces more than Randy Anderson (another employee performing the same job) he would receive a greater financial reward because of his greater productivity under an incentive plan. The straight piecework plan and the standard hour plan are the most commonly used individual plans.

A predetermined amount of money is paid for each unit produced under a **straight piecework plan.** The piece rate is calculated by dividing the standard hourly output into the job's pay rate. For example, if the standard output is .04 hour per unit, or 25 units per hour, and the job's pay rate is $5 per hour, the piece rate would be $.20. In this example, an employee who produced at the rate of 280 units per day would earn $56 in an eight-hour day (280 units × 8 hours × $.20). Most incentive plans in use today have a guaranteed base. In the example above, it would be the $5 per hour rate.

The straight piecework plan is simple and easily understood by employees.[17] One possible weakness (which is minimized by the use of today's computers) is that any change in the overall pay scale necessitates computing new piece rates for every job. The standard hour plan was devised to overcome this problem.

The **standard hour plan** is *an individual incentive plan under which time allowances are calculated for each unit of output.* Again, assume that 25 units per hour, or .04 hour per unit, is the standard output, $5 the hourly job rate and eight hours the time worked per day. Under these assumptions, an employee would have an allowance of .04 hour per unit of output (instead of a piece rate of $.20 per unit).

An employee producing at the rate of 280 units per day would receive an allowance of .04 hour per unit for all units produced in a day. Therefore, in an eight-hour day, this employee would earn 11.2 standard hours (280 units × .04 hour per unit). The pay for the day would be 11.2 standard hours × $5 per hour, or $56.

The standard hour plan has the characteristics of a straight piecework plan. An advantage is that piece rates need not be recalculated for every pay rate change.

---

[17]Belcher, *Compensation Administration*, p. 315.

One potential problem with both the straight piecework plan and the
standard hour plan is related to the output standard. The standard is typically established by industrial engineers and may be distrusted by the
workers. Any change in the standard, although justified in the eyes of
management, may be viewed with considerable skepticism by the employees.

When individual output cannot be easily distinguished, group and companywide plans offer alternatives to individual incentive plans. These approaches will be discussed next.

471

Chapter 13
Benefits and
Other
Compensation
Issues

GROUP INCENTIVE PLANS

As we suggested earlier, it is not always feasible to pay individual incentives. Work is often organized in such a manner that productivity results
from group effort. It is then difficult, if not impossible, to determine each
individual's contribution, so incentives must be provided to the group. For
example, if the group produced 100 units over standard, each member
would receive incentive compensation on a pro rata basis.

There are advantages and disadvantages to group incentives. For instance, in the assembly of electrical transformers, ten employees may be
working on one phase of the operation. They must work together if the
overall task is to be successfully accomplished. If nine employees perform
their tasks but one does not, the productivity of the entire group may suffer.
However, the peer pressure exerted in such a situation can be so great that
the affected individual will either conform to the group's standards or leave
the group. Group incentive plans tend to foster teamwork and often encourage peers to serve as counselors and coaches for new members. Group
members tend to lend a helping hand when it is needed.

COMPANYWIDE PLANS

On a baseball team it does not matter that the pitcher is outstanding or that
the outfield is great. The standard by which the team is evaluated is the
overall won–loss record. Just as with a baseball club, some managers believe
that incentive plans encourage competition among individuals and groups.
Companywide plans then offer a viable alternative. These plans may be
based on the organization's productivity, cost savings, or profitability. To
illustrate the concept of companywide plans, we will discuss profit sharing
plans, employee stock ownership plans, and the Scanlon plan.

Profit sharing. **Profit sharing** is *a compensation plan that results in the
distribution of a predetermined percentage of the firm's profits to employees.* Many organizations use this type of plan to integrate the employee's
interests with those of the company. Profit-sharing plans can aid firms in
recruiting, retaining, and motivating employees to be more productive.

There are three basic forms of profit-sharing plans: current, deferred, and combination.[18]

- *Current plans* provide payment to employees in cash or stock as soon as profits are determined.
- *Deferred plans* involve placing company contributions in an irrevocable trust to be credited to the account of individual employees. The funds are normally invested in securities, and become available to the employee (or his or her survivors) at retirement, termination, or death.
- *Combination plans* permit employees to receive payment of part of their share of profits on a current basis while payment of part of their share is deferred.

Normally, most full-time employees are included in a company's profit-sharing plan after a specified waiting period. Vesting determines the amount of "profit" an employee actually owns in his or her account and is often established on a graduated basis. For example, an employee may become 25 percent vested after being in the plan for two years; 50 percent vested after three years; 75 percent vested after four years; and 100 percent vested after five years. You can see that this approach to vesting may tend to reduce turnover by encouraging employees to remain with the company.

In summarizing the merits and disadvantages of profit sharing, one consultant stated: "Profit sharing has a lot of pluses, but its minus is it's subject to stock market performance and the company's experience, and they are unpredictable."[19] For example, if the company does not make sufficient profits for several years, employees may not benefit from the plan. This may be a special problem when employees have become accustomed to receiving added compensation from profit sharing.

Employee stock ownership plan. *A companywide incentive plan whereby the company provides its employees with common stock* is called an **employee stock ownership plan (ESOP).** Currently, company contributions to ESOPs are tax deductible expenses.

Many of the benefits of profit sharing plans have also been cited for ESOPs. Specifically, ESOP advocates have suggested that employees obtain a stake in the business and become more closely identified with the firm — a relationship that theoretically increases motivation. Also, employees may acquire a second income without increasing the firm's compensation costs. Finally, from a company viewpoint, capital may be raised for expansion.[20]

[18]J. D. Dunn and Frank M. Rachel, *Salary Administration: Total Compensation Systems.* New York: McGraw-Hill, 1971, pp. 261–262.

[19]Kathryn McIntyre Roberts, "Sears, Xerox Acts Spotlight Decline in Profit Sharing," *Business Insurance*, May 2, 1977, p. 34.

[20]Donald E. Sullivan, "ESOP's: Panacea or Placebo?" *California Management Review* 20 (Fall 1977): 55–56.

473

**Chapter 13
Benefits and
Other
Compensation
Issues**

While the potential advantages of ESOPs are impressive, critics point out the dangers of employees having all their eggs in one basket. Employees would be in a vulnerable position should their company fail.

Payroll-based stock ownership plan.   *A special type of ESOP in which stock of a firm is placed into a trust* is called a **payroll-based stock ownership plan (PAYSOP).** In a PAYSOP, the firm's contributions are related to its payroll and employees receive allocations in proportion to their pay. Employees do not pay tax on PAYSOP allocations — which are limited to $100,000 — until they remove the funds. This would occur upon retirement, death, or leaving the organization. PAYSOPs are appealing to businesses because of tax concessions granted by the Economic Recovery Tax Act of 1981 and the general concern about the increasing direct costs of benefits in compensation packages.[21]

The Scanlon plan.   The **Scanlon plan** is *a cost savings plan which, like profit sharing, features participation by the firm's employees.*[22] The plan was developed by Joseph Scanlon in 1937, and it continues to be a successful approach to group incentive, especially in smaller plants. The financial reward provided to employees is based on savings in labor cost, resulting largely from employee suggestions. These suggestions are evaluated by employee–management committees. Calculation of the savings is based on a ratio of payroll costs to the sales value of what that payroll produces. If the company is able to reduce its payroll costs through increased efficiency in operation, the savings are shared with the employees. In reflecting on his company's experience with the Scanlon plan, George Sherman (vice president of human resources for Midland-Ross) stated: "American workers want and, in my judgement, are entitled to a piece of the action when, through their own efforts and ingenuity, they are able to help the company do better."[23]

COMPENSATION FOR MANAGERS

Management performance has a significant impact on a firm's success and survival. For this reason, it is vital for organizations to provide appropriate compensation for their managers. Managerial efficiency and the firm's welfare are closely related. Therefore it is not unusual for a large portion of management compensation — especially for top executives — to be linked to the company's performance.

[21]"Popularity Growing in Use of PAYSOPS," *Pension World* 20 (June 1984): 14.

[22]Dunn and Rachel, *Salary Administration*, p. 253.

[23]"Scanlon Plan Puts Everyone on the Team," *Iron Age* 218 (August 9, 1976): 18.

DETERMINATION OF MANAGERIAL COMPENSATION

A recent survey of "*Fortune 200*" companies indicated that these firms prefer to relate salary growth for the highest level executives to overall corporate performance. For the next management tier, an integration of overall corporate performance with market rates and internal considerations is desired. For lower level managers, the tendency is to determine salaries on the basis of market rates, internal pay relationships, and individual performance.[24] As a generalization, the higher the managerial position, the greater the flexibility managers have in designing their jobs. Management jobs are often difficult to define because of their complexity. And, when they are defined, they are often described in terms of anticipated results rather than tasks or how the work is accomplished. One management consultant has suggested the "entrepreneurial approach," or market pricing, to determine managerial compensation.[25] In this approach, organizations use compensation survey data to determine pay levels for a representative group of jobs. These data may be obtained from such sources as the American Management Association and Sibson & Company, Inc. Some organizations also adapt point and factor comparison methods of job evaluation to determine the relative value of management jobs.

THE HAY GUIDE CHART–PROFILE METHOD

The Hay method has long been an extremely popular compensation approach, and today more than 2000 firms throughout the world use it.[26] This method enables firms to determine the relative difficulty and importance of jobs using these factors: know-how, problem solving, accountability, and, where appropriate, working conditions. Point values are assigned to these factors to determine the final point profile for any job.

The popularity of the Hay method provides it with an important advantage by facilitating comparison of jobs within one firm with those of others. Thus the plan serves not only to permit determination of internal equity — by ascertaining relative worth within the firm — but external equity as well.[27]

TYPES OF MANAGERIAL COMPENSATION

Managers typically prefer to receive the bulk of their compensation in the form of salary. Salary is especially important because it determines their

---

[24]James T. Brinks, APD, "Executive Compensation: Crossroads of the '80s," *Personnel Administrator* 26 (December 1981): 23.

[25]Robert E. Sibson, *Compensation* New York: AMACOM, A Division of American Management Associations, 1974, p. 141.

[26]Richard I. Henderson, *Compensation Management: Rewarding Performance*, 4th ed. Reston, Va.: Reston, 1979, p. 222.

[27]Ibid., p. 225.

475

Chapter 13
Benefits and
Other
Compensation
Issues

standard of living. It also provides the basis for other forms of compensation. For example, an executive might receive life insurance protection at the rate of two and a half times salary. In addition, bonus payments may be related to the executive's salary. These payments supplement the salary; they may be paid on a current or deferred basis. Bonuses are paid by organizations whose managers believe in their incentive value. According to one compensation expert, "average bonus levels range from 80 percent of base salary at the top to 20 percent for the lowest level participant."[28]

The stock option is another form of compensation that is designed to integrate the interests of management with the organization. Although various types of plans exist, the typical **stock option plan** *gives the manager the option to buy a specified amount of stock in the future at or below the current market price.* This form of compensation is advantageous when stock prices are rising. However, there are potential disadvantages to stock option plans. A manager may feel uncomfortable investing money in the same organization in which he or she is building a career. As with profit sharing, this method of compensation is popular when a firm is successful. But, during periods of decline when stock prices fall, the participants may become disenchanted.

Deferred compensation — *pay that is held in trust for a manager until retirement* — is often used to provide a delayed reward for executives. This permits them to receive income when it is taxed at a lower rate.

An interesting, although extreme, case of executive compensation occurred a number of years ago. A large electronics firm allegedly lured a brilliant executive away from a competitor by offering him virtually everything but the "kitchen sink." It was contended that the following inducements were offered: an annual salary of $120,000 (an increase of $30,000), an immediate payment of $250,000 or equivalent stock options, an option to buy 90,000 shares of company stock, and a loan at no interest for ten years of $5.4 million with which to exercise his stock option.[29]

Perquisites (perks) are *any special benefits provided by a firm to an executive that are designed to give the executive something extra.*[30] In addition to status, these benefits provide rewards that either are not considered as earned income or are taxed at a lower level. Some of the more common perks are:

- Company-provided car for both business and personal use.
- Accessible, no cost, parking.
- Limousine service — the chauffeur may also serve as a bodyguard.
- Kidnap and ransom protection.

[28]Belcher, *Compensation Administration*, p. 545.

[29]Reprinted with permission from *Electronics*, August 19, 1968, p. 47. Copyright © by McGraw-Hill, 1968. All rights reserved.

[30]Karen M. Evans, "The Power of Perquisites," *Personnel Administrator* 29 (May 1984): 45.

- Tax assistance and financial counseling.
- Use of company plane and yacht.
- Membership in country clubs.
- Special dining room facilities.
- Season tickets to entertainment and sporting events.
- Use of company credit card.
- College tuition reimbursement for children.[31]

A **"golden parachute" contract** is *an executive perquisite provided for the purpose of protecting executives in the event their firm is acquired by another.* The executive, if negatively affected, may receive maximum permissible payouts under both short- and long-term incentive plans.[32]

Perquisites extend a firm's benefit program on an individual basis. They seem to be more popular in smaller firms than in major organizations.[33]

Some people criticize the high level of executive pay and benefits. In fact, news stories about executives who receive huge pay increases command a great deal of attention. This is especially true when the economy is faring poorly. In response to the question "Are executives overpaid?" the answer is difficult if not impossible to determine. A compensation expert, Robert Sibson, suggests that while there is some overpayment for mediocrity, there is at least an equivalent underpayment for high levels of business performance. He also believes that current executive pay levels show only a slight increase over previous years.[34] It should be remembered that a firm's success depends on executives who possess the ability to utilize the organization's resources effectively. When this is taken into consideration, executive compensation may be better understood.

Some of the special compensation features available for managers apply to other exempt employees in an organization, especially professional employees.

COMPENSATION FOR PROFESSIONALS

People in professional jobs are initially compensated primarily for the knowledge they bring to the organization. Because of this, the administration of compensation programs for professionals is somewhat different than for managers. Many professional employees eventually become managers. For those who do not desire this form of career progression, some organizations have created a dual track of compensation. The dual track provides

---

[31]Henderson, *Compensation Management*, pp. 463–464.

[32]Graef S. Crystal, "Outlook on Compensation and Benefits: To the Rescue of Pay for Performance," *Personnel* 62 (January 1985): 8.

[33]Bruce R. Ellig, "Perquisites: The Intrinsic Form of Pay," *Personnel* 58 (January–February 1981): 23–31.

[34]"In Practice: Overpaying Execs," *Training and Development Journal* 39 (April 1985): 10.

a separate pay structure for professionals, which may overlap a portion of the managerial pay structure. It is indeed a sad situation when professionals who are performing exceptionally well are required to accept management positions in order to increase their compensation. For instance, in some organizations, the only way to increase professionals' pay is to promote them into management. However, a real problem is created when it is discovered that a highly competent and effective professional is not able to perform satisfactorily as a manager.

The professional career curve, shown in Figure 13–4, is an approach that has been developed especially for determining compensation for professional jobs. In preparing career curves, it is assumed that the more experience an individual has, the higher the earnings should be. However, as you can see, career curves may be drawn to reflect varying performance levels. In this particular field a professional employee who has twenty years' experience and performs at a level 10 percent above the average (average = 100) would presumably earn nearly $3200 per month. On the other hand, a person with the same experience but performing only at the 80 percent level would be assumed to earn about $2400 dollars a month.

477

Chapter 13
Benefits and
Other
Compensation
Issues

Figure 13–4. Professional career curves. Source: Adapted, by permission of the publishers from Robert E. Sibson, *Compensation: A Complete Revision of Wages and Salaries.* New York: AMACOM, a division of American Management Associations, 1978.

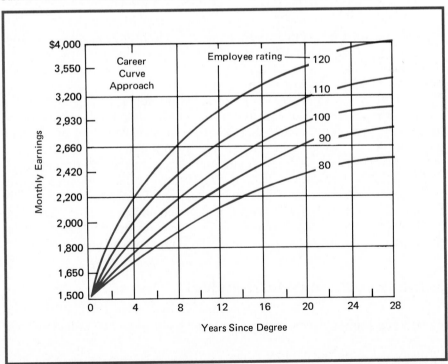

Some type of performance appraisal system is obviously necessary in order to make these productivity distinctions.

SALES COMPENSATION

Because compensation programs for sales employees comprise a unique set of considerations, some organizations assign this responsibility to the sales staff rather than to Personnel. Still, many general compensation practices also apply to sales jobs. For example, job content, relative job worth, and job market value should be determined.

The straight salary approach is at one extreme in sales compensation. This means that salespersons receive a fixed salary regardless of their sales levels. Organizations use this method primarily when continued product service after the sale is stressed.[35] For instance, many sales representatives who deal largely with the federal government are compensated in this manner. At the other extreme, the person whose pay is totally determined as a percentage of sales is on straight commission. An example of a salesperson in this category might be door-to-door salespersons. Richard H. Swanson, director of compensation for General Mills, Inc., has stated that "The only 'pure' nondeferred compensation plan is the 100 percent sales commission plan. This type of pay is probably the most effective one to motivate salespeople. Unfortunately, straight commission is inappropriate for most of the selling that is done today."

Between these extremes, there are endless combinations of part salary–part commission. The possibilities increase when various types of bonuses are added to the basic compensation package. The emphasis given to either commission or salary depends on several factors, including the organization's philosophy toward service, the nature of the product, and the time period required for closing a sale.

In addition to salary, commissions, and bonuses, salespersons often receive other forms of compensation that are intended to serve as added incentives. Sales contests that offer television sets, refrigerators, or expense-paid vacations to exotic locations are not uncommon.

If any one feature sets sales compensation apart from other programs, it is the emphasis placed on incentives. The nature of sales work often simplifies the problem of determining individual output. Sales volume can usually be related to specific individuals, a situation that encourages payment of incentive compensation. Also, experience in sales compensation practices over the years has supported the concept of relating rewards to performance.

NONFINANCIAL COMPENSATION

In recent years, most Americans have been able to satisfy their basic physiological and safety needs, so their interests have tended to shift somewhat

---

[35]Sibson, *Compensation*, p. 141.

away from money as the primary form of compensation. As employees receive sufficient cash to provide for basic necessities (and then stereoes and color televisions), they tend to desire rewards that will satisfy higher order needs. Specifically, social, ego, and self-actualization needs are becoming more important. These needs may be satisfied through the job that employees are given to perform and the environment of that job. The basic nonfinancial elements of the total compensation package are illustrated in Figure 13–5.

479

**Chapter 13
Benefits and
Other
Compensation
Issues**

THE JOB

A major human resource management goal is to satisfactorily match job requirements and employee abilities and aspirations. Although the task of job

Figure 13–5. Nonfinancial elements of a total compensation program.

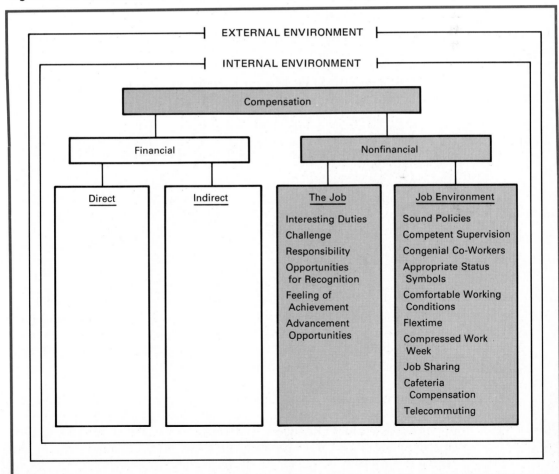

design is typically performed by other organizational units, personnel does have a responsibility in recruiting, selecting, and placing individuals in those jobs. A good case could even be made for directly involving Personnel in the task of job design. Having a "good" job has the potential for becoming an important part of nonfinancial compensation. Because of this, a number of organizations have become actively engaged in job enrichment, as we discussed in chapter 9.

The job is a central issue in many theories of motivation, and we believe that it is also a vital part of a total compensation program. Employees may receive important rewards by performing meaningful jobs. While this type of reward is intrinsic in nature, a firm's management determines job content. Therefore the job's compensation possibilities are to a degree under the organization's control. The selection and placement processes are extremely important in this context. A job that is challenging to one person may be quite boring to another.

THE JOB ENVIRONMENT

The job's environment is also an important part of nonfinancial compensation. The significance of a warm, supportive organizational culture was discussed in chapter 9. While organizations have often paid mere lip service to making jobs more rewarding, a concerted effort has frequently been made to improve many of the factors in the environment that surround the job.

Sound policies.   Personnel policies expressing management's sincerity in its employee relationships can serve as positive rewards. For example, policies and practices related to providing stable employment reflect a company's respect for its human resources. IBM demonstrates this idea. In almost forty years, despite severe recessions and dramatic technological changes, no IBM employee has been laid off because of economic necessity. If a firm's policies show respect — rather than disrespect, fear, doubt, or lack of confidence — the result can be rewarding to both the employees and the organization.

Competent supervision.   Nothing in organizational life can be so demoralizing to employees as to have an incompetent supervisor. Successful organizations have continuing programs that emphasize supervisory and executive development. These programs exist to ensure insofar as possible the continuity of sound leadership and management.

Congenial co-workers.   Although a few individuals in this world may be quite self-sufficient and prefer to be left alone, this attitude is not prevalent. Most of us possess in varying degrees a desire to be accepted by our work group. This acceptance helps us to satisfy basic social needs. Management, in its staffing efforts, should be concerned with developing compatible work groups.

481

Chapter 13
Benefits and
Other
Compensation
Issues

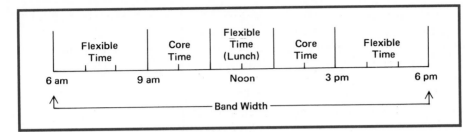

Figure 13–6. An illustration of flextime.

Appropriate status symbols.   Employees may engage in activities such as comparing the size of their offices with those of peers or measuring the distance from their offices to the chief executive's. When this extreme behavior occurs, it is time to examine the firm's policy regarding status symbols. While these symbols may be appropriate in achieving certain purposes — such as providing incentives for employees to progress in the firm — care must be taken to ensure that they are not overemphasized. However, status symbols (such as office size, the size and quality of the desk, other office furnishings, floor covering, office location, title, parking space, or make of company car) can serve as compensation because they often appeal to employees' ego needs. Some organizations tend to minimize the use of status symbols, but other firms use them liberally. A critical point to consider in providing such rewards is that they be provided equitably.

Comfortable working conditions.   Good working conditions are for the most part taken for granted in many organizations today. However, a brief return to nonair-conditioned offices would quickly remind us of their importance. The view that working conditions can be a form of compensation is reinforced by pay plans that increase the financial reward for jobs with relatively poor working conditions.

Flextime.   *The practice of permitting employees to choose, with certain limitations, their own working hours* is referred to as **flextime.** It was introduced in Germany in the late 1960s and has since spread throughout Europe and the United States. In a flextime system, employees work the same number of hours per day as they do on a standard schedule. However, they are permitted to work these hours within what is called a band width, which is the maximum length of the work day (see Figure 13–6). Core time is that part of the day when all employees must be present. Flexible time is the time period within which employees may vary their schedules.[36] A typical schedule per-

[36]Tim Burt, "Making the Most of Time with Flexible Working Hours," *Personnel Executive* 1 (March 1982): 37.

mits employees to begin work between 6:00 A.M. and 9:00 A.M. and complete their workday between 3:00 P.M. and 6:00 P.M.

Perhaps flextime's most important feature is that it allows employees to schedule their time to minimize conflicts between personal needs and job requirements. This advantage would be quite attractive to individuals such as Liz Brown, who have scheduling problems. She now has the opportunity to arrive at work later, after dropping her children off at school. Personal needs can be accommodated without employees resorting to the use of sick leave. Flextime also permits employees to work at hours when they feel they can function best. It caters to those who are early risers or those who prefer to work later in the day. The public also seems to reap benefits from flextime. Transportation services, recreational facilities, medical clinics, and other services can be better utilized as a result of reduced competition for service at conventional peak times.

Flextime is not suitable for all types of organizations. Its use may be severely limited in assembly-line operations and companies utilizing multiple shifts. However, flextime seems feasible in a number of situations. Many organizations that use it feel that both employees and employers benefit. Clearly, the use of plans such as flextime are compatible with desires of employees (especially younger ones) to participate in decisions that affect their work.

The compressed work week. *Any arrangement of work hours that permits employees to fulfill their work obligation in fewer days than the typical five-day work week* is referred to as the **compressed work week.** The most common approach to the compressed work week has been four ten-hour days. Working under this arrangement, some employees have reported an increase in job satisfaction. In addition, the compressed work week offers them the potential for better use of leisure time for family life, personal business, and recreation.[37] Employers in some instances have cited advantages such as increased productivity and reduced turnover and absenteeism.

On the other hand, problems have been encountered in such areas as work scheduling and employee fatigue. In some cases, these problems have resulted in lower quality products and reduced customer service. Some firms have reverted to the conventional five-day week. It seems clear that, overall, acceptance of the compressed work week is not as clear-cut as acceptance of flextime.

Job sharing. A relatively new approach to work — job sharing — is attractive to people who wish to work fewer than forty hours per week. In **job sharing**, *two part-time people split the duties of one job in some agreed on manner and are paid according to their contributions.* From the employer's view-

---

[37]Simcha Ronen and Sophia B. Primps, "The Compressed Work Week as Organizational Change: Behavioral and Attitudinal Outcomes," *Academy of Management Review* 6 (January 1981): 61.

483

**Chapter 13
Benefits and
Other
Compensation
Issues**

point, compensation is paid for only one job, but creativity is obtained from two employees. The total financial compensation cost may be greater because of the additional benefits provided; however, this expense may be offset by increased productivity. Job sharing may be especially attractive to individuals who have substantial family responsibilities and to older workers who wish to move gradually into retirement.

Flexible compensation (cafeteria compensation).   **Flexible compensation plans** *permit employees to choose from among many alternatives how their financial compensation will be allocated.* They are given considerable latitude in determining how much of the financial compensation will be taken in the form of salary, life insurance, and pension contributions, and so on. Cafeteria plans permit flexibility in allowing each employee to determine the compensation package which would best satisfy his or her particular needs.

The rationale behind cafeteria plans is that employees have individual needs and preferences. A sixty-year-old man would probably not desire maternity benefits in an insurance plan. At the same time, a twenty-five year old woman who regularly jogs six miles each day might not place a high value on parking facilities located near the firm's entrance. Some of the possible compensation vehicles utilized in a cafeteria approach are shown in Table 13–2.

Obviously, organizations cannot permit employees to select the forms of all their financial compensation as they choose. The mandatory benefits required by law must be provided. Also, one compensation expert believes that "It is usually best to mandatorily give each employee a basic 'core' of coverage — especially in the medical insurance area."[38] Some guidelines would likely be helpful for most employees in the long run. However, the freedom to select highly desired benefits would seem to maximize the value of an individual's compensation. Involvement in the determination of tailored compensation plans should also effectively communicate the cost of benefits to employees.

TRW, Inc., has had a flexible compensation program since 1974. The program was inspired by a general belief that employees should have more flexibility and self-determination in shaping their compensation package. The plan developed at TRW is based on these principles:

- The core plan will be available to each employee at the company's expense.
- Plans that are better, but more costly than the current plan, will be developed and made available at the employee's expense.
- Plans that provide less coverage, and are less costly than the current plan, will be developed and an employee given credit toward other benefits or given the difference in cash.

[38]David J. Thomsen, "Introducing Cafeteria Compensation in Your Company," *Personnel Journal* 56 (March 1977): 130.

Table 13–2. Compensation vehicles utilized in a cafeteria compensation approach

Accidental death, dismemberment insurance
Birthdays (vacation)
Bonus eligibility
Business and professional memberships
Cash profit sharing
Club memberships
Commissions
Company medical assistance
Company-provided automobile
Company-provided housing
Company-provided or subsidized travel
Day care centers
Deferred bonus
Deferred compensation plan
Deferred profit sharing
Dental and eye care insurance
Discount on company products
Education costs
Educational activities (time off)
Employment contract
Executive dining room
Free checking account
Free or subsidized lunches
Group automobile insurance
Group homeowners insurance
Group life insurance
Health maintenance organization fees
Holidays (extra)
Home health care
Hospital-surgical-medical insurance
Incentive growth fund
Interest-free loans
Layoff pay (S.U.B.)
Legal, estate-planning, and other professional assistance
Loans of company equipment
Long-term disability benefit
Matching educational donations
Nurseries
Nursing home care
Opportunity for travel

Outside medical services
Paid attendance at business, professional, and other outside meetings
Parking facilities
Pension
Personal accident insurance
Personal counseling
Personal credit cards
Personal expense accounts
Physical examinations
Political activities (time off)
Price discount plan
Private office
Professional activities
Psychiatric services
Recreation facilities
Resort facilities
Retirement gratuity
Sabbatical leaves
Salary
Salary continuation
Savings plan
Scholarships for dependents
Severance pay
Shorter or flexible work week
Sickness and accident insurance
Social Security
Social service sabbaticals
Split-dollar life insurance
State disability plans
Stock appreciation rights
Stock bonus plan
Stock options plan (qualified, nonqualified, tandem)
Stock purchase plan
Survivors benefits
Tax assistance
Title
Training programs
Vacations
Wages
Weekly indemnity insurance

Source: "Introducing Cafeteria Compensation in Your Company," by David J. Thomsen. Reprinted with permission *Personnel Journal* Copyright March 1977.

485

Chapter 13
Benefits and
Other
Compensation
Issues

- The core plan will be reviewed annually and will be maintained at a competitive level.
- Additional choices will be added as experience is gained and as new elements of the total compensation package can be defined on a choice basis.

Choices in the current plan include health care, hospital, surgical, maternity, supplemental accident, and major medical benefits. Future possibilities for expanded areas of choice are additional vacation, retirement supplement, group auto and home owners' insurance, and long-term disability compensation.

In spite of new legislative restrictions, the number of flexible compensation programs are increasing. Such plans provide substantial advantages for both employer and employee.[39] For example, the employer can:

- Improve its competitive position in the marketplace by appealing to individual needs.
- Provide a degree of cost control by shifting a portion of the costs to employees — yet, generally in ways that provide them with tax savings.
- Make employees more aware of the value of their compensation.
- Limit contributions to benefits programs without alienating employees.

Advantages to employees that may be highly valued include:

- Having greater control over a significant aspect of their employment.
- Being able to save money by paying a portion of benefit costs with tax-deferred dollars.

Telecommuting.   **Telecommuting** is *an approach to work that permits employees to work at home.* In keeping with this concept and to combat the steady increase in employment costs, Control Data Corporation (CDC) had developed a program it calls HOMEWORK. This innovative approach is a home-based training and employment program for persons seeking a nontraditional work environment.

Using a cathode ray tube (CRT) located in the employee's home and connected by telephone to CDC's computer network, both training and job duties are carried out without reduction in efficiency and quality. An example of a HOMEWORK job is that of business application programmer. Initially, HOMEWORK was available only to a few severely disabled employees. It has now been expanded, and the program has great potential for employees who have no disability. Additional HOMEWORK programs are being developed by CDC that have wide-ranging implications for other

[39]Susan J. Velleman, "Flexible Benefit Packages that Satisfy Employees and the IRS," *Personnel* 62 (March 1985): 33.

employers in both the private and public sectors. The following advantages have been cited for both employee and employer:

- Permits effective use of human resources.
- Eliminates the need for office space.
- Provides flexible working hours.
- Eliminates costs associated with travel to and from work.
- Enhances intellectual functioning.
- Helps establish strong bonds and company loyalty.
- Permits a higher level of self-care for severely disabled employees.
- Reduces costs of health care (CDC's costs decreased 50–75 percent for most of its participants).
- Increases employees' self-concept and confidence levels.
- Provides a means for reentering a traditional work environment.

It has been predicted that programs such as the CDC's HOMEWORK will involve as many as 15 million workers by the mid-1990s.[40] Ties between employees and their firms may be weakened, and successful programs will require a higher degree of trust between employees and their supervisors. However, one thing seems certain: The size of the work force should expand with the increased utilization of handicapped workers and workers with small children.

SUMMARY

Benefits include all financial rewards that generally are not paid directly to the employee. Benefits are provided to employees because of their membership in an organization. Benefits required by law include: Social Security, unemployment compensation, and workers' compensation. There seems to be an endless number of benefits provided voluntarily by organizations. These benefits may be classified as follows: (1) payment for time not worked; (2) employee health and security benefits; (3) service to employees; and (4) premium pay.

Compensation is most often determined by how much time an employee spends at work. However, compensation that encourages organizations to relate pay to productivity is referred to as incentive compensation. Its purpose is to encourage greater productivity in individuals and work groups. The straight piecework plan and the standard hour plan are the most commonly used individual plans. Group incentive plans tend to foster teamwork. Companywide group incentive plans include: profit sharing, employee stock ownership, and the Scanlon plan.

Managerial efficiency and the firm's welfare are closely related. Therefore it is not unusual for a large portion of management compensation —

---

[40]"If Home Is Where the Heart Is,' *Business Week*, May 3, 1982, p. 66.

especially for top executives — to be linked to the company's performance. Managers typically prefer to receive the bulk of their compensation in the form of salary because it determines their standard of living. Salary also provides the basis for indirect compensation such as life insurance. Other forms of compensation designed to integrate the interest of management with the organization include bonuses, stock option plans, deferred compensation, and perks.

487

Chapter 13
Benefits and
Other
Compensation
Issues

People in professional jobs are compensated primarily for the knowledge they bring to the organization. Because of this, the administration of compensation programs for professionals is somewhat different than for managers. Because compensation programs for sales employees constitute a unique set of considerations, some organizations assign this responsibility to the sales staff rather than to Personnel. In addition to salary, commissions, and bonuses, salespersons often receive other forms of compensation that are intended to serve as added incentives.

As employees receive sufficient cash to provide for basic necessities, they tend to desire rewards that will satisfy higher order needs. Specifically, social, ego, and self-actualization needs become more important. These needs may be satisfied through the job that employees are given to perform and the environment of that job.

QUESTIONS FOR REVIEW

1. Define *benefits*. What are the general purposes of benefits?
2. Describe the benefits that are required by law.
3. What are the basic categories of voluntary benefits? Give an example of each type of benefit.
4. Distinguish among overtime pay, hazard pay, and shift differential pay.
5. What is meant by the term *incentive compensation*? When would an individual incentive plan, as opposed to a group incentive plan, be used?
6. Define the following terms:
   (a) Straight piecework
   (b) Standard hour plan
   (c) Profit sharing
   (d) Employee stock ownership plan
   (e) Scanlon plan
7. What are major determinants of compensation for managers? List and define the primary types of managerial compensation.
8. Why are nonfinancial compensation considerations becoming such a major part of an individual's pay?
9. What are some of the basic types of nonfinancial compensation?

TERMS FOR REVIEW

Benefits
Utilization review
Wellness
Premium pay

Hazard pay
Incentive compensation
Straight piecework plan
Standard hour plan

Profit sharing
Employee stock ownership plan (ESOP)
Payroll-based stock ownership plan
(PAYSOP)
Scanlon plan
Stock option plan
Deferred compensation

Perquisites (perks)
"Golden parachute" contract
Flextime
Compressed work week
Job sharing
Flexible compensation plans
Telecommuting

Incident 1

A number of years ago Electrojet Corporation, of Atlanta, Georgia, implemented a comprehensive profit-sharing plan. The company manufactures a group of patented jet engine components, which it sells to companies such as Boeing, Lockheed, and some European companies. The decision to share profits was made after several years of rapidly increasing sales and profits. The decision was based largely on an attitude survey of the employees at Electrojet, which showed that they strongly preferred profit sharing over other fringe benefits.

The compensation plan at Electrojet provides for wages before profit distributions that are about 20 percent below wage levels for similar jobs in Atlanta. Half of company profits are paid out each quarter as a fixed percentage of employee wages. Over the past few years distributed profits have averaged more than 50 percent of base wages. Because of the high total wages, Electrojet has been a popular employer and has been able to take its pick from a long waiting list of applicants.

Other benefits have been kept to a minimum at Electrojet. There is no retirement plan and a very limited medical plan designed to cover catastrophic illnesses only.

The recession of 1981–1982 hit the airline industry especially hard. Profits were down for all major airlines and one, Braniff, even declared bankruptcy. As a result, aircraft sales were greatly depressed. Few new orders were received by the manufacturers and many existing orders were canceled or scaled back. As a supplier to the aircraft manufacturing industry, Electrojet Corporation's sales plummeted.

The profit-sharing bonus for 1981 was only about 25 percent of base wages. Profits declined further for the first two quarters of 1982. By mid-year, it was clear that the company would be in the red for the entire second half. A board meeting was called in late August to discuss the profit-sharing program. One director made it known that he felt the company should drop profit sharing. The personnel director, Vince Harwood, was asked to sit in at the board meeting and to make a presentation suggesting what the company should do about compensation.

QUESTIONS

1. Evaluate the compensation plan at Electrojet.
2. If you were Mr. Harwood, what would you recommend for the short term? For the long term?

Incident 2

Wayne McGraw greeted Robert Peters, his next interviewee, warmly. Robert had an excellent academic record and appeared to be just the kind of person Wayne's company, Beco Electric, was seeking. Wayne is the university recruiter for Beco and had already interviewed six graduating seniors at Centenary College.

Based on the application form, Robert appeared to be the most promising candidate to be interviewed that day. He was twenty-two years old. He had a 3.6 overall grade point average and a 4.0 in his major field, industrial management. He was the vice president of the Student Government Association and was activities chairman for Kappa Alpha Psi, a social fraternity. The reference letters in Robert's file revealed that he was both very active socially and a rather intense and serious student. One of the letters, from Robert's employer the previous summer, expressed satisfaction with Robert's work habits.

Wayne knew that discussion of pay could be an important part of the recruiting interview. But he did not know which aspects of Beco's compensation and benefits program would appeal most to Robert. The company has an excellent profit-sharing plan, although 80 percent of profit distributions are deferred and included in each employee's retirement account. Health benefits are also good. The company's medical and dental plan pays almost 100 percent of costs. A company cafeteria provides meals at about 70 percent of outside prices, although few managers take advantage of this. Employees get one week of paid vacation after the first year and two weeks after ten years with the company. In addition, there are twelve paid holidays each year. Finally, the company encourages advanced educational efforts, paying for tuition and books in full and often allowing time off to attend classes during the day.

QUESTIONS

1. What aspect of Beco's compensation and benefits program are likely to appeal to Robert? Explain.
2. Is the total compensation package likely to be attractive to Robert? Why? Why not?

REFERENCES

Adamache, K. W. "Fringe Benefits: To Tax or Not to Tax?" *National Tax Journal* 38 (March 1985): 47–64.

Akerlof, G. A. "Gift Exchange and Efficiency–Wage Theory: Four Views." *The American Economic Review* 74 (May 1984): 79–83.

Applebaum, Stephen H. and Millard, John B. "Engineering a Compensation Program to Fit the Individual Not the Job." *Personnel Journal* 55 (March 1976): 121–124.

Aschkenasy, J. "Erlenborn Eyes Newly Proposed Taxation of Employee Benefits." *National Underwriter (Life and Health Insurance Edition)* 89 (February 23, 1985): 2.

Bacas, H. "Passing the Buck on Benefits." *Nation's Business* 73 (February 1985): 18–21.

Belcher, David W. *Compensation Administration.* Englewood Cliffs, N.J.: Prentice-Hall, 1974.

"Benefits Important in Costs of Hiring Elderly (Senate Special Committee on Aging Study)." *Employee Benefit Plan Review* 39 (March 1985): 13–16.

Breakwell, Barbara. "Profit-Sharing Schemes Under the New Rules." *Accountancy* 91 (July 1980): 107–109.

Brinks, J. T. "Executive Compensation: Crossroads of the '80s" *Personnel Administrator* 26 (December 1981): 23–26+.

Brooks. L. D. et al. "How Profitable are Employee Stock Ownership Plans?" *Financial Executive* 50 (May 1982): 32–34.

Burt, Tim. "Making the Most of Time with Flexible Working Hours." *Personnel Executive* (March 1982): 37–43.

Bushardt, S. C. and Fowler, A. R. "Compensation and Benefits: Today's Dilemma in Motivation." *Personnel Administrator* 27 (April 1982): 23–26.

Chen, Yung-Ping. "The Growth of Fringe Benefits: Implications for Social Security." *Monthly Labor Review* (November 1981): 3–8.

Cockrum, Robert B. "Has the Time Come for Employee Cafeteria Plans?" *Personnel Administrator* 28 (July 1982): 66–72.

Collins, S. R. "Incentive Programs: Pros and Cons." *Personnel Journal* 60 (July 1981): 571–575.

Coltrin, S. A. and Barendse, B. D. "Is Your Organization a Good Candidate for Flextime?" *Personnel Journal* 60 (September 1981): 712–715.

"Communications as the Marketing of Benefits." *Benefits Plan Review* 39 (March 1985): 79+.

Compflash: News Developments in Employee Compensation and Benefits. New York: AMACOM, a division of American Management Associations, 1981.

Cook, Frederic W. "Long-Term Incentives for Management, Part 1: An Overview." *Compensation Review* 12 (Second Quarter 1980): 15+.

Cooper, G. A. "An Actuary's View of Benefits in the Future." *Risk Management* 32 (March 1985): 34–36+.

Crowder, Robert H., Jr. "The Four-day, Ten-hour Workweek." *Personnel Journal* 61 (January 1981): 26+.

Crystal, Graef S. "Outlook on Compensation and Benefits: To the Rescue of Pay for Performance." *Personnel* 62 (January 1985): 8.

Cumming, Charles M. "Executive Pay and Its New Wrinkles." *Best's Review* 82 (November 1981): 22+.

Curry, Talmer E., Jr. and Haerer, Deane N. "The Positive Impact of Flextime on Employee Relations." *Personnel Administrator* 26 (February 1981): 62–66.

"Defensive Design Has Held Basic Need for Employee Benefit Plans in 1985." *Journal of Accountancy* 159 (March 1985): 23+.

Ellig, Bruce R. "Perquisites, The Intrinsic Form of Pay." *Personnel* 58 (January–February 1981): 23–31.

"Employee Stock Plans: Far Short of Ideal." *Office* 92 (September 1980): 72.

Evans, Karen M. "The Power of Perquisites." *Personnel Administrator* 29 (May 1984): 45.

Fannin, Rebecca A. "American Can Employees Test New Flexible Benefits Programs." *Business Insurance* 12 (March 6, 1978): 1.

Foegen, J. H. "Basing Benefits on Employee Performance." *Administrative Management* 42 (November 1981): 60–63.

Freedmand, S. M. et al. "Compensation Program: Balancing Organizational and Employee Needs." *Compensation Review* 14 (1982): 47–53.

"GAO Study Reveals ESOPs May Adversely Affect Participants." *The Journal of Taxation* 53 (October 1980): 222.

Geisel, J. "Benefit Cost Increases Starting to Slow." *Business Insurance* 19 (January 14, 1985): 1+.

Hamilton, E. K. "How to Set Up Flexible Benefits." *Compensation Review* 14 (1981): 68–74.

Hammer, Edson G., Ahmadi, Mohammad, and Ettkin, Laurence P. "Long-term Forecasting of Employee Benefits: An Impossible Task?" *Personnel Administrator* 26 (December 1981): 30–34+.

Haneberg, Ron. "Cash-Deferred Profit Sharing Plans." *Financial Executive* 48 (July 1980): 36–38.

Harkavy, J. and Kahn, H. R. "Senator Packwood Speaks Out on Employee Benefits." *Risk Management* 32 (March 1985): 7.

Jay, Wendy. "Long-Term Incentives for Management, Part 2: What's New in Stock Option and Appreciation Right Plans." *Compensation Review* 12 (1980): 21–33.

Kenny, John B. "Competency Analysis for Trainers: A Model for Professionalization." *Training and Development Journal* 36 (May 1982): 142–148.

Kerr, J. R. "Diversification Strategies and Managerial Rewards: An Empirical Study." *Academy of Management Journal* 28 (March 1985): 155–179.

Lawler, Edward E. III. "New Approaches to Pay: Innovations That Work." *Personnel* 53 (September–October 1976): 11–23.

Lawyer, M. S. and Gourlay, J. G., Jr. "Having Capital Problems? ESOPs May be the Answer." *ABA Banking Journal* 74 (March 1982): 117+.

"Letting Employees Choose Their Own Fringe Benefits." *International Management* 35 (September 1980): 36–38+.

Littrell, Earl K. "Designing a Profit-Sharing Plan for a Service Company." *Management Accounting* 62 (October 1980): 47+.

McLaughlin, D. J. "Reinforcing Corporate Strategy Through Executive Compensation." *Management Review* 70 (October 1981): 8–15.

Milligan, J. W. "ESOP's: Stock Ownership Plans Grant Companies Pension Flexibility." *Business Insurance* 15 (July 1981): 29 + .

Morehart, Thomas B. and O'Connell, John J. "The Risk Manager's Role in Employee Benefits Administration." *Risk Management* 24 (October 1977): 42–46.

Morris, J. R. "Benefit Growth: Back to the Days of Yore." *Nation's Business* 73 (February 1985): 22–23.

"Popularity Growing in Use of PAYSOPS." *Pension World* 20 (June 1984): 14.

"Post-Retirement Benefits Facing Intense Scrutiny (Life and/or Medical Benefits)." *Employee Benefit Plan Review* 39 (February 1985): 22 + .

"Sales Incentives Get the Job Done." *Sales and Marketing Management* 127 (September 1981): 67–120.

Schuster, M. and Flortowski, G. "Wage Incentive Plans and the Fair Labor Standards Act." *Compensation Review* 14 (1982): 34–46.

Schwartz, Jeffrey D. "Maintaining Merit Compensation in a High Inflation Economy."
Personnel Journal 61 (February 1982): 147–152.

"Social Change Spurs Flexible Benefit Plan Growth." *The National Underwriter* 27 (July 3, 1981): 85–88.

"A Spectacular Debunking of Social Security Critics." *Business Week* (September 22, 1980): 25–26.

Thomas, Edward G. "Update on Alternative Work Methods." *Management World* 11 (January 1982): 30–32.

Tinsley, LaVerne C. "Workers' Compensation: Key Legislation in 1981." *Monthly Labor Review* 105 (February 1982): 24–30.

"Travel as an Incentive." *Dun's Business Month* 119 (April 1982): 26–27.

Villeman, S. J. "Flexible Benefit Packages That Satisfy Employees and the IRS." *Personnel* 62 (March 1985): 33–41.

Weitzul, J. B. "Money Talks Sometimes." *Best's Review Life Edition* 82 (January 1982): 86 + .

Yoder, Dale and Heneman, Herbert G., Jr. eds. *ASPA Handbook of Personnel and Industrial Relations: Motivation and Commitment*, Vol. 2. Washington, D.C.: The Bureau of National Affairs, 1975.

Parma Cycle Company: The Pay Plan

At Parma Cycle Company in Parma, Ohio, wage rates for hourly workers are established by a three-year labor–management agreement. The agreement provides for cost-of-living adjustments (COLA) based on changes in the Federal Consumer Price Index. Wage rates vary according to job class and by seniority within each class. For example, a machine operator with two to four years seniority earns $8.75 per hour. With four to eight years seniority the rate increases to $10.60 an hour. A company-paid health plan provides medical and dental care for employees. The company contributes 6½ percent of wages to a retirement plan administered by the machinists union.

Salaried workers at Parma Cycle are paid straight salaries based on a forty-hour work week. For first- and second-level managers and clerical workers, work beyond forty hours in any week is compensated on a pro rata basis. For managers above the second level there is no additional compensation for work after forty hours per week. Cost of living adjustments are applied semiannually to all wages and salaries.

Only in the sales department at Parma is any kind of incentive compensation program in effect. The sales representatives are paid a commission averaging about 2 percent of sales in addition to straight salary. The sales manager assigns the sales representatives to particular territories; they are generally given a choice of territories according to seniority. Once a sales representative has become accustomed to a given territory, however, requests to change are usually turned down. As older sales representatives have left the company some of the younger ones have moved into the better sales areas. This has caused some of the more senior sales representatives to request changes in territory to increase their sales potential. This has been done in a few cases but no consistent policy has been developed.

Parma Cycle Company was building a new plant in Clarksdale, Mississippi in 1986–1987. The new plant was to employ about 600 people, two-thirds the number working at the main plant in Parma, Ohio. About two months before the new plant was scheduled to open, Jesse Heard, the personnel director, was asked to meet with the president to discuss the compensation policies that would be followed in Clarksdale. Jesse knew that Jim Burgess, the president, tended to take a personal hand in matters relating to pay, so he prepared thoroughly for their meeting.

Mr. Burgess had a reputation for getting right to the heart of the matter. "I'm worried about the pay differentials that we are going to have between this plant and the one in Clarksdale," he began. "As I see it, some of the people down there won't be paid half as much as similar workers here." "That's true," said Jesse, "That really is the main reason for the move to Clarksdale. Without the union and with the low wage rates in that area, we will be able to pay just what the market requires. Most of the helpers and trainees will be available, we think, at minimum wage." "How will the pay classifications down there compare to those up here?" asked Mr. Burgess. "Well," said Jesse, "up here we have 'workers' and 'machine operators' and the pay within classes is by seniority. Down there we plan to have helpers/trainees, grades 1 and 2, and machine operators, grades 1, 2, and 3. Seniority won't count. We will promote workers based on the recommendations of their supervisors and their performance evaluation scores."

"I liked the incentive plan when you told me about it before, Jesse," said Mr. Burgess. "Let's go over it again. As I understand it, we are going to take 30 percent of the cost savings below standard and pay it out as semiannual bonuses." "Yes," said Jesse. "An individual's bonus will be a certain percentage of the gross wages paid during that period. But we will multiply that by the person's performance evaluation score." "Will the standard costs be the same as the ones we have here at the Parma plant?" asked Mr. Burgess. "Yes, at first they will," answered Jesse. "But after a time, it will be the average of costs at the two plants."

Mr. Burgess continued, "The last time we talked I think you said that we would save money in Clarksdale on the benefits package too." "Yes," replied Jesse, "For one thing, the tradition in that area is for the company to pay a health insurance premium for a worker and for the worker to pay the portion applicable to any dependants. Also, we won't have a dental plan down there, just medical. Finally, I don't think that we will even have a retirement program for those workers, at least not for a few years." "I think I know the answer," said Mr. Burgess, "but, what about the ones who transfer down from Parma?" "They'll have the same benefits they have here," replied Jesse. "We will continue to cover them under the same insurance plan and guarantee that their wages will keep pace with those of similar workers here at Parma."

QUESTIONS

1. What are the pros and cons of paying workers on the basis of seniority?
2. How do cost-of-living adjustments (COLA) work?
3. Is anything legally wrong with Parma's plan for paying salaried workers? Explain.
4. Are the pay and benefits differentials between the plants likely to create problems? Why? Why not?

Experiencing Human Resource Management

Job Evaluation by "Points"

The following two job descriptions (Figures IV–1 and IV–2) are for two new jobs created at Parma Cycle Company's Parma, Ohio plant. As a personnel specialist you have been asked to evaluate the jobs according to the company's point system. Study the job descriptions carefully and complete a job evaluation matrix (see Figure IV–3) provided for each job. Assume that each job factor has five degrees and compute the point total for each job.

In actual practice you would normally have more information available than just the job descriptions. In this case, though, you must work with what you have. This information will be used to determine the initial job classification, and therefore the pay rate for the job.

QUESTIONS

1. What additional factors would you include in evaluating clerical jobs?

2. What job factors would you include for machine operators at Parma Cycle?

3. How would you change the relative weights assigned to the job factors? Why?

Figure IV–1. Parma Cycle Company's job description: Personnel office receptionist.

Position Title				Position Number
Personnel Office Receptionist				Approval
Division or Staff Department Personnel	Location	Reports to Assistant Person. Dir.		Effective Date
Department or Activity	Section	Point	Grade	Revises

Job Summary

　　　Greets visitors to the Personnel Office; directs them to the appropriate desks. Operates Personnel Office switchboard, with four incoming lines and twelve extensions. Performs miscellaneous clerical work as directed by Assistant Personnel Director.

Nature of Work

1. Welcome visitors to Personnel Office and direct them to appropriate desk or person.

2. Maintain familiarity with all office procedures to facilitate above.

3. Answer incoming calls politely, switching them to the appropriate desk.

4. Perform miscellaneous clerical and administrative work as directed by Assistant Personnel Director.

5. Type outgoing letters and other correspondence as directed by Assistant Personnel Director.

Qualifications

　　　High school education
　　　Pleasing voice
　　　Typing 60 words per minute
　　　Ability to operate PCD 16 switchboard

Position Title				Position Number
Personnel Clerk, II				
				Approval
Division or Staff Department Personnel	Location	Reports To Records Supervisor		Effective Date
Department or Activity	Section	Point	Grade	Revises

Job Summary

Maintain performance evaluation records and miscellaneous clerical work as required.

Nature of Work

1. Every six months, and as required in special cases, distribute about 800 performance evaluation forms along with form memoranda describing how to complete the performance evaluations to the respective supervisors.

2. File completed forms in respective personnel records.

3. Insure timely completion of performance evaluation forms by follow-up memoranda, phone calls, and personal visits to supervisors.

4. Do miscellaneous typing of forms, reports, and records as directed by supervisor.

5. Fill in for personnel office receptionist when required.

Qualifications

High school education, or equivalency certificate
Typing, 50 words per minute
Familiarity with IBM Selectric III typewriter
Score of 50 or better on company filing and records retrieval test

Figure IV–2. Parma Cycle Company's job description: Personnel clerk, II.

Job Factors	Weight	Requirement for each job factor on this job				
		1	2	3	4	5
Reasoning & Creativity	40%					
Physical skill & Coordination	25%					
Strength & Stamina	15%					
Complexity of Duties	20%					

Total Points: [   ]

Figure IV–3. A job evaluation matrix.

Part Five

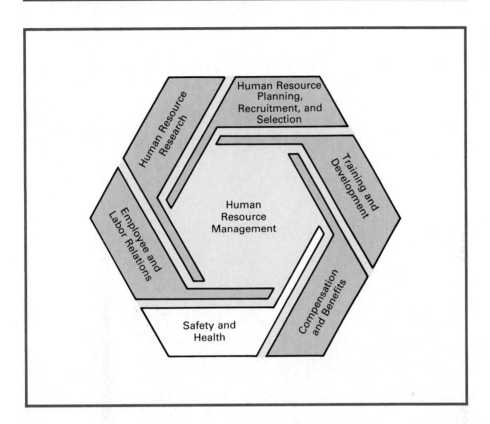

Human Resource Research

Human Resource Planning, Recruitment, and Selection

Training and Development

Human Resource Management

Employee and Labor Relations

Compensation and Benefits

Safety and Health

SAFETY AND HEALTH

CHAPTER OBJECTIVES

1. Describe the nature of the safety and health field and its role in organizations.
2. Describe the Occupational Safety and Health Act and the impact it has had on business operations.
3. State the nature of stress and the importance of stress management in business today.
4. Describe burnout and explain why it is of major concern to management.
5. Identify the various sources of stress.
6. Explain the approaches organizations and individuals take in coping with stress.
7. State the rationale for and the role of physical fitness, alcohol, drug, and employee assistance programs.

Chapter 14

A SAFE AND HEALTHY
WORK ENVIRONMENT

Dionne Martin, safety engineer for Sather Manufacturing, was walking through the plant when she spotted a situation that immediately got her attention. Someone had spilled a large quantity of oil on the floor and had not cleaned it up. Just at that moment, Ron Moore, one of the firm's employees, stepped on the oil. His feet went out from under him and the packages he was carrying scattered everywhere. Ron landed squarely on his back and for a moment did not move. Although he got up slowly, it appeared that Ron was not injured. Dionne was relieved, but became quite disturbed when she realized the many possible consequences of the accident.

Bob Byroms, production foreman for King Electronics, is concerned about the health of one of his best workers, Cecil Weeks. For the past several months Cecil has been relatively ineffective on the job. He has been doing sloppy work and many of his coworkers have complained about his poor disposition. Recently, Bob observed Cecil at his locker during a work break take a bottle from a brown bag and drink from it. The odor on Cecil's breath suggested to Bob the cause of Cecil's changed work habits. Bob believes that Cecil may be an alcoholic. He wonders what should be done.

Dionne and Bob are each involved with but a few of the many critical areas related to employee safety and health. Dionne realizes that safety is a major concern in an organization and that she must constantly work to ensure that accidents such as the one she just witnessed are reduced or eliminated. Bob has just discovered that the poor performance of one of his employees may be caused by a stress-related drinking problem.

In our discussion, **safety** involves *protecting employees from injuries due to work-related accidents*. **Health** refers to *the employees' freedom from physical or emotional illness*. Many people may wonder why Personnel should be concerned with such a wide range of responsibilities. The answer becomes quite clear, however, when you realize that safety and health are a major aspect of human resource management. Problems in these areas can seriously affect productivity. Employee accidents and illnesses can have a dramatic effect on a firm's effectiveness. Although line managers are primarily responsible for safety and health within the firm, Personnel provides needed expertise through its staff assistance. In addition, Personnel is frequently responsible for coordinating and monitoring specific safety and health programs.

The chapter begins with a discussion of the impact of the Occupational Safety and Health Act on today's businesses. Safety and health programs are then discussed. This is followed by a presentation on stress management. Topics included in this section are burnout, physical fitness, alcoholism, drug addiction, and employee assistance programs. Also covered are stress sources and means used to combat stress. The overall purpose of this chapter is to provide you with an understanding of the importance of safety and health in organizations today.

THE OCCUPATIONAL SAFETY AND HEALTH ACT

Industrial safety has, for years, been a major problem that has seemingly resisted solution. The problem's magnitude can best be understood by considering these statistics. During World War II, 292,000 U.S. servicemen were killed in action, and more than 17,000 servicemen lost major limbs. During the same period, approximately 90,000 people were killed in factory accidents; there were approximately 9,000 permanent injuries, 500,000 partial permanent injuries, and 10,000,000 temporary injuries.[1]

Prior to 1971, industrial safety was regulated primarily by the workers' compensation laws of the various states. In 1970, Congress passed the **Occupational Safety and Health Act (OSHA)** *to ensure that insofar as possible*

---

[1]*Handbook of Labor Statistics*, 1947 ed., U.S. Department of Labor, Bureau of Labor Statistics, p. 164.

every man and woman in the nation has a safe and healthy working environment. It quickly became one of the most controversial laws affecting personnel management and has dramatically altered management's role in the area of safety and health. The basic requirements of the Act are summarized in Table 14–1.

CRITICISM OF THE ACT

Critics immediately attacked the law in spite of an apparent need for safety and health legislation. One detractor stated that "The Act wasn't needed,

---

Table 14–1. Job safety and health protection

The Occupational Safety and Health Act of 1970 provides job safety and health protection for workers through the promotion of safe and healthful working conditions throughout the nation. Requirements of the act include the following.

Employers

Each employer must furnish to each of his employees a place of employment free from recognized hazards that are causing or are likely to cause death or serious harm to his employees; and shall comply with occupational safety and health standards issued under the act.

Employees

Each employee shall comply with all occupational safety and health standards, rules, regulations, and orders issued under the act that apply to his own actions and conduct on the job. The Occupational Safety and Health Administration (OSHA) of the Department of Labor has the primary responsibility for administering the act. OSHA issues occupational safety and health standards, and its Compliance Safety and Health Officers conduct jobsite inspections to ensure compliance with the act.

Inspection

The act requires that a representative of the employer and a representative authorized by the employees be given an opportunity to accompany the OSHA inspector for the purpose of aiding the inspection. Where there is no authorized employee representative, the OSHA Compliance Officer must consult with a reasonable number of employees concerning safety and health conditions in the workplace.

Complaint

Employees or their representatives have the right to file a complaint with the nearest OSHA office requesting an inspection if they believe unsafe or unhealthful conditions exist in their workplace. OSHA will withold, on request, names of employees complaining. The act provides that employees may not be discharged or discriminated against in any way for filing safety and health complaints or otherwise exercising their rights under the act. An employee who believes he has been discriminated against may file a complaint with the nearest OSHA office within thirty days of the alleged discrimination.

Table 14–1. Job safety and health protection (continued)

Citation

If upon inspection OSHA believes an employer has violated the act, a citation alleging such violations will be issued to the employer. Each citation will specify a time period within which the alleged violation must be corrected. The OSHA citation must be prominently displayed at or near the place of alleged violation for three days, or until it is corrected, whichever is later, to warn employees of dangers that may exist there.

Proposed penalty

The act provides for mandatory penalties against employers of up to $1,000 for each serious violation and for optional penalties of up to $1,000 for each nonserious violation. Penalties of up to $1,000 per day may be proposed for failure to correct violations within the proposed time period. Also, any employer who willfully or repeatedly violates the act may be assessed penalties of up to $10,000 for each such violation. Criminal penalties are also provided for in the act. Any willful violation resulting in death of an employee, upon conviction, is punishable by a fine of not more than $10,000 or by imprisonment for not more than six months, or by both. Conviction of an employer after a first conviction doubles these maximum penalties.

Voluntary activity

While providing penalties for violations, the act also encourages efforts by labor and management, before an OSHA inspection, to reduce injuries and illnesses arising out of employment. The Department of Labor encourages employers and employees to reduce workplace hazards voluntarily and to develop and improve safety and health programs in all workplaces and industries. Such cooperative action would initially focus on the identification and elimination of hazards that could cause death, injury, or illness to employees and supervisors. There are many public and private organizations that can provide information and assistance in this effort, if requested.

Source: *OSHA Bulletin (poster)*, Washington, D.C.: U.S. Department of Labor, 1977.

it is being implemented too rapidly with a hard hand, and the cost of compliance is so high that it threatens our corporate competitive position."[2] This comment continues to represent many employers' views. However, the Act does have considerable support from unions, public interest groups, and some employers.

The purpose and intent of the Act have rarely been questioned. However, OSHA has received a great deal of criticism. Most of it has dealt with the trivia of some requirements and the general manner in which the law has been administered by the Office of Safety and Health Administration. Note that the acronym OSHA is used to refer to both the act and the federal agency that administers it.

[2]Fred K. Foulkes, "Learning to Live with OSHA," *Harvard Business Review* 51 (November-December 1973): 57.

Horror stories about OSHA abound; some are factual, others fictitious. In one instance, Joe Pinga, who operated a bakery in West Warwick, Rhode Island, was charged by OSHA with twelve violations, including having a safety rail that was four inches too low. Pinga took the case to court where he spent $1500 in legal fees to avoid a $90 fine. During the trial, the young OSHA inspector admitted that her only qualification as an inspector was a forty-hour series of OSHA seminars.[3] Another story involved the owner of a small business in a western state. He was told by an OSHA inspector to install separate men's and women's restrooms for his employees. "He had but one employee: his wife."[4]

One citation was given for "allowing ice to come in direct contact with water." Another story that some still like to tell involves a standard that was strictly enforced. It called for U-shaped toilet seats in workside washroom facilities.[5] The latter two standards have been eliminated, as have a number of other trivial provisions.[6]

CURRENT TRENDS

There is little doubt that OSHA's intent is justified and that many businesses have neglected safety and health. Administrative changes have been made to make the agency more responsive and to overcome its negative image. In the late 1970s, President Jimmy Carter directed OSHA to "get back to basics." Although funding for OSHA has been severely reduced since 1981, the Reagan administration has continued to support a policy involving "counseling employers rather than penalizing them." Injuries and illnesses per 100 full-time workers were cut from 9.5 in 1981 to 7.6 in 1983. While these statistics suggest a positive trend, critics point out that occupational diseases are typically slow to develop and difficult to identify.[7]

The Office of Safety and Health Administration has also begun to concentrate its resources on high risk industries, such as meatpacking, where results will be greater (see Table 14–2). Industries with lower accident and illness rates will not receive as much attention as before. While safety has received the primary emphasis in the past, OSHA has been moving into areas that affect health. Inspectors trained in these areas are now being employed.

Many of OSHA's rules have been simplified. For instance, instead of requiring that a fire extinguisher be a certain number of inches above the floor, the rule now states only that it has to be readily accessible. In addition,

---

[3]"Rage Over Rising Regulations," *Time* 111 (January 2, 1978): 48.
[4]"Why Nobody Wants to Listen to OSHA," *Business Week*, June 14, 1976, p. 64.
[5]Ibid.
[6]"OSHA Drops 928 Nitpicking Standards," *Nation's Business* 66 (December 1978): 17.
[7]"Dead-end Jobs," *The Economist* 295 (June 22, 1985): 26.

Table 14–2. Industries with the highest injury and illness incidence rates in 1982 and percentage changes from 1981

Industry	1982		1981		Percent change
	Rank	Incidence rate*	Rank	Incidence rate*	
Meatpacking plants	1	30.7	1	32.8	−6.4
Mobile homes	2	27.4	3	29.3	−6.5
Structural wood members, n.e.c.†	3	24.8	5	26.0	−4.6
Special product sawmills, n.e.c.	4	24.2	4	27.3	−11.4
Ship building and repairing	5	24.2	7	24.4	−.8
Wines, brandy, and brandy spirits	6	23.8	22	21.6	10.2
Animal and marine fats and oils	7	23.5	13	23.3	.9
Raw cane sugar	8	22.9	2	31.2	−26.6
Automatic merchandising machines	9	22.3	20	21.8	−2.3
Bottled and canned soft drinks	10	22.0	9	24.2	−9.1
Leather tanning and finishing	11	21.7	12	23.6	−8.1
Malt	12	21.5	11	23.8	−9.7
Fabricated structural metal	13	21.5	6	25.3	−15.0
Cottonseed oil mills	14	20.9	15	23.0	−9.1
Reclaimed rubber	15	20.9	39	19.4	7.7
Travel trailers and campers	16	20.6	24	21.4	−3.7
Sanitary services	17	20.5	8	24.3	−15.6
Logging camps and logging contractors	18	20.4	40	19.3	5.7
Truck and bus bodies	19	20.4	31	20.7	−1.4
Cold finishing of steel shapes	20	20.2	17	22.4	−9.8

*The incidence rates represent the number of injuries and illnesses per 100 full-time workers.
†The abbreviation n.e.c. stands for not elsewhere classified.

Source: Occupational Injuries and Illnesses in the United States by Industry, 1982, U.S. Department of Labor, Bureau of Labor Statistics, April 1984, Bulletin 2196, p. 2.

Table 14–3. Work accident costs

Compensation paid to all workers in the nation who are under workers' compensation laws was approximately $13,359,000,000 in 1980 (latest figures reported by the Social Security Administration). Of this amount, $3,860,000,000 was for medical and hospital costs and $9,499,000,000 for wage compensation. These figures are not comparable to Council cost estimates due to differences in coverage of workers and types of cases.

TOTAL COST IN 1982 _____ **$31,400,000,000**

    Direct Costs _____ **$14,700,000,000**

Includes wage losses of $5,200,000,000 insurance administrative costs amounting to about $5,900,000,000 and medical costs of $3,600,000,000.

    Indirect Costs _____ **$14,700,000,000**

Includes the money value of time lost by workers other than those with disabling injuries, who are directly or indirectly involved in accidents. Also included would be the time required to investigate accidents, write up accident reports, etc.

    Fire Losses _____ **$2,000,000,000**

    Cost per Worker _____ **$320**

This figure indicates the value of goods or services each worker must produce to offset the cost of work injuries. It is *not* the average cost of a work injury.

Source: National Safety Council, *Accident Facts* (Washington, D.C.: U.S. Government Printing Office, 1983), p. 24.

almost 1000 inappropriate rules have been eliminated.[8] This trend is expected to continue. The agency's leaders are expected to retain their emphasis on both health and safety, but they appear to be taking a more positive and realistic approach.

SAFETY

Many workers are killed or injured each year as a result of job-related accidents. The cost of these accidents is substantial — $32 billion in 1982 — as you can see in Table 14–3. The cost is often passed along to the consumer in the form of higher prices. Everyone, directly or indirectly, is affected as accident rates go up. Although many forward-looking businesses had elaborate safety programs years before OSHA was passed, a large number of firms established formal safety programs as a result of its enactment.

[8]"OSHA Drops 928 Nitpicking Standards."

Marsha Slaughter-
Kilborn
Division Personnel
Manager
GTE — General
Telephone Company of
the Southwest

A primary reason Marsha Slaughter-Kilborn chose a career in human resource management was that the field is so varied. A career field with six distinct specialties plus a generalist area was very appealing to her. Other professions simply did not seem to present as much challenge or opportunity for diversification.

Slaughter-Kilborn's career began with GTE in labor relations, although as a graduate student she had focused her attention on training and development. She recalls, "I wish I could say that starting in labor relations was my idea because it turned out so well. However, it was actually my employer's decision. I had applied for a generalist position but during the employment interview, the personnel manager decided that I was just what they were looking for in a labor relations assistant." Even though she was a young college graduate, she realized that an entry level position in this specialty would provide invaluable experience and an excellent base for career advancement. The vice president of human resources apparently had the same opinion

and specifically sought a qualified candidate with the ability and drive to rise to any top level human resource position within the GTE system.

Slaughter-Kilborn strongly believes that the experience and knowledge acquired researching and preparing arbitration cases and serving on bargaining committees greatly enhanced her career. She received two promotions during the first two years with GTE. When she was promoted to division personnel manager, she gained additional experience in other areas including staffing, training and development, and compensation and safety. She also learned to work with various government agencies such as the OFCCP, EEOC and OSHA.

To be successful in the HRM field as it exists today, Slaughter-Kilborn believes that one must have exceptional communication, analytical, and perceptual skills. She says, "HRM professionals must be able to work in a constantly changing environment — a world where legal issues or questions arise constantly and new, unforeseen problems crop up daily. It is still amazing to me," she states, "that after almost six years in the field I continue to be faced with new challenges. Since I have a tendency to become bored when I'm not challenged, this works to my advantage."

In college, Slaughter-Kilborn was exposed to many HRM topics. One course in

THE FOCUS OF SAFETY PROGRAMS

Safety programs may be designed to accomplish their purposes in two primary ways. In the first approach to safety program design, the firm works toward creating an environment and attitudes that promote safety. Accidents can be reduced by employees consciously or unconsciously thinking

particular required considerable research and presentation of papers on particular current topics. "At that time," she recalls, "none of us thought we would ever be facing issues such as AIDS in the workplace, transsexual employees, drug testing, or employment-at-will issues. On the other hand, the avant-garde concepts of that period such as quality circles and employee participation teams have now become rather commonplace."

One experience from college always stuck in Slaughter-Kilborn's mind. The East Texas State University ASPA chapter, of which she served as president, often invited guest speakers to campus. One such speaker seemed to concentrate on all of the negative aspects of Personnel as he perceived them. Ms. Slaughter-Kilborn relates, "This talk was so negative that he almost had me convinced I had made a mistake choosing HRM as a major. He told us that Personnel managers always played the adversarial role with the operations people and were, therefore, highly unpopular. He also bemoaned the fact that HRM professionals had little real authority in comparison with line management which made it difficult to enforce Personnel policies."

Slaughter-Kilborn believes that this individual was off base in his way of thinking and probably also in the way he approached line managers. Her response is, "I have had no real problem with lack of authority because I deal with each manager individually, using an approach that is effective with his or her personality type. I try to use influence rather than authority to accomplish my objectives. When a manager's actions are, for example, in violation of the labor agreement or state or federal laws and need to be corrected, I try to handle such situations with finesse — not with heavy-handed hand slapping."

Slaughter-Kilborn believes that HRM professionals should take every opportunity to help educate others who are not well versed in given Personnel areas. This approach, she feels, will result in other managers seeking advice and input prior to taking action involving HRM expertise. "Once you gain the respect of your peers for your competence and knowledge," she adds, "you will not need formal authority because you will have the most potent ability of all — the power to influence and persuade others. When you have developed a strong rapport with your peers, you will be thought of as one of the team, not as an adversary. In my opinion, that's the only way to become a truly effective human resource professional."

about safety. This attitude must permeate each and every phase of the firm's operations. A strong company policy emphasizing safety and health is critical. For example, a major chemical firm's policy states: "It is the policy of the company that every employee be assigned to a safe and healthful place to work. We strongly desire accident prevention in all phases of our

Table 14–4. Office of Safety and Health Administration guidelines for power transmission apparatus

Power Transmission Apparatus

All belts, pulleys, shafts, flywheels, couplings, and other moving power transmission parts must be securely guarded.

A flywheel located so that any part is seven feet or less above a floor or platform must be guarded with an enclosure of sheet, perforated or expanded metal, or woven wire. It must also be fenced in with guard rails.

All exposed parts of horizontal shafting must be enclosed in a metal or wire cage on a frame of angle iron or iron pipe securely fastened to the floor or frame of the machine. If wire mesh forms the enclosure, it should be the type in which the wires are strongly fastened at every cross point, either by welding, soldering, or galvanizing.

Projecting shaft ends must be guarded by nonrotating caps or safety sleeves.

Pulleys or sheaves seven feet or less from the floor must be guarded with metal or wire mesh enclosures.

Horizontal, vertical, and inclined belt, rope, and chain drives must be enclosed in metal or wire mesh cages. The same applies to chains, sprockets, couplings, and gears.

Guards for horizontal overhead belts must run the entire length of the belt and follow the line of the pulley to the ceiling. This also applies to overhead rope and chain drives.

Source: *Essentials of Machine Guarding*, U.S. Department of Labor, Office of Safety and Health Administration, OSHA no. 2227 (July 1975), pp. 10, 12.

operations. Toward this end, the full cooperation of all employees will be required." As the policy infers, no one person is assigned the task of making the workplace safe. It is the job of everyone from top management to the lowest level employee. All members of the firm are encouraged to devise innovative solutions to safety problems.[9] One study found that firms that strengthened the safety function, improved safety committees, or enforced safety rules experienced fewer accident claims.[10]

In the second approach to safety program design, organizations develop and maintain a safe working environment. The previously described approach to accident prevention was more psychological in nature. Here, the physical work environment is altered to prevent accidents. Even if Joe Smith, a machine operator, has been partying all night and can barely open his eyes, the safety devices on his machine will keep him safe. It is in this area that OSHA has had its greatest influence. For instance, the agency's guidelines for power transmission apparatus are shown in Table 14–4.

[9]Jeff Ball, "Do-It-Yourself Safety: A Federal Agency Stresses Worker Participation," *Job Safety and Health* 5 (November 1977): 16.

[10]Barbara Gray Gricar and H. Donald Hopkins, "How Does Your Company Respond to OSHA?" *Personnel Administrator* 28 (April 1983): 53.

Through procedures such as these and those developed by individual organizations, an attempt is made to create a physical environment where accidents cannot occur.

DEVELOPING SAFETY PROGRAMS

Organizational safety programs require planning for prevention of workplace accidents. Plans may be relatively simple, as would be the case for a small retail store. A large automobile assembly plant would likely have a more complex plan and develop a highly sophisticated program. Regardless of the organization's size, top management's support is essential if safety programs are to be effective. The top executives in a firm must be shown how accident prevention can affect the organization's profits. They must recognize the tremendous economic losses that can result from accidents. Some of the logical reasons for top management's support of a safety program are listed in Table 14–5. As you can see, the lost productivity of a single injured worker is not the only factor to consider. Every phase of human resource management is involved. For instance, the firm may have difficulty in recruiting if it gains a reputation for having hazardous working conditions. Employee relations may be seriously hampered if workers do not believe that management cares enough about them to make their workplace safe. Compensation may also be affected if the firm must

---

Table 14–5. Reasons for management's support of a safety program

- *Personal loss.* Most individuals strongly prefer not to be injured. The physical pain and mental anguish associated with injuries is unpleasant. Of much greater concern is the possibility of permanent disablement or even death.

- *Financial loss to injured employees.* Most employees are covered by company insurance plans or personal accident insurance. However, an injury may result in financial losses not covered by the insurance.

- *Lost productivity.* When an employee is injured, there will be a loss of productivity to the firm. In addition to obvious losses, there are often hidden costs. For example, a replacement may need additional training to replace the injured employee. Even when a person can be moved into the injured employee's position, efficiency may suffer.

- *Higher insurance premiums.* Workers' compensation insurance premiums are based on the employer's history of insurance claims. The potential for savings related to employee safety provides a degree of incentive to establish formal programs.

- *Possibility of fines and imprisonment.* Since the enactment of OSHA, a willful and repeated violation of its provisions may result in serious penalties.

- *Social responsibility.* Many executives feel responsible for the safety and health of their employees. A number of firms had excellent safety programs years before OSHA. They understand that safety is in the best interest of the firm.

pay more to attract qualified applicants and retain valued employees. Keeping employees on the job may become a serious problem if the workplace is perceived as hazardous. Managers in unionized firms should recognize that a collective bargaining agreement containing both no-strike and grievance arbitration clauses does not provide protection against a walkout by their employees if objective evidence of abnormally dangerous working conditions exist. Managers in union free firms should be aware that their employees' right to walk out when hazardous working conditions exist is also protected by the Labor Management Relations Act. Whether the firm is unionized or union free, it is an unfair labor practice to interfere with workers' rights with regard to safe working conditions.[11]

Companies with effective safety programs have worked to involve virtually everyone in the firm. Line managers are normally responsible for controlling conditions that cause accidents. As part of this responsibility, they must set the proper safety example for other employees. If a supervisor fails to use safety devices when demonstrating use of the equipment, subordinates may feel that the device is not really necessary. The line manager's attitude can also affect a worker's attitude toward safety training. Comments such as "Let's go to that worthless safety meeting," are not likely to elicit enthusiastic support from subordinates. The supervisor can show support for the safety program by conscientiously enforcing safety rules and cooperating with the staff people who monitor the program.

In many companies, a staff person coordinates the overall safety program. Some major corporations have risk management departments, which anticipate losses associated with safety factors and prepare legal defenses.[12] Titles such as safety director, safety engineer, and safety committee are common. One of the safety director's primary tasks is to provide safety training for company employees. This involves educating line managers as to the merits of safety and teaching them how to recognize and eliminate unsafe situations. Although the safety director operates essentially in an advisory capacity, a well-informed and assertive director may have considerable power in the organization.

ACCIDENT INVESTIGATION

At times accidents happen even in the most safety-conscious firms. Each accident should be carefully evaluated to ensure that it does not recur. Both the safety engineer and the line manager participate in investigating accidents. One of the responsibilities of any supervisor is to prevent accidents. To accomplish this, the supervisor learns — through active participation in the safety program — why accidents occur, how they occur, where they

---

[11]John J. Hoover, "Workers Have New Rights to Health and Safety," *Personnel Administrator* 28 (April 1983): 47.

[12]John L. Pickens, "Effective Loss-Control Management," *Management Review* 66 (December 1977): 41–42.

Table 14–6. Pattern of accident rates by length of service		
Length of service	Men*	Women*
1 month	10.64	8.78
2–3 months	5.90	5.47
4–6 months	3.41	3.31
7–12 months	1.72	1.84
2–3 years	.84	.95
4–5 years	.43	.46
6–10 years	.21	.23
11–25 years	.06	.05
26–35 years	.02	.01

*Rates are expressed as the average percent per month of work injuries, by length of service, for 218,446 men and 52,136 women in ten states, 1976–1977.

Source: Norman Root and Michael Hoefer, "The First Work-Injury Data Available from New BLS Study," *Monthly Labor Review* 102 (January 1979): 77. Reprinted by permission.

occur, and who is involved. Surprisingly, it has been estimated that 10 percent of the work force is responsible for 70 percent of the accidents.[13] Supervisors will gain a great deal of knowledge in the area of accident prevention by assisting in the preparation of accident reports.[14]

A safety program also needs to be reflected in the training and orientation of new employees. The early months of employment are often critical. As Table 14–6 shows, work injuries decrease substantially with length of service.[15] Note that this pattern is consistent for both men and women. Knowledge of the relationship between length of service and accidents should be particularly important to supervisors as they train new employees.

EVALUATION OF SAFETY PROGRAMS

Perhaps the best indicator of the success of any safety program is checking to find out whether accidents have been reduced. But evaluation involves more than counting the number of accidents. The number may have been reduced, but the accidents that occurred may have been more severe. Therefore measures of performance must first be established. Statistics such as frequency rates and severity rates are often used. The **frequency rate** is *expressed by the following formula, which computes the number of lost-time accidents per million people-hours worked:*

$$\text{Frequency rate} = \frac{\text{Number of lost-time accidents} \times 1{,}000{,}000}{\text{Number of people-hours worked during period}}$$

[13]Milton Layden, "Whipping Your Worst Enemy on the Job: Hostility," *Nation's Business* 66 (October 1978): 87.

[14]W. H. Weiss, "Accident Investigation: A Major Responsibility of Supervisors," *Supervision* 40 (July 1978): 1.

[15]Norman Root and Michael Hoefer, "The First Work-Injury Data Available from New BLS Study," *Monthly Labor Review* 102 (January 1979): 77.

Although this above formula is often used, OSHA has developed a formula for frequency rate that is conceptually different.[16] The agency's formula is:

$$\text{Incidence rate} = \frac{\begin{array}{c}\text{Number of injuries}\\\text{and/or illnesses}\end{array}}{\begin{array}{c}\text{Total hours worked}\\\text{by all employees}\\\text{during reference}\\\text{year}\end{array}} \times \begin{array}{l}\text{200,000 (Base for 100 full-time}\\\text{equivalent workers who are}\\\text{working 40 hours per week, 50}\\\text{weeks per year.)}\end{array}$$

The major differences between this formula and the first one are that both injuries and illnesses are considered and that the base for reporting injury frequency rates is 100 full-time employees (as opposed to the million employee-hours in the first formula).

The **severity rate** supplies *an indication of the number of days lost because of accidents per million people-hours worked.* It is expressed by the formula:

$$\text{Severity rate} = \frac{\text{Number of people-days lost} \times 1{,}000{,}000}{\text{Number of people-hours worked during period}}$$

Not only must criteria be available to evaluate the program, but a reporting system must also exist that ensures that accidents will be recorded. At times, when a new safety program is initiated, safety figures show a significant decrease in the number of accidents. However, some supervisors may have failed to report some accidents to make the statistics look better for their units. Proper evaluation of a safety program depends on the reporting and recording of accurate data.

To be of value, the conclusions derived from an evaluation must be used to improve the safety program. Gathering data and permitting them to collect dust on the safety director's desk do not solve problems or prevent accidents. The results of the evaluation must be transmitted upward to top management and downward to line managers in order for improvements to be made.

HEALTH AND WELLNESS PROGRAMS

The reason for a firm to be concerned with its employees' health becomes crystal clear when economic values are placed on employee worth. For instance, how valuable is a highly qualified executive who has developed and implemented a new marketing program? Or, what value could be placed on a skilled engineer trained by the firm for five years? Consider, for example, the bright, forty-year-old executive who succumbs to alcoholism because of job stress; the machinist, who because of job boredom, turns to

[16]Lyne R. Schauer and Thomas S. Ryder, "New Approach to Occupational Safety and Health Statistics," *Monthly Labor Review* 95 (March 1972): 18–19.

drugs to brighten the day; or the designer who pushes herself so hard that she dies of cardiac arrest while walking out of the building. Loss of an individual's productivity because of health problems definitely affects an organization's profitability.

Union support has also hastened the establishment of more effective health programs. Today, unions are placing industrial health issues high on their list of demands in collective bargaining.[17] Rather than concentrating primarily on pay, unions now seek items such as a safer work environment and recreational facilities.

Environmental factors play a major role in the development of physical and mental disorders. The traditional view that health is dependent on medical care and is simply the absence of disease is changing. Today, many more individuals perceive that optimal health can be achieved through environmental safety, organizational changes, and different lifestyles. Infectious diseases, over which the individual has little control, are not the problem they once were. Now, chronic lifestyle diseases are more significant and people do have a great deal of control over them. These are the health problems related to heavy smoking, undue stress, lack of exercise, obesity, and alcohol and drug abuse.[18]

A formal company wellness program involves more than merely dispensing aspirin and bandages. As with the safety program, it should reflect a company philosophy that emphasizes the value of its human assets. Many of the procedures used in establishing a sound safety program are also applicable to a company wellness program. A firm with the reputation of having a healthy work environment is in a stronger position to perform many of the other personnel functions. For instance, recruitment may be easier because applicants want to work for the company. Employee and management relations may be improved when workers believe that the company has their best interests in mind.

A wellness program starts when applicants are initially screened and continues throughout the worker's employment. It typically is concerned with a wide variety of potential health hazards. Certain fumes, dust, gases, liquids, and solids have proven harmful to workers' health. A wellness program may emphasize reducing the noise level in a plant because loss of hearing has resulted from excessive and prolonged exposure to noise. In recent years, a major health concern has been that of workers' exposure to hazardous substances such as asbestos. In addition to monitoring traditional health problems, many organizations have expanded the scope of their health concerns to include a number of problems and programs that are closely related to wellness. The first of these to be discussed is stress management.

---

[17]"The New Activism on Job Health," *Business Week*, September 18, 1978, p. 146.

[18]Robert H. Rosen, "The Picture of Health in the Work Place," *Training and Development Journal* (August 1984): 26.

STRESS MANAGEMENT

A notable trend within U.S. industry is an increasing concern for employees' emotional well-being. Managers are becoming more aware that long-term productivity is largely dependent on the dedication and commitment of the company's employees. Another factor is that workers are now more often holding their employers liable for emotional problems they claim are work related.[19] Regardless of the reason, programs dealing with stress and its related problems are becoming increasingly popular.

Stress is *the body's reaction to any demand made on it.* Perceptions of events, whether positive or negative, activate stress. It is therefore a highly individual matter. Certain events may be quite stressful to one person but not to another. Mild stress actually improves productivity.[20] For example, it can be helpful in developing creative ideas. Everyone lives under a certain amount of stress. In fact, the only people without stress are dead.[21] But, if stress is severe enough and persists for long periods of time, it can be harmful. Stress can be as disruptive to an individual as any accident. It can result in poor attendance, excessive use of alcohol or other drugs, poor performance on the job, or even overall poor health. In fact, there is increasing evidence that undue stress is related to the diseases that are leading causes of death — coronary heart disease, stroke, hypertension, cancer, emphysema, diabetes, and cirrhosis — and also to suicide.[22] The results of stress have been estimated to cost American industry $20–$50 billion each year.[23] The cost to a single firm may account for as much as 6 percent of total sales.[24]

Aside from humanitarian reasons, the economic factor is sufficient to gain management's interest in helping employees manage stress. A legal factor may provide still another reason. One manager recently filed suit against his company charging that his physical ailments, including a heart attack, were caused by the pressure of his job. The man won his case and the company was ordered to make a cash settlement.[25]

The National Institute for Occupational Safety and Health (NIOSH) is one organization that has studied stress as it relates to work. This organi-

[19]Mitchell S. Novit, "Mental Distress: Possible Implications for the Future," *Personnel Administrator* 27 (August 1982): 47.

[20]Michael Pesci, "Stress Management: Separating Myth from Reality," *Personnel Administrator* 27 (January 1982): 59.

[21]Hans Selye, "Secret of Coping with Stress," *U.S. News & World Report* 82 (March 21, 1977): 1.

[22]John M. Ivancevich and Michael T. Matteson, "Optimizing Human Resources: A Case for Preventive Health and Stress Management," *Organizational Dynamics* 9 (Autumn 1980): 5–8.

[23]Oliver L. Niehouse and Karen B. Massoni, "Stress—An Inevitable Part of Change," *Advanced Management Journal* 44 (Spring 1979): 17.

[24]Randy Weigel and Sheldon Pinsky, "Managing Stress: A Model for the Human Resource Staff," *Personnel Administrator* 27 (February 1982): 56.

[25]Ivancevich and Matteson, "Optimizing Human Resources," p. 6.

Table 14-7. Stressful jobs

Where the pressure builds up

12 Jobs with the most stress

1. Laborer
2. Secretary
3. Inspector
4. Clinical lab technician
5. Office manager
6. Foreman
7. Manager/administrator
8. Waitress/waiter
9. Machine operator
10. Farm owner
11. Miner
12. Painter

Other high-stress jobs (in alphabetical order)

- Bank teller
- Clergy
- Computer programmer
- Dental assistant
- Electrician
- Fireman
- Guard/watchman
- Hairdresser
- Health aide
- Health technician
- Machinist
- Meatcutter
- Mechanic
- Musician
- Nurses' aide
- Plumber
- Policeman
- Practical nurse
- Public relations person
- Railroad switchman
- Registered nurse
- Sales manager
- Sales representative
- Social worker
- Structural-metal worker
- Teachers' aide
- Telephone operator
- Warehouse worker

Source: From a ranking of 130 occupations by the federal government's National Institute for Occupational Safety and Health.

zation's research indicates that some jobs are more stressful than others. The twelve most stressful jobs are listed in Table 14–7. The central theme that ties these jobs together is lack of employee control over their work.[26] People in these jobs may feel trapped and that they are more like machines than people. Some of the less stressful jobs involve workers who have more control over their jobs, such as college professors and master craftspersons. The fact that certain jobs are beginning to be identified as more stressful than others has some serious implications for management. Managers must be responsible for recognizing deviant behavior and referring affected subordinates to health professionals for diagnosis and treatment. (Refer to Figure 14–1 for behavior that may indicate problems.) In addition, managers should monitor their employees' progress and provide them with the motivation to succeed.[27] Stress may result in many complex problems, but it

[26]Niehouse and Massoni, "Stress," p. 41.
[27]Pesci, "Stress Management," p. 67.

- Reduced clarity of judgment and effectiveness
- Rigid behavior
- Medical problems
- Strained relationships with others due to irritability
- Increasing excessive absence
- Emerging addictive behaviors (e.g., drugs, alcohol, smoking)
- Expressions of inadequacy and low self-esteem
- Apathy or anger on the job

Figure 14–1. Signs of stress: What managers should look for. Source: Michael Pesci, "Stress Management: Separating Myth from Reality." Reprinted from the January 1982 issue of *Personnel Administrator*. Copyright 1982.

can generally be handled successfully.[28] The following section describes a condition which may result from organizational and individual failure to deal with stress effectively.

BURNOUT

Sheryl Weaver supervised fifty people in the administrative department of a large insurance firm. She was a competent and conscientious manager with a reputation for doing things right and on time. Until recently, Sheryl had been strongly considered as a candidate for the position of vice president — administration. However, things have changed. Sheryl behaves differently. She can't seem to concentrate on her work and appears to be a victim of "battle fatigue." "Oh, Sheryl," a co-worker advised, "You'll make it. You've always been so strong." But Sheryl surprised her associate when she responded, "I don't want to be told I'll make it on my own. I already know I can't."

Sheryl doesn't know exactly what has caused her run-down condition. She senses that she is at her wits end and desperately needs assistance. Sheryl apparently is the victim of an increasingly publicized phenomenon known as burnout. **Burnout** has been described as *a state of fatigue or frustration, which stems from devotion to a cause, way of life, or relationship that did not provide the expected reward.*[29] Burnout is often associated with a mid-life or mid-career crisis, but it can happen at different times to different people.[30] Individuals in the helping professions, such as teachers

---

[28]Ibid., p. 58.

[29]Herbert J. Freudenberger, *Burnout: The High Cost of High Achievement* (Garden City, N.Y.: Anchor Press, Doubleday and Company, 1980), p. 13.

[30]John G. Nelson, "Burn Out—Business's Most Costly Expense," *Personnel Administrator* 25 (August 1980), 82.

and counselors, seem to be susceptible to burnout because of their jobs, whereas others may be vulnerable because of their upbringing, expectations, or their personalities.[31] Burnout is frequently associated with people whose jobs require close relationships with others under stressful and tension-filled conditions.[32] While any employee may experience this condition, perhaps 10 percent of managers and executives are so affected.[33] The dangerous part of burnout is that it is contagious. A highly cynical and pessimistic burnout victim can quickly transform an entire group into burnouts. Therefore, it is important that the problem be dealt with quickly. Once it has begun, it is difficult to stop.[34]

Some of the symptoms of burnout include: (1) chronic fatigue; (2) anger at those making demands; (3) self-criticism for putting up with demands; (4) cynicism, negativism, and irritability; (5) a sense of being besieged; and (6) hair-trigger display of emotions.[35] Other symptoms might include recurring health problems, such as ulcers, back pain, or frequent headaches. The burnout victim is often unable to maintain an even keel emotionally. Unwarranted hostility may occur in totally inappropriate situations.

Burnout is a problem that should be dealt with before it occurs. In order to do so, managers must be aware of potential sources of stress. These sources exist both within and outside the organization and are discussed next.

SOURCES OF STRESS[36]

Regardless of its origin, stress possesses the same devastating potential. Some factors are controllable to varying degrees, whereas others are not. In the following paragraphs we discuss some of the primary sources of stress.

The family.   Although a frequent source of happiness and security, the family can also serve as a significant stressor. Consider that nearly one-half of all marriages end in divorce. Divorce itself is also quite stressful. When it leads to single parenthood, the difficulties may be compounded.

Children are another of life's sources of happiness. Yet, consider the effect of an infant awakening parents in the middle of the night with a

[31]Dick Friedman, "Job Burnout," *Working Woman* 5 (July 1980): 34.

[32]Christina Meslach and Susan E. Jackson, "Burned-Out Cops and Their Families," *Psychology Today* 12 (May 1979): 59.

[33]Beverly Norman, "Career Burnout," *Black Enterprise* 12 (July 1981): 45.

[34]Cary Cherniss, "Job Burnout: Growing Worry for Workers, Bosses," *U.S. News & World Report* 88 (February 1980): 72.

[35]Harry Levinson, "When Executives Burn Out," *Harvard Business Review* 59 (May–June 1981): 76.

[36]Certain portions of this section were adapted from unpublished working papers of Robert M. Smith, Professor and Head of Counseling and Guidance Department, East Texas State University, 1982.

severe asthmatic attack! Anxiety levels rise significantly as the parents watch their child struggle for each breath. Academic problems or extreme social adjustment difficulties for a teenager can also create much anguish for the entire family.

A relatively recent phenomenon is the dual career family. When both husband and wife have job and family responsibilities, traditional roles are altered. What happens when one partner is totally content with a job and the other is offered a sought-after promotion requiring transfer to a distant city? At best, these circumstances are beset with difficulties.

Financial problems. Problems with finances may place an unbearable strain on the family. Such difficulties are frequently related to divorce. For some, these problems are persistent and never quite resolved. Nagging, unpaid bills and bill collectors can create much tension.

Living conditions. Stress levels may also be increased for people who live in densely populated areas. These people face longer lines, endure more hectic traffic jams, and contend with higher levels of air and noise pollution. Metropolitan life has many advantages; however, the benefits provided are not without costs, often in the form of stress.

Life changes. Life change events have been weighted according to the stress they produce. As you can see in Table 14–8, the most stressful life event is the death of a spouse. One study determined that 70 percent of the persons who registered more than 300 life change units (LCUs) in a year had an illness during the following year. It was also noted that they tended to have multiple illnesses.[37]

Organizational culture. Generally speaking, an organizational culture characterized by a lack of freedom is strongly pervaded with stress. The CEO's leadership style often sets the tone. If he or she is autocratic and permits little input from subordinates, a stressful environment may result. If the CEO is too weak, internal conflicts may result as subordinates compete for power. Certain firms have even been cited as having stressful climates because the CEO insists on superior performance.

Even in the healthiest organizational culture, stressful relationships among employees can occur. Employee personality types vary and, combined with differing values and belief systems, they may so impair communication that stressful situations occur. Also, competition encouraged by the organization's reward system for promotion, pay increases, and status may add to the problem.[38]

---

[37]E. K. Eric Gunderson and Richard H. Rahe, eds., *Life Stress and Illness* (Springfield, Ill.: Charles C Thomas, 1974), p. 62.

[38]"Can You Cope with Stress?" *Duns Review* 106 (November 1975): 90.

Table 14–8. Life change events

Type of event		LCU values
Family	Death of spouse	100
	Divorce	73
	Marital separation	65
	Death of close family member	63
	Marriage	50
	Marital reconciliation	45
	Major change in health of family	44
	Pregnancy	40
	Addition of new family member	39
	Major change in arguments with wife	35
	Son or daughter leaving home	29
	In-law troubles	29
	Wife starting or ending work	26
	Major change in family get-togethers	15
Personal	Detention in jail	63
	Major personal injury or illness	53
	Sexual difficulties	39
	Death of a close friend	37
	Outstanding personal achievement	28
	Start or end of formal schooling	26
	Major change in living conditions	25
	Major revision of personal habits	24
	Changing to a new school	20
	Change in residence	20
	Major change in recreation	19
	Major change in church activities	19
	Major change in social activities	18
	Major change in sleeping habits	16
	Major change in eating habits	15
	Vacation	13
	Christmas	12
	Minor violations of the law	11
Work	Being fired from work	47
	Retirement from work	45
	Major business adjustment	39
	Changing to different line of work	36
	Major change in work responsibilities	29
	Trouble with boss	23
	Major change in working conditions	20
Financial	Major change in financial state	38
	Mortgage or loan over $10,000	31
	Mortgage foreclosure	30
	Mortgage or loan less than $10,000	17

Source: From E. K. Eric Gunderson and Richard H. Rahe, eds., *Life Stress and Illness*, Springfield, Ill.: Charles C Thomas, 1974. Courtesy of Publisher.

Role ambiguity and role conflict.   **Role ambiguity** exists *when employees lack clear information about the content of their jobs.* This condition can be quite threatening to an employee and produce feelings of insecurity.

Role conflict.   Role conflict occurs *when an individual is placed in the position of seeking opposing goals.* For example, a manager may be expected to increase production while having to decrease the size of the labor force.[39] When this happens, both objectives may not be reached and stress stems from the resulting conflict. A nationwide survey emphasized the pervasiveness of these problems. It revealed that 35 percent of the respondents had complaints about role ambiguity, and 48 percent felt that they were victims of role conflict.[40]

Job overload.   *When employees are given more work than they can possibly handle,* they become victims of **job overload**. A critical aspect of this problem is that often the best performers in the firm are the ones affected. These individuals have proven that they can perform more so they are given more to do. At its extreme, work overload becomes burnout.

Working conditions.   The physical characteristics of the workplace, including the machines and tools used, can create stress. Overcrowding, excessive noise, poor lighting, and poorly maintained work stations and equipment can all adversely affect employee morale and increase stress levels.

It is important for managers to be aware of sources of stress. It is equally vital that they implement programs to deal with stress effectively. Programs and techniques for coping with stress are discussed next.

COPING WITH STRESS

A number of organizational programs and techniques may be effective in either preventing or relieving excessive stress (see Table 14–9). General organizational programs, while not specifically designed to cope with stress, may nevertheless play a major role. The programs and techniques listed in Table 14–9 are discussed in the chapters of this text as indicated. Effective implementation will achieve these results:

■   An organizational culture is created that holds anxiety and tension to an acceptable level. Employee inputs are sought and valued by all levels of management. Generally, individuals are given greater control over their work. Communication is emphasized.

[39]Arthur P. Brief, "How to Manage Managerial Stress," *Personnel* 57 (September–October 1980): 27.

[40]Peter J. Frost, Vance F. Mitchell, and Walter R. Nord, *Organizational Reality: Reports from the Firing Line,* 2nd ed. (Glenview, Ill.: Scott, Foresman and Company, 1982), p. 446.

Table 14–9. Organizational programs and techniques that can be effective in coping with stress	
General organizational programs	**Chapter**
Job analysis	4
Training and development	8
Effective communication, motivation and leadership styles (corporate culture)	9
Organization development	9
Career planning and development	10
Performance appraisal	11
Compensation	12, 13
Specific techniques	
Hypnosis, transcendental meditation, biofeedback, and relaxation response	14
Specific organizational programs	
Physical fitness, alcohol and drug abuse, and employee assistance programs	14

- Each person's role is defined, yet care is taken not to discourage risk-takers and those who want to take on greater responsibility.
- Individuals are provided with the training and development needed to assist them in the successful performance of current and future jobs. Equal consideration is given to the need for achieving personal as well as organizational goals. Individuals are encouraged to plan and exercise greater control over their own work. They are trained to work as effective team members and to develop an awareness of how they and their work relate to others.
- Employees are assisted in planning for career progression.
- Organizational members participate in making decisions that affect them. They are made aware of their company's plans and their particular role in implementing these plans. They know what is going on in the firm and how well they are performing their jobs.
- Employee needs — financial and nonfinancial — are met through an equitable reward system.

Again, refer to Table 14–9 and note the specific techniques that can be utilized by organizations or individuals in dealing with stress. These methods include hypnosis, biofeedback, transcendental meditation, and the relaxation response.

Hypnosis is "*an altered state of consciousness that is artificially induced and characterized by increased receptiveness to suggestions.*" A person in a hypnotic state may therefore respond to the hypnotist's suggestion to relax.[41] Hypnosis can help many people to cope with stress. The serenity achieved through dissipation of anxieties and fears can restore an

[41]Herbert Benson, *The Relaxation Response* (New York: William Morrow and Company 1975), p. 72.

individual's confidence. A principal benefit of hypnotherapy is that peace of mind continues after awakening from a hypnotic state. This tranquility continues to grow, especially when the person has been trained in self-hypnosis.[42]

Biofeedback is *a method of learning to control involuntary bodily processes such as blood pressure or heart rate.*[43] For example, using equipment to provide a visual display of blood pressure, individuals may learn to lower their systolic blood pressure levels.

Transcendental meditation (TM) is *a stress-reduction technique whereby a secret word or phrase (mantra) provided by a trained instructor is mentally repeated while an individual is comfortably seated.* Repeating the mantra over and over helps prevent distracting thoughts. It has been found to produce these physiologic changes: decreased oxygen consumption, decreased carbon-dioxide elimination, and decreased breathing rate. Transcendental meditation results in a decreased metabolic rate and a restful state.[44]

The relaxation response is another technique for dealing with the stressful consequences of living in our modern society. This approach to dealing with stress was developed at Harvard's Thorndike Memorial Laboratory and Boston's Beth Israel Hospital. The technique has its roots in ancient Eastern and Western religious, cultic, and lay practices such as Yoga. Use of this method was found to produce the same kind of physiologic changes as transcendental meditation. The feelings associated with this altered state of consciousness have been described as ecstatic, beautiful, and totally relaxing. Other individuals have felt a sense of well-being similar to that experienced after exercise, but without the fatigue.[45] Relaxation response technique procedures are shown in Figure 14–2.

Table 14–9 also lists organizational programs that are designed specifically to deal with stress and related problems. These include physical fitness, alcohol and drug abuse, and employee assistance programs. These programs are discussed in the remaining sections of the chapter.

PHYSICAL FITNESS PROGRAMS

Although few organizations have fully staffed facilities, about 50,000 U.S. business firms have exercise programs designed to help keep their workers physically fit.[46] From management's viewpoint, this effort is sensible. Loss

[42]E. M. Cherman, *Stress and the Bottom Line: A Guide to Personal Well-Being and Corporate Health* (New York: AMACOM, a Division of American Management Associations, 1981), p. 273.

[43]Benson, *Relaxation*, pp. 55–56.

[44]Ibid., pp. 60–62.

[45]Ibid., pp. 75, 112–114.

[46]Russell W. Driver and Ronald A. Ratliff, "Employers' Perceptions of Benefits Accrued from Physical Fitness Programs," *Personnel Administrator* 27 (August 1982): 21.

1. Sit quietly in a comfortable position.
2. Close your eyes.
3. Deeply relax all your muscles, beginning at your feet and progressing up to your face. Keep them relaxed.
4. Breathe through your nose. Become aware of your breathing. As you breathe out, say the word, "ONE," silently to yourself. For example, breathe IN . . . OUT, "ONE": IN . . . OUT, "ONE": etc. Breathe easily and naturally.
5. Continue for 10 to 20 minutes, You may open your eyes to check the time, but do not use an alarm. When you finish, sit quietly for several minutes, at first with your eyes closed and later with your eyes opened. Do not stand up for a few minutes.
6. Do not worry about whether you are successful in achieving a deep level of relaxation. Maintain a passive attitude and permit relaxation to occur at its own pace. When distracting thoughts occur, try to ignore them by not dwelling upon them and return to repeating "ONE." With practice, the response should come with little effort. Practice the technique once or twice daily, but not within two hours after any meal, since the digestive processes seem to interfere with the elicitation of the relaxation response.

Figure 14–2. Procedures for the relaxation response. Source: From pp. 114–115 (under the title "Procedures for The Relaxation Response") in *The Relaxation Response* by Herbert Benson, M.D., with Miriam Z. Klipper. Copyright © 1975 by William Morrow and Company, Inc. By permission of the publisher.

of productivity resulting from coronary heart disease totals approximately $32 billion annually.[47] The total cost to society is even higher because of lost tax revenue, health care costs, and the expense involved in finding and training replacements. Absenteeism, accidents, and sick pay are often reduced through company-sponsored fitness programs. Employees who are physically fit are more alert and productive, and their morale is higher.[48]

A number of organizations have developed physical fitness programs for their employees. Xerox Corporation currently has nine in-house physical fitness centers at locations throughout the United States. The Xerox programs are designed to help employees avoid coronary heart diseases and other degenerative disorders. A fitness program, carefully designed for each individual, helps people feel and look better. As an added benefit, it also enhances their self-concept. Jim Post, program manager of executive fitness at Xerox, has stated: "We are concerned about the ever-increasing costs of medical and insurance premiums, but beyond that, we have an obligation to our people as people."

The Xerox executive fitness program emphasizes four areas: (1) cardiovascular fitness; (2) flexibility; (3) relaxation by means of bio-

[47]Robert Kreitner, "Employee Physical Fitness: Protecting an Investment in Human Resources," *Personnel Journal* 55 (July 1976): 340.
[48]Kenneth H. Cooper, *The New Aerobics* (New York: A Bantam Book/Published by arrangement with M. Evans and Company, 1970), p. 13.

feedback; and (4) weight conditioning. In the cardiovascular training program, the motorized treadmill is the primary tool. The bicycle ergometer is also used along with biofeedback training. Biofeedback, which was described earlier, is a process that permits an individual to monitor his or her own physiological states (such as pulse rate, skin temperature, blood pressure, muscular tension, and brain waves) through the use of bioinstruments. Electrodes are placed over selected muscles during exercise. They indicate the level of a person's tension. By listening to an audio tone, individuals can actually measure and relax the tension existing in a specific muscle.

Flexibility (the range of movement in a joint or joints) is achieved by using static methods. Static stretching holds muscles and connective tissues at their greatest length, thus helping to relax them. Joint flexibility helps prevent the aches and pains that are common with aging. Finally, relaxation, by means of biofeedback, is an important aspect of the exercise program. Appropriate exercise has been shown to have a greater effect on relaxation than the use of tranquilizers.

Xerox's weight conditioning program is used to strengthen major muscle groups and joints. The lifting of heavy weights, especially for middle-aged individuals, is carefully avoided; relatively light weights and frequent repetition are emphasized.

At Kimberly-Clark Corporation, approximately 1200 employees participate in a health management program. A staff of twenty-three full-time health care professionals administers this program utilizing a $2.5 million facility. Prior to admission, employees undergo a physical and medical history exam. Each employee then receives an individualized health prescription. The program at Kimberly-Clark was begun after its top management made a commitment to reduce health care costs.[49]

The number of programs such as the ones at Xerox and Kimberly-Clark is expected to increase dramatically in the future. Firms now recognize how healthy workers contribute directly to the profitability of the organization.

Summing up the rationale for fitness programs, one corporate president stated:

> Companies will continue to invest in the health and well-being of their employees, and not just to keep health care costs down. They are now starting to see that there is a direct productivity-related benefit to keeping people healthy. Also, people like to be in a situation where management says: Sure you can jog — there is a jogging track, and here is counseling for how to quit smoking, or whatever. So, the absorption by employers of more health care costs, mostly resulting from making available more health care benefits, is going to rise — not because it's a social requirement but because it makes good business sense.[50]

---

[49]Ivancevich and Matteson, "Optimizing Human Resources," p. 6.
[50]"Today's Trends Suggest Revolutionary Changes for Business in the Future," *Personnel Administrator* 30 (February 1985): 70–71.

ALCOHOL ABUSE PROGRAMS

Alcohol abuse is a significant problem and can result from excessive stress. The American Medical Association defined **alcoholism** as *a treatable disease* in 1956.[51] The disease is characterized by uncontrolled and compulsive drinking that interferes with normal living patterns.

An individual may feel that drinking improves his or her ability to cope. However, alcohol rarely improves performance; rather, it impairs performance. As a person starts to drink excessively, the drinking itself results in greater stress. This increased stress is dealt with by more drinking, making it a most vicious circle.[52] Alcohol abuse affects people at every level of society, from top level managers to the skid row homeless. It is also one of the most difficult conditions to detect. Sometimes a person progresses to advanced stages of alcohol abuse before perceiving that he or she may actually be an alcoholic. By then, the person's career may be on the verge of destruction. Early signs of alcohol abuse are especially difficult to identify. Often the symptoms are nothing more than an increasing number of absences from work. Productivity may, over a period of time, begin to decline. Accidents may occur more frequently.[53] A normally pleasant person can become highly disagreeable.

An increasing number of firms are establishing alcohol abuse programs. From fifty programs in 1950, the number had expanded to nearly 2400 by 1977. Supervisors are being trained to cope with this health problem. No longer does alcohol abuse result in automatic termination. Some of the warning signs that supervisors look for with regard to alcohol abuse are shown in Table 14–10. Any one of these signs taken individually does not suggest the excessive use of alcohol. It is when they are observed as a pattern that potential difficulties may exist.

DRUG ABUSE PROGRAMS

There are indications that drug abuse in industry has increased during the past decade. Society has become more concerned with this health problem. Numerous firms have recognized that drug problems exist and have taken positive action to deal with them. One such formal program is illustrated in Figure 14–3. The program includes: (1) safeguards that identify drug problems or prevent them from occurring; and (2) mechanisms that lead to discharge of drug abusers from the firm.

A major purpose of the program is to ensure that drug abusers are not hired. However, if a person becomes an abuser after employment, a supervisor can use progressive discipline for work-related irregularities such as

---

[51]W. David Gibson, "They're Bringing Problem Drinkers Out of the Closet," *Chemical Week* 123 (November 15, 1978): 85.

[52]Derek Rutherford, "Alcoholic Solution," *The Accountant* 182 (August 21, 1980): 310.

[53]Kenneth P. Camisa, "How Alcoholism Treatment Pays for Itself," *SAM Advanced Management Journal* 47 (Winter 1982): 55.

Table 14–10. Warning signs of alcohol abuse

Warning signs

The New York City Affiliate, Inc., National Council on Alcoholism, considers the following work related problems to be possible indications of alcohol abuse:

- Absenteeism
- Ineffectiveness on the job
- Tardiness (particularly mornings and after lunch)
- Careless and sloppy work
- Accidents on the job
- Unexplained absences from the workplace
- Inability to remember details and commitments
- Leaving work early
- Avoidance of co-workers and supervisors
- Unpredictable and inappropriate behavior
- Customers' complaints
- Co-workers' complaints
- Unreasonable resentment
- Overreaction to criticism
- Borrowing money from co-workers
- Grandiose, aggressive, belligerent behavior
- "Jekyll and Hyde" personality

Source: "They're Bringing Problem Drinkers Out of the Closet," *Chemical Week* 123 (November 15, 1978): 85. Reprinted by permission.

absenteeism and low productivity. A supervisor should be trained to look for signs of drug abuse.

If drug abuse is suspected, the supervisor should require that the employee report to the medical department. Failure to comply may result in discharge. The medical department works with the individual or refers the individual to appropriate agencies for treatment. At all times, there should be an ongoing educational program that constantly advises employees of the dangers of drug abuse.

EMPLOYEE ASSISTANCE PROGRAMS

Chief executive officers are fond of saying, "Employees are our most important asset." Actions speak louder than words, however, and an effective way for a firm to demonstrate concern for its people is to develop and implement an employee assistance program.[54] One comprehensive ap-

[54]Roger K. Good, "What Bechtel Learned Creating an Employee Assistance Program," *Personnel Journal* 63 (September 1984): 80.

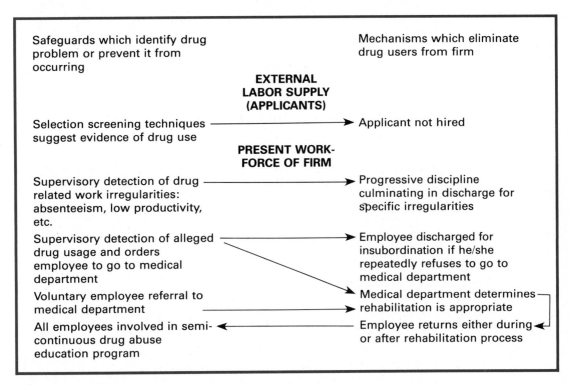

Safeguards which identify drug problem or prevent it from occurring	Mechanisms which eliminate drug users from firm

EXTERNAL LABOR SUPPLY (APPLICANTS)

Selection screening techniques suggest evidence of drug use ——————→ Applicant not hired

PRESENT WORK-FORCE OF FIRM

Supervisory detection of drug related work irregularities: absenteeism, low productivity, etc. ——————→ Progressive discipline culminating in discharge for specific irregularities

Supervisory detection of alleged drug usage and orders employee to go to medical department ——————→ Employee discharged for insubordination if he/she repeatedly refuses to go to medical department

Voluntary employee referral to medical department ——————→ Medical department determines rehabilitation is appropriate

All employees involved in semi-continuous drug abuse education program ←—————— Employee returns either during or after rehabilitation process

Figure 14–3. Some safeguards and mechanisms used to eliminate employee drug use. Source: Ken Jennings, "The Problem of Employee Drug Use and Remedial Alternatives," *Personnel Journal*, November 1977. Copyright © 1977. Reprinted with permission.

proach that many organizations have taken to deal with burnout, alcohol and drug abuse, and other emotional disturbances is through an **employee assistance program (EAP)**. In an EAP, *a firm either provides in-house professional counselors or refers employees to an appropriate community social service agency.* Typically, most or all of the costs are borne by the employer up to a predetermined amount. The EAP concept includes a response to personal psychological problems that interfere with both an employee's well-being and overall productivity.[55] The purpose of EAPs is to provide emotionally troubled employees with the same consideration and assistance given employees having physical illnesses.

Every firm has employees who have personal problems. Over the last ten years, EAPs have grown in number from 400 to well over 5000. They are being adopted primarily to increase worker productivity and reduce costs. For example, an executive of a national benefits consulting firm

[55]Fred Dickman and William G. Emener, "Employee Assistance Programs: Basic Concepts, Attributes and an Evaluation," *Personnel Administrator* 27 (August 1982): 55.

estimates that for every dollar invested in EAPs, about $8–$10 are returned in the form of increased productivity and decreased health care claims.[56]

One such program has been initiated at American Coil Spring Company. L. C. Barry, employee relations director, describes the program by saying, "Its intent is to help employees whose personal problems are affecting their work. Frequently, drinking, drugs, impending divorce, finances, etc., will adversely affect a person's attendance, productivity, or relationship with fellow employees. Often they result in disciplinary action with ultimate termination. The intent of the EAP is to catch these problems early on and refer the employee to counseling before his or her job is in jeopardy."

The Kemper Group also has a well known EAP. At Kemper, the following principles guide the administration of its employee assistance program:

1. We believe that alcoholism, drug addiction, and emotional disturbances are illnesses and should be treated as such.
2. We believe the majority of employees who develop alcoholism, other drug addiction, or emotional illness can be helped to recover, and the company should offer appropriate assistance.
3. We believe the decision to seek diagnosis and accept treatment for any suspected illness is the responsibility of the employee. However, continued refusal of an employee to seek treatment when it appears that substandard performance may be caused by any illness is not tolerated. We believe that alcoholism, or drug addiction, or emotional illness should not be made an exception to this commonly accepted principle.
4. We believe that it is in the best interest of employees and the company that when alcoholism, other drug addiction, or emotional illness is present, it should be diagnosed and treated at the earliest possible date.
5. We believe that the company's concern for individual alcohol drinking, drug taking, and behavioral habits begins only when they result in unsatisfactory job performance, poor attendance, or behavior detrimental to the good reputation of the company.
6. We believe that confidential handling of the diagnosis and treatment of alcoholism, or other drug addiction, or emotional illness is essential.

One survey of 450 U.S. firms showed that 37 percent currently have an EAP. Another 13 percent were either considering or developing a program, and 18 percent provide assistance "as needed." Of the firms included in the survey, only 32 percent provided no assistance. Of those firms with

---

[56]Kay Wyrtzen, "Employee Assistance Programs," *Supervision* 47 (May 1985): 6–7.

EAPs, 42 percent provide services "in-house, 45 percent utilize outside agencies, and 13 percent use a combination."[57]

In emphasizing the potential benefits of EAPs, United States Tobacco Company's EAP brochure cites the program's advantages:

1. Early recognition and resolution of business and personal problems.
2. Retention of valuable employees.
3. Improved productivity and profits.
4. Reduced absenteeism.
5. Improved morale.[58]

Employment assistance programs are justified not only on the basis of helping to improve the quality of life for employees, but also serving to improve an organization's performance. These advantages help account for the rapid growth of EAPs.

To become more effective, however, directors of EAPs need to reexamine their practice of waiting for supervisory referrals. Typically, problems are not dealt with until they have adversely affected job performance. Instead, EAPs should actively promote health improvement and disease prevention programs. Prevention of alcohol and drug abuse is more cost effective than treatment, which is the common EAP practice.[59]

SUMMARY

Safety involves protecting employees from injuries caused by work related accidents. Health refers to the employees' freedom from physical or emotional illness. Industrial safety has been a major problem that has seemingly resisted resolution. In 1970, Congress passed the Occupational Safety and Health Act.

Many workers are killed or injured each year as a result of job-related accidents. Safety programs may be designed to accomplish their purposes in two primary ways: (1) creating an environment and an attitude that promote safety; and (2) developing and maintaining a safe physical working environment.

The reason a firm is concerned with its employees' health becomes clear when economic values are placed on the employees' worth. A formal company health program should reflect a company philosophy that emphasizes the value of its human assets and that has top management support. A health program starts when applicants are initially screened and continues throughout the workers' employment.

---

[57]"Compensation Currents," *Compensation Review* 15 (Second Quarter 1983): 15.

[58]Hermine Zagat Levine, "Employee Assistance Programs," *Personnel* 62 (April 1985): 14.

[59]Keith McClellan, "The Changing Nature of EAP Practice," *Personnel Administrator* 30 (August 1985): 34.

In addition to monitoring traditional health problems, many organizations have expanded the scope of their health concerns to include stress management. Stress refers to greater than usual physiological and psychological reactions to an event or situation. If stress is severe enough and persists for long periods of time, it can be harmful. Stress can be as disruptive to an individual as any accident.

Burnout has been described as a state of fatigue or frustration that stems from devotion to a cause, way of life, or relationship that did not provide the expected reward. Burnout is a problem that should be dealt with before it occurs. In order to do so, managers must be aware of potential sources of undue stress. Some of the primary origins of stress include: the family, financial problems, living conditions, life changes, organizational climate, role ambiguity and role conflict, job overload, and working conditions.

Organizational programs have been designed specifically to deal with stress and related problems. These include physical fitness, alcohol and drug abuse, and employee assistance programs.

QUESTIONS FOR REVIEW

1. Distinguish by definition between safety and health.
2. What are the reasons that the Occupational Safety and Health Act has received so much criticism? What is the current attitude toward OSHA?
3. What are the primary ways in which safety programs are designed? Discuss.
4. What are some measurements that would suggest the success of a firm's safety program?
5. Why should a firm attempt to identify stressful jobs? What could an organization do to reduce stressful situations associated with a job?
6. What are some signs that a supervisor might look for in identifying alcohol abuse?
7. Why should a firm be concerned with employee burnout?
8. Explain why employee assistance programs are being established.

TERMS FOR REVIEW

Safety
Health
Occupational Safety and Health Act (OSHA)
Frequency rate
Severity rate
Stress
Burnout
Role ambiguity

Role conflict
Job overload
Hypnosis
Biofeedback
Transcendental meditation (TM)
Alcoholism
Employee assistance program (EAP)

Incident 1

Wanda Zackery was extremely excited a year ago when she joined Landon Electronics as its first safety engineer. She had graduated from Florida State University with a degree in electrical engineering and a strong desire to enter business. Wanda had selected her job at Landon Electronics over several other offers. She believed that it would provide her with a broad range of experiences, which she could not receive in a strictly engineering job. Also, when she was interviewed by the company president, Mark Lincoln, he promised her that the firm's resources would be at her disposal to correct any safety-related problems.

Her first few months at Landon were hectic but exciting. She immediately identified numerous safety problems. One of the most dangerous involved a failure to install safety guards on all exposed equipment. Wanda carefully prepared her proposal, including expected costs, to make needed minimum changes. She estimated that it would take approximately $50,000 to complete the necessary conversions. Wanda then presented the entire package to Mr. Lincoln. She explained the need for the changes to him and Mr. Lincoln cordially received her presentation. He said that he would like to think it over and would get back to her.

But that was six months ago! Every time Wanda attempted to get some action on her proposal, Mr. Lincoln was friendly but still wanted some more time to consider it. In the meantime, Wanda had become increasingly anxious. Recently, a worker had barely avoided a serious injury. Some workers had also become concerned. She heard through the grapevine that someone had telephoned the regional office of OSHA.

Her suspicions were confirmed the very next week when an OSHA inspector appeared at the plant. No previous visits had ever been made to the company. Although Mr. Lincoln was not overjoyed, he permitted the inspector access to the company. Later he might have wished that he had not been so cooperative. Before the inspector left, he wrote violations for each piece of equipment that did not have the necessary safety guards. The fines would total $5000 if the problems were not corrected right away. The inspector cautioned that repeat violations could cost $50,000 and possible imprisonment.

As the inspector was leaving, Wanda received a phone call. "Wanda, this is Mark. Get up to my office right now. We need to get your project underway."

QUESTIONS

1. Discuss Mr. Lincoln's level of commitment to occupational safety.
2. Is there a necessary tradeoff between Landon's need for low expenses and the workers' need for safe working conditions? Explain.

Incident 2

"Just leave me alone and let me do my job," said Manuel Gomez. Taken aback, Bill Brown, Manuel's supervisor, decided to "count to ten" before responding to Manuel's fury. As he walked back to his office, Bill thought about how Manuel had changed over the past few months. He had been a hard worker and extremely cooperative when he went to work for Bill two years earlier. The company had sent Manuel to two training schools and had received glowing reports about his performance in each of them.

Until about a year ago, Manuel had a perfect attendance record and was a nearly ideal employee. At about that time, however, he began to have personal problems, which resulted in a divorce six months later. Manuel had requested a day off several times to take care of personal problems and Bill had tried to help in every way he could. He tried not to get involved in Manuel's personal affairs. But he was aware of the strain Manuel must have felt as his marriage broke up and he and his wife engaged in the inevitable disputes about child custody, alimony payments, and property.

During the same time period, top management initiated a push for improving productivity. Bill found it necessary to put additional pressure on all of his workers, including Manuel. He tried to be considerate but he had to become much more performance oriented, insisting upon increased output from every worker. As time went on, Manuel began to show up late for work and

actually missed two days without calling Bill in advance. Bill attributed Manuel's behavior to extreme stress and because Manuel had been such a good worker for so long he excused the tardiness and absences, only gently suggesting that Manuel should try to do better.

Sitting at his desk, Bill thought about what might have caused Manuel's outburst of a few minutes earlier. Bill had simply suggested to Manuel that he shut down the machine he was operating and clean up the surrounding area. This was a normal part of Manuel's job and something he had been careful to do in the past. Bill thought that the disorderliness around Manuel's machine might account for the increasing number of defects in the parts he was making. "This is a tough one, I think I'll talk to the boss about it," thought Bill.

QUESTIONS

1. What do you think is likely to be Manuel's problem? Discuss.
2. If you were Bill's boss, what would you recommend that he do?

REFERENCES

Booth, R. "What's New in Health and Safety Management." *Personnel Management* 17 (April 1985): 36–39.

Brief, Arthur P. "How to Manage Managerial Stress." *Personnel* 57 (September–October 1980): 25–30.

Briscoe, D. R. "Learning to Handle Stress — A Matter of Time and Training." *Supervisory Management* 25 (February 1980): 35–38.

Cahan, V. and Dwyer, P. "Formaldehyde Limits: A Continuing Battle." *Chemical Week* 136 (April 17, 1985): 11 +.

Camisa, Kenneth P. "How Alcoholism Treatment Pays for Itself." *SAM Advanced Management Journal* 47 (Winter 1982): 53–57.

Dickens, W. T. "Difference Between Risk Premiums in Union and Nonunion Wages and the Case for Occupational Safety Regulations." *American Economic Review* 74 (May 1984): 320–323.

Foulkes, Fred K. "Learning to Live with OSHA." *Harvard Business Review* 51 (November–December 1973): 57–67.

Freudenberger, Herbert J. "Burnout — An Unnecessary Tax on the Successful." *Administrative Management* XLIII (April 1982): 99.

Good, Roger K. "What Bechtel Learned Creating an Employee Assistance Program." *Personnel Journal* 63 (September 1984): 80.

Grimaldi, Joseph and Schnapper, Bette P. "Managing Employees Stress: Reducing the Costs, Increasing the Benefits." *Management Review* 70 (August 1981): 23–28+.

Hanson, D. "Study Criticizes Federal Protection of Workers from Illness, Injury." *Chemical Engineering News* 63 (April 29, 1985): 14–15.

Herzberg, Frederick. "Putting People Back Together." *Industry Week* 198 (July 24, 1978): 48–50+.

Interview with J. Lightbody, "Safety Valve for Employee Stress." *International Management* 36 (February 1981): 17–18.

Ivancevich, J. M. and Matteson, M. T. "Optimizing Human Resources: A Case for Preventive Health and Stress Management." *Organizational Dynamics* 9 (Autumn 1980): 5–25.

Ivancevich, John M., Matteson, Michael T., and Preston, Cynthia. "Occupational Stress, Type A Behavior, and Physical Well-Being." *Academy of Management* 25 (June 1982): 373–389.

Kahn, R. L. "Work, Stress and Individual Well Being." *Monthly Labor Review* 104 (May 1981): 28–30.

"Keeping Drugs Out of the Workplace." *Human Resources: Journal of the International Association for Personnel Women*, 2(3) (Summer 1985): 8–9.

Kutchins, Albert. "The Most Exclusive Remedy Is No Remedy at All: Workers' Compensation Coverage for Occupational Diseases." *Labor Law Journal* 32 (April 1981): 212–228.

Levine, Hermine Zagat. "Employee Assistance Programs." *Personnel* 62 (April 1985): 14.

Levinson, Harry. "When Executives Burn Out." *Harvard Business Review* 59 (May–June 1981): 73–81.

Lourie, Roger H. "Executive Stress: Pressure In a Grey Flannel Suit." *Direct Marketing* 44 (December 1981): 46–49.

Lundblad, E. C. "Incentive Programs Reduce Accidents, Save Money." *National Safety News* 131 (January 1985): 35–37.

Medman, Alan R. "Self-Health — A Survivor's Guide to Taking Charge and Combatting Stress." *Data Management* 19 (December 1981): 25–26.

Murray, T. H. "The Lethal Paradox in Occupational Health Research." *Business and Society Review* no. 53 (Spring 1985): 20–24.

"NLRB Limits Union Access (Limitations on a Union's Ability to Gather Workplace Information That Could Affect Safety and Health of Workers)." *Engineering News-Record* 214 (February 21, 1985): 50–51.

Nelson, John G. "Burn Out — Businesses' Most Costly Expense." *Personnel Administrator* 25 (August 1980): 81–87.

"OSHA Ordered to Talk About Toxics." *Engineering News-Record* 214 (June 6, 1985): 54.

"OSHA Sued for Failure to Shield Whistle Blowers (Worker Complaints)." *Engineering News-Record* 214 (June 13, 1985): 11–12.

"Persuading Employees to Stop Smoking." *International Management* 36 (April 1981): 26–29.

Pesci, Michael. "Stress Management: Separating Myth From Reality." *Personnel Administrator* 27 (January 1982): 57–67.

"Right to Know: An Ongoing Battle Grows Hotter." *Chemical Week* 136 (January 16, 1985): 8–10.

Robinson, J. C. "Racial Inequality and the Probability of Occupation-Related Injury or Illness." *Milbank Memorial Fund Quarterly Health and Society* 62 (Fall 1984): 567–590.

Rosen, Robert H. "The Picture of Health in the Work Place." *Training and Development Journal* (August 1984): 26.

"Safety Last." *Economist* 294 (February 16, 1985): 69.

Schuler, Randall S. "Occupational Health in Organizations: Strategies for Personnel Effectiveness." *Personnel Administrator* 27 (January 1982): 47–55.

Spencer, J. A. "Health Education Is Required!" *National Safety News* 131 (January 1985): 32–34.

Srachta, B. "Motivation, A Key to Fewer Accidents." *National Safety News* 131 (January 1985): 63–64.

"Today's Trends Suggest Revolutionary Changes for Business in the Future." *Personnel Administrator* 30 (February 1985): 70–71.

Weigel, Randy and Pinsky, Sheldon. "Managing Stress: A Model for the Human Resource Staff." *Personnel Administrator* 27 (February 1982): 56–60.

Wilkerson, Roderick. "Keep That Safety Committee Moving." *Supervision* 40 (March 1978): 24.

"Workplace Hazards Seen Exacerbated by U.S. Policy." *Chemical Marketing Reporter* 227 (January 28, 1985): 63–64.

Yankelovich, Daniel. "Managing in an Age of Anxiety." *Industry Week* 195 (October 24, 1977): 52–58.

Parma Cycle Company: Safety and Health at the New Plant

"I want the new plant to be a model of safety and health," said Mr. Burgess, the president of Parma Cycle Company in Parma, Ohio. "I do too," said Jesse Heard, the personnel director, "but you have to be aware that it's going to cost a lot." "Remember now, Jesse," the president replied, "we're putting the plant in Clarksdale, Mississippi primarily to reduce costs. I believe that the main thing we can do for safety is to train our workers to be safety conscious. That doesn't cost much." "That's the main thing, I know," said Jesse, "but we'll also have to spend some money. There are several areas where safety can be improved by installing hand rails. Also, a good number of the machines will come in without chain and belt guards. We'll have to have those fabricated." "Well," said Mr. Burgess, "let's just try to meet the OSHA requirements on those kinds of things. I'd like to see a cost benefit analysis of anything that goes beyond the OSHA standards."

At about that time, Cliff Brubaker, the chief engineer at Parma, who had also been summoned to the meeting, came in. After a few niceties, Cliff asked, "Mr. Burgess, making sure that all the machinery and the machine layouts meets OSHA requirements has made engineering the new plant a lot more difficult. We won't be able to use our floor space nearly as efficiently at Clarksdale as we do here at Parma. Also, the workflow is going to be less efficient because I had to separate machines to keep the area noise level below the maximum standard. Don't you think we could fudge a little on some

of this? The Parma plant doesn't come close to meeting OSHA requirements and we have only had one $5000 fine since I've been here."

"I don't think you can trade off personal safety against a few dollars of cost savings," Jesse said. "You remember when Joe Blum lost his arm last year? The company came out okay on that because Joe didn't sue us. But what about Joe? How much was his arm worth?" "Don't get upset, Jesse," said Cliff. "I know what you mean and I really feel the same way. But we can go to extremes." Mr. Burgess spoke up, "I don't think that meeting OSHA standards is going to extremes. Besides, if companies like Parma Cycle don't take some initiative in protecting workers, we're going to see even more enforcement efforts in the future. I want to make sure that you both understand my position. Everything in the plant at Clarksdale is to meet OSHA requirements for safety and health as a minimum. If the requirements can be exceeded with no additional cost, I want to opt for maximum safety. If you have to spend extra money to improve safety or health at the Clarksdale plant, I want to see a benefit-cost analysis on each item." "I think that that's clear enough," said Jesse. "Me too," said Cliff, "but I'll have to get back with you on a number of the modifications we had planned."

Questions

1. What do you think of Mr. Burgess' insistence on using OSHA standards as a goal?
2. Do you agree with Jesse that, "you can't trade off personal safety against a few dollars of cost savings?"

This is a role-playing exercise involving Roger Graves, an abrasive cut-off saw operator at Parma Cycle Company's Parma, Ohio plant, and Roy Brinson, his supervisor. The exercise is designed to highlight the kind of problems created when suspected alcohol or drug abuse produces a safety concern.

Role Descriptions

Roger Graves. You have been operating the abrasive cut-off saw for three years. The saw consists of an electric motor with a very thin, 24-inch diameter, reinforced grinding wheel, or "blade," attached. The grinding wheel spins at a high rate of speed, but is covered by a protective guard. You wear goggles as further protection and the vacuum system takes away the dust created by the spinning wheel.

You cut three-fourths-inch to 1-inch diameter steel tubing to various lengths. To do this, you slide a long length of tubing under the cut-off wheel until it contacts a spot that you have set at the appropriate distance from the saw. Then you grasp the handle on the saw and pull it downward until the wheel contacts the metal and cuts through it. You release the handle, allowing the saw to be pulled upward by a heavy spring. Then you move the piece of tubing you have cut and slide the tubing down for another cut. This continues throughout the

day with periodic changes in the diameter and length of the pieces you are cutting.

You don't consider your job particularly dangerous, although you realize that the saw blade would cut through anything coming in contact with it, including a hand or arm. You have also seen a saw blade explode when an operator pulled the handle down rapidly, causing the blade to contact the metal being sawed too sharply. If this should happen and the operator were not wearing safety goggles and a leather apron, the flying pieces of abrasive disk could cause injury.

Recently you have been having family problems. Your wife moved to her mother's home, taking your two children with her. You have tried to keep it from affecting your work. A few times, however, you have stayed up all night trying to work things out, driving to your wife's mother's home, and so forth. Thus you sometimes arrive at work the next day in pretty bad condition. Your supervisor has spoken to you a time or two about looking tired or being careless. You like and respect him; you really want to do a good job; but you think the personal problems you have may last for a long time. Your supervisor came by a little while ago and asked you to come to his office. The woman who operates your saw on the next shift has just shown up. As you head for the supervisor's office you think, "I sure hope there's no problem. All I need now is problems at work too."

Roy Brinson. You have been a supervisor at Parma for eight years and have been working in your present department for four of those years. Recently you have observed Roger Graves with increasing concern. Several times you have seen Roger barely miss his hand when bringing the cut-off saw into contact with the metal he was cutting. The OSHA inspector has complained about the safety of the machine but no way has been found to make it completely safe without seriously hampering productivity. Roger has been a safe operator until very recently. You suspect that he is an alcoholic now. He has come to work a number of times looking disheveled, red-eyed, and uncommunicative. He failed to show up for work one day without even calling. When you questioned him about it, he avoided a direct answer and you didn't press the matter. You think that Roger may need professional help.

Your immediate problem, though, is that you have decided you have to transfer him to a safer job. You have decided to assign him to the frame painter. There he will hang the bicycle frames on a conveyor which moves through a spray painting enclosure where the frames are automatically painted and baked dry. He will be responsible for adjusting the painting equipment, maintaining the conveyors, etc. The job is at the same skill level as his present job but it involves no significant danger. He will have to learn some new skills. You have talked this matter over with the personnel director. He agrees that you have no choice but to transfer Roger immediately. As you see Roger approaching the office you try to think of how you can tell him of your decision.

Questions

1. How should Roy Brinson break the news to Roger?
2. Discuss Roy's decision to transfer Roger. Suggest alternatives.
3. Do you have enough information to suggest that Roger has an alcohol-abuse problem? Defend your answer.

Part Six

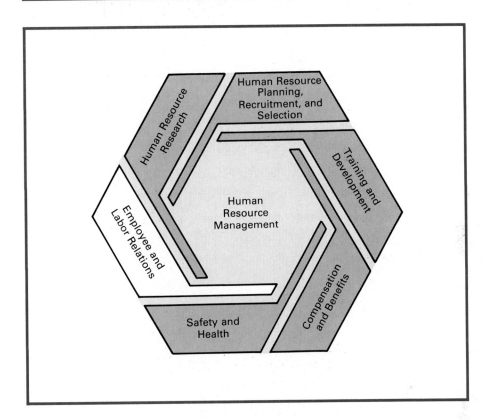

EMPLOYEE AND
LABOR RELATIONS

CHAPTER OBJECTIVES
1. Describe the history of the labor movement.
2. List the most significant union objectives.
3. Identify the reasons why employees join unions.
4. Describe the basic structure of union organization.
5. State the basic steps involved if a union desires to become the bargaining representative.
6. Explain the various strategies that a union may use in gaining bargaining unit recognition.

Chapter 15

THE LABOR UNION

Cameron Tyler and Michael David were having their ritual cup of coffee at the Wide Awake Cafe. They had been friends since high school and enjoyed the early morning visits before going to work. Cameron was operations manager at Capps, Inc., a plastics molding firm. Michael was head of the benefits department at ETC, an electronics assembly and testing firm.

"I just don't understand it," reflected Cameron. "You sound upset," said Michael, "what happened?" "Oh, we got word yesterday that some of our production people have filed a petition with the NLRB to conduct a representation election in our plant," replied Cameron. "What right do they have to do this? Why would they even want to? What's going to happen next? Mike, you've dealt with unions for years. Can you explain to me what's going on?" Michael shook his head and said, "Good luck! I think you had better take a crash course on the background of the union movement and what's involved in establishing a collective bargaining relationship. From the sound of things I think you're going to need all the help you can get."

Cameron's reaction to the NLRB petition is not unexpected. He is frustrated and disappointed to think that his employees would take such an action. He is probably fearful because he has heard about union drives at other companies. Because he is uninformed about the labor movement in the United States and legislation relating to it, Cameron is on the verge of panic and unable to plan and react effectively.

Since the turn of the century, no single factor has exerted more influence on human resource management than organized labor. Through the process of collective bargaining, organized labor has established patterns of employee–management relations that have influenced not only unionized companies but also those that strive to maintain nonunion status. Wage levels, benefits, and working conditions for millions of employees now reflect decisions made jointly by unions and management. Human resource policies and practices can no longer be determined unilaterally by management in many organizations.

Unions have become not only a political force in America, but they are also active in the general social and economic spheres of individual communities and the nation as a whole. They attempt to influence the decisions of state legislatures and Congress in such areas as employee recruitment and selection, training and development, compensation, and health and safety. Because of the prominent role that unions play in many organizations and in the society as a whole, human resource management has become much more complex. An understanding of the labor movement is essential for practitioners and students of HRM.

This chapter begins with a history of the labor movement in the U.S. and the legislation relating to it. Next, the objectives of unions, the reasons why employees join unions, and the multilevel organizational structure of unions are discussed. Finally, the steps that are taken to establish the collective bargaining relationship and some union strategies used to obtain recognition are presented.

THE LABOR MOVEMENT BEFORE 1930

Unions are not a recent development in American history. The earliest unions originated at the end of the eighteenth century about the time of the American Revolution. Although these early associations had few characteristics of present-day labor unions, they did bring workers together to consider problems of mutual concern. These early unions were local in nature and usually existed for only a short time.[1]

---

[1]*Brief History of the American Labor Movement*, U.S. Department of Labor, Bureau of Labor Statistics, Bulletin 1000, 1970 ed., p. 1.

The labor movement has not followed a simple and straightforward line of development. Instead, it has experienced as much failure as success. Employer opposition, the impact of the business cycle, the growth and development of American industry, court rulings, and legislation have exerted their influence in varying degrees at various times. As a result, the labor movement's history has somewhat resembled the swinging of a pendulum. At times, the pendulum has moved in favor of labor and, at other times, it has swung toward the advantage of management.

Prior to the 1930s, the trend definitely favored management. The courts strongly supported employers in their attempts to thwart the organized labor movement. This was first evidenced by use of criminal and civil conspiracy doctrines derived from English common law. A **conspiracy,** generally defined, is *the combination of two or more persons who band together to prejudice the rights of others or of society (e.g., by refusing to work or demanding higher wages).* An important feature of the conspiracy doctrine is that an action by one person, though legal, becomes illegal when carried out by a group. From 1806 to 1842, seventeen cases went to trial charging labor unions with conspiracies.[2] These cases resulted in the demise of several union organizations and certainly discouraged union activities by other groups of employees. The conspiracy doctrine was softened considerably by the decision in the landmark case *Commonwealth v. Hunt* in 1842. In that case Chief Justice Shaw of the Supreme Judicial Court of Massachusetts contended that labor organizations were legal organizations. In order for a union to be convicted under the conspiracy doctrine, it must be shown that the objectives of the union are unlawful or the means employed to gain a lawful end are unlawful.[3]

Other tactics used by employers to stifle union growth were injunctions and yellow-dog contracts. The **injunction** is *a prohibiting legal procedure that was used by employers to prevent certain union activities such as strikes and unionization attempts.* The **yellow-dog contract** was *a written agreement between the employee and the company made at the time of employment, prohibiting a worker from joining a union or engaging in union activities.* Each of these defensive tactics, used by management and supported by the courts, severely limited union growth.

In the latter half of the nineteenth century the American industrial system started to grow and prosper. Factory production began to displace handicraft forms of manufacturing. The Civil War gave the factory system a great boost. Goods were demanded in quantities that only mass production methods could supply. The railroads developed new networks of routes spanning the continent and knitting the country into an economic whole. Employment was high and unions sought to organize workers in both new and expanding enterprises. Most unions during this time were small and rather weak, and many did not survive the economic recession of the 1870s.

[2]Benjamin J. Taylor and Fred Witney, *Labor Relations Law,* 4th ed. Englewood Cliffs, N.J.: Prentice-Hall, 1983, pp. 19–21.

[3]Ibid., p. 24.

Union membership rose to 300,000 by 1872 and then dropped to 50,000 by 1878.[4] This period also marked the rise of radical labor activity and increased industrial strife as unions struggled for recognition and survival.[5]

Out of the turbulence of the 1870s emerged the most substantial labor organization that had yet appeared in the United States. The Noble Order of the Knights of Labor was founded in 1869 as a secret society of the Philadelphia garment workers. After its secrecy was abandoned and other crafts were invited to join, it grew rapidly, reaching a membership of more than 700,000 by the mid-1880s. Internal conflict among the Knights' leadership in 1881 gave rise to the nucleus of a new organization that would soon replace it on the labor scene.[6] That organization was the American Federation of Labor (AFL).

Devoted to "pure and simple unionism," Samuel Gompers, of the Cigarmakers Union, led some twenty-five labor groups representing the skilled trades to found the American Federation of Labor in 1886. Gompers was elected the first president of the AFL, a position he held, except for one year (1894–1895), until his death in 1924. He is probably the single most important individual in American trade union history. The AFL began with a membership of some 138,000 and doubled that number during the next twelve years.[7]

In 1890, Congress passed the Sherman Anti-Trust Act. This marked the entrance of the federal government into the statutory regulation of labor organizations. Although the primary stimulus for this act came from public concern over business's monopoly power, court interpretations soon applied its provisions to organized labor. Later, in 1914, Congress passed the Clayton Act (an amendment to the Sherman Act) with the intent of removing labor from the purview of the Sherman Act. Again, judicial interpretation nullified that intent and left labor even more exposed to lawsuits.[8] Nonetheless, the AFL grew to almost five million members by 1920.[9]

During the 1920s labor faced legal restrictions on union activity and unfavorable court decisions. The one exception to such repressive policies was the passage and approval of the Railway Labor Act of 1926. This was the first time that the government declared without qualification the right of private employees to join unions and bargain collectively through representatives of their own choosing without interference from their employers. It also set up special machinery for the settlement of labor disputes. Although the act covered only employees in the railroad industry (a later amendment extended coverage to the airline industry) it foreshadowed the extension of similar rights to other classes of employees in the 1930s.

[4]*Brief History,* p. 9.

[5]See Foster Rhea Dulles, *Labor in America,* 3rd ed. New York: Crowell, 1966, pp. 114–125.

[6]Ibid., pp. 126–149.

[7]*Brief History,* pp. 15–16.

[8]E. Edward Herman and Alfred Kuhn, *Collective Bargaining and Labor Relations.* Englewood Cliffs, N.J.: Prentice-Hall, 1981, pp. 37–39.

[9]*Brief History,* p. 27.

Art E. Hobbs
Vice President,
Employee Relations/
Administration
E-Systems, Inc.

In 1970, Art E. Hobbs graduated from the University of Texas at Arlington with a degree in business management. Twelve years later he was named vice president, employee relations/administration for E-Systems, Inc., Greenville Division. His meteoric rise in the field of human resource management is a tribute to his pursuit of excellence and the skillful execution of a professional career plan. His first job upon graduation was with Texas Power and Light Company as a field account manager. In this position, he was placed in various assignments of increasing responsibility in the area of field accounting. While with TP&L, Hobbs received training in all facets of district level operations including personnel, accounting, and marketing. That initial training continues to have a major impact on his career. In 1973 he joined Frito-Lay, Inc. as a training specialist and was quickly recognized for his overall grasp of the personnel function. Less than a year later, he was promoted to personnel manager for the Lubbock, Texas and Denver, Colorado operations. Early in 1978, Hobbs returned to the Dallas headquarters of Frito-Lay as employee relations manager and, later, as the manager of Management Institute. In this position he was responsible for developing and implementing a centralized "Institute" approach to management skills training.

When the position of director, employee relations became open at E-Systems, Inc., Hobbs was asked to apply. He did so, and was offered the position which he ac-

cepted in late 1979. In that capacity he was accountable for all employee relations functions including staffing, compensation, benefits, administrative services, labor relations, EEO, and training/management development. One year later he was promoted to director of administration where his responsibility was expanded to include security and public relations in addition to employee relations. In September of 1982, Hobbs was named vice president, employee relations/administration.

When asked to describe a major problem he had encountered in the area of personnel and how he ultimately resolved it, Hobbs replied, "For many years, the working relationship between organized labor and management at the Greenville Division of E-Systems was best described as adversarial. During previous contract negotiations, the adversary, or win-lose approach, had resulted in an extended strike, the results of which have lingered on to the present time. Day-to-day activity involving labor and management were characterized by one-upmanship and very little true problem solving was achieved. I developed a pro-active labor relations program emphasizing problem prevention rather than reaction. Some specific elements of this program include:

- Building a responsible relationship with union representatives.
- Holding regular meetings with union officials to discuss issues and concerns before they become grievance problems.
- Increasing "floor time" for labor relations representatives.
- Striving for win-win solutions to problems.

- Orientation and training for supervisors on how to administer the day-to-day aspects of the labor agreement.
- Communicating with supervisors/managers on a regular basis regarding contract interpretation, grievance settlements, etc.
- Administering a new employee orientation program with a special section on how to resolve problems, questions, and concerns."

Hobbs notes that as a result of implementing this new pro-active labor relations program, several positive results have been achieved. These results include: reduced number of grievances, reduced number of arbitrations, reduced time spent by company and union representatives on grievances, a new labor agreement negotiated with no strike vote taken, and an improved working climate among supervisors and the bargaining unit.

While new challenges lie ahead, he takes great pride in his accomplishments in the field of human resources management. "My only regret," he says, "is that I did not recognize my interest in Personnel while in college. But, there were not that many personnel courses available while I was in school. Today's graduates have a much better opportunity to be exposed to the advantages of a major in personnel and human resource management."

THE LABOR MOVEMENT AFTER 1930

The 1930s found the United States in the midst of the worst depression in its history. The unemployment rate rose as high as 25 percent.[10] The sentiment of the country began to favor organized labor as many people blamed business for the agony that accompanied the Great Depression. The pendulum began to swing away from management and toward labor.

ANTI-INJUNCTION ACT (NORRIS–LAGUARDIA ACT) — 1932

The Great Depression caused a substantial change in the public's thinking about the role of unions in society. Congress reflected this thinking in 1932 with the passage of the Norris–LaGuardia Act. It affirms that U.S. public policy sanctions collective bargaining and approves the formation and effective operation of labor unions.[11] While this act did not outlaw the use

[10]*Historical Statistics of the United States, Colonial Times to 1970, Bicentennial Edition, Part I.* Washington, D.C.: U.S. Bureau of the Census, 1975, p. 126.
[11]Taylor and Witney, *Labor Relations Law*, pp. 90–93.

of injunctions, it severely restricted the federal courts' authority to issue them in labor disputes. It also made yellow-dog contracts unenforceable in the federal courts.[12]

NATIONAL LABOR RELATIONS ACT (WAGNER ACT) — 1935

In 1933 Congress made an abortive attempt to stimulate economic recovery by passing the National Industry Recovery Act (NIRA). Declared unconstitutional by the U.S. Supreme Court in May, 1935, the NIRA did provide the nucleus for legislation that followed it. Section 7a of the NIRA proclaimed the right of workers to organize and bargain collectively. Congress did not, however, provide procedures to enforce these rights.[13]

Undeterred by the Supreme Court decision and strongly supported by organized labor, Congress speedily enacted a comprehensive labor law, the National Labor Relations Act (Wagner Act). This act, approved by President Roosevelt on July 5, 1935, is one of the most significant pieces of labor–management relations legislation ever enacted. Drawing heavily on the experience of the Railway Labor Act of 1926 and Section 7a of NIRA, the act declared legislative support, on a broad scale, of the right of labor to organize and engage in collective bargaining. The spirit of the Wagner Act is stated in Section 7, which defines the substantive rights of employees:

> Employees shall have the right to self-organization, to form, join, or assist labor organizations, to bargain collectively through representatives of their own choosing, and to engage in other concerted activities, for the purpose of collective bargaining or other mutual aid or protection.

The rights defined in Section 7 were protected against employer interference by Section 8, which detailed and prohibited five management practices deemed to be unfair to labor:

1. Interfering with or restraining or coercing employees in the exercise of their right to self-organization.
2. Dominating or interfering in the affairs of a union.
3. Discriminating in regard to hire or tenure or any condition of employment for the purpose of encouraging or discouraging union membership.
4. Discriminating against or discharging an employee who has filed charges or given testimony under the act.
5. Refusing to bargain with chosen representatives of employees.

The **National Labor Relations Board (NLRB)** was created by the Na-tional Labor Relations Act to administer and enforce the provisions of the act. The NLRB has been given two principle functions: (1) to establish procedures for holding bargaining-unit elections and to monitor the election

[12]Ibid., pp. 93–97.
[13]Ibid., pp. 166–167.

procedures; and (2) to investigate complaints and prevent unlawful acts involving unfair labor practices. Much of the NLRB's work is delegated to thirty-three regional offices throughout the country.

Following passage of the Wagner Act, union membership increased from approximately 3 million to 15 million between 1935 and 1947.[14] The increase was most conspicuous in industries utilizing mass production methods. New unions in these industries were organized on an industrial basis rather than a craft basis, and members were primarily unskilled or semi-skilled workers. An internal struggle developed within the AFL over the question of whether unions should be organized to include all workers in an industry or organized strictly on a craft or occupational basis. In 1935 six AFL-affiliated unions and the officers of two other AFL unions formed a "Committee for Industrial Organization" to promote the organization of workers in mass production and unorganized industries. The controversy grew to the point that in May 1938 the AFL expelled the Committee for Industrial Organization unions. In November 1938 the expelled unions held their first convention in Pittsburgh and reorganized as a federation of unions under the name of Congress of Industrial Organizations (CIO). The new federation included nine unions expelled from the AFL and thirty-two other groups established to recruit workers in various industries.[15] John L. Lewis, president of the United Mine Workers, was elected the first president of the CIO.

The rivalry generated by the two large federations stimulated union organizing efforts in both groups. With the ensuing growth, the labor movement gained considerable influence in the United States. However, many individuals and groups began to feel that the Wagner Act was too prolabor. This shift in public sentiment was in part related to costly strikes following World War II. Whether justified or not, the blame for these disruptions fell on the unions.

LABOR MANAGEMENT RELATIONS ACT
(TAFT–HARTLEY ACT) — 1947

In 1947, with public pressure mounting, Congress overrode President Truman's veto and passed the Labor Management Relations Act (Taft–Hartley Act). The Taft–Hartley Act extensively revised the National Labor Relations Act, which became Title I of the new law. A new period in public policy regarding labor began. The pendulum had again begun to swing toward a position that reflected more of a balance between labor and management.

Some of the important changes introduced by the Taft–Hartley Act included:

[14]Bernstein, "The Growth of American Unions," *American Economic Review* 44 (1954): 308–317.

[15]*Brief History,* pp. 31–33.

1. Modification of Section 7 to include the right of employees to refrain from union activity as well as engage in it.
2. Prohibition of the closed shop (the arrangement requiring that all workers be union members at the time they are hired) and narrowed the freedom of the parties to authorize the union shop (the employer may hire anyone he or she chooses, but all new workers must join the union after a stipulated period of time).
3. Broadening of the employer's right of free speech.
4. Provision that employers need not recognize or bargain with unions formed by supervisory personnel.
5. Giving employees the right to initiate decertification petitions.
6. Provision for government intervention in "national emergency strikes."

A significant change in the Act extended the concept of unfair labor practices to unions. Labor organizations were to refrain from:

1. Restraining or coercing employees in the exercise of their guaranteed collective bargaining rights.
2. Causing an employer to discriminate in any way against an employee in order to encourage or discourage union membership.
3. Refusing to bargain in good faith with an employer regarding wages, hours, and other conditions of employment.
4. Engaging in certain types of strikes and boycotts.
5. Requiring employees covered by union-shop contracts to pay initiation fees or dues "in an amount which the Board finds excessive or discriminatory under all circumstances."
6. "Featherbedding", i.e., requiring that an employer pay for services not performed.

One of the most controversial elements of the Taft–Hartley Act is its Section 14b, which permits states to enact right-to-work legislation. **Right-to-work laws** are *laws that prohibit management and unions from developing agreements requiring union membership as a condition of employment.* Twenty-one states, located primarily in the South and West, have adopted such laws, which are a continuing source of irritation between labor and management.[16] Much of the impetus behind the right-to-work movement is provided by the National Right to Work Committee, based in Springfield, Virginia.[17]

For about ten years after the passage of the Taft–Hartley Act, union membership expanded at about the same rate as nonagricultural employ-

[16]In January 1985, Idaho became the twenty-first state. Other states are: Alabama, Arizona, Arkansas, Florida, Georgia, Iowa, Kansas, Louisiana, Mississippi, Nebraska, Nevada, North Carolina, North Dakota, South Carolina, South Dakota, Tennessee, Texas, Utah, Virginia, and Wyoming.
[17]Arthur A. Sloane and Fred Witney, *Labor Relations*, 4th ed. Englewood Cliffs, N.J.: Prentice-Hall, 1981, p. 378.

ment. But all was not well within the organized labor movement. Ever since the creation of the CIO, the two federations had engaged in a bitter and costly rivalry. Both the CIO and the AFL recognized the increasing need for cooperation and reunification. In 1955, following two years of intensive negotiations between the two organizations, a merger agreement was ratified and the AFL-CIO became a reality. In the years following the merger, however, the AFL-CIO faced some of its greatest challenges.

LABOR–MANAGEMENT REPORTING AND DISCLOSURE ACT (LANDRUM–GRIFFIN ACT) — 1959

Corruption had plagued organized labor since the early 1900s. Periodic revelations of graft, violence, extortion, racketeering, and other improper activities aroused public indignation and invited governmental investigation. Even though the number of unions involved was small, every disclosure undermined the public image of organized labor as a whole.[18]

Scrutiny of union activities intensified after World War II and ultimately led to the creation in 1957 of the Senate Select Committee on Improper Activities in the Labor or Management Field, headed by Senator McClellan of Arkansas. Between 1957 and 1959, the McClellan Committee held a series of nationally televised public hearings that shocked and alarmed the entire country. As evidence of improper activities mounted, the AFL-CIO moved to take action.

In 1957, the AFL-CIO expelled three unions (representing approximately 1.6 million members) for their practices. One of them, the Teamsters, was the largest union in the country. In 1959, largely as a result of the recommendations of the McClellan Committee, Congress enacted the Labor–Management Reporting and Disclosure Act (Landrum–Griffin Act). This Act marked a significant turning point in the involvement of the federal government in internal union affairs. The Landrum–Griffin Act spelled out a "Bill of Rights of Members of Labor Organizations" designed to protect certain rights of individuals in their relationships with unions. The Act requires extensive reporting on numerous internal union activities and contains severe penalties for violations. Employers are also required to file reports when they engage in activities or make expenditures that might undermine the collective bargaining process or interfere with protected employee rights. In addition, the Act amended the Taft–Hartley Act by adding additional restrictions on picketing and secondary boycotts.

In 1974, Congress extended coverage of the Taft–Hartley Act to private not-for-profit hospitals and health care institutions. This amendment

---

[18]Dulles, *Labor*, pp. 382–383.

brought within the jurisdiction of the National Labor Relations Board some 2 million employees. Proprietary (profit-making) health care organizations were previously under NLRB jurisdiction. The amendment does not cover government-operated hospitals; it applies only to the private sector.

The labor movement has experienced membership problems since the mid-1950s. In 1968 the second largest union in the country, the United Auto Workers, disaffiliated with the AFL-CIO. The UAW reaffiliated with the AFL-CIO in 1981. Also, between 1950 and 1980, union membership dropped from about one-third of the nonfarm work force to 19 percent. If this trend continues, union membership would be at 1930 levels by the year 2000.[19]

A trend is also developing regarding the ability of unions to gain recognition as collective bargaining agents in companies. In 1968, unions won 57.1 percent of the representation elections held by the NLRB. By 1981, union victories had dropped to 44 percent.[20] The trend for that period is shown in Figure 15–1.

THE PUBLIC SECTOR

Government employees are generally considered a class apart from other workers. This is reflected in their exclusion from the coverage of general labor legislation.[21] However, like their counterparts in private industry, government employees have demonstrated a persistence in organizing in order to gain an effective voice in the manner and terms of their employment.

For many years the federal government had no well-defined policy on labor–management relations regarding its own employees. On January 17, 1962, President John F. Kennedy issued Executive Order 10988. Section 1(a) of the Order stated:

> Employees of the federal government shall have, and shall be protected in the exercise of, the right, freely and without fear of penalty or reprisal, to form, join and assist any employee organization or to refrain from any such activity.

For the first time in the history of the federal civil service, a uniform, comprehensive policy of cooperation between employee organizations

---

[19]"Beyond Unions," *Business Week,* July 8, 1985, p. 72.

[20]Ann M. Reilly, "Big Labor's Crumbling Clout," *Dun's Review* 112 (October 1978): 53; U.S. National Labor Relations Board, *Forty-Sixth Annual Report 1981.* Washington, D.C.: U.S. Government Printing Office, 1981, pp. 18, 205–206.

[21]Examples include the Social Security Act, Fair Labor Standards Act, and the National Labor Relations Act, as amended.

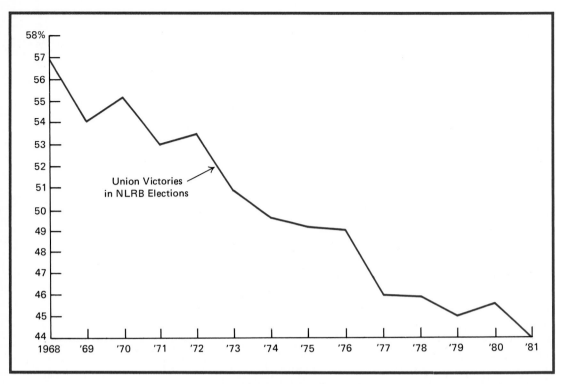

Figure 15–1. Union victories in NLRB elections. Source: National Labor Relations Board.

and management in the executive branch of government was established. Employees were permitted to organize and negotiate personnel policies and practices and matters affecting working conditions that were within the administrative discretion of the agency officials concerned. Employees could not strike, however. Public Law 84-330, passed in 1955, had made it a felony to strike against the U.S. government.[22]

Executive Order 10988 established the basic framework for collective bargaining in federal government agencies. Subsequent EOs revised and improved this framework and brought about a new era of labor relations in the public sector.[23] In fact, the federal government transferred to and codified the provisions of those executive orders in Title VII of the Civil Service Reform Act of 1978. This Act regulates most of the labor–management relations in the federal service. It establishes the Federal Labor Relations Authority (FLRA), which is modeled on the National Labor Relations Board.

[22]Section 305 of the Labor Management Relations Act of 1947 also makes it unlawful for government employees to participate in any strike.

[23]Executive Order 11491 (effective January 1, 1970); EO 11616 (effective November 1971); EO 11636 (effective December 1971); EO 11838 (effective May 1975).

Requirements and mechanisms for recognition and elections, dealing with impasses, and handling grievances are covered in the Act.

The U.S. Postal Service is not subject to Title VII of the Civil Service Reform Act of 1978. It was removed from cabinet status and given independent government agency status by the Postal Reorganization Act of 1970. Postal employees were given collective bargaining rights comparable to those governing private industry. National Labor Relations Board rules and regulations controlling representation issues and elections are applicable to the postal service. Unfair labor practice provisions are also enforced by the NLRB. However, the right to strike is prohibited and union-shop arrangements are not permitted.

There is no uniform pattern to state and local labor relations and bargaining rights. Some states have no policy at all, while a haphazard mixture of statutes, resolutions, ordinances, and civil service procedures exists in others. By 1980, some thirty-eight states had passed some form of legislation that obligates state agencies and local governments to permit their public employees to join unions and to recognize bona fide labor organizations.[24] Prior to 1960, less than a handful of states had such legislation. The diversity of state labor laws makes it difficult to generalize about the legal environment affecting collective bargaining at the state and local levels.

Unilateral determination of the conditions of employment by employers is increasingly being questioned by public employees. Employers are having their decisions questioned not only by their employees, but also by the unions and associations that represent them. Placed in the middle between their employees and the general public, state and local governments are being forced to specify in clearer terms the collective bargaining rights of workers.[25]

EMPLOYEE ASSOCIATIONS[26]

The Bureau of Labor Statistics lists thirty-four major professional and state employee associations, which represent more than 2.6 million people. The largest, the National Education Association, has almost 1,700,000 members. Other major associations include the American Nurses' Association, 187,000 members, and the American Association of Classified School Employees, 150,000. The number of locals (chapters) affiliated with employee associations is 16,689, with 65 percent chartered by the NEA.

[24]Herman and Kuhn, *Collective Bargaining*, p. 93.

[25]Taylor and Witney, *Labor Relations Law*, p. 654.

[26]*Directory of National Unions and Employee Associations*, U.S. Department of Labor, Bureau of Labor Statistics, Bulletin 2079, September 1980.

In the past, employee associations were concerned primarily with the professional aspects of employment and avoided any semblance of unionism. In recent years, this has changed as public and private sector unions have actively organized both professional and government employees. Many employee associations are now enthusiastically pursuing collective bargaining relationships on behalf of employees with employers.

OBJECTIVES OF UNIONS

As previously indicated, the labor movement has a long history in the United States. Yet, each union within the movement is a unique organization seeking its own objectives. However, several broad objectives characterize the labor movement as a whole. These include:

1. To secure and, if possible, improve the living standards and economic status of its members.
2. To enhance and, if possible, guarantee individual security against threats and contingencies that might result from market fluctuations, technological change, or management decisions.
3. To influence power relations in the social system in ways that favor and do not threaten union gains and goals.
4. To advance the welfare of all who work for a living, whether union members or not.[27]

In order to accomplish these objectives, most unions recognize that they must strive for continued growth and power. Although growth and power are related, they will be discussed separately.

GROWTH

To maximize its effectiveness a union must strive for continued growth. Members pay dues, which are vitally needed to promote the union cause. Thus an overall goal of most unions is continued growth. But, as we previously mentioned, the percentage of union members in the work force is declining. Many union leaders are concerned about this trend. Much of a union's ability to accomplish its objectives is derived from strength in numbers. For this reason, unions must continue to explore new sources of potential members. Unions have recently directed much of their attention toward the service industries, professional employees, and government employees.

---

[27]Edwin F. Beal and James P. Begin, *The Practice of Collective Bargaining*, 6th ed. Homewood, Ill.: Richard D. Irwin, 1982, p. 91.

POWER

Power is defined here as the amount of external control an organization is able to exert. As such, a union's power is influenced to a large extent by the size of its membership. However, there are other facts to be considered.

The importance of the jobs held by union members significantly affects union power. For instance, an entire plant may have to be shut down if unionized machinists performing critical jobs decide to strike. A few strategically located union members may exert a disproportionate amount of power. A union's power can also be determined from the type of firm that is unionized. Unionization of such key workers as truckers, steelworkers, or farm workers can affect the entire country. Through control of key industries, a union's power may extend to firms that are not unionized. For instance, in some geographic areas of the country the power of the trucking unions extends well beyond firms that the truckers serve. Firms that depend on deliveries by the trucking industry often yield to union pressures in order to continue receiving services.

By achieving growth and power, a union is capable of exerting its force in the political arena. *The political arm of the AFL-CIO is the* **Committee on Political Education (COPE).** Founded in 1955, its purpose is to support politicians who are friendly to the cause of organized labor. The union recommends and assists candidates who will best serve its interests. Union members also encourage their friends to support those candidates. The larger the voting membership, the greater the union influence with politicians. With "friends" in government, the union is in a much stronger position to maneuver against management.

WHY EMPLOYEES JOIN UNIONS

Individuals join unions for many different reasons, and these reasons tend to change over time. They may involve job, personal, social, or political considerations. It would be impossible to discuss them all, but the following are some of the major reasons: dissatisfaction with management, need for a social outlet, opportunity for leadership, forced unionization, and social pressure from peers.

DISSATISFACTION WITH MANAGEMENT

Every job holds potential for real dissatisfactions. Each individual has a boiling point that can trigger him or her to consider a union as a solution to real or perceived problems. Unions look for problems in organizations and then emphasize the advantages of union membership as a means of solving them. Some of the more common reasons for employee dissatisfaction are described on p. 554.

Compensation. Employees want their compensation to be fair and equitable. Wages are important to them because they provide both the necessities and pleasures of life. If employees are dissatisfied with their wages, they may look to the union for assistance in improving their standard of living.

An important psychological aspect of compensation involves the amount of pay an individual receives in relation to that of other workers performing similar work. If an employee perceives that management has shown favoritism by paying someone else more to perform the same or a lower level job, the employee will likely become dissatisfied. Union members know precisely the basis of their pay and how it compares with others.

Job security. For a young employee, job security is often less important than it is for an older worker. He or she may feel that "If I lose this job, I can always get another." But, if employees see management consistently terminating older employees to make room for younger, more aggressive workers, they may begin to think about job security. If the firm does not provide its employees with a feeling of job security, the workers may turn to a union.

Management's attitude. People like to feel that they are important. They do not like to be considered a commodity that can be bought and sold. In some firms, management's attitude is one of insensitivity to the needs of its employees. When this situation occurs, employees may perceive that they have little or no influence or control in job-related matters. Workers who feel that they are not really part of an organization are prime targets for unionization.

Management's attitude may be reflected in such small actions as how notices on the bulletin board are written. Memos addressed "To All Employees" instead of "To Our Employees" may indicate a management attitude of indifference to employee needs. This attitude will likely stem from top management. But it is initially noticed in the actions of first-line supervisors. Workers may notice that the supervisors are judging people entirely on what they can do, how much they can do, and when they can do it. Because of this attitude, employees may be treated more as machines than people. Supervisors may fail to give reasons for unusual assignments and may expect employees to dedicate their entire lives to the firm without providing adequate rewards. The prevailing philosophy may be: "If you don't like it here, leave." When management does not consider the needs of the employees as individuals, the firm is ripe for unionization.

A SOCIAL OUTLET

People, by nature, have strong social needs. They generally enjoy being around others who have similar interests and desires. Some employees join a union for no other reason than to take advantage of union-sponsored

recreational and social activities that members and their families find
fulfilling.

Some unions now offer day care centers and other services that appeal
to working men and women and increase their sense of solidarity with
other union members. People who develop close personal relationships
will likely stand together in difficult times.

PROVIDING OPPORTUNITY FOR LEADERSHIP

Certain individuals aspire to leadership roles. It is not always easy for an
operative employee to progress into management. Many individuals may
not even desire to enter management of the firm. However, those employees
with leadership aspirations can often satisfy these ambitions through the
union. As with the firm, the union also has a hierarchy of leadership, and
individual members have the opportunity to work their way up through
its various levels. Employers often notice employees who are leaders in the
union and it is not uncommon to find them promoted into managerial ranks
as supervisors.

FORCED UNIONIZATION

It is generally illegal for management to require that an individual join a
union prior to employment. However, in the twenty-nine states without
right-to-work laws, it is legal for an employer to agree with the union that
a new employee must join the union after a certain period of time (generally
thirty days) or be terminated. This is referred to as a union-shop agreement.
Data are not available to indicate the number of employees who become
union members because of these compulsory agreements.

PEER PRESSURE

Many individuals will join a union simply because they are urged to do
so by other members of the work group. Friends and associates may constantly remind an employee that he or she is not a member of the union.
This social pressure from peers is difficult to resist. Failure to join the union
may result in complete rejection of the employee by other workers. In
extreme cases, union members have threatened nonmembers with physical
violence and have sometimes even carried out these threats.

UNION STRUCTURE

The labor movement has developed a multilevel organizational structure
over time. This complex of organizations ranges all the way from local
unions to the principal federation, the AFL-CIO. Each level has its own

officers and ways of managing its operations. Many national unions have intermediate levels between the national and the local levels. In this section, however, we will describe only the three basic elements of union organization: (1) the local union; (2) the national union; and (3) the federation, or AFL-CIO.

THE LOCAL UNION

The basic element in the structure of the American labor movement is the **local union.** To the individual union member, it is the most important level in the structure of organized labor. Through the local, the individual deals with the employer on a day-to-day basis. There are approximately 64,000 local unions in the United States, most of which are affiliated with one of the 174 national unions.[28]

There are two basic kinds of local unions: craft and industrial. **Craft unions,** such as the Carpenters and Joiners, are *typically composed of members of a particular trade or skill in an area or locality.* Members usually acquire their job skills through an apprenticeship training program. **Industrial unions** generally *consist of all the workers in a particular plant or group of plants.* The specific kind of work they do or the level of skill they possess is not a condition for membership in the union. An example of an industrial union is the United Auto Workers.

The local union's functions are many and varied. Administering the collective bargaining agreement and representing the workers in handling grievances are two important activities. Other functions include keeping the membership informed about labor issues, promoting increased membership, maintaining effective contact with the national union, and, when appropriate, negotiating with local level management.

THE NATIONAL (OR INTERNATIONAL) UNION

The most powerful level in the union structure is the national union. As previously stated, most locals are affiliated with national unions. Some national unions are called *international* because they have affiliated locals in Canada.

A **national union** is *composed of local unions, which it charters.* As such, it is the parent organization to the local unions. The local union — not the individual worker — holds membership in the national union. The national union is supported financially by each local union, whose contribution is based on its membership size.

[28]*Directory,* p. 73.

The national union is governed by a national constitution and a national convention of local unions, which usually meets every two to five years. The day-to-day operation of the national is conducted by elected officers, aided by an administrative staff. The national union is active in organizing any unorganized workers within its jurisdiction, engaging in collective bargaining at the national level, and assisting its locals in their negotiations. In addition, the national union may provide numerous educational and research services for its constituent locals, dispense strike funds, publish the union newspaper, provide legal counsel, and actively lobby at national and state levels.

AFL-CIO

The American Federation of Labor and Congress of Industrial Organizations (AFL-CIO) is the central trade union federation in the United States. It represents the interests of labor and its member national unions at the highest level. The federation engages in no collective bargaining; however, it provides the means through which member unions can cooperate to pursue common objectives and attempt to resolve internal problems faced by organized labor. The federation is financed by its member national unions and is governed by a national convention, which meets every two years.

As shown in Figure 15–2, the structure of the AFL-CIO is complex. The federation has state AFL-CIO bodies in all fifty states and Puerto Rico. In addition, national unions can affiliate with one or more of the trade and industrial departments. These departments seek to promote the interests of specific groups of workers who are in different unions but who have common interests. Among the federation's major activities are:

1. Improving the image of organized labor.
2. Extensive lobbying on behalf of labor interests.
3. Political education through COPE (Committee on Political Education).
4. Resolving disputes between national unions.
5. Policing internal affairs of member unions.

The AFL-CIO is a loosely knit organization of some 100 national unions. It has little formal power or control. The member national unions remain completely autonomous and decide their own policies and programs. Not all national unions are members of the federation. In fact, one of the largest unions is not a member; the Teamsters Union was expelled in 1957. In the late 1970s affiliated unions, however, represented approximately 17,024,000 members, or about 78 percent of all union members in the United States.[29]

[29]Ibid.

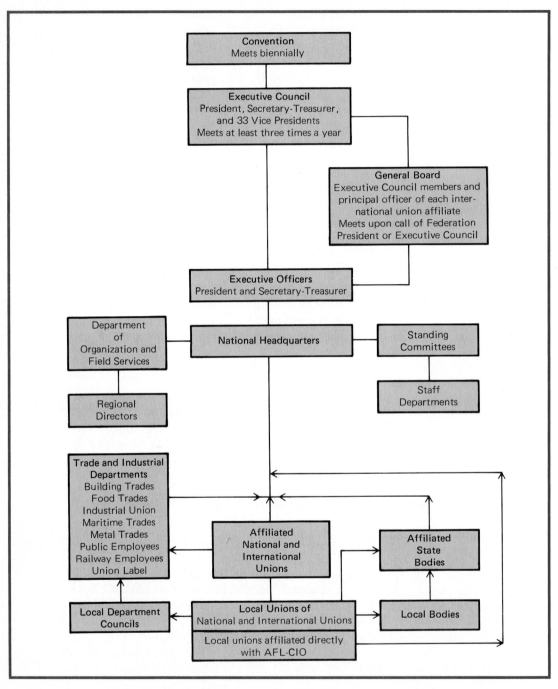

Figure 15–2. The structure of the AFL-CIO. Source: Bureau of Labor Statistics, *Directory of National Unions and Employee Associations*, 1980.

ESTABLISHING THE COLLECTIVE BARGAINING RELATIONSHIP

The primary law governing the relationship of companies and unions is the National Labor Relations Act, as amended.[30] Collective bargaining is one of the key parts of the Act. Section 7 of the Act states that "employees shall have the right to self-organization, to form, join, or assist labor organizations, to bargain collectively through representatives of their own choosing, or to engage in other concerted activities for the purpose of collective bargaining. . . ."

As defined by Section 8(d) of the act, **collective bargaining** is:

> the performance of the mutual obligation of the employer and the representative of the employees to meet at reasonable times and confer in good faith with respect to wages, hours, and other terms and conditions of employment, or the negotiation of an agreement, or any question arising thereunder, and the execution of a written contract incorporating any agreement reached if requested by either party, but such obligation does not compel either party to agree to a proposal or require the making of a concession.

The Act further provides that the designated or selected representative of the employees shall be the exclusive representative for all the employees in the unit for purpose of collective bargaining. A **bargaining unit** consists of *a group of employees, not necessarily union members, recognized by an employer or certified by an administrative agency as appropriate for representation by a labor organization for purposes of collective bargaining.* A unit may cover the employees in one plant of an employer, or it may cover employees in two or more plants of the same employer. Although the Act requires the representative to be selected by the employees, it does not require any particular procedure be used, so long as the choice clearly reflects the desire of the majority of the employees in the bargaining unit. The employee representative is normally chosen in a secret election conducted by the NLRB. When a union desires to become the bargaining representative for a group of employees, several steps leading to certification have to be taken (see Figure 15–3). External and internal factors can affect the process. The primary external factors are legislation and the union; the prevailing organizational culture can affect the internal environment.

SIGNING AUTHORIZATION CARDS

A prerequisite to forming a recognized bargaining unit is to determine whether there is sufficient amount of interest on the part of employees. Evidence of this interest is expressed when at least 30 percent of the employees in a work group sign an authorization card. The **authorization card** is *a document indicating that an employee wants to be represented by a*

---

[30]Common usage is the Labor Management Relations Act of 1947 (Taft–Hartley Act).

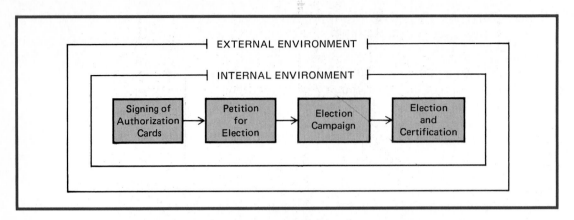

Figure 15–3. The steps that lead to forming a bargaining unit.

labor organization in collective bargaining. Most union organizers will not proceed further unless at least 50 percent of the workers in the group sign cards. An authorization card used by the International Association of Machinists and Aerospace Workers is shown in Figure 15–4.

PETITION FOR ELECTION

After the authorization cards have been signed, a petition for an election may be made to the appropriate regional office of the NLRB. When the petition is filed, the NLRB will conduct an investigation. The purpose of the investigation is to determine, among other things, the following:

1. Whether the Board has jurisdiction to conduct an election.
2. Whether there is a sufficient showing of employee interest to justify an election.
3. Whether a question of representation exists (for example, the employee representative has demanded recognition, which has been denied by the employer).
4. Whether the election will include appropriate employees in the bargaining unit (for instance, the Board is prohibited from including plant guards in the same unit with the other employees).
5. Whether the representative named in the petition is qualified (for example, a supervisor or any other management representative may not be an employee representative).
6. Whether there are any barriers to an election in the form of existing contracts or prior elections held within the past twelve months.[31]

---

[31]*A Guide to Basic Law and Procedures under the National Labor Relations Act.* Washington, D.C.: U.S. Government Printing Office, 1978, pp. 11–13.

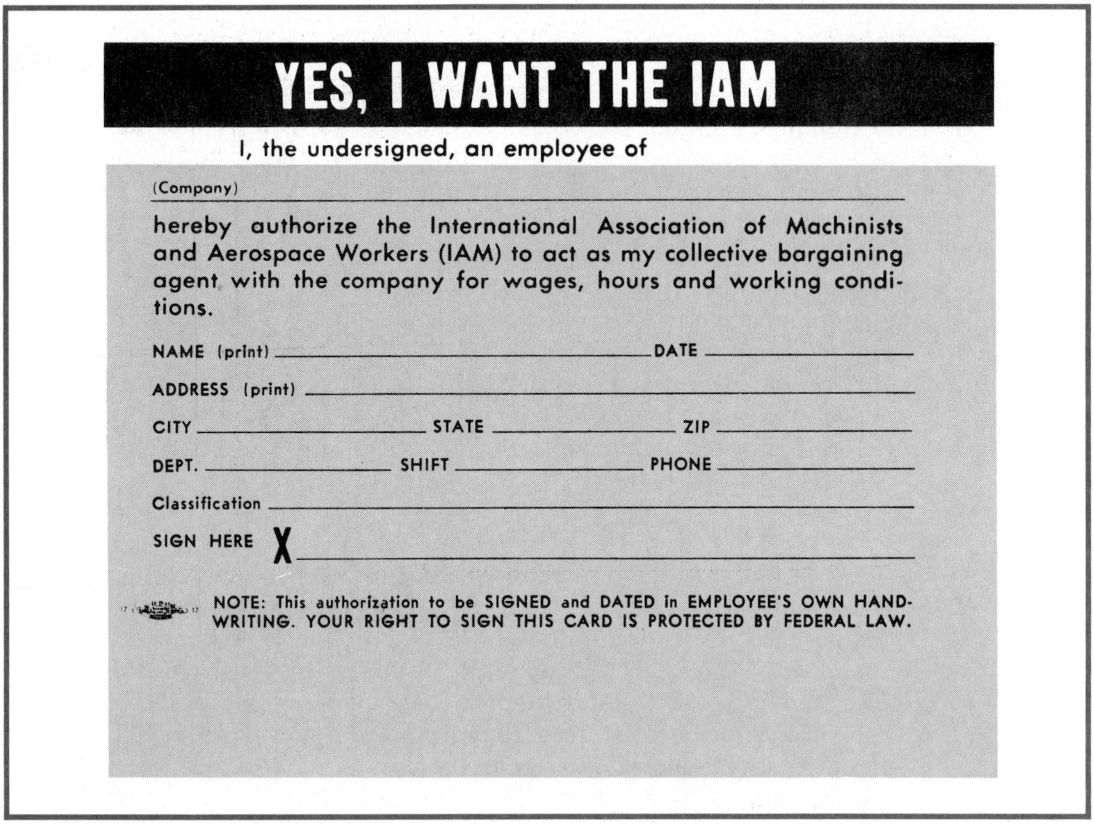

YES, I WANT THE IAM

I, the undersigned, an employee of

(Company) ______________________________

hereby authorize the International Association of Machinists and Aerospace Workers (IAM) to act as my collective bargaining agent with the company for wages, hours and working conditions.

NAME (print) ____________ DATE ____________

ADDRESS (print) ____________

CITY ____________ STATE ____________ ZIP ____________

DEPT. ____________ SHIFT ____________ PHONE ____________

Classification ____________

SIGN HERE X ____________

NOTE: This authorization to be SIGNED and DATED in EMPLOYEE'S OWN HANDWRITING. YOUR RIGHT TO SIGN THIS CARD IS PROTECTED BY FEDERAL LAW.

Figure 15–4. An authorization card. Source: The International Association of Machinists and Aerospace Workers.

Assuming that these conditions are met, the NLRB will ordinarily direct that an election be held within thirty days. Election details are left largely to the regional director. At this time, management is prohibited from making unusual concessions or promises, which would encourage workers to remain union free.

CAMPAIGN

When an election has been ordered, both the union and management will likely make strong attempts to promote their causes. Unions will continue to encourage workers to join the union. Management may begin a campaign to tell workers the benefits of remaining nonunion. Theoretically, both the union and management are permitted to tell their stories without interference from the other side. It is the obligation of the NLRB to monitor the process and prevent illegal activities from occurring. At times, the campaign becomes quite intense. An election will be set aside if it was marked by conduct that the NLRB considers to have interfered with the employee's freedom of choice. Examples of such conduct are:

- An employer or a union threatening loss of jobs or benefits to influence employees' votes or union activities.
- An employer or a union misstating important facts in the election campaign when the other party does not have a chance to reply.
- Either an employer or a union inciting racial or religious prejudice by inflammatory campaign appeals.
- An employer firing employees to discourage or encourage their union activities or a union causing an employer to take such an action.
- An employer or a union making campaign speeches to assembled groups of employees on company time within the twenty-four hour period before an election.

ELECTION AND CERTIFICATION

The NLRB monitors the secret-ballot election on the date set. Its representatives are responsible, first, for seeing that only eligible employees vote and, second, for counting the votes. Where a valid election is held, the Board will issue a certification of the results to the participants. If a union has been chosen by a majority of the employees voting in the bargaining unit, it will receive a certificate showing that it is now the official bargaining representative of the employees in the unit.

UNION STRATEGIES IN BARGAINING UNIT RECOGNITION

Unions may use various strategies to obtain recognition by management. Unions generally try to make the first move. This places management in the position of having to react to union maneuvers. The search for potential firms to organize is a continuous, ongoing effort conducted by union leaders. To begin a drive, unions often look for festering wounds. Union organizers recognize that if management's house is in order the firm will be extremely difficult to organize. Some indications of a firm that is ripe for organizing include:

- A history of unjustified and arbitrary management decisions.
- Compensation below the industry average.
- Lack of concern for the welfare of the firm's employees.

The union does not normally look at isolated conditions of employee unrest. Rather, it attempts to locate general patterns of employee dissatisfaction. Whatever the case, the union will probably not make a major attempt at organizing unless it feels that there is a good chance for success.

The union may take numerous approaches in getting authorization cards signed. One effective technique is to first identify workers who are not only dissatisfied, but who are also influential in the firm's informal organization. These individuals can assist the organizers in developing an effective organizing campaign. Information is obtained through the grapevine regarding such facts as who was hired, who was fired, and management mistakes in general. Such information is beneficial to union organizers as they approach company employees. Statements such as this are common: "I hear Bill Adams was fired today. Understand he was well liked. No way that would have happened if you had a union."

Ultimately, the union must abandon its secret activities. Sooner or later, management will discover the organizing attempt. At this point, union organizers may station themselves and other supporters at company entrances and pass out "throwsheets" or campaign literature proclaiming the benefits of joining the union and emphasizing the weaknesses of management. They will talk to anyone who will listen in their attempt to identify union sympathizers.

Employees who sign an authorization card are then encouraged to convince their friends to sign also. It becomes a mushrooming effort. Often a sufficient number of authorization cards have been signed before management has time to react.

Union efforts continue even after the election petition has been approved by the NLRB. Every attempt is made by the organizers to involve as many workers from the firm as possible. The outside organizers would like to take a backseat and let company employees convince their peers to join the union. Peer pressure typically has much more effect in convincing a person to join a union than outside influence can; peers are the individuals who are most keenly aware of the problems of the firm.

SUMMARY

Since the turn of the century, no single factor has exerted more influence on human resource management than organized labor. Through the process of collective bargaining, organized labor has established patterns of employee–management relations affecting both unionized companies and those that strive to maintain nonunion status. Wage levels, benefits, and working conditions for millions of employees now reflect decisions made jointly by unions and management.

In order to accomplish their objectives, most unions recognize that they must strive to increase their size and power. The reasons individuals join unions are many and varied and they tend to change over time. They may involve dissatisfaction with management, need a social outlet, an opportunity for leadership, forced unionization, and social pressure from peers.

The labor movement has taken on a multilevel organizational structure over time. This complex of organizations ranges from local unions to the principal federation, the AFL-CIO. Each level has its own officers and ways of managing its operations.

Collective bargaining requires an employer and the representative of its employees to meet at reasonable times, to confer in good faith about certain matters, and to put into writing any agreement reached if requested by either party. The series of steps that typically are taken when a union desires to become the bargaining representative includes: (1) signing of authorization cards; (2) petition for election; (3) election campaign; and (4) election and certification. The external environment and internal environment both affect this process.

QUESTIONS FOR REVIEW

1. Describe the development of the labor movement in the United States.
2. List the unfair labor practices by management that were prohibited in the Wagner Act.
3. What union actions were prohibited under the Taft–Hartley Act?
4. In what way does unionization of the public sector differ from unionization of the private sector?
5. Why would unions strive for continued growth and power? Discuss.
6. What are the primary reasons that employees join labor unions?
7. Explain the structure of the AFL-CIO.
8. What steps must a union take in attempting to form a bargaining unit? Briefly describe each step.
9. Describe the ways unions might go about gaining bargaining-unit recognition.

TERMS FOR REVIEW

Conspiracy
Injunction
Yellow-dog contract
National Labor Relations Board (NLRB)
Right-to-work laws
Committee on Political Education (COPE)
Local union

Craft unions
Industrial unions
National union
Collective bargaining
Bargaining unit
Authorization card

REFERENCES

Adams, Larry T. "Changing Employment Patterns of Organized Workers." *Monthly Labor Review* 108(2) (February 1985): 25–30.

Batt, William L., Jr. and Weinberg, Edgar. "Labor-Management Cooperation Today." *Harvard Business Review* 56 (January–February 1978): 96–104.

Bethell, Tom. "Working Man's Fate Ignored by Unions." *Data Management* 16 (July 1978): 28–29.

"Beyond Unions." *Business Week*, July 8, 1985, p. 72.

Brown, T. P. "Appropriate Bargaining Units in Health-Care Institutions: The Disparity of Interests Test." *Employee Relations Law Journal* 10 (Spring 1985) 717–722.

Bureau of National Affairs, *Basic Patterns in Union Contracts*, 8th ed. Washington, D.C.: The Bureau of National Affairs, 1975.

Caruth, Don and Mills, Harry N. "Working Toward Better Union Relations." *Supervisory Management* 30 (February 1985): 7–13.

"Collective Bargaining and Fifty Years of the CIO." *Labor Law Journal* 36 (August 1985): 659–664.

Craver, Charles B. "The Current and Future Status of Labor Organizations. *Labor Law Journal* 36(4) (April 1985): 210–225.

Deligman, Daniel. "Who Needs Unions?" *Fortune,* July 12, 1985, pp. 54–66.

Doyle, P. M. "Area Wage Surveys Shed Light on Decline in Unionization." *Monthly Labor Review* 108 (September 1985): 13–19.

Gennard, J. "What's New in Industrial Relations." *Personnel Management* 17 (March 1985): 19–21 +.

Gray, Robert T. "Where the Public Stands on Union Power Grab." *Nation's Business* 66 (February 1978): 74–79.

"How About an Employees Annual Report?" *CPA Journal* 55 (March 1985): 66–67.

Hughes, M. J. "White-Collar Organizing — We're Not Giving Up." *Management Review* 74 (March 1985): 54–56.

Kilgour, John G. "Responding to the Union Campaign." *Personnel Journal* 57 (May 1978): 238–242.

Krajci, T. J. "Labor Relations in the Public Sector (County-Level Law Enforcement Negotiations)." *Personnel Administrator* 30 (May 1985): 43 +.

Lardaro, Leonard. "Authorization Card Reliability and the Impact of Actions by the NLRB: An Examination of Several Uses." *Labor Law Journal* 35(6) (June 1984): 344–351.

Levenson, Mark. "Big Labor's First Big Defeat: The Taft-Hartley Act." *Dun's Review* 112 (October 1978): 35–36.

Lowenberg, J. Joseph. "Some Aspects of Bargaining in Government Enterprise." *Monthly Labor Review* 101 (April 1978): 32–34.

Marina, Angel. "White-Collar and Professional Unionization." *Labor Law Journal* (February 1982): 82–101.

McCullough, George B. "Transaction Bargaining — Problems and Prospects." *Monthly Labor Review* 101 (March 1978): 33–34.

Moss, Herbert A. "The 24-Hour Rule in NLRB Elections." *Labor Law Journal* (February 1982): 102–108.

"The New Strategies Unions Are Trying." *Business Week,* December 4, 1978, pp. 63–64.

Pestillo, Peter J. "Can Unions Meet the Needs of a 'New' Work Force?" *Monthly Labor Review* 102 (February 1979): 33–36.

Porter, Andrew A. and Murman, Kent F. "A Survey of Employer Union-Avoidance Practices." *Personnel Administrator* 28 (November 1983): 66–71.

"The Promise of the Wagner Act." *American Federationist* 92 (July 6, 1985): 1–3.

Reilly, Ann M. "Big Labor's Crumbling Clout." *Dun's Review* 112 (October 1978): 52–61.

"The Revival of Labor? It's All Up to the AFL-CIO." *Purchasing* 98 (May 23, 1985): 113.

Saltzman, G. M. "Bargaining Laws as a Cause and Consequence of the Growth of Teacher Unionism." *Industrial Labor Relations Review* 38 (April 1985): 335–351.

Schwartz, Stanley J. "The National Labor Relations Board and the Duty of Fair Representation." *Labor Law Journal* (December 1983): 781–789.

Silberman, David M., "Labor Law Turned Upside Down." *American Federationist* 92 (July 6, 1985): 5–7.

"State Employee Bargaining: Policy and Organization." *Monthly Labor Review* 108 (April 1985): 51–56.

Stevens, George E. "Human Resource Management and the Law." *Arizona Business* (Third Quarter, 1983): 8–15.

Tidwell, Gary L. "The Supervisor's Role in a Union Election." *Personnel Journal* 62(8) (August 1983): 640–645.

"2001: A Union Odyssey." *Newsweek,* August 5, 1985, pp. 40–43.

Voos, Paula B. "Does It Pay to Organize? Estimating Costs to Unions." *Monthly Labor Review* 107(6) (June 1984): 43–44.

Wasilewski, E. "BLS Expands Collective Bargaining Series for State and Local Government." *Monthly Labor Review* 108 (May 1985): 36–38.

"Why Unions Lose at Many Companies." *Nation's Business* (August 1982): 50–51.

CHAPTER OBJECTIVES
1. Discuss the collective bargaining process.
2. Describe what is involved as unions and management prepare for negotiation.
3. Name and define the basic topics that are included in virtually all labor agreements.
4. Relate the typical procedure that is involved as union and management attempt to negotiate a new labor agreement.
5. Identify the means through which breakdowns in negotiations may be overcome.
6. Describe current trends in collective bargaining.

Chapter 16

COLLECTIVE BARGAINING

Wayne Sanders, president of Advanced Manufacturing Systems, was angry and disappointed. He had just been informed by the NLRB that a majority of his employees had voted to have the union represent them. He looked at the personnel manager, Max Lewis, and said: "I don't know what to do. The union will demand so much we can't be competitive." Max replied: "Don't forget, Mr. Sanders, just because the union has won the right to be represented doesn't mean that we have to agree to all their terms. I'm sure we can negotiate a good contract."

We saw in the previous chapter how a union gains the right to act as the bargaining representative for a group of employees. But, as Max Lewis told Mr. Sanders, the mere fact that a union has gained this right does not mean that an unfavorable union–management agreement will automatically result. The definition of collective bargaining in chapter 15 describes the basic requirements that union and management negotiators must meet in order to reach a contractual agreement. The way they go about achieving this end is referred to as the collective bargaining process. The purpose of this chapter is to identify and describe the many factors involved in this process.

THE COLLECTIVE BARGAINING PROCESS

Diversity is probably the most prominent characteristic of collective bargaining in the United States. There is no precise format of what to do or how to do it. A generalization of the collective bargaining process is shown in Figure 16–1. As you can see, both external and internal environmental factors can influence the process. For instance, the form of the bargaining structure can affect how collective bargaining is conducted. The four major types of structure are: (1) one company dealing with a single union; (2) several companies dealing with a single union; (3) several unions dealing with a single company; and (4) several companies dealing with several unions. Most contract bargaining is carried out under the first type of structure. The process can become quite complicated when several companies and unions are involved in the negotiations.

Another environmental factor influencing collective bargaining is the type of union–management relationship that exists. When a group of workers decides that it wants union representation, changes occur in the organization. In the absence of a union, management exercises virtually unlimited authority. However, when a union becomes the bargaining representative, management must change its style of decision making to include union representatives. Employees can take collective action that is not always to the liking of management. This can lead to an adversarial relationship with varying degrees of conflict. Sloane and Witney list six types of union–management relations:

1. *Conflict.* Each challenges the other's actions and motivation; cooperation is nonexistent; uncompromising attitude and union militancy are present.
2. *Armed truce.* Each views the other as antagonistic, but tries to avoid head-on conflict; strict interpretation of bargaining obligations and contract interpretations.
3. *Power bargaining.* Management accepts the union; each side tries to gain advantage from the other.

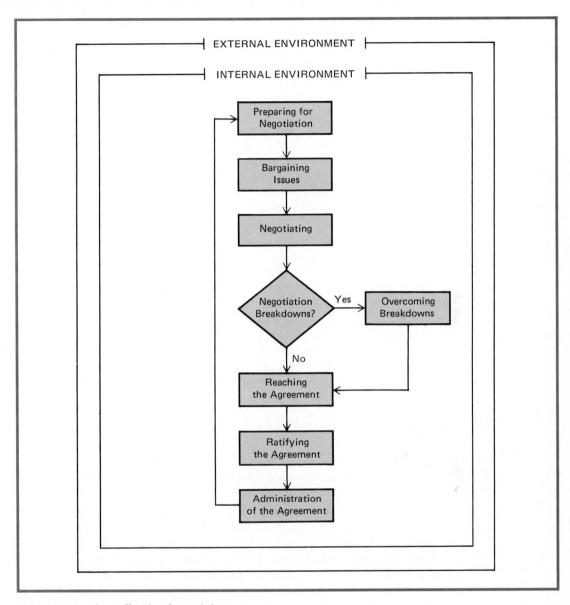

Figure 16–1. The collective bargaining process.

4. *Accommodation.* Each tolerates the other in a live and let live atmosphere, and attempts to reduce conflict without eliminating it.
5. *Cooperation.* Each side accepts the other and works together to resolve personnel and production problems as they occur.
6. *Collusion.* Both "cooperate" to the point of adversely affecting the legitimate interests of employees, other businesses in the industry,

and the consuming public; conniving to control markets, supplies, and prices illegally and/or unethically.[1]

The nature and quality of union–management relations vary over time and at different points in time. The first three types of relationships mentioned are generally unsatisfactory; collusion is not acceptable, and cooperation is rare. The mainstream of U.S. union–management relations appears to be some form of accommodation. Depending on the type of relationship encountered, the collective bargaining process may be relatively simple or it may be a long, tense struggle for both parties.

The first step in the collective bargaining process is preparing for negotiations. This is often an extensive and ongoing process for both union and management. Issues to be negotiated are determined. Negotiating involves the two sides conferring to reach a mutually acceptable contract, but breakdowns in negotiations can occur. Both labor and management have at their disposal tools and arguments that can be used to convince the other side to accept their view. Eventually, however, management and the union reach an agreement that defines the rules of the game for the duration of the contract. The next step is for the union membership to ratify the agreement. Note that there is a feedback loop from administration of the agreement to preparing for negotiations (see Figure 16–1). In many instances, preparing for the next round of negotiations begins virtually from the time the present contract is ratified. The steps depicted for the collective bargaining process form the basic outline for the remainder of this chapter.

PREPARING FOR NEGOTIATIONS

Because of the complex issues facing labor and management today, careful advance preparations must be made before any formal negotiations begin. The length of a typical labor agreement is three years. If an agreement has been in effect, both sides may have discovered a number of things that need to be added, deleted, or modified. These become issues to be addressed in the next round of negotiations.

Bargaining issues can be divided into three categories: mandatory, permissive, and prohibited. **Mandatory bargaining issues** are *those issues that fall within the definition of wages, hours, and other terms and conditions of employment* (see Table 16–1). These issues generally have an immediate and direct effect on workers' jobs. A refusal to bargain in these areas could lead to an unfair labor practice charge. **Permissive** (not mandatory) **bargaining issues** are *those issues that may be raised, but neither side may insist that they be bargained over.* For example, the union may want to bargain over health benefits for retired workers or union participation in

---

[1]Arthur A. Sloane and Fred Witney, *Labor Relations*, 4th ed. Englewood Cliffs, N.J.: Prentice-Hall, 1981, pp. 28–35.

Table 16–1. Mandatory issues for bargaining

Wages

Hours

Discharge

Arbitration

Paid holidays

Paid vacations

Duration of agreement

Grievance procedure

Layoff plan

Reinstatement of economic strikers

Change of payment from hourly base to salary base

Union security and checkoff of dues

Work rules

Merit wage increase

Work schedule

Lunch periods

Rest periods

Pension plan

Retirement age

Bonus payments

Cancellation of seniority upon relocation of plant

Discounts on company products

Shift differentials

Contract clause providing for supervisors keeping seniority in unit

Procedures for income tax withholding

Severance pay

Nondiscriminary hiring hall

Plant rules

Safety

Prohibition against supervisor doing unit work

Superseniority for union stewards

Partial plant closing

Hunting on employer's forest reserve where previously granted

Plant closedown and relocation

Change in operations resulting in reclassifying workers from incentive to straight time, or cut work force, or installation of cost saving machinery

Price of meals provided by company

Group insurance—health, accident, life

Promotions

Seniority

Layoffs

Transfers

Work assignments and transfers

No-strike clause

Piece rates

Stock purchase plan

Workloads

Change of employee status to independent contractors

Motor carrier—union agreement providing that carriers use own equipment before leasing outside equipment

Overtime pay

Agency shop

Sick leave

Employer's insistence on clause giving arbitrator right to enforce award

Management rights clause

Plant closing

Job posting procedures

Plant reopening

Employee physical examination

Bargaining over "bar list"

Truck rentals—minimum rental to be paid by carriers to employee-owned vehicles

Musician price lists

Arrangement for negotiation

Change in insurance carrier and benefits

Profit sharing plan

Company houses

Subcontracting

Discriminatory racial policies

Production ceiling imposed by union

Most favored nation clause

Source: Reed Richardson, ''Positive Collective Bargaining,'' Chapter 7.5 of *ASPA Handbook of Personnel and Industrial Relations,* copyright © 1979 by The Bureau of National Affairs, Inc., Washington, D.C., pp. 7–120, 121. Reprinted by permission.

establishing company pricing policies. **Prohibited** (illegal) **bargaining issues** are *those issues that are statutorily outlawed.* (One such issue is the closed shop.)

The union must constantly gather information regarding membership dissatisfaction. The union steward is normally in the best position to gather this data. Because stewards are elected by their peers, they must be well-informed regarding union members' attitudes. The union steward constantly funnels information up through the union's chain of command where the data are compiled and analyzed. Union leadership attempts to uncover any areas of dissatisfaction because the general union membership must approve any agreement before it becomes final. It would be foolish for union leaders to demand management concessions and have the members reject their proposals. Union leaders will lose their positions if the demands they make of management do not represent the desires of the general membership.

Management also spends long hours preparing for negotiations. The many interrelated tasks that management must accomplish are presented in Figure 16–2. In this illustration the firm allows approximately six months to prepare for negotiations. All aspects of the current contract are considered, including flaws that should be corrected.

When preparing for negotiations, management can obtain a considerable amount of useful information from first-line supervisors. These are the individuals who must administer the labor agreement on a day-to-day basis. They must live with any error that management makes in negotiating the contract. An alert first-line supervisor is also able to inform upper management of the demands unions may make in future negotiations.

Management also attempts periodically to obtain information regarding the attitudes of the work force. Surveys are often administered to workers on a regular basis to determine their feelings toward their jobs and job environment. When union and management representatives sit down at the bargaining table, both sides likely know a great deal about employees' attitudes.

Another part of preparation for negotiations involves identifying various positions that both union and management will take as the negotiations progress. Each takes an initial position representing "Utopia" — the conditions union or management would prefer. It is likely that the two sides will determine an absolute limit to their offers or demands before a breakdown in negotiations occurs. Preparations should include considerable detailed planning because clear minds often do not prevail during the heat of negotiations.

Finally, a major consideration in preparing for negotiations is the selection of the bargaining teams. The makeup of the management bargaining team usually depends on the type of firm and its size. Normally, bargaining is conducted by labor relations specialists, with the advice and assistance of operating managers. In some instances top executives are directly involved, particularly in smaller firms. Larger companies utilize staff spe-

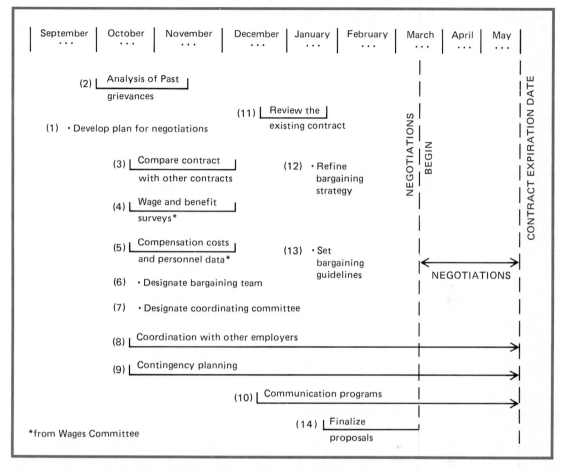

Figure 16–2. An example of company preparations for negotiations. Source: Adapted from "Preparations for Negotiations" by Ronald L. Miller. Reprinted with permission, *Personnel Journal*, copyright January 1978.

cialists (a personnel manager or industrial relations executive), managers of principal operating divisions, and in some cases an outside consultant such as a labor attorney.

The responsibility for conducting negotiations for the union is usually entrusted to union officers. At the local level, the bargaining committee will normally be supplemented by rank-and-file members elected specifically for this purpose. In addition, the national union will often send a representative to act in an advisory capacity or even participate directly in the bargaining sessions. The real task of the union negotiating team is to develop and obtain solutions to the problems raised by the union's membership.

Charles E. Brown
Senior Staff Vice
President, Honeywell,
Inc.

Charles E. Brown says, "My career in employee relations came about quite by accident. After serving as a noncommissioned infantry officer in World War II, I was attached to a personnel unit. It was there that I first encountered the 'personnel business.'"

Returning to Indiana, Brown noted that a number of management schools had a personnel emphasis, which he decided to pursue. Many years later, as head of employee relations for Honeywell, he had personnel responsibilities for 100,000 employees in thirty-five countries.

Upon leaving Indiana University in 1949 with B.S. and M.S. degrees in personnel management, he joined the Glidden Company's corporate personnel staff. In 1959 he became director of industrial relations for the Cleveland Pneumatic Tool Company, and in 1962 accepted an opportunity to join Honeywell, Inc., as director of industrial relations. This decision proved to be a good one, as he progressed steadily through the ranks to the highest personnel position in Honeywell.

He believes that a business enterprise, or a department of a business enterprise, is very much like a professional athletic team. "We are the managers of our teams, and we have players in various positions. We compete with other teams, winning some games and losing some, and we are highly interested in finding ways to improve our win-loss ratio." He suggests that team building starts with the basic task of selection and placement. "When we have big wins or losses they are normally traceable to a small group of managers who were well suited to the task, or vice versa."

Brown believes that managers should devote more time to the selection of new entrants into the department. He says, "We spend a lot of time examining proposals for new buildings and equipment, but we tend to neglect the process of carefully selecting the best qualified candidate for each opening."

When asked about motivation he replies, "What can you and I as managers do to cause people who work for us to apply their very best efforts? You might say, 'Pay them more than they can earn elsewhere,' and it is true that pay is an important factor. More important, however, is the working climate, which is made up of many ingredients. Among these important ingredients is the attitude employees have toward their job and toward the boss. Is the boss basically fair? Does he or she care about the well-being of employees? Is he or she approachable? Can an employee talk with the boss on issues of real concern, both business and personal matters?"

When asked what he would do differently if he were starting over in his chosen field of personnel management Brown replied, "I would learn more about my company's business — its products, customers, financial requirements, etc. I would establish priorities more carefully, concentrating on those items which are most critical to the success of the business. Finally, I would spend more time developing strong interpersonal relationships among employees at all levels so that I knew the organization more from personal contact than from studying reports."

The document that results from the collective bargaining process is called an agreement or contract. It regulates the relationship between the employer and the employees involved for a specified period of time. Each agreement is unique and there is no standard or universal model. Despite dissimilarities, certain topics are included in virtually all labor agreements. These include recognition, management rights, union security, compensation and benefits, grievance procedure, employee security, and job-related factors.

RECOGNITION

This section usually appears at the beginning of the labor agreement. Its purpose is to identify the union that is recognized as the bargaining representative and to describe the bargaining unit, that is, the employees for whom the union speaks. A typical recognition section might read, "The XYZ Company recognizes the ABC Union as the sole and exclusive representative of the bargaining unit employees for the purpose of collective bargaining with regard to wages, hours, and other conditions of employment."

MANAGEMENT RIGHTS

A section that is often, but not always, written into the labor agreement spells out the rights of management. If no management's rights section is included, management may reason that it retains control of all topics not described as bargainable in the contract. The precise content of the management rights section will vary by industry, company, and union. When included, management rights generally involve:

1. Freedom to select the business objectives of the company.
2. Freedom to determine the uses to which the material assets of the enterprise will be devoted.
3. Power to discipline for cause.[2]

In a brochure it publishes for all its first-line supervisors, Southwestern Bell Telephone Company describes management's rights when dealing with the union. The brochure includes the following:

> You should remember that management has all such rights except those restricted by law or by contract with the union. You either make these decisions or carry them out through contact with your people. Some examples of these decisions and actions are:
>
> ■ To determine what work is to be done and where, when, and how it is to be done.
> ■ To determine the number of employees who will do the work.

[2]Edwin F. Beal and James P. Begin, *The Practice of Collective Bargaining*, 6th ed. Homewood, Ill.: Richard D. Irwin, 1982, pp. 295–298.

- To supervise and instruct employees in doing the work.
- To correct employees whose work performance or personal conduct fails to meet reasonable standards. This includes administering discipline.
- To recommend hiring, dismissing, upgrading, or downgrading employees.
- To recommend employees for promotion to management.[3]

UNION SECURITY

Union security is typically one of the first items negotiated in a collective bargaining agreement. The objective of union security provisions is to ensure that the union continues to exist and perform its function. A strong union security provision makes it easier for the union to enroll and retain members. Some basic forms of union security clauses are discussed in the following paragraphs.

Closed shop. A **closed shop** is *an arrangement whereby union membership is a prerequisite to employment.* Such provisions are generally illegal in the United States.

Union shop. As mentioned in chapter 15, a **union shop** is *a requirement that all employees become members of the union after a specified period of employment (usually thirty days) or after a union shop provision has been negotiated.* Employees must remain members of the union as a condition of employment. The union shop is generally legal in the United States except in states that have right-to-work laws.

Maintenance of membership shop. Employees who are members of the union at the time the labor agreement is signed, or who later voluntarily join, must continue their memberships until the termination of the agreement, as a condition of employment. This form of recognition is also prohibited in most states that have right-to-work laws and is rarely utilized anymore.

Agency shop. An **agency shop** provision *does not require employees to join the union; however, the labor agreement requires, as a condition of employment, that each nonunion member of the bargaining unit must* "pay the union the equivalent of membership dues as a kind of tax, or service charge, in return for the union acting as the bargaining agent."[4] The agency shop is outlawed in most states that have right-to-work laws.

[3]*Management/Employee/Union Relations.* Dallas: Southwestern Bell Telephone Company, December 1971, p. 3.
[4]Beal and Begin, *Collective Bargaining,* p. 286.

Exclusive bargaining shop.   Thirteen of the twenty-one states having right-to-work laws allow only exclusive bargaining-shop provisions. Under this form of recognition, the company is legally bound to deal with the union that has achieved recognition, but employees are not obligated to join or maintain membership in the union or to financially contribute to it.

Open shop.   An open shop describes the absence of union security rather than its presence. The **open shop**, strictly defined, is *employment that is open on equal terms to union members and nonmembers alike*. Under this arrangement, no employee is required to join or financially contribute to the union, nor is any union recognized as the bargaining representative.

Dues checkoff.   Another type of security that unions attempt to achieve is the checkoff of dues. A checkoff agreement may be used in addition to any of the previously mentioned "shop" agreements. When the **checkoff of dues** is in effect, *the company agrees to withhold union dues from members' checks and to forward the money directly to the union*. Because of provisions in the Taft–Hartley Act, each union member must voluntarily sign a statement authorizing this deduction. Dues checkoff is important to the union. It eliminates much of the expense and time of collecting dues from each member.

COMPENSATION AND BENEFITS

This section typically constitutes a large portion of most labor agreements. Virtually any item that can affect compensation and benefits may be included. Some of the items frequently covered are:

- *Wage rate schedule:* The base rates to be paid each year of the contract for each job are included in this section. At times, unions are able to include a cost-of-living allowance or escalator clause in the contract in order to protect the purchasing power of employees' earnings. These clauses are generally related to the Consumer Price Index (CPI) prepared by the Bureau of Labor Statistics. Their purpose is to ensure that a worker's real wage to remain relatively constant.
- *Overtime and premium pay:* Provisions covering hours of work, overtime, and premium pay, such as shift differentials, are included in this section.
- *Jury pay:* Some firms pay an employee's entire salary when he or she is serving jury duty. Others pay the difference between jury pay and the compensation that would have been earned. The precise procedure covering jury pay is typically stated in the contract.
- *Layoff or severance pay:* The amount that employees in various jobs and/or seniority levels will be paid if they are laid off or terminated is presented in this section.

- *Holidays:* The holidays to be recognized and the amount of pay that a worker will receive if he or she has to work on a holiday are specified here. In addition, the pay procedure for times when a holiday falls on a worker's normal day off is provided.
- *Vacation:* This section spells out the amount of vacation that a person may take, based on seniority. Any restrictions as to when the vacation may be taken are also stated.

GRIEVANCE PROCEDURE

A major portion of the labor agreement is often devoted to the grievance procedure. It contains the means by which employees can voice dissatisfaction with specific management actions. Also included in this section are the procedures for disciplinary action by management and the termination procedure that must be followed. A portion of chapter 18 is devoted to disciplinary action and the grievance process.

EMPLOYEE SECURITY

This section of the labor-management agreement establishes the procedures that cover the security of individual employees. Seniority and grievance handling procedures are the key topics related to employee security.

Seniority is determined by *the amount of time that an employee has worked in various capacities with the firm.* Seniority may be companywide, by division, by department, or by job. Establishment of a seniority policy in the labor agreement is quite important because the person with the most seniority, as defined in the labor agreement, is typically the last to be laid off and the first to be recalled. The seniority system also provides a basis for promotion decisions. Employees with the greatest seniority will likely be considered first for promotion to higher level jobs.

JOB-RELATED FACTORS

Many of the rules governing employee actions while at work are included here. Some of the more important factors are company work rules, work standards, and rules related to safety. This section varies, depending on the nature of the industry and the product manufactured.

NEGOTIATING

There is no way to ensure speedy and mutually acceptable results from negotiations. At best, the parties can attempt to create an atmosphere that will lend itself to productive results. For example, the two negotiating teams usually meet at an agreed-on neutral site, such as a hotel. It is generally important that a favorable relationship be established early so as to avoid "eleventh hour" bargaining.[5] It is equally important that union and management negotiators strive to develop and maintain clear and open lines of communication. Collective bargaining is a problem-solving activity, so good communication is essential to its success. It is best that negotiations be conducted in the privacy of the conference room, not in the news media. If the negotiators feel publicity is necessary, joint releases to the media may avoid unnecessary conflict.

The negotiating phase of collective bargaining begins with each side presenting its initial demands. Because a collective bargaining settlement can be expensive for a firm, it is important that the cost of the various proposals be estimated as accurately as possible. An example of how one company evaluated a union proposal is shown in Table 16–2. As you can see, there were no changes in some instances, while in others the cost increase was substantial.

---

[5]Eleventh-hour bargaining refers to last-minute settlement attempts just prior to the expiration date of an existing agreement. Failure to reach agreement in this manner frequently results in a strike.

Table 16–2. Estimating the cost of changes in contract terms

Changes in costs	Increased cost
1. Direct payroll — annual	
Straight time earnings — 36¢ per hour general increase	
100 employees × 2080 hours × 36¢	$74,880
Premium earnings — second shift established differential — 10¢ per hour	
30 employees × 2080 hours × 10¢	6,240
Overtime — overtime cost increased by increased straight time rate — average straight time rate increases 39¢	
39¢ × 12,000 overtime hours × .5 overtime rate	2,340
Bonus	None
Other direct payroll cost increases	None
Total increase in direct payroll costs	83,460
2. Added costs directly resulting from higher payroll costs — annual F.I.C.A — 7.15% times increase in average straight-time earnings	
100 employees × 36¢ × 7.15% × 2080 hours	5,353.92
Federal and state unemployment insurance tax	No change
Workers' compensation	No change
Other	No change
Total additional direct payroll costs	5,353.92

Table 16–2. Estimating the cost of changes in contract terms (continued)	
Changes in costs	**Increased cost**
3. Nonpayroll costs — annual	
Insurance — company portion	
Health insurance	No change
Dental insurance	None
Eye care	None
Life insurance — added employer contribution, $100 per year	
$100 × 100 employees	10,000
Pension costs — fully vested pension reduced from 25 years and age 65 to 20 years and age 62	52,000
Miscellaneous	
Tuition reimbursements (addition)	600
Service rewards	No change
Suggestion awards (addition)	350
Loss on employee cafeteria	No change
Overtime meals	No change
Cost of parking lots	No change
Company parties	No change
Personal tools	No change
Personal safety equipment (addition)	1,200
Personal wearing apparel	No change
Profit sharing	No change
Other	No change
Total additional nonpayroll costs — annual	64,150
4a. Changes in nonwork paid time	
Holidays — 2 new holidays added to 6 already in contract	
100 employees × 8 hours × 2 holidays × $3.96 average new wage	6,336
Vacation — new category added — 4 weeks (160 hours annual vacation) with 20 or more years service — former top was 3 weeks after 15 years	
Average number of employees affected annually 15 employees × 40 hours × $3.96 average new wage	2,376
Paid lunch time — paid ½ hour lunch time added to contract	
100 employees × ½ hour × 236 days worked yearly × $3.96 average new wage	46,728
Paid wash-up time	None
Coffee breaks	No change
Paid time off for union activity — new 1 hour per week per shop steward	
10 shop stewards × $4.20 shop steward average new wage × 1 hour × 52 weeks	2,184
Paid sick leave	None
Paid time off over and above workers' compensation paid time	None
Jury service time off	No change
Funeral leave time off	No change
Paid time off for safety or training	No change
Other	None
Total change in hours paid for but not worked — annual	57,624

Table 16–2. Estimating the cost of changes in contract terms (continued)	
Changes in costs	Increased cost

4b. Financial data derived from costing out (Items 1–4, above)	
Total increase in contract costs	
Item 1 + Item 2 + Item 3	152,963.92
Average total increase in contract costs per employee payroll hour	
(Item 1 + Item 2 + Item 3) ÷ 2080 hours	.735
Average total increase in direct payroll costs per employee hour	
(Item 1 + Item 2) ÷ 2080 hours ÷ 100 employees	.427
Average total increase in nonpayroll costs per payroll hour per employee	
Item 3 ÷ 2080 hours ÷ 100 employees	.308
Average total increase in nonwork paid time expense per payroll hour per employee	
Item 4 ÷ 100 employees	576.24
Average total increase in direct payroll costs per productive (worked) hour per employee	
(Item 1 + Item 2) ÷ 1,888 hours ÷ 100 employees	.47
Average total increase in nonpayroll costs per productive (worked) hour per employee	
Item 3 ÷ 1,888 hours ÷ 100 employees	.34

Source: Reprinted by permission from "Positive Collective Bargaining," by Reed C. Richardson, Chapter 7.5 of *ASPA Handbook of Personnel and Industrial Relations*, copyright © 1979 by The Bureau of National Affairs, Inc., Washington, D.C.

The term *negotiating* suggests a certain amount of give and take. An example of the negotiation of wage increases is provided in Figure 16–3. In this illustration, labor initially demands a $.40 per hour increase. Management counters with an offer of only $.10 per hour. Both labor and management — as expected — reject the other side's demands. Plan B for labor calls for lowering its demand to a $.30 per hour increase. Management counters with an offer of $.20. Both positions are feasible to the other side. They are now in the bargaining zone for both labor and management. Wages will be agreed on somewhere between a $.20 and $.30 per hour increase. The exact amount will be determined by the power of the bargaining unit and the skills of the negotiators.

Negotiations at times are similar to a high-stake poker game. A certain amount of bluffing and raising of the ante takes place in many negotiations. The ultimate bluff for the union would be when a negotiator says, "If our demands are not met, we are prepared to strike." Management's version of this bluff would be to threaten a lockout. Each of these tactics will be discussed later. A form of power politics tends to evolve. The party with the greater leverage can expect to extract the most concessions. The realities of negotiation are not for the weak of heart.

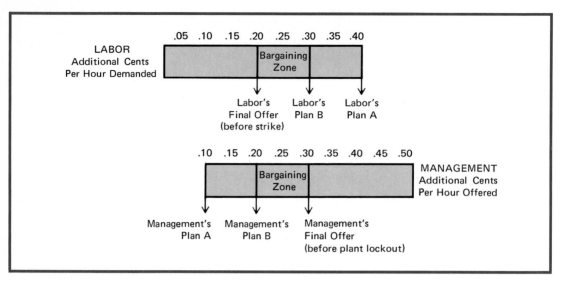

Figure 16–3. An example of negotiation for a wage increase.

Even though one side in the negotiating process may appear to possess the greater power, negotiators often take care to keep the other side from losing face. They recognize that the balance of power may switch rapidly. By the time the next round of negotiations occurs, the pendulum may be swinging in a different direction. Even if management appears to have the upper hand, minor concessions may be made that will allow the labor leader to claim benefit gains for the union. Management may demand that workers pay for grease rags that are lost. (Assume that the loss of these rags had become excessive.) In order to obtain labor's agreement to this demand, management may agree to provide new uniforms for the workers if the cost of these uniforms would be less than the cost of the lost rags. Thus labor leaders, although forced to concede to management's demands, could show their workers that they have obtained concessions from management.

As we mentioned previously, each side likely does not expect to obtain all the demands presented in its first proposal. However, management must remember that if it concedes to a demand from labor, the concession may be difficult to reverse in future negotiations. For instance, if management agrees to provide dental benefits, it will be difficult to withdraw these benefits in the next round of negotiations. Labor, on the other hand, can lose a demand and continue to bring it up in the future. *Demands that the union does not expect to receive when they are first made* are known as **beachhead demands**.

At times negotiations may break down, even though both labor and management may sincerely want to arrive at an equitable contract settlement. Several means of removing roadblocks may be used in order to get negotiations moving again. Breakdowns in negotiations can be overcome through third party intervention, union strategies, and management strategies.

THIRD PARTY INTERVENTION

Often a person from outside both the union and the organization can intervene to provide assistance when an agreement cannot be reached and a breakdown occurs. At this point there is an impasse. The reasons behind each party's position may be quite rational. Or, the breakdown may be related to emotional disputes that tend to become distorted during the heat of negotiating. Regardless of the cause, something must be done to continue the negotiations. The two basic types of third party intervention are mediation and arbitration.

Mediation. **Mediation** is *a process whereby a neutral third party enters a labor dispute when a bargaining impasse has occurred.* The objective of mediation is to persuade the parties to resume negotiations and reach a settlement. A mediator has no power to force a settlement but can help in the search for solutions, make recommendations, and work to open blocked channels of communication. Successful mediation depends to a substantial degree on the tact, diplomacy, patience, and perseverance of the mediator. The mediator's fresh recommendations are used to get discussions going again.

Arbitration. **Arbitration** is *a process in which a dispute is submitted to an impartial third party to make a binding decision.* There are two principal types of union–management disputes: rights cases and interests cases. Those that involve disputes over the interpretation and application of the various provisions of an existing contract are referred to as *rights* arbitration. This type of arbitration is used in settling grievances. Grievance arbitration is common in the United States and will be discussed in chapter 18. The other type of arbitration, *interest* arbitration, involves disputes over the terms of new or proposed collective bargaining *agreements.* In the private sector, the use of interest arbitration as an alternative procedure for impasse resolution has not been a common practice. Unions and employers rarely agree to submit the basic terms of a contract (i.e., wages, hours, and working conditions) to a neutral party for disposition. They prefer to rely on collective bargaining and the threat of economic pressure (i.e., strikes and lockouts) to decide these issues.[6]

---

[6]Raymond A. Smardon, "Arbitration Is No Bargain," *Nation's Business* (October 1974), pp. 80–83.

In the public sector, most governmental jurisdictions prohibit their employees from striking. As a result, interest arbitration has been used to a greater extent than in the private sector. Although there is no uniform application of this method, fourteen states have legislation permitting the use of interest arbitration to settle unresolved issues. In a number of states, compulsory arbitration of interest items is required at various jurisdictional levels.[7] A relatively new procedure used in the public sector is final-offer arbitration, which has two basic forms: package selection and issue-by-issue selection. In package selection, the arbitrator must select one party's entire offer on all issues. In issue-by-issue selection, the arbitrator examines each issue separately and chooses one party's final offer on each issue.[8]

SOURCES OF MEDIATORS AND ARBITRATORS

The principal organization involved in mediation efforts, other than the available state and local agencies, is the Federal Mediation and Conciliation Service (FMCS). The FMCS was established as an independent agency by the Taft–Hartley Act in 1947. Either or both parties involved in negotiations can seek the assistance of the FMCS, or the agency can offer help if it feels that the situation warrants it. Federal law requires that any party wishing to change the contract must give notice of this intention to the other party sixty days prior to the expiration of a contract. If no agreement has been reached thirty days prior to the expiration date, the FMCS must be notified.

In arbitration, the disputants are free to select any person as their arbitrator so long as they both agree on the selection. Most commonly, however, they make a request for an arbitrator to either the American Arbitration Association (AAA) or the FMCS. The AAA is a nonprofit organization with offices in many cities. Both the AAA and the FMCS maintain lists of arbitrators. Only people who can show, through references, experience in labor–management relations and acceptability to both labor and management as neutrals are selected for inclusion.[9] Because of the complexity of many cases, arbitrators are discovering that a legal background is often necessary.

UNION STRATEGIES FOR OVERCOMING
NEGOTIATION BREAKDOWNS

There are times when a union believes that it must revert to extreme measures to exert pressure on management to agree to its bargaining demands.

[7]Benjamin J. Taylor and Fred Witney, *Labor Relations Law*, 4th ed. Englewood Cliffs, N.J.: Prentice-Hall, 1983, pp. 652–653.

[8]Robert E. Allen and Timothy J. Keaveny, *Contemporary Labor Relations*. Reading, Mass.: Addison-Wesley, 1983, pp. 558–559.

[9]Donald Austin Woolf, "Arbitration in One Easy Lesson: A Review of Criteria Used in Arbitration Awards," *Personnel* 55 (September–October 1978): 76.

Strikes and boycotts are the primary means that the union may use to overcome breakdowns in negotiations.

Strikes. *When union members refuse to work in order to exert pressure on management in negotiations,* their action is referred to as a **strike**. When a strike is called, the union attempts to exert pressure — resulting in lost customers and less revenue — that will force management to submit to labor's terms.

The timing of a strike is important in determining its effectiveness. An excellent time is when business is thriving and the demand for the firm's product or services is expanding. On the other hand, the union might be hard-pressed to obtain major concessions from a strike if the firm's sales are down and it has built up a large inventory. In this instance, the company's welfare would not be severely damaged.

Contrary to many opinions, unions prefer to use the strike only as a last resort. Strikes are extremely expensive not only for the employer, but also for the union and its members. A union's treasury is often depleted when strike benefits are paid to its members during the strike. In addition, members suffer because they are not receiving their normal pay. Strike benefits help, but union members certainly cannot maintain a normal standard of living on them. Strike benefits, when paid at all, are minimal, usually less than $50 a week.[10]

Sometimes during negotiations (especially at the beginning) the union may want to strengthen its negotiator's position by taking a strike vote of the membership. The members traditionally give overwhelming approval. This vote does not necessarily mean that there will be a strike, only that the union leaders have the authority to call one if negotiations reach a stalemate. It can add a sense of urgency to efforts to reach an agreement.[11]

Successful passage of a strike vote has additional implications for union members. Virtually every national union's constitution contains a clause requiring the members to support and participate in a strike if one is called. If a union member fails to comply with this requirement, he or she can be fined. Thus union members place themselves in jeopardy if they cross a picket line without the consent of the union. Fines may be as high as 100 percent of wages for as long as the union remains outside the company to advise people that the union is on strike and to encourage all people (employees, delivery people, etc.) to support the union.

Boycotts. The boycott is another of labor's weapons to get management to agree to union demands. A **boycott** involves *an agreement by union members to refuse to use or buy the firm's products.* A boycott exerts economic pressure on management, and the effect often lasts much longer

---

[10]Beal and Begin, *Collective Bargaining,* p. 232.
[11]Ibid., pp. 221–222.

than that of a strike. Once shoppers change their buying habits, their behavior will likely continue long after the boycott has ended. At times, significant pressures can be exerted on a business when union members, their families, and friends refuse to purchase the firm's products and encourage the public not to patronize the firm. This is especially true when the products are sold at retail and are easily identifiable by brand name. For instance, the boycott against Farrah in the 1970s was effective because the product could easily be associated with the company.

The practice of a union attempting to encourage third parties (i.e., suppliers and customers) to stop doing business with the firm is known as a secondary boycott. This type of boycott was declared illegal by the Taft–Hartley Act.

MANAGEMENT'S STRATEGIES FOR OVERCOMING NEGOTIATION BREAKDOWNS

Management may also use various strategies to encourage unions to reconvene negotiations. One form of action that is somewhat analogous to a strike is called a lockout. In a **lockout**, *management temporarily ceases operation of the business.* The employees are unable to work and do not get paid. Although the lockout is used rather infrequently, the fear of a lockout may bring labor back to the bargaining table. A lockout is particularly effective when dealing with a weak union, when the union treasury is depleted, or when the business has excessive inventories.

Another course of action that a company has at its disposal, should the union decide to strike, is to keep the firm operating by placing management and nonunion personnel in the striking workers' jobs. The type of industry involved has considerable effect on the impact of this maneuver. If the firm is not labor intensive and if maintenance demands are not high, such as at a petroleum refinery or a chemical plant, this practice may be quite effective. When it is used, management will likely attempt to show how production actually increases with the use of nonunion employees. At times, management personnel will actually live in the plant and have food and other necessities delivered to them.

Another way management can continue operating a firm during a strike is by hiring replacements for the strikers. The hiring of replacements on either a temporary or a permanent basis by the employer is legal when the employees are engaged in an *economic* strike, i.e., one that is part of a collective bargaining dispute. A company that takes this course of action risks creating bitterness among its employees who are on strike and inviting violence.

RATIFYING THE AGREEMENT

In the vast majority of collective bargaining encounters, the parties reach agreement without experiencing severe breakdowns in negotiations or resorting to disruptive actions. Typically, this is accomplished before the current agreement expires. After the negotiators have reached a tentative agreement on all topics negotiated, they will prepare a written agreement complete with the effective and termination dates. The approval process for management is often easier than for labor. The president or chief executive officer has usually been kept up-to-date regarding the progress of negotiations. Any difficulty that might have stood in the way of obtaining approval has likely already been resolved by the negotiators with top management.

However, the approval process can be more difficult for the union. Until it has received approval by a majority of those voting in a ratification election, the proposed agreement is not final. At times, union members reject the proposed agreement and a new round of negotiations must begin. In recent years, approximately 10 percent of all tentative agreements have been rejected when presented to the union membership. Many of these rejections might not have occurred if union negotiators had been better informed of the desires of the membership.

ADMINISTRATION OF THE AGREEMENT

Negotiating, as it relates to the total collective bargaining process, may be likened to the tip of an iceberg. It is the visible phase, the part that makes the news. The larger and perhaps more important part of collective bargaining is the administration of the agreement, which is seldom viewed by the public.[12] The agreement establishes the union–management relationship for its effective length. Usually no changes in contract language can be made until the expiration date except by mutual consent. Administering the contract is a day-to-day activity. Ideally, the aim of both management and the union is to make the agreement work to the mutual benefit of all concerned. Often, this is not an easy task. In the daily stress of the work environment, terms of the contract are not always uniformly interpreted and applied.

Management is primarily responsible for explaining and implementing the agreement at all affected levels. This could include meetings or training sessions not only to point out significant features, but also to provide a clause-by-clause analysis. Supervisors in particular need to know their responsibilities and what to do when disagreements arise. Additionally, managers can be encouraged to notify top management of any contract provisions that are causing problems so that they can be considered when preparing for the next round of negotiations.

The human resource manager plays a key role in the day-to-day administration of contract provisions. He or she gives advice on matters of dis-

---

[12]Harold W. Davey, *Contemporary Collective Bargaining*, 3rd ed. Englewood Cliffs, N.J.: Prentice-Hall, 1972, p. 141.

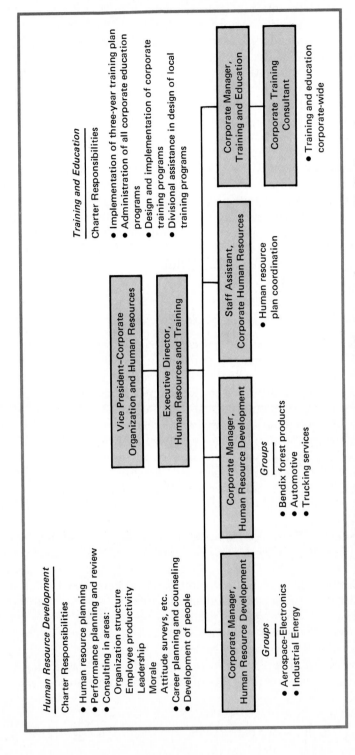

Figure 16–4. The organization of the personnel department at Bendix Corporation. Source: Bendix Corporation.

cipline, works to resolve grievances, and helps first-line managers to establish good working relationships with all employees affected by the terms and conditions of the labor agreement. When a firm is unionized, the role of HRM tends to change rather significantly. In major corporations in which the large majority of the operative employees belong to unions, the HRM function may be divided into separate human resources and industrial relations departments. The Bendix Corporation provides an excellent example of this separation of activities by having both a vice president of human resources and a vice president of industrial relations (see Figures 16–4 and 16–5). In situations such as this, the vice president of human resources may perform all human resource management tasks with the exception of industrial relations. The vice president of industrial relations would likely deal with union-related matters. As one vice president of industrial relations stated:

> My first challenge is, wherever possible, to keep the company union-free and the control of its operations in the hands of corporate management of all levels. Where unions represent our employees, the problem becomes one of negotiating collective bargaining agreements which our company can live with, administering these labor agreements with the company's interests paramount (consistent with good employee relations), and trying to solve all grievances arising under the labor agreement short of their going to arbitration, without giving away the store.

THE FUTURE OF COLLECTIVE BARGAINING

The collective bargaining process and the labor movement have undergone changes in recent years. They no doubt will be altered further in the years ahead by forces of varying magnitudes and conflicting perspectives.

INDUSTRIAL AND OCCUPATIONAL CHANGE

Of the many environmental conditions that shape an organization's labor–management relations, none is more pervasive or dominant than the market conditions for the firm's products and/or services and its own labor markets.[13] In the 1980s, the trend is toward increased competition within product markets. This trend has a strong international dimension, reflecting the growing interdependence of world markets. Competition fosters innovation, opens up new market opportunities, and creates new jobs. Firms in mature markets, however, with fewer opportunities for growth and expansion cannot compete for scarce job opportunities. Employers and employees in such markets need to concern themselves with career transitions, job losses, and organizational restructuring.

[13]Thomas A. Kochan and Thomas A. Barocci, *Human Resource Management and Industrial Relations*. Boston: Little, Brown, 1985, pp. 528–529.

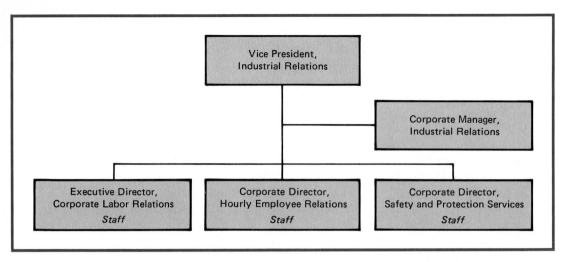

Figure 16–5. The corporate industrial relations department at Bendix Corporation by functional responsibility. Source: Bendix Corporation.

Historically, unions have had their greatest success in the manufacturing, mining, transportation, and construction sectors of the economy. In 1976, workers in these industries comprised 63.5 percent of the union members in the United States.[14] With the relative decline in importance of these industries and the relative growth in importance of service industries, union membership has declined. Major increases in employment have taken place in wholesale and retail trades; finance and insurance; general service industries; and federal, state, and local government. These industries have had low union representation in the past.[15]

The pattern of employment by occupation has also changed markedly over time. Major changes in white-collar occupations have included increases in the number of professional and clerical employees. In blue-collar occupations, the proportion of operative employees increased through 1950; then a long-term decline in the use of laborers and an increase in service occupations occurred.[16] It is also interesting to note that between 1955 and 1984 a larger proportion of employees in the industrial work force were assigned to nonproduction jobs.[17] The shift toward more professional, service-sector, and white-collar occupations implies that different expectations may be present in the workplace. Not only may labor need to rethink

[14]Allen and Keaveny, *Contemporary Labor Relations*, pp. 633–634.

[15]David A. Dilts and Clarence R. Deitsch, *Labor Relations*. New York: Macmillan, 1983, p. 363.

[16]John A. Fossum, *Labor Relations*, 3rd ed. Plano, Texas: Business Publications, Inc., 1985, pp. 472–473.

[17]Ibid., pp. 475–477.

its organizing strategy, but management also needs to sharpen its managerial skills in negotiating and team building.

MULTINATIONALS AND FOREIGN COMPETITION

Unions often point to multinational corporations as an important cause of U.S. economic problems, especially unemployment. Many companies have located part or all of their operations outside the United States to take advantage of lower labor and material costs — and favorable tax laws. Investment funds have been diverted to foreign operations, costing the American economy jobs.[18] However, Japanese and European firms have invested significantly in various U.S. marketing and manufacturing areas, which has created new jobs here in the United States. As these firms hire American workers, some interesting collective bargaining situations will likely be created.

Foreign competition has had major impacts on employment in several U.S. industries already. The shoe, apparel, auto, steel, and rubber industries have lost jobs, and their employees have also felt the effects at the bargaining table in terms of wage and work-rule concessions.[19] Most union members are aware of the balance of payments problems that the United States faces in world trade.

TECHNOLOGY AND PRODUCTIVITY

Several events have occurred in a relatively short period of time to complicate labor relations and the collective bargaining process. One of the most dramatic developments is the science of robotics. The microprocessor and the silicon chip gave robots greater capabilities than had previously been envisioned.[20] Now in their second generation, robots have senses of vision and touch. The use of robots in manufacturing has almost quadrupled between 1979 and 1981 (from 1300 to over 5000). It is predicted that by 1990 the figure will be 120,000.[21]

Not only is this new technology being used in factories, but its use in the office may have an even greater impact. It appears that the new machines will reduce the number of jobs available in the years ahead and could very well alter the nature of the work that is available.[22] The increased use of robots is often supported because of the growing concern for quality control and competitiveness in international markets. The new technology increases productivity in those areas where it is used. Union leaders, however,

---

[18]Dilts and Deitsch, *Labor Relations*, pp. 364–365.

[19]Fossum, *Labor Relations*, p. 481.

[20]Michael R. Carrell and Christina Heavrin, *Collective Bargaining and Labor Relations.* Columbus, Ohio: Charles E. Merrill, 1985, pp. 411–412.

[21]Allen and Keaveny, *Contemporary Labor Relations*, pp. 634–635.

[22]Ibid.

have recently bargained for advance notice of the implementation of robots and for retraining rights so that workers can learn new skills for long-term employment.[23]

Manufacturing productivity rose 3.5 percent in the United States in 1984, ninth place in a survey of ten industrial nations. Japan's 9.5 percent growth in productivity outpaced the increases of the other countries. The United States exceeded only Norway, with its growth of 1.7 percent.[24]

As measured in output per hour, increases in the ten countries were:

Japan	9.5%	Denmark	4.1%
Sweden	6.8	Canada	4.0
Italy	6.3	Britain	3.9
France	5.0	United States	3.5
West Germany	4.7	Norway	1.7

It certainly appears that U.S. management and labor need to find ways to improve cooperation and productivity. Benefits that both management and labor could share include such things as increased competitiveness, improved profits, and better job security.

CONCESSION BARGAINING

Beginning in 1980, a new bargaining process referred to as concession, giveback, or nontraditional bargaining emerged. Many industries were suffering economic hardship brought on by deregulation in some cases and foreign competition in others and reflected in high rates of unemployment and business failures. Employees in a number of industries approved deferral of pay increases, reduced benefits, and work-rule changes. Some of the industries in which workers were involved were railroads, retailing, auto, rubber, airlines, and meat packing. In return for employee concessions, employers agreed to:

- Increased job security.
- Profit-sharing plans.
- Participation in some areas of decision making.
- Equality of sacrifice.[25]

The essence of successful and continued concession bargaining is the development of mutual trust and respect by both parties.

TWO-TIER CONTRACTS[26]

One of the most controversial recent developments in collective bargaining is the two-tier wage system. As we mentioned in chapter 12, several in-

---

[23]Carrell and Heavrin, *Collective Bargaining*, p. 412.

[24]Greenville, *Texas, Herald Banner*, June 11, 1985.

[25]Carrell and Heavrin, *Collective Bargaining*, pp. 420–422.

[26]Based on Irwin Ross, "Employers Win Big in the Move to Two-Tier Contracts," *Fortune*, April 29, 1985, pp. 82–84+.

dustries (airlines, trucking, supermarkets, aerospace, and shipbuilding) are already operating under such contracts. Under this system, newly hired workers are paid less than employees already on the payroll. While the two-tier system basically provides unequal pay for equal work, the system does save organizations a great deal of money in labor costs and at the same time provide more jobs. The system has been accepted by unions in lieu of wage cuts in companies hit hard by deregulation, foreign competition, and aggressive nonunion competitors.

There are two basic types of two-tier scales: temporary and permanent. In a temporary system, the new employees are hired for less than those hired earlier, but they can advance to parity over time. In a permanent system, the new hires will never achieve parity. There are also variations and modifications of these basic types of scales, and some companies have even instituted a third (lower) tier.

Savings in wages and benefits can be significant. American Airlines saved more than $100 million in labor costs in 1984 and looks forward to further cost reductions. Lockheed's Georgia operations are saving some $19 million a year. Although more people have jobs, will the dissatisfaction and poor morale that are generated offset the large savings? Turnover and productivity will be factors to watch in these companies. Labor may well use the discontent with these systems to recruit new members.

CONCLUSIONS

Union membership is dropping; its traditional blue-collar industrial base is melting away. American manufacturers are moving operations outside the United States, and foreign firms are flooding the market with goods. Productivity increases in this country are lagging behind those of most of the industrialized nations, and new technology is taking away jobs. Workers have given up pay raises and benefits in the hope of keeping their jobs. A new wage system of unequal pay for equal work is being negotiated in some companies.

The outlook for organized labor is not very bright, but the truth of the matter is that it does not look any better for many employers. Maybe now is the time for labor and management to take a look at cooperation as the type of union–management relationship for which to strive. They do not have to give up anything — they just need to pool their strengths. Harvard professor D. Quinn Mills knows the turmoil that gave birth to the modern union movement.[27] He sees little trust between management and labor, and envisions a real adversarial system. Collective bargaining is practiced primarily as rule-making, which is self-defeating for both parties. Management needs fewer rules for and willing cooperation from the work force. Unions need company management that is sensitive to the needs of the workers. Mondy and Premeaux came to a similar conclusion when they observed,

[27]See D. Quinn Mills, "Reforming the U.S. System of Collective Bargaining," *Monthly Labor Review* (March 1983): pp. 18–22.

"Now is the time for management to lessen its adversarial relationship with union members and build cooperation between union and management . . . [to] build for the future."[28] Unions must become more sophisticated in their response to management efforts to improve productivity. Management must be prepared to help workers adjust to changes that will be required in the future.

But Ben Fisher, for 30 years a major negotiator for the United Steelworkers of America, notes that "although there is general agreement that job security is at the heart of current bargaining concerns, it is not always admitted that long-run job security first requires that there be jobs."[29] He believes that if the workplace is not competitive, there is no hope for the people involved. The overriding issue for the U.S. economy is jobs; and successful businesses create jobs. American workers need jobs — good and secure jobs in order to improve their real standard of living. If management does not recognize the depth of labor's difficulties, it is likely to compound the problem. Labor relations must target issues that are crucial to workers and managers alike.

SUMMARY

The process through which union and management negotiators reach a contractual agreement is referred to as collective bargaining. Although there is no precise format, the same general collective bargaining process is usually used. External and internal environmental factors have an impact on the process. Depending on these factors, the process may be relatively simple or it may be a long, tension-filled struggle for both parties.

The first step in the collective bargaining process is preparing for negotiations. This is often an extensive and ongoing process for both the union and management, issues to be negotiated are determined. Negotiating involves the two sides attempting to agree on a mutually acceptable contract. But, at times, breakdowns in negotiations occur. Both labor and management have at their disposal tools which can be used to convince the other side to accept their views.

In the next step of the bargaining process, the union membership ratifies the agreement. The labor agreement defines the rules of the game for labor and management to abide by for the duration of the contract. There is also a feedback loop from administration of the agreement to preparation for the next round of negotiations. In many instances, preparing for negotiations begins virtually from the time the contract is ratified.

A number of things are happening that may alter the collective bargaining process in the future. Union membership is dropping as the number

---

[28]R. Wayne Mondy and Shane R. Premeaux, "The Labor/Management Power Relationship Revisited," *Personnel Administrator* 30 (May 1985): 55.

[29]See Ben Fischer, "Labor's Dilemma: Adapting to Post-Recession Unionism," *Industry Week* (August 6, 1984): pp. 41–44.

of service industries is increasing. American firms are moving more operations outside the United States, and foreign companies are increasing the export of their goods to the United States. Lagging productivity increases and increased technological advances are jeopardizing job security. Perhaps a new emphasis on labor–management cooperation is needed to resolve these and other issues of concern to employers and employees alike.

QUESTIONS FOR REVIEW

1. Describe the basic steps involved in the collective bargaining process.
2. Why is it so critical for management to be thoroughly prepared prior to conducting contract negotiations?
3. Why is it said that "at times negotiations are similar to a high-stakes poker game"?
4. Define each of the following:
   (a) management rights
   (b) closed shop
   (c) union shop
   (d) agency shop
   (e) maintenance of membership
   (f) checkoff of dues.
5. What are the primary means by which breakdowns in negotiations may be overcome? Briefly describe each.
6. Describe the role of a human resource manager in a unionized firm.
7. Describe the potential difficulties that might be involved in ratifying a labor agreement.
8. What is involved in the administration of a labor agreement?
9. Discuss some current forces that can influence the collective bargaining process.

TERMS FOR REVIEW

Mandatory bargaining issues
Permissive bargaining issues
Prohibited bargaining issues
Closed shop
Union shop
Agency shop
Open shop
Checkoff of dues

Seniority
Beachhead demands
Mediation
Arbitration
Strike
Boycott
Lockout

Incident 1

Barbara Washington, the chief union negotiator, was meeting with management on a new contract. The union team had been preparing for this encounter for a long time. Barbara felt that she was on top of the situation. Her only worry was whether the union members would support a strike vote if one were called. Due to the recession there was high unemployment in the area. The members' attitude was one of "We are generally pleased, but get what you can for us." She believed, however, that skillful negotiating could keep the union team from being placed in a position where the threat of a strike would be needed.

In the first session, Barbara's team presented its demands to management. Pay was the main issue, and a 30 percent increase spread over three years was demanded. Management countered with an offer of a 10 percent raise over three years. After some discussion, both sides agreed to reevaluate their positions and meet again in two days.

Barbara met with her negotiating team in private, and it was the consensus that they would decrease the salary demand slightly. They felt that the least they could accept was a 25 percent increase.

At the next meeting, Barbara presented the revised demands to management. They were not well received. Bill Thompson, the director of industrial relations, began by saying: "Our final offer is a 15 percent increase over three years. Business has been down and we have a large backlog of inventory. If you feel that it is in your best interest to strike, go ahead."

Barbara's confidence collapsed. She knew that there was no way that a strike vote could be obtained. Management must have accurately read the mood of the workers. She asked for a recess to review the new proposal.

QUESTIONS

1. How important is the threat of a strike to successful union negotiations?
2. What do you recommend that Barbara do when she next confronts management?

Incident 2

Alonzo Alexander, personnel manager for Hyatt Manufacturing, had a problem that he did not know how to handle. His firm was unionized and the relationship between management and the union had generally been good. The firm also had a strong affirmative action program. Hyatt had made major strides in implementing this program throughout the firm, with the notable exception of the machine department. In that department there were no minority or women employees.

Alonzo had recommended many blacks and women to the production manager. Some of them had been hired but they never stayed long. In their exit interviews, they often made comments such as "I just wasn't part of the team. No one would even talk to me." or "They helped one another. But no one would help me." or "I was blamed if I was nearby when something went wrong."

The problem was further complicated by the fact that the union employees were uncooperative. When Alonzo attempted to talk to the workers, he was told in no uncertain terms that if he wanted problems, he could keep sending minority and women employees to the department. He knew that if this department were shut down by a strike, the entire company would have to close. Alonzo wanted to maintain the affirmative action program but also knew the impact that a wildcat strike could have on the company.

QUESTIONS

1. What is the underlying cause of the problem at Hyatt Manufacturing?

2. How would you suggest that Alonzo deal with this situation? Discuss.

3. What should be the union's responsibility in this situation?

REFERENCES

"Arbitration: A Contract Clause That May Keep You Out of Court." *Engineering News-Record* 200 (May 25, 1980): 25.

Baer, Walter E. "Preserving Management's Upper Hand in Negotiations." *Administrative Management* 39 (June 1978): 80–82.

Barbush, Jack. "Do We Really Want Labor on the Ropes? We're Entering a New Era of Industrial Relations and That's Cause for Concern." *Harvard Business Review* 63 (July–August 1985): 10–16.

Berstein, J. "The Evolution of the Use of Management Consultants in Labor Relations: A Labor Perspective." *Labor Law Journal* 36 (May 1985): 292–299.

Cappilli, P. "Theory Construction in Industrial Relations and Some Implications for Research." *Industrial Relations* 24 (Winter 1985): 90–112.

DeMoss, R. C. "Double Breasting — An Intriguing Approach to Business Revitalization." *Employee Relations Today* 12 (Spring 1985): 55–62.

Fischer, Ben. "Labor's Dilemma: Adopting to Post-Recession Unionism." *Industry Week* (August 6, 1984): 41–44.

Flare, Steven. "Pay Cuts Before the Job Even Starts." *Fortune*, January 9, 1984, pp. 75–77.

Freedman, Audrey and Fulmer, William E. "Last Rites for Pattern Bargaining." *Harvard Business Review* 60 (March–April 1982): 39–42 + .

Greenberg, Murray and Harris, Philip. "The Arbitrator's Employment Status as a Factor in the Decision-Making Process." *Human Resource Management* 20 (Winter 1981): 26–29.

Harking, P. J. "Labor Relations: The Fickle Nature of Employment Agreements." *Personnel Journal* 64 (May 1985): 76 + .

Hoerr, J. "Pleading Labor's Case at Japan's U.S. Plants (Union–Management Relations)." *Business Week*, May 13, 1985, pp. 30–31.

Hoover, John J. "Union Organization Attempts: Management's Response." *Personnel Journal* 61 (March 1982): 214–219.

Iteina, J. M. "The Frustrations of Labor, the Revolt of Workers." *Personnel Administrator* 30 (May 1985): 22 + .

Klein, Stuart M. and Rose, Kenneth W. "Formal Policies and Procedures can Forestall Unionization." *Personnel Journal* 61 (April 1982): 275–281.

Kochan, T. A. et al. "U.S. Industrial Relations in Transition." *Monthly Labor Review* 108 (May 1985): 28–29.

Kohl, J. P. and Stephens, D. B. "On Strike: Legal Development in Labor–Management Relations." *Cornell Hotel/Restaurant Administration Quarterly* 25 (February 1985): 71–75.

Kruger, Daniel H. and Jones, Harry E. "Compulsory Interest Arbitration in the Public Sector: An Overview." *Journal of Collective Negotiations in the Public Sector* 10 (1981): 355–380.

"Labor Relations Update." *Personnel* 62 (February 1985): 64–65.

Leonard, J. F. "Striking Harmony with Unions." *Training and Development Journal* 39 (March 1985): 72–74.

Melbinger, M. S. "Negotiating a Profitsharing Plan: A Survey of the Options." *Employee Relations Law Journal* 10 (Spring 1985): 684–701.

Michelson, D. W. "Beware of GAPs in Collective Bargaining (Games, Assumptions and Preconceived Strategies)." *Personnel* 62 (April 1985): 73–76.

Miller, Ronald. "Preparations for Negotiations." *Personnel Journal* 57 (January 1978): 36–39.

Mills, D. Quinn. "Reforming the U.S. System of Collective Bargaining." *Monthly Labor Review* (March 1983): 18–22.

Mondy, R. Wayne and Preameaux, Shane R. "The Labor/Management Power Relationship Revisited." *Personnel Administrator* 30 (May 1985): 51–52 + .

Murray, T. J. "New Union Bargaining Issue (Quality Circles)." *Dun's Review* 118 (September 1981): 119.

Murphy, B. S. et al. "A Successor Employer's Duty to Bargain." *Personnel Journal* 64 (May 1985): 29–30 + .

Murphy, T. W. "Management During Boycott." *Journal of Property Management* 50 (May–June 1985): 76–77.

"Nissan: Rising Sun Over Industrial Relations (Several Unions Have Signed Agreements Designed to Avoid Strikes)." *Economist* 295 (April 27, 1985): 69–70.

Ogden, S. G. "The Reform of Collective Bargaining: A Managerial Revolution?" *Industrial Relations Journal* 12 (September/October 1981): 30–42.

Primeaux, William and Brannen, Dalton. "Why Few Arbitrators are Deemed Acceptable." *Monthly Labor Review* 98 (September 1975): 27–30.

Reisman, B. and Compa, L. "The Case for Adversarial Unions." *Harvard Business Review* 63 (May–June 1985): 22–24+.

Rohan, T. M. "Employee Relations: Do Something Outrageous!" *Industry Week* 224 (January 7, 1985): 49–50.

Rohrer, Robert. "Not the Union . . . the People!" *Supervision* 44 (March 1982): 13.

Ross, Irwin. "Employees Win Big in the Move to Two-Tier Contracts." *Fortune*, April 29, 1985, pp. 82–84+.

Ruben, George. "Airlines Win Wage Concessions." *Monthly Labor Review* 106 (September 1983): 38.

Sorge, M. and Krebs, M. "Saturn Termed Ultimate Test of UAW–GM Labor Relations." *Automotive News*, March 11, 1985, p. 2.

Stundza, Tom. "Labor to Stress Security in Contract Talks: The Main Thrust in This 'Light Year' Will Be Job Security, Not Wage Inflation." *Purchasing* 98 (January 17, 1985): 52–54.

"Unions Move into the Office." *Business Week*, January 25, 1982, 90+.

Woolf, Donald Austin. "Arbitration in One Easy Lesson: A Review of Criteria Used in Arbitration Awards." *Personnel* 55 (September–October 1978): 76.

Chapter 17

UNION FREE ORGANIZATIONS

Wayne Smith, a new production worker for Ampax Manufacturing, recently moved from the North to the Southwest. He was carrying on a conversation with several workers on his shift. "I don't see why we don't have a union here. Who's going to represent us when management puts the screws on?" Wayne's conversation was cut off fast by one of the other workers, who replied, "We don't believe in unions in this plant. The plant management has done a good job. If you believe you need a union to represent you, maybe you don't need to work here." Wayne nodded his head to indicate his understanding and did not mention unionization again to his co-workers.

Brad Carpet, production manager for the Thompson Manufacturing Company, was upset. He had just been walking through the plant and accidentally heard one of his supervisors severely reprimanding an employee in front of his co-workers. Brad called the supervisor aside and said, "We're a union free organization and hope to remain this way. What you just did was one of the fastest ways to create a feeling among our employees that they need a union."

These incidents describe some employee and management attitudes in union free firms. Wayne Smith had just discovered that not all employees feel that they need to be represented by a union. On the other hand, Brad Carpet is quite concerned that the action of one of his supervisors may create an atmosphere where employees feel that they need a union. Union free firms comprise an important part of the industrial scene in the United States. Also, many employees who work under collective bargaining agreements are not union members. The overall purpose of this chapter is to acquaint you with some of the characteristics of union free firms and the factors related to maintaining this status.

WHY EMPLOYEES AVOID JOINING UNIONS

Most employees in the United States do not belong to unions. Their reasons for not joining are many and varied, some of which may be seen in Figure 17–1. In the first place, it costs money to be a union member. There is typically an initiation fee followed by dues that must be paid on a regular basis in order to remain a member. From time to time, there may also be assessments. Although dues typically do not amount to more than two percent of before-tax pay, many individuals would rather use this money in other ways. A worker who makes $24,000 annually would pay dues of approximately $40 per month, in addition to the initiation fee.

Figure 17–1. Why employees do not join unions.

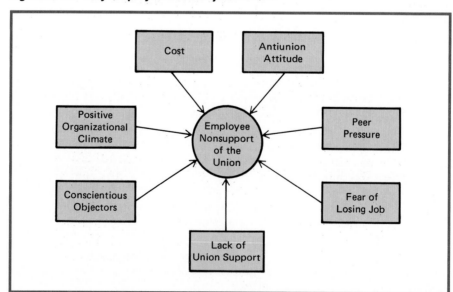

Also, many employees think that unions are unnecessary. It is their belief that they should not have to depend on a third party to help satisfy their needs. These individuals feel that their value to the organization should be judged on an individual basis. If their performance is superior, the reward should be appropriate and direct. They believe that joining a union is an admission that others control their destiny. These individuals feel that joining the union would limit their opportunities for advancement.

In addition, just as there may be peer pressure in some firms to encourage employees to join the union, in other instances there may be as much pressure against union affiliation. Even if an individual might desire to join a union, the informal work group may be powerful enough to preclude even people having the strongest of wills from outwardly supporting a union. As Wayne Smith discovered in the incident at the beginning of the chapter, the prevailing attitude of his co-workers was to maintain a union free status.

Reprisals for union activities are illegal in the United States. Even so, some employees would feel insecure about their jobs if they engaged in union activities. Perhaps they have seen workers who supported the union receive what they perceive as unfair treatment from their employers. If a worker can be easily replaced, the employee may decide not to take a chance on losing his or her job by supporting union activities.

Establishing a union is much like starting a business. The cost to start and maintain a union must be evaluated in relation to the revenue or benefits to be gained. The union may decide to expend minimum or no effort in the establishment of a new bargaining unit. For instance, a union would tend to look more favorably on organizing a section of five hundred skilled workers as opposed to a group of five semiskilled employees. Although the union might like to help the five employees, the cost of organizing and supporting them would likely be excessive.

Unions also recognize that there are certain industries, firms, and locations in the country with a tradition of resisting unions. For instance, even though the Sunbelt states offer unlimited opportunities for unionization, unions have experienced difficulties there. Also, a union may believe that additional attempts to unionize IBM Corporation are a waste of money because previous efforts proved fruitless.

Certain employee groups have religious or moral beliefs that preclude them from joining organizations. Because unions are organizations, these employees refuse to work for a firm where union membership is required.

Finally, there may be factors within the company that keep employees from joining a union. The corporate culture (discussed in chapter 9) may be one that encourages open communication and employee participation. Workers may have excellent relationships with their supervisors. Trust may exist to the point that workers may feel that they do not need a third party to represent them in their dealings with the company. Where this attitude is present, the employees identify strongly with the objectives of the company.

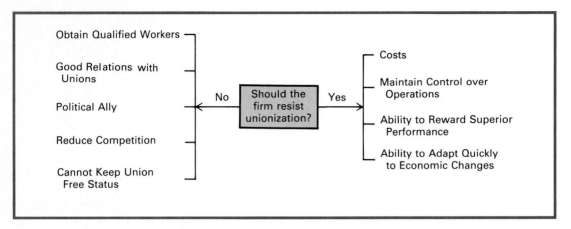

Figure 17–2. Should the firm resist unionization?

COST/BENEFIT ANALYSIS — UNIONIZATION

Valid reasons exist for management's acceptance or rejection of unionization (see Figure 17–2). Rationales for both philosophies will be described next.

ACCEPTANCE OF UNIONIZATION ATTEMPTS

There may be times when resistance to unionization attempts is not advantageous. In these situations, management must set aside personal feelings and make decisions that are in the firm's best interest. For example, the maritime and construction unions often provide a ready source of labor from their hiring halls. A firm operating in one of these industries may find it advantageous to accept unionization in order to obtain qualified workers. In other instances, management may realize benefits by utilizing the political influence of unions. For example, a union's effective lobbying efforts may help a firm obtain contracts that will benefit both the union members and the firm.

In addition, there are situations where the relationship between management and the union is quite good and well established. In these instances, it may be prudent to keep that union. Otherwise, a more demanding union may take its place. Management rationalizes that it can work within the present system; the future with a different union may be uncertain.

Management may also desire unionization of competing organizations. If a competitor attempts to enter the industry by paying lower nonunion wages, the larger established firms operating with greater economy of scale will likely desire unionization of the new firm.[1] Costs to all firms producing similar products remain relatively constant when all are unionized.

[1]John G. Kilgour, "Before the Union Knocks," *Personnel Journal* 57 (April 1978): 186.

R. H. Heil
Senior Vice President–
Personnel
Delta Air Lines, Inc.

Delta Air Lines has always been known as a people oriented company, and as Senior Vice President–Personnel, one of Russ Heil's responsibilities is to make sure it stays that way. Proof that Delta takes personnel relations very seriously can be seen by the fact that Delta was rated as being one of the top three work environments in America by the author of "The One Hundred Best Companies in America to Work For." In 1982, Delta employees presented their company with a rather unique Christmas present — a thirty million dollar B-767 aircraft.

After a tour with the United States Army, Heil began his career at Delta in 1966, joining the company as an aircraft performance engineer. He had graduated from the Georgia Institute of Technology with a degree in aerospace engineering.

"I really didn't choose Personnel as a career," he said. "At the time I joined Delta's engineering department, I decided that one of the things I wanted to do was to go back to school for a masters in business administration. Going to school at night, I graduated in 1969 from Georgia State University with an MBA degree. I felt that an MBA would not only help me perform my duties at the time, but also would better prepare me for whatever opportunities and challenges were presented in the future."

After receiving his MBA, Heil worked for several years for the head of Delta's operations division, where he became involved in many general policy matters as well as in technical projects. Then in 1972, when it was announced that Delta and Northeast Airlines would merge, his career took a major turn. He was asked to join the personnel division to help with the many facets of the merger. He has been in Personnel since then, moving through various positions of increasing responsibility until being promoted to his current position in 1984.

At Delta, Heil sees the role of Personnel as simply to make sure that Delta people are treated fairly and with respect, no matter in what area of the company they work. "I think it is extremely important," he said, "that the personnel implications be considered when major operational decisions are made. Here, the Personnel function is accorded much greater weight in the decision-making process than perhaps exists in many firms. The Personnel function is a separate division having status equal to other divisions of the company. In fact, most major operating decisions are not made until the personnel aspects have been considered, and the personnel division has made its input concerning those decisions. We work very hard to avoid decisions that have an adverse impact on the people of Delta. Our people are, without question, our most valued asset."

When asked what he sees as the biggest challenge he faces as head of the Personnel division, he responded, "My biggest challenge is to ensure that Delta maintains the feeling of family that has characterized the growth and development of the company for over 55 years. We work very hard to preserve that feeling even though we now number almost 40,000 employees. At Delta the individual is recognized as an individual. Each individual can be heard, and the company can respond to the individual's needs. We don't want our people to feel that they have become lost in the bigness of the company."

An additional factor determining whether a firm should resist unionization attempts involves a realistic appraisal of whether it can remain union free. There are numerous instances in which the firm would have little hope of staying union free. For example, there would likely be little chance for a maritime company located in New York City to remain union free. If there is no reasonable way the firm could remain union free, it would likely be in its best interest to begin developing a strategy for working within a unionized environment. The presence of a union will increase the demands made on the firm's human resource management.

RESISTANCE TO UNIONIZATION ATTEMPTS

Although there may be valid reasons for a firm to accept unionization, it is likely that a large percentage of executives would prefer that their companies remain union free. In fact, a major goal for many organizations is to remain union free. Some reasons for a firm desiring to remain union free are described next.

Costs. In most instances, the compensation paid to union members is higher than that for nonunion workers. However, firms realize that they must remain competitive in order to survive. Delta Air Lines, a union free organization, has had considerable success in comparison to its unionized competitors. It is likely that Montgomery Ward would want to remain union free because its primary competition (Sears) is also union free. If Montgomery Ward were unionized, the firm would likely experience higher labor costs. However, because of a highly competitive situation, it could not pass these costs along to the consumer.

It has been estimated that unionization increases labor costs as much as 25–80 percent.[2] Factors that contribute to increased labor cost include: "the high cost of complex, payroll-padding work rules; work stoppages, strikes and slowdowns; lengthy negotiations and the grind of arbitration cases; and layoff by seniority."[3] The type of working relationship between labor and management will have a considerable impact on cost. In general, however, the overall cost of labor is higher in a unionized firm.

Maintaining control over operations. Management typically wants to operate without restrictive union work rules and other provisions that could reduce management's authority.[4] When a firm is unionized, management relinquishes some of its control over the work environment. For example, with People Express, a union free airline, a ticket agent may be seen loading

[2]Jerry Eisen, "Don't Be Complacent about Union Organizing," *Personnel Administrator* 30 (August 1985): 122.

[3]Wiley I. Beavers, "Employee Relations Without a Union," in Dale Yoder and Herbert G. Heneman, Jr. (eds.), *ASPA Handbook of Personnel and Industrial Relations: Employee and Labor Relations*, Vol. III. Washington, D.C.: The Bureau of National Affairs, 1976, p. 7-82.

[4]"What Put Labor on the Defensive," *Business Week*, December 4, 1978, p. 56.

baggage or doing a multitude of other tasks during slow periods. Even top executives, from the chairman on down, have filled in as dispatchers, schedulers, and baggage handlers. This would not happen in a unionized firm where jobs are very structured.

Union free firms do not have strikes, which interfere with operations. A strike during a critical period can be disastrous to a firm. Its competitors can then step in and increase their shares of the market. One of the reasons that the U.S. steel industry has experienced such a decline in sales is because of extended strikes in the past. Manufacturers, needing steel to run their business, tried Japanese and European steel and often kept purchasing from the foreign supplier after the strike was over.

Ability to reward superior performance.   It is often much easier to reward superior performance in a union free firm. A study involving twenty-six nonunion firms revealed that "company executives believe they achieve higher productivity than they would if they were organized.[5] Promotions and salary increases may be based solely on performance instead of seniority. In a unionized firm, the compensation that is paid to each worker is specified by the agreement.

Ability to adapt quickly.   Most organizations experience fluctuations in the demand for their products. Some firms undergo severe business downturns before the cycle is reversed. Union free firms are typically able to respond much more rapidly to changing conditions. If wages must be reduced to remain competitive, the union free firm can generally adjust more rapidly. The unionized firm is bound by the labor agreement and cannot lower wages unless the union agrees to a contract change. When the automobile industry was in severe difficulty because foreign products were less expensive and of better quality, management could not quickly lower wages to be competitive. Any wage concessions had to be negotiated. Often these negotiations were unsuccessful.

When workers must be laid off as a result of declining demand, management in a union free firm is able to terminate employees whose work productivity is marginal. The seniority system determines who will be laid off in a unionized company.

STRATEGIES AND TACTICS FOR MAINTAINING UNION FREE STATUS

Some managers believe that the presence of a union is evidence of management's failure to treat employees fairly.[6] Following this reasoning,

[5]Fred K. Foulkes, "How Top Nonunion Companies Manage Employees," *Harvard Business Review* 59 (September–October 1981): 90.
[6]Beavers, "Employee Relations Without a Union," p. 7-83.

Table 17–1. Factors that reduce the chances for union organizing

1. A conviction by employees that the boss is not taking advantage of them.
2. Employees who have pride in their work.
3. Good performance records kept by the company. Employees feel more secure on their jobs when they know their efforts are recognized and appreciated.
4. No claims of highhanded treatment. Employees respect firm but fair discipline.
5. No claim of favoritism that's not earned through work performance.
6. Supervisors who have good relationships with subordinates. The AFL-CIO maintains that this relationship of supervisors with people under them — above all — stifles organizing attempts.

Source: "What to Do When the Union Knocks," *Nation's Business* 54 (November 1966): 107. Copyright © 1977 by *Nation's Business*. Reprinted by permission.

management insensitivity to the demands of its people often results in unionization. The AFL-CIO lists several factors that, if present in a plant that it is attempting to organize, will significantly reduce chances of unionizing. They are listed in Table 17–1.

If a firm's goal is to remain union free, it must establish its strategy long before a union organizing attempt begins. The development of long-term strategies and effective tactics for the purpose of remaining union free is critical because employees' decisions to consider forming a union are usually not made overnight. Negative attitudes regarding the company are typically formed well in advance of any attempt at unionization.[7]

If a firm desires to remain union free, it must borrow some of the union's philosophy. In fact, unions have done much to improve the conditions of nonunionized employees. Basically, management must be able to offer workers equal or better conditions than they could expect with the union. A total management system is needed to avoid unionization. Weakness in any critical area may develop into an open invitation to the union. As shown in Figure 17–3, all aspects of the firm's operations are involved in maintaining its union free status.

FIRST-LINE SUPERVISORS

Extremely important to a firm's ability to remain union free is the overall effectiveness of management, particularly first-line supervisors. The first-line supervisor represents the first line of defense against unionization. The supervisory ability of these managers often determines whether unionization will be successful. The supervisor assigns work, evaluates each individual's work, and gives out praise and punishment. The manner in

[7]John G. Kilgour, "Responding to the Union Campaign," *Personnel Journal* 57 (May 1978): 242.

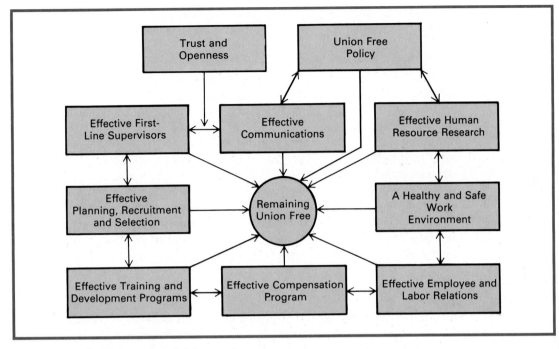

Figure 17–3. Strategies and tactics for remaining union free.

which he or she communicates with the employee in these and other matters can affect the individual's attitude toward the firm. To the employee, the supervisor is management. In the workplace, the supervisor has more influence over employees than any other manager.

The supervisor also must communicate information about the firm to employees. Information regarding profits, sales, how the firm's product compares to competitors', and the like are important. The grapevine may reveal that sales are declining, which would likely disturb many workers. If the supervisor explains that sales are down across the industry but are expected to return to normal in the next quarter, less anxiety might be experienced.

In order for a supervisor to be able to communicate effectively with employees, he or she must possess timely and accurate information. If the employee is aware of company plans before the supervisor, the supervisor's credibility is diminished. For instance, if top management changes a company policy regarding safety hats in a particular area and the supervisor is not advised, the manager might continue to instruct employees to adhere to the old policy. Because of the speed of the grapevine, it is likely that the workers would know of the change soon after it occurred. If disciplinary action resulted from such a situation, the supervisor would be quite embarrassed.

The supervisor must also be adept at interpreting the signals of non-verbal communication. A well-trained supervisor can identify symptoms of unrest among employees. For instance, increasing signs of resentment, where there were none before, may indicate union activity. The recent creation of informal groups may also indicate unrest. The supervisor might notice that workers may stop talking or change the conversation when he or she approaches. A competent supervisor will notice these signs and report them immediately to upper level management. There may be patterns of similar activities in other departments, suggesting an attempt at unionization. This knowledge may assist management in developing appropriate strategies and tactics.

One of the fastest ways to convert a nonunion person into a union advocate is to have an environment that promotes favoritism. To the worker, favoritism is equivalent to discrimination. The supervisor must establish an atmosphere in which the worker believes that he or she can receive fair treatment.

UNION FREE POLICY

As we discussed in chapter 2, effective communication in an organization extends to all employees. The fact that the organization's goal is to remain union free should be clearly and forcefully communicated to all members of the organization. A recommended policy statement might read as follows:

> Our success as a company is founded on the skill and efforts of our employees. Our policy is to deal with employees as effectively as possible, respecting and recognizing each of them as an individual.
>
> In our opinion, unionization would interfere with the individual treatment, respect and recognition the company offers.
>
> Consequently, we believe a union free environment is in the employees' best interest, the company's best interest and the interest of the people served by the corporation.[8]

This type of policy evolves into a philosophy that affects everyone in the firm. All employees, from the lowest paid worker to upper level management, must understand this goal of the firm. It should be so strong that no personnel-related decision is made without asking, "How will this affect our union free status?"

The union free policy should be repeatedly communicated to every worker. Workers must be told why the company advocates the policy and how it affects them. This involves much more than sending a memo each year to all employees stating that the company's objective is to remain union free. All means to ensure effective communication may be needed to convince company employees that the firm intends to remain union free.

---

[8]James F. Rand, "Preventive-Maintenance Techniques for Staying Union-Free," *Personnel Journal* 59 (June 1980): 497.

One of the most important considerations for a firm that wants to remain union free is the establishment of credible communication.[9] Effective communication is essential in maintaining union free status. Employees must be given the information they need to perform their jobs and provided feedback on their performance. Management should aggressively share information with workers concerning activities taking place within the firm. In addition, management must listen to expressions of employee needs and their perceptions of management policies and practices.

In order to sustain employee cooperation in the pursuit of organizational goals, management must consider the needs of employees. Employees want to know things such as:

- Their standing in relation to the official, formal authority structure.
- Their standing in relation to the informal organization with respect to individual status, power, acceptance, and so forth.
- Events that have a bearing on their own and the company's future economic security.
- Operational information that will enable them to develop pride in the job.

One approach taken to encourage open communication is the open-door policy. The **open-door policy** is *a company policy whereby employees have the right to take any grievance to the person next in the chain of command if a satisfactory solution cannot be obtained from their immediate supervisor.* Delta Air Lines is well known for its open-door policy, which enables employees to air any grievances. An effective open-door policy represents an attitude of openness and trust among people within the organization. It is not sufficient to state that an open-door policy exists and then punish the employee for bypassing his or her immediate supervisor. The employee must not fear that talking to the manager next in line will be detrimental to his or her career. Although on the surface it might seem that an open-door policy would result in wasted time for upper and middle level supervisors, in most instances this has not proven to be the case. The mere knowledge that an employee can move up the chain of command with a complaint without fear of retribution often encourages the immediate supervisor and the employee to work out their differences.

TRUST AND OPENNESS

Openness and trust on the part of managers and employees are important factors if a firm desires to remain union free. The old expression that "actions speak louder than words" is certainly valid for a firm that desires

---

[9]Charles L. Hughes, *Making Unions Unnecessary.* New York: Executive Enterprises, 1976, p. 15.

to remain union free. Credibility must exist between labor and management, and this trust only develops over time. When employees feel that openness and trust do not exist, difficulties result. If employees perceive that the manager is being open and receptive to ideas, feedback is encouraged. Managers need this feedback to do their jobs effectively. On the other hand, if managers give the impression that their directives should never be questioned, communication tends to be stifled.

One of the major factors in the success of Japanese businesses is said to be that managers trust not only their workers but also their peers and superiors. As a result, a simpler organizational structure than that generally used in the United States is possible. Toyota, for example, has only six levels of management between a factory worker and the chief executive officer; Ford Motor Company has eleven. More levels of management result in higher overhead costs and more time-consuming decision making. Japanese firms assume that personnel at all levels are competent and trustworthy and thus do not have to employ highly paid executives to review the work of other highly paid executives.[10]

HUMAN RESOURCE PLANNING, RECRUITMENT, AND SELECTION

A firm's ability to remain union free relates closely to its human resource planning, recruitment, and selection practices. For instance, if a firm used only word of mouth from current employees as a recruiting source, a very homogeneous work force of friends and relatives could develop. Such a work force would likely have strong interpersonal relationships. Should management take action against any worker, the work group might perceive this as a negative action affecting them all. For this reason, Personnel will likely wish to recruit from a wide variety of sources.

A firm's method of human resource planning can have a major impact on its susceptibility to unionization. If the firm is constantly hiring and terminating employees in reaction to the demand for its products, the firm may face unionization. A firm can often maintain employment stability with adequate planning.

Personnel policies also have a major impact on remaining union free. Delta Airline's promotion-from-within policy is credited with giving employees a feeling of security. All of the company's top managers have been with the company for over two decades, and no one at Delta expects to be denied a promotion by someone being hired from outside.

TRAINING AND DEVELOPMENT PROGRAMS

Many employees want the opportunity to grow and advance within the company. Often it is through training and development that these goals can be obtained. A philosophy that is genuinely supportive of T&D would

[10]"Trust: The New Ingredient of Management," *Business Week*, July 6, 1981, p. 104.

extend all the way from top management to the lowest level employee. As we discussed in chapter 8, the success of any companywide training program depends on the support and interest shown by top management. Management support is crucial because its attitude will filter down and influence employees at the lower levels of the organization.

One important requirement of training and development is for employees to have a genuine desire for self-improvement. Some employees are content in their present positions, while others desire to develop their potential. More employees will wish to improve their skills if they are able to see a relationship between increased training, higher pay, and other rewards. A firm takes a giant step to remain union free when it provides avenues for advancement in skill and status. The seniority system often hinders union employees in these opportunities.

Supervisors also need training to prepare them for union organizing attempts. If the union knows that a firm's supervisors have been thoroughly trained in tactics to deal with the union, it may decide against organizing attempts. This type of training will also assist in preventing costly mistakes that could lead to charges of unfair labor practices. Training is necessary because the supervisor's actions can actually bind the employer. Ignorance on the part of the supervisor is no excuse.

COMPENSATION PROGRAMS

The financial compensation that employees receive is the most tangible measure they have of their worth to the firm. If an individual's salary is substantially below that paid by other firms in the area of similar work, dissatisfaction will surely occur. Compensation must remain competitive if the company expects to stay union free.[11]

The compensation program in a union free firm should be intelligently planned and communicated to all employees. They must understand what they are being compensated for and how the system works. The firm is a prospect for unionizing activities if employees perceive the system as being unfair.

The same approach should be followed in regard to the benefits area. The firm need not have the best benefits in a geographic area or an industry to protect its nonunion status. However, the benefits package must be competitive. Employees must know what benefits they are actually receiving. Too often, firms do not inform their employees about their benefits. When such a situation exists, the financial resources of the company are being wasted and its union free status is jeopardized.

A SAFE AND HEALTHY WORK ENVIRONMENT

A firm that has gained a reputation for failure to maintain a safe and healthy work environment leaves itself wide open for unionization. For years unions

---

[11]Rand, "Preventive-Maintenance Techniques," p. 498.

have campaigned successfully by convincing workers that the union will provide them with a safer work environment. In fact, labor unions were leading advocates of OSHA and continue to support this type of legislation.

EFFECTIVE EMPLOYEE RELATIONS

A means of resolving employee complaints, whether actual or perceived, should be available. A systematic process that permits employees to complain about matters affecting them is needed. The **grievance procedure** is *a mechanism that gives subordinates the opportunity of complaining to and carrying appeals beyond their immediate supervisors.* Most unions have negotiated formal grievance procedures, but such procedures are not so common in union free firms. When employees do not have ways to voice their complaints and have them resolved, even small gripes may grow into major problems.

The grievance procedure is a way of keeping problems from becoming serious. Total commitment to such a policy needs to start with top management and be instilled in every manager. Supervisors should develop an attitude of wanting to resolve problems before they become formal complaints.[12] Employees who believe that management is concerned with attempting to resolve their problems lack a major reason for needing a union.

A means of resolving grievances in union free organizations is through the use of ombudspersons. Ombudspersons have been used for some time in Europe, and the practice is becoming more popular in the United States. Ombudspersons act as top management's eyes and ears. An **ombudsperson** is *a complaint officer with access to top management, who hears employee complaints, investigates them, and sometimes recommends appropriate action.* Because of their access to top management, ombudspersons can often resolve problems swiftly. In many cases, the ombudsperson simply helps employees locate people who can solve their problems. Sometimes ombudspersons recommend specific actions to managers. The Singer Company uses an ombudsperson system. In a recent company newsletter, Harry P. Hancock, Jr., senior director, employee relations program, described its program (Figure 17–4).

HUMAN RESOURCE RESEARCH

Human resource research can reveal changes in attitudes within the organization that could ultimately lead to unionization. Ignored problems often lead to attitudes that encourage unionization. One purpose of human resource research is to identify personnel problems at an early date. Corrective action should be taken before workers feel a need for a union to solve their problems.

Research may reveal symptoms of worker unrest. For instance, turnover statistics may reveal an alarming trend in a department within the company. When general employee dissatisfaction exists, the turnover rate normally

---

[12]Foulkes, "Nonunion Companies," p. 95.

See the Ombudsman

An employee is fired for cause, disciplined or preceives himself or herself a victim of discrimination. To reverse the decision or remedy the situation, the employee tries normal channels—but remains dissatisfied with the results.

In many organizations, the story would end here. At Singer, because of the Corporate Ombudsman program started in 1976, the story can have another chapter or two. And, although the story may not necessarily have a happy ending, employees are guaranteed that they won't be subjected to harrassment or retribution for contacting the Ombudsman.

A concept borrowed from Scandinavia, the Ombudsman function entails an impartial investigation of and assistance in equitably settling complaints. At Singer this corporate-wide function is the responsibility of Harry P. Hancock, Jr., senior director, employee relations programs. "Because the program is informal rather than formal and the range of cases is varied," explains Mr. Hancock, "there is really no single modus operandi. I handle each case as it presents itself."

The range of cases include grievances about performance appraisals, involuntary discharge, sexual harrassment, sexual discrimination, denial of promotion, formal reprimand and conflict with or unfair treatment by a supervisor.

For the purpose of illustrating the thoroughness of the Ombudsman proceedings, Mr. Hancock describes how he might deal with a discharge-for-cause case brought to his attention by an employee who had exhausted all normal channels and remained dissatisfied.

"In the investigation and evaluation," he explains, "we rely heavily on the division personnel staff. Our objective is to make sure that:

- The rule or policy allegedly broken by the employee has been published, posted or otherwise made known to employees.

- The employee has been warned about any earlier infractions and given counseling.
- The employee has given a reasonable length of time to improve performance.
- The proposed disciplinary action is appropriate to the infraction.
- Other employees charged with similar infractions have been treated in a similar manner."

If it is determined that the employee has been unfairly discharged, the case is discussed with the immediate supervisor who initiated the action. If the decision is not reversed or amended at this level—which it usually is—then the discussion is brought to successively higher levels. On the other hand, if it is judged that the decision was appropriate, the employee is so advised and the case is closed.

Most problems are resolved, of course, through Singer's normal channels. Resolving a problem via normal channels includes an initial discussion with the immediate supervisor. If the issue is not settled at that level, then the matter is taken to higher levels, in the specific unit. Equal Opportunity coordinators, industrial relations personnel and other employee relations specialists may become involved.

In cases of terminations of employees with more than ten years of continuous service, standard procedure requires that those terminations be approved by members of the Management Committee.

If employees, after having gone through normal channels, still believe that they have received unfair treatment then they can bring the matter to the attention of the Ombudsman.

Figure 17–4. A description of an ombudsman program. Source: Used with permission of The Singer Company.

increases. Good exit interviews, as part of the research effort, can assist management in identifying problems before they become critical.[13]

Another indicator of employee dissatisfaction is the number of customer complaints received. For example, research reveals that customer

[13]Wanda R. Embrey, R. Wayne Mondy, and Robert M. Noe, "Exit Interview: A Tool for Personnel Development," *Personnel Administrator* 24 (May 1979): 48.

complaints are increasing because of reduced quality, it might mean that the employees have problems which need resolving. Accident frequency, maintenance costs, and theft are other indicators of employee dissatisfaction.[14]

UNION DECERTIFICATION

Until 1947, once a union was certified, it was certified forever.[15] However, the Taft–Hartley Act made it possible for employees to decertify a union. *When a union loses its right to act as the exclusive bargaining representative of a group of employees, this is referred to as* **decertification.** The process is essentially the reverse of what a union must accomplish to be recognized as an official bargaining unit. In recent years, many decertification elections have been held. By 1979, employee groups favoring removal of the union were winning 75 percent of the elections. Of the 777 decertification elections, only 194 resulted in union victories.[16]

The Adolph Coors Company is one major firm that has become union free through decertification. Because of a company policy of requiring employees to take lie detector tests, the company's brewery workers walked out in April 1977. A week later the AFL-CIO announced a nationwide boycott of the company's beer. The Coors family, which still controlled the majority of the common stock, would not budge and eventually broke the strike. A decertification election was held July 20, 1978, and 71 percent of the workers voted to oust the union.[17] Factors other than wages caused the employees to want to rid themselves of the union. Coors wage rates were much higher than in other nearby industries. Coors simply wanted the freedom to run its organization without union interference.[18]

Decertification elections have also been won in such well-known firms as Holiday Inn, Goodyear, Dow Chemical, Sears, American Airlines, and The Washington Post. However, smaller firms appear to be achieving the greatest won–lost record (see Table 17–2). Perhaps this is because it is easier for management to reestablish trust with employees in smaller firms.

Decertification procedure. The rules established by the NLRB are specific in stating the prerequisites for filing a decertification petition. In order for the NLRB to conduct a decertification election, at least 30 percent of the bargaining unit members must petition for an election. As might be expected, this task by itself may be difficult because prounion supporters are likely to strongly oppose the move. Although the petitioners' names are

[14]Beavers, "Employee Relations Without a Union," pp. 7-69–7-70.

[15]93 Daily Congressional Record 3954 (23 April 1947).

[16]William E. Fulmer, "Decertification: Is the Current Trend a Threat to Collective Bargaining?" *California Management Review* 24 (Fall 1981): 16.

[17]"Coors Undercuts Its Last Big Union," *Business Week*, July 24, 1978, p. 47.

[18]"Coors Brewery Says Workers Vote to Decertify the Union," *The Wall Street Journal*, December 15, 1978, p. 23.

Table 17–2. Decertification elections by unit size		
Employees	Number of elections	Number company won (% won)
1– 49	2,209	1,715 (78)
50– 99	391	205 (52)
100–149	129	65 (50)
150–199	77	39 (51)
200–499	96	41 (43)
500 or more	21	8 (38)

Source: Reprinted, by permission of the publisher, from "How to Win a Decertification Election," by Woodruff Imberman, MANAGEMENT REVIEW, September 1977, p. 27, © 1977 by AMACOM, a division of American Management Associations. All rights reserved.

supposed to remain confidential, many union members are fearful that they will be discovered to have signed the petition.

Timing of the NLRB's receipt of the decertification petition is also critical. It must be submitted between sixty and ninety days prior to the expiration of the current contract. When all these conditions have been met, the NLRB regional director will schedule a decertification election by secret ballot.

The NLRB carefully monitors the events leading up to the election. If the NLRB determines that management initiated the election, it will likely not certify the election. Current employees must initiate the request for the election. After the petition has been accepted, management can support the decertification election attempt. If a majority of the votes cast are against the union, the employees will be free from that union. However, strong union supporters are all likely to vote. If a substantial number of employees are indifferent to the union and choose not to vote, decertification may not be approved.

Management and decertification. When management senses employee discontent with the union, it often does not know how to react. Many times management decides to do nothing, reasoning that it is best not to get involved. Some managers even believe that it is illegal to participate. But, if it does want to get involved, management can use a variety of tactics. Basically, if a firm really wants the union decertified, it must learn how to be active rather than passive.

Meeting with union members to discuss the benefits of becoming union free have proven beneficial. In fact, they are often cited as being the most effective campaign tactic. These meeting may be with individual employees, small groups or even entire units. Management explains the benefits of being union free and answers questions that may arise in these meetings.[19]

[19]William E. Fulmer, "When Employees Want to Oust Their Unions," *Harvard Business Review* 56 (March–April 1978): 167–168.

Management may also provide workers with legal assistance in preparing for decertification. Because the workers have likely never experienced a decertification election, this assistance may prove invaluable. The NLRB may not permit an election if the paperwork has not been properly completed. A major point to remember is that management cannot initiate the decertification action; it is entirely the workers' responsibility.

The most effective means through which decertification can be accomplished is to improve the firm's organizational culture so that workers will no longer feel the need to have a union. This cannot be done overnight. Mutual trust and confidence must be developed between worker and employer.

If decertification is to succeed, management must eliminate the problems that initially led to unionization. Although many corporate executives believe that pay and benefits are the primary reasons for union sentiments, these factors likely are not the real cause.[20] Failure to treat employees as individuals is often the primary reason for unionization. The *real* problems often stem from practices such as failing to listen to employees' opinions or treating workers unfairly and dishonestly. It is extremely difficult for employees to remain loyal to a firm with managers who know them only as numbers and not by name. Many organizational attitudes and actions indicate to employees how the firm feels toward them. Some of these indicators are:

- Poor housekeeping.
- Poor supervision.
- Inadequate wage differentials among the various skill levels.
- Inadequate preventive maintenance.
- Arbitrary company policies.
- Unfair promotional policies.
- An ineffective complaint and discipline procedure.[21]

Naturally, this list is far from complete. However, existence of these problems in organizations may have led initially to the firm's unionization. Even if a firm truly desires to become union free it cannot accomplish this objective immediately. Elimination of the unsatisfactory conditions will take time.

THE ROLE OF HUMAN RESOURCE MANAGEMENT IN A UNION FREE ORGANIZATION

The human resource manager in a union free firm has a slightly different role than his or her counterpart in a unionized company. The tasks of the

---

[20]Woodruff Imberman, "How to Win a Decertification Election," *Management Review* 66 (September 1977): 38.
[21]Ibid.

human resource manager in a unionized firm often revolve around contract negotiations and grievance handling. The human resource manager in a union free firm must work toward creating an atmosphere in which the workers will not feel a need for union representation. Human resource managers serve as the catalyst for developing and maintaining nonunion attitudes. The human resource manager, therefore, must ensure that all managers are trained to work with their employees in a positive manner so that workers can maintain their self-esteem.

In union free organizations, the human resource professional is often assigned a role with greater responsibility. This executive more often reports directly to the president and is often a member of the board of directors.[22] In addition, the ratio of personnel professionals to employees is usually higher than in union organizations — perhaps one per 100 employees as opposed to one per 200 employees.

SUMMARY

Union free firms comprise an important part of the industrial scene in the United States. Many employees who work under collective bargaining agreements are not union members. Some of the reasons that employees do not belong to unions include: (1) cost; (2) antiunion attitude; (3) peer pressure; (4) fear of job loss; (5) lack of union support; (6) conscientious objections; and (7) positive organizational culture.

If a firm desires to remain union free, a total management system is needed. The primary factors in maintaining a union free status are: (1) effective first-line supervisors; (2) clearly stated union free policy; (3) effective communication; (4) climate of trust and openness; (5) effective human resource planning, recruitment, and selection; (6) effective training and development programs; (7) effective compensation program; (8) safe and healthy work environment; (9) effective employee relations; and (10) effective human resource research.

Decertification occurs when a union loses its right to act as the exclusive bargaining representative of a group of employees. The process is essentially the reverse of what a union must accomplish to be recognized as an official bargaining unit.

QUESTIONS FOR REVIEW

1. What do you believe are the most important reasons for employees not joining a union? Discuss.

2. There are reasons both for and against a firm resisting unionization attempts. What are they?

---

[22]Foulkes, "Nonunion Companies," p. 93.

3. If you were developing strategies and tactics to remain union free which ones would you use? Briefly describe each.
4. What role does the first-line supervisor play to help a firm remain union free?

5. Describe the process of decertification.
6. How might the role of a personnel manager change if he or she moves from a unionized firm to a union free firm? Discuss.

TERMS FOR REVIEW

Open-door policy
Grievance procedure

Ombudsperson
Decertification

Incident 1

Ed Davis is a supervisor at the Paxma Manufacturing Company, a manufacturer of a special kind of filler material for packaging. Ed was transferred to his present job from another plant. He accepted the transfer because he felt it would provide a better opportunity for promotion. Ed's new section includes fifteen workers whose jobs are essentially identical. The workload at Paxma often fluctuates, requiring extensive use of overtime. This overtime is very popular among the workers and Ed's predecessor had distributed it on a simple rotation basis.

When Ed took over, he felt that overtime should be a reward for excellent performance. He also felt that certain workers needed the overtime more than others. Ed did not discuss this with the workers but simply began to assign the overtime as he saw fit.

Everything seemed to be going well until the day Ed was called to the office of Mary Donnelly, the personnel manager. After a brief greeting Mary said, "Ed, I hear through the grapevine that there's a good deal of dissension in your crew. Some of the workers feel they're not being given their fair share of overtime." Ed replied, "I assign everybody their fair share. It's just not always an equal share." "That may be true, Ed," said Mary, "but at least a couple of the workers believe that most of the overtime has been going to the three new people you've hired." "Who told you that?" asked Ed. "I don't think that should be important," Mary answered, "but you need to think about whether there's any substance to the impression your workers have." "You may be right," said Ed. "I suppose I could unconsciously have favored the people I selected."

QUESTIONS

1. Do you think the personnel manager was correct in getting involved in the line function of assigning overtime? Explain.
2. What would you do if you were Ed?

Incident 2

Barney Cline, the new personnel manager for Ampex Utilities, was just getting settled in his new office. He had recently moved from another firm to take over his new job. Barney had been selected over several in-house candidates and numerous other applicants because of his record of getting things done. He had a good reputation for working through people to get the job accomplished.

Just then his phone rang. The person on the other end of the line said, "Mr. Cline, could I set up an appointment to talk with you?" "Certainly," Barney said, "when do you want to get together?" "How about after work? It might be bad if certain people saw me speaking to anyone in management."

Barney was a bit puzzled, but he set up an appointment for 5:30 P.M., when nearly everyone would be gone. At the designated time there was a knock on his door; it was Mark Johnson, a senior maintenance worker who had been with the firm for more than ten years.

After the initial welcome, Mark began by saying, "Mr. Cline, several of the workers asked me to talk to you. The grapevine has it that you're a fair person. The company says it has an open-door policy. We're afraid to use it. Roy Edwards, one of the best maintenance men in our section, tried it several months ago. They hassled him so much that he quit only last week. We just don't know what to do to get any problems settled. There have been talks of organizing a union. We really don't want that, but something has to give."

Barney thanked Mark for his honesty and promised not to reveal the conversation. In the weeks following the conversation with Mark, Barney was able to verify that the situation existed as Mark had described it. There was considerable mistrust between managers and the operative employees.

QUESTIONS

1. What are the basic causes of the problems confronting Ampex Utilities?
2. How do you feel that Barney should attempt to resolve this problem?

REFERENCES

Adams, C. T. "Changing Employment Patterns of Organized Workers." *Monthly Labor Review* 108 (February 1985): 25–31.

Anderson, John C., O Reilly, Charles A. III, and Busman, Gloria. "Union Decertification in the U.S.: 1947–1977." *Industrial Relations* 19 (Winter 1980): 100–107.

Arnold, B. "Paychecks Won't Get Much Fatter." *Business Week*, December 24, 1984, pp. 20–21.

Bacas, H. "In Unions There Is Weakness." *Nation's Business* (April 1983): 25–30 +.

Bethell, Tom. "Working Man's Fate Ignored by Unions." *Data Management* 16 (July 1978): 28–29.

Bleiberg, R. M. "Organized Labor's Future: More Today May Be Less, But There's a Lot Up for Grabs." *Barrons*, February 25, 1985, p. 9.

Bohlander, George W. "Employee Protected Concerted Activity: The Nonunion Setting." *Labor Law Journal* (June 1982): 344–351.

Carney, Christopher F. "What Supervisors Can Do about Union Organizing." *Supervisory Management* 26 (January 1981): 10–15.

Clark, K. B. "Unionization and Firm Performance: The Impact on Profits, Growth, and Productivity." *American Economic Review* 74 (December 1984): 893–919.

Eisen, Jerry. "Don't Be Complacent about Union Organizing." *Personnel Administrator* 30 (August 1985): 122.

Foulkes, Fred K. "How Top Nonunion Companies Manage Employees." *Harvard Business Review* 59 (September–October 1981): 90–96.

Fulmer, William E. "When Employees Want to Oust Their Union." *Harvard Business Review* 56 (March–April 1978): 163–170.

———. "Decertification: Is the Current Trend a Threat to Collective Bargaining?" *California Management Review* 24 (Fall 1981): 14–22.

Harrison, Edward L.; Johnson, Douglas and Rachel, Frank M. "The Role of The Supervisor in Representation Elections." *Personnel Administrator* 26 (September 1981): 67–71.

Hoerr, John. "Beyond Unions." *Business Week*, July 8, 1985, pp. 72–77.

Hoover, John J. "Union Organization Attempts: Management's Response." *Personnel Journal* 61 (March 1982): 214–219.

Hughes, Charles L. *Making Unions Unnecessary*. New York: Executive Enterprises, 1976.

Imberman, Woodruff. "How to Win a Decertification Election." *Management Review* 66 (September 1977): 26–39.

Lewis, Ephraim. "BW/Harris Poll: Confidence in Unions Is Crumbling." *Business Week*, July 8, 1985, p. 76.

Markham, S. and Scott, D. "Controlling Absenteeism: Union and Nonunion Differences." *Personnel Administrator* 30 (February 1985): 87–88 +.

McCollum, J. K. and Norris, D. R. "Nonunion Grievance Machinery in Southern Industry." *Personnel Administrator* 29 (November 1984): 106–112.

McCracken, P. W. "Giving Unions Their Due." *Across the Board* 21 (November 1984): 59–60.

Mooney, Marta "Let's Use Job Security as a Productivity Builder." *Personnel Administrator* 29 (January 1984): 38–44.

Pfeffer, Jeffrey and Ross, Jerry. "Union–Nonunion Effects on Wage and Status Attainment." *Industrial Relations* 19 (Spring 1980): 140–150.

Rand, James F. "Preventive-Maintenance Techniques for Staying Union-Free." *Personnel Journal* 59 (June 1980): 497–499.

Sappir, Mark Z. "The Employer's Obligation Not to Bargain When the Issue of Decertification is Present." *Personnel Administrator* 27 (February 1982): 41–45.

Stokes, A. "What to Do When the Union First Appears." *Food Service Marketing* 43 (April 1981): 18.

Swann, James P., Jr. "Formal Grievance Procedures in Nonunion Plants." *Personnel Administrator* 26 (August 1981): 66–70.

Tidwell, G. L. "The Meaning of the No-Strike Clause." *Personnel Administrator* 29 (November 1984): 51–53 +.

Voos, P. B. "Trends in Union Organize Expenditures." *Industrial Labor Relations Review* 38 (October 1984): 52–63.

CHAPTER OBJECTIVES
1. Distinguish between discipline and disciplinary action.
2. Identify and describe the steps involved in the disciplinary process.
3. Describe the steps involved in progressive discipline.
4. Explain how grievance handling is typically conducted under a collective bargaining agreement and with nonunion firms.
5. State how termination conditions may differ when operative employees, executives, managers, or professionals are involved.
6. Explain the concept of employment at will.
7. Describe the difficulties involved with resignations and what should be done when resignations occur.
8. Explain the role of internal employee relations with regard to demotions, layoffs, transfers, promotions, and retirements.

Chapter 18

INTERNAL EMPLOYEE RELATIONS

Bob Halmes, the production supervisor for American Manufacturing, was mad at the world when he arrived at work. The automobile mechanic had not repaired his car on time the day before, so he had been forced to take a taxi to work this morning. No one was safe around Bob today and it was not the time for Phillip Martin, a member of Local 264, to report for work late. Without hesitation, Bob said: "You know our company can't tolerate this type of behavior. I don't want to see you around here anymore. You're fired." Just as quickly, Phillip replied, "You're way off base. Our contract calls for three warnings. My steward will hear about this."

Bill Morton, a ten-year employee at Ketro Productions, arrived at Personnel to turn in his letter of resignation. He was obviously upset at his supervisor. When the personnel manager, Robert Noll, asked what was wrong, Bill replied: "Yesterday, I made a mistake and set my machine up wrong. It was the first time in years that I've done that. My supervisor chewed me out in front of my friends. I wouldn't take that from the president, much less a two-bit straw boss!"

These situations suggest only a few of the problems associated with internal employee relations. Bob Halmes has just been reminded that certain factors limit his power to fire Phillip Morton. The resignation of Bill Martin might have been avoided if his supervisor had not shown poor judgment and disciplined him in front of his friends.

The status of most workers is not fixed within an organization. There is constant movement upward, laterally, downward, and out of the firm. In order to ensure that workers with the proper skills and experience are available at all levels, constant and concerted efforts are required to maintain good internal employee relations. In this chapter we focus on topics related to discipline and the grievance process, terminations, resignations, demotions, layoffs, transfers, promotions, and retirements.

DISCIPLINARY ACTION

A necessary, but often trying, aspect of internal employee relations is taking disciplinary action. A firm needs a program to administer disciplinary action when violations of company policies or rules occur. Not only is there a need for such policies, but a process should also exist to assist employees in appealing disciplinary actions. Unjustified disciplinary action has contributed to the loss of union free status by many firms. It has also resulted in unauthorized wildcat strikes, walkouts, and slowdowns in unionized firms.[1] The effect of these actions can result in unnecessary expense and loss of production time.

Discipline is *the state of employee self-control and orderly conduct present within an organization.* It indicates the extent of genuine teamwork. **Disciplinary action** occurs *"when standards are maintained by invoking a penalty against an employee who fails to meet them."* Effective disciplinary action condemns the employee's wrongful act, not the employee as a person.[2]

In spite of a firm's desire to solve its employee problems in a positive manner, at times this is not possible. A major purpose of disciplinary action is to ensure that employee behavior is consistent with the firm's goals. Rules are established to assist the organization in accomplishing its objectives. When a rule is violated, the effectiveness of the organization is diminished to some degree, depending on the severity of the infraction. For instance, if a worker reports late to work, the loss to the firm may be minimal. However, if a worker fails to use the safety guard on a machine

---

[1]Richard F. Gibson, "Discipline: Search for New Solutions," *Industry Week* 182 (July 15, 1974): 52.

[2]Keith Davis, *Human Behavior at Work.* New York: McGraw–Hill, 1977, p. 261.

and is severely injured, the loss may be substantial. Supervisors must realize that disciplinary action can be a positive force for the company. The firm benefits from developing and implementing effective disciplinary action policies. Without a healthy state of discipline, or the threat of disciplinary action, the firm's effectiveness may be severely limited.

Disciplinary action can also help the employee become more effective. For example, if a worker is disciplined because of failure to monitor the quality of his or her output, and the quality improves after the disciplinary action, it has been useful in the worker's development. Because of improved performance the individual may receive a promotion or pay increase. The individual is reminded of what is expected and fulfills these requirements better. Effective disciplinary action can thus encourage the individual to improve his or her performance.

THE DISCIPLINARY ACTION PROCESS

The disciplinary action process is dynamic and ongoing. One person's actions can affect others in the group. For instance, if a worker is disciplined, it is likely that this action would influence other workers when they learn that such mistakes will not be tolerated.

The disciplinary action process is shown in Figure 18–1. The external environment affects every area of human resource management, including disciplinary policies and actions. Changes in technology may render a rule inappropriate. Or, it may necessitate the establishment of new rules. For instance, a firm may purchase a modern piece of equipment that has new and different maintenance requirements. Laws that affect company policies and rules are also constantly changing. For instance, OSHA has caused many firms to establish new safety rules. Unions are another external factor. Specific punishment for rule violations are subject to negotiation. For instance, the union may negotiate three written warnings for tardiness instead of the two warnings a present contract might require.

Changes in the internal environment of the firm can also alter the disciplinary process. Through organizational development, the firm may alter its culture. This change may result in first-line supervisors handling disciplinary action in a more positive manner. Organization policies can also have an impact on the disciplinary process. For instance, a policy of treating employees as if they were mature human beings would significantly affect the process.

The disciplinary action process deals largely with infractions of rules. Rules — specific guides to action — are created to facilitate the accomplishment of organizational goals. The do's and don'ts associated with accomplishing tasks are highly inflexible. A company rule may prohibit smoking in a given area. Or, it may require that hard hats be worn in hazardous areas.

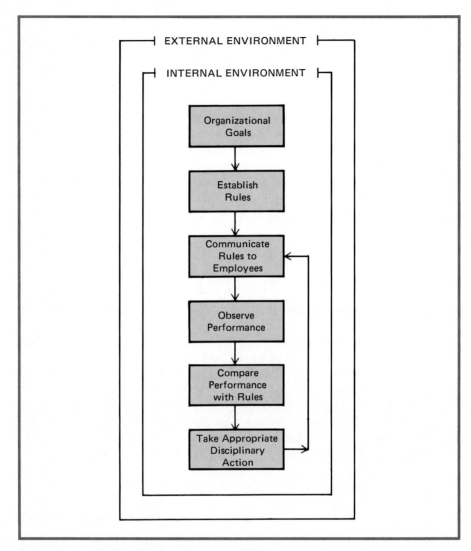

Figure 18–1. The disciplinary action process.

After rules have been established, they must be communicated to the affected employees. Individuals cannot obey a rule if they do not know it exists. As long as employee behavior does not vary from acceptable practices, there will be no need for disciplinary action. But, when an employee's behavior violates a rule, corrective action may be taken. The purpose of this action is to alter the types of behavior that can have a negative impact on achievement of organizational goals.

Note that Figure 18–1 shows a feedback loop from take appropriate disciplinary action to communicate rules to employees. Some employees find out that a rule is being enforced only when a peer receives disciplinary action. The employee may then conform to the rule because he or she chooses not to receive similar disciplinary action.

APPROACHES TO DISCIPLINE

Several concepts regarding the administration of disciplinary action have been developed. Two of these — the hot stove rule and progressive discipline — will be discussed next. We believe that the progressive discipline approach is preferable. However, knowledge of the hot stove rule is helpful because some of its principles are incorporated in the progressive discipline approach.

THE HOT STOVE RULE

One view of administering disciplinary action is referred to as the *hot stove rule*. According to this approach, disciplinary action should have the following consequences:

1. *Burns immediately:* If disciplinary action is to be taken, it must occur immediately so the individual will understand the reason for it. With the passage of time, people have the tendency to convince themselves that they are not at fault.
2. *Provides warning:* It is also extremely important to provide advance warning that punishment will follow unacceptable behavior. As you move closer to a hot stove, you are warned by its heat that you will be burned if you touch it.
3. *Gives consistent punishment:* Disciplinary action should also be consistent in that everyone who performs the same act will be punished accordingly. As with a hot stove, each person who touches it is burned the same.
4. *Burns impersonally:* Disciplinary action should be impersonal. There are no favorites when this approach is applied.

Although the hot stove approach has some merit, it also has weaknesses. If the circumstances surrounding all disciplinary situations were the same, there would be no problem with this approach. However, they are often quite different. For instance, does the organization penalize a loyal, twenty-year employee the same as an individual who has been with the firm less than six weeks? Many variables may be present in a disciplinary case. Therefore a supervisor often finds that he or she cannot be completely consistent and impersonal in the action taken. Because situations do vary, the progressive discipline philosophy may be more realistic.

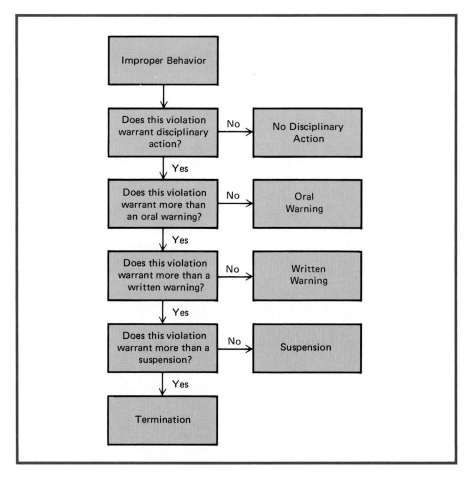

Figure 18–2. The progressive discipline approach.

PROGRESSIVE DISCIPLINE

Progressive discipline is *an approach to imposing disciplinary action designed to ensure that the minimum penalty appropriate to the offense is imposed and involves answering a series of questions about the severity of the offense.* When the progressive discipline approach is followed, an attempt is made to make penalties appropriate to the violation (or accumulated violations). The manager must ask a series of questions — in sequence — to determine the proper disciplinary action (see Figure 18–2). After it has been determined that disciplinary action is appropriate, the question is asked: "Does the violation warrant more than an oral warning?" If the improper behavior is minor and has not previously occurred, perhaps only an oral warning will be sufficient. Also, an individual may receive several written warnings before a "yes" answer might apply to the question,

"Does this violation warrant more than a written warning?" The manager does not consider termination until each lower level question is answered "yes." However, major violations, such as hitting a supervisor, may justify the immediate termination of the employee.

In order to assist a manager to recognize the proper level of disciplinary action, some firms have formalized the procedure. One approach in the establishment of progressive disciplinary action is shown in Table 18–1. In this example, a worker who is tardy will receive an oral warning the first time it happens and a written warning the second time; the third time, the employee will be terminated. Fighting on the job is an offense that normally results in immediate termination. However, specific guidelines for various offenses should be developed to meet the needs of the industry and the organization. For instance, smoking in an unauthorized area may be grounds for immediate dismissal in an explosives factory. On the other hand, the same violation may be less serious in a plant producing concrete products.

THE ADMINISTRATION OF DISCIPLINARY ACTION

As might be expected, disciplinary actions are not pleasant supervisory tasks. Many people find it difficult to punish another worker. Reasons for managers wanting to avoid disciplinary action include:

1. *Lack of training:* Some supervisors do not have the knowledge and skill necessary to handle disciplinary problems.
2. *Fear:* There may be concern that top management will not support a disciplinary action.
3. *The only one:* The supervisor may feel that "No one else is disciplining employees, so why should I?"
4. *Guilt:* The manager may think: "How can I discipline someone if I've done the same thing?"
5. *Loss of friendship:* The supervisor may believe that disciplinary action will damage friendship with an employee or the employee's associates.
6. *Time loss:* The interview takes valuable time.
7. *Loss of temper:* The supervisor may be afraid of losing his or her temper when talking to an employee about a rule violation.
8. *Rationalization:* The manager may reason that "The employee knows it was the wrong thing to do, so why do we need to talk about it?"[3]

These reasons apply to all forms of disciplinary action — from an oral warning to termination. There are, however, some additional reasons that should be mentioned regarding termination. Managers often avoid this form

[3]Wallace Wohlking, "Effective Discipline in Employee Relations," *Personnel Journal* 54 (September 1975): 489.

Table 18–1. Suggested guidelines for disciplinary action

A. Examples of offenses resulting in immediate discharge:

1. Intoxication or use of drugs
2. Fighting
3. Refusal to work
4. Theft
5. Willful destruction of property
6. Gross insubordination
7. Gross misconduct unbecoming an employee
8. Conviction of a felony charged by court of proper jurisdiction, provided the felony is relevant to the position
9. Falsifying time cards
10. Use of undue influence to gain or attempt to gain promotion, leave, favorable assignment, or other individual benefit
11. Falsification, fraud, or omission of information in applying for a position
12. Failure to report to work without notification for a period of three days
13. Failure or inability to complete a required training program that is a part of a job assignment
14. Failure to obtain or maintain a current license or certificate required by law or organizational standards as a condition of employment
15. Any other act which endangers the safety, health, or well-being of another person, or which is of sufficient magnitude that the consequences cause or act to cause disruption of work or gross discredit to the organization

B. Examples of offenses resulting in first, a written warning; and second, an immediate discharge:

1. Gambling
2. Careless, negligent, or improper use of property
3. Unauthorized or improper use of any type of leave
4. Failure to report to work without notification for a period of one or two days
5. Releasing confidential information without proper authority
6. Sleeping on job
7. The violation of, or failure to comply with, an executive order, or published rules and regulations of the organization

C. Examples of offenses resulting in first, an oral warning; second, a written warning; and third, an immediate discharge:

1. Uncivil conduct
2. Tardiness
3. Unauthorized absence from the job
4. Failure to maintain satisfactory and harmonious working relationships with the public or other employees
5. Smoking in an unauthorized area
6. Failure to punch the time clock
7. Foul and abusive language
8. Inefficiency, incompetency, or negligence in the performance of duties

Source: Rodney L. Oberle, "Administering Disciplinary Actions," *Personnel Journal*, January 1978. Copyright © 1978. Reprinted with permission.

of disciplinary action even when it is in the company's best interests. This problem often stems from breakdowns in other areas of the human resource function. For instance, if the performance appraisal system is not valid, managers may be in a weak position to terminate a worker. It is embarrassing to decide to fire a worker and then be asked why this individual was rated so high on the previous evaluation.

Another problem related to managers' reluctance to fire employees for cause is lack of record keeping. When no documentation is maintained, it may be difficult to justify to upper level management that a person should be terminated. Rather than run the risk of a decision being overturned, the manager retains the ineffective worker.

Finally, some managers have come to believe that it is useless even to attempt to terminate members of protected groups. This view is inaccurate. Anyone whose performance is consistently below standard can be terminated. However, managers must conduct performance appraisals so that they distinguish between levels of productivity, keep good records, and provide even-handed treatment of all workers.

A supervisor may be perfectly justified in administering discipline. However, he or she may create considerable dissension among other employees by the improper handling of the disciplinary action. The old philosophy of reprimanding in private and praising in public remains as valid today as ever. Disciplining a worker in the presence of others may embarrass the worker and actually defeat the purpose of the discipline. Employees have a desire to save face in front of their peers. Even if they are wrong, they resent the disciplinary action if it is in public. The incident at the beginning of the chapter in which Bill Morton quit his job because of being disciplined before his peers provides an excellent illustration.

In addition, many managers may be too lenient early in the disciplinary process and too strict in later stages. This lack of consistency does not permit the worker to gain a true understanding of the precise punishment associated with the action. As Robert F. Garrett, manager, labor relations, Georgia-Pacific Corporation, stated: "A supervisor will often endure an unacceptable situation for an extended period of time. Then, when the supervisor finally does take action, he or she is apt to overreact and come down excessively hard." Consistency does not necessarily mean that the same penalty must be applied to two different workers for the same offense. For instance, employers would be consistent if they always considered the worker's past record and length of service. A long-term employee might only receive a suspension. A worker with only a few months' seniority might be terminated for the same act. This type of action could be reasonably viewed as being consistent.[4]

---

[4]John E. Tobin, "How Arbitrators Decide to Reject or Uphold an Employee Discharge," *Supervisory Management* 21 (June 1976): 21.

Joyce Lawson
Consultant, Human
Resources Management
Consulting

Human resource management has become increasingly complex, particularly in the past two decades. This complexity is reflected in the types of questions, concerns, and problems raised by management and employees, such as:

- Some of our businesses have job posting systems. Should we consider expanding open promotion systems to all businesses? What kinds of jobs should be included: hourly only, nonexempt and exempt salaried, some management, etc.? What are the key elements for a successful system?
- Turnover is increasing on job X. Why are employees leaving? Are there selection procedures we can use to identify those employees who will stay and those who will leave? Can a test publisher send something for us to use? What do the government's selection guidelines say about this?
- Companies with performance appraisal systems for professional employees usually have only *one* system. Our many businesses have developed their own, so we have *many* systems. Should we establish one system to be applied com-

panywide? Are the various systems working? Can they work more effectively?
- The cost of transferring an employee has increased dramatically; the cost to the employee has increased as well. "Quality of life" issues are affecting employees' willingness to transfer. Are these factors influencing the company's ability to transfer required skills? Should we be doing anything more or different?

These questions, and many others like them, are often asked of Joyce Lawson, a consultant in human resource management, by operating business managers, personnel professionals, and corporate management. Her responses are based on twenty-five years of experience in virtually every aspect of human resource management, both with the General Electric Company and as an independent consultant. As a generalist, she advises businesses on such diverse procedures as reduction in force, performance appraisal systems, appeals procedures for employees, selection and promotion systems, and employee transfers. Lawson says, "In the past few years, the questions that have demanded most of my time are the ones related to appeals procedures or problem-solving procedures for professional employees, performance appraisals, and employee relocation."

She cites a particular instance from the

early 1980s, when changes in the economy and the housing market made the transfer of employees a significant cost of doing business: "One large company had established a reputation for having one of the best transfer policies among its peers, and had introduced a new home sale assistance program and a mortgage interest differential allowance to increase its assistance to transferring employees. Despite the new program, recruiters told us they were not getting their first choices for jobs and that employees were turning down transfer opportunities. We had to find out why. The finance and relocation people were as interested as the employee relations managers. So we went to recently transferred employees and asked them about their relocation experiences. What we found was that moving was a stressful experience, created by a volatile housing market, high mortgage rates, a perceived lack of adequate information about the transfer process, and a need for spouse employment assistance.

"So the finance and relocation people made improvements in the home sale assistance program, and mortgage interest differential allowance. Additionally, we assigned the coordinating responsibility for a transfer to the employee relations managers — many parties are involved and we had to ensure that they all work effectively. We established a checklist to help them do the coordinating job.

"We published an employee relocation information package spelling out what the company policy was all about, the important parts of the program, and what was expected of the employees. And we established guidelines for spouse employment assistance for operating divisions to follow. We did not leave it there; we surveyed employees after their transfer for a period of time to ensure that the company was on top of their experiences, good and bad," she concludes.

"The one thing," Lawson says, "we can be sure of in the human resource management business is that it never gets boring. As soon as one concern is resolved, another interesting question comes along, which cannot be answered without a lot of research. That is what makes this a fascinating, worthwhile profession."

She has served as a member of various employer group committees and currently is a member of the Board of the American Society for Personnel Administration Foundation. The professional association that receives most of her attention is the International Association of Personnel Women; she has served as a member of the executive board for a number of years and is a past president. "This organization has offered great opportunities for women to develop as professionals in their chosen career and, as the organization grows, so do the members — personally and professionally. I feel I have contributed a lot, but I have received more through my participation." she relates.

Table 18-2. Code on discipline procedure

- All employees should be given a copy of the employer's rules on disciplinary procedures. The procedures should specify which employees they cover and what disciplinary actions may be taken, and should allow matters to be dealt with quickly.

- Employees should be told of complaints against them and given an opportunity to state their case. They should have the right to be accompanied by a trade union representative or fellow employee of their choice.

- Disciplinary action should not be taken until the case has been fully investigated. Immediate superiors should not have the power to dismiss without reference to senior management, and, except for gross misconduct, no employee should be dismissed for a first breach of discipline.

- Employees should be given an explanation for any penalty imposed, and they should have a right of appeal, with specified procedures to be followed.

- When disciplinary action other than summary dismissal is needed, supervisors should give a formal oral warning in the case of minor offenses, or a written warning in more serious cases.

Source: "Code on Discipline Procedure," *Industrial Management* 7 (August 1977): 7. Used with permission.

In order to assist management in administering discipline properly, a *Code on Discipline Procedure* has been prepared by the Advisory, Conciliation and Arbitration Service. The purpose of the code is to give practical guidance on how to draw up disciplinary rules and procedures and how to use them effectively. The code recommends actions as shown in Table 18–2. As you can see, the code stresses communication of rules, telling the employee of the complaint, conducting a full investigation, and giving an opportunity for the employee to tell his or her side of the story.

GRIEVANCE HANDLING UNDER A COLLECTIVE BARGAINING AGREEMENT

If the employees in an organization are represented by a union, workers who believe that they have been disciplined or dealt with unjustly can appeal through the grievance and arbitration procedures of the collective bargaining agreement. The grievance procedure has been described as "one of the truly great accomplishments of American industrial relations. For all its defects . . . it constitutes a social invention of great importance."[5] The grievance system encourages and facilitates the settlement of disputes between labor and management. A grievance procedure permits employees to express a complaint without jeopardizing their jobs. It also assists management in seeking out the underlying causes and solutions to grievances.

[5]Neil W. Chamberlain, *The Labor Sector*. New York: McGraw–Hill, 1955, p. 240.

THE GRIEVANCE PROCEDURE

637

Chapter 18
Internal
Employee
Relations

Virtually all labor agreements include some form of grievance procedure.[6] A **grievance** can be broadly defined as *an employee's dissatisfaction or feeling of personal injustice relating to his or her employment relationship.* A grievance under a collective bargaining agreement is generally well-defined. It is usually restricted to violations of the terms and conditions of the agreement. Other conditions that may give rise to a grievance are:

- A violation of law.
- A violation of the intent of the parties as stipulated during contract negotiations.
- A violation of company rules.
- A change in working conditions or past company practices.
- A violation of health and/or safety standards.[7]

Procedures through which disputes involving aggrieved employees may be resolved have many common features. However, variations may result from differences in organizational or decision-making structures or the size of a plant or company. Larger organizations tend to have more formal procedures, involving a succession of steps. Some general principles that have gained widespread support and can serve as guidelines in establishing a system of positive grievance administration are:

- Grievances should be adjusted promptly.
- Procedures and forms airing grievances must be easy to utilize and well-understood by employees and their supervisors.
- Direct and timely avenues of appeal from rulings of line supervision must exist.[8]

The most common type of grievance procedure is shown in Figure 18–3. The first step usually entails an informal oral presentation of the employee's grievance to the immediate supervisor in the presence of the union steward. This step offers the greatest potential for improved labor relations. A large majority of grievances are settled here.

The procedure ends if the grievance can be resolved at the first step. If it remains unresolved, the next step consists of the plant manager or personnel manager meeting with higher level union officials, such as the grievance committee or the business agent or manager. Prior to this meeting the grievance is written out, dated, and signed by the employee involved

---

[6]U.S. Department of Labor, Bureau of Labor Statistics, *Characteristics of Major Collective Bargaining Agreements*, July 1, 1975. Washington, D.C.: U.S. Government Printing Office, Bureau of Labor Statistics Bulletin 1957, 1977.

[7]K. L. Sovereign and Mario Bognanno, "Positive Contract Administration," in Dale Yoder and Herbert G. Heneman, Jr. (eds.), *ASPA Handbook of Personnel and Industrial Relations: Employee and Labor Relations*, Vol. III. Washington, D.C.: The Bureau of National Affairs, 1976, pp. 7-161–7-162.

[8]Ibid., p. 7-164.

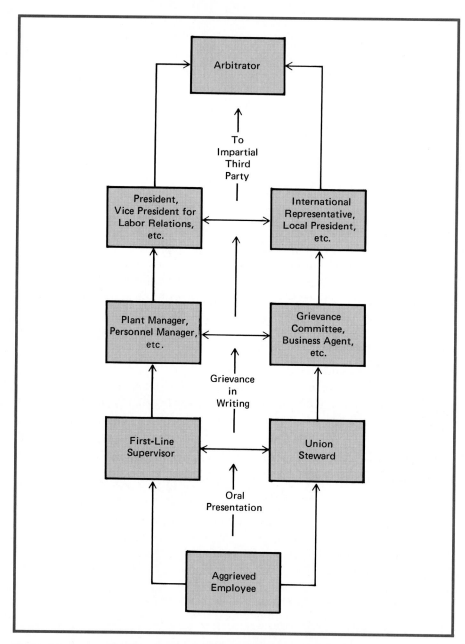

Figure 18–3. A multiple-step grievance procedure. Source: Robert W. Eckles et al., *Essentials of Management for First-Line Supervision*, New York: John Wiley & Sons, 1974, p. 529. Reprinted by permission of John Wiley & Sons, Inc.

and the union steward. Events are stated as they are perceived, identifying the portion of the contract that allegedly has been violated and the settlement desired. If the grievance is not settled at this meeting, it is appealed to the third step. This step typically involves the firm's top labor representative (such as the vice president of industrial relations) and high level union officials. At times, depending on the severity of the grievance, the president may represent the firm. A grievance that still remains unresolved at the conclusion of the third step may go to arbitration if it is provided for in the contract and the union decides to proceed that far.

Labor-relations problems can become major ones when the supervisor is not equipped to handle grievances at the first step. While the first step is usually handled informally by the union steward, the aggrieved party, and the supervisor, the supervisor must be prepared. The supervisor should obtain as many facts as possible before the meeting because the union steward is likely to have done his or her homework.

The supervisor needs to recognize that the grievance may not reflect the real problem. For instance, the employee might be mad at the company for modifying the pay policies, even though the change was approved by the union. In order to voice discontent, the worker may file a grievance for a minor violation of the contract. The idea of hidden causes of grievances has been referred to as the "iceberg theory."[9]

ARBITRATION

The grievance procedure has been a successful instrument for the peaceful resolution of labor–management problems. However, most grievance procedures provide a final step, arbitration, to resolve any issues that remain unresolved.[10] **Arbitration** is *the process that allows the parties to submit their dispute to an impartial third party for resolution.* Most agreements restrict the arbitrator's decision to application and interpretation of the agreement, and the decision is final and binding on the parties. While arbitration at times is used to settle conflicts in contract negotiations, its primary use has been in settling grievances.

If the union decides to go to arbitration, it notifies management. At this point, the union and the company must select an arbitrator. Most agreements make provision for the method of selection. The selection is usually made from a list supplied by the Federal Mediation and Conciliation Service (FMCS) or the American Arbitration Association (AAA), discussed in chapter 16. When considering potential arbitrators, both management and labor will study the candidates' previous decisions in an attempt to detect any biases. Neither party wants to select an arbitrator who might tend to favor the other's position.

[9]Ibid., p. 7-159.
[10]Of the 1514 agreements studied, 1455 provided for arbitration. U.S. Department of Labor, Bureau of Labor Statistics Bulletin, 1957.

When arbitration is used to settle a grievance, a variety of factors may be used to evaluate the fairness of the management actions that caused the grievance. Some of these factors include:

- Nature of the offense.
- Due process and procedural correctness.
- Double jeopardy.
- Grievant's past record.
- Length of service with the company.
- Knowledge of rules.
- Warnings.
- Lax enforcement of rules.
- Discriminatory treatment.[11]

The large number of interacting variables in each case makes the arbitration process difficult. High degrees of patience and judgment on the part of the arbitrator are required.

After the arbitrator has been selected and he or she has agreed to serve, a time and place for a hearing will be determined. The issue to be resolved will be presented to the arbitrator in a document that summarizes the question or questions to be decided and any contract restrictions that prohibit the arbitrator from making an award that would change the terms of the existing contract.

At the hearing each side presents its case. Arbitration is an adversary proceeding, so a case may be lost because of poor preparation and presentation. The arbitrator may conduct the hearing much like a courtroom proceeding. Witnesses, cross-examination, transcripts, and legal counsel may all be used. The parties may also submit or be asked by the arbitrator to submit formal written statements (so-called briefs). After the hearing, the arbitrator studies the material submitted and testimony given and reaches a decision within thirty to sixty days. The decision is usually accompanied by a written opinion giving the reasons supporting the decision.

The courts will generally enforce an arbitrator's decision unless: (1) the arbitrator's decision is shown to be unreasonable or capricious in that it did not address the issues; (2) the arbitrator exceeded his or her authority; or (3) the award or decision violated a federal or state law.

PROOF THAT DISCIPLINE WAS NEEDED

When discipline is administered, it is possible that it will ultimately be taken to arbitration. Employers have learned that they must prepare records that will constitute proof before an arbitrator.[12]

---

[11]F. Elkouri and E. A. Elkouri, *How Arbitration Works*, 3rd ed. Washington, D.C.: The Bureau of National Affairs, 1973.
[12]William E. Lissy, "Necessity of Proof to Support Disciplinary Action," *Supervision* 40 (June 1978): 13.

Interdepartmental
Correspondence

DATE: July 1, 1987

TO: J. Jones
FROM: J. Doe
SUBJECT: *Written Warning*

On this date, you were thirty minutes late to
work with no justification for your tardiness. A
similar offense occurred last Friday. At that time
you were told that failure to report to work on
schedule would not be condoned. I now find it
necessary to tell you in writing that you must
report to work on time. Failure to do so will result
in the termination of your employment. Please
sign below that you have read and that you
understand this written warning.

_____

NAME

_____

DATE

Figure 18–4. An example of a written warning. Source: "Administering Disciplinary Actions" by Rodney L. Oberle. Reprinted with permission *Personnel Journal* copyright January 1978.

The supervisor should document any actions that suggest that disciplinary action may ultimately be required. Since the burden of proof is on the employer, the supervisor should collect information regarding events, circumstances, places, and witnesses. It is not sufficient to allege that the employee is incompetent; the arbitrator will demand clear proof.

Although the format of a written warning may vary, the following information should be included:

1. Statement of facts concerning the offense.
2. Identification of the rule that was violated.
3. Statement of what resulted or could have resulted because of the violation.
4. Identification of any previous similar violations by this individual.
5. Statement of possible future consequences should the violation occur again.
6. Signature and date.[13]

An example of a written warning is shown in Figure 18–4. In this instance, the worker has already received an oral warning. The individual is also

[13]Adapted from Robert D. Buchanan, "How to Apply Constructive Discipline," *Food Service Marketing* 40 (October 1978): 64.

warned that continued tardiness could lead to termination. It is important to document oral warnings since they may be the first step in disciplinary action leading ultimately to arbitration.

WEAKNESSES OF ARBITRATION

Arbitration has achieved a certain degree of success in resolving grievances between labor and management. However, it is not without weaknesses. There are those who say that arbitration is losing its effectiveness because of the long time lapse between the first step and the settlement of the grievance. Often, 100–250 days may pass before a decision is made.[14] The reason for the initial filing of the grievance may actually be forgotten before it is finally settled.

Another problem is the cost of arbitration, which have been rising at an alarming rate. The cost of settling even a simple arbitration case can be quite high. These expenditures are typically shared by labor and management. Forcing every grievance to arbitration may be used to place either management or the union in a difficult financial position.

GRIEVANCE HANDLING FOR UNION FREE EMPLOYEES

While the step-by-step procedure for handling union grievances is common practice, the means of resolving complaints in union free firms varies.[15] These companies can set up an organizational appeal system, although this is not typically done. Scott in his study found that only 11 percent of responding organizations (91 of 793) had any kind of procedure.[16] A consideration of these procedures is important because more than 80 percent of the work force in the United States is nonunion. In union free firms, employers have more flexibility in designing a grievance procedure to satisfy both management and employee needs.

The grievance procedure must be viewed by management and employees as being comprehensive and impartial. As such, there are many versions that may prove to be acceptable. The grievance procedure may consist of an informal dialogue between employee and supervisor or it may, as a last resort, involve calling in an arbitrator to settle disputes.

A well-designed union free grievance procedure ensures that the worker has ample opportunity to make complaints without fear of reprisal. If the system is to work, employees must be well-informed about the program

---

[14]Lawrence Stessin, "Expedited Arbitration: Less Grief Over Grievances," *Harvard Business Review* 55 (January–February 1977): 129.

[15]Ronald L. Miller, "Grievance Procedures for Non-Union Employees," *Public Personnel Management* 7 (September–October 1978): 302.

[16]William G. Scott, *The Management of Conflict: Appeal System in Organizations.* Homewood, Ill.: Richard D. Irwin, 1977, pp. 56–80.

and be convinced that management wants them to use it. "Most employees are hesitant to formalize their complaints and must be constantly urged to avail themselves of the arrangement."[17] The fact that a manager says, "Our workers must be happy because I have received no complaints," does not indicate that grievances do not exist. In a closed, threatening organizational culture workers may be afraid to voice their dissatisfaction to management.

Typically, an employee initiates a complaint with his or her immediate supervisor. However, if the complaint involves the supervisor, the individual is permitted to bypass the immediate supervisor and proceed to the employee-relations specialist or the manager at the next level. The grievance ultimately may be taken to the organization's top executive for a final decision.

TERMINATION

Termination is the most severe penalty that an organization can impose on its employees. The experience of being terminated is traumatic for employees regardless of their position in the organization. Feelings of failure, fear, disappointment, and anger can all hit the employee at the same time. It is also an uneasy time for the person making the termination decision. Knowing that termination may affect not only the employee but an entire family increases the tension. Not knowing how the terminated employee will react also may create considerable anxiety for the manager who must do the firing. Regardless of the similarities in the termination of employees at various levels, distinct differences exist with regard to operative employees, executives, managers, and professionals.

TERMINATION OF OPERATIVE EMPLOYEES

The procedure used to terminate operative employees is typically well-defined. Specific violations that could lead to termination are normally spelled out in the labor agreement. For example, drinking on the job might be identified as a reason for termination. Excessive absences may require three written warnings by the supervisor before termination action is taken. When no union is present, the violations justifying termination are often included in the firm's employee handbook.

Some organizations direct the personnel department to assist terminated employees in locating new jobs. However, the reason for the termination will likely determine the amount of effort devoted to employment assistance. If the individual was terminated because of a reduction in the work force, more effort will likely follow. For instance, when a major meat packing company in the southwest closed, a massive effort was made to

[17]James P. Swann, Jr., "Formal Grievance Procedures in Non-Union Plants," *Personnel Administrator* 26 (August 1981): 67.

find jobs for the workers who had been terminated. On the other hand, a person who is terminated for theft will likely receive little if any support from management in finding a new job.

TERMINATION OF EXECUTIVES

Executive termination must be viewed from a different perspective. There is likely no formal appeals procedure for executives. The decision to terminate an executive has probably been approved by the chief executive officer in the organization. In addition, the reasons for termination may not be as clear as with lower level employees. Some of the reasons include:

1. *Economic:* At times, business conditions may force a reduction in the number of executives.
2. *Reorganization:* In order to improve efficiency, a firm may reorganize, resulting in the elimination of some executive positions.
3. *Philosophical differences:* A difference in philosophy of conducting business may develop between an executive and other key company officials. In order to maintain consistency in management philosophy, the executive may have to be replaced.
4. *Decline in productivity:* The executive may have been capable of performing satisfactorily in the past, but, for various reasons, he or she can no longer perform the job as required.

This list does not include factors related to illegal activities or actions taken that are not in the best interests of the firm. Under those circumstances, the firm has no moral obligation to the terminated executive.

In recent years, the practice of firing employees has become more acceptable, and the number of executives who are terminated annually has increased significantly. It has been estimated that approximately 6 percent of all executives in major corporations lose their jobs through terminations.[18] While an organization may derive positive benefits from executive terminations, they also present "a potentially hazardous situation for the organization."[19] Many corporations are concerned about developing a negative public image that reflects insensitivity to the needs of their employees. They fear that such a reputation would impede their efforts to recruit high quality managers. Also, terminated executives have at times made public statements detrimental to the reputation of the firm.

Many organizations have established a systematic means of executive outplacement. **Outplacement** is *a process whereby a terminated executive is given assistance in finding employment elsewhere.* In instances where

---

[18]Morton Yarmon, "Fired Executives Try a New Tactic," *Parade*, July 22, 1979.

[19]"Outplacement Counseling." Pamphlet developed by Drake Bean Morin, Inc., consultants in human resources management, 1979.

Table 18–3. Typical services provided by outplacement consulting firms

- Pretermination counseling for the manager who is doing the termination.
- Travel to the place where the termination will occur. (No extra fee should be charged for this service, but travel expenses for the consultant should be reimbursed by the company or organization.)
- Vocational counseling by a trained psychologist.
- Resume development, printing, and distribution.
- Training on how to be interviewed (preferably using closed circuit TV).
- Consultation for the wife or husband of the terminated individual.
- Feedback to the client corporation or organization on the status of the individual.
- Continuous consultation available to the individual until placement.

Source: William J. Morin, "Outplacement Counseling: What Is It?" *The Personnel and Guidance Journal* 55 (May 1977): 555. Used with permission.

such services exist, an outside consultant often is employed to aid the terminated executive in finding appropriate employment elsewhere. In executive termination, the use of outside consultants may be superior to the use of in-house personnel. The released executive may not trust internal personnel and may be more open with an outsider.

Outplacement consultants provide the executive with a wide variety of services. Some typical services are shown in Table 18–3. Consultants may initially assist the executive in performing a thorough self-assessment to determine his or her future career interests. The consultant will also instruct the executive in proper interviewing techniques. Since it may have been many years since the executive had an interview, the consultant can be helpful in preparing the individual for the job market. The outplacement consultant also may assist the executive in identifying firms that could best use his or her qualifications. Through outplacement, the firm strives to reduce the trauma associated with termination of an executive who has been with the firm for a long time.

TERMINATION OF MID-LEVEL AND LOWER LEVEL MANAGERS AND PROFESSIONALS

In the past, the most vulnerable and perhaps the most neglected group of employees with regard to termination has been mid-level and lower level managers and professionals, who are generally neither members of a union nor protected by a labor agreement. Nor do they have the political clout that a terminated executive may have. The reasons for their termination may be based solely on the attitude of their immediate superior on a given day.

EMPLOYMENT AT WILL

Approximately two of every three American workers' jobs depend almost entirely on the continued good will of their employers. Individuals falling into this category are known as "at-will employees." Generally, the U.S. legal system presumes that the jobs of such employees may be terminated at the will of their employer and that these employees have a similar right to leave their jobs at any time.[20] **Employment at will** is *an unwritten contract that is created when an employee agrees to work for an employer, but there is no agreement as to how long the parties expect the employment to last.* Because of a century-old common law rule in the United States, employment of indefinite duration can, in general, be terminated at the whim of either party.

With the exception of South Dakota, the employment-at-will rule is the current standard everywhere in the country. However, a trend appears to be developing that could afford workers greater job security. Some courts have decided that terminations of at-will employees are unlawful if they are contrary to general notions of "public policy" or if they are done in "bad faith."[21]

Although the concept of employment at will remains strong, judges, legislators, and employees are increasingly willing to challenge rigid notions of unlimited employer discretion. This is particularly true in the area of public policy concern. However, employers can do certain things to protect themselves against litigation for wrongful discharge based on a breach of implied employment contract. For example, application blanks that contain statements suggesting job security or permanent employment should be avoided.[22]

RESIGNATION

Even when organizations are totally committed to making their environments good places in which to work, workers will still resign. Some employees cannot see promotional opportunities, or at least not enough, for themselves. If excessive numbers of a firm's highly qualified and competent workers are leaving, means must be found to reverse the trend.

A frequently given reason for resignation is to obtain a better salary and/or benefits. However, most firms conduct salary surveys or otherwise keep in touch with what competitors are paying. Research has shown that, when workers mention pay as a reason for resignation, there are often other, deeper reasons for their decisions to leave. Management should identify

---

[20]Lawrence Z. Lorber, J. Robert Kirk, Kenneth H. Kirschner, and Charlene R. Handorf, *Fear of Firing: A Legal and Personnel Analysis of Employment at Will.* Alexandria, Va.: The ASPA Foundation, 1984, p. 1.

[21]Ibid., p. 1.

[22]Ibid., p. 20.

the causes and correct them. The cause may be a department manager with whom no one can work or an organizational culture that is stifling creative employees.

A certain amount of turnover is healthy for an organization. New people bring new ideas and fresh approaches to an organization. But, when turnover becomes excessive, something must be done. The most qualified employees are often the ones who resign because they are more mobile. On the other hand, marginally qualified workers seemingly never leave.

ANALYZING VOLUNTARY RESIGNATIONS

When a firm wants to determine the real reasons that individuals decide to leave the organization, it can use the exit interview and/or the post-exit questionnaire. Both techniques may be used.

The exit interview is conducted while the individual is still employed; it is typically the last major contact the employee has with the company. The exit interview encourages the employee to tell his or her resignation story openly and freely. The personnel department is usually responsible for conducting this interview. An employee would likely not respond as freely during an interview with the supervisor, reasoning that he or she may need a letter of recommendation from the supervisor in the future. The typical exit interview involves the following:

- Establishment of rapport.
- Purpose of the interview.
- Attitudes regarding the old job.
- Exploration of reasons for leaving.
- Comparison of the old and new job.
- Changes recommended.
- Conclusion.[23]

Specific topics that might be covered by the interviewer are listed in Figure 18–5. Note that the interviewer is focusing on job-related factors and is attempting to probe in depth to determine the real reason that the person is leaving. Over a period of time, properly conducted exit interviews may provide considerable insight into why employees are leaving. Patterns are often identified that uncover weaknesses in the firm's human resource management system. Knowledge of the problem then permits corrective action to be taken.

Another means of determining why an individual left the firm is the postexit questionnaire. When this approach is used, former employees are sent a questionnaire several weeks after they leave the organization. Usually, departed workers are already in place at their new company. The questionnaire is structured to draw out the real reason that the employee left

---

[23]Wanda R. Embrey, R. Wayne Mondy, and Robert M. Noe, "Exit Interview: A Tool for Personnel Development," *Personnel Administration* 24 (May 1979): 46.

1. Let's begin by your outlining briefly some of the duties of your job.
2. Of the duties you just outlined, tell me three or four that are crucial to the performance of your job.
3. Tell me about some of the duties you liked the most and what you liked about performing those duties.
4. Now, tell me about some of the duties you liked least and what you did not like about performing those duties.
5. Suppose you describe the amount of variety in your job.
6. Let's talk a little bit now about the amount of work assigned to you. For example, was the amount assigned not enough at times, perhaps too much at times, or was it fairly stable and even overall?
7. Suppose you give me an example of an incident that occurred on your job that was especially satisfying to you. What about an incident that was a little less satisfying.
8. Let's talk now about the extent to which you feel you were given the opportunity to use your educational background, skills, and abilities on your job.
9. Tell me how you would assess the quality of training on your job.
10. Suppose you describe the promotional opportunities open to you in your job.

Figure 18–5. Questions related to general job factors. Source: Wanda R. Embrey, R. Wayne Mondy, and Robert M. Noe, "Exit Interview: A Tool for Personnel Development." Reprinted from the May 1979 issue of *Personnel Administrator*.

the organization. Ample blank space is also provided so that former employees can express their feelings about and perceptions of the job and the organization. One strength of this approach is that the individual is no longer with the firm and may respond more freely to the questions. A weakness is that the interviewer is not present to interpret and conduct an in-depth probe for the real reason for leaving.

ADVANCE NOTICE OF RESIGNATION

Most firms would like to have a two-week notice of resignation from departing clerical and operative employees. A month's notice may be desired from professional and managerial employees who are leaving the firm. When notice is desired by the firm, the policy should be clearly communicated to all employees.

If firms want departing employees to give advance notice, the company must fulfill certain obligations. For instance, suppose that a worker does

the right thing and submits advance notice — then is terminated immediately. Word of this action will spread rapidly to other employees. And,
should they decide to resign, they will not give any advance notice.

Permitting a resigned worker to remain on the job once a resignation
has been submitted may create some problems; if bad feelings exist between
the employee and the supervisor or the company, the departing worker may
be a disruptive force. On a selective basis, the firm may wish to pay the
employee for the notice time and ask him or her to leave the premises
immediately. However, this action should not often be necessary because
most workers are ethical about what they say and do during the advance
notice time.

DEMOTION

Termination often is the solution when a person is not able to perform his
or her job. But, at times, a demotion may provide a better alternative.
Demotion is *the process of moving a worker to a lower level of duties and
responsibilities, which typically involves a cut in pay.* Management is often
at fault when a demotion becomes necessary. Perhaps the individual had
been performing quite satisfactorily at one level in the organization. As a
result, the employee had been promoted. But the individual could not cope
with the additional responsibilities and failed in the new job. Rather than
terminate a productive worker, management demotes the employee to a job
that he or she can perform well.

Emotions often run high when an individual is demoted. Loss of respect
among peers, embarrassment, anger, and disappointment may occur. The
employee's productivity may also decrease. For these reasons, demotion
should be used very cautiously. One means of reducing the trauma associated with a demotion is to establish a probationary period in which a
promoted worker is permitted to try out the new job. Should the person
not work out in the job, the individual will not view moving back to the
old job so negatively.

At times demotions are used as an alternative to discharge, especially
when a long-time employee is involved. The worker may have performed
satisfactorily at a particular level for many years. The individual's productivity may then begin to decline for a variety of reasons. Perhaps the
worker is just not physically capable of performing the duties that he or
she once could. Or, the individual may no longer be willing to work the
number of hours that the job requires.

If demotion is chosen over termination, efforts must be made to preserve
the self-esteem of the individual. The person may be asked how he or she
would like to handle the demotion announcement. A positive image of the
value of this worker to the company needs to be projected.

The handling of demotions in a unionized organization are typically
spelled out quite clearly in the labor–management agreement. Should a

decision be made to demote a worker for poor performance, the union should be notified of this intent and the specific reasons for the demotion. Often the demotion will be challenged and carried through the formal grievance procedure. Precise documentation is necessary for the demotion to be upheld. Even with the problems of demotion for cause, it is often easier to carry out than termination would be.

LAYOFF

The economic success of many companies rises and falls in cycles. At times a firm may experience a high demand for its products and/or services, and at other times the demand may fall. Often when the firm is experiencing lowered demand, it has no other choice but to lay off workers. Although being laid off is not the same thing as being fired, it has the same short-term effect: The worker is no longer employed.

Being laid off can be more psychologically debilitating to a person than being terminated. With termination, the relationship with the firm is severed, and the former employee can go ahead and look for another job. This is not the case with a layoff. Here, the worker still has ties to the firm, although not as an active participant in the organization. In many instances, the laid-off worker does not even have a general idea of when he or she will be recalled. The worker's financial resources dwindle as he or she waits. The longer the layoff, the more frustrating it becomes. Lifestyles may change and tension builds up.

Whether the firm is union free or unionized, well-thought-out layoff/recall procedures should be developed. Workers should understand when they are hired how the system will work in the event of a layoff. When the firm is unionized, the layoff procedures are usually stated clearly in the labor–management agreement. Seniority usually is the basis for layoff. The agreement also likely has a clearly spelled out *bumping* procedure. When senior level positions are eliminated, the people occupying them have the right to bump workers from lower level positions, assuming that they have the proper qualifications for the lower level job. When bumping occurs, the composition of the work force is altered.

Procedures for recalling laid-off employees are also usually spelled out in labor–management agreements. Again, seniority is typically the basis for worker recall with the most senior employee being recalled first.

Union free firms also need to establish layoff procedures prior to facing a layoff. In union free firms, seniority should be an integral part of any layoff procedure. But, frequently, other factors should be considered. Productivity of the employee is typically a most important consideration. When productivity is a factor, management must be careful to see to it that productivity, not favoritism, is the actual basis. Workers generally have an accurate perception of their own productivity level and that of their fellow employees. Therefore it is important to accurately define both seniority and productivity considerations well in advance of any layoff.

TRANSFER

The lateral movement of a worker within an organization is called a **transfer**. A transfer may be initiated by the firm or by an employee. Transfers do not, and should not, infer that a person is being promoted or demoted.

Transfers serve several purposes. First, firms often find it necessary to reorganize. Offices and departments are created and abolished in response to the needs of the company. In order to fill positions created by a reorganization, employee moves not entailing promotion may be necessary. The same is true when an office or department is shut down. Rather than terminate valued employees, management may transfer them to other areas within the organization.

A second reason for transfers is to make positions available in the primary promotion channels. Firms are typically organized in a hierarchy. Each promotion is more difficult to obtain than the previous one because there are fewer positions available. At times, very productive but unpromotable workers may clog promotion channels. Other workers who are qualified to move upward in the organization may find their opportunities for promotion blocked. When this happens, a firm's most capable future managers may seek employment elsewhere. In order to keep primary promotion channels open, the firm may decide to transfer employees who are unpromotable but productive at their present levels.

Another reason for transfers is to satisfy the personal desires of employees. The reasons for wanting a transfer are numerous. It may be that an individual needs to work closer to home to take care of aging parents. Or, the worker may dislike long commuting trips to and from work. A worker may resign if the requested transfer is not approved. Rather than risk losing a valued employee, the firm may agree to the transfer.

Transfers may also be an effective means of dealing with personality clashes. Some people just cannot get along with each other. Because each of the individuals may be a valued employee, transfer is an appropriate solution to the problem. But human resource managers must be cautious regarding the "grass is greener on the other side of the fence" syndrome. When some workers encounter a temporary setback, they immediately ask for a transfer — before they even attempt to work through the problem.

Before any worker's request for transfer is approved, it should be analyzed in terms of the best interests of both the firm and the individual. Disruptions may occur when the worker is transferred. For example, a qualified worker must be available to step in and fill the position being vacated.

It is advisable for management to establish policies regarding transfers. Such policies will permit workers to know in advance when there is a likelihood of having a request for transfer approved. If the transfer is for personal reasons, some firms do not pay the moving costs. Whether the organization will or will not pay should be clearly spelled out.

PROMOTION

A **promotion** is *the movement of a person to a higher level position in the company*. The term *promotion* is one of the most emotionally charged terms in the field of human resource management. An individual who receives a promotion normally receives additional financial rewards and the ego boost associated with achievement and accomplishment. Most employees have a positive feeling about being promoted. But, for every individual who gains a promotion, there likely are others who were not selected. If these individuals wanted the promotion badly enough, their egos may be deflated, perhaps resulting in reduced productivity or even in resignations. If the general consensus is that the wrong person was promoted, resentment, at least, may occur.

Promotions in the future may not be as available as in the past. For one thing, in cost reduction programs many organizations are reducing the number of management positions. International competition has also slowed the growth of many firms, which might otherwise have necessitated more management positions. Also, women and minorities are now vying for positions that were not available to them in the past. The effect of these changes is that more people will be striving for fewer promotion opportunities. Consequently, organizations must look for ways other than promotion to reward deserving employees.

RETIREMENT

Most long-term employees leave an organization through retirement. Retirement may occur at a certain age or after a certain number of years, or it may be based on both of these factors. Upon retirement, former employees usually receive a pension each month for the remainder of their lives.

In the past there were too many instances of retirement-plan failure. Workers would retire believing that they would receive lifelong pensions only to find that retirement programs were insufficiently funded. In 1974, the Employee Retirement Income Security Act (ERISA) was passed with the purpose of protecting employees participating in company-sponsored retirement plans.

EARLY RETIREMENT

Sometimes employees will retire before reaching the age or length of service requirement. Often the retirement pay is reduced for each year that the retirement date is advanced. From an organization's viewpoint, early retirement of employees has both positive and negative aspects.

From a positive viewpoint, a long-term worker may have begun performing below expectations. Rather than fire this faithful worker of many years, early retirement may be offered. Also, even though a worker is performing adequately in his or her present job, this individual may be blocking a promotion channel for highly qualified workers. Further, if an extended layoff is expected, a product line is being discontinued, or a plant is being closed, early retirement may provide the solution to having a surplus of employees.

From a negative viewpoint, valued employees may leave the organization. Individuals that the firm does not want to lose may take early retirement. In addition, early retirement is often more expensive to the company than normal retirement. And early retirement decisions are often made on short notice, resulting in a disruption of operations.

There appears to be a growing trend toward early retirement. Second careers are becoming more and more common. Human resource planning must take these trends into consideration.

RETIREMENT PLANNING

Anticipation of retirement is often filled with strong emotions. Questions such as, "Do I have enough money?" "What will I do?" "Will I be able to adjust?" and many more often haunt the individual as retirement approaches. Just as a well-planned orientation program eases the transition of a new hire into the organization, a company-sponsored retirement planning program eases the transition of a long-term employee from work to leisure.

Often a firm devotes time, staff, and money to provide useful information to workers approaching retirement. Typically, such information relates to finances, housing, relocation, family relations, attitude adjustment, and legal affairs.[24]

Some firms have taken retirement planning a step further. At times firms consider both the social and psychological implication of the retirement and change process. Adaptation to retirement living is the focus of this form of planning. Individuals who have already retired are brought to meetings to speak and to answer questions regarding retirement life. Managing the change in lifestyle is often a topic for discussion.[25] Retirement is a major event in an individual's life, and employers can often help to make the transition a much smoother one.

[24]Marilyn Merikangas, "Retirement Planning with a Difference," *Personnel Journal* 62 (May 1983): 420.
[25]Ibid.

LEGAL IMPLICATIONS OF EEO FOR INTERNAL EMPLOYEE RELATIONS

Most people believe that equal employment opportunity (EEO) legislation primarily affects individuals entering the company for the first time. Nothing could be further from the truth. Virtually all phases of internal employee relations are affected. Of special concern to the EEOC are decisions relating to promotion. The Household Finance Corporation paid more than $125,000 to white-collar female employees who charged that they were denied promotion because of their gender. Under terms of a consent decree, the company also agreed to hire women for 20 percent of the branch representative openings (subject to availability) until women comprised 20 percent of such representatives. They also were required to hire 20 percent of their new employees from specified minority groups for clerical, credit and branch representative jobs, until the total of such employees reached 65 percent of their population in the labor area. Household Finance Corporation also agreed to train women and minority employees to help them qualify for better jobs where they are underrepresented.[26]

One of the largest payments ever made was under an agreement signed by AT&T with EEOC and the Department of Labor. It provided for payment of approximately $15 million to employees allegedly discriminated against. The agreement also called for additional affirmative actions and for an estimated $50 million in yearly payments for promotion and wage adjustments to minority and women employees.[27]

Termination of workers when they reach a certain age is a major concern in enforcement of the Age Discrimination Act. In *EEOC v. Leggett and Myers*, the commission alleged that age was a factor in the discharge of approximately 10 percent of the employees during a reduction in force. The court ruled against the company, and back pay recovery is estimated at $20 million. In *Hagman and EEOC v. United Airlines*, a jury awarded $18.2 million to 112 pilots who had been forced to retire at age sixty. In *EEOC v. Home Insurance Company*, an age discrimination case was won on behalf of 143 employees who had been forced to retire at age sixty-two, back pay recovery has been estimated to be $6–$8 million.

Some employers have systematically terminated workers when they reach a certain age, say fifty-five. The problem in many cases is that prior to termination, high performance evaluations were often given to the employees involved. These evaluations provided the terminated employees with the data needed to develop valid cases contending that the reason for termination was age, not a decline in performance.

[26]*U.S. v. Household Finance Corporation*, 4 EPD para. 7680 (N.D. Ill., 1972) — Consent decree.

[27]U.S. Equal Employment Opportunity Commission, *Affirmative Action and Equal Employment: A Guidebook for Employers*, Vol. 1. Washington, D.C.: U.S. Government Printing Office, January 1974, p. 10.

10. Distinguish between demotions, transfers, and promotions.

11. What are some EEO legal implications affecting internal employee relations?

TERMS FOR REVIEW

Discipline
Disciplinary action
Progressive discipline
Grievance
Arbitration

Outplacement
Employment at will
Demotion
Transfer
Promotion

Incident 1

Quality Business Forms, Inc., has a policy stating that employee absenteeism should not exceed four days during a ninety-day work period without medical verification. If an employee does not have medical reasons for excessive absences, he or she may be subject to disciplinary action.

Ed Thompson has been employed by Quality for over twenty-one years. In the past three years he has had an abnormal number of absences, which his supervisor chose to ignore due to Ed's long tenure with the company. When Ed's supervisor was transferred and another individual in the department, Alice Randall, assumed the supervisory position, she immediately advised Ed that his absenteeism was excessive and that it would have to cease or disciplinary action would be taken. Ed claimed that he was injured five years previously on his job and that his absences were a result of that injury. A review of Ed's health records was undertaken; no such injury had ever been reported.

Ed's attendance improved during the first six months under Randall's supervision but began to deteriorate during the latter part of the year. Ed, warned again about the absenteeism, came back with his previous excuse. At this point, Randall contacted the personnel manager for assistance in dealing with Ed. She was told that further disciplinary steps should be taken along with a complete physical evaluation by the corporate medical doctor. The physical exam was conducted immediately and no physical abnormalities were found.

This information was given to Ed verbally by the doctor, but Ed did not accept the findings. He was then counseled by the personnel manager, his supervisor, and his department manager. Ed listened very intently to what was being said and took notes. Ed was told that the next step in the disciplinary procedure would be dismissal if his absenteeism continued. He said he understood and he would work when he felt good and would not work when he did not feel good.

Thirty days later Ed and his supervisor were called in to the personnel office at 7:00 A.M., and Ed was terminated. Ed was shocked at actually being fired, since it was necessary for the president of the company to approve the termination of an employee with a long service record. A discrimination charge was filed but was dropped after no grounds could be established. A workers' compensation claim was received but could not be substantiated. And, finally, an unemployment claim was submitted, but it was dismissed.

Incident 2

As Norman Blankenship came into the mine office at Consolidated Coal Company's Rowland mine, near Clear Creek, West Virginia, he told the mine dispatcher not to tell anyone of his presence. Norman was the general superintendent of the Rowland operation. He had been with Consolidated for more than 23 years, having started out as a coal digger.

Norman had heard that one of his section bosses, Tom Serinsky, had been sleeping on the job. Tom had been hired two months earlier and assigned to the Rowland mine by the regional personnel office. He went to work as section boss, working the midnight to 8:00 A.M. shift. Because of his age and experience, he was the senior person in the mine on his shift.

Norman took one of the battery-operated jeeps used to transport personnel and supplies in and out of the mine and proceeded to the area where Tom was assigned. Upon arriving, he saw Tom lying on an emergency stretcher. Norman stopped his jeep a few yards away from where Tom was sleeping and approached him. "Hey, you asleep?" Norman asked. Tom awakened with a start and said, "No, I wasn't sleeping."

Norman waited a moment for Tom to collect his senses and then said, "I could tell that you were sleeping. But that's beside the point. You weren't at your work station.

You know that I have no choice but to fire you." After Tom had left, Norman called his mine foreman, who had accompanied him to the dispatcher's office, and asked him to complete the remainder of Tom's shift.

The next morning, Norman had the mine personnel officer officially terminate Tom. As part of the standard procedure, the mine personnel officer notified the regional personnel director that Tom had been fired and the reasons for firing him. The regional personnel director asked the personnel officer to get Norman on the line. When he did so, Norman was told, "You know that Tom is the brother-in-law of our regional vice president, Eustus Frederick?" "No, I didn't know that," replied Norman, "but it doesn't matter. The rules are clear. I wouldn't care if he was the regional vice president's son."

The next day, the regional personnel director showed up at the mine just as Norman was getting ready to make a routine tour of the mine. "I guess you know what I'm here for," said the personnel director. "Yeah, you're here to take away my authority," replied Norman. "No, I'm just here to investigate," said the personnel director.

When Norman returned to the mine office after his tour, the personnel director had finished his interviews. He told Norman, "I think we're going to have to put Tom back to work. If we decide to do that,

658

can you let him work for you?" "No, absolutely not," said Norman. "In fact, if he works here, I go." A week later, Norman learned that Tom had gone to work as section boss at another Consolidated coal mine in the region.

QUESTIONS

1. What would you do now if you were Norman?
2. Do you believe that the personnel director handled the matter in an ethical manner? Explain.

REFERENCES

Apcar, Leonard M. "Postal Ruling Is Designed to Realign Pay." *The Wall Street Journal*, December 26, 1984, p. 2.

Barkhaus, Robert S. and Meek, Carol L. "A Practical View of Outplacement Counseling." *Personnel Administrator* 27 (March 1982): 77–81.

Baxter, John D. "Mid-Manager Morale Sinks to a Low Level." *Iron Age* 228 (April 19, 1985): 61–67.

Bearak, Joel A. "Termination Made Easier: Is Outplacement Really the Answer?" *Personnel Administrator* 27 (April 1982): 63–71.

Beitner, E. I. "Justice and Dignity: A New Approach to Discipline." *Labor Law Journal* 35 (August 1984): 500–505.

Benfield, Clifford J. "Problem Performers: The Third-Party Solution." *Personnel Journal* 64 (August 1985): 96–101.

Beyer, J. M. and Trice, H. M. "A Field Study of the Use and Perceived Effects of Discipline in Controlling Work Performance." *Academy of Management Journal* 27 (December 1984): 743–764.

Bradshaw, David A. and Deacon, Linda Van Winkle "Wrongful Discharge: The Tip of the Iceberg?" *Personnel Administrator* 30 (November 1985): 74–76.

Bryant, Alan W. "Replacing Punitive Discipline with a Positive Approach." *Personnel Journal* 29 (February 1984): 79–87.

Camden, Thomas M. "Use Outplacement as a Career Planning Tool." *Personnel Administrator* 27 (January 1982): 35–37.

Cameron, D. "The When, Why, and How of Discipline." *Personnel Journal* 63 (July 1984): 37–39.

Cohen, S. L. and Prestor, J. "Solving the Promotion Puzzle." *Management World* 14 (February 1985): 16–18.

Dalton, Dan R. and Todar, William D. "Win, Lose, Draw: The Grievance Process in Practice." *Personnel Administrator* 26 (March 1981): 25–29.

Discenza, Richard and Smith, Howard L. "Is Employee Discipline Obsolete?" *Personnel Administrator* 30 (June 1985): 175–186.

Dreyer, R. S. "The Slightly Breakable Rule." *Supervision* XLIII (May 1981): 11–13.

Engel, Paul G. "Preserving the Right to Fire." *Industry Week* 224 (March 18, 1985): 39–40.

Himes, Gary K. "Handling Gripes and Grievances." *Supervision* XLIII (February 1981): 3–6.

Huberman, John. "Discipline Without Punishment Lives." *Harvard Business Review* 53 (July–August 1975): 6–8.

Kleiman, Lawrence S. and Clark, Kimberly J. "Users' Satisfaction with Job Posting." *Personnel Journal* 29 (September 1984): 104–108.

Lissy, William E. "Necessity of Proof to Support Disciplinary Action." *Supervision* 40 (June 1978): 13.

Lo Bosco, M. "Consensus on Nonunion Grievance Procedures." *Personnel* 62 (January 1985): 61–64.

Lorber, Lawrence Z., Kirk, J. Robert, Kirschner, Kenneth H., and Handorf, Charlene R. *Fear of Firing*. Alexandria, Va.: The ASPA Foundation, 1984.

McClellan, Keith. "The Changing Nature of EAP Practice." *Personnel Administrator* 30 (August 1985): 29–37.

Moore, Perry. "The Problems and Prospects of Cutback Management." *Personnel Journal* 30 (January 1985): 91–95.

O'Brien, F. P. and Drost, D. A. "Non-union Grievance Procedures: Not Just an Anti-Union Strategy." *Personnel* (September–October 1984): 61–69.

Olson, F. C. "How Peer Review Works at Control Data." *Harvard Business Review* 62 (November–December 1984): 58–59.

———. "Outplacement Helps Ease Termination for Employee and Employer." *Savings Institution* 105 (December 1984): 127.

Pingpank, Jeffrey C. and Mooney, Thomas B. "Wrongful Discharge: A New Danger for

Employers." *Personnel Administration* 26 (March 1981): 31–35.

Powell, Jon T. "Listening to Help the Hostile Employee." *Supervisory Management* 26 (November 1981): 2–5.

Scott, Dow and Markham, Steve. "Absenteeism Control Methods: A Survey of Practices and Results." *Personnel Administrator* (June 1982): 73–84.

Shane, Joseph. "Due Process and Probationary Employees." *Public Personnel Management* 2 (May–June 1973): 171–178.

Shore, Harvey, "SMR Forum: Employee Assistance Programs — Reaping the Benefits." *Sloan Management Review* 25 (Spring 1984): 69–73.

Stessin, Lawrence. "Expedited Arbitration: Less Grief Over Grievances." *Harvard Business Review* 55 (January–February 1977): 128–134.

Stoeberl, Philipp A. and Schneiderjans, Marc J. "The Ineffective Subordinate: A Management Survey." *Personnel Administrator* 26 (February 1981): 72–76.

Trisler, S. "Grievance Procedures: Refining the Open-Door Policy." *Employment Relations Today* 11 (Autumn 1984): 323–327.

Veglahn, Peter A. "Making the Grievance Procedure Work." *Personnel Journal* 56 (March 1977): 122–123.

Vernon-Gerstenfeld, Susan and Burke, Edmund. "Affirmative Action in Nine Large Companies: A Field Study." *Personnel Journal* 62 (April 1985): 54–60.

Weiss, Bernard, "Constructing Your Criticism." *Supervisory Management* 26 (May 1981): 12–18.

Welch, Barry. "Keeping the Discipliners in Line." *Personnel Management* 10 (August 1978): 21–24.

The Clarksdale, Mississippi plant of Parma Cycle Company had been open for only six months when the first efforts at unionization became apparent. A known union organizer was in town and prounion leaflets began to appear around the factory. As the personnel director at Clarksdale, Edward Deal had been expecting this to occur. He knew that the workers who had been brought down from the main plant in Parma, Ohio had a strong union tradition. He also knew that the wage and benefits package at Clarksdale was far less liberal than that at the Cleveland plant. So far, this had created no major problem. Most of the workers recruited from the Clarksdale area felt that they were well paid in comparison with others in that area.

In the plant that same day, Janice Snively was thinking about whether she should talk to the personnel director. Janice had been hired by Parma two weeks prior to start-up time. She had previously worked as a maintenance supervisor at a garment factory about sixty miles from Clarksdale. She had taken a slight pay cut in order to take what she thought would be a better job in the long run and to be nearer her family, who lived in Clarksdale.

Janice's crew of ten machine operators and two parts handlers was among the best in the plant. Janice had made friends with each of them and they obviously respected her. She felt that one reason she was a good leader was her willingness to "get her hands dirty." Because of her experience in maintenance she was able to repair the machines herself when they broke down. When an operator was absent, she would simply take over that machine in order to keep the workflow going.

Lately she had noticed a change. The workers seemed to be shutting her out. In a couple of instances, when several of her crew were congregated at one table in the lunch room, the conversation stopped as she approached and then awkwardly began again. The change of topic was obvious. For the first time, too, she began to hear complaints from the employees. For example, the operator of the cut-off machine, which cuts certain frame members to size, complained of the speed with which the machine operated. "I have less than one second to move the cut off piece before the tubing feeds through to start another cut. I'll be lucky not to lose an arm," he said. There had been a number of similar complaints, many of them related to safety, some to working conditions, and a number of workers had asked about when their next raise was coming.

Janice just thought that handling all of these kinds of problems was part of the supervisor's job and so she wasn't too concerned. Because of something that had happened this morning, though, Janice decided it was time to talk to the personnel director.

Janice walked in as Ed was thinking about the advantages and disadvantages of having a union. "Ed," she said, "I want you to look at this. One of the workers gave it to me and asked if it is true. I didn't know how to answer." Janice handed Ed the mimeographed sheet, which is reproduced on p. 662. After studying the sheet for a moment Ed said, "It's basically true, but I wish it weren't."

QUESTIONS

1. What do you think caused the unionizing attempt at Parma Cycle's Clarksdale plant?
2. What sequence of events is likely to occur before the Clarksdale plant becomes unionized?
3. Assuming that Parma Cycle wishes to prevent unionization of the Clarksdale plant, what might the union and management legally do before and after a union representation election is ordered by the NLRB?

Experiencing Human Resource Management

Advice for the Supervisor

A major part of the personnel director's job is to advise managers at all levels regarding personnel matters, particularly matters related to dealing with a union. In this exercise you will play the role of a personnel director who has been asked for advice by a supervisor, Larry Bradley.

ROLE DESCRIPTIONS

Larry Bradley. You have been with Parma Cycle Company for twelve years, the last four as a supervisor at the Parma, Ohio, plant. You are a very safety-conscious supervisor with a reputation for strictly enforcing the rules. Because of this, you believe, you have not had a lost time accident in your division since you became supervisor. There is a rule in the plant, well known to everyone, that every intersection is a "4-way stop" for fork-lift trucks. According to the labor–management agreement, even minor safety violations justify a three-day suspension and a written warning.

Tuesday you asked for a volunteer to stay late and move some pallets of materials using a small fork-lift truck. Charlie Fox volunteered. While he was moving materials that evening, you worked in your office, getting caught up on some paperwork. You had only about an hour's work to do. When you finished, you started walking back to the area where Charlie was working. You saw the fork-lift truck with Charlie at the wheel round the corner at a high speed and without stopping. You informed Charlie Fox that you were suspending him for three days and placing a written warning in his personnel folder. You told him not to bother reporting for work the next morning. Charlie appeared upset but that did not concern you particularly. You have a job to do and you want it to be done safely. That night, a friend called you and warned you to be ready because the union steward, Eugene Wilson, is upset about your treatment of Charlie. Early the next morning you call the personnel director, Jesse Heard, for advice. You know you will soon have to confront Charlie and Eugene.

Charlie Fox. You have been with Parma only two years. You are twenty-two years old, married, and have a new child. You want to move into management one day and do not want any bad marks on your record. You also need every dime you can get just to keep up with monthly bills and the expenses of a new child. You realize that in a technical sense Larry is correct in imposing the penalty. You think it is unreasonable, however, because there was no one else in the plant except the night watchman. Larry had told you he'd be ready to leave in about an hour. So you were hurrying to complete the work before that hour was up just to keep from delaying him. You wanted to explain, but he didn't give you a chance; just told you that you that you were suspended. When you spoke to the union steward about it, he actually seemed eager to help, immediately taking your side. You hope that you can convince Larry to change his mind about punishing you.

Eugene Wilson. You were elected union steward for the Wheel Assembly Division last year. There have been few grievances since then and you have had a rather uneventful year as steward. A couple of times workers have brought complaints to you but you thought that management was correct in each case and you told the workers so. You like being the union steward but feel that you might not be elected next time unless you are able to make a "show." The situation involving Charlie Fox gives you your chance. Your believe Larry Bradley was unreasonable in suspending Charlie. The purpose of the traffic rule in the plant is to keep people from getting run over by forklift trucks. Because there was practically nobody in the plant, there was really no danger. You hope you can convince Larry to back down.

QUESTIONS

1. How might your advice differ depending on whether you have heard Charlie's side of the story?
2. If Larry does not back down, what are the steps that may have to be taken to resolve the disagreement?
3. What is likely to be the impact of Larry's authority over the workers if he backs down?

Part Seven

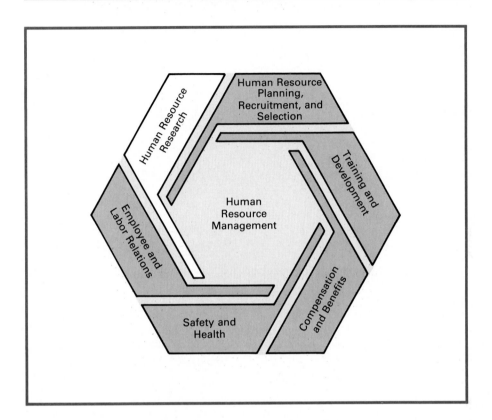

HUMAN RESOURCE
RESEARCH

CHAPTER OBJECTIVES
1. Describe why human resource research must consider the productivity challenge.
2. Explain the importance of research to human resource management.
3. Identify the basic methods of inquiry for research.
4. Describe the steps that need to be accomplished in the research process.
5. Describe how quantitative methods may be used in human resource research.

Chapter 19

PRODUCTIVITY AND HUMAN RESOURCE RESEARCH

Mary Carter, personnel manager for Ajax, Inc., noted that the turnover rate in the research and development department was approaching 200 percent. She knew that the loss of qualified researchers could have a serious impact on the success of Ajax, which was known for its leadership in developing new products. Mary decided to propose a confidential questionnaire to be administered to all employees in the department in an attempt to identify reasons for the excessive turnover.

Bob Stephens, president of Queens Manufacturing Company, was concerned as he viewed profit figures for the year. Sales had been good but he had been hearing rumblings of discontent throughout the organization. Somehow, people at Queens did not appear to be happy. Because the company employed approximately 5000 workers, he wondered how he could uncover the problems facing the organization.

Additional information provided through human resource research could benefit both Bob and Mary. Mary might be able to determine the reason for the high turnover rate. Bob could try to uncover the problems that appear to pervade the entire organization. Human resource research may be able to assist both managers in their endeavors.

The personnel manager's job, as discussed in chapter 1, is vastly different from only a few years ago. In order to contend with mounting responsibilities, the personnel manager has discovered that information derived from research is constantly required. **Human resource research** is *the systematic study of human resources for the purpose of maximizing personal and organizational goal achievement.*

Unless an organization possesses the resources to afford a human resource research function, it is likely that each human resource manager or specialist will, at one time or another, be called on to conduct research. This chapter provides an overview of the research function as it pertains to human resource management.

THE PRODUCTIVITY CHALLENGE

A major focus of human resource research is to determine ways to increase a firm's productivity. Historically, the United States has had the highest level of productivity of any major country. **Productivity** is *a measure of the relationship between inputs (labor, capital, natural resources, energy) and the quality and quantity of outputs (goods and services).* Note from this definition that outputs must be measured in terms of both quality and quantity. For example, the Chevrolet Vega was produced in the United States in quantities and at a cost approximating those of the Toyota Corolla (made in Japan). The output of Vegas may have been the same in terms of quantity but the Corolla was clearly superior in terms of quality. In general, U.S. auto industry productivity has not been as high as that of Japanese automakers in recent years.

Productivity is usually expressed in terms of output per person-hour or output per employed person. What causes it to be high or low? Productivity is affected not only by the capability and motivation of workers but also by technology, capital investment, capacity utilization, scale of production, and many other factors.

How does productivity in the United States compare with that in other countries? Figure 19–1 shows the relative levels of productivity in terms of output per employed person in the major industrial countries since 1960. Note that although the United States has a commanding lead over most of

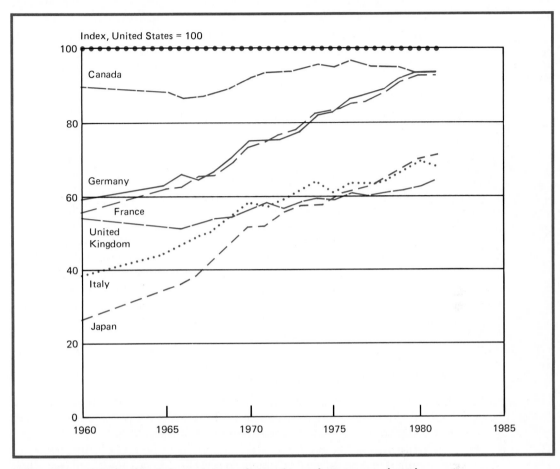

Index, United States = 100

Figure 19–1. Relative levels in real gross domestic product per employed person for selected countries, 1960–1981. Source: U.S. Department of Labor, Bureau of Labor Statistics, 1983.

these other countries, the lead is narrowing. In 1982, the United States held about an 8 percent productivity advantage over its nearest competitor.

In the 1980s there is much concern in the United States because the *rate of growth* in productivity is less than that of other industrial nations. Table 19–1 illustrates this point for the countries shown in Figure 19–1. Table 19–1, however, does not show productivity levels but the *rates of growth* in productivity. Note that in 1965–1973 productivity in the United States grew more slowly than in any of the other countries. During the period 1973–1981, only Canada's productivity growth was lower than that of the United States. This is not a recent phenomenon, however, and it exists in part because the United States started from a higher base. For example, in 1960, when Japanese productivity was less than one-fourth of that in the United States, the same *absolute* increase in productivity for both countries would have represented a *percentage* increase four times higher for Japan. Still, the major challenge facing American management during the 1980s and 1990s will be to attain levels of productivity growth that will ensure that the United States remains, as it has always been, the most productive major nation in the world. This can be accomplished only through improvements in all aspects of production. If management has a single societal goal, increasing productivity has to be it. Remember, as we have defined the term, *productivity* includes a measure of both the quality and quantity of output.

Several authorities — such as John Naisbitt, author of *Megatrends* and Thomas Peters and Robert Waterman, authors of *In Search of Excellence* — have noted the shift in the United States from an industrial to a service and information economy. As this occurs, productivity becomes more difficult to measure. For example, it is harder to calculate the output of a computer programmer or a financial adviser than that of a person who works on an assembly line at General Motors. Nevertheless, improvements in productivity remains a central objective of human endeavor. Human resource research has an important role to play in this endeavor.

BENEFITS OF HUMAN RESOURCE RESEARCH

Applications of human resource research are numerous and increasing rapidly. However, a major difficulty, and therefore a cost, is that personnel professionals are often not qualified in this area. Although this human resource function is not highly developed, it is potentially beneficial to companies. Personnel professionals may need to take the time and effort to upgrade themselves in this area. Human resource managers who desire

Table 19–1. Rate of growth of productivity in real gross domestic product per employed person for selected countries, 1965–1981.		
	Real gross domestic product per employed person*	
Country	**1965–73**	**1973–81**
United States	1.6	0.2
Canada	2.4	0.1
France	4.6	2.4
Germany	4.3	2.5
Japan	8.2	2.9
United Kingdom	3.2	1.3

*Rates are expressed as average annual percent change.

Source: U.S. Department of Commerce.

671

Chapter 19
Productivity
and Human
Resource
Research

Table 19–2. Areas of human resource research use

Company	Research area
Atlantic Richfield Company	■ Selection test validation Assessment center validation Survey research
Fleming Companies, Inc.	■ Specific emphasis on turnover, turnover reasons, turnover costs Identification of high potential employees for accelerated development Impact of union contracts on compensation Improving performance appraisal
Control Data Corporation	■ Staffing, compensation, interviewing, performance appraisal, management training, surveys of employee attitudes, productivity enhancement, employee development, selection
Ashland Oil, Inc.	■ Selection at both the exempt and nonexempt levels and also in the early identification of people with potential to become high level managers
Ford Motor Company	■ Selection, opinion surveys, career progress, performance appraisal, quality motivation, management potential, organization

to conduct research may find it necessary to recruit specialists in statistics and computer science to provide the expertise.

The potential benefits of sound human resource research far exceed the costs. Organizations only recently have begun to realize the full significance of the human component on their ability to achieve goals. This realization has occurred at a time when the competitive nature of business is making it increasingly difficult to obtain and retain qualified individuals. Many of the traditional concepts regarding human resource management have been questioned, and new ideas are needed if today's complex tasks are to be effectively accomplished.[1] Workers no longer feel compelled to remain with a firm for life. Other options are available, such as beginning a second career or taking a job with a competitor. Large firms use human resource research extensively. But the benefits have yet to be realized in many other organizations.

Specific applications of human resource research depend to a large extent on a firm's needs. As you can see in Table 19–2, there is considerable

[1]Kenneth Knight, "The Role of Personnel Research in the Real World," *Personnel Management* 7 (December 1975): 14.

overlap in the type of research presently being conducted, but differences do exist. These variations are attributable to such factors as the size, goals, and particular problems of the individual organization.

EFFECTIVE MANAGEMENT

Many human resource management practices have been questioned because of recent laws and government regulations.[2] For instance, it is no longer acceptable to use job specifications containing arbitrary requirements as a basis for recruiting and selecting employees. Managers are now called upon to prove that their employment decisions are based on valid requirements. However, as Walter Tornow, executive consultant and director of personnel research for Control Data Corporation, states, "On the whole, government regulations have had a positive effect because they cause organizations to examine and document their practices in ways that heretofore were not deemed necessary for some."

Another reason for the increased need for human resource research relates to the rapid changes that have occurred in the work environment. Because of the current rapid rate of change, management may need to alter its approach in adapting to new conditions. In the last twenty years the nature and composition of the work force has been significantly altered. Protected groups are entering the work force in ever-increasing numbers. Research is required to identify how the goals of these new work force members can be integrated with the needs and goals of the firm.

Largely because of increased educational opportunities, both managers and nonmanagers have become more sophisticated in their employment expectations. Management styles may need modification to achieve optimum results. While a highly autocratic manager may have been successful in the past, a similar style in today's organizations may lead to resentment and, in the long run, lower productivity. Also, the nature of the organizational structure may need modification. The means of identifying appropriate managerial styles and organizational structure will continue to be a major task of human resource research.

The actual nature of the work has also been changing rapidly. This has caused firms to continuously strive to upgrade their work forces. One of management's most difficult tasks is to get employees to accept change resulting from technological advances. The use of robotics in automobile assembly plants has created a tremendous need for retraining. The new General Motors Saturn plant to be located in Tennessee will likely require many new skills. It is not easy for a person to be told that his or her skill is no longer needed and that a new skill must be learned. Research may well provide the means by which people may learn to accept change more readily and thereby continue to be productive members of the work force.

[2]Richard W. Beatley, "Research Needs of PAIR Professions in the Near Future," *The Personnel Administrator* 23 (September 1978): 17.

Executive Insights

Walter W. Tornow,
SPHR
Vice President &
Executive Consultant
Control Data Business
Advisors

Walter Tornow's first jobs included being a "bag boy" at a supermarket, an inventory clerk at a sports shop, and an orderly at a cancer hospital. It even included being a Santa's helper at a department store — a job he regretted was very seasonal.

In his undergraduate training, Tornow's academic interests were quite eclectic, ranging from pre-med, philosophy, humanities, and economics to psychology. In graduate school he continued his interest in philosophy but became more and more attracted to industrial and organizational psychology. It was here — in courses such as differential psychology and social psychology — that he learned to appreciate individual differences and interpersonal dynamics, and their importance to the workplace. He received his Ph.D. in industrial-organizational psychology in 1970 from the University of Minnesota, with a minor in statistics and industrial relations.

While finishing his degree, Tornow directed employee survey programs for the Industrial Relations Center, while also working part-time at Control Data Corporation. Upon graduation in 1970, he received a full-time offer from Control Data. Since then he has enjoyed an interesting career with the company that has carried him through many varied roles, responsibilities, and areas of concentration.

He started as an associate personnel administrator in personnel research, then advanced through the ranks of staff specialist, personnel consultant, senior personnel consultant, manager of personnel research, director of personnel research, and vice president and executive consultant, human resources research. His functions have included job analysis, selection and validation research, job classification and evaluation, performance appraisal, program evaluation, employee surveys and survey research, training needs analysis and training evaluation, productivity improvement, health habit assessment, organization culture change, and integrated tool development for key human resource functions.

His work involvements have been equally many and varied. They have included developing an inmate behavior description system for evaluating prisoners at a large midwestern prison, directing the development of a computer-based system for diagnosing and treating learning disabled children, evaluating the impact of alcoholism and treatment on employee productivity and health care utilization, developing a "quality of service" index for evaluating psychological staff services at a midwestern clinic, and directing the development of the employee case against unwanted company take-overs.

As a major proponent for the practical value of personnel research, Tornow defines personnel research in three ways — as an activity, as a responsibility, and as an organizational unit. As an activity, personnel research is the strategic asking of answerable questions concerning HR tools and programs, collecting and analyzing the appropriate information, and then providing answers that are valuable, that is, answers that can be applied by practitioners toward more effective employee utilization and relations.

As a responsibility, personnel research is really conducted, however informally, by all personnel and line management people. As such, it is done continuously as an integral and necessary part of sound human resource management.

As an organizational unit, personnel research can represent a basic and multipurpose resource to other functions in the organization by providing research, development, and evaluation support.

In his role as head of the personnel research function at Control Data, Tornow supported the graduate training of many graduate students and their thesis research. He holds the rank of clinical associate professor from the University of Minnesota in recognition of the contribution he and his company have made to the training and experience of the graduate students.

In his current role, Tornow heads the advanced product development function for Control Data Business Advisors. He helps define new product concepts and opportunities by leveraging emerging professional, technology, and marketplace trends. In his current position, he is able to blend his academic training and practitioner orientation with the P&L perspective for new business development.

Finally, Tornow has been active in professional affairs. He is a licensed consulting psychologist and accredited by ASPA's Personnel Accreditation Institute as a senior professional in human resources (SPHR). He is national chairperson of the Personnel Accreditation Institute's functional standards committee on personnel research. Also, he has been an active member of the American Psychological Association's Society for Industrial-Organizational Psychology. For PAI, Tornow has directed a major professional effort aimed at codifying the body of knowledge standards for the personnel profession.

HUMAN RESOURCE PLANNING, RECRUITMENT, AND SELECTION

Plans must be made to recruit, select, and retain the type of employees who are capable of working toward achievement of organizational objectives. An organization possesses a distinct personality as does an individual. Just as each of us has observed personalities with whom we feel uncomfortable, organizations must seek to find the best match between the needs of the firm and its employees. An individual may be considered an excellent worker in one firm and a poor producer in another, even though similar tasks are performed.

Recruitment research is directed toward determining how individuals with high potential can be encouraged to apply for jobs with the firm. For instance, firms need to determine the most likely source of qualified candidates for the sales force. It does little good to know the qualities that prospective employees should possess and not know where and how to recruit these individuals.

675

Chapter 19
Productivity
and Human
Resource
Research

The goal of employee selection research is to identify prospective employees with the greatest potential for achieving success. As might be expected, the definition of a successful employee varies from organization to organization. This research often attempts to identify factors such as background and experience, education, hobbies, and test scores associated with differentiating between successful and less successful applicants.[3] Complicating these efforts are variations in the profiles of successful workers by geographic location and gender. For instance, in one study, a profile of successful men and women was developed for a firm. Although there were as many successful women as men, the profiles based upon biographical data were essentially different.[4]

TRAINING AND DEVELOPMENT

Human resource research is also quite important in the area of training and development. In the past, there have been numerous instances of improper allocation of training dollars. Studies may identify the firm's employees who can benefit from training. For instance, a high error rate associated with certain employees might indicate that they need additional training.

Also, research into the usefulness of the training program may be needed. Are workers better prepared to do their jobs after training, or is the training an exercise in futility? Training and development is expensive and its cost must be justified.

In addition, the type of training and development that is needed may be identified through human resource research. The productivity level of different departments may suggest that certain managers require development in the areas of managerial concepts and practices. Finally, an analysis of employee performance may suggest additional areas of training and development.

COMPENSATION

Both actual and perceived inequities in the firm's compensation system can create problems. Managers must be able to identify the actual inequalities and make the needed corrections, as well as be able to provide information to employees that will help to solve the problems. In order to maintain a fair compensation policy, it is not uncommon for firms to conduct extensive outside comparability surveys. In addition, surveys are often conducted in-house to determine employees' attitudes regarding their pay.

[3]R. Wayne Mondy and Frank N. Edens, "An Empirical Test of the Decision to Participate Model," *Journal of Management* 2(2) (Fall 1977): 11–16.
[4]"Job Longevity Differs by Sex," *Convenience Store News* 11(9) (May 2, 1975): 1.

Compensation research is widely used to identify potential problems before they get out of hand. In an inflationary era, firms constantly bid for skilled employees, and an organization's compensation program can rapidly become outdated.

EMPLOYEE AND LABOR RELATIONS

When research is used in the area of employee and labor relations, its focus is on topics that can affect individual job performance. Some of this research may be needed to identify factors that will permit the firm to remain union free. Factors within the environment, such as working conditions, may be found to have a detrimental effect on employee productivity and job satisfaction. This type of information would likely be beneficial in maintaining union free status. When problems are left unsolved, the worker may believe that the only remedy to the situation is to join the union.

SAFETY AND HEALTH

The primary task of research in health and safety relates to identification of problem areas before they become critical. For instance, research may be conducted to analyze the locations and causes of accidents.[5] It also can be used to identify characteristics of workers with higher probabilities of having accidents. Accident patterns may be identified and changes recommended to prevent their occurrence.

METHODS OF INQUIRY IN HUMAN RESOURCE RESEARCH

The type of problem confronting human resource managers determines, to a large extent, the method of inquiry that will be used. The use of each method or combination of methods depends on the particular needs of the organization. Specific research methods — the case study, the survey feedback method, and the experiment — will be described next.

THE CASE STUDY

The **case study** is *a research method that attempts to uncover the underlying reasons for occurrence of a problem in such areas as plants, departments, or sections.* The problem confronting Mary Carter (described at the beginning of the chapter) may well be solved through use of the case study. Employees in the research and development department likely are experiencing problems entirely different from those of other departments. Mary

---

[5]W. H. Weiss, "Accident Investigation: A Major Responsibility of Supervisors," *Supervision* 40 (July 1978): 1–3.

must work with the department head to determine the underlying cause of the difficulty. Solutions to problems associated with a plant, department, or section are sought through the use of the case study. When using this method, the researcher attempts to identify causes of specific problems. Typical problems for which the case study might be used include identifying the reason for:

677

Chapter 19
Productivity
and Human
Resource
Research

- An excessively high turnover rate at a particular plant.
- A high absenteeism rate in a specific department.
- A high accident rate at a certain building site.
- Low morale in a particular department.
- The low number of minority members in a certain plant.
- The underlying reasons for a wildcat strike at a particular location.

Naturally, there are many more situations in which the case study method may be used. No conscious attempt is made to develop new theories or make broad generalizations, although possible new management approaches may be suggested from the study.

THE SURVEY FEEDBACK METHOD

A major function of human resource research is to periodically determine the attitudes of employees toward their jobs, pay, and supervision. Responses to questions may also reveal ways by which productivity can be improved.[6] The **survey feedback method** is *a research technique that bases change efforts on the systematic collection and measurement of employee attitudes with the use of anonymous questionnaires.* For instance, Ford Motor Company uses the survey to obtain the opinions of its salaried personnel. Every other year, Ford administers a salaried personnel opinion survey. The results are published in Ford's in-house publication, *The American Road.* With information such as this, management is in a position to correct problems before they become too serious.

When surveys are used, they may be either the objective multiple choice type (see Figure 19–2) or a scaled answer to suggest agreement or disagreement to a particular question (see Figure 19–3). Objective analysis of survey results often requires a more detailed study. Possible bases for comparison of survey results might be by:

1. Section or department.
2. Age.
3. Gender.
4. Seniority.
5. Job level or degree of responsibility.
6. Changes in attitudes from a previous survey.

---

[6]Robert Loffreda, "Employee Attitude Surveys: A Valuable Motivation Tool," *The Personnel Administrator* 24 (July 1979): 42.

Why did you decide to do what you are now doing?

a. Desire to aid or assist others
b. Influenced by another person or situation
c. Always wanted to be in this vocation
d. Lack of opportunity or interest in other vocational fields
e. Opportunities provided by this vocation
f. Personal satisfaction from doing this work

What do you like least about your job?

a. Nothing
b. Pay
c. Supervisor relations
d. Problems with fellow workers
e. Facilities
f. Paper work and reports

Figure 19–2. Examples of multiple choice responses to survey questions.

Considering all aspects of your job, evaluate your compensation with regard to your contributions to the needs of the organization. Circle the number that best describes how you feel.

Pay Too Low		Pay Low		Pay Average		Pay Above Average		Pay Too High	
1	2	3	4	5	6	7	8	9	10

What are your feelings about overtime work requirements? Circle the number that best indicates how you feel.

Unnecessary				Necessary on Occasion			Necessary		
1	2	3	4	5	6	7	8	9	10

Figure 19–3. Examples of scaled responses to survey questions.

7. Comparison with other divisions, departments, etc.
8. Comparison with a standardized score if a validated instrument is being used.

The information becomes more meaningful to management when survey data are analyzed by various subgroups. A major point to consider is that survey responses often identify symptoms rather than causes. When surveys are administered, the researcher should avoid concentrating on isolated

679

Chapter 19
Productivity
and Human
Resource
Research

responses. Instead, the data should be viewed from a broader perspective. A pattern depicting a general trend may be found. Responses will likely reflect this trend if there are difficulties in the organization. For instance, even if the compensation and benefits program is quite competitive, a low evaluation in this area may reflect — not an inadequate compensation system — but general dissatisfaction.

When surveys are used to identify employee attitudes and opinions, certain cautions must be observed. First, confidentiality of responses must be assured.[7] Employees must believe that their specific responses will not be communicated to management. It is for this reason that outside consultants are often employed to administer the questionnaire. Even if members of the personnel department are quite ethical, employees may still perceive the department as being a tool of management. Rightly or wrongly, the employee may always wonder whether Personnel would succumb to management pressure to reveal responses given by specific employees.

Confidentiality means more than merely omitting a worker's name on the questionnaire. Even in a large firm, numerous sections consist of only a small number of employees. Or, in a large department, a characteristic of a particular worker may make identification easy. For instance, one large department of fifty workers may have only one woman in it. Protection of such a person's confidentiality is crucial to obtaining accurate results. The researcher must constantly be alert to these situations and be prepared to consolidate groups when necessary to ensure that anonymity is preserved.

The results of the surveys must be communicated to the various affected groups. Employees need to see that their responses are being heard. If surveys are to be used continually, management must take some action on the results.

When survey results are communicated to management, it is often best for each department or section head to be contacted individually.[8] For instance, if the survey suggests that problems exist in the marketing department, the department head will likely be more receptive to criticism if his or her peers are not listening. Just as workers do not like to be disciplined in the presence of their co-workers, managers do not like to receive survey results in the presence of others. Superior results are typically obtained when the data are discussed with each person or group separately.

At times, surveying every employee is not feasible because of time or cost restraints. **Sampling** is the *process by which only a portion of the total number of individuals are studied, from which conclusions are drawn for the entire group.* Bob Stephens, the president of Queens Manufacturing Company, might ask his personnel manager to administer a questionnaire to a sample of the workers. As shown in Figure 19–4, the total number of

---

[7]R. Wayne Mondy and Wallace F. Nelson, "Job Satisfaction Among Radiologic Technologies," *Applied Radiology* 7 (July–August 1978): 66.

[8]"A Productive Way to Vent Employee Gripes," *Business Week*, October 16, 1978, 169.

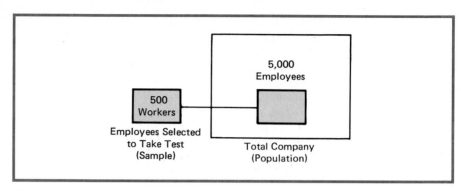

Figure 19–4. The distinction between population and sample.

workers in the firm is 5000. The time, effort, and cost necessary to survey all 5000 workers may be prohibitive. The researcher then decides on a sample size of 500, selects at random this number of workers, administers the questionnaire to them, and draws conclusions based on the responses from the employees comprising the sample.

THE EXPERIMENT

A method of inquiry that involves the manipulation of certain variables while others are held constant is referred to as an **experiment.** With this method, there is both a control group and an experimental group. The control group remains constant and operates as it did under the old environment, whereas selected variables are manipulated for the experimental group. For instance, a manager may desire to determine the effect that a new training program will have on productivity. The control group would continue to perform tasks in the conventional manner. The experimental group would receive the training. It is assumed that if a change in productivity occurs in the experimental group, it results from the training. On the surface, the experiment would appear to be an excellent means of inquiry. In actuality, it is sometimes difficult to isolate the many interrelated variables affecting people and their performance.

THE RESEARCH PROCESS

In order to accomplish human resource research, a firm needs to develop a systematic approach. You have likely discovered that you make better grades when you follow a systematic procedure for studying. Likewise, the most fruitful research is accomplished by following a logical process. The research process consists of six basic steps and is subjected to external and internal environmental constraints (see Figure 19–5).

RECOGNIZE THE PROBLEM

681

**Chapter 19
Productivity
and Human
Resource
Research**

One of the difficult tasks in the research process is to recognize that a problem exists. For instance, at what point does absenteeism become excessive? When does a turnover problem actually exist? A certain amount of turnover may be healthy for an organization. However, it often becomes convenient to explain away a potential problem. A manager may state, "Even though turnover is high, we really don't have a problem because those people didn't fit in the organization anyway." Such a comment would lead a researcher to suspect that this manager may not be open to problem

Figure 19–5. Personnel and the research process.

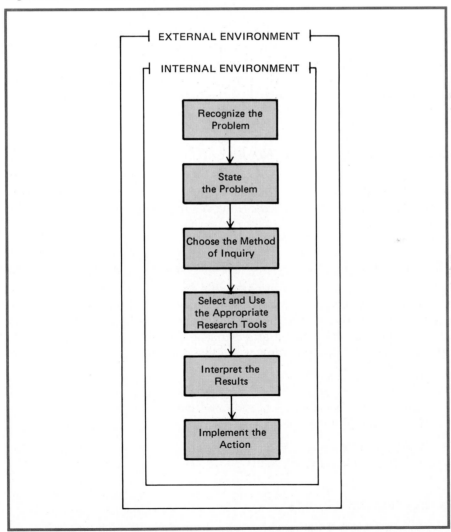

recognition. In actuality, the problem may be caused by an inadequate selection process, insufficient managerial training, or a multitude of other reasons. Or, as the manager suggests, there may be no problem. Regardless of the situation, openness on the part of the manager is the cornerstone of problem recognition.

STATE THE PROBLEM

The next step in the process is to clearly state the purpose of the research. The major hurdle to overcome is that the problem — not the symptoms — must be identified. Research should not focus on symptoms but should concentrate instead upon solving problems. As you might expect, this may prove difficult. For instance, a manager might maintain that the cause of decreased production is low employee morale when, in fact, this is not the real problem. Research may determine that dictatorial supervisors have been exerting so much pressure on employees that they could care less about productivity. If the manager attempted to solve the morale problem through means such as increasing benefits, it is unlikely that conditions would improve. A clear definition of the problem is essential for effective research.

CHOOSE THE METHOD OF INQUIRY

The method of inquiry chosen depends to a large extent on the nature of the research. The case study, the survey, and the experiment are all viable alternatives as methods of inquiry. However, most human resource research involves either the case method or the survey.

SELECT AND USE THE APPROPRIATE RESEARCH TOOL

Numerous quantitative tools are available for use by the human resource researcher. Specific techniques will be reviewed later in this chapter. These quantitative approaches are merely tools, and we do not suggest that all managers must be experts in mathematics and statistical theory in order to take advantage of their use. However, managers do need to know:

- Availability of quantitative tools.
- Circumstances under which these tools should be used.
- Strengths and weaknesses of each method.
- How to interpret the results.

The selection of a tool depends on the particular purpose for which the research is being conducted.

INTERPRET THE RESULTS

The person closest to the problem should participate in interpreting the results. When outsiders alone attempt to interpret the results, they often

683

Chapter 19
Productivity
and Human
Resource
Research

arrive at strange conclusions. For instance, the survey may suggest that major dissatisfaction exists in the engineering department. A person not close to the situation might mistakenly identify the problem as one of inadequate supervision. Actually, the engineers may have voiced their dissatisfaction over the poor facilities in which they work.

IMPLEMENT THE NECESSARY ACTION

The most difficult phase of the research process is to implement the necessary action based on the research conclusions. The research results may have identified areas where changes need to be made. Personnel now becomes the catalyst to convince line management that a change is necessary. In many instances, this task is quite difficult. Telling a manager that his or her managerial style is causing excessive turnover can be uncomfortable. However, the benefits of the research begin to be realized at this point in the process.

QUANTITATIVE METHODS IN HUMAN RESOURCE RESEARCH

When faced with the prospect of using quantitative methods, many people throw up their hands in frustration and say, "I can't do it." A mystique surrounds quantitative methods, which often tends to place a barrier between those who conduct research and those who make decisions in the so-called real world. This need not be the case. An effective human resource manager knows that quantitative methods are needed if many of the problems associated with human resource management are to be solved. The manager needs to know the limitations of the various methods and how to interpret their results, leaving the actual technical details to the researcher. Quantitative tools available for use in human resource research will next be briefly discussed.

CORRELATION ANALYSIS

Many times a researcher would like to know the relative strength of the relationships between two or more variables. **Correlation analysis** *measures the degree of association, or correlation, that exists between two or more variables.*[9] For instance, is there a relationship between job satisfaction and employee absenteeism? Figure 19–6 shows a high negative relationship between job satisfaction and employee absenteeism: As job satisfaction goes down, absenteeism goes up. On the other hand, Figure 19–7 shows a high positive correlation between the level of employee

[9]Charles T. Clark and Lawrence L. Schkade, *Statistical Analysis for Administrative Decisions*, 3rd ed. Cincinnati: Southwestern, 1979, pp. 386–387.

education and productivity: The higher the education level is, the greater the productivity. However, these correlations might not hold for another firm and thus cannot be universally applied.

The benefits of correlation analysis are considerable, but it must be used with caution. A correlation can be deceptive when the relationship does not reflect cause and effect. A high correlation may exist, but it might be meaningless. For instance, one study indicated a high positive correlation between the number of grey squirrels in north Louisiana and political activity in Washington, D.C. Here, a high relationship existed but the two variables were obviously unrelated. Personnel should be alert to this potential problem, and not make decisions based on inappropriate interpretations.

REGRESSION ANALYSIS

Regression analysis was described in chapter 5 as a technique that has proven useful in human resource planning. It has also proven beneficial in personnel research. Recall that the purpose of **regression analysis** is to "utilize the relation between two or more quantitative variables so that

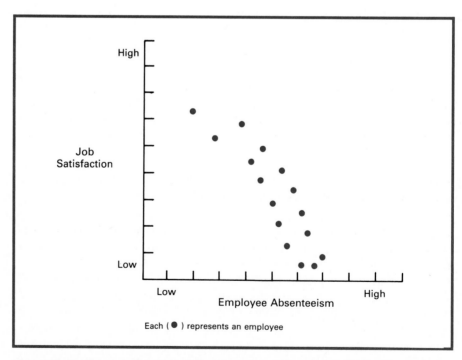

Figure 19–6. The negative correlation between job satisfaction and employee absenteeism at a particular firm.

685

Chapter 19
Productivity
and Human
Resource
Research

Figure 19–7. The positive correlation between education level and level of productivity at a particular firm.

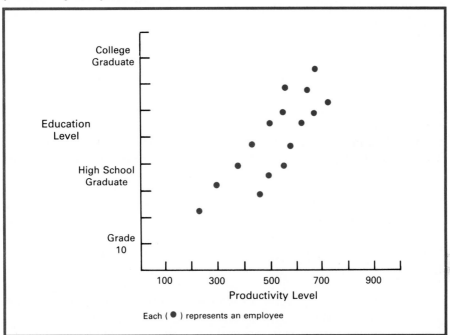

one variable can be predicted from the other, or others."[10] Suppose, for instance, that you would like to determine whether employee productivity can be estimated from their educational attainment (refer to Figure 19–7). In regression analysis terminology, the productivity level is referred to as the dependent variable. The education level used to estimate the level of productivity is called the independent variable. In this example, there is only one independent variable, so the process is referred to as simple linear regression. The use of two or more independent variables is termed multiple regression.

When regression analysis is used in human resource research, some possible dependent variables might be:

- Satisfaction level of employees.
- Length of employment of employees.
- Productivity level of employees.
- Accident rate of employees.

[10]John Netter and William Wasserman, *Applied Linear Statistical Models.* Homewood, Ill.: Richard D. Irwin, 1974, p. 21.

Personnel data that might be used as the independent variable include:

- Background and biographical data.
- Work history with the firm.
- Personal goals and aspirations.
- Test scores.

The use of biographical data in screening is expected to increase in the future.[11]

The researcher might attempt to determine through regression analysis which of the independent variables aid in differentiating between productive and less productive workers. The regression model developed using these variables may assist the manager in identifying prospective employees who will become successful workers, thereby improving selection decisions. The model's accuracy must be validated through other statistical means. But, if the model proves appropriate, it can be useful in the selection process.

DISCRIMINANT ANALYSIS

The purpose of **discriminant analysis** is to *identify factors that differentiate between two or more groups in a population.*[12] This statistical technique is being used more frequently in human resource research. When two-group discriminant analysis is used, an attempt might be made to identify factors that differentiate between some of the following:

- Satisfied versus less satisfied employees.
- Long-term versus short-term employees.
- Productive versus less productive employees.
- Accident-prone versus less accident-prone workers.

Only the imagination of the researcher limits the factors that can be used. Some of the potential factors that the researcher might use to differentiate between two groups include:

- Background and biographical data.
- Work history with the firm.
- Personal goals and aspirations.
- Test scores.

For instance, suppose the researcher was attempting to determine whether certain background or biographical factors differentiated between satisfied and less satisfied workers. Much as with regression analysis, the level of satisfaction becomes the dependent variable. However, unlike regression, individuals in the two groups are identified as either satisfied

---

[11]Beatley, "PAIR Professions," p. 19.

[12]For an in-depth look at discriminant analysis, see Donald F. Morrison, *Multivariate Statistical Methods,* 2nd ed. New York: McGraw-Hill, 1976, pp. 230–245.

687

**Chapter 19
Productivity
and Human
Resource
Research**

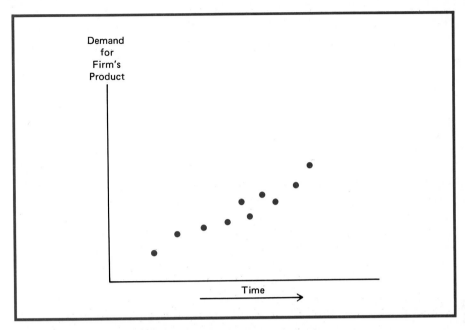

Figure 19–8. A scatter diagram for time series analysis.

or less satisfied. Through the use of discriminant analysis, independent variables capable of distinguishing between the two selected groups are identified. The mechanics of discriminant analysis also permit determining the reliability of the model developed.

TIME SERIES ANALYSIS

A technique that has proven quite helpful in making projections over time is time series analysis. **Time series analysis** is *a variation of regression analysis in which the independent variable is expressed in units of time.* As in regression analysis, both a dependent variable and an independent variable are required. However, the independent variable is now associated with time and the dependent variable is associated with demand.[13] In Figure 19–8 the dependent variable is the demand for the firm's product. When the number of employees required in a company is closely associated with demand for the firm's product, time series analysis may prove useful in forecasting the organization's human resource needs. Using the same general mathematical procedure as in regression analysis, a time series equation can be calculated and estimates of future demand can be made.

[13]Joseph G. Monks, *Operations Management: Theory and Problems.* New York: McGraw-Hill, 1977, pp. 277–278.

HUMAN RESOURCE RESEARCH: AN ILLUSTRATION

In order to illustrate how human resource research may be used in an organization, an actual example will be described next. At the firm's request, it will not be identified. The techniques used and the benefits achieved are factual. The organization, a regional medical center in the southwest, had experienced rapid growth and the accompanying growing pains. The personnel director and the hospital administrator recognized that difficulties were developing and called on an outside consultant. He was to work with them in identifying and solving problems before they became critical.

The consultant first talked with numerous employees to get a general view of the situation. Refusal of employees to talk about certain subjects and their apparent nervousness during the informal interviews suggested that problems did exist.

The next phase of the research project involved developing a survey tailored specifically to the hospital. Sample questions, which are shown in Figure 19–9, were developed. As you can see, topics ranged from managerial style to compensation. Administration of the questionnaire to all hospital personnel was a critical step. Because problems appeared to exist, maintaining each participant's confidentiality was crucial. The hospital administrator's role was to notify each employee that the survey was to be made. From that point on, the employees would have no further contact with any member of the administration regarding the survey.

Groups of employees met with the consultant in the room where the survey was to be administered. He first explained the survey's purpose and then assured the employees of confidentiality. Employees were told that summary results only would be provided to the administration. At this point it became even more obvious that problems did exist. Many employees wanted to know in detail the relationship between the consultant and the administration. Continuous assurances of confidentiality had to be made. Because of the nature of hospital work, the researcher had to administer the questionnaire over a 48-hour period. To ensure further confidentiality, the respondents were told that they should put their completed questionnaires in blank envelopes so they could not be identified. Some employees even chose to mail their responses to the consultant rather than risk having the questionnaire get lost at the hospital.

The next phase entailed analyzing the results. Data from each employee were coded on a general purpose computer card and were analyzed for the entire hospital and for each of its departments.

Statistics for the entire hospital proved inconclusive. However, when the survey results were evaluated by departments, some obvious problems began to surface. Employees in certain departments appeared to be much more discontented than other workers. For instance, the levels of satisfaction in the radiology and lab departments appeared to be consistently below the satisfaction level of the hospital in general. Figure 19–10 shows the summary of responses by department regarding the overall working environment.

What do you like most about your job?
a. Helping or providing service for others
b. Learning opportunities
c. Personal satisfaction
d. Being around people
e. The work you perform at this hospital at this job
f. Nothing
g. Other (Specify)
h. Other (Specify)

What do you like least about your job?
a. Nothing
b. Pay
c. Supervisor relations
d. Problems with fellow workers
e. Facilities
f. Paper work and reports
g. Patient related problems
h. Doctor related problems
i. Other (Specify)
j. Other (Specify)

How would you describe your overall working environment? Circle the number that best describes how you feel.

Extremely Frustrating		Frustrating		Acceptable		Above Average		Excellent Work	
1	2	3	4	5	6	7	8	9	10

What do you think of strikes in the health care field? Circle the number which indicates how you feel.

Strongly Favor		Favor		Neutral		Opposed		Strongly Opposed	
1	2	3	4	5	6	7	8	9	10

What do you think about the system of giving pay increases at this hospital? Circle the number that best describes how you feel.

Very Bad		Poor		Satisfied		Good		Excellent	
1	2	3	4	5	6	7	8	9	10

Considering all aspects of your job, evaluate your compensation with regard to your contributions to the needs of the hospital. Circle the number that best describes how you feel.

Pay Too Low		Pay Low		Pay Average		Pay Above Average		Pay Too High	
1	2	3	4	5	6	7	8	9	10

Figure 19–9. Sample survey questions.

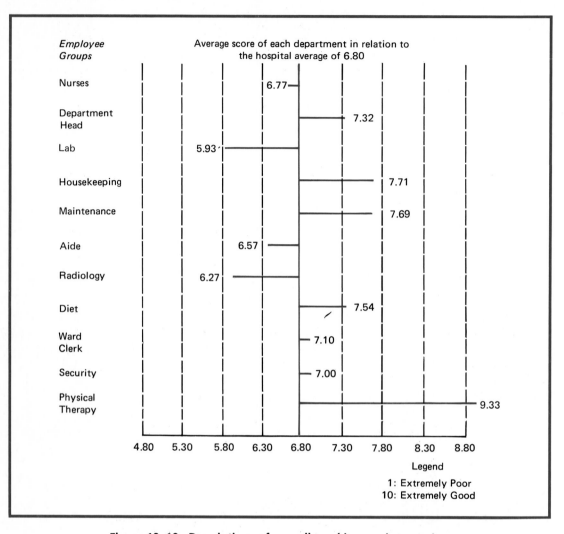

Figure 19–10. Descriptions of overall working environments.

At this point, however, only symptoms had been uncovered. The next phase entailed identification of specific problems. The results of the survey were presented to each department head individually. They reviewed the results, discussed what the symptoms revealed, and participated in the identification of problems.

The analysis of the radiology department provides an excellent illustration of the difference between the identification of symptoms and the identification of problems. The hospital had experienced rapid growth during the past few years, and, while other departments had increased staff to handle the increased workload, the radiology department had not. This

691

**Chapter 19
Productivity
and Human
Resource
Research**

caused employees and the department head to work overtime. Also, questioning of other supervisors revealed that the salary level of this department had not kept pace with radiology departments in nearby hospitals. The combination of these two factors — understaffing and unrealistic salary level — resulted in considerable job dissatisfaction. The cause of the dissatisfaction had now been determined. The same procedure was used with the other departments in which there was low satisfaction.

The consultant was now able to provide the hospital administrator with not only the survey results but also some sound recommendations. Suggestions for improvement were made to each department, as well as for the entire hospital. They included:

1. Implementation of a management training program emphasizing communication skills, leadership, motivation, and other human relation techniques.
2. Reevaluation of the hospital's compensation program, including reacquainting employees with their fringe benefits package, clarifying the method of granting pay increases, and evaluating new benefits.

The timing of the research and resulting implementation of the recommendations later proved to be critical. Within a year, a major attempt at unionizing the hospital was made but failed. The research study, which identified these human resource problems and proposed solutions, was credited with being the major factor in preparing the hospital for its successful efforts in resisting unionization.[14]

CHALLENGES OF THE FUTURE

"There are no problems, only challenges." Even if this statement is not entirely true, HRM problems must be considered challenges or at least situations that can and will be met. Personnel has experienced rapid growth as a profession. This is due, in part, to progressive-thinking firms which have recognized the need for effective human resource management. Personnel's responsibilities will continue to expand because human resources will be increasingly recognized as a critical factor in an organization. Human resource managers' tasks will likely impact the entire culture of organizations because of their potential to impact the firm's profitability.

Business organizations have many different objectives, not the least of which is to make a profit. However, organizations that plan to survive must

[14]R. Wayne Mondy and Wallace F. Nelson, "Job Satisfaction Among Radiologic Technologies," *Applied Radiology* 7(4) (July–August 1978): 65–67. Copyright © by Barrington Publications, Inc., 825 S. Barrington Avenue, Los Angeles, California 90049. Reprinted by permission.

establish goals which relate to social responsibility. In the past, the federal government has responded to deficiencies in this area by enacting legislation to fill the gaps. A large part of the responsibility of maintaining an organization's social conscience will be borne by human resource professionals.

The free enterprise system has proven to be the most effective in the world. Capable people must be employed and motivated toward increased productivity in order for the system to function properly. Human resource professionals must ensure that people with high potential are selected by their firms. Competent employees are vital not only to an individual firm but also to the survival of our entire economy. One personnel director stated, "The survival of business in a free economy will be determined by the influence and use of the human resources, but they must be relevant and productive, and they must pay off in long-range objectives." Personnel must take the leadership role in providing policies and programs for more fully realizing human potential in the workplace as a means of increasing both productivity and the quality of work life. Of special concern are the untapped resources represented by females and minority groups. Although women constitute approximately 50 percent of the population, their full capabilities remain underutilized. Black, Mexican-American, and other protected groups have only realized some of the benefits of the free enterprise system. If maximum productivity is to be achieved, all people in our society must be fully utilized.

Throughout the past few decades, government regulation of business was greatly expanded. Overseeing implementation of the various laws and regulations has typically been placed in the hands of the human resource executive. More and more government injected into employment relations has required more expertise in the form of qualified personnel executives. Because legislation can have such a major influence, sometimes even affecting the survival of the firm, the importance of the personnel function has greatly increased.

Human resource managers will have the opportunity to counteract the trend toward increased government intervention. Government regulation of business often results from the public belief that business has not been socially responsible. Personnel managers must be aware of societal values. They must be at the leading edge of organizational change. Human resource managers are the experts in this area and must initiate changes which balance the needs of individuals, employers, and society.

SUMMARY

Human resource research involves the systematic study of human resources for the purpose of maximizing personal and organizational goal achievement. The specific applications of human resource research depend to a large extent on the needs of a particular firm. From time to time, all of the personnel functions have needs for human resource research.

693

Chapter 19
Productivity
and Human
Resource
Research

The type of problem confronting the personnel manager determines, to a large extent, the method of inquiry that will be used. When the personnel manager is called on to uncover the underlying reasons for a particular occurrence, the case method is often used. The survey feedback method is used to determine employee attitudes. A method of inquiry that involves certain the manipulation of while others are held constant is referred to as the experiment.

In order to accomplish human resource research, a systematic approach needs to be used. The six basic steps in the research process are: (1) recognizing the problem; (2) stating the problem; (3) choosing the method of inquiry; (4) selecting and using the appropriate research tool; (5) interpreting the results; and (6) implementing the action.

Numerous quantitative tools are available for use by human resource managers. The purpose of correlation analysis is to measure the degree of association between two or more variables. The purpose of regression analysis is to determine the relationship between two or more variables so that one variable can be predicted from the others. The purpose of discriminant analysis is to identify factors that differentiate between two or more groups in a population. Time series analysis permits projections to be made over time.

QUESTIONS FOR REVIEW

1. Describe the general methods of inquiry available for use by the human resource researcher.
2. Why would the experiment as a method of research often not provide an excellent means of inquiry in the area of human resources?
3. Identify the basic steps that should be accomplished in the research process.
4. Why have firms begun to realize that they can benefit from effective human resource research?
5. Briefly define each of the following quantitative tools as they may be used in human resource:
   (a) correlation analysis
   (b) regression analysis
   (c) discriminant analysis
   (d) time series analysis

TERMS FOR REVIEW

Human resource research
Productivity
Case study
Survey feedback method
Sampling

Experiment
Correlation analysis
Regression analysis
Discriminant analysis
Time series analysis

Mike Manton is president of Lewis Milling Company of Muncie, Indiana. The company has about 100 employees and Mike has owned and managed the company since he founded it in the 1950s. Mike has always taken a good deal of pride in knowing every employee by name. To him the company is just one big happy family.

Last year, however, Mike sensed a growing level of dissatisfaction. Turnover increased and the workers just didn't seem as happy anymore. When Mike mentioned it to his office manager, Jeffry Wilson, Jeffry agreed that there had been a change. "I don't know what has caused it," said Jeffry, "but I do know that things are getting worse." Jeffry suggested a professionally conducted attitude survey to identify the problem. Mike approved this, and the survey was conducted with the assistance of a professor from the state university. Employees were encouraged to give honest answers and were given the usual assurances of anonymity. They were told that the company management would receive only generalized summaries of the survey results.

Mike found the results shocking. It was evident that a large number of his people were dissatisfied with various aspects of their jobs. Some thought the pay was too low. Others felt the supervision was inad-

equate or arbitrary. Many objected to the harsh working conditions. A few even mentioned the "high and mighty" attitude of the "big boss."

Mike demanded and received the individual questionnaire results from the consultant. As Mike studied the individual questionnaires he became even more disturbed. By noting certain demographic data, he felt he could identify some of the respondents. He simply could not believe that trusted employees could be so unappreciative of the jobs he had provided them over the years.

He called in his department heads and gave them the names of workers whose questionnaire responses showed the most dissatisfaction. He ended the meeting with the following statement: "If they aren't happy with this company they can leave. If you find anyone else who isn't happy here, I want to know about it."

QUESTIONS

1. What critical mistakes were made in conducting and using the attitude survey?
2. Do you feel that Mike's attitude toward disgruntled employees was justified? Discuss.

Isabelle Anderson is plant manager for Hall Manufacturing Company in Alexandria, Louisiana, a company that produces a line of relatively inexpensive painted wood furniture. Six months ago, Isabelle became concerned about the turnover rate among workers in the painting department. Man-

ufacturing plant turnover rates in that area of the South generally average about 30 percent and this was true at Hall. The painting department, however, had experienced a turnover of nearly 200 percent in each of the last two years. Because of the limited number of skilled workers in the area, Hall had an extensive training program for new painters, and Isabelle knew that the high turnover rate was extremely costly.

Isabelle conducted exit interviews with many of the departing painters. Some of them said they were leaving for more money, others for better benefits, and most cited some kind of "personal reasons" for quitting. Isabelle checked and found that Hall's wages and fringe benefits were competitive with, if not better than, those of other manufacturers in the area. She then called in Nelson Able, the painting supervisor, to discuss the problem. Nelson's response was, "You know how this younger generation is. They work to get enough money to live on for a few weeks and then quit. I don't worry

about it. Our old timers can take up the slack." "But Nelson," Isabelle replied, "we have to worry about the turnover rates. It's really costing the company a lot of money. I'm going to ask Joe Swan to administer a survey to get to the bottom of this." Nelson replied, "Do whatever you think is right. I don't see any problem."

QUESTIONS

1. Do you agree that a survey of employees is the best way to identify the problem? Explain.
2. What kind of survey would you conduct and how would you analyze the results?

REFERENCES

Barrett, G. V. "The Concept of Dynamic Criteria: A Critical Reanalysis." *Personnel Psychology* 38 (Spring 1985): 41–56.

Bass, B. M. and Barrett, G. V. *People, Work and Organizations: An Introduction to Industrial and Organizational Psychology*, 2nd ed. Boston: Allyn and Bacon, 1981.

Bennis, Warren G. *Changing Organizations*. New York: McGraw-Hill, 1966.

Bownas, D. A. "A Quantitative Approach to Evaluating Training Curriculum Content Sampling Adequacy." *Personnel Psychology* 38 (Spring 1985): 117–131.

Faley, R. H. "Age Discrimination and Synthesis of the Legal Literature with Implications for Future Research." *Personnel Psychology* 37 (Summer 1984): 327–350.

Gordon, Michael E. and Kleiman, Lawrence M. "The Prediction of Trainability Using a Work Sample Test and an Aptitude Test: A Direct Comparison." *Personnel Psychology* 29 (Summer 1976): 243–253.

Harkman, J. Richard and Oldham, Greg R. "Motivation Through the Design of Work: Test of a Theory." *Organizational Behavior and Human Performance* 16 (August 1976): 250–279.

Herzberg, Frederick. *Work and the Nature of Man*. Cleveland: World, 1966.

Jones, R. R. "1984 was a Good Year for R&D Salaries." *Research & Development* 27 (March 1985): 67–70.

Keller, R. T. "A Cross-National Validation Study Toward the Development of a Selection Battery for R&D Professional Employees. *Trans Engineering Management* 31 (November 1984): 162–165.

Knight, Kenneth. "The Role of Personnel Research in the Real World." *Personnel Management* 7 (December 1975): 14–17.

Likert, Rensis. *The Human Organization*. New York: McGraw-Hill, 1967.

Martin, David C. and Bartol, Kathryn M. "Managing Turnover Strategically." *Personnel Administrator* 30 (November 1985): 63–73.

Mondy, R. Wayne and Mills, Harry N. "Choice Not Chance in Nurse Selection." *Supervisor Nurse* 9 (November 1978): 35–39.

Pajer, Robert G. "Finding Selection Research Data: Federal Agencies as a Source." *Public Personnel Management* 6 (November–December 1977): 442–446.

Peters, William S. and Chanpous, Joseph E. "The Use of Moderated Regression in Job Redesign

Decisions." *Decision Sciences* 10 (January 1979): 85–95.

Pucik, V. "White Collar HRM: A Comparison of the U.S. and Japanese Automobile Industries. *The Columbia Journal of World Business* 19 (Fall 1984): 87–94.

Purcell, John "Is A Listening to the Corporate Personnel Department?" *Personnel Management* (September 1985): 28–31.

Sharplin, A. D. "Coercive Power: Indispensable or Inconsequential." *Northeast Louisiana Business Review* (Spring–Summer 1982): 10–14.

Thurstone, L. L. "What is Personnel Research? (Part II)." *Personnel Journal* 61 (May 1982): 371.

Tung, Rosaline L. "Strategic Management of Human Resources in the Multinational Enterprise." *Human Resource Management* 23 (Summer 1984): 129–141.

Wehrenberg, Stephen B. "The Exit Interview: Why Bother?" *Supervisory Management* 25 (May 1980): 20–25.

Williams, D. R. "Employment in Recession and Recovery: A Demographic Flow Analysis." *Monthly Labor Review* 108 (March 1985): 35–42.

Yerkes, Robert M. "What is Personnel Research? (Part I)." *Personnel Journal* 61 (May 1982): 370.

Zarandona, J. L. and Camuso, M. A. "A Study of Exit Interviews: Does the Last Word Count?" *Personnel* 62 (March 1985): 47–48.

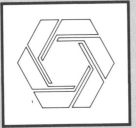

Parma Cycle Company: Looking Ahead

Edward Deal was jubilant. He had just received notification from the National Labor Relations Board that the union representation election at Parma Cycle's Clarksdale, Mississippi, plant had gone against the union. The margin was small, only 53 percent to 47 percent, but Ed considered it a significant victory. As personnel director at Clarksdale, he had done everything within his power to prevent the plant from becoming unionized. For example, wages and benefits at Clarksdale had started far below those at the Parma, Ohio plant. At Edward's insistence, the package had been made competitive in the labor market. His recommendation for this had not been approved until top management was convinced that a unionizing effort was underway at Clarksdale.

With the new wage and benefits package, Parma Cycle became the highest paying employer in the Clarksdale area. From Ed's vantage point, morale seemed to be quite high in the plant. Jobs with Parma were much sought after. An average day saw twenty or thirty new job applicants. In fact, the rush of job applicants had forced Edward to post a sign reading "No Jobs Available."

There were still a couple of things that concerned Edward, though. First, the representation election had been extremely close. Twenty-five more votes would have swung it in the union's favor. Ed thus felt a certain insecurity about the prospects for future unionization attempts at the plant. He knew that the company would have to live up to workers' expectations in order to keep the union out. He was also concerned about the qualifications of the workers he had hired. During the recruiting process, all that Ed had been able to offer to new trainees was minimum wage. The average wage for beginning workers at Parma's Clarksdale plant had been only $5.20 an hour. Consequently, only very young, mostly unskilled workers had applied. They had been trained to some degree but were certainly no match for the work force at Parma's Ohio plant.

He decided to call Jesse Heard, his old boss and the personnel director at the Parma Ohio plant. After a friendly greeting, Ed got right to the point. "Jesse," he said, "I thought we were surely going to lose the represention tation election and I'd have been thrilled to get even a 1 percent victory margin. But, let's not kid ourselves. If we don't do a super job of keeping our workers satisfied, the union will get those extra 25 votes next time." "You're right," replied Jesse, "and even if you do, the result might be the same in the long run." "Why is that?" asked Ed. Jesse answered, "There has been a good deal of pressure by the union up here for us to recognize a bargaining unit at Clarksdale. I don't know how long top management will have the will to resist." "You really know how to let the air out of a fella's balloon," said Ed. "I don't mean to do that," Jesse replied, "but I do think we need to take a realistic view."

"Speaking of being realistic," continued Ed, "let's face it. We started the plant in Clarksdale to reduce labor costs and we hired a full complement of employees here at very low rates compared to those we are paying now. We have raised the wages and we still have the same workers. The only way we can really have lower costs now is for the workers here to produce more than those at Parma." "I see what you mean," said

Jesse, "I'll be down for a visit in a couple of months. I don't know if I can help in any way, but we can sure talk about it."

A few weeks later Ed decided that it was time to find out a little more about his work force. He called Jules Cagney, a professor of personnel administration at Mississippi State University in Starksville, and asked him to recommend a research design. "Professor Cagney," said Edward, "I am not as concerned about keeping the union out as I am about treating our people fairly and maintaining a high level of motivation. I mainly want to know what their attitudes and concerns are so that we can design the personnel program around that." "I'll do some thinking about that," said Cagney, "and be back in touch with you within a day or two."

QUESTIONS

1. What kind of study do you think that Cagney will recommend? Explain.
2. What are the trends in personnel administration that Edward should consider in designing or redesigning the personnel program at Clarksdale?

Experiencing Human Resource Management

Looking Ahead

Human resource research is conducted to determine what has happened in the past as well as to determine certain things about the present, such as personal attitudes of employees. This has been done at Parma Cycle Company's Clarksdale, Mississippi plant by Jules Cagney. Information developed from such studies as that conducted by Professor Cagney form the foundations of personnel strategic planning. Implied in making plans is some assumption about what the future holds. Consequently, it is worthwhile for personnel managers to try to judge the human resource management environment at least a year or two ahead of time. Based on what you have learned about Parma Cycle Company and the trends in human resource management, consider the questions below and write or discuss your answers.

QUESTIONS

1. Will the Clarksdale plant be unionized two years from now? Why or why not?
2. How will worker productivity at Clarksdale compare to that of Parma, Ohio? Explain.
3. What national or regional trends will affect personnel management at the Ohio plant? The Mississippi plant?

Glossary

Adverse impact: A concept established by the Uniform Guidelines, which occurs if protected groups are not hired at the rate of at least 80 percent of the best achieving group. (6)

Advertising: A way of communicating the employment needs within the firm to the public through media such as radio, newspaper, or industry publications. (6)

Affirmative action program (AAP): A type of program that certain organizations must develop to demonstrate that protected group members are employed in proportion to their representation in the firm's relevant recruitment area. (6)

Agency shop: Employees are not required to join the union; however, the labor agreement requires, as a condition of employment, nonunion members of the bargaining unit to "pay the union the equivalent of membership dues as a kind of tax, or service charge, in return for the union acting as the bargaining agent." (16)

Aiming: The ability to move the hands quickly and accurately from one spot to another. (7)

Alcoholism: A treatable disease characterized by uncontrolled and compulsive drinking. (14)

Apprenticeship training: A method that combines classroom and on-the-job training. (8)

Arbitration: The process of submitting a contract negotiation dispute or an un-resolved grievance to an impartial third party for a binding decision. (16, 18)

Assessment center method: An appraisal approach that requires employees to participate in a series of activities similar to those that they might be expected to do in an actual job. (11)

Authorization card: A document indicating that an employee wants to be represented by a labor organization in collective bargaining. (15)

Bargaining unit: A group of employees, not necessarily union members, recognized by an employer or certified by a government agency as appropriate for representation by a labor organization for purposes of collective bargaining. (15)

Beachhead demands: Demands that the union does not expect to receive when they are first made. (16)

Behavior modeling: Utilization of videotapes prepared specifically to illustrate how managers function in various situations in order to develop managerial interpersonal skills. (8)

Behaviorally anchored rating scale (BARS): A performance appraisal method that combines elements of traditional rating scales and critical incidents methods. (11)

Benefits: All financial rewards that are not paid directly to the employee. (13)

Biofeedback: A method of learning to control involuntary bodily processes such as blood pressure or heart rate. (14)

Note: The numbers in parentheses at the end of definitions indicate the chapter in which the term is first used and defined and, in some cases, subsequent chapters in which it is emphasized again as a key term.

Board interview: An interview in which one candidate is quizzed by several interviewers. (7)

Bottom-up approach: A forecasting method that proceeds upward in the organization from small units to ultimately provide an aggregate forecast of employment needs. (5)

Boycott: An agreement by union members to refuse to use or buy the firm's products. (16)

Burnout: A state of fatigue or frustration that stems from devotion to a cause, way of life, or relationship that did not provide the expected reward. (14)

Business games: Simulations that represent actual business situations. (8)

Career: A general course of action that a person chooses to pursue throughout his or her working life. (10)

Career anchors: Five different motives that account for the way people select and prepare for a career. (10)

Career development: A formalized approach taken by an organization to ensure that people with the proper qualifications and experience are available when needed. (10)

Career paths: Flexible lines of progression through which employees typically move. (10)

Career planning: A process whereby an individual sets career goals and establishes the means to achieve them. (10)

Case study: A training method that utilizes actual or simulated business problems for students to solve; a research method that attempts to uncover the underlying reasons for the occurrence of problems in a segment of an organization (such as a plant, department, or section). (8, 19)

Central tendency: A common error that occurs when employees are incorrectly rated near the average or middle of the scale. (11)

Checkoff of dues: Agreement by the company to withhold union dues from members' checks and to forward the money directly to the union. (16)

Classification method: A job evaluation method by which a number of classes, or grades, are defined to describe a group of jobs. (12)

Closed shop: An arrangement whereby union membership is a prerequisite to employment. (16)

Coaching: An on-the-job approach to management development in which the manager—on a one-to-one basis—is given an opportunity to teach by example. (8)

Cognitive aptitude tests: Tests to measure an individual's ability to learn as well as perform a job. (7)

Collective bargaining: The performance of the mutual obligation of the employer and the representative of the employees to meet at reasonable times and confer in good faith with respect to wages, hours, and other terms and conditions of employment, and the execution of a written contract incorporating any agreement reached, if requested by either party. Such obligation does not compel either party to agree to a proposal or require the making of a concession. (15)

Committee on Political Education (COPE): The political arm of the AFL-CIO. (15)

Comparable worth: The value of dissimilar jobs (e.g., company nurse and welder) as determined through some form of job evaluation, with pay rates assigned according to their relative values. (12)

Computer-assisted instruction (CAI): An extension of programmed instruction (PI) that takes advantage of the speed, memory, and data manipulation capabilities of the computer for greater flexibility. (8)

Concurrent validity: A test validation method in which scores and criterion data are obtained at essentially the same time. (7)

Conference method: A widely used instructional approach that brings together individuals with common interests to discuss and attempt to solve problems. (8)

Conspiracy: The combination of two or more persons who band together to prejudice the rights of others or of society (e.g., by refusing to work or demanding higher wages). (15)

Construct validity: A test validation method used to determine whether a test measures certain traits or qualities identified as important in performing a job. (7)

Content validity: A test validation method whereby a person performs certain tasks that are actual samples of the kind of work the job requires or completes a paper-and-pencil test that measures relevant job knowledge. (7)

Controlling: Comparing what is happening with what should be happening and taking corrective action, if necessary. (1)

Corporate culture: The system of shared values, beliefs, and habits within an organization that interacts with the formal organizational structure to produce behavioral norms. (2, 9)

Correlation analysis: A method of measuring the degree of association, or correlation, that exists between two or more variables. (19)

Cost-of-living allowance (COLA): An escalator clause in a labor agreement that automatically increases wages as the Bureau of Labor Statistics' cost of living index rises. (12)

Craft unions: Unions that are typically composed of members of a particular trade or skill in an area or locality. (15)

Criterion-related validity: A test validation method that compares the scores on selection tests to some aspect of job performance, for example, by performance appraisal (PA). (7)

Critical incident method: A performance appraisal technique that requires written records to be kept of highly favorable and highly unfavorable actions that occur in an employee's work. (11)

Cut-off score: The test score below which an applicant will not be selected. (7)

Cyclical variation: A reasonably predictable movement about the trend line that occurs over a period of more than a year. (5)

Decertification: Loss of a union's right to act as the exclusive bargaining representative of a group of employees. (17)

Deferred compensation: Pay that is held in trust for a manager until retirement. (13)

Delphi technique: A formal procedure for obtaining consensus among a number of experts through the use of a series of questionnaires. (5)

Demotion: The process of moving a worker to a lower level of duties and responsibilities, which typically involves a cut in pay. (18)

Direct financial compensation: The pay that a person receives directly in the form of wages, salaries, bonuses, and commissions. (12)

Disciplinary action: The invoking of a penalty against an employee who fails to meet company standards. (18)

Discipline: The state of employee self-control and orderly conduct within an organization. (18)

Discriminant analysis: A quantitative method of identifying factors that differentiate between two or more groups in a population. (19)

Employee assistance program (EAP): A program in which firms deal with problems of burnout, alcohol and drug abuse, and other emotional disturbances. (14)

Employee equity: A condition which exists when individuals performing similar jobs for the same firm are paid commensurate with factors unique to the employee. (12)

Employee stock ownership plan (ESOP): A companywide incentive plan whereby the company provides its employees with common stock. (13)

Employment agency: An organization that assists firms in recruiting employees and, at the same time, aids individuals in their attempts to locate jobs. (6)

Employment at will: An unwritten contract that is created when an employee agrees to work for an employer, but there is no agreement as to how long the parties expect the employment to last. (18)

Employment interview: The final interview before a job offer is made, a goal-oriented conversation in which the interviewer and applicant exchange information. (7)

Equivalent forms: A method of determining selection test reliability by correlating the results of tests that are similar but not identical. (7)

Essay method: A performance appraisal method whereby the rater writes a brief narrative statement describing the employee's performance. (11)

Executive: A top level manager. (1)

Executive search firm: Organizations that are retained to search for the most qualified executive available for a specific position and are only on assignment from the company seeking a specific type of individual. (6)

Exempt employees: Executive, administrative, and professional employees and outside salespersons. (12)

Experiment: A method of inquiry that involves the manipulation of certain variables while others are held constant. (19)

External environment: Those factors that affect a firm's human resources from outside the organization. (2)

External equity: A condition which exists when pay for employees performing jobs in a firm that is comparable to that for similar jobs in other firms. (12)

Factor comparison method: A job evaluation technique in which (1) raters need not keep the entire job in mind as they evaluate; (2) raters make decisions on separate aspects, or factors, of the job; and (3) the method assumes the existence of five universal job factors. (12)

Finger dexterity: The ability to make precise, coordinated finger movements such as those performed by an electronics assembler or a watchmaker. (7)

Flexible compensation plans: Employees are permitted to choose from among many alternatives the way their financial compensation will be allocated. (13)

Flextime: The practice of permitting employees to choose, with certain limitations, their own working hours. (13)

Forced-choice performance reports: A performance appraisal technique whereby the appraiser is given a series of statements about an individual and the rater indicates which items are most or least descriptive of the employee. (11)

Forced distribution: An appraisal approach in which the rater is required to assign individuals in the work group to a limited number of categories similar to a normal frequency distribution. (11)

Frequency rate: The number of lost-time accidents per million people-hours worked. (14)

Functional job analysis (FJA): A comprehensive job analysis approach that concentrates on the interactions among work, worker, and organization. (4)

Generalist: A person who performs tasks in a wide variety of personnel-related activities. (1)

Going rate: The average wage that most employers pay for the same job in a particular area or industry. (12)

"Golden parachute" contract: An executive perquisite provided for the purpose of protecting executives in the event their firm is acquired by another. (13)

Grievance: An employee's dissatisfaction or feeling of personal injustice relating to his or her employment relationship. (18)

Grievance procedure: A mechanism that gives subordinates the opportunity of complaining to and carrying appeals beyond their immediate supervisors. (17)

Group appraisal: The use of two or more managers who are familiar with an employee's performance and, as a team, appraise his or her performance. (11)

Group interview: An interview consisting of several applicants who interact in the presence of one or more company representatives. (7)

Guidelines oriented job analysis (GOJA): A method developed to respond to the growing number of legislation affecting staffing and which involves a step-by-step procedure for describing the work of a particular job classification. (4)

Halo error: The type of appraisal error that occurs when an evaluator perceives one factor as being of paramount importance and gives a good overall rating to an employee who rates high on this factor. (11)

Hazard pay: Additional pay provided to employees who work under extremely dangerous conditions. (13)

Health: The employee's freedom from physical or emotional illness. (14)

Human resource information system (HRIS): Any organized method for obtaining information on which to base human resource decisions. (5)

Human resource planning (HRP): A management process that involves analyzing an organization's human resource needs under changing conditions and then developing policies and systems to satisfy those needs. (5)

Human resource research: The systematic study of human resources for the purpose of maximizing personal and organizational goal achievement. (19)

Hypnosis: An altered state of consciousness, which is artificially induced and characterized by increased receptiveness to suggestions. (14)

In-basket training: A simulation in which the participant is given a number of business papers such as memoranda, reports, and telephone messages that would typically come across a manager's desk and is asked to assign priorities to them. (8)

Incentive compensation: Compensation that relates pay to productivity. (13)

Indirect financial compensation: All financial rewards that are not paid directly to the employee. (12)

Industrial unions: Unions that are composed of all the workers in a particular plant or group of plants. (15)

Influencing: The act of determining or affecting the behavior of others. (1)

Injunction: A prohibiting legal procedure that was used by employers to prevent certain union activities such as strikes and unionization attempts. (15)

Internal environment: Those factors that affect a firm's human resources from inside the organization. (2)

Internal equity: A condition which exists when employees performing jobs for a company are paid according to their job's relative value within that organization. (12)

Internship: A special form of recruiting that involves placing a student in a temporary job in the company with no obligation on the part of the company to permanently hire the student and no obligation on the part of the student to accept a permanent position with the firm; a training approach whereby university students divide their time between attending classes and working for an organization. (6, 8)

Job analysis: The systematic process of determining the duties and skills required for performing jobs in an organization. (4)

Job bidding: A technique that permits individuals in the organization who believe that they possess the required qualifications to apply for the posted job. (6)

Job description: A document that provides information regarding the tasks and responsibilities of the job. (4)

Job design: The process of determining the specific tasks to be performed, the methods used in performing the tasks, and how the job relates to other work in the organization. (4)

Job enlargement: Changes in the scope of a job so as to provide greater variety to the worker. (4)

Job enrichment: Restructuring the content and level of responsibility of a job to make it more challenging, meaningful, and interesting to the employee. (4, 9)

Job evaluation: That part of a compensation system in which a firm determines the relative value of one job in comparison with others. (12)

Job knowledge questions: Questions that assess the knowledge required for performing the job and which must be possessed prior to filling the job. (7)

Job knowledge tests: Tests designed to measure a candidate's knowledge about duties of the position being applied for. (7)

Job overload: A situation which exists when employees are given more work than they can possibly handle. (14)

Job posting: A procedure for communicating to company employees the fact that job openings exist. (6)

Job pricing: The act of placing a monetary value on the worth of a job. (12)

Job rotation: Moving employees from one job to another for the purpose of providing them with broader experiences. (8)

Job sample simulation questions: Situations whereby an applicant may be required to actually perform a sample task from the job. (7)

Job sharing: An employment situation in which two part-time people split the duties of one job and are paid according to the amount of time they work. (13)

Job specification: The minimum acceptable qualifications that a person should possess to perform a job. (4)

Key job: A job that is well known in the company and industry and one that can be easily defined. (12)

Labor market: The geographical area from which employees are recruited for a particular job. (12)

Leadership: The directing and influencing of other individuals' activities. (9)

Leniency: The giving of undeserved high ratings. (11)

Likes and dislikes analysis: A tool for assessing certain factors that could have an impact on the development of a career path. (10)

Local union: The basic element in the structure of the American labor movement. (15)

Lockout: Temporary cessation of business operations by management. (16)

Long-run trend: A projection of the demand for a firm's products and/or services, typically five years or more into the future. (5)

Management: The process of getting things done through the efforts of other people. (1)

Management by objectives: A philosophy of management that emphasizes the setting of agreed-on objectives by superior and subordinate managers and the use of these objectives as the primary basis of motivation, evaluation, and control efforts. (9)

Management development: All learning experiences provided by an organization for the purpose of providing and upgrading skills and knowledge required in current and future managerial positions. (8)

Management inventory: Detailed data regarding each manager to be used in identifying individuals possessing the potential to move into higher level positions. (5)

Management position description questionnaire (MPDQ): A form of job analysis designed for management positions, which uses a checklist method to analyze jobs. (4)

Mandatory bargaining issues: Those issues that fall within the definition of wages, hours, and other terms and conditions of employment. (16)

Manual dexterity: The coordinated movement of both hands and arms, such as those required by large assembly jobs. (7)

Media: Special methods of communicating ideas and concepts in training and development. (8)

Mediation: A process whereby a neutral third party enters a labor dispute when a bargaining impasse has occurred. (16)

Mission: The organization's continuing purpose or reason for being. (2)

Motivation: The willingness to put forth effort in the pursuit of goals. (9)

Multinational company (MNC): A company that conducts a large part of its business outside the country in which it is headquartered and has a significant percentage of physical facilities and employees in other countries. (2)

National Labor Relations Board (NLRB): Created by the National Labor Relations Act to administer and enforce the provisions of the act. (15)

National union: Composed of local unions, which it charters. (15)

Nondirective interview: An interview where probing, open-ended questions are asked. (7)

Nonfinancial compensation: The satisfaction that a person receives by performing meaningful job tasks or from the psychological or physical environment in which the job is performed. (12)

Norms: A distribution of many scores obtained from people similar in nature to the applicants being tested. (7)

Objectivity: The process of ensuring that all individuals scoring a given test will obtain the same results. (7)

Occupational Safety and Health Act (OSHA): A federal act passed in 1970 to ensure that insofar as possible every man and woman in the nation has a safe and healthy working environment. (14)

Ombudsperson: A complaint officer with access to top management, who hears employee complaints, investigates them, and sometimes recommends appropriate action. (17)

On-the-job training (OJT): An informal approach to training in which a person learns job tasks by actually performing them. (8)

Open-door policy: A company policy whereby employees have the right to take any grievance to the person next in the chain of command if a satisfactory solution cannot be obtained from their immediate supervisor. (17)

Open shop: Employment that is open on equal terms to union members and nonmembers alike. (16)

Organization development (OD): An organizationwide application of behavioral science knowledge to the planned development and reinforcement of a firm's strategies, structures, and processes for improving its effectiveness. (9)

Organizational equity: A balancing of the needs of operative employees, managers, and shareholders. (12)

Organizational structure: The manner in which the human resources of the firm are organized or arranged. (9)

Organizing: The acquisition of human, material, and financial resources and specifying the relationships among them in order to get things done. (1)

Orientation: The guided adjustment of new employees to their company, jobs, and work group. (8)

Outplacement: The use of a consulting firm to assist terminated employees find appropriate employment elsewhere. (18)

Paired comparison: A variation of the ranking method that involves comparing the performance of each employee with every other employee in the group. (11)

Pay compression: The perception by workers that the pay differential between their pay and that of employees in jobs above or below them is too small. (12)

Pay grade: The grouping of similar jobs to simplify the job pricing process. (12)

Pay range: A minimum and maximum pay rate with enough variance between the two to allow some significant pay difference. (12)

Payroll-based stock ownership plan (PAY-SOP): A special type of ESOP in which stock of a firm is placed in a trust for employees. (13)

Performance appraisal (PA): A system that provides a periodic review and evaluation of an individual's job performance. (11)

Permissive bargaining issues: Those issues that may be raised, but neither side

may insist that they be bargained over. (16)

Perquisites (perks): Any special benefits provided by a firm to an executive that are designed to give him or her something extra. (13)

Personnel managers: Individuals who normally act in an advisory (staff) capacity when working with other managers regarding human resource matters. (1)

Planning: Determining in advance what should be accomplished and how it should be done. (1)

Plateauing: A career condition that occurs when job functions and work content remain the same. (12)

Point method: A job evaluation method that requires that job factors be selected according to the nature of the specific group of jobs being evaluated. (12)

Policy: A predetermined guide established to provide direction in decision making. (2)

Position: The collection of tasks and responsibilities performed by one person. There is a position for every individual in an organization. (4)

Position analysis questionnaire (PAQ): A structured job analysis questionnaire that distinguishes between job-oriented elements and worker-oriented elements. (4)

Predictive validity: A test validation method in which a test is administered and criterion information is obtained later. (7)

Premium pay: Compensation given to employees for working long periods of time or working under dangerous or undesirable conditions. (13)

Productivity: A measure of the relationship between inputs (labor, capital, natural resources, energy) and the quality and quantity of outputs (goods and services). (19)

Profession: Characterized by the existence of a common body of knowledge and a procedure for certifying membership. (1)

Profit sharing: A compensation plan that results in the distribution of a predetermined percentage of the firm's profits to employees. (13)

Programmed instruction (PI): A teaching method that provides instruction without the intervention of an instructor. (8)

Progressive discipline: An approach to imposing disciplinary action designed to ensure that the minimum penalty appropriate to the offense is imposed and involves answering a series of questions about the severity of the offense. (18)

Prohibited bargaining issues: Those issues that are statutorily outlawed. (16)

Promotion: The movement of a person to a higher level position in the company. (18)

Promotion from within: The policy of filling vacancies above entry-level positions with present employees. (6)

Psychomotor abilities tests: The measurement of strength, coordination, and dexterity. (7)

Quality circles: Groups of employees who meet regularly with their supervisors to identify production problems and recommend solutions. (9)

Quality of work life (QWL): The extent to which employees satisfy significant personal needs through their organizational experiences. (9)

Random variations: Changes for which there is no pattern. (5)

Ranking method: A performance appraisal method in which a rater ranks all employees in a given group on the basis of their overall performance; a job evaluation method by which raters examine the descriptions of jobs being evaluated and arrange them in order according to their relative value to the company. (11, 12)

Rating scale: A widely used appraisal method that rates employees according to defined factors. (11)

Realistic job preview (RJP): The conveying of important information about a job to an applicant in an unbiased manner, including both positive and negative factors. (7)

Recruitment: The process of attracting individuals on a timely basis, in sufficient numbers and with appropriate qualifications, to apply for jobs with an organization. (6)

Reference checks: Means of providing additional insight into information provided by an applicant and to verify the accuracy of the information provided. (7)

Regression analysis: A quantitative method that utilizes the relationship between two or more variables to predict one item (known as the dependent variable) based on knowledge of the other item(s) (known as the independent variables). (5, 19)

Reliability: The extent to which a selection test provides consistent results. (7)

Requisition: A document that specifies various details including job title, department, and the date the employee is needed for work. (6)

Right-to-work laws: Laws that prohibit management and unions from developing agreements requiring union membership as a condition of employment. (15)

Role ambiguity: The lack of a clear understanding on the part of employees about the content of their jobs. (14)

Role conflict: A condition which exists when individuals are placed in the position of seeking opposing goals. (14)

Role playing: A technique in which some problem—real or imaginary—involving human interaction is presented and then spontaneously acted out. (8)

Safety: Protection of employees from injuries caused by work-related accidents. (14)

Sampling: The process by which only a portion of the total number of individuals are studied, from which conclusions are drawn for the entire group. (19)

Scanlon plan: A cost savings plan which, like profit sharing, features participation by the firm's employees. (13)

Seasonal variation: Reasonably predictable changes that occur over a period of a year. (5)

Selection: The process of choosing from among a group of applicants those individuals best suited for a particular position. (7)

Selection ratio: The number of people hired for a particular job compared to the number of individuals in the applicant pool. (7)

Seniority: The amount of time that an employee has worked in various capacities with the firm. (16)

Sensitivity training: An organization development technique that is designed to make employees aware of themselves and their impact on others. (9)

Severity rate: An indication of the number of days lost because of accidents per million people-hours worked. (14)

Simulation: The computer is used to assist in performing experiments on a model of a real system. (5)

Simulators: Training devices of varying degrees of complexity that duplicate the "real world." (8)

Situational questions: Questions that pose a hypothetical job situation to determine what the applicant would do in such a situation. (7)

Social responsibility: An organization's basic obligation to ensure that its decisions and operations meet the needs and interests of society. (2)

Special events: A recruiting method that involves an effort on the part of a single employer, or group of employers, to attract a large number of applicants for interviews. (6)

Specialist: An individual who may be either a top executive, a middle manager, or a nonmanager who is typically concerned with only one of the six functional areas of human resource management. (1)

Split-halves method: A method of determining selection test reliability whereby a test is administered and then divided into two parts, and the two sets are then correlated with each other. (7)

Standard-hour plan: An individual incentive plan where time allowances are calculated for each unit of output. (13)

Standardization: The uniformity of the procedures and conditions related to the administering of tests. (7)

Stockholder: An owner of a corporation. (2)

Stock-option plan: An executive compensation plan in which managers are given the opportunity for a manager to buy a specified amount of stock in the future at or below the current market price. (13)

Straight piecework plan: Payment of a predetermined amount for each unit produced. (13)

Strategic plan: A plan designed to help the firm achieve its primary objectives. (5)

Strengths/weaknesses balance sheet (SWBS): A technique that was developed to assist in making career path decisions. (10)

Stress: The body's reaction to any demand made on it. (14)

Stress interview: A form of interview that intentionally creates anxiety to determine how an applicant will react in certain types of environments. (7)

Strike: The refusal of union members to work in order to exert pressure on management in negotiations. (16)

Structured interview: An interview consisting of a series of job-related questions that are consistently asked of each applicant for a particular job. (7)

Survey feedback method: A research technique that assists change efforts by the systematic collection and measurement of employee attitudes with the use of anonymous questionnaires. (9, 19)

Team building: A conscious effort to develop effective work groups throughout the organization. (9)

Telecommuting: An approach to work that permits employees to perform their job duties at home through the use of a computer terminal. (13)

Teletraining: A training method used for training people more efficiently and more effectively utilizing teleconferencing. (8)

Test-retest method: A method of determining selection test reliability by giving the test twice to the same group of individuals and correlating the two sets of scores. (7)

Time series analysis: A variation of regression analysis in which the independent variable is expressed in units of time. (19)

Training and development (T&D): Planned continuous effort by management to improve employee competency levels and organizational performance. (8)

Transactional analysis (TA): An OD method that considers the three ego states of the "Parent," the "Adult," and the "Child" in understanding interpersonal relations and assists in improving an organization's effectiveness. (9)

Transcendental meditation (TM): A stress reduction technique whereby a secret word or phrase (mantra) provided by a trained instructor is mentally repeated while an individual is comfortably seated. (14)

Transfer: The lateral movement of a worker within an organization. (18)

Two-tier wage system: A wage structure reflecting lower pay rates for newly hired employees than those received by established employees performing similar jobs. (12, 15)

Union: A group of employees who have joined together for the purpose of dealing with their employer. (2)

Union shop: A requirement that all employees become members of the union after a specified period of employment (usually thirty days) or after a union shop provision has been negotiated. (16)

Utility analysis: The determination of the ratio of benefits to costs for any selection technique. (7)

Utilization review: The process of scrutinizing medical diagnoses, hospitalization, surgery, and other medical treatment and care prescribed by doctors. (13)

Validity: The extent to which a test measures what it is supposed to measure. (7)

Vestibule training: Training that takes place away from the production area on equipment that closely resembles the actual equipment used on the job. (8)

Vocational interest tests: Tests to indicate the occupation in which a person has the greatest interest and is most likely to receive satisfaction. (7)

Wage curve: The fitting of a curve to plotted points in order to create a smooth progression between pay grades. (12)

Weighted application blank (WAB): An approach that attempts to identify factors on the application blank that differentiate between such criteria variables as long-term and short-term employees, productive and less productive workers, and satisfied and less satisfied employees. (7)

Weighted checklist method: A performance appraisal technique whereby the rater completes a form similar to the forced-choice performance report but in which the various responses have been assigned different weights. (11)

Wellness: A concept that focuses on the prevention of illness and disease. (13)

Work-sample tests: Identification of a task or set of tasks that are representative of a job and the use of these tasks for selection testing. (7)

Work standards method: A performance appraisal method that compares each employee's performance to a predetermined standard or expected level of output. (11)

Worker requirements questions: Questions that seek to determine an applicant's willingness to conform to the requirements of a job. (7)

Wrist-finger speed: The ability to rapidly make wrist and finger movements. (7)

Yellow-dog contract: A written agreement between the employee and the company made at the time of employment prohibiting a worker from joining a union or engaging in union activities. (15)

Zero-base forecasting: Use of the organization's current level of employment as the starting point for determining future staffing needs. (5)

Index

Myers, David C., 110n
Myers, Donald W., 92n, 114n

Nadler, Leonard, 263n
Naisbitt, John, 670
National Child state, 322
National Education Association, 552
National Industrial Recovery Act
    (NIRA), 545
National Institute for Occupational
    Safety and Health (NIOSH), 514–
    515
National Labor Relations Act (NLRA) of
    1935, 61, 421, 545, 559
National Labor Relations Board (NLRB),
    61, 545–546, 548
    petition for election and role of, 561
    on union decertification, 616–617
National norms for testing, 214
National origin, discrimination on basis
    of, 84, 200
National Right to Work Committee, 547
National union, 556–557. See also La-
    bor unions
Neher, William R., 277n
Nelson, John G., 516n
Nelson, Wallace F., 679n, 691n
Nemec, Margaret M., 175n
Netter, John, 685n
New employee checklist, 269
Newman, Jerry M., 415n, 425n
Newspaper help-wanted advertising,
    174–175
Newstrom, John W., 285n
Niehouse, Oliver L., 514n, 515n
Nikkel, Deborah, 146n
No probable cause statement, 66
Noe, Robert M., 615n, 647n, 648n
Noer, David M., 51n
Nonfinancial compensation, 414, 478–
    479
    employee involvement in job design
        as form of, 479–480
    job environment as form of, 480–486
Nontraditional bargaining, 592
Nonverbal communication, during job
    interview, 242, 243
Nord, Walter R., 520n
Normal probability curve, 214
Norman, Beverly, 517n
Norms in testing, 214
Norris, Dwight R., 216n
Norris-LaGuardia Act, 61, 544–545
Novack, Stanley R., 208n
Novit, Mitchell S., 514n

Oakar, Pendleton, 435n
Oberle, Rodney L., 632n
Objectivity in testing, 213
Observation method, used for job analy-
    sis, 97, 100
Occupational Measurement System
    (OMS), 112–114
Occupational Safety and Health Act
    (OSHA) of 1970, 9n, 67, 115, 500–
    501
    criticism of, 501–503
    requirements of, 501–502
Occupational Safety and Health Admin-
    istration, 67

Odiorne, George, 264n
Office of Federal Contract Compliance
    Programs (OFCCP), 67, 71–73,
    184
    Order No. 14, 184
    Revised Order No. 4, 184, 185
Office of Personnel Management, 69
Office of Safety and Health Administra-
    tion, 502–503
    sample guidelines of, 508
Office size, 481
Oldham, Greg R., 115
Olson, Howard C., 110n
Ombudsperson, 614, 615
On-the-job training (OJT), 283
Open-door policy, 611
Operational analysis, 264, 265
Operational level accreditation for
    professional in human resources
    (PHR), 29–30
Operative employee training programs,
    282–284
Order No. 14, 184
Organization change, 252
    reasons for resistance to, 254–255
    reduced resistance to, 255–256
    sequence, 252–254
Organization development, 308–309
    program evaluation, 327–328
    use of consultant for, 326–327
Organization development techniques
    job enrichment, 318–319
    management by objectives (MBO),
        313–316
    quality circles, 311–313
    sensitivity training, 324–325
    survey feedback, 319–321
    team building, 309–311
    transactional analysis, 320, 322–324
Organizational analysis, 264–265
Organizational career planning, 344–
    347, 349
Organizational change, 326
Organizational characteristics, 302
Organizational culture, as potential
    source of stress, 518
Organizational equity, 415–416
Organizational goals, 143
Organizational membership, 438
Organizational structure, 302–303
Orientation
    purposes of, 267–268
    stages in effective, 268–271
O'Sullivan, Devin, 287n
O'Toole, Thomas, 43n
Ottemann, Robert L., 387n
Otts, Herbert A., 257n
Ouchi, William G., 12–13, 299n
Outplacement, 644–645
Output standard, 466, 470
Overpayment, 444
Overtime, 163
    payment for, 577
Ozley, Lee M., 307n

Paired comparison, 384–385
Parent country nationals (PCNs), 49,
    50
Parent ego state, 320
Paris, Ellen, 458n

Parks, Largent, Jr., 395n
Participative culture, 304, 306–308
Patten, Thomas H., Jr., 309n, 327n
Patterned interview guide, 225, 226
Patton, John A., 427n, 432n
Paxton, Dan R., 258n
Pay compression, 445
Pay range, 441–443
Pay secrecy, 444–445
Payroll based stock ownership plan
    (PAYSOP), 473
Pearlman, Kenneth, 234n
Peers, performance appraisal by, 374
Pendleton, Clarence, 435
Pera, Gina, 12n
Performance. See Employee
    performance
Performance appraisal (PA)
    assessment center method, 398, 400–
        401
    career planning and, 351–352
    characteristics of effective, 392–396
    defined, 366
    interview, 396–399
    legal implications of, 396
    methods of, 376–390. See also Perfor-
        mance appraisal methods
    objectives of, 367–369
    period of, 375
    problems in, 390–392
    process of, 369–372
    responsibility for, 372, 374–375
    use of, 369, 370
Performance appraisal methods, 376
    actual use of, 388–390
    behaviorally anchored rating scales,
        386, 387
    critical incidents, 378, 384
    essay, 384
    forced distribution, 385
    forced-choice and weighted checklist
        performance report, 385
    management by objectives, 386–388
    ranking, 384–385
    rating scales, 376–383
    work standards, 384
Performance expectations, 393
Perks. See Perquisites
Permissive bargaining issues, 570, 572
Perquisites (perks), 475–476
Personal bias, 392
Personality tests, 220
Personnel Accreditation Institute (PAI),
    21–22, 29
    accreditation requirements of, 29–31
Personnel executives, 14–17
Personnel function, 17–20
Personnel management, beginning a ca-
    reer in, 355–358
Personnel manager, 4–5
Personnel surplus, 142–143
Pesci, Michael, 514n, 515n
Peters, Thomas J., 299n, 670n
Phillips v. Martin Marietta Corporation,
    77–78
Physical examination, as part of hiring
    processes, 232
Physical fitness programs, 522–524
Physical handicap, discrimination on
    basis of, 200